EDITED BY KRISTINA BORJESSON

FEET TO THE FIRE

THE MEDIA AFTER 9/11

TOP
JOURNALISTS
SPEAK
OUT

Prometheus Books

59 John Glenn Drive
Amherst, New York 14228-2197

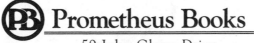

Published 2005 by Prometheus Books

Inquiries should be addressed to
Prometheus Books
59 John Glenn Drive
Amherst, New York 14228–2197
VOICE: 716–691–0133, ext. 207
FAX: 716–564–2711
WWW.PROMETHEUSBOOKS.COM

09 08 07 06 05   5 4 3 2 1

Library of Congress Cataloging-in-Publication Data

Feet to the fire : the media after 9/11 : top journalists speak out / edited by Kristina Borjesson.
    p. cm.
Includes bibliographical references and index.
ISBN 1–59102–343–2 (hardcover : alk. paper)
1. Press and politics—United States. I. Borjesson, Kristina.

PN4888.P6F44 2005
070.4'49320973090511—dc22

2005017814

Printed in the United States of America on acid-free paper

For the US Soldiers Who Have Died in Iraq and for Their Families,
Who Deserve to Know

إلى المواطنين الابرياء الذين قتلوا في العراق و إلى أسرهم الذين لهم الحق لمعرفة لماذا

[For the Innocent Civilians Who Have Died in Iraq
and for Their Families, Who Deserve to Know]

For Americans Who Need and Deserve to Know

For Aspiring and Working Journalists Who Need Good Role Models

CONTENTS

ACKNOWLEDGMENTS

My deepest gratitude goes to those who participated in this book:

Hannah Allam
Jon Alpert
Deborah Amos
Peter Arnett
James Bamford
Juan Cole
Thomas Curley
Barton Gellman
Christopher Hedges
Ted Koppel
Paul Krugman
Jonathan Landay
Tom Lasseter
John MacArthur
David Martin
Walter Pincus
Anthony Shadid
Warren Strobel
Ronald Suskind
Helen Thomas
John Walcott
Tom Yellin

Special Thanks to Editorial Consultant Patricia Hartwell

Without Patricia Hartwell, *Feet to the Fire* would have been a different book.

She helped me make fundamental decisions for this project, including selecting the candidates to put in the book. A brilliant researcher and analyst, Patricia knows as much if not more about what's going on in American politics and the press than any well-known pundit I can think of. Beyond her long experience as a journalist and television producer, she also brought the added dimension of great passion to the project. Our daily discussions about issues and events kept me on top of things and informed my interview questions. I've known Hartwell for more than a decade now and was well aware while we were at *CBS Reports* producing documentaries that she possessed more intellectual wattage than virtually anyone else in the unit—senior management included. I am truly fortunate and privileged to have had her as a close collaborator on *Feet to the Fire*. Her input took the book to much higher levels than I could have alone.

Thanks to Prometheus Books and particularly to Editor in Chief Steven Mitchell for being infinitely patient.

My everlasting gratitude to my husband and children; their love and understanding are everything to me.

Interviews with Ted Koppel, Helen Thomas, Tom Curley, Tom Yellin, John MacArthur, Jon Alpert, and Christopher Hedges have been included in this book with the kind permission of the Arte Channel in France and Philippe Alfonsi, executive producer of API Productions. The interviews were originally conducted for a documentary on the American press entitled *USA Media Blues*, which was produced by API and Arte and directed by Yves Boisset. The film premiered on Arte in September 2004.

INTRODUCTION

*F*eet to the Fire is the product of acts of generosity, courage, and care on the part of twenty-one of this nation's most distinguished journalists. They took the time to talk to me, to answer difficult questions, and then to review and return their edited transcripts. They didn't do it as a personal favor. I had never met most of them and none of them are personal friends. I think that first and foremost, they did it for the American people. I think, too, they did it for the rest of the world. Finally, they did it for the record.

I don't know of any other record like this one. In a time of full-blown crisis, the last superpower's greatest messengers are allowing the world to walk in their shoes and see events through their eyes. Again, I say it is an act of courage. It takes guts, particularly when you are well known, to share your thoughts and to speak candidly about your profession. Several people I interviewed didn't go through with it, either because they didn't like what they said or they wouldn't make the time to review and return their edited transcripts. So here and there you'll read, "We interviewed X" or "X said," and you'll not find X's transcript in the book. I bear no grudges against any of the Xs. Only those who are meant to be in this book are in it.

Many of the reporters I talked to would ask, "Have you spoken to

_____?" I decided that if three different interviewees mentioned the same name, I had to interview that person for the book. This was how the best of the best within American journalism's arena of excellence was revealed to me. By far and away, the most often mentioned and most highly recommended news source was Knight Ridder. That's why there is a preponderance of Knight Ridder reporters in this book. Their reporting is indeed excellent, but don't take my word for it. Check them out at www.realcities.com/mld/krwashington/.

"Have you spoken to _____" also built the story arc for this book. The first group of reporters give insider tours of news and government power centers. Then, those on the front lines of post-9/11 crisis reporting —national security reporters and foreign/war correspondents—take us deep into their worlds.

Inside the corporate media, the heavy hitters are clear about the fact that the public interest is now defined as what the public is interested in. News as a public service takes a backseat to news as a product. In June 2004, I interviewed Ted Koppel. His *Nightline* program is one of the rare, really good news shows still standing, although it has lost half its audience over the years and has always lived in a Siberian time slot. Koppel made this disheartening comment about the public interest: "If I wanted to do a program on the basketball player Kobe Bryant, and the allegations that he raped a young woman while he was out in Colorado, that would get more of an audience than what *Nightline* does, because night after night what we do is cover developing events in Iraq. And by and large, the American public is not interested in that right now." Associated Press president and CEO Tom Curley, who is leading an unprecedented and much-needed campaign against government secrecy, says: "It follows a pattern. When there is more interest, we provide more, editors ask more questions, the graphics get more compelling, and the understanding becomes more complete." It's undeniable that audience demand has a firm grip on TV news providers. But the fact is, the information offerings from which the public gets to pick and choose to create that demand are, to put it mildly, limited. The myriad reasons for that are explained by a number of people in this book from the ultimate insider's perspective. But television's sins, says *Harper's* publisher John MacArthur, go way beyond limited coverage. He gives examples where television has played the role of propaganda arm for the US government. He cites a "fabricated story about Iraqi soldiers in occupied Kuwait pulling babies out of incubators and leaving them on the floor to die." MacArthur goes on to say that the story had been manufactured by George H. W. Bush's administration in conjunction with the Kuwaitis and the public relations agency Hill & Knowlton. The purpose of this lie was to help garner the necessary Senate votes to send the US military to Iraq for the first Gulf War.

The bottom line is that in this era of twenty-four-hour cable news, there is less hard news and real information than ever on television about what is going on in this nation's arena of power and around the world. There is also more entertainment and advertisement disguised as news. Finally, there is propaganda and fake news masquerading as real news, courtesy of the US government. *Feet to the Fire* shows what is happening to journalism as a result of this surfeit of junk information and misinformation. The book also shows that the relationship between the government and the governed, and the government and the press, has fundamentally changed.

There is some really significant reporting out there that simply isn't punching through to the public consciousness because it is not on television. Here again, I must mention Knight Ridder. I wonder what would have happened if Knight Ridder's prewar reporting had hit the national airwaves at the same time that it was hitting newsstands in cities and towns outside of Washington and New York City. There are profound, multidimensional consequences to the lack of public awareness about what the nation's leadership is deciding and doing. There are deadly consequences, too.

Covering the arena of power without fear or favor has always been one of the hardest jobs a reporter can take on. Today, it is an almost impossible task. Walter Pincus of the *Washington Post* really put his finger on why this is when he said, "When it comes to government, we moved into a PR society a long time ago. Now, it's the PR that counts, not the policy. They can make any policy seem like the right thing or the wrong thing, depending on what information they put out." The press is not viewed as a watchdog; it is viewed as a conduit for getting information to the public. Journalists who won't accept the job are punished. Veteran White House reporter Helen Thomas earned her current persona non grata status with the administration after asking White House spokesman Ari Fleischer why, if the president deplored a suicide bombing in Israel, he wanted to "bomb and kill thousands of innocent Iraqis, including women and children."

In addition, Walter Pincus is concerned about the press's failure to cover government's mistakes and malfeasance. "It creates a feeling in the public that government's continually corrupt and can't be changed," he says. Pincus thinks that the lack of coverage and accountability is ultimately resulting in the Constitution "being short-circuited."

On very rare occasions, a reporter will lift the veil and expose the heart of power. Author Ron Suskind provided a breathtaking view inside the Bush administration in his best-selling book *The Price of Loyalty*. His interview in this book contains a series of intimate portraits of President Bush, Vice President Dick Cheney, and White House adviser Karl Rove. The president, Suskind says, "believes in the near-mystical powers of his instincts. He is unempirical. He is not particularly curious. He is driven by the dictates of a vivid personality—and personality is destiny in this model of leadership. . . . It's a very improvisational model for leadership. There are parts of it that people are surprised to see have panned out." Suskind's descriptions of how this president and his closest advisers make decisions are gripping. Following Suskind, *New York Times* columnist Paul Krugman takes the bird's-eye view of the administration, examining President Bush's agenda and assessing its impact on Americans and the rest of the world.

The most profound decision President Bush and his administration have made was to invade Iraq. Documenting that decision-making process fell most directly within the purview of national security reporters. Here in particular, Knight Ridder took the lead before any other news outlet and continues to break new ground. Given the consequences of the decision to go to war, it is not an overstatement to say that a debt of gratitude is owed to John Walcott, Jonathan Landay, and Warren Strobel for their prewar reporting. They have created an unparalleled examination of how the administration made its case for going to Iraq. The examination continues as I write this. In early May 2005 they reported a story about a leaked memo on US-British prewar discussions that clearly showed that the administration had decided to go to war by at least July 2002. In the memo, the head of the United Kingdom's foreign intelligence service is quoted as saying, "The intelligence and facts were being fixed around the policy."

The *Washington Post*'s Barton Gellman and Walter Pincus are also owed the same debt of gratitude. Pincus's dead-on reporting often landed on the paper's back pages, but he was undeterred. He pushes on, too. On May 28, 2005, he added this report to the record: "Two army analysts whose work has been cited as part of a key intelligence failure on Iraq— the claim that aluminum tubes sought by the Baghdad government were probably meant for a nuclear weapons program rather than for rockets—have received job performance awards in each of the past three years, officials said." Pincus went on to report that the analysts, George Norris and Robert Campos, received lump-sum cash payments.

Of all the national security reporters I interviewed, I think that CBS's national security correspondent, David Martin, has the toughest job. He works for a high-profile network, lives among his sources, and has to be excruciatingly careful about his reporting, not just because the subjects he covers are sensitive but because of the nature of television as a medium. Before talking to him, I had never considered how even in a meticulously reported piece the interplay between sound bites and narration can undermine the truth that a broadcast reporter is trying to get across to an audience.

Jim Bamford's critique of the prewar reporting is, perhaps, the most unvarnished. A brilliant, independent national security reporter, Bamford lays out a disturbing case against the Bush administration in his book *A Pretext for War: 9/11, Iraq, and the Abuse of America's Intelligence Agencies*. Bamford's comments, along with those of the other national security reporters in this book, raise one key question: Were laws broken and, if so, what laws? Knight Ridder's Jonathan Landay is looking for the answer. "There's a law that prohibits the American government from propagandizing its own people," he says, and "there are laws that make it a crime for a public official to willfully or knowingly mislead or lie to Congress. It's a high crime under the Constitution's impeachment clause to manipulate or deliberately misuse national security intelligence data. And under federal criminal law, it's a felony to 'defraud the United States or any agency thereof, in any manner or for any purpose.'"

The details of how the United States wound up in Iraq are as troubling as the fact that, after interviewing almost two dozen of this country's best journalists, I discovered that there is no consensus among them regarding why America preemptively invaded Iraq. This, I think, is profound.

Equally profound is the level of ignorance among the American leadership in Washington and the military in the Middle East about the region in general and Iraq in particular. The lack of postinvasion planning has been catastrophic, particularly for innocent Iraqi civilians. So many fundamental mistakes have been made that it is hard to select only one as the most egregious. There is, however, one that bothers me more than any other. I find the fact that the United States doesn't even bother to keep an Iraqi civilian death count grotesquely disrespectful and wrong. I don't think that anything could more clearly send the message that these innocent people are viewed as expendable. The rage this engenders, of course, falls most heavily on American soldiers who—all the hype and formal statements of praise aside —barely escape finding themselves in the same category.

The level of ignorance about the Middle East and Iraq being what it is puts the *Washington Post*'s Anthony Shadid and historian/blogger Juan Cole into a class by themselves as precious assets. Shadid's understanding of the cultural, social, and political dynamics at play in the Middle East and Iraq is reflected in his interview for this book. Anyone who truly wants to understand what's going on over there or anyone who needs confirmation that real people with real names and real families live there should make reading Shadid's reporting a priority. Juan Cole's "Informed Comment" blog is no less important and provides literally up-to-the-minute information and background on unfolding events. Professor Cole is an expert on the Middle East, Islamic movements, and Muslim radicalism. The history, the context, the consequences, they're all there, en vivo, on "Informed Comment."

Finally, there are the war correspondents who document the wages of death and other consequences of military engagement. Peter Arnett is the most experienced living war correspondent I know of. The old adage "the more things change, they more they stay the same" is the distressing theme that runs through his interview. His fascinating personal accounts eventually point to a coverage cycle for this war that looks very much like what he experienced during the Vietnam War: a pretext for war is created. Initially, the press and public are prowar and "patriotic." As the war bogs down, the tide begins to turn and more unfavorable reporting emerges. Finally, the reporting is decidedly negative, but only after a critical mass of dead American soldiers has accumulated.

Former *New York Times* war correspondent Christopher Hedges's interview amounts to a meditation on the horrors of war, beginning with an examination of the process of rallying public support for it. "What happens is you create this kind of invisible crowd of the dead [9/11 victims] and you use death to sanctify the war, and to question the enterprise of the war is to dishonor the memory of the dead. It's a kind of sacrilege against the dead. This is also a very good technique for keeping at bay any kind of criticism of the war." Hedges was in the field for twenty years and carries heavy memories of carnage in his head, some of which he shares here.

Independent videojournalist Jon Alpert's narrative about outsmarting Iraqi censors and holding hands with death to capture rare footage during the first Gulf War reads like a thriller. The thriller turns into a Kafka novel when Alpert tries to get the footage on the air upon his return to the United States. His story more than most reveals broadcast television's limitations as a viable provider of controversial and important news. Another veteran of reporting on conflict in the Middle East, National Public Radio's Deborah Amos, speaks in disheartening detail of the tragic and deadly missteps made by young American soldiers who lack cultural sensitivity training and are "scared witless."

Knight Ridder's correspondents Hannah Allam and Tom Lasseter are by far the youngest of those I interviewed. Lasseter says that what he knows to be true about issues and events in Iraq is that what is true today could very easily be the opposite tomorrow. When I spoke to Allam, she was particularly distressed about the disconnect between Middle America's perception of events in Iraq and what she was reporting from Baghdad.

I can't possibly do justice to *Feet to the Fire* in an introduction. It has too many layers; it is too rich in information, characters, and events. But upon reading the book, perhaps more people will realize that some areas of reporting are incredibly difficult and that television should not be anyone's sole source of news. For those who have turned mainstream media bashing into a full-time blood sport, this book is proof that gifted reporters, doing very important work, do reside there. Finally, if this book does anything, it makes this abundantly clear: the United States cannot hope to fulfill the role it wants to assume as the planet's great superpower unless its leaders and the citizens they represent know and care much more about the planet. Our continued collective ignorance can only lead to global-scale catastrophe. Our press gets some of the blame for this, but I also think the problem is far more fundamental than negligent journalism. The idea that our educational system should get as much if not *more* attention than our military system is not just some warm, fuzzy notion. It is a matter of survival. Imagine if our educational system were literally tied to our national security needs. Imagine, for example, that children in schools across the country were learning Chinese right now, beginning in kindergarten—the best time to learn a foreign language. Twenty years hence, when this nation will really have to reckon with China, we actually might have enough reporters and diplomats and other people so familiar with the culture and the language that we won't be victims of disastrous "intelligence failures" and other colossal stupidities resulting in war and death. This, frankly, is my greatest hope.

EXECUTIVE IMPRESSIONS

I

CRISIS COVERAGE AND THE CANDY BAR IMPERATIVE

ABC Archives

TED KOPPEL
Anchor and Managing Editor,
ABC News *Nightline*
Interviewed June 2004

Of all the star TV journalists of his generation, Ted Koppel has arguably done the most important work, most consistently. Unlike his colleagues, he's had a vehicle, *Nightline*, that has maintained its reputation for taking hard looks at important issues. Although *Nightline* doesn't have the audience it used to have, the program has grown more important by virtue of the fact that real news and serious, informed analysis of important issues on television are now down to practically zero. Virtually no other host of any current affairs show on television today conducts interviews with the grace, wit, and intelligence that Koppel has displayed over the years. He is, without a doubt, a master interviewer.

Koppel appeared for his interview looking neat as a pin and very much like the high-powered accountant of big-issue whos, whats, whens, wheres, and whys that he is. He has a very firm handshake and an intense but friendly gaze. At first, he took a professorial tone with me, forcing me to whittle down my first question so that it could be more easily, accurately, and, perhaps, more politically correctly answered. He loosened up as time went on, but clearly he was as good at deflecting some of my questions as he is at nailing *Nightline* subjects with his. He has a sense of humor, which I admire in anyone but think is absolutely necessary for someone in his position. At times I had the feeling that I was talking to a restrained version of another person, but that was understandable given the fact that he's Ted Koppel and that the camera he was looking into was recording an interview slated for viewing by a fairly large European audience. It is, I think, axiomatic that the more power you have, the harder it is to be brutally frank in public because what you do and say has more impact on more people, things, and events. Having said that, Koppel made some provocative comments about his definition of censorship, his audience, and American journalism. I disagree with him on some of the issues we discussed, but ultimately I was impressed by the fact that he is a man who understands exactly what role he is playing and the limitations of that role:

> Here's how the system works and you know it. I create one candy bar. Mr. Jones creates another candy bar. Mr. Smith creates a third candy bar. We put our candy bars out there and we say to you, "Buy our candy bar." And you pick. Maybe you pick mine. Maybe you pick Mr. Smith's. Maybe you pick Mr. Jones's. Or maybe you don't like candy bars. I can't force you to buy it. All I can do is put the product out there. All right? The product is there. You've been talking to me about American journalism, and I have conceded to you that in many aspects American journalism is going through difficult times. Nevertheless, it's all there if people want to look for it. It can be found, but we can't hold a gun to their heads and say, "You must read the *New York Times*. Or you must watch *Nightline*." No they mustn't. They do whatever they damned well please. And if the consequence of that is going to be that the United States goes through some difficult times over the next five, or ten, or twenty, or fifty years, then eventually if not they, then their children will say, "You know something, we need to pay a little more attention to what is going on overseas."

As I mentioned, the interview began with a lesson in formulating an answerable question:

Assess the prewar coverage leading up to going into Iraq.

When you assess prewar coverage, what are we assessing? Are we assessing the *New York Times* and *USA Today*, or are we assessing the *Wall Street Journal*? Are we assessing the Bill O'Reilly program, are we assessing CNN, MSNBC, *Nightline*, ABC as a whole? They all did it their own way.

Assess the main networks, because they reach the largest audience.

True. Even there, I'm not being argumentative with you, but what is unique about American media is that there is so much of it. If people were watching Fox News in the run-up to the war, they will have gotten one impression. If they were watching *Nightline*, they might have gotten a somewhat different impression. If they were watching Jim Lehrer's broadcast on PBS, they might have gotten a different impression yet again. I just feel terribly uncomfortable giving an across-the-board assessment of how American television did.

Let's make it more specific then. Can you assess the broadcast coverage of the reasons given for going to war? Assess your own network's coverage.

It ranges from the sort of fragmentary coverage that comes with a program that does reports in one-and-a-half- and two-minute pieces to an hour and a half. Six weeks before the war began, we did a program on *Nightline* that was a town meeting that asked the simple question: Why now? Why do we need to go to war? What are the causes behind it? We actually did it over at the Church of the Presidents, and we had a largely military audience. I still remember Senator Carl Levin was on one side and Senator John McCain was on the other side, but the issue that I was raising at the time was "I understand all the reasons that have been given, but what's magic about now? Why not six months from now? Why not a year from now? Why not two years from now?" Does that constitute the totality of our coverage? Of course not, but we were raising questions like that. For *Nightline* to raise questions, that's our bread and butter. That's what we do. So if you want to be critical of the coverage of what the American media did, it's going to be a little more difficult if you limit yourself to *Nightline* because we reflected some of the doubts that people were raising at the time. But again, if I were doing our evening news broadcast or doing *Good Morning America* or doing some other program that deals in shorter pieces, it would have been much more difficult for me to do that.

What do you think of the criticism that the American press is getting because of the weapons of mass destruction, for example? People are criticizing the media saying that the tough questions weren't asked. Dan Rather told the BBC that even he refrained from asking the tough questions and from putting people's feet to the fire about that. What do you think?

I think that if we had waited a year, do you think that our friends in France or in Germany or in Russia would then have been satisfied and said, "OK, you waited a year. A year is reasonable." What would have happened in that year? At the end of that year, we would have been precisely where we are today. No weapons of mass destruction would have been found. The only difference, of course, would have been that the Bush administration would have adamantly said, "All right, we waited a year, quite clearly the Saddam regime has been very skilled, Iraq is a large country, there are many places to hide these weapons of mass destruction, the inspectors have not been able to find them." They would have simply argued that the rationale for war was even greater after a year than it was before. The response would not have been "Well, we've waited a year, the inspectors have done another year's worth of inspecting, they still haven't found any weapons of mass destruction, I guess we were wrong." We have been in Iraq now with 150,000 or 135,000 American troops for fifteen months and they have found nothing. And there are still people within the administration who are saying, "Ah yes, but we're not finished yet. We haven't looked everywhere yet." You think it would have been any different if the troops had been replaced by UN inspectors during that time?

I guess people are expecting a process. The process would be that the president says we have to go to war because of this, and then that rationale is looked into. That raison de guerre or causus belli would be checked out. Is it true that Saddam has weapons of mass destruction? Is it true or not that Saddam Hussein is connected to al Qaeda?

When you ask the question, you imply that there is an easily attainable answer. The question was: are there weapons of mass destruction? My point is we have now been in Iraq for over a year and those who were inclined to believe that there were weapons of mass destruction in the first place are insisting that they still believe it to this day, despite all the evidence to the contrary. Those who believe that Saddam had a relationship with al Qaeda, with Osama bin Laden, continue to believe it to this day, despite all the evidence to the contrary. It hasn't changed the true believers on either side. Quite frankly, I must tell you that I don't believe that there has been an adequate discussion of the real reasons for the war, which I think have little or nothing to do with al Qaeda, little or nothing to do with weapons of mass destruction, and everything to do with the fear that instability and chaos in the Persian Gulf would be devastating. When people talk about oil having been the reason for the war, I think they are correct. Not in the limited sense in which they sometimes say it. Not in the sense that America is trying to acquire for itself access to Iraq's oil wells. They could have had that access at any time simply by saying to Saddam Hussein, "OK, we raise the embargo. The embargo is lifted, we will now buy your oil." We could have had the oil all along; that wasn't the problem. The great fear is that America has lost its surrogate, who was once the shah of Iran. We no longer have Iran. America is in danger of losing its surrogate in Saudi Arabia. The Saudi royal family is in danger of losing its control. America needs to have a place from which it can assure the stability of the Persian Gulf. Ironically, I would think that that would be of as much interest to our friends in France and our friends in Germany and our friends in Japan as it should be to the American public. Stability in the Persian Gulf is one of the few genuine strategic interests that we and the Europeans and the Japanese have in common.

Now why is it that that can't be reported to the American public in a way that really sinks in?

I've said it many times. I've said it on the air many times. It sure shows how little influence I really have.

I have heard some comments from high-level colleagues like *Harper's* publisher John MacArthur, who told us he thinks there's a problem of no demand for the kind of analysis and questioning in a timely fashion because the educational level in this country is sinking and sinking fast. People don't read anymore and they don't want to watch anything complicated on television. Do you agree with that?

Oh, sure. It's not true of all Americans and not true of the country across the board, but I don't think that you can have had the sort of explosion in television that has existed in this country over the past ten years, I don't think you can have the sort of downward spiral of appealing to the worst instincts of people both in terms of sex and violence, without some negative results. Having said that, I think there's more good material available on television today, certainly more than there was some forty-odd years ago when I began in this business.

Are you talking in terms of journalism?

I'm talking in terms of everything.

> **I just read your book, in which you said American television is floating in crap, literally, that's what you said.**

I didn't say that literally.

> **Well, I read that in your book.**

You may have read only part of what I said, because if memory serves, and I did write it, I think what I have been saying all along is the bad television is worse than anything we've ever had, and the good television is better than the best of what we've ever had. Look, when I joined ABC forty-one years ago, we had one black-and-white, fifteen-minute newscast every night. That was it. That was the extent of our news coverage. Now we have two hours of *Good Morning America* in the morning, we have half an hour of *World News Tonight*, we have half an hour of *Nightline*, we have *20/20*, we have *Primetime*, we have *This Week with George Stephanopoulos*. Just the sheer volume of news coverage that is available on ABC today is, conservatively speaking, ten or fifteen times what it was in 1963. And some of that is pretty damned good.

> **Are you saying that the amount of quality information has also increased with the volume?**

What I'm saying is the volume of crap and the volume of quality have both increased.

> **So if people really have access to good information, why do you think there was a *Washington Post* poll[1] that came out after we'd gone into Iraq that showed that almost half of the American population believed that Saddam Hussein was connected to 9/11?**

Let me tell you a little story. Where are we here?

> **Where are we?**

Yes, where are we?

> **What, in America?**

No, no, no, no.

> **Here literally?**

Right here.

Right here at ABC News?

Which city are we in?

Washington, DC.

Washington, DC. Amazing. I have been doing *Nightline* now for twenty-four and a half years. At the beginning of each program, an announcer says, "And now, joining us *from Washington* is Ted Koppel. At the end of each program I say, "For all of us here at ABC News *in Washington*, I'm Ted Koppel, goodnight." All right?

OK.

Twenty-four years of doing that, two hundred fifty-six times a year, it works out to about six thousand programs times two, once at the beginning and once at the end, and that's twelve thousand times. You know what happens to me down here every day? Someone runs into me at the supermarket and says, "Ted, what are you doing down here in Washington?" I say, "Well, I live here in Washington." "Oh, and you commute to New York?" "No," I say, "I do the program from Washington." "I didn't realize you did the program from Washington." And you are surprised that simply because something is reported on television people don't automatically internalize it? That they don't take it in and understand it and examine it critically? With people, it goes in one ear and comes out the other. People watch television while they're brushing their teeth, taking a shower, taking care of other bodily functions, making love to their wives or their girlfriends. They don't pay very much attention to television. It's not an activity.

Are you kidding?

I'm not kidding.

I think Americans are intravenously connected to their TVs.

Oh, they have it on all the time. It's there all the time. But do they really hear what's going on? Unless of course it's *American Idol* and they're . . . as to which song, which young woman's . . . there they can tell you every last detail. But put them in front of the television set with a newscast on and ask them at the end of that newscast what was reported, and for most part, they pay little or no attention.

Do you realize how disconcerting that is to the rest of the world who look at the United States as the nine-hundred-pound gorilla on the

planet? There's a concern here about American people not really being aware of the American presence around the world.

Oh, and you're surprised by that?

No, I'm not surprised. Essentially, what you're saying to me is, "Look we're doing our job, they're just not paying attention."

I don't want to suggest that we did a perfect job before the war. I'm simply saying to the degree that people are saying now, "How come you didn't raise any questions about the weapons of mass destruction? The connection to al Qaeda?" Whatever it is. We did. Did we raise them as forcefully as we should have? Did we raise them night after night after night after night? No, we didn't. And I must tell you quite frankly, if you ask me did I believe that there were weapons of mass destruction in Iraq, absolutely I believed it. I believed it because I knew that when UNSCOM[2] left Iraq back in 1998, they were still reporting, and defectors who defected to Jordan from Saddam Hussein's government were reporting that there were still weapons of mass destruction. There was no evidence that they had been destroyed. Saddam should have known that if those weapons had not been destroyed that he was in real danger of being invaded again by the United States, and yet he continued to refuse to give the evidence of having disposed of those weapons. Do we know to this day what happened to those weapons? We know they existed at one time. There was no question about that. It's not that that was made up. Hallabjah is not a figment of the American government's imagination. Back in 1988, when he was our guy, when we were giving him satellite photographs so that he could better fight the Iranians, Saddam Hussein used chemical weapons against the Kurds in Hallabjah. We know he had them; we know he used them. What happened to them? We still don't know.

The weapons of mass destruction is kind of a long discussion, too, because it started out with weapons of mass destruction being nuclear weapons and then it sort of morphed into nuclear weapons and chemical weapons.

No, it didn't morph. There were aspects of the story, which, I must say, are difficult. First of all, there would be rhetorical questions raised by people like Dr. Condoleezza Rice:[3] "Do we want our first indication of a terrorist attack to be a mushroom cloud?" Well, let me think about that. No, I don't think I want the first indication of a terrorist attack to be a mushroom cloud. Is what you're saying that Saddam Hussein has nuclear weapons? "No, but we think that he could have them fairly soon." "How soon?" "Well, maybe within a year or two." All right, is that a "raison de guerre" as you put it? Is that a causus belli? Is that reason enough for us to go to war?

Well, you do know about the International Atomic Energy Agency report that Tony Blair cited in a joint press conference with President Bush on September 7, 2002. John MacArthur and his guys at *Harper's Magazine* did some research and two days later said that this report didn't even exist.

Do you know what happened after Desert Storm?[4] After the first operation against Iraq when the CIA had reported that Saddam had nothing in terms of developments for nuclear weapons? And then after the war? One of his sons-in-law defected to the Jordanians and all of a sudden we discovered that he was quite far along in his nuclear development. It is not, after all, a new process.

It's not a perfect science, no.

A, it's not a perfect science and B, the Israelis bombed their nuclear reactors in Iraq back in June 1981,[5] so it's not as though this is something new that Saddam was after.

Yes, but was that the causus belli?

I've already told you what I thought was the causus belli. But when everyone in the administration tells you one thing, two things, three things . . .

You don't just take their word for it, do you?

No, I don't just take their word for it. But when they tell me why they're going to war, I certainly have to give proper deference to . . . if the president says I'm going to war for reasons A, B and C, I can't very well stand there and say, "The president is not telling you the truth, the actual reason that he's going to war is some reason he hasn't even mentioned." I as a reporter at least have to say, "Here's what the president is saying. Here's what the secretary of defense is saying. Here's what the director of the CIA is saying. Here's what the members of Congress are saying." And indeed, when everyone at that point who has access to the classified information is with more or less one voice agreeing that, yes, there appears to be evidence that Saddam Hussein still has weapons of mass destruction—maybe not nuclear, but certainly chemical and probably biological—are you suggesting that the entire American press corps then say, "Well, horse manure."

Well, they've been lied to before. A lot.

Yes we have.

By presidents about causus belli.

Sure. Absolutely.

The Vietnam War comes to mind.

You know, we do not have a separate role in the framework of American government that says no matter what anyone in the US government is telling you, if your instinct tells you that it's horse manure, every day say, horse manure, horse manure, horse manure.

Well, it has to be checked out as quickly as possible.

Yes.

Then horse manure comments.

Where would you have checked it out? Because British intelligence was telling Tony Blair the same thing. German intelligence was telling . . .

Well, doesn't referring to a nonexistent International Atomic Agency Report raise red flags?

Yes, when it finally becomes known.

That was two days later . . .

All right. Just this morning I saw Dr. Condoleezza Rice on the air talking about Mr. Ahmed Chalabi[6] as though "He was never our guy. We don't have a horse or a dog in this fight. If the Iraqi people want him, that's fine, if they don't want him, that's fine with us, too." Is there no sense of embarrassment sometimes about what was said before or what was done before? Clearly not. I mean, she is able to go on American television and say this with a completely straight face, "We, you know, the president never supported Ahmed Chalabi anymore than we supported anybody else," when in point of fact he was flown into Iraq aboard an American military plane with several hundred of his own military supporters equipped with American uniforms and American weapons.

Right. And did anybody say to her, "With all due respect that's not true"?

No, nobody did this morning because it was Katie Couric who was interviewing her on the *Today Show*. Now, one question for you: Why do you think that so many members of the Bush cabinet are more than happy to go on the *Today Show* and not happy to come on *Nightline*?

Because you're going to . . .

Because I'm going to ask her that question, that's right. On a morning program when you've only got two and a half minutes for the interview or three minutes for the interview, it's probably not going to get asked.

Have you ever been censored, Ted?

No.

You've been able to ask any question, do any show you wanted to do.

Anything I want to do.

Throughout your entire career.

Throughout my entire career. I have never been censored. I've been at ABC News for forty-one years, and throughout that time I have never been censored. I have always been allowed to do whatever programs I want to do. I have only once been asked by the secretary of state not to carry a story, and that was for good and sufficient reason. I'm happy to tell you what that was. It was back when I was diplomatic correspondent. The American hostages had been taken in Tehran and I got wind of the story that some of the hostages had escaped from the US Embassy and had made it to the Canadian Embassy. And the secretary of state called me and asked me not to run the story on what seemed to me to be the reasonable predicate that if the Iranians knew that these Americans were in the Canadian Embassy, they would probably storm the Canadian Embassy and take them.

Well, that's reasonable.

So I didn't run it. But that's the only time in forty-one years that I've ever been asked not to run a story.

Now, you did something recently that got your show pulled off a few stations. Could you talk about that?

Sure. We made a decision to read the names and show the photographs of what at that point was I believe the seven hundred and twenty-one Americans—military—who had been killed in Iraq up to that day. And a group called the Sinclair Broadcasting Company, which owns a lot of television stations—seven or eight of which are ABC stations—ordered its ABC stations not to carry that program because they thought that running the photographs and giving the names was intended as a political statement on our behalf, that it was an antiwar statement, that it was unpatriotic and therefore they were not going to carry it. That's the bad news. The good news was that the public response was overwhelmingly in favor of what we did. We received somewhere in the neighborhood of eighty thousand e-mails the next day, of which some seventy-odd thousand were positive. We got very strong support from Senator John McCain, who wrote an angry letter denouncing the president of this organization, and within very short order some reporting was done on him and it turned out that he and his group were major contributors to the Bush administration. All in all, I think it worked out quite fairly.

> **What would you say to a European audience that thinks that a lot of censorship goes on in the networks and at the top media outlets that reach large audiences and that there is corporate business pressure as well as pressure from the government that results in censorship on important issues?**

I think you have to be very careful when you use the word censorship. Censorship has a very clear meaning to me. Censorship has the force of law. Censorship involves the government saying, "You cannot report what you want to report. You have to show us everything that you intend to put on the air and we will then decide whether you can or whether you can't." That's censorship. The fact that the Bush administration, like the Clinton administration before it, like every administration I've known in the thirty-two years that I've been working in Washington, tries to influence what gets on the air and what doesn't get on the air—that's not censorship. That's political influence. To the best of my knowledge, that exists in the best of families. That exists in France, in Germany, in Great Britain. There are always people who will try to influence what does get on the air and what doesn't get on the air. What I think ultimately still makes the United States a rather remarkable place in terms of its journalism is that the consumer has a lot of options. If he doesn't like the sort of pro–Bush administration, pro-American tilt of the Fox Network, no one is holding a gun to his head saying, "You have to watch the Fox Network." You can watch PBS, you can listen to NPR, you can watch ABC, NBC, CBS, MSNBC, CNN, the National Geographic Channel—whatever you want. There are scores of newspapers, hundreds of magazines, thousands of books, and they're all available.

Do you think, though, that the network coverage is that different from network to network?

No. I don't. But I don't think that has anything to do with censorship. I think that has to do with commercialism. I think that has to do with what my colleagues and I have learned, to our enormous regret, the American public wants to see. So that if, for example, I wanted to see *Nightline*'s ratings rise dramatically tonight, I know how to do it.

Sit here in your underwear.

No, frankly, that would not do it. I think people would be calling up saying "Put your clothes back on again." But if I were to do tonight's program on the Scott and Laci Peterson case, where this young man stands accused of having murdered his pregnant wife, that would get more people watching. If I were to do a hard-hitting ten-part series on Michael Jackson and his apparent affinity for young boys, that would improve the ratings. If I wanted to do a program on the basketball player Kobe Bryant, and the allegations that he raped a young woman while he was out in Colorado, that would get more of an audience than what *Nightline* does, because night after night after night what we do is cover developing events in Iraq. And by and large, the American public is not terribly interested in that right now. And the fact that we continue to do it has damaged our ratings, and yet, surprise, the Disney Corporation which owns the Disney Company, which owns ABC, and the president of ABC News have been enormously supportive of us doing what we are doing because they feel it's the right thing to do. But where does the pressure come from? The pressure comes from the ratings not doing well. When the ratings don't do well, sponsors don't want to pay as much money for each thirty-second commercial any more, and if the sponsors don't pay as much money anymore, then the Disney Company doesn't earn as much any more.

Does that worry you?

Of course it worries me . . .

That there's no interest in substantive issues . . .

To say there is no interest is a misstatement. After all, we still have four and a half to five million people who watch this program every night. The

Larry King Show, for example, on CNN has roughly one million people who watch it every night. CNN, although it gets a lot of publicity for being the network that everybody watches, on average has about 330,000 people who watch it. There are still a lot of folks—I mean five million people every night is a lot of people. Would I prefer that it were ten million? You bet. Once upon a time, it used to be.

What happened?

What happened is CNN, MSNBC, Fox, HBO, Arts and Entertainment, Showtime.

What's your assessment of Fox?

My assessment is that it was absolutely needed at the time, that indeed there was too much homogeneity, that what was on the other networks did tend, as you suggested with one of your questions a moment ago, to reflect too much what was on all the other networks. Not because we go to the same ideological school, but there was a certain laziness there. Fox came along and said, "We sense an appetite for more conservative coverage, more patriotic coverage, for giving people a reflection of what is really in their hearts, rather than what these elitists in Washington want to report." Lo and behold, they've done very well. So clearly there was a need for it.

Talk to us about being embedded. You were the only one who seemed to have the guts to do it.

There were a lot of guys who were embedded.

Of your stature, let me add.

Age, is what you're saying, of my age.

OK, you caught me.

What about it?

Tell me about the experience. There's been a lot of discussion about it, and I wanted to hear whether you think it was a valuable way of covering the war.

Sure. Look, I've heard all the same criticism you have and will talk about it. One of the problems with the criticism is that it takes each slice of embedded coverage and treats it as though that slice existed alone, in a vacuum. I was with the division command of the Third Infantry Division.

They occupied what was called the "Point of the Spear." They were the first big outfit into Iraq, the first big outfit into Baghdad. My coverage reflected what I was getting with that particular unit. But my coverage was augmented by what colleagues of mine were doing with other outfits, what colleagues of mine were doing covering the State Department, covering the White House, covering what Europeans were saying, what Asians were saying. The coverage that ABC got as a whole was not dependent on what this one embed had.

Was it terrifying?

Sure, there were terrifying moments. But the point I want to make is, I had access. . . . I've been covering wars, after all, since 1966. I covered the Vietnam War for three and a half years. I've covered about ten other wars since then. I have never had better access. It was possible for me to go into the command tent when the commanding general of the Third Infantry Division was getting his intelligence briefing in the morning, when he was on the radio with his battalion commanders every morning getting their battlefield reports of what was happening. I heard them as he heard them. I heard what he was saying to them, I heard what they were saying to him, and I was about as well informed as I've ever been in my life. Now, did I see a lot of dead Iraqis? No. You know why? Because most of them were killed forty miles away by rockets that travel forty miles before they explode. Or because the unit would be calling in close air support and these people would be killed by planes, and by the time we had moved those forty miles through the desert, what we saw were burned-out cars, burned-out trucks, burned-out tanks, every once in a while a body, but most of the time the bodies had already been removed. So again, the criticism is, when you're embedded, you're not showing the casualties of the Iraqis. True enough. Never saw them. If I'd seen them, I would have shown them.

Do you think there has been enough coverage of that angle?

No. But, you know, again, you just asked me a moment ago, was I scared. And yes there were times when I was scared. It's a lot less scary to be with twenty thousand members of a heavy armored division than it is before the war to say, "OK, I volunteer to stay in . . ."—where are you going to stay—Baghdad was probably the only place, unless you were working for Al Arabiya.[7] And even that was a pretty gutsy choice. "I'll stay in Baghdad and see what happens when the United States starts firing its cruise missiles at Baghdad." Those guys would have been in a position to show the casualties. The guys who were coming up with the invading force, they're going to see what the troops see. And we did.

Your assessment then is that there wasn't really any pressure put on the networks to refrain from showing dead bodies, either dead Americans or . . .

I had what became a rather well-known discussion with my colleague Charlie Gibson, because one day Charlie said on the air, "You know, I don't think we should be showing the bodies of the dead, or for that matter, showing the wounded." And I said, "I'm sorry, but I disagree. I think it's absolutely essential that we show the bodies of the dead and of the wounded. I'm not saying that we show the faces of the American dead. We should be very careful that we are not the ones to inform the families back home by showing the body of one of their loved ones, but to pretend to be covering a war without showing the consequences of war is not to cover it at all." We got into a lively debate and there was a lot of newspaper coverage of that afterward, so yes, of course I believe that you show the dead and the wounded.

What do you think of that flap over the pictures of the coffins?

Ludicrous.

Talk about your experiences in Vietnam and the Gulf War in terms of coverage. Do you think there was a difference in terms of access and quality of the coverage?

A couple of observations. Number one, I was forty years younger when I covered the Vietnam War than when I covered this latest war. And, I'm managing editor and anchor of this program now, so I have a certain access to senior officers now that I didn't have when I was in my mid to late twenties. So in that sense the access was a lot greater this time around. But back in Vietnam we had total access. I mean access in terms of traveling with the troops, going to the front with the troops, being there while the troops were fighting and sitting on the helicopter as the wounded were being evacuated. We were with them more or less everywhere they went. There were certain restrictions put on us in terms of covering Special Forces because they were going on forays into Cambodia and that wasn't supposed to be happening. But we got around that. I walked into Cambodia from Thailand at a time when we were not supposed to be in Cambodia. I reported for the first time that American planes were on bombing missions and I had video of it both in Laos and in Cambodia. But to do that I had to cross the Mekong in a Pirogue Motor and leave my soundman behind as a hostage with the Thai authorities who wanted to be sure that we were coming back again. So there were things that you had to do to cover the stories in those days that frankly as a man in my sixties I'm not going to be doing anymore. But access? Yes, we had access.

And you would say that the access to the Iraq war is comparable for the young reporters?

In some respects it was better in Vietnam, because in Vietnam there were no limitations put on you. The embedding process entails saying, "OK, you're going to be with that unit and you have to stay with that unit until the fighting is over." In Vietnam, you stayed with a unit for as long as you wanted to and then you got out any way that you could. Usually that meant getting out on a helicopter that was bringing out the dead and the wounded. That's how you got out.

What about the Gulf War?

The Gulf War was sort of a fiasco from the point of view of coverage because basically the Pentagon denied access most of the time. The people who really got access during the Gulf War were those who had the courage and the creativity to go off and travel with the Egyptian army or travel with the Saudis. You weren't getting much access by traveling with the Americans. The upshot of that—and one of the reasons that the embedding procedure was created—was here was the Gulf War, which was a huge military success, and the Pentagon suddenly looked around and said, "Hey, we did great, right? Where are the pictures? Oh, that's right. We wouldn't allow the press to go with us." A lot of the generals who were commanding that operation came out and said, "That was a mistake. We needed to have people there to record what we did, because it was really good." The more sophisticated among them said, "Even when we do something wrong, it's useful to have the press there, because there are going to be charges flying from all over the world that what we did was not only wrong but was far worse than it was. And it's helpful to have somebody on the scene who is relatively objective, who can say, 'Yes, the American troops made a mistake, but they did it because of A, B, C, and D.'" So the decision was made the second time around of invading the Persian Gulf that the press was going to be there. That's another reason why I'm absolutely convinced that the administration genuinely believed that there were weapons of mass destruction. They wanted us there to show that. They thought they were going to be there. I thought they were going to be there.

So what do you say to Helen Thomas[8] who says that she thinks the press was in a coma before we went to war?

I love Helen and you're not going to draw me into a fight with Helen. Helen is a grande dame of American journalism and she is entitled to whatever opinion she holds. I don't think we were in a coma. I think it was perfectly legitimate to believe—as I started to say before—as French intelligence believed, as German intelligence believed, as Russian intelligence believed—that there were weapons of mass destruction. I know of no intelligence outfit in the world . . .

The Israelis, too?

The Israelis, too. Now, did the Israelis believe it or were the Israelis simply saying it because they wanted to encourage the Americans to come in? I don't know. But I'm inclined to believe that, yes, the Israelis believed it. Why did they believe it? Because there had been weapons of mass destruction there. We knew they were there and there was no evidence that they had been destroyed. And if after all Saddam wanted to avoid an invasion, the easiest way of doing that would be to say, "Yes, we have a few tons of weapons of mass destruction. Here, take them out. Look anywhere you want to look."

Do you really think that would have stopped the invasion?

Yes. If he had done that early enough, I don't think that the United States could have gone ahead with it then. I really don't.

I sort of wonder if something else wouldn't have popped up. Some other raison de guerre.

Would have been tough beforehand. Would have been very, very difficult. But as I say, the problem that I see is those who say, "We should have given it another six months so that the inspectors could do their work." At the end of six months, the administration would have said, "We haven't proved anything yet, all we've proved is that they're well hidden."

I know you hate sweeping questions so I hesitate to ask, but I'm going to ask anyway. . . .

You ask whatever you want and I'll answer whatever I want.

If you were to say, "American journalism falls short here, generally speaking, and it's great there." Can you answer that question?

Sure. Over the course of a long lifetime in journalism I've covered events in about eighty-seven different countries. Roughly speaking, journalism operates under one of three systems or a combination of the three. It either operates under a dictatorship, as, for example, it did under Saddam Hussein, or as it does today under Kim Jong Il in North Korea. It operates in a theocracy as it does today, for example, in Iran. Or it operates under the capitalist umbrella. Sometimes you get a combination of those things. There can be a partial dictatorship, which is also materialistic and capitalistic. But by and large it's one of those three systems. Of the three systems, all have their—well, I don't know that there are any advantages under dictatorship or theocracy. But all have their disadvantages. The one that has the fewest disadvantages is capitalism. Under capitalism, in the marketplace, all of these operations that we work for have to make a profit. If they don't make a profit, they either go out of business or we go off the air. Usually what happens is we go off the air. The fact that the marketplace has become even more competitive than it has ever been in the past simply means that there is more and more pressure to produce programming that will hold on to a smaller and smaller share of the audience. That's a problem. That is a major problem for the United States. But again, you can find interesting, thoughtful, provocative news more easily here in the United States than I think you can find it anywhere in the world. The best of French television may be better than the best of American television. The best of French journalism may be better in newspapers than the best of American journalism. Forgive me if I'm chauvinistic enough to say I don't think so. I frankly think the best in American journalism is as good as any in the world. But the fact of the matter is you can find it anywhere, including, I might add, if you want to, and if you speak French, you can buy *France Soir* or *Paris Match*, or you can watch French television via satellite. It's all available. If people don't watch or read it, it's because they don't choose to or they don't want to go to the trouble. But one thing that still exists in this country is the freedom of choice to read, or watch, or listen to whatever you want to.

What's your assessment of the state of investigative journalism and foreign affairs reporting?

Investigative reporting as you know is time-consuming and expensive. So again, here we are talking about how every large organization has become a little smaller because it has been fragmented. There is less money available. That tends to reduce the amount of investigative journalism that is done by the traditional sources. Having said that, what people can do today that they could never do when I was a young reporter is they can go out on their own. My son or one of my daughters can go out with a small video camera, shoot her own story, come back, edit it on her own computer, put it on the Internet, hit the send button, and it is available to everyone in the world who wants to watch it. That's a network.

Yes, but can she air it on her dad's show that has five million people?

No, no.

That's a critical mass audience.

No, no, no. What I'm saying is that what we have lost in terms of the relative power of the networks and the relative willingness of the networks to do investigative journalism has been compensated for in part by the Internet, by the capacity now of individuals or small groups if they want to set up a blog site on the Internet and communicate with like-minded people about issues that they're interested in. That didn't exist twenty years ago. What they can do is create their own documentaries. I could have gone out with a film camera when I was twenty-five years old and shot some film and written a script and edited it together and then I would have walked around with my little package of film and said, "Please sir, would somebody put this on the air?" And nobody would have put it on the air.

Yes, but you realize that unless it hits a critical mass, it's a work in a paper bag.

Exactly. But what I'm saying is that at least today you can put it out there, and if a very talented twenty-five-year-old comes along and puts out a piece of video and people say, "Wow! Did you see that?" then eventually, you know what's going to happen? Ted Koppel is going to pick up the phone and call that person and say, "Can we buy that from you, because that was really good and I'd like to put it on *Nightline*." And that person very quickly . . . in other words, it's simply an avenue that is available today that was not available twenty years ago.

What about foreign affairs reporting?

Americans have always been a little bit narrow-minded about foreign reporting. When I say Americans, I realize I'm generalizing. You can pick up the *New York Times*, the *Los Angeles Times*, the *Wall Street Journal*, or the *Washington Post* every day and you will see that foreign reporting is alive and well and flourishing. By the same token, I'm working for a network—and it wouldn't make any difference if I was working for CBS or NBC, because they've all done the same thing—who have a fraction of the people overseas today that we had overseas when I was a foreign correspondent. Back in those days we might have had twenty or more; now we may have five. And again, why? Because it's expensive. Because it's time-consuming. And because in the final analysis, if we are not at war, Americans tend to be a little bit chauvinistic and view the world with blinders and are not terribly sophisticated about how what happens in a certain part of Europe can have an impact on what happens in Latin America or on what happens in the United States. In this age of international terrorism, I think that is changing, but only in a very narrow fashion.

Well, is that a good headspace for the nine-hundred-pound gorilla on this planet to be in?

By nine-hundred-pound gorilla you mean what?

America. I just feel that the lack of interest on the part of American citizens in world affairs or their lack of involvement in world affairs via influencing government leaders is problematic given the power of this nation.

Sure. Here's how the system works and you know it. I create one candy bar. Mr. Jones creates another candy bar. Mr. Smith creates a third candy bar. We put our candy bars out there and we say to you, "Buy our candy bar." And you pick. Maybe you pick mine. Maybe you pick Mr. Smith's. Maybe you pick Mr. Jones's. Or maybe you don't like candy bars. I can't force you to buy it. All I can do is put the product out there. All right? The product is there. You've been talking to me about American journalism and I have conceded to you that in many aspects American journalism is going through difficult times. Nevertheless, it's all there if people want to look for it. It can be found, but we can't hold a gun to their heads and say, "You must read the *New York Times*. Or you must watch *Nightline*." No they mustn't. They do whatever they damned well please. And if the consequence of that is going to be that the United States goes through some difficult times over the next five or ten or twenty or fifty years, then eventually if not they, then their children will say, "You know something, we need to pay a little more attention to what is going on overseas." It will be like every other product that is sold in America. When people perceive a need for it, they will buy it. When they perceive a desire for it, they will buy it. But you can't force them to. All we can do is put it out there.

Twenty years down the line, do you see American journalism changed at all?

Oh, absolutely. Radically changed, because the technology is radically changing. Again, today you have tens of thousands of people. Let me put it another way. In theory, all Americans have a right to be journalists. Every single one. When I was a kid, that was the theory—everyone could be a journalist, but you still had to be able to communicate that. You had to be able to transmit the message, and if you didn't have a printing press or a television network or a radio network, you could go and turn out a few mimeographs in your garage and stand on the street corner and pass it out but you didn't really have the means of communicating that to a mass audience. Today, you do. That's a huge difference. Now, every American not only has the theoretical right and capacity to be a journalist, they also have the technological availability to get it out there. Wherever they want to. That's huge.

If you were to pose the question to me personally, I would confess to you that much of what has always made me want to do what I do has been the adrenaline rush. The adventures of covering a war are clearly a part of that. I don't think that's why most people get into it anymore. I think here, too, there has been a change among young people. Many people today want to get into journalism because they perceive it as a way to become famous and make a lot of money. It's not of course. It really isn't. Probably 95 percent of the men and women who work in journalism in the United States are barely making a living. They're not doing very well at it. Those are actually the people I admire the most. You should get into journalism because you love it, because you can't believe that there is anything else in the world that is more exiting, more interesting, more fascinating. That's not necessarily the way things are today.

TED KOPPEL, a forty-two-year veteran of ABC News, was named anchor of *Nightline* when the broadcast was introduced in March 1980. In his anchor role, Mr. Koppel is the principal on-air reporter and inter-viewer for television's first late-night network news program. In addition Mr. Koppel is the program's managing editor.

Each weekday evening, from 11:35 PM to 12:05 AM (ET), *Nightline* provides in-depth reporting on one or more of the major stories in the news through a combination of live interviews with newsmakers and background reports from *Nightline* reporters in the field. In its twenty-fourth year on the air, *Nightline* is still considered one of the finest inno-vations in broadcast news. In 1993 the *Philadelphia Inquirer* said ". . . '*Nightline*,' frequently a beacon of responsibility in a frequently irre-sponsible medium, proves that television can be an invaluable part of the American system."

Nightline's success is due in large part to the exemplary Ted Koppel, who has established a reputation among viewers, critics, and his peers as a journalist par excellence. Mr. Koppel has been cited by the *Wall Street Journal* as "the preeminent TV interviewer in America," while the *Los Angeles Times* refers to him as "the undisputed reigning lion of tough TV interview journalism."

In March 2003 Mr. Koppel was embedded with the army's Third Infantry Division for five weeks, reporting first from Kuwait, and then moving with the division across the border into Iraq and finally into Baghdad, chronicling the fall of the city. The *New York Times* said, "Mr. Koppel brings a cool intelligence and perspective to war coverage." Mr. Koppel and the *Nightline* team also reported the division's move through Kuwait, across the border into Iraq, and to Baghdad in a one-hour prime-time ABC News special, "Tip of the Spear," in April 2003.

Mr. Koppel has won every major broadcasting award, including forty-one Emmy Awards, eleven George Foster Peabody Awards, twelve duPont-Columbia Awards, ten Overseas Press Club Awards, two George Polk Awards, and two Sigma Delta Chi Awards, the highest honor bestowed for public service by the Society of Professional Journalists. In addition, in 2002 the George Foster Peabody Awards for Broadcast Excel-lence recognized *Nightline* with a Lifetime Achievement Award, citing outstanding long-form news presentations for more than twenty years.

Mr. Koppel was honored with the first Goldsmith Lifetime Achieve-ment Award for Excellence in Journalism by the Joan Shorenstein Barone Center on the Press, Politics, and Public Policy at Harvard University. In 1997 he was awarded the Fred Friendly First Amendment Award from Quinnipiac College. In addition, he was the recipient of the prestigious

Gabriel Personal Achievement Award from the National Catholic Association of Broadcasters and Communicators. In 1985 Mr. Koppel was honored with the first Gold Baton in the history of the duPont-Columbia Awards for *Nightline*'s week-long series originating from South Africa.

Mr. Koppel was named the first recipient of the Sol Taishoff Award presented by *Broadcasting Magazine*. He was voted best interviewer on radio or TV by the *Washington Journalism Review* in 1987 and was named Broadcaster of the Year by the International Television and Radio Society. In January 2002 he was awarded the Fred Friendly Award for Excellence in Television Journalism from Amnesty International. Mr. Koppel is an inductee of the Broadcasting Hall of Fame.

In 1994 Mr. Koppel was named a Chevalier de l'Ordre des Arts et des Lettres from the Republic of France. He has received honorary degrees from Syracuse University, Colgate University, University of South Carolina, American University, New England School of Law, Fairfield University, Middlebury College, Georgetown School of Law, Dartmouth College, Knox College, Howard University, Duke University, Saint Louis University, University of Pennsylvania, Tufts University, Loyola University, Johns Hopkins University, Catholic University, Brandeis University, and Fordham University.

Mr. Koppel is the author of three books: *Off Camera: Private Thoughts Made Public* was published in 2000; in 1996 he coauthored *Nightline: History and the Making of Television* with Kyle Gibson; and in 1977 he coauthored, with Marvin Kalb, the best-selling novel *In the National Interest*.

Before his *Nightline* assignment, Mr. Koppel worked as an anchor, foreign and domestic correspondent, and bureau chief for ABC News.

From 1971 to 1980 he was ABC News's chief diplomatic correspondent and for a two-year period, beginning in 1975, he anchored the *ABC Saturday Night News*. His diplomatic assignment included covering former secretary of state Henry Kissinger, a tour of duty during which Mr. Koppel traveled more than a quarter of a million miles in the days of Kissinger's "shuttle diplomacy."

Before being named diplomatic correspondent, Mr. Koppel was ABC News's Hong Kong bureau chief from 1969 to 1971. In 1968 he became Miami bureau chief for ABC News, where his assignments included covering Latin America. On the political beat, he has had a major reporting role in every presidential campaign since 1964.

Mr. Koppel joined ABC News in New York in 1963 as a full-time general assignment correspondent, at the age of twenty-three. Prior to joining ABC News, he worked at WMCA Radio in New York City, where he was a desk assistant and an occasional off-air reporter.

A native of Lancashire, England, Mr. Koppel moved to the United States with his parents when he was thirteen years old. He holds a BS from Syracuse University and an MA in mass communications research and political science from Stanford. He is married to the former Grace Anne Dorney of New York City. They reside in Potomac, Maryland, and have four children.

NOTES

1. In a September 6, 2003, article on the poll titled "Hussein Link to 9/11 Lingers in Many Minds," *Washington Post* reporters Dana Milbank and Claudia Deane wrote: "Sixty-nine percent of Americans said they thought it at least likely that Hussein was involved in the attacks on the World Trade Center and the Pentagon." http://www .washingtonpost.com/wpsrv/politics/polls/vault/stories/data082303.htm.

2. This is the United Nations Special Commission, which was mandated to "carry out immediate on-site inspections of Iraq's biological, chemical and missile capabilities" and to "assist the Director General of the IAEA [International Atomic Energy Agency]" to do the same with respect to "the nuclear field." http://www.un.org/Depts/unscom/ unscom.htm#MANDATE.

3. Rice was national security advisor to President Bush at that time.

4. "Operation Desert Storm" was the name given to the first Gulf War in which an international coalition led by the US military attacked Iraq in January 1991 to drive Saddam Hussein out of Kuwait. Hussein attacked Kuwait after claiming that the Kuwaitis were overproducing oil and thereby destroying Iraq's economy and that they were stealing oil via slant drilling into Iraq's Rumaila oil field.

5. It was called Operation Babylon. On June 7, 1981, Israeli F-16s bombed Iraq's Tammuz-1 nuclear reactor.

6. A British-educated former banker, Ahmed Chalabi has been the leader of the anti-Saddam Iraqi National Congress, which was started with US government funding in the early 1990s for the purpose of overthrowing Saddam. Chalabi received large sums of money from the US government for his activities and was a source of faulty prewar intelligence. Although he has no industry experience, he is currently acting oil minister for the new Iraqi government.

7. Al Arabiya is a twenty-four-hour news channel that was launched in March 2003 and is based in Dubai Media City.

8. Once considered "the dean of the White House press corps," Thomas is now a columnist for Hearst Newspapers. See chapter 5 in this book.

2

INSIDE THE
RATINGS VISE

Courtesy of Tom Yellin

TOM YELLIN
President and
Executive Producer,
P.J. Productions
Interviewed May 2004

You don't survive in the shark-tank environment of a television network for three decades and then wind up with the plum assignment
of executive producer of documentaries for ABC's star correspondent,
Peter Jennings, without a certain set of skills. Tom Yellin is a quintessential network guy: smart, Ivy League–educated (Harvard), politically
astute, tough, and accustomed to working under pressure. He comes
across as very affable, and as the forty-something father of four daughters, I imagine that serves him well at home. Professionally, Yellin lives
in a vise where he is constantly squeezed between meeting the highest
possible standards of journalism via producing programs of public

48

interest and importance, and delivering programming that grabs a big audience and makes money for ABC Television. In this interview, he speaks openly and in detail about the pressures he faces as a production executive, giving the reader a chance to sit in his seat and vicariously experience his circumstances. As you will see, the job is prestigious and pays well, but it is far from easy. Yellin doesn't ask for sympathy. He has a very practical attitude about dealing with what he doesn't like about network television, and he makes no excuses for anybody or anything in the network news business, including the fact that it is a business. When he talks about network audiences, he sometimes refers to them as consumers. Having said that, Yellin clearly loves his job, cares deeply about his profession, and feels strongly about wanting to deliver real journalism to his audience. He also honestly admits that it's a struggle to do so. I began by asking him to assess the press's post-9/11 coverage. As any self-respecting executive would, he started by accentuating the positive.

Regarding the reporting on the current war in Iraq, I think there have been highlights and lowlights. During the combat phase of the war, both print and television correspondents did some wonderful reporting. Because of what had happened in the previous Gulf War,[1] the military was much more open and gave reporters much more access than they had back then. I thought that was, in some cases, used really, really well. In the immediate postwar period, I also thought there was some very, very good reporting from the field about how quickly the situation on the ground changed, particularly given the expectations that had been created by a bunch of American officials about how the coalition forces would be greeted after the war. In this current phase, when the situation is so uncertain, there has also been some excellent reporting. The whole problem with the Abu Ghraib prison abuse scandal[2] would not have come to light if it weren't for Seymour Hersh and the people at *60 Minutes II* and some other American journalists. So I think there's been some excellent, excellent reporting. On the other hand, from the very beginning, I think the great challenge for the American press has been to figure out how to cover this in a way that doesn't compromise their journalistic principles but is consistent with what some people view as their patriotic duty. I think that's really been the problem in many instances.

During the combat phase of the war, a lot of journalists working for television companies—not so much the networks, but some of the smaller companies—felt pressure from their management and other people in their organizations to be more patriotic and to wear American flag lapel pins. I think most people who covered combat realized that was inappropriate. But the pressure was definitely there, and I don't think that was right. I think that's a misunderstanding of the role of the press in a free society, particularly when journalists are in combat and their lives are at stake. In the aftermath of the combat, some reporters have been reluctant to talk about how difficult things have become in Iraq for the very same reasons. There are those who believe that bad news is bad news and really shouldn't be reported. Some of the people who are controlling journalistic entities now aren't as comfortable with the real role of the press, which is to ask questions, to expose mistakes, to talk about problems, and to deliver news which, in the case of war, is often not particularly wonderful. Some people aren't comfortable with that, and, to me, this is the greatest problem with this war.

Who specifically isn't comfortable in your mind?

I'm talking about some of the people who own journalistic entities who aren't traditional owners of newspapers or TV news companies and who have a political agenda themselves. A lot of people talk about Fox News. There's no question that as a journalistic entity they've done some excellent work, but they also project an image that's much more pro-American than I think most journalists feel comfortable with. Having done that, they've had great success. It's hard to say whether it's because of their pro-American coverage or because of some other aspect of what they do, but their success spawns competitive pressures that a lot of people feel. A very, very difficult circumstance in which to find yourself in the cable world is to be losing the ratings war and feeling as though one reason why may be that your coverage isn't as patriotic as that of some of the people who are doing better. There's a lot of pressure in that world. I don't work there myself, so I don't have firsthand knowledge of that, but my sense from colleagues of mine who do is that that's a real issue.

I remember Dan Rather at CBS making a comment about pressure coming from the Bush administration and CNN correspondent Christiane Amanpour talking about pressure coming from the administration and their "foot soldiers at Fox." What's your reaction to Dan Rather's comment?

I don't actually remember it.

He compared—he said it was an obscene comparison—but he compared the pressure to dissidents being necklaced in South Africa.

Well, I'll leave that to Dan.

> But then Christiane Amanpour was on the *"Topic A"* show telling Tina Brown that the press censored itself. She said, "even at my own network," meaning CNN, there was censorship as a result of pressure from the Bush administration and their "foot soldiers at Fox."

I don't know that the Bush administration actually has foot soldiers at Fox. I can only speak for ABC News where I sometimes work. I worked there during the actual combat phase of the war for quite some time, and I didn't feel that. There's a long tradition of covering combat within ABC News, and we, I thought, did a pretty good job. There are things I wish that we had done differently, but that's always true with a big, giant story like this. There were times when we discussed the appropriate tone to take and the proper way to label the whole war, because all television entities like to brand these things with an overall name. We talked about that in the context of what's patriotic and what's appropriate journalistically and we opted for the journalistically appropriate title "War in Iraq." I think there was a lot of pressure to balance the coverage in a way that was appropriate. There were great critics of the war at the time, and when they appeared, we made an effort to find people who were strong supporters of the war, and I think we struck the appropriate balance. But it is also true that you could look on your screen and see what Fox and some of the other cable networks were doing and wonder whether or not they were feeling pressure.

> Let's talk about the coverage before the war, coverage of the reasons given for going to war. What's your assessment of that?

Obviously, we missed the story. There's no question about it. But the world press missed the story in that sense, because there haven't been any weapons of mass destruction. That was the logic the Bush administration and their coalition partners used to launch the war, and though it was challenged, presumably everyone in the press could have challenged it more.

I don't think just journalists missed it. Congress missed it. The intelligence community apparently had great debates about this subject. The administration missed it. You're only as good as your sources of information, and had we had even better sources inside the intelligence community, I think we would have been able to report on the dissent that we now know occurred within that community. But at the time, I still think we would have relied on what the administration said publicly was their rationale for the war. We didn't have sources inside Iraq who could search the whole country in a comprehensive way. Of all the weapons inspectors who'd been in Iraq, not one was saying, "There are no weapons of mass destruction here, we completely disagree with this logic." They were saying, "We don't know." Could we have hit the "we don't know" question harder, I'm sure we could have. I think everyone regrets that that wasn't done better. But I don't fault the press for missing that story. I think it was pursued aggressively, and I think journalists fight the next war better than the one before and learn the lessons from the one before. I think the next time, if there is a next time, if there's anything comparable, whatever the assumptions are that are underlying the logic of an American military mission somewhere in the world, those assumptions will be much more aggressively challenged than they were in this war.

> **We interviewed Carl Bernstein and John MacArthur [publisher of *Harper's Magazine*]. Regarding not discovering earlier that the weapons of mass destruction never really existed, Bernstein said, in effect, "What sources were we going to use that were going to tell us definitively?" John MacArthur, however, talked about how two days after President Bush and Britain's prime minister, Tony Blair, held a press conference citing an International Atomic Energy Agency report as a source of proof that Saddam could reconstitute his nuclear weapons in a matter of months, *Harper's Magazine* researchers found out that that report didn't even exist.**

Did they report that?

> **Yes, they reported it. But here's the problem, it's not television.**

Right.

> **It's not the mass consciousness media.**

That's one important piece of evidence, and in retrospect I think it stands out. If what you say is right . . . I'm just not sure, given the weight of . . . I mean, Colin Powell went in front of the United Nations and said, "These weapons of mass destruction exist, look at this, look at this, look at this." After that performance, a lot of people criticized the evidence he used as being a little less definitive than perhaps he had led us all to believe. But when you have Secretary of State Colin Powell, Secretary of Defense Donald Rumsfeld, the president of the United States, all kinds of people inside the United States government and the British government making the same point, and all the former weapons inspectors not being able to contradict that in a definitive way, it's a very tough call to make. I think it would have been bad journalism, frankly, to go out on a limb and say, before knowing what we know now, that weapons of mass destruction did not exist in Iraq. I don't think you could have said that then in any convincing way, and it would have been bad reporting. It turns out that there aren't. But I don't think that it would have been appropriate to report at the time.

Do you think that there was an attempt to make a connection between Saddam Hussein and 9/11?

I think President Bush tried very hard to make that connection, and lots of people did stories suggesting that that connection was tenuous at best. I know that in the programs that I supervised at ABC, we did those stories a number of times before and during the combat phase of the operation. Interestingly, the poll numbers didn't change in terms of what people believed. You could report that and report that and report that and the power of the president's bully pulpit, which he used to make that suggestion, overwhelmed any reporting that was done by others. So I think that story was actually well reported. Certainly anyone who has experience with Iraq and the Middle East recognizes that it was a very tenuous claim that wasn't logical based on the relationships between those two groups. There was no evidence to support it. So I think that was well reported. The reporting didn't stick, however.

I want to discuss the issue of official sources. You're an experienced newsman as well as a news executive, and you know probably better than I that in sensitive circumstances your official sources are going to lie to you.

Yes. Yes.

Do you really think that we held the official sources' feet to the fire enough?

In retrospect, obviously not on some crucial questions about the logic that underlay the war. But I think that within the press, it's important to make distinctions among the different reporters and different organizations. There's a wide range of skills and resources. There's just a tremendous range of work that was done and I'm reluctant to characterize all of it in one fell swoop. As I said, I think some excellent reporting was done before, during, and after the combat phase of the war, and some of that reporting continues to this day. One of the things that was heavily reported before the war was the deep disagreements that existed within the military about the logic for the war: whether or not it could be waged effectively, whether there were enough troops, and whether or not there was a plan to deal with the aftermath of successful combat, not to mention whether or not they were well prepared for the weapons of mass destruction that they presumed Saddam Hussein had. There was a great deal of reporting about that, and I thought some of it was really, really excellent. I would cite Seymour Hersh[3] as an example. Some of it was done on ABC. So it's not as though the press as a group marched uniformly behind President Bush and the civilians in his administration who were arguing for the war. One of the most interesting stories that we reported heavily before the war was the fact that a lot of military people didn't want to fight it and thought it was a bad idea. But some reporters weren't as aggressive as others. I think that's the nature of the business.

I was shocked by that June 22, 2004, ABC–*Washington Post*[4] poll indicating that more than half of the people they talked to thought Saddam had provided support to al Qaeda. I was also very surprised when Christiane Amanpour, Dan Rather, and CNN International's executive vice president and general manager, Rena Golden, all said essentially the same things about censorship and the pressure to be patriotic. Do you feel that this administration has a much better handle on presenting and manipulating information, because how does this happen, this whole misperception in the beginning and after we've prosecuted the war that people have about Saddam Hussein being connected to 9/11? How does that happen?

That I can't explain. I don't understand it. I don't have an explanation.

Is there not enough context being reported in news?

I think that some of the responsibility for understanding how the world really works lies with the consumer. I think people need to make an effort to understand their world. It's a very complicated world we live in, and as a journalist, all I can do is put things out there. People either pay attention or they don't. They get it or they don't. I don't think it's appropriate to put all the responsibility for educating people and having them understand what's going on upon the people who create the information flow. The public has to show an interest in the information. People have to be willing to absorb it.

Americans are traditionally inward-looking. Historically, as a group, they don't have a broad worldview. I don't think that has changed particularly. Maybe they are a little more globally oriented now than they were fifteen or twenty years ago, but they're not nearly as globally oriented as the people of so many other countries around the world. There's no awareness of various parts of the world and different cultures, and I think that affects the way Americans absorb information about things like whether or not there's a connection between Saddam Hussein and al Qaeda. I think it's easy for them to confuse those two things—"Wait, they're both over there, they both speak Arabic, they both sort of look funny, they're both dangerous, they must be friends." It's easy for them to fail to recognize that there could be vast differences among people in that part of the world who have a common interest in opposing United States policy. So I think a lot of responsibility for the confusion over what is and isn't true rests with consumers. People have to want to know, and I'm not sure Americans always really do want to know.

Where is the line between information or education and entertainment in news?

That's a very, very interesting question. As a television producer, I feel a profound responsibility to keep the audience that is watching or considering watching a program that I've created interested during every second of it. It's arrogant and irresponsible for a television producer to think that he or she can afford to bore people. To do that is a mistake you make at your own peril, and it will affect your career and the information you're trying to convey. So I think it's very important to compel people. That is different from compromising your journalistic values for entertainment values. There is tremendous pressure now in American television to get as many people to watch as possible. Anything that will get people to watch is considered something that people in the news business ought to think about doing. There is pressure to compromise journalistic values from time to time that I think the best people withstand and others don't.

No responsible network executive producer can afford to not know what the ratings are for the programs he or she produces. It's impossible to not be aware of how those ratings go up and down and to not make the connection between that and what you do. If you keep doing something over and over again because you think it's journalistically responsible and the ratings keep going down, there's a problem. If you aren't doing something that someone else is doing and their ratings are going up, then you're going to feel natural pressure to do what they do. I think those competitive pressures can be healthy. If you assume that people actually do want to know the truth and that the person or organization that provides it the best will be the most successful, then that pressure is healthy. For example, in the run-up to this war, a tremendous amount of time, effort, energy, and money was spent inside ABC News on the technology that was going to be used to report the war: how were we going to get a live signal from the battlefront to viewers' homes as often as possible and in the best way possible? That's good pressure because it forced us to upgrade everything we did, to rethink how we did things, to come up with new ways to convey information, to get people, and to be as aggressive as possible in the field. So the pressure to be successful is good pressure. At the same time, there's bad pressure. There's bad pressure when you see someone doing something wrong that you wouldn't do and you have to make a decision whether you're going to do that yourself or not. I don't want to sound like a Pollyanna, but I honestly believe that the three main networks, ABC, CBS, and NBC, resist that pressure pretty successfully when it comes to reporting stories like war. They don't do things that compromise their appropriate journalistic values in the service of getting a bigger audience. Having said that, the prime-time arena outside of big stories like war has changed radically. You can debate whether or not what happens now in prime time on network news programs is news. Some people think it is and some think it isn't. But that's very different from the war coverage.

As a news manager and a journalist, do you sometimes feel that you're operating between a rock and a hard place?

Yes. I think there's no question that when you're in a position of responsibility in American television journalism, you sometimes feel tremendous conflict between the purist journalistic instinct and the pressure from the people for whom you ultimately work to produce the highest possible rating. But I'd like to think that the reason that these jobs pay pretty well is because I can figure out how to manage that pressure effectively.

During this war, I was running the prime-time news area during the combat phase, and we did a bunch of programs in prime time. The people who worked on those programs were so happy to be covering this war because it was so different from the kinds of things that normally go into the programs they produce for American prime-time television, where the pressure for ratings sometimes comes close to overwhelming what you might think of as the best journalistic judgment. But on a big story like this, what's going to win is getting the best information out most quickly in front of the most number of people. So ironically, when you're in the middle of combat, you're going to be most successful if you do the best job, journalistically speaking. This war was no exception to that rule, particularly at the major networks. So, in a funny way, for a manager responsible for editorial content and generating high ratings, the pressure is less extreme in a war situation.

In the asymmetrical warfare period we're in right now, where there's no raging combat or war front but where people are still getting killed all the time and it just looks ugly and terrible and unpleasant, that situation inverts itself, because it is very difficult to report on this period in a new way every day. People get sick of low-intensity combat. The sense you have as someone who manages this period is, "I've heard that story already. I really don't want to hear anymore about that, thank you very much. Isn't there something else you can tell me?" It's frustrating to feel that there's a giant story out there that is difficult to report because people's appetite for it has gone down, but it's impossible to work in American network or cable television and not be sensitive to the appetites of your viewers. The great question is: Do you try to lead viewers to the right story or do you respond to what they want to hear and want to know about? Again, I think you have to do both, but on a big story like a war, all the good people I know at every place I know would not feel like they were facing a crisis if they had to choose between reporting an important story or set of facts and giving in to commercial pressure. The position you take as a journalist is that this should be reported, and if someone up the line doesn't want to air it, that's a decision that you don't have to confront. I personally have never had to choose between something that would be commercially successful and something that was really, really important. If something's really important, I push to report it, and if someone else doesn't want to air it, that's their decision.

Walter Cronkite[5] made a comment about how the ravages of war have gone unreported because of Pentagon control. Tom Curley, president and CEO of the Associated Press, is starting a media advocacy group to try and deal with secrecy in government because he feels that there's so much withholding of information going on. I think there's a connection between control of information, control of visuals, and missing the big story, don't you?

I disagree. I covered the first Gulf War extensively. I was in Saudi Arabia and then in Kuwait City after the Americans went in there. The Pentagon shut us out and did everything they could to keep us as far away from anything as possible. We hated it. A couple of ABC reporters and I tried to go around them and we succeeded. We got into Kuwait City without a military escort at the same time that the Americans were arriving.

There definitely was a Pentagon blackout. They wanted only the pictures they wanted, when they wanted them, and they wanted to control everything. That was a form of military censorship that I thought was wrong in a democracy and bad for everybody. Ultimately, it didn't serve their interests because it made us their enemies. This time, I think that they were open. You cannot argue that they didn't put reporters with almost every unit out there. People saw all kinds of things. In terms of seeing the battle when there was a battle, I don't think that the Pentagon denied access. I think they learned a lesson from the first Gulf War and behaved very, very differently and were much, much more open this time. So I don't think that was an issue.

In terms of controlling information, that's a very different question. I think this particular administration is immensely secretive. They clearly have people with a very aggressive political agenda who believe that their agenda is not well served by openness. Look at how long they sat on the information surrounding this prisoner abuse scandal in Iraq. Look how that story is spreading. I think that speaks to a misunderstanding on their part of the real role a free press plays in an open society, which is to let information out and let things happen, because if you try to cover things up, they always get worse. That's the great lesson of the second half of the twentieth century, in my opinion. From Vietnam to Watergate and beyond, cover-ups are what get you in trouble. Everyone makes mistakes. People do things that go wrong. The press's job is to expose that, but if you are someone in power and you try to cover it up, you're going to get into trouble. I think it remains to be seen where that leads with this particular administration, but they certainly are not open and sharing when it comes to information.

What I question is this reporting of what the official sources said before the war. If the president comes out and says, "If you're not for us, you're against us," how do you, even as a legitimate journalist or a great journalistic enterprise, question those official sources openly on a regular basis? That's what was missing from the prewar coverage: skepticism. It was just ripped away by this whole patriotic environment.

I think in the wake of 9/11, during the run-up to this war and with the success of the American effort in Afghanistan, there was a different environment. Each time there is a war, the press struggles to find its role.

This was a war that was hung on 9/11.

That's right.

There's a huge logical disconnect between 9/11 and going to Afghanistan and 9/11 and going to Iraq. It's a huge logical disconnect. And that's what I didn't see in the press.

It's interesting, because Peter Jennings and I did a documentary in 1997, *Unfinished Business: The CIA and Saddam Hussein*, about the Clinton administration's greatest foreign policy failure. It was about their failure to take advantage of the opportunity presented by the Iraqi National Congress [INC] led by Ahmed Chalabi[6] to overthrow Saddam Hussein. Just as the INC and a group of people they had gotten together were prepared to try to take on Saddam Hussein from the north, the Clinton administration pulled the plug on providing air support, just like Kennedy did at the Bay of Pigs.[7] It was one of the Clinton administration's darker moments. Chalabi, as you know, became the darling of the conservatives and now is being attacked by the CIA. The whole Chalabi story is quite interesting. As journalists, we felt that this was a terrific story about the Clinton administration's failure to deal effectively with Saddam Hussein and Iraq when they had the opportunity to do so. It's important to keep in mind that Saddam Hussein was a really bad guy.

You're right. The logic for this war was directly related to 9/11. But there are a lot of thinking, thoughtful, smart, caring people who believe that ridding the world of Saddam Hussein is a good thing and that Saddam's behavior certainly justified his being got rid of.

Who are we to get rid of Hussein?

Well, that's a question. I think as journalists we're supposed to raise those questions, but in the case of the Clinton administration, they had encouraged these Iraqi dissidents and people living inside and outside of Iraq to do this and then walked away from it at the last minute. That is what our program was about, and I think it's a dark chapter in Clinton's history. In this case, you had people in the Bush administration who were deeply committed to getting rid of Saddam Hussein. Our job as journalists is to report on their behavior. And I disagree with you a little bit about whether or not the story was missed in the beginning. There were lots and lots of stories in every responsible journalistic organization about the disconnect between the logic of September 11 and going into Iraq. There were lots of stories about the military's reluctance to prosecute this war. There were lots of stories about the firing of the secretary of the army and the chief of staff of the army when they were putting out information about what the prowar partisans at the Pentagon didn't like about the number of troops it would take to deal with the situation after the war was over. It's something that was well reported on. It may have been overwhelmed by what the president said, and certainly we didn't get at the issue of weapons of mass destruction at all. We the press didn't get at that at all. We missed that completely. But as I said, so did a lot of other people.

I think it's easy in hindsight to criticize the press in general for the prewar coverage. I think that misses what's most interesting here. What's most interesting to me in retrospect and what I would be most critical of about the role the press played is whether or not we reported properly on the context in which all this was occurring and how that affected people's judgment. What I see now when I look back is a country that was filled with frustration, anger, and pain and that wanted to do things. And it gave people who had an agenda the opportunity to take advantage of that. There's no question that long before September 11, there were people inside the Bush administration who from the moment they went to work were thinking, How do I get into Iraq? And they saw an opportunity—a legitimate opportunity from their point of view—after September 11 to move in that direction and they pushed very hard to do it. I think that's the story we missed reporting as effectively as we might: the connection between the prior belief system of a whole group of people who are in very important positions in the Bush administration and what they actually did. Would that have led us to report the story more aggressively? Again, there was some good reporting on this subject, but overall, if you have to consider the press as a whole, I think we missed that story.

I don't know if you agree with me or not, but primarily what was missing during the run-up to the war were pieces that did provide context. Pieces that made people understand the history of the situation, because how can you be critical if you don't know?

One of things that we reported on heavily before the war was how long it was going to take, and how the administration had a timetable that was X number of days, and how a lot of people believed that they were wildly optimistic and that Saddam's elite Republican Guard units were going to be a much tougher opponent than we thought. There were people inside the military who thought that this was not going to be the cakewalk that Bush and some of his people believed that it was going to be. It turns out that Bush was right. I supervised many stories about the difficulties of urban combat and how hard it was going to be to take Baghdad and how once they got to the cities, they'd rush through the south, but Basra was going to be a problem, and that there were all these other cities that nobody knew about and that are now quite familiar, and blah, blah, blah, blah. Well, that was wrong. The problem with speculative storytelling in journalism is that it is often wrong. I think the best you can hope for is to be effective at reporting what you can see in front of you and to do it in a way that does produce some context and that is skeptical.

I'm not talking about speculation, I'm talking about history. The United States is the nine-hundred-pound gorilla on this planet, and most Americans don't even know what we have done and are doing out there, right?

I think that was true in Vietnam, which is not a great model to use. One of the things that strikes me about this war is how similar it's becoming in some ways to Vietnam. Reporters on the ground are seeing a disaster unfolding in front of them and they are reporting on it as best they can, but somehow it doesn't seem to sink in back home. In some ways, the press is being blamed for reporting bad news all the time. You see that on the right-wing talk shows. You see that among certain American politicians, who are saying that we aren't supporting our troops enough and are asking why we aren't telling the good news and the good stories. There have been stories about how the soldiers on the ground are doing a wonderful job in very difficult circumstances. They're not just doing a good job at fighting against bad guys, but they're also nation building, which is something the president said he never wanted to do before he got into office.

Journalists come back from Iraq and talk about how difficult the situation is and what the problems are, and it sounds like Vietnam all over again. You see it in their reporting, yet the coverage does not seem to be having as much of an impact on the American population as one would expect. With Vietnam, it took time. It lagged, and eventually Americans turned against the war. I think it's very possible that that could happen here as the experiences that the reporters are having translate more and more clearly into the reporting that you see in print and on the air. I think as more and more Americans die there, the probability of the tide turning goes up. The death toll is really what turns Americans against things like this. The numbers are going up and that doesn't show signs of changing.

Do you think the reporting is better now than it was before, during the run-up to the war?

I'm very reluctant, as I've said a couple of times, to generally characterize the reporting. I think it varies widely. I think some people do exceptionally well and some don't. Seymour Hersh has done an extraordinary job from the very beginning. Hersh has great sources in the military. I know him. He's a colleague and we've worked together. I think he's a brilliant reporter and I hope he wins a bunch of Pulitzer Prizes for his work. John Burns of the *New York Times* did some really good reporting before and during the war. I think a number of television reporters have had a harder time because they aren't in Iraq as long. They tend be rotated out more quickly. I think that in a situation like the one in Iraq right now, you've got to spend a long time in the country to be successful at developing your own sources and doing original reporting. Also, television reporting tends to be a little bit more reactive because there's less of it. You're covering the news of the day.

During the war a lot of embedded television reporters did pretty well given the circumstances they were in. I don't think that reporters were out there doing poorly. I think organizations were showing some reluctance to report bad news. I wouldn't challenge the work of individual reporters. I would challenge whether or not the pressures people who manage news organizations and television companies feel allow them to report the story as fully as they might if those pressures were not as great. You don't see within the networks or the cable channels competitive pressure for a wide breadth of reporting showing every aspect of what's going on in Iraq right now. What you see is a limited public appetite for a certain amount of stuff. More than that, people say to themselves, "You know what, I really don't want to know. If I want to know more, I'll read the *Economist*, I'll read the *New York Times*, or I'll read something else." So, accomplishing a wide breadth of reporting under those circumstances poses a challenge for television.

I think there are real problems with the way that American television journalism is moving now. I think there are tremendous pressures for ratings and audience size that inevitably run up against the judgments people have to make about what to do. But ironically, I think those pressures evaporate on the big stories, because it's on the big stories that you tend to define your identity. It's on the big stories that you make your mark. What is much more troubling to me is that things around the edges that deserve coverage are much more affected by ratings pressures. If there's a big story like a September 11 or combat in Iraq or a presidential election, the best reporters will be sent out to cover it aggressively and the television news organizations will put it on the air effectively. But once they simmer down to a lower intensity, even those stories will be subject to the competitive pressures that are very much a part of reality in American television today.

Other stories that don't appear to have the same level of importance are the ones that don't get the coverage they deserve. Ironically, my concern about the direction in which American journalism—particularly on television—is headed is not as great when it comes to a story like the war in Iraq as when it comes to a lot of other things.

What's happening in American television is that the world is segregated into a very hard-news-oriented group of programs, particularly the evening news, and a very soft-news world consisting primarily of the prime-time newsmagazines. Prime-time newsmagazines aren't really newsmagazines anymore, except in periods of tremendous stress or when there's a really big story. They're lighter, feature-oriented programs designed to attract a large audience. They're not meant to be vehicles for serious reporting. Occasionally, the networks air documentaries that are designed to showcase serious reporting, but there aren't very many of them and they're not considered particularly important in the grand scheme of things. So you have a world that's dividing more than ever before into a hard-news world and a soft-news world. In the soft-news world, the economic pressures are enormous. They're also enormous in the hard-news world, but I think people are discovering that if you're going to be in that world, real hard news is the route to success.

Is our press as free as it can be? Is there censorship, or is there self-censorship in your experience?

Those are two very different questions. Is there censorship from the government? No. There absolutely is not. I've never seen it. I've never heard of it. Any attempt to censor the free press in this country would, I think, produce an outcry from all journalists and from the American public. I just think there's nothing like that. Now, is there information that public officials keep secret from journalists? Absolutely. That's the nature of the beast. The goal of the journalists is to discover what they don't know in spite of people in positions of power not wanting them to know it.

Is there self-censorship? I think there's always been self-censorship in journalism. The pressures come from a variety of different sources. At the moment, the self-censorship that I'm most concerned about comes from the commercial pressures that particularly television broadcasters feel to generate as big an audience as possible in every part of the day possible with every program that they do. Some people believe that the proper way to generate the largest possible audience is by figuring out what people want to see and then putting that on TV. I believe that the proper way to be successful is to tell people things they don't know, because by definition, if they don't know it, they don't know whether or not they want to see it. The difference between those two philosophies is very much in play right now in American television. There are lots of people who believe that you want to find out what people want to know and then tell them that. There are also lots of people like me who believe that you want to figure out what's important and tell that in a way that will be interesting to an audience. Just because you're telling people things they don't know doesn't mean that you're absolved of the responsibility of telling it in a very, very compelling way. I believe telling people things they don't know is much more likely to get them to watch you regularly than telling them things that they think they want to know and already know a great deal about. But I think that, at the moment, I'm in the minority in commercial television. I think the other view, that you want to figure out what people want to know about and go tell them that, is much more prevalent.

> **Do you think that certain stories are avoided because they're too sensitive or they might attract a lawsuit or they take too long to report—like investigative reporting?**

I think there are lots of lawyers who look at things now that they wouldn't have looked at twenty years ago. That's true across the board in all of journalism because we live in a much more litigious culture now in America. It's terrible. I hate it. It's awful. Most American journalists are doing their absolute best, but it's very difficult sometimes to get access to the audience, either in print or in television, with the stories you want to tell.

I think that investigative reporting is the core work of good journalists and that there aren't nearly as many resources put into investigative reporting as I would like to see. Is there a lack of investigative reporting because a lot of journalists work for companies that have large corporate interests? I don't believe that. I just don't think that investigative journalism is valued as much. It's just not the fashion in journalism right now. These things ebb and flow. Investigative journalism will be rediscovered in X number of years and become all the rage again. Having said that, some great work has been done recently. Look at what happened with the prison scandals in Iraq. That was discovered by some very good investigative reporters.

I'm not sure that investigative journalism was the rage in the early seventies when Watergate[8] came out. You had two guys who stumbled onto a story. The real point with journalism is that it's sort of accidental all the time anyway. By definition you're going after something that's unknown or not well known and so you never quite know what you're going to get. I think that's still true now. I personally don't spend a lot of time wringing my hands about how terrible journalism is and how the American media is not doing its job. I think we live in a complicated environment. My goal as a journalist is to figure out how to do good work in that environment. That's what most reporters I know do. I don't have a lot of time for people who sit around and complain about how terrible things are. Things are always good or bad, and you have to figure out how to do good work in that environment. I'm never going to own the television network or the newspaper that I work for, and most good journalists I know are in the same situation. So most good reporters figure out how to do good work in the environment in which they find themselves. You just have to be persistent and determined and it will happen. I've also never had a story killed or experienced any sort of government or self-censorship. Big stories get reported. That's what happens. Sometimes it's more difficult in the initial phases than others, but they get reported and they get well reported.

Do you think the American audience trusts the press?

I don't know if Americans trust the press. The surveys I've seen show that they trust journalists more than they trust government officials and many other professionals. But I think trust is a really big issue. As a journalist I feel, and I think most of my colleagues feel, that the only thing we've got going for us is our credibility and if we violate that trust, if we get things wrong, then we're completely screwed. Once you've lost your credibility, you have nothing to offer. One way to do that is to report a story incorrectly. Another way to do it is to let your credibility gradually erode by not doing your job. The question now is whether or not, in this very difficult environment in which we work, the credibility of the American press is being gradually eroded because reporters are not working hard enough. I hope that's not the case. I don't believe it is the case. I think the war in Iraq presents a real opportunity for people to do some great work.

I think the greatest strength of the American press as a whole is that there is so much of it. There are just enormous numbers of journalists wandering around of all types and stripes, and there's a natural competitiveness among them that is impossible to suppress no matter how many big corporations take over how many networks and no matter how many newspapers are owned by the same company. Journalists are competitive by nature or they wouldn't have the job. The great virtue of American journalism is that it's like the country itself—it's just all over the place. There are so many different kinds of people with all kinds of different ideas of what they ought to do. They're on the Internet, they're in newspapers, and they're on television and radio. They are documentary makers and pseudo-documentary makers, like this guy Michael Moore.[9] The complexity and diversity of American journalism is its greatest strength. Out of that diversity comes a lot of stuff, and stuff produces more stuff. People follow up and follow up and follow up and eventually big stories do get reported and they get well reported. The prison scandal in Iraq is a very, very good example of that. That story is not going to go away until it's been reported to death. In my opinion, the great challenge for the American press in the future is for the people who own the organizations to overcome the kinds of competitive pressures that are brought to bear upon them and that are inevitably passed on to the journalists who work for them.

We shouldn't succumb to the temptation to make people feel better. That's not a journalist's job. The pressure to tell people things that they want to hear—that will make them feel better, more secure, more comfortable, happier, and safer—is enormous. It doesn't just come from the companies that people work for; it comes from your neighbors. It comes from your friends. It comes from your family. We live in a very changeable and dangerous world at the moment and everyone wants to feel better. But I think that especially because the United States is the most powerful country in the world and has tremendous global responsibilities, we American journalists have to remember that our role is to make people uncomfortable. Our role is to make people nervous. Our role is to find out bad things that are happening and to expose things that have gone wrong. As long as we keep doing that, we'll be fine. But it's a harder and harder and harder thing to do, not just because of the commercial pressures that all journalistic organizations feel, but also because of the nature of the world. It's a very dangerous world.

TOM YELLIN brings to P.J. Productions fifteen years of experience as an executive producer at ABC News and almost three decades in network television. Tom has been executive producer of *Peter Jennings Reporting* since its inception in 1990. He was also the executive producer of numerous award-winning programs and series, including "The Century" and "In Search of America," "ABC 2000"—a twenty-three-hour broadcast marking the millennium—and several of Jennings's children's programs, town meetings, and breaking news specials.

From 1992 to 1995, Tom was the executive producer of the prime-time newsmagazine *Day One*, which he created and which, under his direction, broadcast a landmark series of investigative reports on the tobacco industry. Tom first came to ABC News in 1980 as a New York–based producer for *Nightline*, followed by two years as *Nightline*'s senior producer in London. He returned to New York and was a senior producer for *World News Tonight* with Peter Jennings until 1985, when he became the senior producer of CBS News's weekly series *West 57th*. He moved back to ABC News in 1989.

Tom's programs have won many prestigious awards, among them the duPont-Columbia, the Peabody, the Emmy, and the Polk awards.

NOTES

1. On August 2, 1990, Iraq invaded Kuwait after Saddam accused Kuwait of ruining Iraq's economy by overproducing oil and stealing oil from Iraq's Rumaila oil field via slant drilling. On November 29, 1990, the UN Security Council decided that all necessary means should be used to get Iraq out of Kuwait. On January 12, 1991, Congress authorized the United States to attack. On January 16, 1991, Operation Desert Storm, a military operation involving an allied coalition led by the United States, began attacking Iraq. The war officially ended on April 6, 1991. During Desert Storm, the military took drastic steps to control press coverage of the conflict.

2. At the Abu Ghraib prison in Iraq, American soldiers from a US military intelligence unit, US military police, and some civilian contractors abused and tortured prisoners. Shocking photos of their activities were released showing naked prisoners being forced into humiliating sexual and other poses, while their captors were pictured with them giving "thumbs-up" signs and, in at least one case, holding a leash with a prisoner on the other end.

3. Seymour Hersh is a well-known investigative reporter and author. In his most recent book, *Chain of Command: The Road from 9/11 to Abu Ghraib* (New York: Harper-Collins, 2004), Hersh "takes an unflinching look behind the public story of President Bush's 'war on terror' and into the lies and obsessions that led America into Iraq." Quote from the front flap of *Chain of Command*'s dust jacket.

4. The poll question and answer can be found at http://www.washingtonpost.com/ac3/ContentServer?pagename=polls&nextstep=displayQuestion&interactive=n&pollid=2004169&pripollid=&varname=q25a&privarname=&questCategoryType=n&questCategory=Variables.questCategory&keyword=Variables.keyword&pollDateRange=Variable.

5. "Walter Cronkite is the former CBS News anchorman whose commentary defined

issues and events in America for almost two decades." A major poll once named him "The most trusted man in America." Cronkite joined CBS in 1950 and retired in 1981. Museum of Broadcast Communications. http://www.museum.tv/archives/etv/C/htmlC/cronkite wal/cronkitewal.htm.

6. A British-educated former banker, Ahmed Chalabi has been the leader of the anti-Saddam Iraqi National Congress, which was started with US government funding in the early 1990s for the purpose of overthrowing Saddam. Chalabi received large sums of money from the US government for his activities and was a source of faulty prewar intelligence. Although he has no industry experience, he is currently acting oil minister for the new Iraqi government.

7. President Kennedy approved an April 1961 invasion of Cuba by a CIA-trained militia of Cuban exiles to oust Fidel Castro but refused to lend critical air support when the militia requested it. The invasion failed.

8. *Washington Post* reporters Bob Woodward and Carl Bernstein became famous in the early 1970s as a result of their investigation of the Watergate scandal, which involved members of President Nixon's Committee to Re-Elect the President burglarizing and attempting to wiretap Democratic Party headquarters located in a building complex in Washington called Watergate. Woodward and Bernstein's investigation eventually led to the resignation of President Nixon.

9. Michael Moore is an award-winning author and filmmaker who examines hard issues with humor. His Web site is http://www.michaelmoore.com/.

3

CHASING EYEBALLS AND REMEMBERING JESSICA LYNCH

Jim Cooper/AP Photo

THOMAS CURLEY
President and
Chief Executive Officer,
Associated Press
Interviewed May 2004

Tom Curley looks like a man in charge of an organization reaching more than one billion eyeballs and ears a day. He's tall and lanky and moves around in an easy, self-assured manner. He looks you straight in the eye, has a good, strong handshake and a deep voice. When he speaks, he sounds exactly like what he is: the CEO of a huge news-selling business (albeit a nonprofit one). He is voluble on the issues he wants to discuss and diplomatic or even evasive on what he perceives as more controversial issues, like criticizing the press. His discretion, while perfectly understandable, was, at times, exasperating. Having said that, the most consistent impression I had of him was of a person who is very smart, honest, and utterly decent.

As with all big journalism outfits, the Associated Press is, from one day to another, worthy of both praise and criticism for all kinds of things. But the fact is, one of the key services that a wire service provides—first on-the-scene reports on breaking news stories—is one of the hardest things to do in journalism. In terms of reporting, it truly is where the rubber meets the road in the hardest, fastest way. Getting a story and getting it out quickly and accurately is not only nerve-racking and difficult, it is very, very easy to get wrong for a lot of reasons, not all of them having to do with the reporter's skills. In his interview, Curley cited the Jessica Lynch story as an example. At first, the story out of the Pentagon was that Pvt. Jessica Lynch was captured by Iraqis and saved by US Special Forces who found her with stab and bullet wounds. It was also reported that she had been slapped and interrogated while in her hospital bed. Later, among other things, it turned out that she had no bullet or stab wounds and had been treated well by Iraqi physicians at the hospital. Curley said that "Remember Jessica Lynch" became a mantra for AP reporters after that.

Curley's opening comments in this interview clearly indicate that the business end of his job is, in a very profound sense, just the half of it. He is deeply committed to excellence in journalism and, unlike others in positions similar to his, is willing to dedicate his time and resources to fighting against major obstacles to that. The first thing he did when he arrived at the AP was tour the organization's bureaus around the country and, essentially, take the AP's pulse. What he discovered turned him into a man on a mission.

———————

Traveling around the United States over the last year, I noticed that there seemed to be a reluctance to go after information as aggressively as the industry had in the past. So we began surveying the bureau chiefs of the Associated Press in every state to get some feel for where we are on access issues and what's going on with the government. And we confirmed a thesis that at the state, federal, and local levels, whether it's in the executive branches or in the courts, there has been a move toward more secrecy. Part of this is in response to the aftermath of September 11 and the attacks. Some of that is understandable; we didn't know what the threat was, we didn't know where it was coming from, so you could imagine the press stepping back for a period of time. But clearly, this has operated at several levels and it's gone beyond September 11. At the federal level, John Ashcroft, the attorney general, put out a memo that said, "We presume all government information to be secret unless proven otherwise." When we went back over that, there was a September 2003 General Accounting Office survey of the officers whose duty it is to make public information available to the public, and fully a third of them said that they were able to keep more information from the public a year after Ashcroft's order.

Is that legal?

He worked it very smoothly and it wasn't on a legal basis. There is a Freedom of Information Act, and he said, "We're just turning it around." What he did was raise the barrier. In so doing, he created some obstacles, but he also created some momentum and that momentum carried beyond. We saw it at the court level, so it wasn't just the executive branch. We saw it in a most pronounced way at local offices; the smaller the town, the more someone was likely to presume the information was his or hers and not the people's information. So there has been a change, and you don't really need to have your notebook snatched by a policeman to know it's getting harder to get information in this country.

Has anybody accused you of being unpatriotic because you're pushing on this government secrecy issue?

No, that has not really been a criticism that's come back. One proposal was to consider setting up a federal lobbying effort—that's how the game's played these days—and there are some journalists who are quite nervous about getting into any advocacy role, so I think we need to have a good debate about that. We anticipated that ahead of time. Some people saw it as a partisan initiative, and I've been very careful to point out how all the administrations have a duty to get their side heard and that it wasn't about that and to try to put it in some perspective. The Kennedys were very good at creating a myth around themselves. President Reagan was a great communicator. Everybody gives him credit for that, and we almost look at those who fail to get their side out as fools. So we would expect the government to try its best to get its position heard, and it's our duty to weave through all that and present the facts. So I've tried to give that a bigger perspective and get it beyond any partisan politics.

The reason why I asked is because a Justice Department spokesperson came back and said, "Look, we're fighting this war on terror and we

need to have this secrecy" and the logical thought after that is don't push the government when it's under fire from the terrorists.

There has been no comeback like that yet and I would be surprised. I think where the rubber meets the road is on the detaining of people of Middle Eastern descent and the disposition of the court cases. The press has taken a step back and hasn't initiated a lot of efforts to find out why these people are being held and what the issue is. So part of this was a call to arms for us to do what we should do and ask the questions we should have been asking all along. It was more of a challenge to the press, rather than an assault on the administration. I tried to say, "Look, this is our role. We are not impartial here. We are not a referee who says yes this time and no next time. It's our job to fight for information on behalf of everybody, not just ourselves."

What are the details of this lobbying effort? How exactly are you setting it up and how's it going to work?

It's a very measured approach to make sure we have consensus. There have been a number of journalism organizations in the United States that have worked for a number of years and have done a lot of things right and so we don't want to alienate anybody; we really want to try to build consensus. So the first step for this is just to have a meeting to try to see the scope of the problem. Before I gave the speech, we did talk to just about everybody to make sure that there was consensus that the bar has been raised, that we need to take a stronger approach, and that we need to be more aggressive at fighting for our position. So far we've had unanimous support. If this holds at a real meeting, then we'll look at what's the best way to set it up. Obviously, the Associated Press [AP] is in a good position here because we already spend a lot on First Amendment initiatives. We're organized in every state in the United States, so that gives us a very good footprint.

I have heard from some US senators who have applauded our initiative, so technically the question is: Can we set up the center and under what auspices in Washington to pursue an agenda and also to be sure that there are no more initiatives that would prevent information from coming out? Each day there are a number of those that we do find out about.

But isn't it very difficult to set up alliances among persons who have different concepts of what a journalist should be?

Yes, getting journalists to agree is always a wonderful challenge, and I am very humble about what we will be able to accomplish. It has been clear for a number of months what the issue is, and if we don't fight for it, if we aren't aggressive, and if we don't put some money out there, we risk further setbacks. If you look at what's happened around the court cases of the people who may or may not have been involved in any way around September 11, or about people who may or may not have been detained for the right reason, we haven't been aggressive there. So I think there's a widespread realization that we need to examine it. I'm not sure if we'll get consensus. It is indeed a challenge, but we want to try to do our best to build a consensus.

> **Walter Cronkite said that Pentagon secrecy was one of the great travesties of the war in Iraq in terms of the press and getting information out to people. Do you agree with that?**

I'd be a little more measured. My view is a little different. I am reminded of a McLuhan[1] quote from the late sixties that the amplification of a position often is greater than the position. That wasn't exactly McLuhan's quote, but it was along those same lines, and I think we are dealing with people who are very skilled in making a point. I remember meeting with a group of editorial page editors on the eve of the war and we were going through a period of self-examination: Did we ask the right questions? Were we tough enough? And one of the points that we agreed on was that the administration had moved the agenda, and by the time you understood what the line of thinking was, it had moved on. By the time you understood which experts you might contact, the reason, the raison d'étre, had moved again. So it was hard for us to keep up. Was that an excuse or not? When I went back and reread the history of the Vietnam War, I was struck with one major thought. In 1968 the world was filled with student protests. They were in Prague. They were in Paris. They were in New York. They were in Chicago. They were in Mexico City. Yet the Vietnam War continued for five more years. And there was a lot of protest in the United States. So how long does it take to get people to ask the right questions or to understand a situation? It can take a long period of time. That's the way democracy works. I do think in a way that we moved faster through the information land mines this time, so I've been feeling a little bit better about our role and the questions that we've asked. I do think that if you look back on twelve or fifteen months, we really have gone through a lot of the issues, vetted them, and come up with answers. So I think we have performed a service.

> **We've been talking to a lot of leading journalists and we've had some very mixed comments. Carl Bernstein, for example, feels that for the last**

twenty-five years the media has done a good job and throughout the various wars did as well as could be expected. John MacArthur of *Harper's Magazine* reserves his biggest criticism for the prewar coverage, when the war was being sold to the American public. He said that he doesn't understand how the weapons of mass destruction [WMDs] argument was allowed to slide for so long because literally a couple of days after the first announcement was made, he discovered that the International Atomic Energy Agency report[2] that was being quoted to present the WMD argument didn't exist. He was saying he didn't understand why the press didn't pick up on that. And I said, "Do you think it's an official source problem?" and he had no answer. Once you go to war, you're committed and then it's a different set of problems. But before the war, that's a very critical time. So I'd like your assessment of the coverage before the war in Iraq and what you think of what MacArthur said.

I'm reminded of a recent study that came out about the Holocaust and World War II and when it was known in the US government; of the depth of the report about the Gulf of Tonkin[3] and what happened there in Vietnam; of the first Gulf War, when the accuracy of the weapons looked to be so precise and was probably about one-tenth of what it was perceived to be; and of one incident from this war that was so famous, which was the saga of Pvt. Jessica Lynch[4] from West Virginia. So there are always these issues and in the short run it is really hard to know. And what is the timetable by which we come up with the answers when we know for sure? I think if it's measured against the past, we move faster than we ever have at understanding. And I think that says many good things about the role of the press in our society and also the discussion that we can have with the American people. So the discussion has moved. Was it as fast as some people liked? Absolutely not. Was it as precise as it could have been? No, but there were some pretty famous people saying these weapons existed. Secretary of State Colin Powell and UK prime minister Tony Blair made pretty dramatic statements. I know if you talk to people in the press, they were swayed by some of those statements. Or they were brought to the point of saying, "OK, that's a position." We now know things differently. And we really learned that six or eight months later.

Do you think we're too quick to believe our political leaders or anybody who's making announcements about sensitive issues?

I think that it depends on the quality of the announcement and the spokesperson at any given time. I think you have to be careful, but, overall, the truth comes out and the truth is coming out faster, and I think this is a moment where we should take more credit and do less beating up of ourselves. I think where we would have a greater shortfall is on economic stories. If you look at the savings and loan crisis in the United States in the late eighties, early nineties, that went on for a long period of time—a lot of information was there. The corporate scandals went on for a long period of time and a lot of that information was there. So on economic reporting I would say that we're not doing as good a job as we should. On government and political reporting, there are a lot of journalists there and there are a lot of stories that are looked at pretty carefully, so I'm more nuanced in my view of what we've done.

My interest in asking the question is not about beating up on the press. It's more about how you better prepare yourself to not be spun, to not be lied to. How do you arm yourself better?

There are some very timely incidents to look at. We put out an advisory about Jessica Lynch and then every time there was a report we said, "Remember Jessica Lynch." There's an advisory almost every day at the Associated Press: "Remember this, check that, you don't know." Very recently there was the report that we filed first of the American military attacking what was a wedding party. And then the military came back and said, "No, this was a staging area for bad people and weapons," and came up with some weapons. What is the truth? We have pictures of weapons and we have pictures of dead people from the wedding, and we had a band that was pictured at the wedding party. We sent a lot of reporters to the scene to try to get the facts. Often, in times of chaos, any of us who have been out there reporting in these types of situations knows it is really hard to see beyond what's immediately in front of you. The larger picture does have to emerge from more careful digging or asking questions. So when a story becomes significant, put more reporters out there. Try not to get caught short in anybody's pronouncement. Try to source where the story is coming from so that everybody can make a judgment of "Well, maybe" or "Wow, this one looks pretty strong." So more information, more people when necessary, and constant reminders. You have to work at this just about every day to make sure that you don't want to believe something that turns out not to be true.

The AP, you guys are the first line of defense journalistically. Everywhere. Before the network and cable camera crews come in, before a lot of the papers come in, the wire services are on the ground and running already, so you really have, I think, the toughest job in terms of what

we're talking about. I'm going back to this official source thing, because I just feel like, from my own personal experience, that we report without question too much sometimes what our official sources say.

Absolutely.

How do we fix that?

I think first of all when an official makes a statement, he or she gets the right to make the statement and it does deserve to be reported. If on further review or further information, it turns out not to be true, they will pay an enormous price. If you go back to what happened in Vietnam, it was very clear that everything, many things, were based on a big lie. And the entire country turned against the administration—two administrations as a result. So those who would risk that make a big wish that they're going to get away with it, and history has shown they don't.

So you can go now and pay later.

It's amazing to me how the American people understand that politicians or officials get a certain amount of spin in the same way as when you look at an ad that says, "lowest possible price for this auto." You know, maybe. But if you work at it, you probably can get a lower price. So we're pretty conditioned to cut through some of the flack. When it gets to be a very serious story or when someone has done a very cold, calculated "let's change what really happened in this incident to rewrite history," that is a much more serious issue and perhaps only 10 percent will ever come to really appreciate what they try to do, but once it's exposed, you pay the price.

Do you think journalists are up to the task of penetrating in a timely manner the veils and smoke and mirrors put up by PR firms like Hill & Knowlton[5] that some of the more powerful members of our government hire to devise public relations campaigns that spin information and sometimes create false impressions?

I think we do and I think that history has shown that we do and I think in the last year you've seen some stories that have proven the fact that we can move fast, that we will get to the bottom of it. But it's not just us. The accounting scandal showed that there were other safeguards that are necessary. Audit committees of boards, boards themselves, auditors themselves. If all safeguards drop, then you have the big incidents and the big problems. All we can do is the best possible job for ourselves and on behalf of what we believe in. Around the Associated Press, the best thing we have going for us is that our content is vetted by fifteen thousand users every day around the world. So if we say something that doesn't look to be true in France, or doesn't look to be true in China, somebody will say something. Or within the United States, if it looks to be biased in one direction or another, we have watchers of all shades and we get some pretty instant feedback.

Your fifteen thousand outlets reach over a billion people?

That's right.

That's huge.

You get a certain amount of scrutiny, and I think that's the best thing that can happen.

There's a certain art to telling the story, and as we well know, some stories just have to get out quickly. But there are other ways to report the news. I remember being at a writing seminar once and somebody saying there are seventy-two ways to write a story, and you'd better try the second version. Stories about people and how they interact are fascinating. There's no shortage of interest or readers or viewers. There is something to the packaging, but I think our technology now and our ability to provide the information that people want in a very directed way makes it much easier for us to tell stories. We really do have the technology to assemble facts quickly and to communicate them around the world in seconds. I think the bigger challenge that we face is we also have the ability to put a story on the air before we know what the story is. You saw that on the night of the Supreme Court ruling in 2000. Some people in television were handed the decision and went out and started reading and said, "On page nine it says this, and on page thirty-five it says that." They could go live, but maybe they shouldn't have until they knew what the ruling said. So, I would say that's the bigger safeguard that I'm concerned about. There's any number of ways of telling the story, and these days with the technology it's very easy to assemble facts in a way that reach people at a number of levels, and I mean local or national or international. The SARS [Severe Acute Respiratory Syndrome][6] story was a gripping example of this, I think. Today we could go global in a second. The disease could go global and so can the stories about the response and where the shortfall was and how we got into the SARS problem. But what a story. The epic picture for me was these little ballet dancers in Beijing with masks on their faces. They were still practicing. So, good pictures tell the stories, too.

I don't recall precisely how the Associated Press covered this, but was there election fraud in the 2000 election, according to what your reporters found?

No. What we have to take a look at is that the election in 2000 was decided by point zero, zero, zero, zero, zero, nine, ninth of a percent. Our system, where elections are conducted in firehouses and city halls and schools across the country, is really not designed to be that precise. I think, overall, the results are pretty clear. The Democrats won the popular vote by 540,000. The Republicans won in the Electoral College by a handful. The Republicans won in the House by a couple handfuls. The Senate was split. The Supreme Court ruled five to four Republican. This is a divided nation and it remains a divided nation for the 2004 election.

Let's compare the coverage of the Gulf War to the coverage of the Iraq war. I also want to compare the pressures on journalists during both conflicts. It's not just the competence of journalists that we have to look at. We have to look at what pressures come to bear. Talk about the differences in the problems of reporting on this conflict and the Gulf War conflict. Also, everybody has this fabulous memory of the Vietnam era as being a time when journalists were really free to go around and cover the war. I'd like you to address whether you think that's true or not.

In every war up until the Gulf War, we had access, and that access was everything. In Vietnam the war went on for a long time, but whenever there was a battle, the reporters had access. They would hop on the helicopters and they would get to the battle. A number of journalists were killed in Vietnam. AP lost several people. In World War II, Korea, and Vietnam, it was all the same. But the military grew cynical and the press grew cynical through the Vietnam War, and it was a great nightmare for our country. So new rules were invented for the Gulf War. And we thought it was a disaster. We now know that some of the video was scripted in a way to look as if it were better than it was. And what was denied to the public was those compelling stories of soldiers making sacrifices or engaging in day-to-day heroism, the acts of kindness and mercy. Their stories were denied. So we don't have a very complete record of the Gulf War. And I think the real losers are the people who served and actually performed the acts on the ground. In the more recent Middle East conflict in Iraq, it has been different. We've had the embeds. I think it was a fabulous program. They only see out the window of their Humvee or their tank or their jeep, so they don't have a complete picture. But if you have enough, and AP had dozens, you do get a picture and you can put it together. You also need people who are not in the Humvees, people who are out, able to see other angles and other views. So that's how you put together a complete picture. On my wall, I have a picture of soldiers rescuing an old woman on a bridge. We have that story of a heroic effort by US soldiers because an AP photographer and an AP reporter were there to bring that story back. If they hadn't been there, that effort, that picture, would not have been captured.

To some extent, the view of the embedded journalist is only as good as the view—it goes without saying. But if you look at what happened over the period of weeks that they were embedded, they got a number of stories that went beyond the view outside the window, and you got a real sense and feel for how a unit was behaving. I also know people who had all the action they could deal with. We really have to remember, though, a larger point about this war and the wars we're in today. It's not the same as World War II, where you knew which side you were on and the lines moved in a cohesive fashion and you were with a particular unit. Journalists are often the targets and are often shot at by both sides. It's not clear whose side someone is on in these conflicts. So it's very, very different these days. To think that you can have the romance of freelancing and going wherever you want is really nonsense. And the notion of these weapons being perfectly accurate is above and beyond belief. The accuracy rates are ten times greater in Iraq than they were in the Gulf War, but TNT is also ten times more explosive in the way it's being applied by the terrorists and the roadside bombers. So the risks are fantastic. A lot of caution has to be exercised. It's not as if there's unlimited access. Or you know where the next battle is going to occur. They occur in buildings. They occur in schools and mosques and places of worship. These are difficult times. Covering war is the most dangerous thing a journalist can do, normally. These days, I think the level of danger has increased immeasurably.

There's a lot of criticism about the embedded system. People are saying, "How can you report objectively when you're literally depending on these guys for your life." What's your response to that?

We do this every day. The truth is, if you're covering a sports team, you can't go in there and be an idiot. You can't go in there and call every player a jerk; you can't say the coach is the dumbest coach you've ever seen, every day. Maybe by the end of the season you've reached that conclusion, but you can't do that. You can't go to City Hall and say, "You're a corrupt official." You've really got to be measured. And you've got to get along with people. This is how it works every day, in every locality, and so you do. But look at the stories. Look at the reports that came from Iraq. When somebody didn't secure a perimeter and people died, those incidents were reported. When people made mistakes, they were reported. When they saved old ladies on bridges, those incidents were reported as well. Look at the output, it's all there.

> **In modern warfare it seems like what's happened—certainly in the Gulf War and in this war and in some of the other, smaller constabulary exchanges like Panama and Grenada—is more civilians get killed than combat people. And yet there seems to be a greater reluctance to report or a greater control on the reporting of—at least certainly in the broadcast arena—that side of the story, the dead bodies, the ravages, the human toll.**

We provide 62 percent of the world's video feed. We make these decisions every day. When there's a beheading or a hanging, we make the feed available and we sell to other media. It's a business-to-business sell; it's not directly to consumers. We put out very strict advisories saying, "What you're about to see . . ." and "You might want to think about it" and "Here's an edited version," but we make that material available. These are tough decisions and dead bodies are not used routinely. Occasionally they are. They have to be used with a reason, for all the obvious reasons. I remember seeing a picture of an injured girl in a Scud attack during the Gulf War in Tel Aviv or Jerusalem and the newspaper getting hundreds of complaints. It was a picture printed in color, and the blood was pretty omnipresent—it was all over her face. And it resonated with readers, so people know the horrors of war. I think we do have a duty to make sure we cover it, but often less is more and they get the story.

Television stations or newspapers have a relationship with their audience that they know and that they want to preserve over a period of time. They make decisions on what they see on any given day. Occasionally they will run pictures of bodies because they believe the story deserves to be told that way. But you don't run body pictures every day. And you could. If you travel to certain parts of Asia and Thailand, auto accidents in their gripping horror are shown in great detail, in graphic detail. I don't believe you could do that so much in the United States. I remember reading a French newspaper that was aimed at middle school students. There was a picture of condoms on the front cover and it was about the growing problem of teen pregnancy. That might be difficult to do in the United States, but culturally, for the French, it probably was a very direct and effective use of art. So people have to make those calls based on the facts. You make hundreds of them on any given day. Whether it's cultural, or war, or what have you, it's about the long-term relationship you want with your viewers and the type of publication you seek to be.

During the time of the Clinton-Lewinsky depositions[7] and the release of the conversations, I advocated less as more. People knew what we were talking about here. They really didn't have to go to the very specific inclusion of that, and if you wanted it, you knew where to go. You knew to jump on the Internet. So it's really about communicating the story and how that's done. It's about telling a story accurately. As long as we present a story accurately and completely, I think we've fulfilled our mission. That doesn't mean you have to print a picture of a crushed body or report every word of a deposition about oral sex.

A recent example that created quite the brouhaha was the photos of the coffins coming in to Dover.[8] What's your assessment of not allowing photos of the coffins of US soldiers killed in Iraq to be shown?

I think to deny us access to those pictures is a terrible thing. I think these people who have given their lives to the United States deserve our coverage. They deserve, if they're coming back in a coffin with the American flag on it, to have all of us know that, look at that picture, and pause and reflect on what they've done. To deny that, I think, is the wrong thing to do.

Why the denial of these photos? There's nothing obscene about them.

In fairness, there are some families who believe that it's private grief and they don't want their loved ones to be swept up in that.

But nobody knows who's in there. You saw those pictures.

On some days you would. On some days there might be two or three and they would be identified. When it was a bad week, when there were a couple of dozen coffins, it was the overall picture that told the story. There would be instances where names got out, so in fairness, it's one that if you're going to have a policy, you need to be consistent. But I think it's one that the American people ought to see.

Besides this government secrecy initiative that you started—which is great, I think—are there other areas that create pressures on journalists that would force you ever to make a decision to kill a story or to not include certain information or to engage, frankly, in self-censorship or any kind of censorship? Have you ever experienced this in your career?

You make decisions every day on whether or not to hold stories, and clearly there are times when stories must be held. They must be sent back for additional reporting, for example. There are any number of stories that are pending now that have been sent back for a new top, a new lead that's more significant to try to advance the story, to say something that hasn't been said so it doesn't look like it's just somebody pushing an agenda and repeating something that's already out there. There are any number of decisions that you make like that all the time. It is not a problem in my view to hold up a story for better writing, better reporting, more detail, better sourcing. Then there's been one other particular area these days of challenges, the so-called HIPAA, the notorious Health Insurance Portability and Accountability Act.[9] It has really complicated not only journalist's lives but the medical community's lives, and there's a lot of paranoia that has come up, so you get into a situation where a former president faints while playing golf, and it's a Saturday, his staff is not immediately available, and hours go by and we don't know and we can't find out if he's OK or what his condition is one way or the other. That's not right.

What is your assessment of the broadcast press? Just take the networks as they come to mind and tell me what you think.

Performance is variable and it has grown more variable, regrettably, because I think the public does get a lot of its news from the broadcast media, and at the local level there seems to have been a cutback on the street reporting resources. I think that's a bad thing. I think the public gets shortchanged for that. I think there's ever more reliance on the newspapers as a result, and for the newspapers that's wonderful. But you're at a point where the stories are going on the air and people should be doing original reporting and advancing a story, adding perspective and telling it the way you need to tell it for the visual medium, and I think there has been a cutback there. In terms of the networks, I think they give a lot of their resources to the prime-time news programs and in many ways have had soaring success with that. There are fewer people watching in the late evening and more people watching in the early morning and I think there's been an increase in the resources in the morning, and I think those programs are getting better. At least the first part of them are very substantive and often much more hard-hitting than they were ten or twenty years ago. So it's not all one way or the other. Often we want to just say it's all good or it's all bad, but it's really nuanced. There's more news all the time from all the places, and some of that's good and sometimes we put the story on the air before we really know what it is.

I think potentially the media today are far more free. I think they have greater resources. I think they have the ability to report with better technology, to edit in a more timely way, to have more impact. Do they always use it? Probably not, but we have that ability today to be more free. I think you've seen that in what's happened in the last year in terms of the story around Iraq and the reasons for or for not going to war. I think we've gotten to that story sooner than we would have in the late sixties.

What's your assessment of Fox?

Media in the United States have been founded on political orientations so that if one has a political orientation and it eventually comes to broadcast I think it's foolish to think anyone should be surprised. I think the programming there has been brilliant. I think they have been very smart about how they have positioned themselves, and I think it's another voice. And more voices make for a fuller report. So God bless them. They're out there putting it on the air every day in a very competitive environment and they have picked up a lot of viewers, so there have been a lot of smart decisions made. In terms of politics, I'll leave that to the others, but I'm for more voices, and if voices want to be positioned in a different way, frankly, I think that's part of the free communications structure of this country.

So you don't think that the conflict between business mandates and journalism is real? Some people are saying there are certain areas of reporting that don't get done because they're not in the interest of the companies that own them or the media corporations don't want to upset the powers that be in Washington and so on. You don't think those conflicts exist?

Yes, I think those conflicts exist. But I think there are enough journalists and companies and voices out there that someone breaks through the fog. Within any company or medium on any given day for some issue, yes, there are possibilities and, frankly, you see it. But the scope of reporting is still large enough to ensure that things get covered.

If that soldier had come to you instead of Dan Rather and given you those pictures of the Abu Ghraib prisoners,[10] would you have held them if the Pentagon called you and told you to hold on to them for two weeks before you reported on them or released them?

In terms of a specific ask like that, I think we want to back up and say we have to know the nature of the ask and be sure that we've made any number of agreements over time. We don't report troop movements and positions and those kinds of things, so there are some nuances here. We tried very hard to get those pictures. AP reported abuses from the prison in October 2003. Brigadier General Karpinski, who was in charge of the prison, denied those abuses. We had a story. We never were able to get the pictures. We tried and tried and tried. We wanted those pictures, we wanted to make them available, we wish we had gotten those pictures, but somebody else did and that's the way it goes.

Do you think the American public trusts the media?

That question, I think, has to go to a whole range of questions, such as Do you like your medical situation these days? Do you trust your doctor? Absolutely. Do you trust you newspaper? Do you trust the magazine that you subscribe to? Do you trust the television station that you watch for your national or local news? The answers come back with very high satisfaction. If you want to have a broad-blanket question about the medical profession or the media, the scores come lower, there's no question.

Why is that?

Oh, I think the global desire to be cranky.

Usually, people trust local information because they have the feeling they can check it. But about what is happening in China or even in Iraq, they are much less sure. Usually people trust information on foreign events much less.

I think there have been some studies that have suggested that the closer people are to a story, they're more likely to trust it, and the more difficult a story or the further it is from where they live, whether geographically or intellectually, the harder it is to accept. So there's probably a strong element of truth to that. But I still think that you can tell a story in a different way and you can illustrate it and bring it home. Also, people who are seeking out news do want both stimulation and facts, so in some of these surveys that you're talking about we have to separate news users from non–news users, and I think your trust and your dependence go way up from people who routinely use news.

The pollsters keep coming out with these reports that give me pause. Even after we went to war, the *Washington Post* came out with a poll [11]

showing that more than 40 percent of the American public still thought that Saddam Hussein was connected to 9/11. Now, you know, of course, everybody blames the press. Does the press have a role in creating the public's misperceptions? Why do you think the public has these misconceptions?

A lot of people were going around saying there was a connection to Saddam Hussein, so it's possible that people wanted to believe it and some believed it because they did believe it. So you have to say that that exists and that's true. If we had run a thousand more stories, would that have changed those positions? Absolutely not. I used to beat myself up over the years about what we could have done better and what we could not. I've become a little more relaxed and more willing to celebrate our successes and what we have gotten right. Again, if you look back on the last year, we've really done pretty well in getting a lot of answers to very difficult questions in a short amount of time.

Do you think that our journalists need to be better trained or that our news consumers need to be better educated? Or do you think the two should happen? I'm concerned about that Pew poll.

I don't know if I can solve your problem. There are some things you can worry about and some things you don't worry about. I think, first of all, journalists do need more training, and in specific areas. We need to do a lot better, and again I would come back to economics and business as an example, but certain specialty skills are lacking, particularly now as the world has seemingly become more interested in technology and as a lot of situations have changed, whether it's an aging society and how you deal with health care issues, the basic federal budget, or what have you. There have been a lot of federal budgets presented in my lifetime that have been myths, and most administrations have almost always gotten a pass on that. Why is that? Well, we can blame ourselves. We can do more training, but people have got to be interested in an issue before something moves. It's pretty interesting, the price of gas has been going up for a long time, but suddenly at above two dollars a gallon, the price of gas is a lot more interesting and those stories are getting much more detailed. So it follows a pattern. When there is more interest, we provide more, editors ask more questions, the graphics get more compelling, and the understanding becomes more complete. There are so many issues on any given day, how much is somebody really going to fight through? I sit in the AP international story conference in the morning, when bureaus from around the world are calling in with their stories. We select for the United States a handful of stories that we'll make available to our members, a few of whom will actually run them. And you really want to cry and say, "Does anybody care about what's going on in Zimbabwe this morning?" The story today hasn't risen enough to a point where it deserves to get more attention than Venezuela, or Singapore, or some other place that has made more dramatic news. You try to capture that on a weekend piece with perspective. You try to make sure that at least before the month is out, that story is written in a way that more people will use it and more people will see the light of day. And if you look at all the columns that are out there and all the pages and all the news content, there really is a lot more, and the great thing about the Internet is, if you're interested in Venezuela, you can just type in the word and get stories on Venezuela that you couldn't get access to before.

Yes, but the average American is a tired person who comes home and wants to turn on the TV or read a newspaper and know what's going on. It's interesting, too, that you're saying that the American people set the agenda for news. Is that what you're saying?

Absolutely. We are an audience-driven culture. We are very competitive. If we don't have what they want, they can vote with their eyeballs pretty quickly.

That explains a lot. Do you think other areas where reporters need more training are foreign reporting, international affairs, and national security affairs?

I'm not sure we need to worry about training. We need to have interest. The interest needs to be higher. When I go around and do the state meetings and meet with the state press associations, I usually ask if they would take a look at anything that's on the wire and put something in the paper that they otherwise wouldn't that interests them. It can be on any subject, but look at the world a little differently. Now I'm getting some really wonderful stories about reporting being done on sister cities in different countries that has led to circulation growth in US towns because it appealed to local ethnic groups that the newspaper hadn't paid as much attention to. So there have been some nice anecdotes, but it is a quick, global, fluid world and I think people understand that.

The story has moved though. The story used to be told in terms of the cold war—good guys and bad guys. And it's moved. It's moved to sports. It's moved to culture. It's moved to economics. Now it's moved to war, but it's different, and it's coming from many places, so it's harder to understand.

Some hard-core journalists say it's moved to entertainment.

There is an entertainment culture. It's been emerging for thirty years. Look at *People* magazine and the success of *People* magazine. When I go around and people say, "It's a great thing what you're doing with all the coverage of Iraq, but can you give me more pictures on the celebrities?" well, that's part of it and that's OK, and it's always been OK. The first correspondent in Nevada for the Associated Press was put there to do divorce stories and wedding stories, so this is an element of the human condition, too: how we get along and how we behave toward each other. You can't just deal with war and budgets all the time.

The perception from the outside world—and I'm sure you probably already know this—is that the United States is the nine-hundred-pound gorilla on the planet and all this stuff is going on, the world is blowing up, and where is the American press? Why aren't they reporting this to the American people? Why don't the American people know what's going on out here in the rest of the world, because we're affected by It?

Yes, that's the real story. I think that's the essence of what's really happened here. If you go back after 9/11 and listen to European broadcasts in the morning as I did on the way to work at the time, people said you could never go into Afghanistan, you would get lost in a morass the way the Russians did in Afghanistan, the way the United States did in Vietnam. It could not happen. Six weeks later, poof, it was gone and the weapons were totally different, and that really rearranged the planet and the game. That's something we haven't talked about. That's really core here. So you can be upset with Iraq for a lot of reasons and you can be for Iraq for a lot of reasons, but in terms of weapons and military and what the United States has done, it has really moved into a league of its own, and it did that without bringing in its allies and that's where the point of friction really began and where, if you will, competition began where there used to be allies and cooperation. That's a real story and I think there's no question that, at that point, political leaders started looking for things, and, being politicians, it was easy for them to find things. Some of it has worked and some of it hasn't worked over there. There have been some economic consequences to not supporting US policies, as well. These are all issues that should be discussed and discussed openly. These are the significant issues that need to be resolved, once you get beneath the surface of the noise over Iraq and what happened.

American journalism is a huge target just like America is a huge target and American journalism is very powerful all over the world, and that's why they're saying, "My God, why aren't the Americans better informed? Well, it's the press's fault." And the American journalists are telling us, "Well, the American people set the agenda." But some reporters have said, "No, no, no, no, our job is not to give them what they want, it's to give them what they need to know." What do you think of that?

That's a deep problem. It is an audience-driven culture. And audiences are going in many different directions. People are competing vigorously to hold viewers or readers. There is no question about that. The pressures are great these days. Everyone is looking for the formula. But there is more news consumption now than there ever has been. It's just going in a lot of different media and much of that is good news. But for legacy media, it's also a great challenge.

There's a lot of news but the question is, what kind of news? That's where the argument is.

No, I think there's a lot of substance and a lot of depth and a lot of perspective. You can get access to great thinkers, you can get easy access to what people are saying in Europe or other places, and to opinions from around the world. Again, it's flowing in a way that does try to shape it and the AP works really hard to try to bring what Europeans or Asians are saying about the United States to the United States.

So do you think the American population needs to grow up as news consumers then?

Oh, no.

Do you think it would be a good idea if the American population were more informed given our position in the world and given some of the more dangerous things that are happening now, post-9/11?

I've listened to the hand-wringing and I have a different view. The American people are informed. They may not be informed on a specific thing at a given moment, but very soon they are informed. They work hard, they are able to process, they are able to make judgments. I've been out there and I've had a lot of conversations with a lot of people, but you can't deny the amount of news media that are providing information. From when you get up in the morning until you go to bed, you can look at your Palm Pilots or Blackberries and get instant news alerts these days.

You have access to incredible amounts of information at any level of depth, and it's not just the dailies or twenty-four-hour cable. You have the magazines weighing in with perspective and depth. It's really tough to make the case that we're dumb and uninformed.

THOMAS CURLEY became president and chief executive officer of the Associated Press on June 1, 2003. He is the twelfth person to lead the AP since its founding in 1848. Under Curley's leadership, the AP is evolving from a wire service to an interactive global news network geared to meet the content needs and marketplace demands of members and customers worldwide.

Curley has restructured senior AP management, created an international division to drive content and new business overseas, charted the development of technology to create a multimedia database for all AP content, and encouraged initiatives to celebrate exceptional and distinctive AP journalism.

Curley says the company's initiatives are aimed at making the Associated Press the essential global news network. "We intend for the Associated Press to be the first words people say when they think of news," he says.

Curley was previously president and publisher of *USA Today*, the nation's largest-selling daily newspaper. Since 1998 he has been senior vice president of the newspaper's owner, Gannett Co., Inc., publisher of one hundred daily newspapers in the United States. *USA Today*'s circulation under Curley grew to more than 2.3 million copies a day.

Curley was the original news staffer on the project that led to the creation of *USA Today*. He was assigned in 1979 by then Gannett chairman Al Neuharth to study the feasibility of a national newspaper. He later worked in every department of the newspaper. In 1986 he became the newspaper's sixth president and in 1991 added the title of publisher.

At the age of fifteen, Curley began his journalism career covering high school basketball for his hometown *Easton (PA) Express*. He continued working for newspapers during college and joined Gannett's *Rochester (NY) Times-Union* in 1972 as night city/suburban editor. He became director of information for Gannett in 1976 and began coordinating Gannett's newspaper research projects, which produced more than fifty thousand interviews on media use. He became editor of Gannett's *Norwich (CT) Bulletin* in 1982 and publisher of the *Courier-News* in Bridgewater, New Jersey, in 1983 before returning to *USA Today* in 1985.

Curley holds a political science degree from Philadelphia's La Salle University and a master's degree in business administration from Rochester Institute of Technology. He is a vice chairman of the boards at both schools.

Curley is married to Marsha Stanley, a former newspaper reporter and freelance writer. They have two daughters.

NOTES

1. Herbert Marshall McLuhan (1911–1980) was known as the Oracle of the Electronic Age or the "guru" of media culture. On his estate's official Web site, http://www.marshallmcluhan.com/main.html, McLuhan is said to have "articulated his perceptions of media as extensions of the human body, and of electronic media, in particular, as extensions of the nervous system, imposing, like poetry, their own assumptions on the psyche of the user."

2. In a September 7, 2002, joint press conference, President Bush and British prime minister Tony Blair both mentioned an International Atomic Energy Agency report that Blair said came out "this morning" and that Bush said showed that Saddam Hussein was "six months away from developing a weapon." There was no such report. According to the *Washington Post*'s Walter Pincus, the leaders misspoke and were actually referring to a recent report put out by the International Institute for Strategic Studies in London. (See chapter 9 in this book.)

3. In a July 27, 1997, article for Fairness and Accuracy in Reporting titled "Thirty Year Anniversary: Gulf of Tonkin Lie Launched Vietnam War," Norman Solomon wrote: "The official story was that North Vietnamese torpedo boats launched an 'unprovoked attack' against a U.S. destroyer 'on routine patrol' in the Tonkin Gulf on August 2 [1964]—and that North Vietnamese PT boats followed up with a 'deliberate attack' on a pair of U.S. ships two days later. The truth was different. Rather than being on routine patrol on August 2, the U.S. destroyer *Maddox* was actually engaged in aggressive intelligence-gathering maneuvers—in sync with coordinated attacks on North Vietnam by the South Vietnamese navy and the Laotian air force." President Johnson ordered US bombers to retaliate, and the Gulf of Tonkin Resolution essentially declaring war on North Vietnam passed through Congress easily. http://www.fair.org/index.php?page=2261.

4. In April 2003 nineteen-year-old Pvt. Jessica Lynch was captured when her company took a wrong turn and was ambushed near Nassiriya, Iraq. Nine of her fellow soldiers were killed. She was taken to a hospital by Iraqi soldiers where she was held for eight days with a broken thigh, broken arm, and dislocated ankle. The Pentagon falsely claimed to the press that she had stab and bullet wounds and had been slapped in her hospital bed. They released footage of a daring raid on the hospital to rescue Lynch and talked about "brave souls putting their lives on the line to make it happen." Lynch had been treated well at the hospital, and there were no soldiers there when her rescuers arrived with cameras rolling to take her away. In his May 15, 2003, article for the UK's *Guardian*, John Kampfner described Lynch's rescue as "one of the most stunning pieces of news management yet conceived."

5. Hill & Knowlton (H&K) is one of the oldest PR firms in the United States. According to the Center for Media and Democracy's SourceWatch, in 1990 H&K went to work for the government of Kuwait, organizing PR in support of the war with Iraq. During the Nayirah affair in the first Gulf War, Victoria Clarke was general manager of Hill & Knowlton's Washington, DC, office. Clarke would later become assistant secretary of defense for public affairs for the George W. Bush administration. http://www.sourcewatch.org/index.php?title=Hill_%26_Knowlton.

6. SARS (Severe Acute Respiratory Syndrome), according to the Centers for Disease Control, "is a viral respiratory illness caused by a coronavirus. . . . SARS was first reported in Asia in February 2003." Over the next few months, the illness spread to more than two dozen countries in North America, South America, Europe, and Asia before the SARS global outbreak of 2003 was contained. http://www.cdc.gov/ncidod/sars/factsheet.htm.

7. Monica Lewinsky was an intern at the White House with whom President Bill Clinton initially denied having sexual relations. He said this in a televised statement on January 26, 1998. Later, in August 1998, Clinton admitted he'd had an inappropriate relationship with Lewinsky. Less than one month later, after conducting an investigation into the matter, independent counsel Kenneth Starr delivered a report to Congress outlining a case for impeaching Clinton on eleven grounds, including lying under oath to a federal grand jury, obstructing justice, and witness-tampering. The House approved impeaching the president for lying under oath to a federal grand jury and obstruction of justice. On February 12, 1999, the Senate voted to acquit the president on both charges.

8. The Associated Press reported on April 23, 2004, that photos taken at Dover Air Force Base of flag-draped coffins of US war dead from Iraq had been released to First Amendment–activist Russ Kick, who had filed a request under the Freedom of Information Act. Defense Department officials said releasing the photos was against a policy prohibiting media coverage of human remains. In the article, the AP reported that "President Bush . . . believes that family privacy should be respected" while "some activists argue that the photos . . . underscore the war's human cost." http://www.msnbc.msn.com/id/4807865/.

9. The Health Insurance Portability and Accountability Act (HIPAA) was passed on August 21, 1996, and is designed to protect the medical privacy of patients by giving them more control over their health information and limiting the use and release of their health records to third parties. According to the Reporters Committee for Freedom of the Press, "doctors, hospitals and other health care providers [must] obtain a patient's written consent before using or disclosing the patient's personal health information." The use of such records for marketing and research purposes is also restricted. http://www.rcfp.org/pullouts/medicalprivacy/particulars.html.

10. At the Abu Ghraib prison in Iraq, American soldiers from a US military intelligence unit, US military police, and some civilian contractors abused and tortured their prisoners. Shocking photos of their activities were released, showing naked prisoners being forced into humiliating sexual and other poses, while their captors were pictured with them giving "thumbs-up" signs and, in at least one case, holding a leash with a prisoner on the other end.

11. In a September 6, 2003, article on the poll titled "Hussein Link to 9/11 Lingers in Many Minds," *Washington Post* reporters Dana Milbank and Claudia Deane wrote: "Sixty-nine percent of Americans said they thought it at least likely that Hussein was involved in the attacks on the World Trade Center and the Pentagon." http://www.washingtonpost.com/wpsrv/politics/polls/vault/stories/data082303.htm.

4
"EVERYBODY WANTS TO BE AT VERSAILLES"

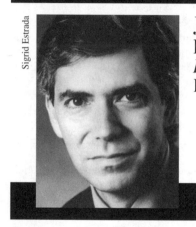

Sigrid Estrada

JOHN MacARTHUR
President and Publisher,
Harper's Magazine
Interviewed May 2004

S ome might find John MacArthur's candor about the problems of the press and the shortcomings of some of journalism's best-known icons shocking. I think it's refreshing. In fact, it is a whole new order of refreshing to hear a journalist and executive in the news business speak so fearlessly. Obviously, neither he nor his magazine has to kowtow to anyone to survive and, indeed, thrive. This is a privilege and, of course, John MacArthur comes from privilege. As the grandson of self-made billionaire John D. MacArthur and the son of self-made millionaire and civil liberties advocate Roderick MacArthur, John MacArthur is genetically programmed to be successful and of public service. Scions of wealthy families like his are often reared to have a strong sense of noblesse oblige about giving back to the country or society that has given so much to them. *Harper's Magazine* is MacArthur's public service. On one hand, it is a journal of literature, culture, and the arts. On the other hand, *Harper's* coverage of politics and current events regularly kicks the powerful and corrupt in the teeth.

John looks and dresses like the standard American preppie, but that's deceptive. He speaks fluent French and is far more cosmopolitan than his appearance conveys. His salt-and-pepper hair and boyish features give the impression of a young man in his thirties gone prematurely gray. Actually, as I write this, he's a couple of years shy of fifty. When you meet him, you think you're going to be dealing with Mr. Mild-Mannered. The minute he starts talking, you realize you're wrong. You realize, too, that his sense of mission goes back a long way: "A lot of us got into journalism because we thought it was our role and our responsibility to never again accept the lies that were told during Vietnam." Now, as the United States is embroiled in a conflict bearing earmarks of the Vietnam War, MacArthur is more riled than ever. He talks about the "courtier press" in Washington. He compares the nation's capital to Versailles during the reign of the *roi soleil* (sun king), Louis IV. "Everybody wants to be in Versailles," he said, close to the power structure and to the current sun king, George W. Bush. MacArthur began with a devastating riff on the press's post-9/11 performance.

The performance of the American press leading up to the second Gulf War or the invasion of Iraq was *meprisable* [despicable]. It was just pathetic. It was the worst it's been since before Vietnam. The American press swallowed and regurgitated and amplified just about every lie the Bush administration put forward, starting with a press conference on September 7, 2002, featuring Tony Blair and George Bush, where they spoke about a new report from the International Atomic Energy Agency[1] that supposedly said that Saddam was six months away from building a nuclear weapon. There was no new report. Few in the press pointed it out immediately. This is major news; "President cites nonexistent report menacing nuclear holocaust," and practically no one reports it.

Curiously, the most thorough account of the fact that there was no International Atomic Energy Agency report appeared about three weeks later in the *Washington Times*, a right-wing, prowar newspaper. The article, "Iraq Report Cited by Bush Does Not Exist: Agency Disavows Report on Iraq Arms," came out on September 27, 2002. From there to October 11 and 12, 2002, which was when the US Congress authorized the war or the invasion of Iraq and gave Bush carte blanche, you had a series of scare stories that appeared in the press. Some of them were based on the *New York Times'* Judith Miller's reporting on the aluminum tubes, which were supposed to be part of a revived atomic bomb program. In the first story, which appeared on September 8, 2002, under Judith Miller and Michael Gordon's byline, you had a quote that stayed with a lot of people—a great piece of propaganda—in which they quoted a senior administration official who was probably Vice President Cheney saying, "If we wait too long to find the smoking gun, the smoking gun may well turn into a mushroom cloud." So you couldn't have a more explicit scare story, a more explicit piece of propaganda than that: if you don't invade Iraq, if you don't attack or disarm Saddam Hussein, he may bring nuclear holocaust to the United States. This story was absolutely false from beginning to end. It was utterly fraudulent. The aluminum tubes, as the International Atomic Energy Agency later pointed out, were meant for conventional rockets, not for the gas centrifuges that are required for making nuclear weapons. But that's just one part of the scare story. Nowhere in that crucial period between September 7 and October 12 did the American press stand up to this tidal wave of nonsense. Again, the great exceptions are the *Washington Times*, me, and Scott Ritter, the weapons inspector from the UN who has since disappeared. He's now been vindicated beyond his wildest imagination, and have you heard anything about Scott Ritter? Has anybody borne him aloft on their shoulders and celebrated his prescience on the war? Has he been permitted to say "I told you so" on all those national TV shows that ridiculed him and called him a friend of Saddam on the take from Iraq? It's just astonishing.

There was an atmosphere in New York and Washington of subservience mixed with a kind of panic among the press corps. They didn't really know which end was up, so they just reported the administration line. Then there were some reporters like Judith Miller who did extra work, got extra credit, and amplified the story. To this day, I don't understand why people are saying that her source was Ahmed Chalabi.[2] A lot of people say that she got a lot of her information about the weapons of mass destruction from Chalabi. It's clear that she got most of her information from the White House directly from Cheney, because the technique for propaganda is to leak the story to the *New York Times*, where it appears on the front page;

then on the talk shows on Sunday morning when the story appears, Vice President Cheney or whoever from the administration cites the story in the *New York Times* as evidence for going to war against Saddam.

There's a second important point about this. The term "weapons of mass destruction" is a nonexpression. It's Orwellian. The distinctions are absurd. If you're talking about weapons of mass destruction, well, conventional bombs used in Dresden and Tokyo were weapons of mass destruction. Ask anybody who was there. There are plenty of survivors who can tell you about it. They deliberately used this meaningless expression "weapons of mass destruction" to conflate atomic bombs, chemical weapons, and biological weapons. Virtually nobody in the American press took the trouble to make the distinction among these three things. The scare story, the threat that was sold by the Bush administration before October 12, was an atomic bomb threat—that Saddam was going to have an atomic bomb—not a chemical weapons or a biological weapons threat. Reasonable people could disagree on these things, but anybody knows that an atomic bomb is far more lethal and will kill far more people than chemical or biological weapons. The latter depends on which way the wind's blowing and how many you drop. You're talking about tens of thousands or hundreds of thousands versus hundreds and thousands perhaps. Sometimes they misfire and they don't kill anybody. So as soon as the vote was finished, as soon as Congress authorized the invasion, they switched from atomic bomb scare stories to weapons of mass destruction stories because they knew, if the atomic bomb story fell apart, which it did, they could still confuse the American public and the world public by referring to weapons of mass destruction, knowing that many people would assume they were still talking about atom bombs, which is what happened.

> **We interviewed Carl Bernstein yesterday, who feels that now and in the last twenty-five years the press has done a good job. I asked him the same question I just asked you about the weapons of mass destruction: how come this was reported no questions asked, and so on? And he essentially said to me, "The administration's remarks about weapons of mass destruction has to be reported, but how do you go and confirm it? You can't go over there and do a physical inventory." Now you just said to me that you managed to check out the reference to the IAEA report within a reasonable amount of time. What did you do that nobody else was able to do?**

I just read the newspapers and somebody here at *Harper's* said, "You know, there is no IAEA report." When I found out there was no IAEA report on Saddam's nuclear capabilities, and I saw Scott Ritter saying, "Look, we think we took care of it by December 1998," I just put two and two together and I said, "This is obviously hokum. It's propaganda; it's a scare story." These are unsourced stories; Judith Miller never names anybody. Then—I do feel a little guilty, I should have been more aggressive, but in addition to being a journalist, I have a full-time job as a publisher— *60 Minutes* and I finally got around to finding an alternative source, which was David Albright, a former UNSCOM[3] weapons inspector who said that in his community of former weapons inspectors and arms experts it was well known that the aluminum tube story was nonsense.

David Albright said on national television on December 8, 2002, that it was well known in his community of former UNSCOM people and weapons inspectors that the aluminum tube story was nonsense and that the aluminum tubes had nothing to do with a revived atomic bomb program. Even then, the print press, the liberal press, did nothing.

Why?

They didn't bother to go find alternative sources. These people were all over the place. Any reporter knows that if there's one weapons inspector speaking publicly, there are others who aren't. Bureaucrats are timid people. They're civil servants. They worry about their next job. They worry about their pensions, like weapons expert Dr. David Kelly[4] in England. They're not bold people. They're not bold the way politicians are bold. The way some journalists are bold. You have to go find them. But if there's one Scott Ritter saying this, that means there are ten or twenty Scott Ritters quietly saying it. You just have to go find them. It doesn't take much work.

Why do you think people like Bernstein, like Judith Miller . . . these are big people.

Carl Bernstein is covering for the establishment press. That's what he comes from. He comes from the *Washington Post* and he's covering for the Washington press. These are institutional people with institutional loyalties. Their loyalties are to the institution first and to the people who read the newspaper second. They don't see their responsibilities the same way that, say, Seymour Hersh[5] sees them.

That's too mind-blowing for me because I feel these are journalists. What is the definition of a journalist? There's a huge disconnect here between "Oh, I'm going to just go ahead and perpetuate a humongous lie" and being a journalist.

The journalists don't know for sure it's a humongous lie, but they see their role as following the party line and repeating or accurately reporting what the government is saying. In the case of someone like Judith Miller, who has a private agenda of overthrowing Saddam Hussein, she really wants to get in on the act; she wants to help amplify the story. But most reporters are not that active. They're just passive. They take the feed and they repeat it.

The *Washington Post* has some very good reporters—Barton Gellman[6] and White House reporter Dana Milbank—and they have good sources. Walter Pincus,[7] another good reporter for the *Washington Post*, has said that if you went into the newsroom and said, "I've got a story that contradicts the official line. I've got a story that says that the weapons threat from Saddam is greatly exaggerated," that maybe one story would appear and get buried on page sixteen or twenty. And if you kept it up, if you kept saying, "I want to do more on this," you would get shut out. They would tell you to shut up and go back to your desk. If you kept pressing it, you would find yourself reassigned to the dog-catching beat. That's the way journalism works in an official journalism town like Washington with one newspaper, basically, and with reporters who are largely dependent on official sources for patronage and for leaks. They can't operate without being part of the system. Or they feel they can't operate without being part of the governmental system of leaks. Nobody in top management encourages them to think otherwise. Donald Graham, the publisher of the *Washington Post*, is a very conservative man. He doesn't want to upset the applecart. He doesn't want to challenge power. He is power. He's part of the establishment in Washington.

But isn't it a fundamental rule of journalism that you check what you're told and if it's not true you report that it's not true?

Not anymore. It's not a fundamental rule anymore. It was when I was coming up. I've told this story a hundred times to reporters who are out of daily journalism, and they say, "Gee, I would have gotten fired for not checking that aluminum tube story or the IAEA report." Not anymore. Nobody asks you to check anything. What you have to check is your guts and your independent thinking at the door when you go in the front door of your newspaper. And you have to check with power. You have to check with the top people in authority before you run anything.

It's true also that in Washington itself a marshal kind of military spirit develops among the press corps. They want to be part of it. To say "This is crazy to invade Iraq. First of all, Saddam's flat on his back. There's been an embargo on for eight years; he's a paper tiger, as we saw in the last war. The idea that he could do any damage to us or to anybody now is absurd. What are we doing?" puts you out of step with 95 percent of your colleagues and you don't feel good personally. You feel left out. And the next thing you know, you stop getting invited to parties, and people say you're a crank and a weirdo. You're not part of the team anymore.

What you are saying is that we have a press that is basically a collection of stenographers.

It depends on what period of history you're talking about. Sometimes the press is a stenographer pool. It was most definitely a stenographer pool in the run-up to this war. Sometimes it's more combative, like it was in the latter stages of Vietnam and in the early- to mid-seventies when investigative reporting was fashionable and Woodward and Bernstein were at the height of their fame. Seymour Hersh was making waves with his reporting on the CIA. Newspapers can and have been very aggressive in this country, but we also go through periods where the press is, strictly speaking, not acting. It is acted upon by Congress and by the president and it just becomes a propaganda arm for the government.

I wonder about whether the increasing concentration of power within corporations, whether more and more mergers of newspapers and television networks has contributed to this cautiousness. This is very much a left-wing analysis, one that probably Noam Chomsky[8] and other left-wing media critics would subscribe to. I've always been cautious about that because I see it more as a social problem. I remember Christopher Hitchens[9] who used to be a great left-winger and is now a famous right-winger saying that the American press is generally passive because they take the Constitution seriously. And in the Constitution we are sovereign, including the reporters. It's our government. So to attack the government very aggressively, to really say they're liars, they're terrible, in a sense is to attack ourselves, our very own Constitution. The British press has no such illusions. They know it's not their government. They know they're outside of the power structure, so they don't have any illusions about it. The reporters and the editors in Washington flatter themselves that they are part of the constitutional apparatus and that gives them a special responsibility to be polite to politicians. That's one theory. My theory is more along the lines of the social one: that nobody likes to be isolated socially. Everybody wants to be at Versailles. Washington is Versailles. They want to be

close to *le roi soleil* [the sun king], they want to be part of the power structure, and if taking the official leak from the official source gets you credit
within your news organization, getting close to Cheney, getting close to
Rumsfeld, getting their story across to the American people—if that brings
you credit and more invitations and more promotions, it's a great way to
live. If you go contrary to that, you wind up back in Cleveland.

That sounds like corruption.

It's a kind of corruption. I don't think it's about money, although some of
it is becoming more and more about money in the sense that if you can
get on a talk show and spout the conventional wisdom on a TV show,
you're more likely to be hired as the speaker for the national widget convention in Des Moines where there is real money. You get paid twenty,
twenty-five thousand dollars for that.

**What are the implications for our society if we have a press like that? If
our elite press, particularly those who reach the mass public consciousness—because that's the era that we're in now—is like that?**

You've seen the implications. You've seen the result. We're now embroiled in a disaster in Iraq, an absolute, unmitigated disaster with thousands of people getting killed for no good reason, no strategy for getting
out, Iraqi society in chaos—worse than it was, I think, under Saddam
Hussein—I'm prepared to say that now. Besides which, as a moral question which I posed to Bernard-Henri Levy,[10] I said, "Is it really worth the
lives of ten thousand, fifteen thousand Iraqis to establish a democracy if
you could?" Because I don't think we can there. I say no, it's not worth
it. I don't think it was worth it. We weren't invited to do it. And these
polls about did we do the right thing or not, or do you want the Americans here . . . well, you can't ask the dead what they think. Are they better
off than they were before the Americans came? It's insane. And that's the
implication, that's the result of an uninformed, passive press. You saw it
right up to the minute before we invaded. Bush was a royal presence. In
his last so-called press conference, it looked like Versailles. He came
down a very wide corridor and came up to the lectern and the press was
there, very respectful, very polite, almost terrified, like a bunch of
courtiers. They had truly become a courtier press.

　　To give a good example of the American press at its worst, we can
look at the toppling of the Saddam statue right after the supposed liberation of Baghdad. Everybody who looked at the picture on the Internet

could see that there were very few people in the square, that this had to be done by the American army, and that it was essentially staged for the American army and for the reelection campaign of George W. Bush. People said there was a miniscandal about the soldier putting first the American flag up and then, "Oh, I made a mistake, I've got to put the Iraq flag up." That wasn't a mistake; it was deliberate. They wanted two takes for the television commercial that they thought they would be able to run for Bush's reelection campaign. They didn't know whether they would use the Iraqi flag or the American flag or both, so they wanted the choice.

Everybody in the square knew that this was a put-up job, that this was a staged-for-TV, fake event. Yet everybody reported it as if there was tremendous enthusiasm and that mobs of people were cheering the liberation of Baghdad and the toppling of Saddam. You have to ask yourself: is it because of fear or is it routine self-censorship? I think it's more banal. It's a bureaucratic sort of automatic self-censorship: "Am I going to fight with my desk back in New York? Am I going to fight with my editors back in New York and say, 'this is ridiculous, this was a staged event for public relations purposes,' and get into a big fight when everybody else says it's the liberation of Baghdad and everybody's cheering? I don't want to get into a fight with my bosses."

I'll give you an example. A reporter for a Canadian newspaper, *La Presse* of Montreal, reported the truth, which was that this was a put-up job; it was staged. His editors back in Montreal said, "It can't be, everybody says it's a mob and they're cheering." He says, "No, it's not," and he filed a story. They killed it. They wouldn't run it. Days later, they apologized to him. They realized they'd been wrong and he'd been right, but they never ran his original version of the story. I have it.

In my book *Second Front: Censorship and Propaganda in the 1991 Gulf War* I talk about the difference in the approach of the French—at least the television journalists I know—and the American press. There's the example of Vincent Nguyen of France 2, who was far from the heaviest fighting, but he was up in Kurdistan and he was confronted with media-trained American soldiers who were trained, as he said, to say nothing in as many words as possible. They wouldn't let him and some other reporters into their temporary base that they'd set up, so they sent out about ten soldiers with their rifles and pretended to answer questions. Vincent, instead of just filming it straight the way an American TV crew would, was literally just quoting them and pretending like they were interesting. He backed away and shot it wide so you could see the sort of absurd circuslike atmosphere of it—that it was a kind of chorus line of soldiers trained to say nothing in front of a mob of reporters who were, in this case, incapable of asking anything substantive. They couldn't get a substantive question asked or answered. So that's a difference in culture, and I do think that the European culture of war coverage is now fundamentally different from the American one.

We used to have very good war correspondents and we had great war photographers. We still have a few, but for the most part, we've subcontracted our war reporting—the real stuff—to foreigners. And when the foreigners bring back the goods, we don't want to show it in many cases. All you would have to do is run Al Jazeera[11] footage and have Americans comment on it and you would do better than anything CBS, NBC, ABC, or CNN are now doing in Iraq, because the reporters at Al Jazeera speak Arabic and they're trusted by the Iraqis, so they can get in places we can't get into, and they show the actual face of war. They show the violence, and they show the corpses. We don't show that. We didn't show it during the run-up to the war.

I certainly agree with those who say that the press of all countries have a tendency to fall into line in wartime when the interests of their own government, their own country, are at stake. The French are no different from the Belgians, the Russians, or the Americans. But I would make the exception when it comes to the British press because the British press was majority prowar, but there was a significant minority that was antiwar and challenged the official line, including the *Daily Mirror*, the *Spectator*, the *Guardian*, the *Observer*, and reporters like Patrick Cockburn, John Pilger, and John Simpson of the BBC. The British press did a better job than the American press of covering their own war in this case. They have a more ferocious sense of skepticism than the American press has, and they take risks. They're not as easily cowed as we are. These are people who see themselves as reporters first and spokesmen for the government last. It's not their job to carry political water for the government. I can't think of more than about one or two American reporters on mainstream television and in newspapers who saw themselves the way John Simpson sees himself at the BBC.

What American reporters?

There was a reporter for *Newsday* named Letta Taylor who was embedded. She's not a war correspondent, just a reporter who got in with everybody else. She goes and travels with a marine unit that saw some action. She quotes the marines the way they really talk. All the other reporters are cleaning up all the bad language. She just reports it. They put little bleeps and dashes and so on, but she has them talking about the Arabs the way soldiers really talk about the Arabs, which is to say, "These are inferior people, they're ragheads. We're not here to liberate anybody, we don't care if they give us a hard time, we'll turn their village into a parking lot." This is the way soldiers talk. They're not sensitive, politically correct public relations agents; they're soldiers. So just her reporting on the way they talked and how they felt after killing people, which was also very good, was better than anything I saw during the Gulf War.

I have to compare the pool system of 1991 to the embedded system of 2003. The embedded system was less bad because it did afford some reporters the opportunity to see something, which was better than nothing. In 1991 there was nothing. There were just videotapes released by the Pentagon and secondhand stories. And Peter Arnett in Baghdad. That's all there was. In this war, you had a few reporters who took advantage of the embedding and actually did a pretty good job.

There's one other example, and it goes to the point that you don't necessarily have to be there to be a good war reporter. Seymour Hersh proved that with My Lai, for example. William Brannigan of the *Washington Post* did the best story on a shoot-up of an Iraqi car that went through a checkpoint where a bunch of civilians were killed, because he heard it on the radio in the tank he was in. He didn't see it. He was far away from it, but he heard the whole exchange between the officer who ordered the shooting and the poor guy who did the shooting who felt terrible after he did it, and they realized they'd made a mess of the first order and that was good. But these were the exceptions. Most of the broadcast reporting showed people loading trucks and zooming through the desert and firing rockets and virtually no corpses on either side. Ted Koppel[12] did show a couple of corpses, but he was more like a big-game hunter putting his foot on a lion than a journalist covering real combat or real horror. The print press was very squeamish about showing pictures of dead bodies or wounded people as well. There were almost no pictures of civilians, and we know they were stacked up in hospitals. We know this from the French and British presses. We know from the Canadian press. We don't know it from the American press. The *New York Times*, at the very end of the war, ran one horrible picture of civilian corpses stacked up in a hospital. But by and large the American people saw nothing of the real face of war, which isn't to say that a few embedded reporters didn't do a pretty good job under the circumstances.

I don't know who had the brilliant idea to do embedding, but they knew that self-censorship would achieve most of what overt censorship achieved in the 1991 Gulf War. These people are brilliant at public relations and at manipulation; that's what they know. They don't know politics, they don't know foreign languages, and they don't know anything about history. They really know public relations. That's what they're good at—advertising and public relations.

Who are these people?

People in the Defense Department, people who work for Defense Secretary Rumsfeld, public relations people from Hill & Knowlton. Victoria Clarke, the spokeswoman for the Pentagon, comes out of Hill & Knowlton. It's no surprise, no coincidence that Hill & Knowlton was the quarterback of the White House public relations campaign and the propaganda campaign in 1991 when they faked the baby incubator atrocity. It's not a coincidence that the best people in public relations come out of companies like Hill & Knowlton and go to work for the government and go back into public relations. They go back and forth and back and forth. They know what they're doing. I don't know who thought of embedding, but it was brilliant.

Since you mentioned the Kuwaiti baby incident, could you go into that?

I've said that the causus belli for the first Gulf War was human rights in the end. A lot of people who would have voted against going to war against Saddam Hussein to evict him from Kuwait voted for it because they said, "Well, in the end, this guy is Hitler; he's an equivalent of Hitler. He's killing babies in incubators and we have to get rid of him. You wouldn't let Hitler stay in power in Germany, would you?" Remember, it was a very close vote in the Senate anyway, to go to war, and the first Bush administration knew they were losing steam in the months running up to the war. The argument "no blood for oil," that the war was about oil and not about liberating Kuwait and that Kuwait wasn't free to begin with, was starting to catch fire. People were starting to think, "Is it really worth getting anybody killed to liberate a bunch of oil wells owned by a little oligarchy called the al-Sabahs?[13] Maybe there's some other way around this. Maybe sanctions are better. Maybe we shouldn't do it. Maybe there's a better way to handle this. After all, Saddam Hussein is our monster. We created him. Let's wait a little bit."

Knowing this, the Bush administration, in conjunction with the

Kuwaitis and their joint public relations agency, Hill & Knowlton, fabricated a story about Iraqi soldiers in occupied Kuwait pulling newborn babies out of incubators and leaving them on the floor to die and then looting the incubators to take them back to Baghdad. The principal witness for this story was a young fifteen-year-old girl who testified in front of the congressional human rights congress. She identified herself only as Nayirah. Nayirah told a hair-raising story about personally witnessing fifteen or sixteen babies being pulled from incubators and left to die on the cold floor. That's what she said in the press release. In person, she said babies. She didn't specify the number of babies and she cried, famously, on national television while she told this horrible tale. She presented herself as a refugee from Kuwait who had to keep her identity anonymous for fear of reprisals against her family back in Kuwait.

I learned and reported later in the *New York Times*, ironically, that Nayirah was the daughter of the Kuwaiti ambassador to the United States. It's very unlikely she was in Kuwait at the time that she said she was, and certainly she was not a disinterested witness. Subsequently, more reporting was done. It turned out that the Iraqis pulled no babies from incubators. There's not a single documented case of a baby being pulled from an incubator and dying during the occupation of Kuwait. It just didn't happen. It's a fabrication. But it had a tremendous influence on public opinion here, and it clearly influenced the vote of several senators who otherwise might not have voted for the war. The Senate resolution passed by only five votes. Many senators talked about human rights and several mentioned the baby incubator atrocity specifically as a reason for voting for the Gulf War. So this is like what happened in World War I with the propaganda about the Germans bayoneting Belgian babies. In this case, it got us into a war that might not have happened otherwise. The Gulf War in 1991 is much closer to Vietnam, so people are still very skeptical. You've got more Vietnam veterans in Congress; you've got both Kerrys. It could have gone the other way without the propaganda. This time, the aluminum tubes or the fake nuclear rearmament campaign are, I think, the equivalent of the baby incubator story.

Why does propaganda still have legs?

People want to believe what the government tells them. They have a tendency to believe what authority tells them, I guess. You have to have independent-minded people and reporters and citizens; a well-educated citizenry is the best defense against this kind of thing. America has been media-trained to death. There's not enough competing information on television and in the newspapers. They've been trained to watch television, and television is very superficial. Newspapers are also very superficial. They can't just blame television. In fact, as I said, *60 Minutes* and French television, which also did a very good story on the propaganda campaign with me, did better than print. It's like Hermann Goering[14] said during the Nuremberg war trials, "All you have to do is tell people that they're threatened by a foreign enemy and they'll follow. It happens the same way in a democracy as in a dictatorship, you just have to scare them. But you do need the help of the press to scare them."

Talk about Fox and the war coverage and Fox's rapid rise in audience share.

I think the Fox effect is terribly exaggerated. Fox television is a circus. It's not news; it's entertainment. It's not a news source. People who believe that stuff believe other wild, inane stuff coming from other sources before. I'm sure they all read other things or got information from other sources that were equally preposterous. It's just a circus. Their ratings are still not big enough to really be able to blame them for what's happened in the country. It's certainly a symptom of what's wrong with the American press, but it's not the cause. *CBS Evening News* with Dan Rather, the supposedly liberal CBS, got a more favorable rating than Fox for its Iraq war reporting from the Media Research Center,[15] a right-wing, prowar media watchdog group. They got a higher grade. They got a B+. Fox got a B. Dan Rather was particularly disgraceful before, during, and after the war. He was just a cheerleader for power, a cheerleader for the administration. Even now, when he goes to redeem himself with the pictures of Abu Ghraib prison, he sits on the story for two weeks. Nobody's called him on this. Because the chairman of the Joint Chiefs of Staff asked him to sit on the story? And then he says, essentially, "We only broke the story because we had to. We didn't break the story because we should, or because it's the right thing to do for the American people or for the world. We broke the story because somebody else was going to break it. It was going to come out on the Internet." This is just utter cowardice on his part.

He's kind of an interesting case because Dan was very aggressive with Nixon, he was very aggressive with George H. W. Bush on the Iran-Contra stuff, and then all of a sudden it's a new era and seemingly a new Dan. How do you account for that?

I interviewed him twelve years ago and he talks a good game and he makes the speech about being tough and independent, but then you look at his ten-million-dollar salary, and you see the theatrical mirror in his dressing room, and you realize this guy is a showbiz hack who makes a lot of money. He's not a journalist anymore. He's a media celebrity. He hasn't done journalism in a long time.

I've forgotten to say the obvious thing, which is that Dan Rather is not his own boss. Whatever Dan Rather really thinks, we don't know. We do know that the owners of CBS are very conservative people. As the journalist and author A. J. Liebling famously said, "Freedom of the press is guaranteed only to those who own one." So the owners of the press set the tone for the reporters. If the chairman of Viacom,[16] Mel Karmazin, wanted aggressive, challenging, controversial opposition journalism, he could get it. But the people working for Mel Karmazin don't think that's what he wants. They assume that's what he doesn't want. We know over the years that there are so many examples of reporters trying to go up against their bosses and being crushed. The owners decide what kind of journalism we get. By and large the owners are very conservative, go-along-to-get-along establishment figures.

Some left-wing analysts argue that the media conglomerates are further stifling independent reporting within big news organizations; too many mergers, too much money at stake. They may have a point as far as they go because I think we're better off with independent press barons—very rich men or women—who are answerable only to themselves as opposed to stockholders or public stockholders where huge amounts of money are at stake and where the CEO is really in charge of protecting the stock, not the company. Controversy, in his or her mind, could hurt the stock price—he/she doesn't want it. That could send a message of cautiousness through the ranks of journalists, and I think the story of CNN supports that notion. Ted Turner was our last real press baron. Ted Turner was a guy with no politics, no ideology. He's a businessman. He's interested in making money, he's interested in being a big man, he may have an interest in the environment, but he's not an ideologue. He's just a guy who thinks, "I do what I want because it's my network and if I want Peter Arnett in Baghdad, nobody's going to tell me not to do it. Not the president of the United States, nobody." I think he sent Peter Arnett to Baghdad because he thought it was good for CNN as a business. He didn't do it out of principle. Better that than the cautious bureaucrat at a publicly held corporation who says, "Oh, I don't want a lot of letters from the stockholders saying, 'What are you opposing the president for? Why are you sending a reporter to Baghdad when the president says not to?'" Turner felt empowered to do what he wanted because he owned it. Now CNN is owned by a massive publicly held corporation and, during the Iraq war, they were cautious and as bad as they were good in the first war.

How come CNN was the only network allowed to stay in Baghdad during the first Gulf War?

We know that CNN made a business deal with Saddam Hussein. They said, "You let us stay and we'll guarantee that what you say makes it to the outside world. I also get to report what I see, up to a point—we'll negotiate that later." CNN made a business arrangement to run a four-line cable all the way from Baghdad to Jordan. For CNN, it was exclusively a business arrangement. For Saddam Hussein, it was a political arrangement. They realized it was in their interest to have some way of getting their message out to the rest of the world, and Ted Turner was smart enough to say, "Let me be the one."

You've painted such a troubling picture here, is there something about America or its culture that doesn't foster or cultivate the development of superior, aggressive, truth-seeking journalists?

America used to have a culture of opposition, but it was a different country. There was a labor movement. We don't have a labor movement anymore. There was a Left. We don't have a Left anymore. Money wasn't the only way to acquire status in the country. Journalists themselves identified more with the working class than with the upper classes. Now, the average journalist on a big newspaper, big TV network, can make an upper-middle-class salary and live in a suburban house. They can live much better than they lived thirty, forty, fifty years ago. Reporters used to be poorly paid and they did it for the glamour or for the glory or because it gave them more self-respect or because they wanted to be writers. They didn't want to stay reporters their whole lives. They didn't see themselves as part of the power structure or part of the upper class the way I think a lot of reporters see themselves now. There is no working-class consciousness anymore among reporters. It's gone. And that's unhealthy.

With the decline of the labor movement and with the upgrading of the status and income of reporters, there's now a tremendous divide between the typical reporter and the typical lower-middle-class American who gets sent off to fight the war. The typical reporter doesn't know anybody who's in the army. He's never been in the army. He's not going to be in the army. He went to college, he was smart enough to stay out of the army or his parents could afford to pay his college tuition, so he has no sense of responsibility anymore to the working class. One of things that offends me the most is that we make the decision to go to war and the only people who have to take responsibility for it really are the people too poor to buy their way out of it. They join the army to get free tuition or a job. They're the ones getting sent off to get killed or wounded or maimed in Iraq. Not the brothers and sisters and relatives of the Washington press corps. I think there were a couple of examples, but very few reporters this go-around have any relatives or any connections in the military.

Why do you think we went to this war?

I think we went to war because George W. Bush's political advisers told him this was an easy way to get reelected. After 9/11 he had to do something to look like he was fighting terrorism. People in this country don't make very good distinctions between Arabs and terrorists and Arab countries. If we invaded Iraq and said Iraq was one of the places fomenting terror, most people would believe us. Even the ones who didn't would say, "We don't like Saddam Hussein, let's get rid of him. It's OK with us." By going to war, Bush would get credit for doing something aggressive while the ideologues in the administration, like Wolfowitz,[17] could try out their mad scheme to reform the Middle East.

I don't know how many of them believed they could turn these places into democracies. This is an idea that was first put forth by Woodrow Wilson, and it's as preposterous today as it was in 1919, but it still has a real hold in the United States. We're a Calvinist country and Calvin spoke of an "elect people."[18] We think we are an elect people with a special role in the world, a special mission to democratize the world, to bring freedom and enlightenment to the heathens. This reform impulse is still a powerful impulse in this country. Some members of the administration really believe in it. I think Wolfowitz actually believes in it. Others are cynical and they say, "Well, if it makes you feel better about doing it, we'll say it's about turning Iraq into a democracy. But our real interest here is in getting our guy reelected in 2004 and looking tough. It's going to be easy." And here's where the delusion sets in. They said it was going to be easy. And it was easy, up to a point.

But what was the logical thread that led to Iraq?

There is no logical thread. As I said, it's a political strategy to get yourself reelected. They knew they weren't going to catch Osama bin Laden easily. They didn't get him in Afghanistan; they missed him. So they had to appear to be doing something substantial about fighting terrorism. Iraq was an easy target that also meshed with their interest in the oil, their interest in getting rid of Saddam, and their delusions about the possibility of democratizing a country that has no interest in democracy. Here they're listening to their friends in the Iraqi National Congress and they're all telling each other, "Yeah, it's going to be easy, it's going to be great and Chalabi's our man." Now, he's not our man anymore, but then he was our man and the American people are going to love it because Saddam is already a real bad guy. Everyone thinks he's terrible. No one's going to cry over the demise of Saddam Hussein, and we're going to ride a wave of patriotic fervor to victory in 2004. Of course, this was idiotic because they didn't think about what people in Iraq wanted or didn't want. They didn't know anything about Arab culture, about Sunnis and Shiites. They don't know the difference. Most Americans don't know that Iranians are not Arabs. They think they're all the same people. So it's an ignorant country on this level. The ignorance extends up fairly high in the administration. They think they can do anything with military power, and they can't. This isn't to say that they don't have other more specific motives, like the money, the oil, and making common cause with Israel, even though Iraq and Israel are two completely different countries and two completely different situations. There are subcategories within this broader idea, but I think these are short-term people and their main interest was getting Bush reelected. Of course it may bring Bush down. These are people who believe in public relations and advertising. They think you can get away with anything if you do the PR and advertising correctly. They're right, up to a point, but then reality intrudes. Reality always trumps public relations and advertising. It has to eventually. You can only suspend reality for so long. You can only have so many photo ops in the square with the statue coming down before reality intrudes and real Iraqis and real Arabs present themselves and say, "Well, we don't want the Americans here." Or "This isn't what we had in mind." Or they start killing each other. This is not something that the American administration understands very well.

So basically you're saying that we're victims of our own provincialism and this is going to continue.

I'd say we're victims of our own Protestant, Calvinist hubris. There's a tremendous arrogance and presumptuousness that comes along with this.

Graham Greene says it very well in his book *The Quiet American*. He says—and he's speaking of Americans—"Innocence is like a leper who has lost his bell, wandering the world meaning no harm." That's what we are. We're just running around killing people by the hundreds, by the thousands, getting our own people killed, and saying, "But why is everyone angry? We're trying to do good. We're here to do good. We're trying to help the world." That's a fundamentally Protestant idea: "We're here, we're not evil, we're innocent. We're here to cleanse the world of evil and why are you angry at us?" I think there are a lot of Americans who are genuinely shocked that the Iraqis don't want us there.

Well, the press had a hand in that.

Yes, sure.

What is your ideal journalist and how would you create a press corps that would be equal to the power that this country wields in the world?

To do what I want to do you have to be an owner, you have to be a publisher, which I am, so I tell my editors to tell their writers that we don't run stuff that regurgitates the government line. If you don't ask questions, if you don't challenge the conventional wisdom or the official wisdom, if you don't tell the truth as best you know it to us and to the readers, you don't get published in *Harper's Magazine*. It's simple. Believe me, there are a lot of people out there who want to do their jobs correctly, a lot of talented reporters out there who'd like to do the right thing. There are fewer than there used to be because their elders aren't setting a very good example. But there are still a lot of young people who want to do the right thing. I meet them. But there's very little money in it. I can't support somebody and their family for very long with what I pay freelancers. CBS, the *New York Times*, and the *Washington Post* can support you and your family. You can live a very comfortable life, but the publishers of those newspapers, the heads of those organizations, are not saying what I'm saying to people. They're saying, "Go slow, be cautious, make sure you check with the government. Make sure the government point of view is represented correctly before you do anything else."

I had this when I interviewed Katharine Graham,[19] heroine of Watergate who supposedly stood up to Nixon and so on. I said, "Why didn't you stand up to the Gulf War censorship system? Why didn't you protest? You're famous. You're identified with the First Amendment, you and Ben Bradlee.[20] You're the cat's pajamas as far as press freedom goes." And she said, "I have to say that this issue was not on my screen. Maybe it should have been on my screen, but it wasn't." She also said she wanted me to be fair to the military, because it was concerned about "valid security issues." And I said, "Well, what about Ben Bradlee?" She said, "You know, Ben has not been involved in the [First Amendment] issues as much as he is in [specific cases]. All his life he really hasn't." Then she tried to take back what she had said. Of course, I wrote it and published it.[21] But that's basically her attitude.

You think she changed between Watergate and the years prior to her death in 2001?

Yes, she changed. I think she went back to the way she really was. You've got to remember, things were much worse in 1973 than they are now. We're not yet as far gone as we were in 1973. In 1973 we'd just lost almost sixty thousand people. We'd killed a million Vietnamese. We'd had race riots that had destroyed a third of our cities. We had this scandal, Watergate, which was like no scandal anybody had ever experienced before. You had profound corruption and Watergate. The impeachment of Nixon has to be seen as the coup de grâce to Vietnam. It's also a reaction to Vietnam. It's not just the scandal itself, but all those things together were too much even for the American establishment and somebody had to call a halt to it. If there's any hope in the current situation with Iraq, it's not going to come from the Democratic Party or from the press, it's got to come from within the Republican Party. The conservatives in the Republican Party are going to have to say, "Wait a minute, this has gone too far, it's time to give Bush the hook."

You said in your book that the last time that the press did its job was in Vietnam.

Right. The argument could also be made that that was because American reporters were following the prevailing opinions. They're not independent. They don't like to go against the prevailing current of opinion. When public opinion turns against the war, at least they follow. They don't defend the war; they follow public opinion. In Vietnam, the press did its job correctly toward the end because American opinion turned against the war. It made it safe for people like anchorman Walter Cronkite on CBS and big newspapers to do the right thing. Even so, Seymour Hersh, a freelancer, broke the My Lai story,[22] thanks to Ron Ridenhour, a brave soldier who wrote many letters to Congress. Ridenhour deserved the Pulitzer Prize as much as Seymour Hersh did. Sy Hersh would say the same thing. But you had to break the story through an independent channel like Seymour Hersh even when the press was doing its job better than it's doing it now. You will still see Vietnam veterans in the press, like Bob Simon on *60 Minutes* who did the segment "Selling the Iraq War to the U.S." with me back in December 2002. He's still a real reporter. He doesn't believe anything the government says. You shouldn't believe anything the government says until you've checked it out. Now you've got most reporters saying, "If the government says it, or if my high official source says it, it must be true or at least I have to report it as if it were true." I don't have any great ideas about how to change the culture except to criticize it and to try to set a good example as a publisher because I know that the power still resides with the owners.

I used to say that private ownership was the only thing that could work because by definition a government press doesn't work. I'm not so sure anymore because the BBC certainly made us look bad. They weren't great during the war, but they were better than American television. Their former director general, Greg Dyke, criticized the American television media for being so prowar as to be absurd. BBC reporter Andrew Gilligan's story about the UK government "sexing up" documents on Iraq's nuclear weapons capability to promote going to war, even though it had some mistakes in it, was essentially true. And that's a government-owned broadcasting system doing a better job reporting on the government than anybody in the United States has done. Certainly I give credit to CBS for finally doing the story on Abu Ghraib,[23] but Abu Ghraib was handed to them. It was thanks to this kid, Joe Darby, who complained to his officers and then the story got out and somebody handed the pictures to CBS. Meanwhile, they're not really covering the real war. As bad as Abu Ghraib is, it's an easy story. It's too easy. You just keep running the pictures over and over again. The same ones. Meanwhile, women and children are being killed in the crossfire in Fallujah and Karbala and nobody's showing anything. Nobody's doing anything on those stories. That story has basically disappeared.

Although you say you feel that Vietnam was the last time the press was doing its job, are you trying to say that the press wasn't out ahead of American public opinion during the Vietnam War at any time?

The Vietnam press corps is overrated as an antiwar, skeptical press corps. The reporters would all tell you that themselves. The big reporters from those days, Neil Sheehan, David Halberstam, Peter Arnett, and Morley

Safer, they were all prowar. They all supported the basic premise of the Vietnam War from the American point of view. They only started to turn against it when they saw how crazy it was and how futile and bloody it was and when American opinion started to shift in late 1967 thanks to Eugene McCarthy[24] and a growing antiwar movement. The press got much better because it got much safer. As late as 1966, Martha Gellhorn, Ernest Hemingway's third wife, a very well-known writer and journalist, goes to Vietnam to report on the bombing campaign and comes back with these horrific stories. She does it as a freelancer and she figures, "I'm Martha Gellhorn, I can sell this to *Life* magazine or some big paper." She couldn't sell it to anybody but her old hometown newspaper, the *St. Louis Post Dispatch*. This was 1966. Everybody knew it was true. We were bombing indiscriminately. We were carpet-bombing in the south and in the north and killing civilians by the thousands—whoever was in the way.

As late as December 1966, Harris Salisbury went to Hanoi for the *New York Times* and reported the truth, which was that the Johnson administration was saying, "No civilians are being killed by American bombs. All our bombing is precision, we're just bombing strategic targets—bridges, ammunition dumps, airfields, and so on; no civilians are being killed."

Salisbury got into Vietnam and went to Hanoi in December of 1966. On Christmas Day he took a walk around Hanoi. He looked around and met people who said, "Actually, there have been some civilians killed. The bombs aimed for the bridge over the Red River were dropped a little short of their target and they hit this densely populated neighborhood and killed five people." He reported this in the fourth or fifth paragraph of a leisurely feature story about walking around Hanoi on Christmas Day, and all hell broke loose. He was denounced as a Communist. They called him "Hanoi Harrison Salisbury." The vitriol that was thrown at him by the administration was unbelievable. And he didn't win the Pulitzer Prize in 1967 for this series of stories because the Pulitzer Prize committee was divided strictly along prowar and antiwar lines and the prowar votes had the day. He was denied the Pulitzer Prize. Clearly he deserved it.

It could be argued that Harrison Salisbury's story about the five civilians killed in Hanoi by errant bombs in December of 1966 really got the antiwar movement going, because it was the first time that Johnson had been caught in an absolute lie, a real falsification. They flatly stated no civilians were being killed and here some civilians were killed. It wasn't terrible, five people, it was not thousands, but they were caught in a lie.

I was so interested in this that I went and rereported the story because when I was in Vietnam in 1994 I realized, "What if he did get it wrong?" I wanted to be absolutely sure he got it right, because it is an absolutely key moment in the history of American journalism. One of our best moments, actually, and one of the best moments in the history of the *New York Times*, which I now think has lost most of its moral authority.

I went to the house and I found the guy whose house was destroyed, whose pregnant wife was killed. I verified it all. The Communists had put up a little plaque in front of his house to reward him. They didn't give him any money. He had to get the money to rebuild his house from his brother who moved to London and opened a restaurant. But it was real. Salisbury got the story right, but he wasn't rewarded for it. He was punished for it.

I'll give you one more example. Jon Alpert was a freelancer for NBC who went over to Iraq in the first Gulf War with Ramsey Clark[25] and took pictures of civilian victims of the bombing. He came back and NBC wouldn't air the footage because he went with Ramsey Clark. It was considered pro-Iraqi, pro-Saddam propaganda. But none of this is surprising to me anymore that you don't score any points with your colleagues or with the establishment if you do your job. After my book *Second Front: Censorship and Propaganda in the 1991 Gulf War* came out, it got tremendous amounts of mainstream attention. I was on *60 Minutes* and got a front-page review in the *New York Times*. How many journalism schools do you think invited me to speak to their students? Zero. The only people who invited me to speak were the US military academy at West Point, to an English class, and the School for Public Relations at Fort Benjamin Harrison in Indiana, the army and military school for public relations.

So all these old lions of journalism, are they all co-opted? Is Woodward co-opted?

Yes, Woodward's co-opted. Woodward is now the official recipient of the official leak at a very high level. His book *Bush at War*[26] was very flattering to the Bush administration. He made a straight business deal, "You give me the minutes of the National Security Council meetings, and I'll make you look good in the months after 9/11." So he painted a portrait of Bush as decisive, in control, and statesmanlike, and in exchange he got the minutes of the National Security Council. That's a business deal, not journalism. His latest book, *Plan of Attack*,[27] is just him taking the feed from Colin Powell. Colin Powell is a very bad actor. He's a hypocrite and a liar. If you go back to My Lai, he was one of the officers responsible for investigating what the American division was doing. He managed not to find anything, which you can read in the *Figaro*, which did a very, very fine story on this a few days ago, but which you will not read in the American press.

He lied in front of the UN Security Council on behalf of his masters in the White House, and now he basically says, "Oh, I'm so appalled to find out that we were lied to. Chalabi lied to us. They misinformed us." This is nonsense. Then he uses Bob Woodward to help clean up his image. This notion of making him defense secretary is idiotic. He's as compromised as the rest of them. But he is Bob Woodward's principal source on *Plan of Attack*, and it's all an attempt to make Colin Powell look like he wasn't there when they made the bad decisions and that he was really against it. He did the same thing after the first Gulf War. And Woodward performed the same service for him.

Powell said in *Plan of Attack* that he opposed the Iraq war, but then he went along because he felt he had to be a good soldier. This was big news. Finally, Bob Edwards on NPR had the intelligence to say to Woodward, "But if you could have published this stuff at the time you learned it, it has much more impact—it's like your Watergate reporting; every new element that you published produced a turn in the story." Woodward said, "In Watergate we were talking about crimes. In this case, we're talking about no crimes."[28] Obviously he had made a deal with Powell that he wouldn't report it until after the war: "You talk to me, you give me the sexy story, and I'll hold it until after the war so I won't make you look bad." That's the way journalism works.

What about David Halberstam? What's your assessment of him?

He's overrated as a Vietnam critic. He was taking leaks from CIA officials and Col. John Paul Vann who were basically saying, "We're not fighting the war correctly." They weren't saying, "The war is a mistake" or "We can't win it." They were saying, "The South Vietnamese Army refuses to fight. They won't go out at night. If we want to win against the Communists, we have to put on black face and we have to go out and fight in the night like the Communists. Unless we take on the Viet Cong mano-a-mano, the way they fight, we can't win it. I'm just telling you that the South Vietnamese army is not up to the task." That's the core of Halberstam's reporting. Is it coming from an interested party who wants greater American involvement in Vietnam? Now, it so happens it was the truth. The South Vietnamese army didn't want to fight. They were afraid to go out. They didn't want to follow orders from their leadership, which they knew was corrupt. They were ambivalent about fighting their fellow Vietnamese. That was all true, so Halberstam gets credit and the *New York Times* gets credit for at least saying that much. But to say that Halberstam is the great critic who predicted the quagmire is an overstatement. From another point of view, you could say that he helped bring on the quagmire because the Johnson administration said to itself and to the world, "We have to send five hundred thousand American troops to do the job that the South Vietnamese can't do by themselves."

Now the question in Iraq is: Are they going to say the same thing? Are they going to escalate or de-escalate? I don't know.

Are there any lions of journalism today?

Seymour Hersh is still great. After Seymour Hersh it's hard to think of anybody who's really doing a good job. Bob Simon is still doing a good job on TV, when he's allowed to do it. So are some of the producers at *60 Minutes*. There are a couple of newspaper columnists who are trying, but they're not reporters, like Paul Krugman.[29] He's not a journalist; he's a PhD economist. Bob Herbert is still trying at the *New York Times*. Barton Gellman[30] is a wonderful reporter at the *Washington Post*. I think he probably knew what was going on during the run-up to the war, and he and Walter Pincus at the *Washington Post* figured out that they couldn't do much.

The reason I have the attitude I have is because of Vietnam. It's all about Vietnam. If you grew up in the atmosphere of Vietnam believing that the government lies and the government obfuscates and the government will sacrifice peoples' lives for no good reason, you are going to be more skeptical than someone who didn't grow up in that atmosphere. What's amazing to me is that people who know better, people who grew up in the Vietnam era or became reporters during the Vietnam era, have been silenced for the most part. You've got Hersh, you've got CBS correspondent Morley Safer still, but he's not doing that much anymore. You don't have very many reporters of that era still practicing journalism. The bosses who went on to become editors and producers are scared. I talked to a congressman from Oklahoma the other day. His reference point is Lebanon, 1983. Not Saigon, 1975. He thinks we can't leave Iraq and that we can't cut and run because it was a mistake to flee Lebanon after the marine barracks were blown up. It sent a message to the terrorists that they could push us around. So it's partly generational. But I get it from Vietnam. It's Vietnam even more than Watergate. I didn't want to go to Vietnam, I didn't want see my brother go, I didn't want to see anybody go, because I knew it was a lie. A lot of us got into journalism because we thought it was our role and our responsibility to never again accept the lies that were told during Vietnam.

> I remember several things about my personal experience working at the networks. One is, all the producers are under talent contracts, so nobody particularly wants to pitch stories that are going to be problematic, either businesswise for the company or that will upset any powerful government institution or corporation that could cause problems for the company. The other thing is that investigating costs a lot of money and takes a lot of time, so you're in your office and people are wondering what the hell you're doing in there for so long while spending all this money. So there are all these pressures that have nothing to do with journalism that affect the bottom line. A lot of really important stories don't even get out of the box because they could be very problematic for you personally, in terms of your career and paying your bills, because all you have to do is get burned once and you're radioactive for a very long time.

Right.

> So that's the pressure inside the networks. I don't know in print, but I guess the pressures are similar.

There's less money at stake in print.

> But it's still the same pressure. You don't want to cause problems for your paper.

So you learn to self-censor. Or you learn to lay off.

> Exactly. And the thing is that when you come up against these barriers, then you have to ask yourself the personal question: "Am I a journalist, in which case I've got to cross that line and I most likely will blow myself up," because if you don't then you become the one who self-censors automatically, and then, frankly, are you a journalist then? What are you at that point?

It's not always black and white. When I worked for big newspapers I also lived to fight another day. I would take it and say, "Well, I'll get the next one. Maybe this one isn't so important that I want to blow up my career over it." But I have to say, the ones where I took it, I eventually got the story out; one way or another, I got the story out. You've got to be up for it. For me, this is the fun of journalism. Getting everybody mad is what we're supposed to do. It's the whole point of it: getting a big reaction, everybody yelling at you, press agents calling you, and politicians complaining and denouncing you. What could be better? I don't understand why they don't have the stomach for it, because it's the whole point for me.

JOHN R. (RICK) MACARTHUR, president and publisher of *Harper's Magazine*, is an award-winning journalist and author. He writes a monthly column for the *Providence Journal* and for Canada's national newspaper, the *Globe & Mail*. Mr. MacArthur's first book, *Second Front: Censorship and Propaganda in the Gulf War,* was a finalist for the 1993 Mencken Award for books and won the Illinois ACLU's 1992 Harry Kalven Freedom of Expression Award. His critically acclaimed follow-up, *The Selling of Free Trade: NAFTA, Washington, and the Subversion of Democracy,* was published in the spring of 2000.

Under MacArthur's stewardship, *Harper's Magazine* has received numerous awards, including nine National Magazine Awards, the industry's highest recognition. In 2003 *Harper's* won a National Magazine Award for feature writing and was a finalist in the categories of general excellence, public interest, reviews and criticism, and profile writing.

Before joining *Harper's Magazine,* Mr. MacArthur was an assistant foreign editor at United Press International (1982) and a reporter for the *Chicago Sun-Times* (1979–1982), *Bergen Record* (1978–1979), *Washington Star* (1978), and *Wall Street Journal* (1977). He writes for newspapers and magazines, including the *New York Times*, the *Wall Street Journal*, the *Washington Post*, the *Boston Globe*, the *Los Angeles Times*, the *Philadelphia Inquirer*, *Le Temps* (Geneva), the *Progressive*, the *Nation*, and the *Columbia Journalism Review.* Mr. MacArthur received the 1993 Mencken Award for best editorial/op-ed column for his *New York Times* expose of "Nayirah," the Kuwaiti diplomat's daughter who helped fake the Iraqi baby incubator atrocity.

A tireless advocate for international human rights, Mr. MacArthur founded and serves on the board of directors of the Death Penalty Information Center and the MacArthur Justice Center. Along with members of his family, he founded Article 19, the International Center on Censorship, based in London, and in 1989 he initiated and helped organize the PEN/Article 19/Author's Guild rally for Salman Rushdie. He is also on the board of directors of the Author's Guild and the Overseas Press Club, and he is a fellow at the New York Institute for the Humanities.

NOTES

1. On its Web site, http://www.iaea.org/About/index.html, the International Atomic Energy Agency describes itself as "the world's center of cooperation in the nuclear field. It was set up as the world's 'Atoms for Peace' organization in 1957 within the United Nations family. The Agency works with its Member States and multiple partners worldwide to promote safe, secure and peaceful nuclear technologies." The IAEA is also considered the UN watchdog organization for monitoring nuclear proliferation.

2. A British-educated former banker, Ahmed Chalabi has been the leader of the anti-Saddam Iraqi National Congress. He received large sums of money from the US government for his activities and was a source of faulty prewar intelligence. Although he has no industry experience, he is currently acting oil minister for the new Iraqi government.

3. The United Nations Special Commission (UNSCOM) was set up to implement the "non-nuclear provisions" of UN resolution 687 of April 3, 1991, which called for "the elimination, under international supervision, of Iraq's weapons of mass destruction and ballistic missiles with a range greater than 150 kilometers, together with related items and production facilities." UNSCOM was also "to assist the International Atomic Energy Agency (IAEA) in the nuclear areas."

4. In May 2003 the BBC identified British government weapons expert Dr. David Kelly as their source who had said that the British government had "sexed up" a report with false claims about Iraqi weapons of mass destruction, including stating that the weapons could be deployed within forty-five minutes. On July 17, 2003, Kelly was found dead. Subsequently, Lord Hutton was charged with investigating Kelly's death. Hutton's investigation, which was disputed, ruled Kelly's death a suicide.

5. Seymour Hersh is arguably the most renowned independent investigative journalist in the United States. He is also an author.

6. See chapter 8 in this book.

7. See chapter 9 in this book.

8. According to the online encyclopedia Wikipedia, Avram Noam Chomsky is an "Institute Professor Emeritus of linguistics" at MIT. "Outside of his linguistic work, Chomsky is also widely known for his political activism and his criticism of the foreign policy of the United States and other governments. Chomsky describes himself as a libertarian socialist and sympathizer of anarcho-syndicalism." http://en.wikipedia.org/wiki/Noam_Chomsky.

9. Christopher Hitchens is a journalist and author born in the United Kingdom who is known for his iconoclastic political views.

10. On the jacket of his 2003 book, *Who Killed Daniel Pearl?* (Hoboken, NJ: Melville House), Levy is described as "France's leading philosopher and one of the most esteemed and best-selling writers in Europe. He has also served on diplomatic missions for the French government—most recently to Afghanistan after the fall of the Taliban."

11. Founded in 1996 and based in Qatar, Al Jazeera is the largest Arabic news channel in the Middle East and provides twenty-four-hour news coverage.

12. See chapter 1 in this book.

13. According to the state of Kuwait's Web site, http://demo.sakhr.com/diwan/emain/Story_Of_Kuwait/Kuwait_before_Oil/political/political.html#1, the al-Sabah family has been ruling Kuwait since at least sometime during the 1700s.

14. Nazi German political leader and head of the German air force.

15. On April 23, 2003, Brent Baker and Rich Noyes of the Media Research Center put out a report, "Grading TV's War News," that assessed the war reporting done by Fox, CBS, NBC/MSNBC, CNN, and ABC. The report can be found at http://www.mrc.org/SpecialReports/2003/pdf/Gulf_War_Special_Report.pdf.

16. Viacom owns CBS, UPN, and more than two hundred radio and TV stations across the United States.

17. Former deputy secretary of defense (now head of the World Bank) Paul Wolfowitz is viewed as a neoconservative or "neocon." The *Christian Science Monitor* article "Neocon 101" states: "'Neocons believe that the United States should not be ashamed to use its unrivaled power—forcefully if necessary—to promote its values around the world." http://www.csmonitor.com/specials/neocon/neocon101.html.

18. Protestant reformer John Calvin (1509–1564), whose ideas are thought by many to be at the heart of American culture, believed in living by a strict moral code that adhered to Christian scriptures. One of his beliefs was that salvation was not a choice but was predetermined by God and that people were "elected" for salvation.

19. As board chairman and CEO of the Washington Post Company from 1973 to 1991 and publisher of the *Washington Post* from 1969 to 1979, Katherine Graham (1917–2001) was one of American media's most powerful women. Under her stewardship, Bob Woodward and Carl Bernstein pursued their investigation of the famous Watergate scandal that led to President Nixon's resignation.

20. Ben Bradlee was editor of the *Washington Post* under Katherine Graham.

21. John MacArthur, *Second Front: Censorship and Propaganda in the 1991 Gulf War* (Berkeley: University of California Press, 2004), p. 208.

22. The massacre at My Lai of five hundred unarmed men, women, and children by US soldiers occurred in South Vietnam on March 16, 1968. Lt. William Calley initiated the massacre. Army photographer Ronald Haeberle was there and took photos of the dead.

23. At the Abu Ghraib prison in Iraq, American soldiers from a US military intelligence unit, US military police, and some civilian contractors abused and tortured prisoners. Shocking photos of their activities were released, showing naked prisoners being forced into humiliating sexual and other poses, while their captors were pictured with them giving "thumbs-up" signs and, in at least one case, holding a leash with a prisoner on the other end.

24. Eugene Joseph McCarthy served Minnesota as a Democratic congressman from 1949 to 1959 and as a senator from 1959 to 1971. He was a strong opponent of President Lyndon Johnson's policies in Vietnam.

25. Ramsey Clark is a former attorney general under President Lyndon Johnson who wrote *The Fire This Time: U.S. War Crimes in the Gulf* (New York: International Action Center, 1991). Clark founded the nonprofit International Action Center, which is devoted to "Information, Activism and Resistance to US Militarism, War and Corporate Greed, Linking with Struggles against Racism and Oppression within the United States." http://www.iacenter.org/.

26. Bob Woodward, *Bush at War* (New York: Simon & Schuster, 2002).

27. Bob Woodward, *Plan of Attack* (New York: Simon & Schuster, 2004).

28. MacArthur, *Second Front*, p. 204.

29. Economist Paul Krugman is a columnist for the *New York Times*. See chapter 7 in this book.

30. See chapter 8 in this book.

THE ARENA OF POWER

5

GRANDE DAME, PERSONA NON GRATA

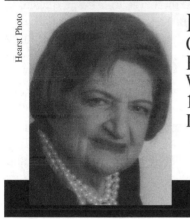

HELEN THOMAS
Columnist,
Hearst Newspapers;
White House Correspondent,
1961–2000
Interviewed June 2004

While waiting in the reception area of the Hearst Newspaper offices for Helen Thomas to come out, I contemplated her amazing career. Thomas is, after all, a living historical figure in American journalism. She is, arguably, a pioneering woman reporter in more ways than any other female journalist alive or dead. She is also the tribe's memory for the White House press corps—a collection of fiercely competitive news-hounds. Helen has earned her position as the grande dame of this group not just by virtue of her longevity—she's been covering US presidents since Kennedy—but because time and again she asks the tough questions that her colleagues won't dare to. Given her legendary career and no-nonsense reputation, I confess that I was caught a little off guard when a smallish woman with a big smile and piercing brown eyes came out, greeted my film crew and me, and immediately offered to get us coffee.

Helen Thomas reminds me of I. F. Stone. She is of strong mind and heart and not afraid to show it. When White House spokesman Ari Fleischer announced that President Bush deplored a suicide bombing in Tel Aviv, Thomas stood up and said: "Ari, this morning you said that the president deplores this terrible act. Why does he want to bomb and kill thousands of Iraqis, including women and children?" I can think of no one else covering the White House right now who would have the nerve to ask that question.

Helen also has the confidence to admit her shortcomings. When I asked her if she thought the American people were as aware as they should be of what goes on in the arena of power and how it operates, she said, "No, and I don't think I am either." Like Stone, Thomas knows in every fiber of her being that she is a public servant and that her role is to stand in the shoes of the American people and demand accountability of this nation's leaders. Past presidents expected this of the press, and while exchanges could get contentious, there was rarely any outright incivility.

Things have changed. The relationship between this White House and the press is very different. This administration is far less tolerant than its predecessors of inconvenient journalists asking tough questions. Nonetheless, Thomas did what she had to do and asked pointed questions about the war in Iraq. Shortly thereafter, she paid the price. My interview with her took place before the 2004 election and began with a discussion of the issues and circumstances that surrounded her recently acquired "persona non grata" status.

I've had several encounters with the White House people. I think some basic questions should be asked for the American people. I really do think it's bizarre that, in one year and in the months and run-up to going to war in Iraq, they've changed their story so many times. The original reason was weapons of mass destruction; we were under imminent threat. The Brits said forty-five minutes, didn't they? And that there were terrorist ties between al Qaeda[1] and Saddam Hussein. None of that has been proved to be true, although they keep hinting and returning to it.

Now Iraq is the central front in the war on terrorism. It wasn't before. It well could be now that some of the policies have added to the recruitment for al Qaeda. But in a briefing, I simply asked Condoleezza Rice,[2] "What is today's rationale for the war?" because it's been so evanescent, so changing. She was not happy with my question, and she fell back on her past statements, that Saddam Hussein had gassed the Kurds and that he had aggressed against neighbors in Kuwait, and I said, "But, this was twelve years ago and we won that war, we punished him, we've had tightest economic sanctions, have a chokehold on—*had* a chokehold on Saddam Hussein—satellite surveillance, bombing them every night in the run-up certainly, in the no-fly zone." No reporter was there, of course, to check on how much they were bombing or how far they went in to Iraq and whether it was limited to parameters of that. Anyway, this was the dialogue.

There ought to be a public debate. Maybe it wouldn't be considered proper protocol right now while you're still in a war or getting out of a war, but at some point, I think the American people should be asking the questions. There may have been a legitimacy to going in, but I didn't hear it and I don't think they used it if they have it.

Let's talk about the era before we went to war, when they were presenting the rationale for going to war. What is your assessment of the press's performance during that time?

From day one, President Bush entered the White House and all of a sudden out of the blue, after lo these many years from the first Gulf War,[3] Saddam Hussein is on the radar screen. Why? What had he done in the intervening times? Suddenly we knew the Bush administration had an agenda, and so everyone started to call up the "Project for A New American Century,"[4] which is on everyone's computer. Once you realized that his advisers were all in this realm of what they call the neoconservatives . . . that was the agenda they tried to sell to Reagan—couldn't do it. Tried to sell it to George H. W. Bush, couldn't do it. Tried to sell it to Clinton. But they obviously had sold it to George W. Bush.

Do you think the press was aware of that at the time?

I think everybody began to get an inkling and of course a lot of them bought into it because the neoconservatives[5] in the administration began tying it up with these tremendous weapons, these caches, these arsenals that Saddam Hussein had. The press had no proof except that Secretary of State Colin Powell, undoubtedly, when he laid his prestige on the line at the United Nations, people believed in him. He had tremendous stature in our country and some very, very professional journalists said that's when they bought into the whole argument that we should go to war.

How do you explain the general enthusiasm of the American press after Colin Powell's presentation at the United Nations? [6]

From 9/11 on, the American press suddenly had to be the superpatriots, or patriots anyway, and they were afraid of being called un-American, unpatriotic, especially if they were on television. The briefings were on television and the reporters were asking questions. They were afraid, I think to some extent, that the American people would not understand. Then you would get this sense that you were jeopardizing the troops after it segued into war itself. So because of both those things, the press went into a coma. But they're coming out of it now, thank God.

So you're basically saying that the American public does exert a certain amount of pressure on journalists.

Oh, definitely. It wasn't just the American public, it was the administration taking advantage of these scare tactics. I'm not saying that we shouldn't be afraid of terrorists. Yes, we certainly should be on our guard. We certainly should do everything except invading our privacy and wiping out our civil liberties and putting people at Guantanamo with no recourse to counsel and no contact with their families. They disappear from the face of the earth. This is not us. This is not us under any circumstances. I mean, due process, we have to follow the Constitution no matter what. That's what makes us different—allegedly.

Talk about this administration and its relationship with the press and if the press's attitude has changed and how toward this administration.

I think that you always give a new administration the benefit of the doubt. You give them a clean shave. You start new. I think there's always this tendency. When you get to be president of the United States, that's the top of the mark. Ain't no other place to go and it seems to me you'd only want to do the right thing and you certainly would want to tell the truth. I think that we all want to believe this. One day, I had a big dialogue with Ari Fleischer, Bush's first press secretary. He came to the "morning gaggle," which is fifteen minutes where you shoot questions at him. The gaggle is not televised. The main briefing is usually around 12:30 and this is televised. They take advantage of that. They want the television.

There had been a horrifying suicide bombing in Israel and Fleischer came out and said, "The president deplores this terrible act." So I said to him, "Ari, this morning you said that the president deplored the suicide bombing. Why does he want to bomb and kill thousands of innocent

Iraqis, including women and children?" Well, you could imagine [laughs]. I laugh now, but it wasn't funny at the time. He was so stunned. He said: "They have a dictator." And I said, "But why does the president want to bomb them?" And Fleischer responded, "They have no control over their lives, they have no say in their government." And I said, "And neither do we." From then on, it was war.

Were there consequences to that, Helen?

The consequences? I think I was persona non grata. Still am. But we are so privileged to ask a question of a president, or his pinch-hitter, or spokesperson, or surrogate. People don't understand that the presidential news conference is the only forum, the only institution in our society, where a president can be questioned. We don't have the British system where the prime minister goes before the House of Commons. If we don't ask the questions, a president can rule by executive order, by edict, unquestioned. Congress can subpoena him, but they won't do it unless it's absolutely dire, the end of the road. So we should never default on our privilege to lay it on the line. Courtesy is very required, but after that, I think, you say, "thank you, yes sir," and then ask the question.

During the whole run-up to the war, I got so much, one, hate mail, and, two, many, many messages saying, "Where is the press?" The American people were thinking, too, and they heard what the White House was saying, and they would write, "Why don't you ask about this?" They thought we weren't tough enough. They thought we were asking too many softballs and playing along when we should have been much more inquiring. We really laid down on the job.

Why do you think the press laid down on the job in the run-up to the Iraq war?

Fear. The fear card was very important. Everybody felt the tension of 9/11, 9/11, 9/11, and then going into a war you don't want to rock any boats. It's not "my country, may she always be right," but "my country right or wrong." Nobody wants to be considered unpatriotic or un-American in these crises.

You've covered a lot of presidencies, a lot of administrations. Is this administration different in some way?

It's more secretive. They're all secretive. All information that I believe belongs in the public domain they think is their private secret and they will dole it out on their own terms, whatever it is. But this is one of the most secretive. They walk in lockstep. It's pretty tight. There's been some leakage lately, but it's only been lately.

Do you think there's malfeasance attached to that secretiveness, and how does the press crack that nut to see what's behind it?

I don't think it's malfeasance. This president hates leaks and he's laid down the law, "You're with us or against us," for his team. You're onboard, or you're not. I think they all got that message very quickly. What it takes is a whistle-blower. It takes somebody who finally throws the dice and says, "No, I'm sorry, this is hurting the country." Like the man who revealed that the cost of the Medicare plan, the so-called reform, was $150 billion more than they had said the cost would be—that kind of thing. Richard Clarke,[7] of course, revealed that the president took him aside and said, "Find me a reason. Find me a tie that connects Saddam Hussein with the terrorists." He had to have more justification. "Find it." Clarke got the message, all right.

What is your assessment of the Iraq war?

I think it was not necessary. I've never covered a president who wanted a war before. And to have a war of choice. Of choice? Wars that I believe in are necessities, when we're attacked. It's absolutely against international law to attack a country without any provocation, which is what we did. It's a violation of international law and the United Nations charter, but I think it's being ignored.

Why do you think it's being ignored?

I think that the president was able to sell the American people. He got Congress to support the war. I would say that the major newspapers in this country certainly supported it. With that kind of backing, the man on the street, even if he had some doubts, has no real say.

Why do you think the major papers supported this war?

The *Washington Post* went all out every day practically for two years. You tell me. Most of their columnists are conservative and believed in it. Same way with the *Wall Street Journal*. The *New York Times* was on the fence for a long time, but it must have felt the pressure, too. I don't know whether they ever really went all out. Not like some of the other papers. But you always want to believe in the authorities, in the White House.

You would never think you would be led down a garden path when the country's at stake—it's war and peace, life and death.

But we have a history of presidents doing that to us. Helen, you've had that experience before.

Not in the same way. Most of the presidents really have some justification. But a war of choice? Don't they know what war is?

What about the Vietnam War?

Yes. You're right to that extent. But I think that one president after another felt that it was part of the cold war and part of fighting the Soviet Union and China. I was against that war even before we went to Vietnam, from the forties, because right after World War II, I thought it was wrong for the colonial powers—the French—to go back into Southeast Asia. They went on to North Africa, Morocco, Tunisia, Algeria—every country that we had promised self-determination. Every one of those countries had to fight independently for its own self-determination and did. The French finally had to pull out of all those places, and the British, too. Even Dien Bien Phu[8] seemed to be the watershed where we should have realized it was wrong to go into Vietnam. French president Charles de Gaulle tried to tell Kennedy, "No," you know. But Eisenhower had promised the South Vietnamese that we would help them. So one promise led to another and the escalation. You're absolutely right, that was wrong. I hated that war.

Compare the coverage of the war in Vietnam to the coverage of the war in the Gulf and Iraq.

The coverage was fabulous of Vietnam. The coverage killed the war, really. In fact, President Johnson, who had escalated and escalated, kept listening to the generals, "If you drop more bombs on North Vietnam, we'll win the war." When he was forced to give up the presidency because of the protests and the division in the country, he gave his first interview to CBS anchorman Walter Cronkite and he told Cronkite that the Vietnam War coming into everybody's living room every night killed his presidency or hurt him so that he couldn't run again. The coverage was absolutely great. Take, for example, Peter Arnett getting this fantastic quote, "We had to destroy the village to save it." And then seeing that little girl running down the street with the napalm.[9] And the shooting of the Viet Cong in the temple by the police chief.[10] All these things added to a horror: "What are we doing there?"

That was great coverage. A correspondent—and there were many women who were terrific there—could jump on a helicopter and go to the front, wherever it was. That doesn't happen now.

What do you think of the coverage of the first Gulf War and the war in Iraq?

The Gulf War was very bad, very, very suppressed, and this was terrible. With embedding during the Iraq war, you got only a soupçon, one slice of the war.

But do you think that embedding could have been considered one part of the coverage and just coverage as opposed to reporting, because reporting is covering all sides?

But we weren't getting all sides. Let me tell you right now what really irritates me. When I'm writing a column and I think that I should be up-to-date on how many casualties we've suffered in this war with Iraq, I'll call the Pentagon and say, "How many fatalities have there been now in the war?" And they'll give me the tally and then they will tell me how many were in combat and how many noncombatants, and reluctantly they'll tell me how many wounded when I ask. And I'll say, "How many Iraqi fatalities?" "Oh, we don't track that, they don't count." Once I called back, and I said, "What do you mean they don't count, we're supposed to be liberating them aren't we?" I said, "I'd like a rationale on that." So they called back a couple hours later and basically said, "Look, it's not our intention to kill people, but if there is resistance, then the numbers don't count."

What do you think of that response?

I think it was so sad, so sad. I know that after Vietnam they made a command decision on this body count business, which was so horrifying. They said, "No more body counts." That is total control of the news. This is a two-sided story, and I'm very unhappy at some of the wire services that every day put out a box on the deaths and wounded. It seems to me those boxes rate one little sentence saying, "The Pentagon does not keep track of—they're not enemy are they?—Iraqi fatalities.'

Chris Hedges spoke to us about that and he was basically calling it a sort of racism.

I don't think it's racism so much as just trying to control the news and conveying to reporters, "Go about your business, this is not your business.

This is war and we're taking care of it. There, there. Don't get the American people too involved and worrying about this. Otherwise, they might be against the war." When the reality of the prison abuses came in, people said, "What is this?" The administration could not control the whistle-blowers who were brave enough to finally make the photographs public.

We spoke to some vets and conservative journalists who say, "Look, these people are trying to prosecute a war, they're trying to get through it and all this negative reporting on dead Iraqis, and all this refusing to report the good things that the Americans are doing over there is not good."

Like what good things?

Well, the coalition forces building schools, for example.

They had schools. They put six women in the new governing council and I wanted to say, "When were they educated enough to take these jobs?" Obviously they're educated; they're doctors, they're professors. I'm not holding a brief for the horrifying, brutal Saddam Hussein, but we act like we went into some sort of primitive culture. They have five thousand years of civilization.

I think it's very difficult to get an independent view. Obviously Iraq was a totally brutal dictatorship and it was impossible to get free information. So we had to rely on our leaders in that respect. In terms of people saying, "Tell the good side," I think you have to tell the truth. In the first place, people have to know war is killing and being killed. That's what it is. That's war. Peace is another story, and if you want to emphasize peace, you also have to emphasize how you got there. I think the truth is the most important thing. That's the only way you can advance civilization and humanity. We don't want the twenty-first century to be a repetition of the twentieth century: two world wars, Korea, Vietnam, the Gulf War, the Spanish-American War. During that whole century it was either you were going to war, just getting out of a war, or trying to prevent a war. What is this? Is that the only way that mankind can live?

What is the press's role?

To tell the truth, to find the truth and to be bold enough to ask the questions that should be asked. To challenge, to keep challenging, and to be adversarial. If you're going to roll over and play dead, you don't do anything. You don't do democracy any good. Congress didn't ask the questions, and we didn't ask the questions enough.

Are there other pressures besides the patriotism and fear?

I do feel that journalism has changed to some extent from the days of Robert Sarnoff and William Paley,[11] who really allowed their networks to keep the news division neutral and successful but didn't expect them to be big moneymakers. I think there's a different corporate view now in terms of the bottom line, making a profit, and putting great correspondents out to pasture if they reach a certain age. You have to have a certain glamour; you're playing to a certain audience. I think that's very sad for the news business. The news business should prevail and news should be loved, and these original people that I mentioned, Sarnoff and Paley, had a great respect for news and they helped democracy. You can't have a democracy without an informed people.

Can you say today that the American press is entirely free?

No, it's never been entirely free. I would say it's less free. I think that there is a free press in this country, but I don't think it's as free as people think.

Do you think the press is performing better or worse than it did in the sixties?

Worse, because it's been too subjected to corporate rules on the profit business. I've never thought of a newspaper as a question of making money. You paid a quarter for a newspaper. But I suppose you should think of the economics, and it's sad that we've become a country of one-newspaper towns. There's no question that economics, that advertising has drifted to television. I guess they think about it as very important, but I don't think about it. I think about, "Oh, we're after the truth." But I guess I have to remember it takes money, too.

It was reported that you said, "Bush is the worst president ever."

I said that off the record. I left out the fact that there's always room for improvement.

Are there things that are going on in the Middle East that the American public just doesn't get information on that would have helped them have a better understanding and be more critical about what's going on?

I think they're getting the coverage, but they don't understand the context. They don't understand why these people are fighting and they don't understand the holocaust and I think that there is so little knowledge about the Middle East. But I think the reporters there are trying to do a good job day to day covering what's happening. The American people do not know the Middle East at all.

Do you think that the American people are as aware as they should be of what goes on in the arena of power and how it operates?

No, and I don't think I am either. During the Kennedy and Johnson and Carter eras, we could walk down the street with the president of the United States and we really had a sort of human instinct about what was happening to them. They would even tell you things, either off the record or just pour it out. Now, I think there is a wall where we really don't understand the machinations. For example, on the Abu Ghraib prison scandal,[12] the president gave an interview to an Iraqi paper and he said, "This is not the American people and you know that." So the correspondent pressed and said, "Well, do you think higher ups were involved besides the MPs, the lower-ranking soldiers?" And the president said, "We're trying to find that out. We want the truth. We're going to get at the truth." He's the president of the United States. All he has to do is call Rumsfeld, Sanchez, Pappas, and Miller[13] and say, "Who gave this order? How did this come about?" "We're trying to find the truth." I'm sorry. All he's got to do is call these people in and say, "How did this happen?" You think they're all going to blame the MPs and say they were all just free-lancers and having fun? That's what they're saying.

How do you think television has affected the news?

Badly. Sound bites. I love television. Nothing can replace seeing with your own eyes. That's television. But when everything is reduced to "blah, blah, blah" and you hear the most important news just being shouted at you in some brief sound bite—nothing can replace seeing the hearings that we've seen and the actualities—but the other side is that there's this compulsion to give you the news in a rat-a-tat-tat. Is that the news? I like newspapers. I like to be engulfed. That's what a newspaper does. It engulfs you and you have to read some of the things you never intended to read. I want us to be totally informed and I do think TV could do a better job.

But do you think that TV news is better now than it was?

I don't think it's necessarily better, no. Nothing can beat Sevareid[14] or Cronkite[15] and people who had some stature and that you felt thought about things. And Murrow.[16] They gave some weight and context to what was really going on.

Why don't we have a new crop of those people?

Because they were not twenty years old and blond.

Is there a training problem, too, do you think? We're the nine-hundred-pound gorilla on this planet, so whatever we do affects the whole wide world. Do you think that puts an additional dimension of pressure and responsibility on the American press? And are we up to the task?

I think we have great reporters, but I think they're not given enough time to think and to really do the job that they can. I have seen correspondents come to the White House at 5:30 in the morning. They will work on a story, dying to get on. Nirvana is to get on the six o'clock or seven o'clock news. And then they're limited. If they get a minute and a half, I mean, it's dreams come true. This is ridiculous.

So you think the system needs to be reformed?

Sure, I don't think it should be a twenty-minute package. I think it deserves more time, more weighty thinking.

We've been told that one of the reasons why good analysis is lacking is because the public doesn't demand it. What do you think?

I don't agree. I'm always told what the public demands and I say, "Prove it." Hollywood says they love violence, that everybody wants to kill, to be shooting up. I don't believe that. I believe there are great stories to be told and everything isn't violent. I think people want to know, they want to know more, and to know the whys. "Why" is totally ignored. I think that we're being shortchanged. But I don't have my finger on the pulse of the nation and know what they want and why they want it. I just know that I think it's important that they be told what's going on, because their lives are all affected by it.

I think the job of a reporter is to find out the truth and then try to convey it in the best way possible. I know that there are always limitations—for example, there is tremendous secrecy in government, it's endemic. I think that's the constant struggle, and it would be nice if the American people understood how difficult it is to get the information, to get to the truth. Every once in a while, somebody decides they should know the truth and this is when you have your breakthroughs. But spokespeople for government are paid by us. If a president wants a flack, let him pay for it. My point is, when they come out on that podium, they should tell the truth and nothing but, and they shouldn't spin.

What is your vision of the future given the past that you have experienced?

My vision is pretty cloudy because I really think that the business pressures are wrong. I think there definitely has to be outlets for the truth unvarnished, let the chips fall where they may.

Who do you think are some of the best living journalists today?

I don't like to name names, but I think there are a lot of good ones.

Even when you're complimenting them?

Yes, sure, but it's singling them out. I'm a good politician. [Laughs] I think Sy Hersh[17] is one of the best. I love Peter Arnett.[18] I think he did a fantastic job. All these people have really known the ups and downs of journalism. There are so many out there. The *New York Times* has so many good ones, and the *Washington Post*, but I can't say the same thing for the columnists. Sam Donaldson of ABC TV is great.

Do you think journalists are more political now than they used to be?

Not in the White House press room. I'm a columnist, so nobody doubts that I'm a liberal—will be from the day I was born to the day I die—but I think that they pretty well play just the facts, which is what they're supposed to do. But I do think that TV polarizes you. If you're on television and you say, "Well, on the other hand" and "As a matter of fact," you don't get invited back. You have to take an extreme position—yes or no. That's what TV does. TV is drama. You can't just sit there like a lump on a log.

If you are a major journalist and you have a large audience and you expose a lie, if the president lies and you expose that, isn't your access cut off?

They don't like it, yes, probably. They don't exactly want to give you another interview or anything else like that. Yes, there's power, power is used, but I don't think that should deter you. It's usually the outsider, not someone on a regular beat, who will be able to work on such stories. In the case of Watergate,[19] we were there and we didn't do a good job at all. It's the outside reporters from the *Post* who were able to go after an interview. The *Washington Post* and the *New York Times* each had about eighteen people covering the Watergate scandal.

I want to get your impression of the war presidents. How would you characterize President Nixon in terms of how he dealt with the press and how honest he was?

I think he was candid and that outside forces really put him on the defense in a way. How he operated in politics was he always had two roads to go and he always took the wrong road. I think there was a lack of trust, maybe from his childhood. But in terms of the press, he was very reserved and he felt he had been burned so many times. He felt that the press was with Kennedy when he ran against Kennedy in 1960 and lost, and when he ran for governor: "You won't have Richard Nixon to kick around anymore." It wasn't his last news conference, but he thought it was. So I think that he was extremely wary of the press. He tried once in a while to smooth the way, but it didn't quite work. At the same time, I think that he was terrific in a press conference. He could stand up just holding a mike, instead of standing behind a podium, with no notes or anything else. He certainly knew American politics, but of course the Watergate scandal was his denouement.

Do you think the press did a good job of covering him?

I don't think that I did a good job of covering him when I didn't find out about Watergate and it took outsiders. But I do think we saw that it was all over almost a year ahead of time and that nothing he could do could resurrect his presidency. You knew that every day, could see it in his face, you could see it in the happenings, much as he and his administration tried. So from that aspect, I felt I was covering.

What about the press coverage of how he was dealing with the Vietnam War? You had some encounters with him, didn't you, on his secret plans to end the Vietnam War?

I had encounters with all of them. All of them tried to put the best face on the war, and they were always upbeat, saying peace was at hand when you knew it wasn't, and you never felt you were getting the whole truth at the White House on the war. In terms of Johnson, I thought that he did a tremendous job on the domestic side, and he really had this great sense of humanity; got through Medicare, the Civil Rights Act, the voting rights for blacks for the first time in the South, federal aid to education, so you knew where his heart was on the domestic side.

What about the war?

The war was bad and Johnson kept trying to put the best face on it, and the officers were telling him what he wanted to hear until he realized that, when General Westmoreland had to ask for 240,000 more troops and the whole country was blowing up with the protests, he couldn't go out. He couldn't go anywhere but to a military base or an aircraft carrier because everywhere he went he would be booed and heckled. Then I think he realized that it was impossible, although he still thought, even when he announced that he wasn't going to run again, that there was a chance that he would be drafted as the Democratic presidential nominee. But when things blew up in Grant Park in Chicago at the Democratic National Committee convention in 1968, it was all over.

What about the upcoming election and this administration—what do you see unfolding?

I see that the election will be a referendum on this war. Anything can happen. You could have another horror of terrorism or find bin Laden. All these things will be something, but I really think that no matter what happens, we still have troops there being shot at. I think that even when there's a government there, there's still going to be some violence, because Americans are going to stand out, they're going to still be around. I think the election will depend on the war.

Why did we go to war?

I don't know. I don't think the president has leveled in terms of telling us why. He said "weapons of mass destruction" but they're nonexistent, really. Ties to terrorism. There may be terrorism now, because it became a great recruiting ground after the invasion. And then there was everything else. Sure, Saddam didn't obey any sanctions he was under, but we had a chokehold on him, he couldn't make a move. Israel has had some sixty resolutions against her, does she obey them? There's been speculation that it could be oil and avenging George W. Bush's father.[20] Well, his father didn't want to go to war. There wasn't one Arab country—even Kuwait and Iran, which had been invaded by Saddam—that wanted to go to war against Iraq. So none of these things stack up. Someday we'll find out why we went to war.

Yes, but isn't timing important in journalism?

The American people should be clamoring to find out why. When it turns out and becomes very clear there are no weapons of mass destruction, why aren't they saying, "Why are we there?"

Why do you think?

Because the American people are in the same coma as the press and Congress. Nobody wants to rock the boat when you're in a war. Now it comes that we're there to support the troops. We're really in Iraq to support the troops. That's how far-fetched we get. So I think that there's always this question of patriotism, but there's a lot of moving away from that. You have to have a reason to send people to die, it seems to me.

What induced the press's coma, do you think?

Fear. The fear card. Not wanting to appear unpatriotic and un-American.

That blows me away to hear that.

Yes, well, I didn't feel that way. I felt I was a good American to be asking the questions. I thought it was my job to keep asking and pressing. Why? The whys.

How do you see the future of the American press?

I think you see so much soul-searching going on now, "Mea Culpa, mea culpa," all over the place, which would never have been necessary if they had done the job. The *New York Times* put out an unprecedented editor's note. Every newspaper that pushed for this war should do soul-searching and go back to the other issues. Columnists who said we should go to war should be asking themselves if they should have supported the war. Instead, they move along with this floating crap game of "Well, now it's to save civilization."

Every administration that goes to war has to have the backing of the people, and every administration that's taken us into war for two hundred years has certainly had to put out their own spin or propaganda to do it. Before, we would have had to wait fifty years, until they opened the archives, to find out all the reasons for anything that happened. Now, there's instancy. It's in the air, there's no control really. Much as countries or governments might want to control the information, they can't. Every once in a while, somebody decides to tell the truth.

After Watergate, we realized that we had really defaulted, and we became much more skeptical, much more hard-driving. In fact, the press secretaries used to come into the pressroom and think they were in the lion's den. We became more important in the sense that we knew that we had not done a good job on Watergate. I think it was a turning point, but we've lost a lot of that now. I think we'll go back to being much more skeptical. Not cynical, but skeptical. We're asking tougher questions now.

Do you think that the press asked tough enough questions before the first Gulf War?

No. They went along, obviously, because there was an attack on a country, an invasion of Kuwait. But what was so odd were the instructions from our State Department for the first Gulf War to the US ambassador in Baghdad, April Glasby, who took the fall for all of this. She essentially told Saddam two or three days before the first Gulf War, "The United States does not intervene in third world disputes. The United States does not intervene in Arab-to-Arab disputes." The next day, forty-four hours later, the instructions were changed. By this time, Saddam was on his way. I'm not saying that she gave him the green light. But certainly he didn't know that the United States would attack him. And anyway, the dispute with Kuwait was that the Kuwaitis were supposed to be slant drilling into Iraq. So those kinds of things never come out at the time. I think because the Iraqis invaded Kuwait we could support that war, because we're against invading countries, aren't we? We're supposed to be.

Before the Iraq war, one of the things that really struck me was this logical disconnect; we went to Afghanistan, OK, there was a certain sense there—that's where those guys were being trained. What I thought was interesting was the logical disconnect when President Bush was trying to connect 9/11 to Saddam Hussein. There seemed to be no . . .

Questioning. That's true. They wanted you to believe that it was Iraq, even though they had no proof of that. About four days before we went in to the war, Bush said, "There's no connection," but they had built it up; it was subliminal by this time.

After graduating from Wayne State University, **HELEN THOMAS** went to Washington, DC, in 1943 and began working for United Press International (UPI), a newswire service providing articles to newspapers around the world. Thomas was hired to write stories of interest to women. She broke into political reporting in 1961, when she began filing stories about the Kennedy administration. Since then, she has covered nine presidents. In 1970 she became UPI's White House correspondent and in 1972 she was the only woman journalist to go on President Nixon's historic trip to China. She also traveled with presidents Ford, Carter, Reagan, and George H. W. Bush.

Thomas was the first woman officer of the National Press Club, the first woman president of the White House Correspondents Association, and the first woman president of the Gridiron Club. She became the first female White House bureau chief of a wire service in 1974. As her career advanced, Thomas came to be considered the "dean of the Washington press corps," and thereafter, in deference to her position, presidential press conferences always began with her question. At the end of her first presidential press conference in 1961, Thomas said, "Thank you, Mr. President." With these words that became the signature sign-off at presidential press conferences, Thomas was carrying on a tradition that was actually established in the FDR era. She has written three books, *Dateline: White House*, *And Thanks for the Memories, Mr. President*, and *Front Row at the White House: My Life and Times*. In 2000 Thomas left UPI to become a Hearst Newspapers columnist.

NOTES

1. An Arabic word meaning "the base," al Qaeda is an international terrorist group headed by a Saudi, Osama bin Laden, which aims to oppose non-Islamic governments with force and violence and seek retribution for force and violence used against Muslims.

2. At the time, Rice was national security advisor for the Bush administration.

3. "Operation Desert Storm" was the name given to the first Gulf War in which an international coalition led by the US military attacked Iraq in January 1991 to drive Saddam Hussein out of Kuwait. Hussein attacked Kuwait after claiming that the Kuwaitis were overproducing oil and thereby destroying Iraq's economy and that they were stealing oil via slant drilling into Iraq's Rumaila oil field.

4. The Project for a New American Century (PNAC) says on its Web site that it "intends, through issue briefs, research papers, advocacy journalism, conferences, and seminars, to explain what American world leadership entails." It is generally seen as a neoconservative take on the role the United States should play in the world. PNAC says it is a nonprofit educational organization dedicated to the propositions "that American leadership is good both for America and the world; and that such leadership requires military strength, diplomatic energy and commitment to moral principle." http://www.newamericancentury.org/.

5. The *Christian Science Monitor*'s article "Neocon 101" states: "'Neocons believe that the United States should not be ashamed to use its unrivaled power—forcefully if necessary—to promote its values around the world. . . . Neoconservatives believe modern threats facing the US can no longer be reliably contained and therefore must be prevented, sometimes through preemptive military action. . . . Most neocons share unwavering support for Israel, which they see as crucial to US military sufficiency in a volatile region. . . . The original neocons were a small group of mostly Jewish liberal intellectuals who, in the 1960s and 70s, grew disenchanted with what they saw as the American left's social excesses and reluctance to spend adequately on defense." http://www.csmonitor.com/specials/neocon/neocon101.html.

6. On February 5, 2003, then secretary of state Colin Powell made a presentation

to the UN Security Council that, he said, had two purposes: "to support the core assessments made by [UN weapons inspector] Dr. Blix and [International Atomic Energy Agency head] Dr. ElBaradei." Powell quoted Blix as saying, "Iraq appears not to have come to a genuine acceptance, not even today, of the disarmament which was demanded of it." Powell said his second purpose was "to provide you with additional information, to share with you what the United States knows about Iraq's weapons of mass destruction as well as Iraq's involvement in terrorism, which is the subject of Resolution 1441 and other earlier resolutions." http://www.whitehouse.gov/news/releases/2003/02/20030205-1 .html./ Later reports showed that Powell's presentation contained errors.

7. Richard A. Clarke was appointed President Clinton's national coordinator for security, infrastructure protection, and counterterrorism and continued in that position under President Bush. He also served as deputy assistant secretary of state for intelligence under President Reagan. In *Against All Enemies: Inside America's War on Terror* (New York: Free Press, 2004), Clarke writes a scathing account of the current President Bush's handling of the war on terrorism.

8. According to the online encyclopedia Nationmaster.com, "the Battle of Dien Bien Phu occurred in 1954 between Viet Minh forces and French airborne and Foreign Legion forces. The battle . . . became the last battle between the French and the Vietnamese in the first Indochina War, which had begun in 1946." http://www.nationmaster .com/encyclopedia/Battle-of-Dien-Bien-Phu.

9. Associated Press photographer Nick Ut took the photo of the girl, Phan Thi Kim Phuc, in June 1972. The two were reunited in 1995.

10. Associated Press photographer Eddie Adams took the photo of South Vietnamese police chief Nguyen Ngoc Loan executing Vietcong member Nguyen Van Lam in Saigon on February 1, 1968, during the Tet offensive (a coordinated surprise attack by the Vietcong on hundreds of towns, villages, and cities throughout Vietnam).

11. Robert Sarnoff was chairman of NBC from 1955 to 1966. William S. Paley developed CBS Radio and CBS Television, running them for more than fifty years, beginning in 1928.

12. At the Abu Ghraib prison in Iraq, American soldiers from a US military intelligence unit, US military police, and some civilian contractors abused and tortured their prisoners. Shocking photos of their activities were released, showing naked prisoners being forced into humiliating sexual and other poses, while their captors were pictured with them giving "thumbs-up" signs and, in at least one case, holding a leash with a prisoner on the other end.

13. Donald H. Rumsfeld is secretary of defense for the United States. Lt. Gen. Ricardo S. Sanchez was the top army general in Iraq at the time the Abu Ghraib scandal broke. Journalist/author Sy Hersh reported in his book *Chain of Command: The Road from 9/11 to Abu Ghraib* (New York: HarperCollins, 2004) that Sanchez ordered a secret investigation into Abu Ghraib on January 1, 2004, as well as an earlier study of military prisons in Iraq. Hersh wrote that a senior Pentagon official told him that "many generals believe that, along with the civilians in Rumsfeld's office, General Sanchez and General John Abizaid, who was in charge of U.S. Central Command in Tampa, Florida, had done their best to keep the issue quiet for the first months of the year [2004]" (p. 41). In May 2005 Sanchez was cleared of wrongdoing in the Abu Ghraib scandal. Col. Thomas M. Pappas was the commander-in-charge of the intelligence unit at Abu Ghraib at the time the scandal broke. Army Maj. General Geoffrey Miller, who, according to Hersh in his

New Yorker article "Chain of Command" (May 17, 2004), was "commander of the task force in charge of the prison at Guantanamo," went to Iraq in September 2003 with a team of experts to review the army's prison program there. Miller assumed the position of deputy commander for detainee operations in Iraq in April 2004. Miller was replaced in that position in November 2004.

14. Eric Sevareid was a pioneering television journalist who retired in 1977. His last job was as a commentator for the CBS Evening News. He died in 1992.

15. Walter Cronkite joined CBS in 1950 and rose to become a household figure and arguably the most influential network anchorman in the history of broadcast television. He resigned from CBS in 1981.

16. Edward R. Murrow, who is considered by many a TV journalism legend, was a broadcast reporter for CBS from 1935 to 1961, after which he became director of the United States Information Agency during the Kennedy era.

17. Seymour Hersh is a well-known investigative reporter and author. In his most recent book, *Chain of Command*, Hersh "takes an unflinching look behind the public story of President Bush's 'war on terror' and into the lies and obsessions that led America into Iraq." Quoted from the front flap of *Chain of Command*'s dust jacket.

18. See chapter 16 in this book.

19. In 1972 *Washington Post* journalists Bob Woodward and Carl Bernstein, with the help of a confidential source named "Deep Throat" (then FBI deputy director Mark Felt), connected a break-in at the Democratic National Committee headquarters located in the Watergate hotel and office complex in Washington, DC, to high-ranking sources in the Nixon administration and the Committee to Re-Elect the President. Their investigation eventually led to President Nixon's resignation in 1974.

20. Allegations that Saddam Hussein had ordered Iraqi intelligence to assassinate President George H. W. Bush in April 1993 during his visit to Kuwait to commemorate the victory of the first Gulf War eventually led President Clinton to order an attack on Mukhabarat, Iraqi intelligence headquarters, which resulted in the deaths of eight civilians when some of the missiles launched landed on nearby homes. In a November 1, 1993, *New Yorker* article titled "Case Not Closed," reporter Seymour Hersh wrote, "But my own investigations have uncovered circumstantial evidence, at least as compelling as the Administration's, that suggests that the American government's case against Iraq—as it has been outlined in public, anyway—is seriously flawed."

6

INSIDE THE HOUSE OF POWER

A GATHERER OF UNMANAGED GLIMPSES

Marion Ettinger

RON SUSKIND
Author and Journalist
Interviewed April 2005

L ifting the veil on the arena of power may not be as life threatening as writing an exposé of the Hell's Angels, but it's almost as hard. What Ron Suskind has achieved with one book and two *Esquire* articles is rare even under the best of circumstances. But the fact that he has managed to gather such an intimate, multidimensional view of the characters and goings-on within a presidential administration that is famous—or infamous—for shrouding itself in deep secrecy is nothing short of miraculous.

I interviewed Suskind over the phone. I haven't met him personally, but it only took a few minutes of conversation for me to figure out why former treasury secretary Paul O'Neill would feel comfortable entrusting the story of his tenure in the Bush administration to Suskind. Ron is warm and engaging. He has a genuine air about him. And a sense of humor. You feel like you're talking to someone you can trust. He speaks the way he writes, like a man who loves language and literature and wants to convey things not just accurately but with energy and color so that they come alive. As an analogy, Vivaldi's music comes to mind. So letting Ron in doesn't seem like a dangerous thing to do. Indeed, he is fair to his subjects, balancing the good with the bad.

Suskind describes his extraordinary collection of "unmanaged glimpses" of the top people in the Bush administration as "a study of power and its uses." It is, I think, a psychoanalysis of power too, and a fascinating one at that. In this interview, he explains how his profiles of those around the president eventually amounted to a portrait of Bush himself. He provides startling analyses of Bush, Rove, and Cheney, as well as the direction in which they are taking this nation. Suskind begins by talking about his *Esquire* articles and a fateful conversation with Paul O'Neill.

The two *Esquire* pieces that I wrote, "Why Are These Men Laughing?" and "Mrs. Hughes Takes Her Leave,"[1] created quite a bit of a stir, because there was almost nothing else at that point that was quite like them, where we had an unmanaged glimpse inside of the big white building which is ever more the beginning, the middle, and the end in the guidance of the ship of state. Not that White Houses ever are much less than that, but I think the way that power has been so centralized throughout the executive branch of government and because so much of President Bush's time is about America's use of power, that the intensity of pertinence of the goings-on in an incredibly small piece of real estate is, I think, rather unique.

In a large measure, what I've felt like I've been really doing is a kind of study in power and its uses. "Why Are These Men Laughing?" and "Mrs. Hughes Takes Her Leave" were really about the president. These *Esquire* articles and my book, *The Price of Loyalty*,[2] about former treasury secretary Paul O'Neill's experiences—are all about the president. "Mrs. Hughes Takes Her Leave" is ostensibly a profile of Bush's former White House counselor Karen Hughes, but we care about her because she has a direct line to the president and was first among equals at that point, even with Karl Rove[3] in consideration. That's why we're interested in the advisers. "Why Are These Men Laughing?" is ostensibly about Karl Rove, but again, it's really about the decision maker, the president, because Karl, like Karen, has what I would call a "Herodotus" perch. The

Greek historian Herodotus of Halicarnassus had this great idea about the Parthenon, which was completed in 432 BCE, just a few years before he died in 425 BCE. He said that there was an ideal place to view the Parthenon in its fine detail—to see the brilliant workmanship of it—while also taking in its broader context of sweeping hills. The analogy within the context of the White House is that you find advisers who are playing their own roles as well as actually helping to steer the ship of state. Through them, we get a sense of how the president as the duly elected leader does what he does and why, as well as what drives him, what his intent is, and how that flows into action.

After I'd done the two *Esquire* articles on Hughes and Rove, Paul O'Neill presented himself. Actually, I presented myself to him. He had read "Why Are These Men Laughing?" and was particularly interested in what I'd written about White House adviser John DiIulio, who had spoken frankly to me about what was going on at the White House: "There is no precedent in any modern White House for what is going on in this one: a complete lack of policy apparatus. What you've got is everything—and I mean everything—being run by the political reign of the Mayberry Machiavellis." That was the first thing O'Neill and I talked about.

He and I were having a fascinating conversation because of what I had written and what he had experienced. John DiIulio was extremely relevant because of the way the White House had treated O'Neill. DiIulio was the first person to leave and to speak, I think, with genuine candor, and without caring how the president would react to what he said. O'Neill was intensely interested in DiIulio and how the White House had come down on him so stridently and so effectively that John caved in public. The White House called him, and he was swiftly apologizing. He didn't take back what he'd said—he knew that was untenable—but he said, essentially, he didn't intend to offend anyone and that he was sorry. That was in the morning of the day the piece broke. At the midday briefing, Ari Fleischer said only that DiIulio's statements in the story were "baseless and groundless." By the late afternoon, the University of Pennsylvania released a statement in which DiIulio further apologized, saying he would never again speak about his tenure in the White House and that his statements were "groundless and baseless"—same words as Ari.

For DiIulio, one of the country's most dynamic public intellectuals, to say his own observations—remember the core of his testimony was a three-thousand-word on-the-record memo he sent me—were essentially meaningless, stunned people. It was a strange, ugly turn. The administration's desire, clearly, was to make an example of John, the first guy to leave the administration and speak with real frankness, so others would not exhibit similar temerity. Tactically, though, it seemed to backfire. This "overreach" created its own reaction, where journalists were opining about what they had done to John, whether he'd soon be at Guantanamo Bay[4] and whatnot, that kept the whole story alive for weeks. The DiIulio memo stands, ever more clearly, as a first lightning bolt about what makes this administration different from some of its predecessors.

I think that President Bush is a uniquely forceful presence at this moment of history. In some ways, a moment shapes an individual, and in this case, I think an individual has also shaped his moment. I think the match of these dramatic times with Bush's personality has shaped a real change in the way America does what it does, the way it views itself, and the way it commands and creates events in the world community. Bush does not present his abilities in many of the traditional ways that we expect not only of presidents but generally of high achievers in American life. I think that causes quite a bit of confusion in some cases for people who are in close and work for him, like cabinet-level officials. The kinds of qualities that we have generally come to expect from presidents are in some cases not particularly vivid or important to this president. Other qualities that we frankly don't often see are quite strongly ladled into this man. He's very action oriented. He is not contemplative. He does not enjoy the process of search and find, of deliberation, of "let's call in all the competing voices and make sure that we are very sound analytically in knowing everything that is possible to know." He is not, and has not, been particularly attuned to the analytical arts. Anyone who has looked at his life sees that this is the case. He did not prosper or, for the most part, succeed by virtue of the standards of the so-called meritocracy. That doesn't portend that he is a man without extraordinary abilities at the time needed.

To understand George Bush you have to understand a man who for decades sat at seminar tables at colleges or mahogany tables in boardrooms with virtually nothing to offer. So-called experts or folks who study well and who rest their confidence on study, experience, and intellectual journeys of left-brain consequence hold forth at these tables with great success. By contrast, Bush is a man who by virtue of a kind of default discovered the path to his success by relying more and more on instinct, on his gut. Think about George Bush arriving at the presidency, a place where even polymaths like Jimmy Carter, or the wonk-president Bill Clinton, felt themselves getting sucked into a vortex of complexity, a realm where a person simply needs to know more than almost any human being can know. How can you know all that you need to know to make certain types of decisions for which there may not be a clear right answer? This is the dilemma that presidents have faced. Some of them have faced it by diving right into the muck and saying, "I am just going to fight my way through and I'm going to stay up late at night and I'm going to get up early in the morning and I'm going to grill people one after another and I'm going to call in folks that frankly don't agree with me and I'm going to hear what they have to say and I'm going to look at it critically." That's the way most presidents have gone about it because they're afraid, they're afraid in some very, very personal corner of their psyche of making mistakes. If you make a mistake at this level, the consequences can be vast.

It's a rational fear that has created what would be called the reasonable doubts and conventional hesitations. Every president of the modern era has faced it. The office is beyond human scale. George Bush's remedy to that problem has not been to wade into the complexities of a host of incredibly dense and nuanced issues. Remember, no issue that gets to the Oval Office is uncomplicated. They're all complex. George Bush's remedy in the first part of his term was to fight his way through it a bit and then pull back. He's not a man who reads. He often doesn't even read short memos he gets. They used to talk about Ronald Reagan saying, "Keep it to a page." There are cases where George Bush has not even read single-page memos on certain key issues. What George Bush feels clearly is his métier is getting people who are generally trusted around him and poking at them. They come in and make presentations after which he throws off a few zingers. Then he throws a question at them that they're not expecting to see how they react. He knows that he cannot know all that this person across the room, or others in the neighboring rooms, knows about a particular issue. Many of them are lifelong experts. So what he does is he throws a few questions at them and watches their reaction. He is a master—as many folks who are not particularly verbal are— at nonverbal communication and body language. That's why he talks so much about body language. He wanted the 9/11 Commission to see him and Dick Cheney together so they could see their body language with one another. Most people don't place a whole lot of stock in body language, but then most people don't see the world the way this president does. What you say may be important. How you say it is almost as important. How you comport yourself while you're saying it, that's important, too.

The president doesn't feel there's any value to being particularly well understood—he says, judge me by my actions—but the more I study him, the more I hear from people who say that "there are a variety of moving parts here, so mix in this part or don't forget that part." There were meetings that the president had with O'Neill where he spoke with a great instinctual clarity about the uses of power, with almost a brazen quality. I think he is especially attuned to power and its uses because, at heart, I don't think Bush trusts that there are necessarily right answers to many issues of public policy.

There's a moment that I think is very telling when, early in Bush's administration, Paul O'Neill sits with him and it's clear that the big giant federal budget surplus is vanishing and that so many of the administration's economic assumptions were based on the idea that there would be a significant surplus to work with. At that point, it was clear that the economy was in the early stages of a significant downdraft and that the surplus wouldn't be there. So O'Neill sits down with Bush and makes the case for adding a provision for "triggers" to his tax cut plan. The triggers were indicators or red flags that would, as Federal Reserve chairman Alan Greenspan put it, "limit surplus-reducing actions if specified targets for the budge surplus and federal debt were not satisfied."

O'Neill and Greenspan had already agreed about this and, frankly, so did most prudent conservative economists, most of them Republicans. O'Neill had studied this issue for many years. So at his meeting with the president, O'Neill made his case for the triggers, telling him that while they would "blunt the tax cut's stimulus," that the president would eventually be rewarded by lowered long-term bond rates and rising equities prices in the capital markets, and that he would also win praise from many quarters for "continuing and advancing the virtues of fiscal prudence." And the president looks at O'Neill and says, "I won't negotiate with myself. It's that simple. If someone comes to me with a plan for this, and they have a significant amount of political backing, I'll sit down with them—talk it out. But until then, it's a closed issue." I think that's a very, very clear rendition of how George Bush sees many policies. For him, it's not a matter of getting the best minds to agree on a right answer. It's a matter of certain answers being the best insofar as the situation can be gauged by people he trusts, whether they are experts or not, and that if those answers are forcefully supported, forcefully carried forward with genuine confidence—and unflinching confidence is maybe the president's key offering to the equation—those answers will be proven right.

To me, he's putting the emphasis on whether or not there's enough political capital to be gained from an alternative proposal. He's saying that if a powerful enough group gets behind an alternative plan, then he'll consider changing his mind. He seems to base his decisions not on whether they're good or not from a standard of expertise, but from the perspective of political gain and whether it serves his base, which I once heard him say were the "haves and have mores." The base is what matters.

I think a big part of his political calculation is whether the base will be served, because the president is very, very focused on winning. The idea is win first; the rest is for later, or for a time of our choosing. By the same token, his view essentially is, "I am not going to have an intellectual, empirical 'let's search for the best answer' challenge to my confidence. It is already decided, but if someone comes with sufficient political capital, they can attempt to challenge my confidence. Frankly, in most cases, I'll just look at them and smile because I am that confident and I will show confidence. If I show confidence it can all but bend laws of physics. If I'm absolutely confident, matched with the authority I constitutionally possess, the combination will mean that even a reasonable case from the other side or a case supported by political capital will probably crumble under that force. Having said that, I will not even entertain the discussion short of somebody coming to me with the actual capital in the opposition. I don't even feel it's worthy of you to question why I've made a certain decision."

I think he is more in charge than people first thought. I think he has grown more and more in charge as his administration and his tenure has unfolded. At the start, he was less convincingly in charge. Presidents run up against a learning curve, and this president was no exception. Having said that, I think he is more and more in charge in the way that he exercises authority, which is often with very little explanation. He will not show his mind. This is one of the ways this president does what he does. Generally, senior advisers say, "I'm here to serve you. After we go through a policy debate"—which the president doesn't do a whole lot of—"I need to really know, once you've made your decision, what your thinking is." This is important. This is the way a president generally exerts influence and authority over senior advisers. Many of these advisers come to the administration as people of great consequence in American life and are already very accomplished in their realms. These are folks that have their own constituencies.

The way it usually works is that the president has to earn their loyalty. The way he does it is when a debate arises, he calls groups into the Oval Office and they have it out. At some point during this fight among three-hundred-pound gorillas, the president shows that he, too, has a mastery of the issue. What the president then does at the end of the day is he says, "Here's why I'm doing what I'm doing," and he shows his mind. He shows his senior advisers that he's thought through the issues and is making his decision for sound and discernable reasons. And then his advisers might say, "I may disagree, but I like the way he thinks."

This president doesn't do that. This president does something that leaves many advisers feeling confused. He says, "I went with my gut, I went on instinct and this is what I've decided and, frankly, I'm not going to give you any more explanation than that. You're here to execute my will." That's a very different model of leadership and it's a more naked show of authority than most folks, including those who have served under other presidents, are used to.

O'Neill is a guy who people, including many presidents, have trusted for good reason for a long, long time. That's why when he described those meetings with the president where Bush remained expressionless and asked no questions, people went, "Hummmmm," and then perhaps they said to themselves, "Well, then again, the president is a horse of a different color. Other presidents wouldn't do that. Other presidents would call in the treasury secretary and say, 'Let's talk about economic policy.' But not this president."

In your book *The Price of Loyalty* over and over you were describing these debates on issues, say Social Security or the energy policy, where there would be what I'd describe as a "stacked-deck" group that would be making the decisions. Take the energy policy issue. Let's face it, Cheney was just talking to industry people, and there were no environmentalists or other people with opposing views hashing out energy policy. So essentially, his inner circle decides what the policy is going to be.

Yes. The president is still not deeply engaged in the particulars of most domestic and foreign policies. He was not engaged in them prior to 9/11, for the most part. What I wrote in my book about how policy is made is an accurate rendition of what really happens. The president will often have a very cursory meeting where he'll be given the broad points. Then he'll say, "That sounds good to me," and then the particulars will be handled by Dick Cheney or driven by Karl Rove. After 9/11, the president became focused on a very few things, and in those areas he has been single-minded in saying, essentially, "I am going to spend the lion's share of my time focused, often very tactically, in these few areas." The biggest area is protecting America and getting bad guys. He wants to be seen as forcefully showing offense. His basic view is offensive, and post-9/11

he's driving a kind of ethos of continuous action to place our enemies per-
petually on the defensive and in a situation where we act and they have
to react. I'm not saying this is necessarily a sound, or complete, strategy.
I'm saying this is the president's strategy, and it's driven in some measure
by a kind of impulsive engagement.

**Talk about his top people—Vice President Dick Cheney, Secretary of
State Condoleezza Rice, Presidential Adviser Karl Rove, and so on—
what are they looking to do in their positions of power? Does the president serve as some sort of vehicle for them?**

I think you can safely say that the vice president is the most powerful vice
president of modern times. Karl is the most powerful political adviser of
any modern president, and they are first among all those folks around the
president. They are the president's left and right hands. During her tenure
as national security advisor, Condoleezza Rice played the role of Bush's
confidante and comfort factor. They would go behind closed doors and talk
through issues together. But the authority and latitude that the president
has given Rove and Cheney is dramatic. Does that mean that they're driving the ship of state? Sometimes, day to day, they kind of are. The president might say, "We want to go toward that island or be charted by this
particular constellation, and tell me how things work out after that." Some
people would say that the devil is in the details, and if you don't go get the
devil, the devil's going to come get you, and that to be essentially sepa-
rated from the how-do-we-get-there-from-here issues is not a reasonable
way to manage the US government. I think the president is in on the discussions about deciding where we want to get to. How-do-we-get-there-
from-here is left to lots of other people and that may mean that there is a
wide disparity between the goals you agreed upon and the outcomes that
the country ultimately has to face. I think that that's what we're seeing.

**With respect to his foreign policy, Bush didn't come up with that. It
seems to me that Wolfowitz, Rumsfeld,[5] and others came up with that
foreign policy way before he was even in office.**

Absolutely. They seemed to think about it long before he did. They came
up with much of the architecture for that back in 1992. Before they left
office with the first President Bush, they were already thinking about
these demonstration model issues having to do with deterring attacks on
US soil and assets abroad by launching preemptive strikes on nations that
were perceived to be threats as a way of sending a message to other
potential attackers. In 1998, when Wolfowitz and Condi were handling

the tutorials to brief candidate Bush on foreign policy, they had to convince him that there was no way to stop the spread of WMDs, that most are carried, after all, by available civil technology, and that we would be facing so-called asymmetrical threats, and that the key would be to set from the start a new direction, a new tone, globally. The president didn't fully act on those ideas, I don't think, until after 9/11, although I think that even before he came into office, he was subscribing to their philosophy on how to guide our relations with other nations.

But whether or not Wolfowitz came up with the president's foreign policy agenda, Bush is accountable for that policy. There are lots of good, bad, and indifferent ideas out there, and the president basically decides which idea he likes and off he goes. Some people would challenge him and say, "You like that idea but you haven't heard or been convincingly exposed to other ideas." And the president will respond, "If you want to amass a lot of political capital and come to me and talk about it, that's fine with me, but until then I've made up my mind." This is the George Bush way. I think he says, "I've made my decision, I'm going to go with it, and my basic confidence in that idea and the application of power behind it will make it right." There's a "might makes right" quality that drives him.

Vice President Cheney, on the other hand, is a mystery to lots of people. He has always kept his cards very close to his vest and has worked hard not to show himself, even though he has moved up, up, up through various stations of the government. Cheney is very good at creating the bureaucratic version of the media event—a crafted episode that seems to be occurring in an impromptu fashion, but is, in fact, very often ingeniously calculated and staged.

Look at global warming. That's an example that everybody felt was a Dick Cheney special. Former EPA [Environmental Protection Agency] administrator Christie Whitman and O'Neill both thought it had Dick Cheney's fingerprints on it. In February 2001 a group of senators sent a letter to the president asking him to clarify his position on global warming. Various folks in the White House responded that sending the letter was a good thing and that the president was going to create his response.

Bush had dealt with global warming during his first presidential campaign. He actually got a great deal of political capital out of it. In a few areas, he was even more of an activist in terms of certain environmental issues than his Democratic opponent, Al Gore. Fast-forward to February 2001. Bush is in office a month and somehow a reappraisal of this important policy is being orchestrated. This was before 9/11, when people had very strong feelings about the environment and global warming. All of a sudden, it's announced that the president will look anew at the issue, which seemed odd because, for the most part, presidents stick to their guns on important campaign promises, particularly in the first one hundred days or couple of years in office.

So O'Neill and Whitman and members of their senior staff went about a significant process of due diligence—because that's the school that they're from—to figure out the truth on global warming, to figure out what was known, what facts could be relied on, and what still needed to be known. They pulled together their various reports and made a presentation. Whitman went in to make that presentation to the president, and he told her, "I've already made up my mind." A letter went back to the senior senators conveying the president's decisions on global warming. Essentially, he had gutted much of what he said he supported and had boldly trumpeted during his campaign. Dick Cheney was delighted. The suspicion is that he had orchestrated the senators' letter to the White House, the "reappraisal," and Bush's response to the letter. It was a perfect Cheney moment. But the key is to make sure there are no fingerprints. Dick is very, very good at this. The vice president has always been good at this.

No fingerprints. Could you clarify that?

No fingerprints means making sure that, beneath the surface of a seemingly impromptu episode and incident, there is no evidence of premeditation, calculation, or manipulation.

What you've described is a situation where one position is taken during the campaign to get votes and then, once in office, a "reappraisal" situation is orchestrated so that the diametrically opposite position can replace the campaign position because that's what works for the people who paid the big bucks for his election.

Some people have made a very convincing case on that score. Paul O'Neill does in my book. He says, "During the campaign they said A and as soon as they got into office, they started working on Z." O'Neill says he felt that he, Whitman, Colin Powell, and other so-called pragmatists or realists in the administration were brought in as cover so that the administration could swiftly, quietly, and almost invisibly move in directions that went against what they said they supported during the campaign. That's O'Neill's position.

My assessment is that the president has never been clear on many of these issues, and I think that he profits from not being clear on them. On its face, it seems as though what Paul O'Neill and others claim is correct. Neither the president nor anyone else in the White House has effectively offered a counterpoint to it.

Talk about Cheney's areas of interest.

Energy, foreign affairs, all sorts of things. Dick has been in government a long time, and he has strong feelings about a variety of issues. He feels especially competent about dealing with energy issues, because he ran an energy company. He basically felt that there was nothing more that he really needed to know on that issue and that he is pretty much best-of-breed in terms of his expertise, so he moved forward pretty much unilaterally on that. The president also has experience with energy, so clearly the two of them talked it through, made their decisions, and off he went.

By the time the Bush administration assumed office, the "why" questions were, for the most part, already answered. The remaining questions had to do with "how" or implementation. What's interesting about Cheney is that he has been an effective number two man for others, acting as a consigliere and adviser, a person who is there to cover your back. I think one of the things that has been a new frontier for Cheney as this president's number two man is that his authority is often more akin to that of a number one. Serving Bush has been one of those "be careful what you wish for" moments for this quintessential number two man. In some ways, the last thing Cheney might want is a number one who gives him more power than a number two ought to have. It presents a real challenge to him as a number two and to his definition of what a number two man is and what he happens to be capable of.

There are many instances where Cheney took the ball and it didn't work out. The energy policy scandal is an example. Cheney was driving much of what we now call prewar intelligence; clearly his fingerprints were all over it. I think he probably understands that history will not judge him favorably on that score. It's an academic discussion, but it is an interesting dilemma when the number two is granted powers that are customarily reserved for a number one. It challenges one's definition of oneself as the loyal number two. There is an old saying along the lines of: Sometimes number twos have enough power to get into trouble, but not enough to get out of it. Cheney was given wide latitude across an enormous shoreline of foreign and domestic policy, and there are even folks in the conservative camp who say, "Boy, that might have been handled better."

Why does the president delegate so much authority to Cheney? Only the president can explain that. Was he overwhelmed? Did he feel he was not capable of handling these issues or some of the complexities of these debates? Was it a matter of him ceding authority to, or investing authority in, Cheney so that he could have a kind of plausible deniability when things went wrong? Those are things that George Bush has never explained. Will he ever explain? Who can say? That's one of the problems. When the president doesn't want you to know his mind, it makes you question whether or not he has thought through the issues with clarity and depth.

I am not ready to make history's judgment and nor, I think, is anyone else in this era who is close to events. I just try to find out what can be demonstrably shown so that people can have all of the pertinent information available to exercise informed judgments and, ultimately, informed consent.

How far can you go? What are you willing to say on that issue?

The president believes in the near-mystical powers of his instincts. He is unempirical. He is not particularly curious. He is driven by the dictates of a vivid personality—and personality is destiny in this model of leadership. You have some of this with every president—a sort of cult of personality at the center of things—but I think it's particularly dramatic with this president. In some cases, I don't think even he knows exactly why he makes certain decisions. He's very faith based and reads scripture for an hour each morning. He engages with people in funny push-and-shove exchanges that might not even be about the issue being discussed but rather about many other things, like sizing them up and looking at their body language to see if he can trust them and have confidence in what they say. It's a very improvisational model for leadership. There are parts of it that people are surprised to see have panned out. Not in every case, but you watch this president do what he does, and sometimes you just kind of shake your head, and say, "Goodness gracious, that seems to have worked."

Let me tell you about Karl Rove. The president has these codes of loyalty, which often are driven by very stark personal judgments like: friend or foe. Karen Hughes and Karl have formed a kind of bond with the president where he feels comfortable around them and feels like they can talk at a level that allows him to build his self-confidence. I think that's the best way to put it. There's a line from Anne Tyler's book *The Accidental Tourist*, which I think is pertinent. She says that in terms of relationships, it's not enough to just love the other person, the fundamental question is who are you when you're with them, because we're different with different people. I think that when the president is with Karl, or Karen, or Condi, he feels like himself. What that means is that he can be comfortable as himself and that they allow or help him to be that way. The president can often be something of a bully, and he can turn pretty quickly on you. That's just his history, but if he feels good about himself when he's with you, that intimacy can give you an enormous amount of influence over him. There are only a few people who are in this innermost circle.

Karl is a very interesting character because what he has done is blur the traditional lines between the political adviser and the policy chief. He is a political adviser. He has focused with incredible ferocity on tactics. At the same time, he is one of these self-made, self-educated men who ranges around quite a bit and has developed a span of interests that has resulted in his wielding dramatic influence on a lot of policies and issues. When a guy like John DiIulio, who is a real expert in various areas of domestic policy, sits with Karl, it sometimes creates discomfort because DiIulio knows that Karl is not really an expert. He knows what an expert is: somebody who has invested extraordinary amounts of effort to really understand the lights and subtleties of a particular issue. Karl is seen as a very, very light-footed, very diversely interested polymath. A polymath is not somebody who can profess having genuine depth on any particular issue, but who has an ability to give you a great thirty minutes on thirty issues. That's Karl. So for this president, who himself has a sort of impro-visational—"I'm focused on this issue, what do I need to know, give me the information now in bold declarative sentences"—urge, a guy like Karl is a perfect match.

Karl also performs functions on the order of, "I will do things, Mr. President, that you don't need to know about. I'll make sure that the out-comes are what you want." Karl is a very, very forceful "ends justifies the means" player. He will do whatever is necessary.

He is a bright guy. Like Cheney, he is very good at "no fingerprint" operations and often carries them out elegantly through subordinates or surrogates. The mob hit orchestrated in South Carolina against John McCain is a perfect example of the kinds of things that Karl will do. It wasn't a little "oh, by the way" thing; it was a significant effort by the Bush campaign. Lots of people in phone banks were calling up a very valuable call list of Republican supporters and push polling McCain, asking questions like: Would it change your view of Senator McCain if you knew that his wife was a drug addict? Would it change your view of Senator McCain if you knew that people in the government or in the Pentagon think he may be mentally unstable from his years in captivity? Would it change your view of Senator McCain to know that he sired a black baby out of wedlock? The diabolical ingenuity of the last question is that McCain has a daughter, Bridget, who he and his wife adopted from Bangladesh, and she does have a dark complexion. The McCains don't really advertise this; they don't want their daughter to feel in any way singled out. And this admirable thing that they have done left open a vulnerability to someone like Karl. So now Karl could, in a place like South Carolina, use this to encourage the perception that "Oh, there's the black baby that they're talking about in the push poll." Karl, of course, denies that he was involved in this. I think that's not plausible. It's not plausible to say that Karl was not involved, and that who knows what crazy things people will do in support of President Bush, and what's a busy manager to do? Maybe somebody will come out and say it someday.

All the important things that happen in the Bush campaign in some way go across Karl's desk. This was an extremely important thing that happened. It's an example of the kinds of things that Karl will do at the behest of the president. "Mr. President, I can and will do things to make sure that we end up where we need to be, and whether you're involved or not is almost not pertinent."

Various organizations have reportedly been crushed by a phone call from Karl. He makes certain that people know when the president disagrees with something they've done and that they will feel genuine consequences because of it. That's an important thing that Karl does for the president. The president believes that people should understand that the choices they make will have consequences. This is a big part of the president's view of effective and appropriate behaviorism. Karl, through surrogates, makes sure that the actual individuals know that they will face consequences for not doing what they're told.

What about your book; did you face consequences after that came out?

Sure. Before the book was written, they tried to dissuade O'Neill several times from cooperating with me. A few weeks after Paul agreed to cooperate with my book, he bumped into a reporter from the *Washington Post*, Glenn Kessler, the White House correspondent, and told him, "Ron Suskind has taken me on as his next project." This was early 2003 and O'Neill had been officially out of office for about a month or so. O'Neill told me about it and I said, "Oh, my gosh, did you have to tell the reporter that?" Of course, it was in the paper the next day. But Paul is blissfully unmanageable, which is one of his charms, and he said, "What do we have to fear from the truth?" which is my philosophy, so he had me there. Then I told him, "The response from the White House will be coming in probably the next twenty-four hours," and he said, "Oh, that's ridiculous." Sure enough, Rumsfeld calls him up, and says, "We think this is a bad idea." Essentially, Don Rumsfeld is the representative of folks in the White House. He has known O'Neill for thirty-five years. They're friendly and their wives are friendly. And Rumsfeld says, "Look, I think you know you shouldn't cooperate with this Suskind guy." And O'Neill says, "He seems like a bright enough guy and he's been doing this a long time and I trust him. Don, you and I have disagreed about plenty of things over the years and this will just have to be another one of them." Soon after, O'Neill got an invitation from Rumsfeld to come to the Pentagon to talk to a senior group of officials about reordering the assets of the vast Department of Defense. It was to be a big think on the matter. So O'Neill went to the Pentagon and they handed him a big sheaf of papers and they said, "Oh, before we start, you have to sign these things." Paul looked at it, and it was a nondisclosure agreement that essentially said that nothing O'Neill ever thought since he was nine years old could ever be made public or some such thing, and O'Neill said, "I can't sign this, but I will take it to my son, who is a lawyer, and let him look at it. Do you still want to go forward with the meeting?" At which point they said, "Yes, we guess so." Another week or so passed and Paul got a similar call from the CIA asking him to come in and help them rethink the world and what intelligence assets ought to be developed and how to build them. And when he arrived, they give him another pile of nondisclosure agreements to sign. And he said, "I really can't sign these things, thanks anyway. Do you still want to have the meeting?"

The White House charted my progress, I think, throughout the year because dozens of people in various parts of the administration did cooperate with the book. O'Neill gave me nineteen thousand documents on disks. He basically gave me everything that touched his desk during his time as treasury secretary, except for classified documents. The thing that makes O'Neill so unique is he is a zealot about transparency. He had always been that way when he was in the government. He was able to create a company based on these ideas at the aluminum giant Alcoa. When he returned to government, he entered Dick Cheney's dome of silence, and his response to that was to conduct a from-my-head-right-to-my-mouth public seminar as treasury secretary.

So he said to me, "Here's everything I have, do with it what you will, Ron. I trust you and know you'll figure it out. You can talk to everyone you can find on any of those lists." There were 7,630 entries in his log, which was all computerized. He gave me his schedule in which was recorded every phone call and who called whom, as well as every meeting and who attended at what time and date. His first minute as treasury secretary to his last minute were recorded in detail.

I started calling people on his lists. When you have a document with someone's name on the top, it's amazing how cooperative he or she can be, because, essentially, I already knew almost everything that was important when I dialed the number. Lots of people just shrugged and said, "What do we have to fear about the truth? It's going to come out anyway, so let me see if I can at least be a part of having my voice represented therein." That's why the book generally works as a narrative that has some historical value, because it was an unmanaged process of investigation and disclosure that ultimately rendered an accurate portrait of the occupants of this White House.

Flash-forward to mid-January 2004—the publication date—and you could hear them try to improvise their strategy the weekend before the book came out. O'Neill and I went on *60 Minutes* and went through the key points of the book with Lesley Stahl. One of the things that flashed on the screen during the *60 Minutes* piece was the cover sheet for a packet of top-secret documents that principals of the National Security Council [NSC][6] received for a meeting on February 1, 2001. Several of the items dealt with Iraq. One of them was an executive summary of a political and military plan for the post-Saddam Iraq crisis. The rest was about what to do once we seized the country. "Secret Classified" was stamped on the cover sheet. I didn't have the underlying documents. But *60 Minutes* flashed that cover sheet on TV without this qualification, and the next day the White House was demanding that the inspector general conduct an investigation into whether O'Neill and I had made off with classified materials.

They launched a formal investigation. They did that on a Monday and it was out there on the Internet, cable, and network evening news. The next day the book appeared in bookstores—a day when this story about the documents was on the front page of newspapers around the country. At that point I said to myself, "Tactically that probably wasn't the smartest thing they could've done." As somebody said to me, "How many of your books does Karl Rove want to sell? The morning the book comes out they say, 'Suskind used classified material to write this book which is now at your bookstores and you can get it today.'"

But it all became rather serious. To be investigated by the full force of the United States government with real penalties attached if it were decided that I had made off with classified government documents is no small matter. There are serious felony penalties, like ten years in prison and a one-hundred-thousand-dollar fine.

The first thing I did was to call Paul. He and I were together doing book tour stuff for the first few days after the investigation was announced. I said, "Look, I'm protected by the First Amendment but you're not, so I'll take it from here." He had given me the documents at the start of the project, and I'd been using them and had them all set up in search indexes. So I told him, "You can just wash your hands of it. I'll handle the lawyers." I ended up with an esteemed Washington law firm, Covington and Burling, to represent me, and they agreed to do the work pro bono, thank goodness. That was an admirable thing to do. A lot of firms wouldn't have touched it. They feel that there are important principles in play, involving some of our cherished freedoms, and so do I.

A few weeks after publication, as I had promised on the book jacket, I began to put on my Web site documents from the nineteen-thousand-document trove. That began happening while the government was actively involved in its investigation. There was a bit of havoc at that point inside the government because they were concerned that I was going to post some of the documents that they were worried about on the Web site. I got a few panicked calls the night before the site went online. I told them not to worry, that I wasn't posting anything with national security implications. So I just kept posting documents in weekly or monthly installments throughout the election year. The docs helped drive news and were used as the foundation for various stories throughout the election and afterward. I put up a big memo on taxes that then assistant treasury secretary Pamela Olson had written just after the election. It was pretty much the full blueprint of choices and consequences. The document swiftly became a key element in the debate to reform the US tax code—on K Street they just called it "the memo"—and it may be a contributing reason why tax reform was soon tabled in favor of reforming Social Security.

Meanwhile, the president's surrogates, Rumsfeld and others, were busy going after O'Neill. Their line was that he was disgruntled and that this was his book. It was not his book. O'Neill provided the central role, but as anyone who reads *The Price of Loyalty* can see, many people were involved in the book. O'Neill provided the book's key point of view; it's like he had a camera poised in the corner of his glasses and you got to be in the key rooms and see the president and all the key players going about their business. That's why the book is one that people read and cite. The White House tried to turn O'Neill's cooperation with the book into a character issue by saying that it was a matter of Paul O'Neill versus the president. It never was. O'Neill never expressed one word of ill will toward the president. He just said, "Here's what's true and what people ought to know."

So they went after O'Neill and then they came after me, and there was all this innuendo and there were personal attacks, but at some point they realized it wasn't going to be worthwhile. Once people saw that *The Price of Loyalty* is very sober, very, very carefully sourced, supported by nineteen thousand documents and the testimony of dozens of people who were actually sitting in various rooms in the government during the moments that are described in the book as well as in government transcripts, it became clear to everybody that the book was not particularly partisan. A month or two after it came out, I started getting calls from Republicans saying, "Look, this is our story." *The Price of Loyalty* is full of the Republican song of prudence in domestic affairs and pragmatism abroad. Increasingly, I think, both sides of the political spectrum have embraced the book at least in some measure by virtue of the fact that it is not written as a partisan document. It's written to offer a basic and, I think, level-headed view of how our government is run at this time of enormous change.

Besides *60 Minutes*, what was the press's response to the book? How did Fox treat you?

Fox interviewed Larry Sabato, who was my professor at the University of Virginia, and asked what kind of student I was and what were my political leanings, and Larry told them, "I think he was a liberal Democrat." I believe he was on Fox's *The O'Reilly Factor*, and Bill O'Reilly said, "Aha!" On balance, the media covered the book as a news event with clear-eyed probity. Reporters all over town were saying, "Thank goodness, this book is a buffet table with a lot of plates on it and the food is free, so let me go dine." The book ended up being cited in stories and discussions on a wide spectrum of issues, including Iraq, weapons of mass destruction, and domestic policy on taxes, Social Security, energy, corporate governance, and the environment. I think it is among the most cited books of the year because of all the disclosures about the president and the issues he was handling. People—folks from the business pages and folks writing about national affairs, foreign affairs, or about the president and his character—just kept coming back to it over and over again, because a fairly wide shoreline is covered. In this environment in which many reporters are starved for sound, double-blind, peer-reviewed, supportable facts, this book gave facts. It disclosed irrefutable facts about many issues that reporters had been digging futilely for over several years. It's not because we don't have the greatest reporters on the planet, because I think that we do, but the White House's message discipline machine is one that basically says, "We don't feel there's an inherent value to public dialogue based on the pertinent facts. We don't. Strategically, there isn't much value to it in our minds and the question is: 'Will we be penalized for not engaging the way other White Houses have generally engaged? Let's see.'"

What are the implications of a White House that doesn't communicate with the press, that is so secretive?

We're seeing the implications right now. The question in politics and the question in managing, preserving, and expanding power is simply: *Does it work or not?* If it works, it will be repeated. If it doesn't, it will be abandoned. Right now, on balance, it has worked. I had a conversation with Karen Hughes during the time that I was visiting the White House on and off for a couple of months in early 2002 while I was working on a story. I said to her, essentially, "Wow, this is such a successful machine you guys have here. Virtually no one has been in here." At that point, the United States had gone into Afghanistan, and Bob Woodward and Dan Balz had written their series, "Ten Days in September: Inside the Bush War Cabinet."[7] Tom Brokaw was there at the White House to do an NBC report, which was, frankly, a Hallmark card. I was about the third reporter to spend significant time in the West Wing. I had a desk across from Karen's office. So we're there and I say, "You really have managed to go around the traditional mainstream press, around the leaders of the Fourth Estate and the national press." Clearly, they had kept the president away from us. They had not done press conferences; fourteen or fifteen press conferences in a first term is historically low. The president's father did something like seventy-five solo press conferences. And I said to Karen that in my view her trying to manage something as ethereal as the truth with such force and precision was like Nixon's wage price freezes. You know, where Nixon tried to control the elemental forces of the economy by freezing and capping them. It works for a while, but then the dam breaks. And she kind of laughed and said, "Well, it seems to be working up to now. We're not worried."

What are the implications if indeed it is successful and it will be repeated? What are the implications for our democracy?

The implications are profound for a host of ideals and standards that I think have proved their worth throughout the modern era of American democracy. One of those standards is that the public does have a right to know and understand what the government is doing and why it is doing it. It is what I call the "good reason" standard. People do what they do for good enough reasons, good enough that intent flows to action. They may not be your reasons or mine, but they are good enough to have resulted in a decision being made. If you know those good enough reasons, you know, for the most part, the things that are most important about what drives individuals and, in some cases, institutions. I think it is a basic obligation that is knit into the very core of American democracy that we understand the good enough reasons upon which our leaders rely to make the decisions that affect all our lives. I think that this standard is increasingly viewed as quaint and part of the arcana of our past because it runs right into the current counterethos, which is message discipline and message control. The pertinent idea is that saying something over and over again—through as many different venues and portals as possible—and just sticking to the script, is a strategy that ultimately wins out.

This problem is compounded by that fact that message control is being exercised in an environment that is increasingly fact-starved. Fact-starved, not necessarily because there aren't some facts out there, but because each side has its own set and in many cases the sides won't even agree on the basics, that, say, the sun rises in the east. They do not share or agree upon any facts. Without mutually agreed-upon facts, what you get is a tyranny of who can be more confident and unflinching and precise in sticking to the script. I think that ultimately creates problems for a sacred principle of informed consent. If the administration had their druthers, they would rather it be consent that is as uninformed as possible.

What role is the press playing in all this?

The press is doing what it has always done. The press is working around the clock trying to keep up with the pace of events and trying to come up with a response to these strategies. What they face are more and more people who say, "I don't see any reason why it in any way benefits me or is worthwhile for me to talk to you. In fact, in this administration, if I speak to you in an unmanaged way without proper authorization, I could face real consequences. My bosses have made that clear to me."

Let me ask you: Why did we go to war?

Why did we go to war? At this point, astonishingly enough, I do not think the public yet understands fully why we went to war in Iraq.

I know that. But why do you think we went to war?

I'll tell you why I think we went to war. Look at Donald Rumsfeld's talking points memo that I put in the beginning of my book. It is a very apt distillation of longer memos that Rumsfeld wrote explaining what he, the neocon community, and others who have been driving US foreign policy truly believe. What do they believe? They think that we cannot stop the spread of weapons of mass destruction because they're carried in large measure by civil private-sector technology that is as ubiquitous as the wind, and that the free market spreads these weapons like spores. So if the spread of weapons of mass destruction cannot be stopped, what do you do? If weapons of mass destruction spread as the memo indicates, then we in the United States will be denied access to regions of the globe, because we will run into so-called asymmetric competitors who are not as big and strong as we are, and who can't and aren't willing to go out on the field of battle and pit their divisions against our divisions. Asymmetric competitors possessing weapons with enormous destructive capacities will deny the United States access to regions of the globe and thwart our various global plans. What do we do about it? Well, part of what we do is transform the US military, to make it a lighter, leaner fighting force for the battles ahead. Then we need to *dissuade*—this is the key word in the memo; it's right near the end on page eight, but it's really another word for *preemption*—these rogue states and in some cases transnational movements from trying to get their hands on the destructive weapons. How do you do that? What you do is you set up a demonstration model showing exactly what will befall a country or a leader who attempts to flout the authority of the United States, either by having weapons of mass destruction, or in some cases, just by wanting them. And they decided that invading Iraq and taking out Saddam Hussein would be a good demonstration model. This was decided before the administration ever was in the corridors of power, before the neocon community ever got back into the big white building.

Why was Saddam Hussein the big choice?

Because they thought he was an easy mark.

So oil had nothing to do with it.

Oil was part of it, but mostly they thought Saddam Hussein would be an easy mark. He was an attractive target for a variety of reasons, again, oil was one of them, but he was also an ideal demonstration model for showing what would happen if you attempt to challenge the authority of the United States of America or even if you harbor desires for weapons of mass destruction. Now the fact is, all those things were justifications that were generally cobbled together. The weapons of mass destruction rationale was front and center because as Wolfowitz, in essence, said, "That's the only thing everyone could agree about." Ultimately, the key thing to understand is that we are engaging in a global experiment in behavioralism. The purpose of the dramatic demonstration like the one we're doing in Iraq is to encourage, coerce, dissuade, and guide other sovereign nations in the decisions that they make. That's the key. The spread of weapons of mass destruction can't be stopped; there are too many countries that have them, and you can't to go to war all over the planet. So what you need to do is show misbehaving nations what will happen if they act in a certain way. That, it was so decided, would be the fate of Saddam Hussein. He would be the example. That's the core of the preemption idea. I think that the companion ideal of bringing democracy to the nations of this region—as a way to thwart terrorism and do something that is obviously for humanity's general good—was a latter-stage, follow-on idea. It is admirable. Though it is not clear that it would do much to reduce the terrorist threat, everyone would, of course, love to see democracy bloom in this region. But I don't think that idea connects to US national interests with an indelible clarity that, say, the mother of a dead soldier can hold tight to. That's generally the test presidents rely on: "What do I say to the families of the fallen?" and "Will the goal match the sacrifice?" I think that's why support of the war has steadily declined. In that way, it's a problem this is not dissimilar to Vietnam.

One of the reasons I asked you why you thought we went to war is because I've interviewed almost two dozen of this nation's top journalists, top messengers, and what's fascinating to me is that there's no consensus on why we went to war. Why is that?

Because this administration, by virtue of playing find-a-justification-for-this-preordained-thing, lost credibility on this issue and never clearly explained to the American public why it was in our national interest to go to war in this country halfway around the world.

They said it was weapons of mass destruction and connections to al Qaeda.

Right

Wasn't that clear?

There were no connections to al Qaeda.

Whether it's true or not is a separate issue from what they said.

They offered all manner of justifications. The fact is that the administration in large measure within itself knew that many of them were hollow.

But what about the press?

What about the press? Why didn't we get it? We still haven't gotten it.

Why?

Why haven't we . . . 'cause it . . .

I have to make a note here that there's a long pause, a long silence on your end.

I think the answer is the one I offer. Look, it is a sacred, solemn duty of the leaders of a nation to explain to the true sovereigns—the voters, the citizens—why we should go to war against another nation. There is a long history of this being a solemn and sober obligation. It can't just be a good reason. It has to be a reason that Americans, on balance, think is worthy of the ultimate sacrifice.

Well, we've been lied to before on this same issue.

Over history, leaders have sometimes flouted this solemn obligation and they've done it at great peril. Ultimately, it is the role of leaders to say, "Here are the clear-as-an-unmuddied-lake reasons why we will now to go war and why young men and women will lose their lives.

But what is the press's role in this exchange?

The press's role was to try to figure this out, but the press was up against a strategic model to keep not just them but the American public and their representatives in Congress from seeing clearly the true reasons and motivations that ultimately drove us to war.

So by implementing their strategic model of message control and management, the administration was going five hundred miles an hour and the press was going fifty. What strategy should the press be using to catch up with them?

I don't have any stunning remedies. I just know the modest thing I've done, which is to say, "I need to find someone with firsthand experience in the innermost councils of state. I need to get them outside of the building and to talk to them about the indispensable role of truth in the American experiment in self-governance. If I can do that, we can engage in a kind of truth therapy where, at least in some cases, they'll come to their senses and say, 'at the end of the day, the truth is all we have. It's all we have in what works in our personal relationships, in what works in our relationships between citizens and their government. And I will be a part of that grand tradition by saying this is what I know because I saw it with my own eyes and I will speak it.'"

In your *New York Times* essay "Without a Doubt,"[8] you wrote that a senior Bush adviser told you, "We're an empire now and when we act, we create our own reality and when you're studying that reality, judiciously as you will, we'll act again creating other new realities which you can study, too. We're history's actors and you, all of you, will be left to just study what we do." So what role are they relegating the press to here?

They view the press as another special interest in Washington, just like the prescription drug people. They say that they don't think it is good to offer lots of access and disclosure, to let people see what they do and why they do it, and to let anyone outside their inner circle know about the key debates that ultimately drive and precipitate policy. Essentially, the press is there to record their decisions.

It strikes me that they're treating the press like a bunch of cobwebby historians recording events after the fact.

What they're saying is that the arc of history bends toward those who have the confidence to act, and that even though the issues may be complex almost to the point of being imponderable, they have the confidence to act, and so they will act. And the press can watch once they've acted. The president and Karl have said this in various ways. People have said to me directly, "I want to be judged on my actions. Judge the president on his actions and their outcomes, not on what he said and not on how we arrive at decisions. You can watch us act like everyone else; you play no special role."

So everybody, including Congress, is excluded from participating in deciding what action is going to be taken.

Absolutely right. That's the whole idea. The whole idea is that they will leave no other alternative other than a kind of default, where you'll simply watch them act after they've decided by themselves what to do.

Then, Ron, we're not living in a democracy anymore.

Well, it's different.

What does that mean?

It's a different place than the country you and I grew up in. Look, tactics matter. They mattered at Waterloo, they mattered in North Africa and at the Battle of the Bulge.[9] They matter. Sometimes history turns on those who are more tactically forceful and effective. In this administration's case, certain tactics have made a real difference in the primacy or relevance of underlying principles.

"Without a Doubt" appeared on the cover of the *New York Times Magazine* two weeks before the election, and it got almost as much coverage as *The Price of Loyalty*. There was a debate inside the *New York Times* where people said, "We know we'll be criticized for engineering an October surprise because we're having you write a cover story in the *New York Times Magazine* right before the election, but we're willing to take that heat." After the story came out, John Kerry ran for a whole week with the part where the president said he wanted to privatize Social Security. Even though that was the centerpiece of what Bush did as soon as he was reelected, his camp didn't want people to be talking about it in the last two weeks of the campaign. The piece stated that this was the first "faith-based presidency" and went on to discuss what that meant for the administration and the country. I think it was clarifying for readers to read those quotes where they said that while they were creating new realities, the press—and really the whole so-called reality-based community, which includes Republicans, Democrats, and, I think, most Americans—would be left in their wake, examining the old realities already behind them. After reading those quotes, Garry Wills and Niall Ferguson[10] and others wrote that we were debating Enlightenment principles in this election. I think we were.

I interviewed Paul Krugman and in the introduction to his book, *The Great Unraveling*,[11] he wrote about the Bush administration within the context of a revolutionary government, which is a government that

assumes power via a prevailing system and then proceeds to dismantle that system. Krugman wrote about how the system was being dismantled on the domestic side via doing away with all the New Deal programs and on the international side via a foreign policy based on preemption rather than retaliation. So I asked Krugman, "If it's a revolutionary government, what kind of a government is it going to be in the end?" He didn't have an answer. Nobody wants to answer that question.

Well, I think people are trying to be reasonable and to see all sides and to not be shrill. As soon as you start becoming shrill, you are, tactically speaking, vulnerable to being attacked for being unreasonable, and it can result in a loss of credibility, or even more specifically, audience. And that's a problem. The fact is, lots of folks who do have some concerns are, on balance, reality based. So they are ever searching across the terrain of what is discernable, and they are withholding judgments until they can find irrefutable support for such judgments. Again, it's a very different way of operating than the more improvisational, often swiftly judgmental model of leadership right now.

The president's fundamentalist Christian supporters are very comfortable with judgment, even for people they've never met. Liberals and conservatives in the reality-based community realize that lots of folks in the White House believe that the system before the Bush administration came into power is part of a receding past and that it doesn't work the way it used to anymore.

Krugman did mention the emerging theocratic character of the current system.

Right. The *Times* piece examines the intellectual architecture for this, and Niall Ferguson uses it as the epigram of his new book. Everybody said, "There it is, clearly."

There's a battle going on around the globe between modernists and fundamentalists, between folks who are more pragmatic and discursive, and a counterethos that is often exhausted with modernity and distrustful of it, and holding fiercely to all manner of fundamentalist literalisms and certainties. That sort of passionate intensity allows, in so many cases, a kind of easy ferocious certainty that the world is divisible into the good people and all the others and that it is manifest destiny that those self-designated good people will triumph.

With respect to the Bush administration, I think it's more complicated than that. There are three parts to their base: the fundamentalist Chris-

tians, the wealthy right-wing and corporate Americans, and the pro-Israeli group. Those are the three base groups, would you agree?

Yes, I think it's a reasonable distillation.

The fundamentalists aren't rich people. A lot of those good Christians are actually middle class and lower. Their interests are inimical to those of the rich. Dismantling the New Deal isn't good for them. So his base consists of groups with directly opposing interests.

I don't think there is rationalists' perfection in the political marketplace any more than there is in the economic marketplace. Sometimes people act in ways that are not aligned with their best interests. But having said that, people underestimate this president and the way he has been able, even though he is a man of privilege, to connect with a wide array of Americans in almost nonverbal ways and to speak to the architecture of "us versus them."

But connecting with people and doing for them are two different things.

Right. The good people say he's a good man and a man of faith, and we have these explosions of faith during times of either great prosperity or great fear, and right now we have both.

But do you think one base is more a priority than another?

I think instinctively he knows the fundamentalist Christians. He understands them. He also understands with great alacrity how to harness these subterranean powers, these enormous forces that roil beneath the surface of American life. He understands the appeal of faith and certainty in these times of modernity fatigue and terrorism and nonspecific fear.

I'm actually asking a much simpler question. Who's he serving the most?

Clearly the wealthy are being served by much of the domestic policy, but the Christian base feels it's being served by a different kind of domestic policy, which is the president's moral certainty, as they call it. They say to themselves: "What do we know? Well, the president is not really going to affect the US economy that much anyway. Once presidents get into office they realize that the economy ebbs and flows in cycles, and I'm out here as a member of the base and I get more or less what I need. There's food on the table. I might want an economic uptick sometime soon, but it's my job to make that happen. I get that this man is in a conversation with God and that what he does is part of some broader plan, maybe one

I cannot discern, but one that I trust and that is divinely affirmed as best as we can know on this earth." The administration gets an awful lot out of that, especially when people are afraid and can't make sense of what's going on. Faith-based people tell me, "No one even agrees on the most basic things. It's just one long noisy argument without solution. History's an argument that never ends. So I wash my hands of it, and what I want is a man who says, 'I'm going to do this because I'm carrying forward the broader timeless law of God's will.'"

The press has a long history of marginalizing these people.

You bet. They have felt very marginalized for a long time. It was easy for folks in the press to dismiss them because the press tends to be reality based in terms of its assessments and analyses. After a while, some of the folks in the faith-based community said to themselves, "Whatever everyone else does, we're bringing to the table another element: the faith-based certainties and satisfactions for which you in the Fourth Estate have no regard. It doesn't seem to fit onto your screen of relevance."

So it's the press's turn to be marginalized.

You bet and the new guard is doing a whale of a job. But I think there are ebbs and flows to that, too. There's no doubt that those in power have won some very significant victories in the last five years. Very significant. I'm hoping to be a counterpoint to that, but I cannot deny what is, on it's face, a string of wins. They have won some victories in marginalizing those who do what I do. But I have great faith in the reality-based power of America's good sense. It always asserts itself eventually.

The question at the heart of the *Price of Loyalty* and the *Times* piece is whether or not the self-correcting features of America's great unfinished experiment in self-governance are functioning properly. I think that of late, some of these features have been damaged or diminished and are not working optimally. If you start changing the fundamental architecture of the way we do what we do and have done it for a long time, certainly the fear is that some of the self-correcting features won't work when we need them.

As I said to Karen Hughes, "Once the dam breaks, it breaks." I think eventually people will say, "Hold on a minute, I'm tired of being treated like a kid and being told what's going on and what my leaders are up to on a strictly need-to-know basis."

It's like when parents tell a kid something that the kid doesn't want to hear and the kid says, "Why do I have to do that?" And the parent says, "It's enough that I told you to do it." That's not enough for the citizens of the world's greatest democracy.

RON SUSKIND is one of America's leading authors and journalists. His latest book, *The Price of Loyalty: George W. Bush, the White House and the Education of Paul O'Neill*, is a sweeping tour of the inner working of the Bush administration. The *New York Times* #1 best-seller follows the two-year arc of Paul O'Neill, the former treasury secretary and a principal of the National Security Council, as he and other senior officials assess the conduct and character of this presidency. The book, which is based on unprecedented access to senior officials and nineteen thousand internal government documents given to the author by Mr. O'Neill, is sure to stand unchallenged as the most explosive and historically significant book of the 2004 election year. The *New York Times* called it "an invaluable contribution both to the historical record and to the fierce public debate over the nature of the Bush administration's true views and motivations on issues of war and peace." The *Los Angeles Times* termed it "incandescent"; *Business Week* called it "eye-popping." It will stand, said novelist Ward Just in the *New York Observer*, "as a first-rate piece of work" and "the best we're likely to have for some time" about the Bush presidency. *Forbes* selected *The Price of Loyalty* as the "Business Book of the Year," *Fortune* cited it as one of the seventy-five "smartest" books ever written, and it was awarded first prize as Best Book of 2004 by Investigative Reporters and Editors, Inc.

Mr. Suskind is also the author of *A Hope in the Unseen: An American Odyssey from the Inner City to the Ivy League* (New York: Doubleday/Broadway, 1998), which follows the two-year journey of a prickly, religious honor student as he escapes from a blighted Washington, DC, terrain to find a home at Brown University. The book, which was launched by a series in the *Wall Street Journal* that won him the 1995 Pulitzer Prize for Feature Writing, has been a favorite on US campuses and in book clubs.

From 1993 to 2000, Mr. Suskind was the senior national affairs writer for the *Wall Street Journal*. He was a contributor to Caroline Kennedy's collection *Profiles in Courage for Our Times* (New York: Hyperion, 2002), along with other prize-winning authors. He currently writes for various national magazines, including the *New York Times Magazine* and

Esquire magazine. His October 17, 2004, cover story in the *New York Times Magazine*, "Without a Doubt: Faith, Certainty, and the Presidency of George W. Bush," is widely cited among the most definitive articles about President Bush in recent times.

Mr. Suskind has appeared on various network news programs as a correspondent or essayist and is a distinguished visiting scholar at Dartmouth College. He is a graduate of the University of Virginia and of Columbia University Graduate School of Journalism. He lives in Washington with his wife, Cornelia Kennedy Suskind, and their two sons.

NOTES

1. "Why Are These Men Laughing?" was in *Esquire*'s January 2003 issue and "Mrs. Hughes Takes Her Leave" was in *Esquire*'s July 2002 issue. Both can be read at Suskind's Web site: http://www.ronsuskind.com/newsite/articles/archives/000005.html.

2. Ron Suskind, *The Price of Loyalty: George W. Bush, the White House, and the Education of Paul O'Neill* (New York: Simon & Schuster, 2004).

3. Karl Rove is a political consultant and President Bush's senior adviser and chief political strategist. In February 2005 he was appointed deputy chief of staff in charge of policy. http://en.wikipedia.org/wiki/Karl_Rove.

4. This is a reference to a US military–run prison at Guantanamo where "enemy combatants" from the "war on terror" are being detained.

5. Paul Wolfowitz was deputy secretary of defense in the Bush administration until he assumed his new position as head of the World Bank in June 2005. Donald Rumsfeld is secretary of defense.

6. On its Web site, http://www.whitehouse.gov/nsc/, the National Security Council is defined as "the President's principal forum for considering national security and foreign policy matters with his senior national security advisors and cabinet officials. . . . The function of the Council has been to assist the President on national and security policies. The Council also serves as the President's principal arm for coordinating these policies among various government agencies."

7. *Washington Post* staff writers Woodward and Balz wrote the eight-part series "Ten Days in September: Inside the Bush War Cabinet," which can be accessed at http://www.washingtonpost.com/wp-dyn/politics/news/postseries/tendaysinseptember/. The first of the series, "America's Chaotic Road to War," came out on January 27, 2002, followed by "We Will Rally the World" (January 28, 2002), "Afghan Campaign's Blueprint Emerges" (January 29, 2002), "A Day to Speak of Anger and Grief" (January 30, 2002), "At Camp David, Advise and Dissent" (January 31, 2002), "Combatting Terrorism: 'It Starts Today'" (February 1, 2002), "A Presidency Defined in One Speech" (February 2, 2002), and "Bush Awaits History's Judgment" (February 3, 2002).

8. "Without a Doubt" by Ron Suskind can be read at http://cscs.umich.edu/~crshalizi/sloth/2004-10-16b.html.

9. Napoleon Bonaparte's defeat on June 18, 1815, at Waterloo, Belgium, at the

hands of Allied armies led by Britain's duke of Wellington and General Blucher from Prussia brought an end to twenty-three years of war. http://en.wikipedia.org/wiki/Battle _of_Waterloo. The 1940–1943 North African campaign, or "Desert War," began with Italian attacks on British occupied areas, which escalated to Italian and German Axis forces fighting US and British Allied forces. The Allies eventually drove the Axis forces out. The Battle of the Bulge (also known as the German Ardennes Offensive) started in December 1944 and was the last major German offensive on the Western Front during World War II. http://en.wikipedia.org/wiki/Battle_of_the_Bulge.

10. A cultural historian, Garry Wills is an author and adjunct professor at Northwestern University in Evanston, Illinois. Niall Ferguson is a professor of history at Harvard University in Cambridge, Massachusetts, and the author of *Colossus: The Price of America's Empire* (New York: Penguin, 2004).

11. Paul Krugman, *The Great Unraveling: Losing Our Way in the New Century* (New York: W. W. Norton, 2003). Also, see chapter 7 in this book.

7

THE **REVOLUTION IS BEING TELEVISED**

YOU JUST DON'T WANT TO BELIEVE WHAT YOU'RE SEEING

Dan Deitch

PAUL KRUGMAN
Op-Ed Columnist,
New York Times
Interviewed March 2005

F or Paul Krugman, who describes himself as an economist moon-lighting as a journalist, there just aren't enough hours in the day. He shoehorned me into his jam-packed schedule by agreeing to be inter-viewed during lunch. In person, he definitely looks like the Princeton pro-fessor that he is. He speaks at a fairly fast clip, and when he's talking, he raises his eyebrows and wears a wide-eyed look that makes you feel like you really should be taking in everything he's telling you because it's very important. He also talks like a man desperate for America to wake up and smell the coffee.

What's so compelling about the reporting Krugman does in his op-ed columns for the *New York Times* are his sources: people don't talk to him, numbers do, and numbers don't lie. When he does the math, Krugman discovers all kinds of disquieting things that he shares with a sizable readership that is really a fan base. But his reporting also elicits lots of hostile reactions, including major attack campaigns via e-mail. Krugman persists, however, and openly admits that he couldn't do what he's doing at the *New York Times* if he didn't have a solid day job teaching.

On the day I interviewed him, the Bush administration's plan to privatize Social Security was weighing heavily on Krugman's mind. But this was just one aspect of a larger picture I wanted him to bring into focus. What I wanted this numbers man and star *New York Times* columnist to do was talk about an epiphany he had had about the definition of the term "revolution" and how that fit into, as he put it, "the whole story of what's going on in the United States right now." As it turns out, Mrs. Krugman had the epiphany first.

I'd been writing from various sides about what's been going on during the Bush administration's tenure. My wife was reading Henry Kissinger's first book, *A World Restored: Metternich, Castlereagh and the Problems of Peace 1812–22*, and she showed me this opening passage about revolutionary power and how people have trouble dealing with it, and she said, "You've got to read this, this is exactly what you've been trying to talk about." Kissinger was saying that when there's a new power on the scene that doesn't accept the legitimacy of the system in which it came to power, people have difficulty dealing with it. People who have been living in a stable system where the balance of conflict is running in fairly narrow channels just cannot accept it, even if the power says outright, "We want to make a revolution. We've got to destroy the system." People react by saying, "Oh, they don't really mean it." They simply cannot acknowledge that the rules have changed and they cannot acknowledge the ambition.

Another feature of revolutionary power that Kissinger wrote about is that it is a power that doesn't accept the idea that opposition is legitimate and seeks to eliminate all opposition. That's the whole story of what's going on in the United States right now. We have this right-wing movement that is pretty up-front about wanting to radically change the system. They weren't so open about it when they ran for office, but if you look at what their think tanks have been saying, or what they say when they're not in front of a crowd trying to look moderate, they're pretty frank about their revolutionary ambitions. In fact, people like Newt Gingrich[1] and Richard Armey[2] talk a lot about "We're making a revolution."

It's pretty clear that on the domestic side they want to roll back all of the New Deal institutions and get rid of the social insurance systems. If you look at the cultural issues, they think that the theory of evolution is evil and that we need to get rid of it. They want a religiously inspired government.

Kissinger makes this wonderful remark about how those who warn about the danger are considered alarmists and how those who downplay it are considered sane. That's exactly what's happening now. Back in 2002 I wrote about how the ideologues on the Right really wanted to get rid of Social Security. I quoted the Heritage Foundation[3] saying, "Don't forget that our goal is to get rid of the New Deal and the Great Society,"[4] which is really Social Security and Medicare. I got a lot of grief for that column because people said, "That's silly, they don't want to do that."

I got letters from friends, and Mickey Kaus, a conservative blogger, wrote something like, "There goes Krugman off his meds again." We now know that the Bush plan would essentially eliminate Social Security. If you look at the numbers for the plan, by the 2050s there would basically be no Social Security left. This information has been very hard to get across to the public.

Social Security is a pay-as-you-go system in which each generation pays taxes that support the previous generation's retirement. If you tell the people who are currently paying into Social Security that they can now take that money and invest it for themselves, who is going to take care of their parents? Any proposal for private accounts is going to lead to huge borrowing to make up for the money that's no longer being paid in to Social Security for the previous generation to collect. It's going to raise all sorts of questions about how you manage the system, particularly since it's a lot more than just a retirement system.

In 2000 candidate Bush said things that were just untrue, like "You can get a higher return on your money by buying bonds than you can from investing in Social Security." As soon as you think it through, it doesn't make any sense at all because it's pretending that there are no debts and no obligations to take care of previous generations.

This radicalized me on two levels. First, here was the candidate of a major political party saying stuff that was just an outright lie, and no one would say it. I tried again and again during the campaign to point this out in my pieces.

Why would no one say it, because they didn't understand it, because they were too lazy, or because they couldn't believe it?

All of the above. They didn't understand it back then, and even now, they're too lazy to figure it out. I just wrote this morning about Bush talking about the Social Security trustees report saying something that it does not say, but apparently nobody in the punditocracy picked up on it. Bush said that according to the trustees, for every year that goes by, the cost of not fixing Social Security is six hundred billion dollars. If you actually read the passage in the trustees report, it doesn't say anything like that. What the trustees were doing was something like a statement of how much you would have to pay to prepay a loan that isn't due for another ten years. Each year you wait makes that number bigger, because the due date gets closer; but that says nothing at all about the advantages or disadvantages of paying sooner rather than later. And it has nothing at all to do with the benefits of Bush-type plans, which don't even involve any prepayment.

Why isn't this properly reported?

Nobody does the homework. When Bush says the trustees said such a thing, apparently nobody thinks to actually go and read the trustees report to see if they actually did say anything like that. Also, the report is a little technical and most pundits aren't good at arithmetic. They know people who put out numbers, but there is a sense among the punditocracy that one guy's numbers are as good as another guy's numbers. I've seen people who are moderates talk about all the useful, interesting research that comes out of the Heritage Foundation. If they did even a little bit of homework, they'd know that the foundation's stuff is totally political and often blatantly dishonest.

By the way, another thing about the 2000 campaign was that it was the only time that I've been prohibited at the *New York Times* from using the word "lie." Howell Raines, the executive editor, said to me, "You can't use that word."

Why?

It sounded too partisan. It's a funny thing—and again, this is part of the story, to say, "the candidate or the president is lying," is considered a partisan statement even if you can document that he's lying, unless it involves a private matter, like a consensual affair. But if he's lying about a public matter, a number or a policy or a rationale for war, it's unacceptably partisan to say that.

What's the logic behind that?

I'm less solid on this than I am on the fact that the lies are going on. But if you're a pundit and you admit that we're living in a world where at least one political side routinely lies about the most important things, like the rationale for huge tax cuts, the rationale for a war, and the rationale for a complete overhaul of the most important social program in America, then you are admitting that we're not living in a world that you aspire to be at the top of. So you don't want to believe it because it makes you too unhappy. Also, if you do admit that's what's happening, then clearly you have a moral obligation to try and stop it, and that's kind of scary. The third thing is that there is enormous pressure. Just before doing this interview, I got around a couple of thousand postcards—identical postcards—denouncing my stand on Social Security. The first time this happened, I actually checked to see where they were coming from, and it turned out that they had come from Brent Bozell's Media Research Center.[5] A different person signed each postcard, but the center organized the campaign.

I think the people on the Right seem to be angrier than ever, judging at least from my mail. They seem more hysterical than ever because they thought, "We've won the election, that's it, there will be no more dissent." And they're totally shocked that people who think they're going in the wrong direction haven't given up. That wasn't part of the script.

I get enormous numbers of hostile e-mails. The editors at the *Times* get hostile e-mails about my columns too. Recently I wrote a column about the head of Medicare threatening to fire the chief actuary if he gave columnists full information. A barrage of e-mails came to my editor saying, "Where's the evidence for that? Why is Krugman saying that? Why is he writing for the *Times* when he makes unsupported statements like that?" The statement was supported by the conclusion of an internal investigation at the Department of Health and Human Services that was published in all the mainstream newspapers.

I get this reputation for being extreme just because I say what's obvious. Columbia University organized a panel to talk about the media's performance and *Atlantic Monthly*'s national correspondent, James Fallows, was there. Fallows is certainly much more of a government intervention markets guy than I ever was, but now I come across as radical compared to him because I say, "Gee, something's happening here." Except for me, everyone on that panel talked as if it was just business as usual—which it isn't.

A lot of journalists want to believe that they're still living in the age of Walter Cronkite. They've ascended to the higher ranks of the profession and their goal was to be a pundit in a high-minded conversation among gentlemen and they don't want to believe that this isn't where we are anymore. I have to say it does kind of amaze me, but just look at Social Security. This is the issue of the moment and the issue that originally radicalized me during the 2000 campaign. Back then, when Bush was laying out his Social Security proposal, I realized that we were dealing with people who were not playing by any rules that I understood. The problems that are sinking it now didn't add up back then.

Do you think the administration sold the tax cut on false pretenses, too?

Oh, yes. I wrote about it. It was clear from the beginning that it was sold on false pretenses on multiple levels. The budget surpluses they projected were junk estimates and we knew that. We didn't know how junky they were, but they were certainly wrong and all biased in an upward direction. The administration lied repeatedly about the nature of the tax cut, pretending that it was a populist thing when it was not, and they're still doing that. They lied about the motivation, claiming that it was about returning excess money to ordinary people, that it was about fighting recession, whatever, when it was obvious if you did a bit of background research that it was all part of the plan to "starve the beast"—to shrink the government by depriving it of revenue. Their sales pitch was kind of like one of those the old late night TV ads, "It slices, it dices, it purees, it does everything"; whatever your problem was, the tax cut was going to be the answer to it.

Where was the press on that one?

The press was terrible on that. Some economics reporters—I'm not going to name names—are conspicuously unable to get the numbers right. There is this thing with news organizations; they specifically don't like to have reporters who have expertise in a field because they're afraid that their writing will be too technical for the public. So a lot of economic reporters don't know the stuff.

There's also the "he said she said" aspect to reporting. Sometimes they'll say, "Well, if you read the story very carefully, you can understand that one side is really wrong." But people don't have time to do that, so it doesn't come through. I've become increasingly happy with the economics reporting of the *Times*. Ed Andrews is actually very good. He does understand how all the stuff works and his stories are pretty clear-cut.

What kind of government are the neoconservatives[6] trying to build?

It really is a coalition on the Right; there is the cultural religious right, and the economic right. There are people who are part of both. I think in some ways Tom DeLay is the quintessential figure here. He's a fanatical supporter of tax cuts who hates the theory of evolution, and unlike Bush, there was nothing accidental about his rise. DeLay,[7] or someone like him, was inevitable.

But among rank-and-file citizens, these are very different groups. There are the malefactors of great wealth and the preachers, and the malefactors of great wealth lead lives that are very different from the preachers, or at least different from what the preachers preach. Actually, it may be an unstable coalition at some level, although not yet.

What the cultural right wants is a more or less theocratic society. They don't want the theory of evolution to be taught in school because that's not the way it is in the Bible. They want to live in a society in which religion pervades public life and personal morality is strongly emphasized.

The economic right wants the welfare state to be dismantled. They want to get rid of the social insurance institutions, and they want to get rid of taxes on capital income.

Isn't privatizing all the various functions of government part of the economic right's agenda? What does that lead to?

It leads back to the good old days when the *London Economist* was bitterly opposed to building the London sewer system because they regarded it as an unwarranted government intervention in life. I think if the neocons get what they want, people will be desperately unhappy, and in the end, the welfare state will be reinvented.

What's funny is that some of the very wealthiest people in the country lean against dismantling the social insurance institutions because they appreciate the virtues of a stable, decent society. But people who have a mere fifty million dollars think it would be great if they didn't have to pay taxes. There's a network of think tanks full of professional privatizers and tax cutters who are working toward that goal on their behalf.

How is this going to affect the average American?

This is hugely negative for the average American because it means cutting benefits and in some cases actually raising taxes on middle- and lower-middle-income families while handing privileges out to the people at the top. If you are, say, a big investment banker, you can look forward not only to minimal taxes but to earning big fees mismanaging Social Security funds, with no nasty questions from government regulators.

We have a system now in which Social Security, Medicare, and Medicaid are safety net programs for working people in case something goes wrong. If you lose your job or your pension, or get sick, all these things are there. If the neocons get what they want, we're back to a society in which you don't have that safety net, and if you're not rich and you get seriously ill, you die. It's really what it comes down to.

The other thing is, of course, the new bankruptcy law they want to pass. Things that happen that cause people to go bankrupt are primarily medical expenses, losing a job, or the intersection of the two, and with the new law, you'll find yourself in debt purgatory indefinitely because it will become very hard to declare bankruptcy and write off your debt.

Is this sort of the third worldization of the United States?

Yes, or the Latin Americanization. It's making us into something more like the classic Latin American nation in terms of the inequalities between the rich and the poor. Now Bush made a tactical error with respect to Social Security, because this is an issue that goes right to the heart of the latent conflict between the cultural right, who tend to be poorer, and the economic right, who tend to be richer. He may be bringing it out into the open because all those people out in the red states, being on average poor are, also on average, more dependent on Social Security than people from the blue states.

When you talk about the "economic right" you're talking about corporations and industries. There seems to be a lot of decision making going on behind closed doors that benefits them. Cheney and his energy policy-making group was one big example of that.

They don't like the idea of anybody having a view of what's going on. The same thing happened with mercury regulations. Bush basically had the industry groups writing the regulations over the protests of the actual scientific experts at the Environmental Protection Agency [EPA]. The fact is that the economic analysis suggests that if you just look at the health costs of mercury poisoning, there are very good reasons for stiff restrictions on the industry, but they more or less forced the EPA not to include those factors. So it's really about favoring the industry over the public. At least this was a case where sunlight got through, but what's happening in all the places where there is no sunlight?

There's a more lax environment in terms of everything. We had the private securities litigation reform act in the nineties that was passed over Clinton's veto, which basically much reduced the ability of individual stockholders to sue executives over the kind of malfeasance that eventually brought down Enron and WorldCom.[8]

What's really grimly funny is that during the Asian financial crisis, American officials would give lectures to the Asians saying, "Your problem is that you don't have an honest system and you don't have proper corporate accounting and you have the managers of companies exploiting their positions for personal gain at the expense of workers and stockholders and we're different, we solved those problems."

What about foreign policy; what's the revolutionary aspect of that?

If you took a look at the neocon group Project for a New American Century,[9] it is not a figment of someone's imagination, it's not a crazy conspiracy theory; these are people who said basically, "We want a force-based foreign policy, starting with a war in Iraq." They didn't say it quite that boldly, but that's what it comes out to. If you say that the real reasons for this war were not the ostensible ones they used to sell it—which shouldn't even be a controversial position because the record is right there—and if you say, "The selling of this war looked a whole lot like the selling of tax cuts"—clearly the ulterior purposes for both were not the expressed ones—people will tell you that you're extreme or you're crazy. Even now, people still go on as if there's some kind of silly conspiracy theory in talking about the influence of the neocons. Some of my colleagues at the *New York Times* have even tried to deny that there really is such a thing as the neocons.

David Brooks wrote a column saying that these people barely know each other. It's a very strange thing.

How does the War on Terrorism fit into this paradigm?

It's wonderful for a cover. It's ideal from their point of view because they can hide everything under the flag. They can appeal to the public on the grounds of patriotism; they can say that criticism of any sort is unpatriotic. We actually had Republican members of Congress saying, "We have to support Social Security privatization because the president wants this and if he doesn't get what he wants it will diminish his authority, which will hamper his ability to fight the War on Terrorism." So it became, "If we don't privatize Social Security, the terrorists have won."

Thomas Frank wrote about this kind of logic in his book *What's the Matter with Kansas?*[10] He wrote that the best way to get the people in Kansas to vote for a party that's actually undermining their security net economically is to say, "But we're the people who keep you safe from the gay married terrorists."

What's really wonderful about the War on Terrorism from the neocon point of view is that, by its nature, nobody from the outside can actually say how it's going. How big is al Qaeda actually? How big a threat is it? Is the administration actually doing a good job countering it? It's all in the shadows, so we have no way of knowing. We have this amorphous enemy, amorphous struggle, and of course when there's some bad political news, they can always raise the terror alert level, and who's to say that they aren't justified?

Meanwhile, Iraq is costing an enormous amount of money. About eight billion is unaccounted for, which doesn't mean that eight billion was stolen, but it means that eight billion was spent with no controls. We know a lot of it was actually handed out in bags of hundred dollar bills. And we get little peeks suggesting that there must have been enormous corruption on the part of the Iraqis whom we put in charge, and a lot of very dubious business deals. Then there's Halliburton,[11] and people say, "Oh, that's too crude, the vice president wouldn't be steering money toward his former company," in which he happens to own hundreds of thousands of shares. The press won't accuse him of personal corruption because it's considered too partisan.

Why?

Because again, that would be saying that we're not in this world that journalists want to be living in. Also, if there's one thing that generates hysterical attacks on you personally as a journalist, it is any suggestion that there are character problems or that anybody, particularly Bush or Cheney, is engaging in personal malfeasance. They will race to find some way to discredit you and attack you and call you corrupt. So for the press, it becomes a learned aversion; they just don't want to talk about it.

You know what's fascinating about this is how much control they have on the mind-set. Who am I talking about when I say "they"?

There's a small group of right-wing think tanks and media organizations, an even smaller set of basic funders, and there's the Republican National Committee. You can identify a pretty tight network from publicly available information. Then, if you have your fantasy, which is that every day the people at Fox News get a memo that tells them how to slant the news today . . .

But that's not a fantasy.

That's the point, it's called "the memo," and they get it every morning. And if you have a fantasy that right-wing pundits get e-mails telling them what issue they're supposed to highlight—well, that's actually how it works, and a few of them have said that a lot of them are on the administration's payroll. Again, I would have said no way, but it turns out it's true.

What's it going to take to penetrate this?

I think you need to have large numbers of people understand that they're under threat.

But that's the press's job.

Yes. Look, I'm actually very heartened by the Social Security debate because in fact this is one where, aside from everything else, the media in the initial phases of this debate was very much pro. You had *Good Morning America* bringing Michael Tanner of the Cato Institute[12] on alone and identifying him simply as an expert and not as an obvious advocate for Bush's plan. There wasn't even the usual "he said, she said" exchange, just Tanner from the Cato Institute selling privatization all by himself. I wish I could track this down, but somebody said that the media aren't just more in favor of privatizing Social Security than the average American, they're more in favor of it than the average Republican member of Congress. Yet, the plan appears to be going down in flames at the time of this interview. This issue clearly touches people's lives.

There's nothing more primal than money.

This was the first time that there was an actual hint from the administration that you were going to be asked to give something up. Everything else had been sold as a pure free lunch.

There must be people in the Social Security administration who know this plan is not good for the public. Where are they?

We know that co-option and intimidation goes on. Exactly how it happens, I don't know. You should talk to Ron Suskind.[13] He's a mainstream journalist. Ron and I have had conversations where he's said, "Just once, I'd like to actually be able to see or hear how it's done, how they force or bully some official into"—I'm not quite sure what words he used—"stopping being a civil servant and becoming a partisan for them."

Look at Federal Reserve Board chairman Alan Greenspan.

Greenspan is a different story. Greenspan was always a hard-line right-winger, and he decided to indulge that, although at enormous cost to his reputation. What struck me was what was going on at the lower level in some of the government offices. The Treasury Department has an office called the Office of Tax Analysis, and from day one they stopped providing the information that they had provided in the past about the distribution of tax cuts by income level. They started providing misleading presentations designed to make the tax cuts look populist in a way they weren't. How did that happen?

Isn't that illegal?

I would have thought so. There are a lot of things that I think are illegal. How can the Treasury Department be creating a war room to sell Social Security privatization and using our money to hire Bush-Cheney campaign operatives? The point is, Bush was elected in a disputed election with fewer votes than his opponent, and yet from day one you had civil servants at the Treasury Department consenting to put their names on partisan distortions of the evidence. All I can say is that you have to understand that there's a machine there. You can see the sum of it. A moderate senator—what now passes for a moderate senator—is told, "Not only will we make sure that you have a primary challenger, but don't think you're going to get any consulting work after you lose." We have the famous Karl Rove phone conversation where he's yelling out, "We will fuck him. Do you hear me? We will fuck him. We will ruin him. Like no one has ever fucked him!"[14] I think the sheer wrongness of it is something that people have a hard time dealing with. When people are confronted with it, they find it very hard to stand up to it.

I find the press's unwillingness to report on this stuff difficult to accept.

Well, it's also partly because the public doesn't rally. They tried to do some reporting on Harken[15] long after it should have been happening, but in the end it didn't get enough resonance because the public didn't want to believe it. Imagine if the Jeff Gannon affair[16] had occurred under Clinton. Just imagine. Why don't we have screaming headlines about a gay hooker in the White House press room? I would have thought at the very least that you could sell a lot of newspapers with that story.

I think there's a fear of that story.

I know. But it was bizarre. There were three front-page *Washington Post* stories about the White House travel office under Clinton when there was, in fact, no malfeasance. But there was virtual press silence on Jeff Gannon.

A little closer to home, as it has become clear that the Social Security thing is going badly, the overwhelming reaction from the right-leaning pundits has been to ascribe all kinds of nasty ulterior motives to skeptics, calling them closet Marxists and paternalists who distrust people. The straightforward "This is a really bad idea according to my analysis" doesn't cut it with them. What's really funny in my mind is the conspiracy theory charge that is almost always made against liberals. If you say that there was political pressure to find a case for war in Iraq, you're accused of being a crazy conspiracy theorist even though it's sort of obvious. My impression is that if you went through and looked at the middle-of-the road pundits at the *Washington Post* and even to some extent my paper, there's an instinctive desire to treat anyone charging that the official version of events isn't true as being off their rockers. My favorite real conspiracy theorist right now is Oklahoma's Senator Inhofe, who believes that the whole world scientific community is conspiring to sell a hoax about global warming, which is, if you think about it, completely crazy.

The other thing that really amazes me is the way that people who served in the administration remain compelled in their mind to be partisan defenders afterward. I don't know how the pressure is brought to bear but we know about John DiIulio,[17] and look at former White House economic adviser Larry Lindsey. He was fired with a minimum of grace and should have been hopping mad. Instead he continues to be a slavish defender of whatever the administration is up to. Think about what the incentives for him to do that are.

Do you think anybody has done a good job of covering anything the administration's been up to?

Actually, with respect to the war, when all these supposed revelations about everything from aluminum tubes to mobile biological weapons vans came out, I said, "I knew all that beforehand, why did I know all that? It was because I'd been reading Knight Ridder all along, and the guys at Knight Ridder had been reporting on the doubts among the midlevel people in the intelligence community. Even though Knight Ridder is a large newspaper chain, it's low prestige because it doesn't have outlets in either Washington, DC, or New York. The point is, according to the journalists who were reporting this stuff, they were getting this information because they had to deal with low and midlevel people because they were a low-prestige chain. They didn't get the one-on-one backgrounder with Condi Rice. So they were doing real legwork. Presumably, that means that the reporters who were getting the champagne access weren't interested in talking to midlevel people, much less actually cultivating those channels. The other thing was that Knight Ridder was able to do this for quite a while because it was flying under the White House's radar.

Speaking of flying *on* the radar, are e-mail campaigns the greatest pressure that you ever felt?

No, the greatest pressure was the attempt to drum up a scandal. I once got paid to tell Enron about the East Asian financial crisis, so I've been called corrupt in papers like the *Washington Times*, the *National Review*, and the *New York Post*, and on Fox News. They constantly referred to me as "Enron consultant." If you actually look at this panel that I served on, the other members included Larry Lindsey[18] and Robert Zoellick[19]—he's now the number two at the State Department—but you never see that mentioned. William Kristol[20] was on the panel for several years. I've also seen articles saying that I personally am responsible for the fall of Enron. Crazy stuff.

What about people who say you don't use humans, you only use numbers as sources?

That's who I am; it's what I know. I have no expertise at investigative reporting or face-to-face reporting. You do need people who do the one-on-one stuff, certainly you need investigative reporting—Ron Suskind, I'm in awe of what he does, but I also know that I should do what I can, and it so happens that the people who can actually do the numbers are pretty scarce.

Where do you see reporting deficits?

In almost everything technical. Even military. When Knight Ridder's military correspondent Joe Galloway writes, which he doesn't very often, I always want to know because he actually knows his stuff. With respect to economics reporting, the budget is technical. Social Security is not. You don't have to be able to understand Nobel-quality work to report on it, but you do need to understand how the system works. You need to know something about rates of return and structure.

With economics reporting, you primarily need to know enough to be able to identify reliable sources. I didn't know a blessed thing about the US budget when I started, but I did know that the Center on Budget and Policy Priorities [CBPP] was totally reliable and that the Cato Institute wasn't.

On information about the Middle East, I like to read stuff by people who actually speak Arabic. I read blogger Juan Cole[21] every morning because at least he can read the local newspapers over there. The blog I have the most fun reading is Duncan Black's Atrios.blogspot.com. It's really funny and he's often obscene and the style is kind of wild, but the positions actually are not. When he was anonymous, I kept on saying, "You know, when he's writing about economics, he sounds awfully like he knows what he's talking about." Sure enough, the guy's a damned economist.

Who are your readers?

A large number of moderate and liberal people who feel like, "What the hell is going on in this country?" For a long time, I was the only mainstream voice articulating that question.

PAUL KRUGMAN is both professor of economics and international affairs at Princeton University and op-ed columnist for the *New York Times*. His is the first regular *New York Times* op-ed column devoted to economics, business, and finance. He is also the Centenary Professor at the London School of Economics. The *Asia Times* recently called him "the Mick Jagger of political/economic punditry."

Called "the most important political columnist in America" by the *Washington Monthly* and "the most celebrated economist of his generation" by the *Economist*, Mr. Krugman was named columnist of the year for 2002 by *Editor and Publisher*. He won the 2004 Asturias Award given by the king of Spain, often called the European Pulitzer.

Mr. Krugman is the author or editor of twenty books and more than two hundred professional journal articles, many of them on international trade and finance. In recognition of his work, he received the John Bates Clark Medal in 1991 from the American Economic Association. It is an award given every two years to the top economist under the age of forty.

Since 1988 Krugman has written extensively for noneconomists, including a monthly column, "The Dismal Science," for the online magazine *Slate*. He has also been a columnist for *Fortune* and has published articles in the *New Republic, Foreign Policy, Newsweek*, and the *New York Times Magazine* before joining the *New York Times*.

Prior to his appointment at Princeton, Krugman served on the faculty of MIT from 1979 until 1999; his last post was Ford International Professor of Economics. He has also taught at Yale and Stanford universities, and from 1982 to 1983 he was the senior international economist for the president's Council of Economic Advisers during the Reagan administration. He is a Fellow of the Econometric Society, a Research Associate of the National Bureau of Economic Research, and a member of the Group of Thirty. He has served as a consultant to the Federal Reserve Bank of New York, the World Bank, the International Monetary Fund, the United Nations, and the European Commission, as well as to a number of countries including Portugal and the Philippines.

His most recent book is the paperback edition of his hardcover bestseller *The Great Unraveling: Losing Our Way in the New Century*, a collection of his *New York Times* columns and other writings. Mr. Krugman and his wife, Robin Wells, write college textbooks about economics. *Microeconomics* was published in October 2004, and *Macroeconomics* is due out in the fall of 2005.

NOTES

1. Newt Gingrich is former Speaker of the House and currently CEO of the Gingrich Group, a communications and management consulting firm. According to a Fox News biography of Gingrich, he is known as "the chief architect of the Republican Contract with America and a key player in the Republican Party's regaining control of Congress after 40 years." http://www.foxnews.com/story/0,2933,2119,00.html.

2. The Columbia Electronic Encyclopedia describes Richard Keith Armey as a former US congressman, former House majority leader, and a "conservative and political ally of [former] House Speaker Newt Gingrich. Armey has advocated the phasing out of Social Security and farm subsidies." http://www.infoplease.com/ce6/people/A0804760.html.

3. A conservative think tank that publishes research on domestic, economic, foreign, and defense policy. http://www.heritage.org/.

4. President Franklin D. Roosevelt's New Deal program was a response to the Great Depression, when millions of people were unemployed and almost every bank in the country was closed. His program established the Tennessee Valley Authority (to help in industrial and agricultural development, improve marginal farm lands, etc.), Social Security, and other programs to create a social safety net and provide work relief to the unemployed and help businesses and agriculture recover. He also taxed the wealthy more heavily and established new controls over banks and public utilities. President Johnson's Great Society program "became Johnson's agenda for Congress in January 1965: aid to education, attack on disease, Medicare, urban renewal, beautification, conservation, development of depressed regions, a wide-scale fight against poverty, control and pre-

vention of crime and delinquency, removal of obstacles to the right to vote." http://www
.whitehouse.gov/history/presidents/lj36.html.

5. On its Web site, http://www.mediaresearch.org/, the Media Research Center
(MRC) describes itself as "America's Media Watchdog" and "The Leader in Documenting, Exposing and Neutralizing Liberal Media Bias." MRC founder and president L.
Brent Bozell III is described as a "lecturer, syndicated columnist, television commentator,
debater, marketer, businessman, publisher and activist" and "one of the most outspoken
and effective national leaders in the conservative movement today."

6. An explanatory column titled "Neocon 101" in the *Christian Science Monitor*
provides information on neoconservative thought: "Neocons believe that the United
States should not be ashamed to use its unrivaled power—forcefully if necessary—to promote its values around the world. . . . Neoconservatives believe modern threats facing the
US can no longer be reliably contained and therefore must be prevented, sometimes
through preemptive military action. . . . Most neocons share unwavering support for
Israel, which they see as crucial to US military sufficiency in a volatile region. . . . The
original neocons were a group of mostly Jewish liberal intellectuals who, in the 1960s and
70s, grew disenchanted with what they saw as the American left's social excesses and
reluctance to spend adequately on defense." http://www.csmonitor.com/specials/neocon/
neocon101.html.

7. On his Web site, http://tomdelay.house.gov/biography.html, Tom Delay, a US
congressman from Texas, is described as "majority leader [and] the second ranking leader
in the United States House of Representatives. He is responsible for developing issues and
policies that form the Republican agenda."

8. "Enron Corporation is an energy trading, natural gas and electric utilities company based in Houston, Texas, that employed around 21,000 people by mid-2001, before
it went bankrupt in December 2001. Fraudulent accounting techniques allowed it to be
listed as the seventh largest company in the United States. . . . It became the largest corporate failure in history and became emblematic of institutionalized and well-planned corporate fraud." http://en.wikipedia.org/wiki/Enron. Thousands of Enron employees lost
their life savings in pension plans tied to Enron stocks. Enron was also found to have engineered an energy crisis in California that drove up the price of electricity ninefold.
Worldcom, a telecommunications company, declared bankruptcy and then admitted in
June 2002 that it had inflated profits by more than four billion dollars through deceptive
accounting.

9. The Project for a New American Century (PNAC) says on its Web site that it
"intends, through issue briefs, research papers, advocacy journalism, conferences, and
seminars, to explain what American world leadership entails." It is generally seen as a
neoconservative take on the role the United States should play in the world. PNAC says
it is a nonprofit educational organization dedicated to the propositions "that American
leadership is good both for America and the world; and that such leadership requires military strength, diplomatic energy and commitment to moral principle." http://www.new
americancentury.org/.

10. Thomas Frank, *What's the Matter with Kansas: How the Conservatives Won the
Heart of America* (New York: Metropolitan Books, 2004).

11. Halliburton is "one of the world's largest providers of products and services to
the oil and gas industries." http://www.halliburton.com/. It is the largest recipient of contracts awarded for postwar work in Afghanistan and Iraq, according to Center for Public

Integrity reporters Andre Verloy and Daniel Politi in their August 1, 2004, article "Halliburton Contracts Balloon." Halliburton, "where Vice President Dick Cheney served as CEO from 1995 to 2000, has come under increased scrutiny because of allegations of overcharging on food service and fuel distribution contracts, poor management and close ties to the administration." http://www.publicintegrity.org/wow/report.aspx?aid=366&sid =100.

12. On its Web site, http://www.cato.org/about/about.html, the Cato Institute describes itself as a "nonprofit public policy research foundation" and says it "seeks to broaden the parameters of public policy debate to allow consideration of traditional American principles of limited government, individual liberty, free markets and peace." Michael Tanner is Cato's director of health and welfare studies. He is credited with launching Project Social Security Choice, described on Cato's Web site as being considered "the leading impetus for transforming the national retirement program into a private savings program."

13. See chapter 6 in this book.

14. See Ron Suskind's January 2003 *Esquire* article "Why Are These Men Laughing?" http://www.ronsuskind.com/newsite/articles/archives/000032.html.

15. According to a special report titled "Bush and Harken Energy" (July 10, 2002), the UK's *Guardian* reported that "on June 22, 1990, George Bush, then a director with a company called Harken Energy, sold 212,140 shares for $848,000. Almost exactly two months later, on August 20, Harken announced a $23.2 million dollar loss, which caused its shares to drop to $2.375 from $3. The next day, Harken returned to $3, but fell to $1 at the end of 1990. Although the law requires prompt disclosure of what are called insider sales or sales by senior executives, Mr. Bush did not inform the Securities and Exchange Commission (SEC), the U.S. market regulator, until 34 weeks later. So technically Mr. Bush was at fault."

16. Jeff Gannon is apparently a pseudonym used by a man whose name appears to be James Dale Guckert. Gannon, whose nude pictures were posted on the Internet and who was linked to male prostitution, was given press credentials by the White House as a reporter for Talon News, which seemed to be more of a political organization than a news outlet. Gannon was well known for asking pro–Bush administration questions, and there were allegations that he was a fake reporter planted at briefings to ask favorable questions. Once exposed, he resigned from Talon News. http://en.wikipedia.org/wiki/Jeff_Gannon.

17. John DiIulio, former domestic policy adviser to the Bush administration, described the administration as the "reign of the Mayberry Machiavellis" and said, "There is no precedent in any modern White House for what is going on in this one: a complete lack of policy apparatus." DiIulio later apologized for his remarks. Also, see chapter 6 in this book.

18. Larry Lindsey was President Bush's assistant to the president for economic policy until he resigned along with Treasury Secretary Paul O'Neill in December 2002.

19. Robert B. Zoellick is deputy secretary of state under Secretary of State Condoleezza Rice.

20. William Kristol is the editor of the *Weekly Standard*, a Washington-based conservative political magazine. http://www.weeklystandard.com/weekly/weekly.asp.

21. Juan Cole's "Informed Comment" blog can be found at http://www.juancole .com/. See chapter 14 in this book.

NATIONAL SECURITY
AND INTELLIGENCE

8

ACCOUNTABILITY'S CORONER

Courtesy of Barton Gellman

BARTON GELLMAN
Special Projects Reporter,
Washington Post
Interviewed March 2005

Barton Gellman has the intensity of a serious scholar, which he certainly could have been if he hadn't chosen to be a reporter. Now in his midforties, he came to journalism with spectacular academic credentials. He graduated summa cum laude from Princeton's Woodrow Wilson School of Public and International Affairs. His college thesis on diplomat George Kennan won him the prestigious Myron T. Herrick Prize and, upon being published, was hailed by *Foreign Affairs* as "extraordinarily well-balanced and perceptive" and by the *New York Times Book Review* as "an astonishing tour de force." Gellman is also a Rhodes Scholar with a master's degree in politics from Oxford. Frankly, this combination of brains and stellar academic formation is rare in journalism. When you read Gellman's articles, the superior quality of his reporting and analysis are immediately apparent. But as you'll see in this interview, even for Barton Gellman, some stories are slippery slopes.

Gellman has a prestigious job at the *Washington Post*, but that doesn't mean it's easy. On the day I met him, he looked stressed out. His eyes were a little red-rimmed, like he had been reading or staring at a computer for a long time. Even so, he still looked much younger than his forty-five years. As I walked into his cluttered office to set up my recording equipment, I was immediately struck by the sight of a big plastic bust of Barbie sitting on what I think was a small credenza. It was a gift for his niece that he kept meaning to remember to take home with him. Besides Barbie, most of the other personal touches in Gellman's office have to do with his family. There are some photos on a shelf overhanging his desk and a couple of children's drawings on the wall.

"I like reconstruction stories that look back on large events," he told me. "You can do better journalism after the fact." When I suggested that looking into the reasons given for going to war *after* the invasion was an exercise in examining a moot issue, he replied, "Holding people accountable for what they say means finding the truth whenever you can find it." For Gellman, the truth and accountability are never dead. They often lie in the evidentiary remains of past events and stories, waiting to be discovered. Like a coroner, he conducts forensic examinations of these remains, bringing the past into focus and documenting who did what to whom when, where, why, and how. The interview began with a discussion of just such an examination to answer a key post-9/11 question.

One of the first things that we started to think about after 9/11 was how did we get into this mess and what were we doing about it. If there's a new war on terrorism, what did the old one look like? I normally do projects, and the first project I did was a three-part series[1] on the war on terrorism under the Clinton administration and in the first eight months of George Bush. We found out a lot about what the United States government knew about bin Laden over the years, what it tried to do, what warnings it had, and where both presidents flinched from taking further action. There were places or subject areas where they knew what they had to do if they wanted to break the Taliban–al Qaeda connection, but the cost was so high that they decided it wasn't worth paying. It would have required—did ultimately require—a full-scale war. They didn't think they could get Pakistan's president, Pervez Musharraf, to wrest control of the ISI [Inter-Services Intelligence, Pakistan's military intelligence] and quell its support for al Qaeda without making it a much higher priority—and thereby jeopardizing democratization, subcontinental stability, nuclear proliferation, and so on. All the usual trade-offs that every government faces.

I don't understand how Musharraf could be expected to be helpful at all, given the fact that he is between a rock and a hard place, between the United States and al Qaeda, two mortal enemies that he has to cater to.

Look, there are a lot of allies of convenience. Musharraf needed Pakistan's frontier with Afghanistan to be friendly and quiet if he was going to defend himself on Pakistan's other frontier against a much more powerful enemy, India. Internally, he had to mollify a strongly Islamist security establishment. So his motivations for friendship with the Taliban were clear enough. What the United States government was saying under Clinton as well as Bush was, "These guys in al Qaeda are trying to kill us and if you help them, directly or indirectly, you are participating in attacks on us, and we will treat it that way." But Clinton didn't quite mean it. He stopped short of treating it that way. What was interesting to me was that the Clinton administration turned out to have done much more against al Qaeda than the public knew. It dramatically increased resources against terrorism, paid much higher prices, and took many more aggressive secret actions. Clinton tried, in a fairly concerted way, to kill bin Laden after 1998, failing several times and coming very close several times to launching missions that might have killed bin Laden.

One the other hand, Clinton did stop short in other areas. I wrote a story that said that there was a chance for the United States to get bin Laden from Sudan in 1996. There was an opportunity, at least on the face of it, when Sudan seemed to be making an offer, although it wasn't very explicit. There were a lot of reasons for doubting whether Sudan would actually come through with handing over bin Laden, and it was not at all clear to whom they would hand him over. Egypt didn't want him, the Saudis didn't want him, and the US government didn't have any charge to file against him, so Clinton's people didn't fully test whether Sudan would have delivered. It's one of those tantalizing, alternative history, might-have-been stories, and it wasn't in the public record so I was glad to get it. Once it got to the punditocracy and TV talkers, it became part of the public indictment against Clinton; he could have captured bin Laden and he didn't do it. But people on the Left read my stories and said, "Look at this, Clinton fought much harder than anybody knew." A faithful portrait of events is always going to provide ammunition to a pretty broad range of political combatants.

In part three of the series, I looked at George Bush during his first eight months in office. Arguably, he did less than Clinton had, and I was able to document what he did and didn't do. He put all the recommendations about al Qaeda on hold and didn't treat it as a top priority. This story was a very granular inside look at what was happening then. What I really wanted to know was, before 9/11 happened, what could have been done, what was done, what was known, what was done about it, and what wasn't done about it? It's very similar territory to what the 9/11 Commission ultimately explored, and they cited some of my stories. I know from the staffers that they were able to use some of those stories to wrestle classified information out of the Bush administration and publish it in their final report on grounds that it had already been made public.

Did you examine the lead-up to 9/11 and look at whether cumulatively all the signals did or did not clearly spell something?

I'm not that sympathetic to arguments that intelligence should have known exactly what was coming.

I'm asking about your reporting. What I'm interested in are the context and analysis that you drew from the facts that you gathered.

I did not examine so much whether the evidence was sufficient to predict the time, place, or manner of the attack. It was very plain that, the summer before the attack, all the indicators of an imminent attack were up. The people most responsible for warding it off, like then CIA director George Tenet and then chief of counterterrorism Richard Clarke, were extremely worried and were tugging on the sleeves of the president and his top advisers and saying, "We've got to do something." It's also clear that in that July before the September 11 attack, they did a number of extraordinary things in terms of battening down the hatches: setting fleets off to sail, changing the security arrangements for Bush's meeting with the pope, making extraordinary requests from foreign governments, recalling staffers from vacations, and so on. But then weeks went by, July became August, and they got tired of it. You can't be on this kind of any-second-now footing forever, and the president's closest advisers—though not his terrorism experts—began to think it was a false alarm. I explored very concretely what did they do, on which days, to demonstrate that they believed that something was imminent, but I didn't try to access whether they could have predicted this attack.

Do you think your other colleagues at other papers were tracking this well?

I like reconstruction stories that look back on large events. I think you can learn a lot from it, but it takes a lot of time and effort and newspaper resources and not everybody does it. The *New York Times* did a pretty good run at this same story. They started on it after I did and they knew I was doing it and they put three reporters on it. Theirs came out between the first two parts of my series and they got a good chunk of it. They were interested in the same questions of who was doing what when. I was glad to have gotten most of mine in sooner. You win some, you lose some. I thought I came out all right on that one.

Do you watch TV at all, Bart?

Sometimes, but I'm not watching too much of the commentary side of it, and that's more and more dominant as you know.

How much news is there in the news part of it?

News is expensive, opinions cheap. They don't do much reporting anymore.

I want to talk about the WMD issue because that was presented as the reason for going to war. What's your assessment of the reporting on that?

I am conflicted on this one. It's clear that a central mission of the press in the run-up to the war was to assess the truth of everything that was being said about the war's likely consequences, about the factual predicate for the war, and so on. WMDs would have been the largest part of that. We now know in retrospect that much of what was said about WMDs was not true. So you would want the press to have turned that up before the war. That would be our ambition. It was a very, very, very hard thing to do. I am bothered by the arrival of a kind of conventional wisdom that says that we collectively didn't try, didn't care, were intimidated, and bought into the case without examining it. I really don't think there's too much to that. I think that there were places and times where we would have wanted to put more resources into the question or give more attention to those doubts, but we couldn't get the smoking gun.

What places and times?

We had some pretty good stories in my paper and elsewhere that had unnamed analysts saying the case was weaker than was being made publicly, but without saying *how* it was weaker. So you could neither name the person speaking nor adduce any evidence. Now critics of our performance say what we should have done was to give those officials equal billing with the president of the United States, who was saying, "I know, and here's the evidence, and here's the secretary of state, and here are the slides." We couldn't do that. We shouldn't do that. If we can't get people who are willing to be named or who at the very least can demonstrate their standing to know what they're talking about, and if at the same time we can't get the evidence behind their dissent, then we can't give it that kind of prominence.

> **I'm going to cite one example: Bush and Blair held a joint press conference in September 2002 and mentioned that a new International Atomic Energy Agency report showed that Saddam was six months away from developing a nuclear weapon. There was no such report.**

Right, that was all wrong. *Washington Post* reporter Dana Milbank wrote a front-page story a few weeks later on October 22, 2002, leading exactly with the incident you're talking about. The headline was "For Bush, Facts Are Malleable." In it, Milbank said flatly, "There is no such report from IAEA." It was a very in-your-face story. He cited that moment as one of several in which the president had said stuff that was just plain false and showed how little that seemed to matter in the ensuing public debate.

> **There didn't seem to be enough reporting countering what Bush was saying. Certainly there were statements in the past by then secretary of state Colin Powell and then national security advisor Condoleezza Rice saying that Saddam had been defanged. Lying on these critical issues sometimes seems almost to be a modus operandus. I'm not interested in the politics of the thing; I'm just talking about the need for the press to get to the bottom of whether or not such critical claims are true. A lie puts its boots on and goes twelve thousand miles around the world and then the truth just goes nowhere, even if it's spoken after the lie. Ted Koppel and Helen Thomas said to me, "Well, when the president stands up and says something, you have to report it."**

You certainly do have to report what the president says and then, at a minimum, you have to say whether he has demonstrated that to be true or not. I guess I would have liked to see it more, but I wasn't involved in the coverage. I think a lot of our stories did say, "He says he knows it for a fact and has proof, but the public record doesn't show that." I want to emphasize: the public record, and our best efforts to penetrate further, didn't show that the president was wrong, either. The pundits who claim now that they "knew" all along are full of crap. They didn't know. They believed. There's too much faith masquerading as fact across the board in our political debate. We can't substitute one faith for another.

Our coverage of the Powell-UN briefing[2] had quite a lot of skeptical stories. There was one on each of the major subjects of the briefing that accompanied the main story. In a story about an audiotape that Powell presented, claiming it was a recording of Iraqi officers conspiring to deceive weapons inspectors, we said, "He's played a tape but experts say that the audio is ambiguous in its meaning and that there is not enough context to know whether in fact they're talking about WMDs or not." What we couldn't do at the time and were able to do later—I was able to do some of it later—was to show specifically what was wrong with the case that they were making before the war, and in some cases to show that they were making it in bad faith. Now I have a certain respect for my own abilities in this area and I think that those stories came out pretty well, but I know that I could not have done those stories before the war.

First of all, I wasn't assigned to them, but if I had been, and if I'd given everything I had to that, it's extremely unlikely I could have got those stories. There are very good reasons why you can get something like that after the fact and not in the heat of it. In the heat of it, there is a maximum clampdown on sources. It's a period of maximum risk for your sources. If what a source tells you can embarrass the president after the fact, that source is taking a risk. If what the source discloses has the potential to thwart the president from achieving his number one policy intention, to derail it, the source is taking a much bigger risk. People I was talking to while the weapons hunt was under way were coming considerably further out of their shells after the war began than they would have dared to before the war. I was trying to talk to those guys before the war to prepare for my WMD coverage, and they were all essentially in hiding; even people I'd known well for years. That's number one.

Number two, you could have your own doubts as an analyst and say, "I think that they're going too far with this," but the confidence of the doubters obviously grew greater every day that passed during the weapons hunt and weapons weren't found. At a certain point, you start to get a shift from "Everyone's saying there are weapons but I'm not so sure

I agree" to "I knew all along the weapons weren't there." Retrospectively, your own position gets a little stronger, and even if it doesn't, your confidence and your willingness to speak out get greater.

Third of all, I have classified information in many of my stories, but there are certain categories of classified information, especially relating to future operations, that are hardest to get and that we're not going to publish. For example, I was able to get proof after the fact that they thought a certain place was going to be a storage site for chemical weapons and that it belonged to Saddam's Special Security Organization, the SSO. In fact, it turned out that they stored vacuum cleaners there, but I couldn't get that earlier on. For me to be able to publish in advance a story about this facility which was listed as site 26 on the US Central Command's priority list would not have been possible, even though some analysts were saying internally that there were reasons for doubting it was an SSO facility. Had they told me about it before they had checked it out, which they didn't, they would have been giving away a site of future interest. After the thing was searched and found to be garbage, writing about it could no longer damage the operation and so then I could start to get at the kinds of granular proof that I was looking for to show how the WMD case was falling apart. My story, "Odyssey of Frustration," came out on May 18, 2003.

But you understand how presenting this evidence after the war instead of while the case for war is being made is totally moot.

I understand that it doesn't affect a national or international societal decision like whether to go to war; that horse is out of the barn. But I don't think it's moot at all. Holding powerful people accountable for what they say and do means finding out the truth whenever you can find it. And though the war decision was made by then, lots of other decisions were not. One relevant decision, for a democracy, was who should be president for the following four years. We gave voters more information to consider. Look, we'd like to get everything in real time, but we just can't.

Is there any way that can be changed? It happens over and over.

It happens over and over for the same reason: you can do better journalism after the fact. It's the same reason why historians know more than journalists do and why I hope that one hundred years from now, they'll know even more than we know now about what happened in this administration, in this White House. To some extent, the problem is not solvable. The problem is inherent in the nature of events and the unfolding of a historical record. But greater determination on our part can help, as can a reminder of the mission of subjecting these kinds of claims to scrutiny. For example, look at our coverage of the Iran nuclear issue right now. I think my colleagues at the *Washington Post* are leading the charge and that we're way ahead on that story. You are seeing claims being made, and on the same day, the next day, or the day after that, you'll find major revelations on our front page about the basis for those claims and whether those claims stand up. We're doing that better now than we did before the Iraq war, partly because we're more conscious of the need to, partly because our sources are less inhibited. There's a sense among people who know secrets in this government, in foreign governments, and in private industry that they ought not to sit on them, that it matters *when* those secrets get talked about. So I'm also finding that there's greater willingness on the part of sources to take risks now and to see the relevance of public debate.

And the reason for that is Iraq, right?

Iraq is clearly the reason. Let's take another case. There are a lot of countries in the world that want to get along with the United States. There are a lot of allies and partial allies and want-to-be allies that just don't want to risk getting between George Bush and Saddam Hussein when it's clear to everyone that Bush intends to go to war. What's the percentage in it? Now you're seeing a different set of behaviors on Iran. Foreign governments and international organizations and US government dissenters are willing to say more sooner than they did before Iraq, and it's plainly because of Iraq.

You wrote an article on December 12, 2002, "U.S. Suspects al Qaeda Got Nerve Agent from Iraqis." You got this story from sources who couldn't tell you who their sources were, and you report in the article that there was really no way of backing this up with real evidence. Why did you report this?

This is a complicated one; it's one of the tougher calls that we had to make. First of all, in the context of looking back on making a case against Iraq and prewar coverage and subjecting the president's claims to scrutiny, this article is getting wrapped into something that it's not. This is not a claim that the US government ever made about Iraq. This was not made as a claim that al Qaeda had possibly received nerve agent from Iraq, and it was not part of the administration's public case. My sources, as I state in the story, were not advocates for the war in Iraq and were not, in fact, policymakers.

This is paradoxical, but I believe that I made the right decision to publish the story even though I now believe that the underlying report is incorrect. First of all, the motivations of my sources, which a lot of people assume they can guess because it looks like it helps make a case against Iraq, were not to try to justify a war with Iraq. About that they were either indifferent or, in one case, highly skeptical. My sources were people who followed terrorism and WMD terrorism, which is what I was doing throughout 2002. They received from a single source a report that was unconfirmed but also quite plausible, and they were very worried about it. We put it in the paper because one official whom we quoted and who is a career counterterrorism official, not a political appointee, told me they get enormous numbers of these threat reports and ninety-nine out of one hundred of them get thrown in the trash. This one was in the 1 percent category. They thought it looked serious, and they were putting resources into trying to confirm it. When career officials tell me a piece of intelligence is in the top 1 percent of credible threats and that they're pouring new resources, meaning technological and human resources, into trying to confirm a report that al Qaeda transported nerve agents out of Iraq and to intercept those weapons if the report is true, then I think that should be reported. I put every caveat into the story: single source, unconfirmed. Now our own ombudsman, Michael Getler, said the story was so hedged that we ought to have waited. I respectfully disagree.

When you started answering the question, you were saying sort of in your defense that the Bush administration never said this, but it does seem to fall under the umbrella of the Bush administration trying to connect al Qaeda and Saddam Hussein.

The administration was doing that. So it falls under that umbrella. But it was not doing that here. A lot of things fall under a lot of umbrellas, but what I'm saying is that this story was not overtly or covertly, sotto voce, or wink-wink, nod-nod, or in any other way part of the political case the Bush administration was making against Iraq. Whether it served that purpose or served another purpose I just can't care. As it happened, White House and CIA spokesmen tried hard to dissuade me from publishing this story.

I still have one more thing to say about the story. Ted Koppel gave us a very interesting interview in which he was talking about how the public doesn't pay attention. Every night he comes on *Nightline* and

says, "I'm Ted in Washington," and closes the show with, "I'm Ted in Washington," and people still stop him in the street and say, "What are you doing in Washington?" The reason I bring this up is because there's a sort of fog where people see the headlines and don't read the stories, so in this case, they could easily get the impression that Saddam gave al Qaeda nerve gas.

By the way, it doesn't say Saddam, it doesn't even say the government of Iraq. It says the intelligence suggests al Qaeda obtained nerve agents "in Iraq" the place, not "from Iraq" the government. And it specifies that even if al Qaeda did obtain the weapons, it's not known whether that happened with the complicity of the Iraqi government.

I'm talking about the headline "U.S. Suspects al Qaeda Got Nerve Agent from Iraqis." The public might consider it a given that it's the Iraqi leadership. I'm just explaining to you the perception.

I knew very well what the perception was going to be. We sat around talking about it in the newsroom and I said, "Everyone's going to think that this has been leaked to us as part of making an inflammatory case against Saddam Hussein and it hasn't been." The story was more transparent about sourcing and more transparent about qualifiers and doubts than almost anything I've ever written because it was at this sensitive political moment, but I didn't think we should withhold it for that reason or even because the US government didn't know it to be true. Hardly anything is nailed down to a certainty.

But this is more highly speculative.

Right. When they say, "It gets through our top 1 percent threshold and this is scary to us and we're pouring resources into blocking it and trying to confirm it"—when career people, who I took seriously and knew well for a long time, said that this was a threat they were taking seriously even though they thought the great majority of threat reports are bullshit—then I thought it passed our threshold for publication.

Now, Bart, you don't think that some of your high-level sources or your deep-in-the-closet sources from time to time might not give you information that they want you to put out there, in other words, try to manipulate you?

Absolutely, but it's not nearly as simple as that. It's very important to me to know what the motivations of my sources are. I know about who they are and where they stand in their career path and what kind of interagency fights they are having, whether they like their boss or not, whether they are near retirement or looking for a promotion, and all those other things. I figure out what their motivations are and I have frank conversations in which I ask them, "Why are you telling me this? You didn't tell me this last week. You didn't tell me this other thing that I wanted to know, so why are you telling me this?" And I test it and then I figure out—sometimes I can only guess—what are some possible motivations here and who might have opposite motivations, who might have doubts about those motivations and what kind of qualifier am I going to get from those other sources. So of course I expect people to try to manipulate me. However, I believe that I know very well what the motivations of my sources were in this case. I can say that these were career people who believed that this was a significant threat, that they weren't sure it was getting sufficient attention inside the US government while everyone was focusing on the forthcoming Iraq war, and that they were worried that al Qaeda was getting underfocused. They wanted to make sure that all available means were being used to track this threat. That was their concern.

> **Let's talk about the postwar era since you're writing some important stuff, like the piece on the Strategic Support Branch. Now that we're in the retrospective phase for examining the reasons for going to war and now that we are in the post, well, we're not de facto in the postwar phase, but we're . . .**

Postconquest.

> **Postconquest. Thank you. I'd like you to talk about your piece, which I think is really important because everybody's complaining about the growing secrecy, and now whole new bureaucracies are being built to conduct secret missions and everything seems to be moving into the Pentagon. Could you just talk about the report that you did and assess what it all means and where it's all going?**

The story you're talking about says that Defense Secretary Rumsfeld has created a new clandestine intelligence-gathering arm inside the Defense Department and has reinterpreted his existing legal authority in ways that none of his predecessors interpreted it. He considers himself to have, in effect, inherent authority to do clandestine human intelligence gathering anywhere in the world, anytime, and that because of the War on Terrorism and because of his inherent powers, he doesn't need to ask the CIA to do this stuff. He can do it himself, and for various legal reasons, he doesn't need to tell Congress as much about it as some people used to think he did.

So he's created this thing that he's calling the Strategic Support Branch and he's integrating it with newly empowered special operating forces.

We have two kinds of Special Forces in this country. There are the ones that they talk about and that are in the budget, and they're sometimes called white Special Forces. Then there are the black Special Forces, which are in the classified budget, and their existence is not officially acknowledged. It's this latter bunch that are called Special Mission Units, and they include the unit that is popularly known as Delta Force, though it hasn't been called that for twenty years. Rumsfeld is giving Delta and these Special Mission Units, along with a newly created intelligence branch, missions that would enable them to go clandestinely anywhere in the world to find out information that he wants found out and possibly to conduct direct operations.

Is Congress becoming ever more beside the point on these matters?

Congress didn't know about this for the first two years it was happening. There is ambiguous evidence about whether certain committee members in Congress were informed about part of it for the fiscal year 2005 budget. When the story came out, people like Senator John McCain of Arizona and a number of Republicans and Democrats made public statements saying they didn't appreciate learning about this kind of thing in the *Washington Post* and they should have been informed and they were going to have hearings. Very quickly the Republican majority asserted itself on the Hill and said, "Well, we've now been briefed and we're satisfied with the assurances we've received, and this is all on the up and up and case closed." So when you have the majority party in the White House and in both houses of Congress in an exceedingly partisan environment, there isn't a whole lot of accountability being demanded or provided on Capitol Hill.

What does that imply?

It makes us in the newspaper business feel like we have all the more reason to be focusing on accountability, meaning are they doing what they say they're doing, are they doing things they're not saying they're doing, is what they say true, how well are they doing it, and so on. That's why Len Downie, the executive editor of the *Washington Post*, calls accountability reporting our highest mission. It's what we think is most important, what matters most about what we do. I think it probably matters more now than it has mattered in certain other periods when there were other institutions that provided stronger means of accountability on their own. But it's important to understand, and here I think we disappoint a lot of people, that we are not and should not be "the opposition," just because the traditional venues of opposition are dormant. We're about what is, not what should be.

> **Prewar, a lot of people were talking about the pressure to not ask tough questions out of fear of being viewed as unpatriotic. Did you ever get any sense of that going on in your paper?**

I give you a flat no on that one. I really didn't. I get so many e-mails and so many questions about this, and I know people don't believe me. I've seen no evidence, ever, that the *Washington Post* flinched from the most skeptical, hardest-hitting journalism it could do because it was afraid either of being considered unpatriotic or angering readers or because of fears of retribution from the White House. When the White House makes threats against certain news organizations, it really just triggers a very strong reflex of "Don't push me, Jack." I've got to tell you that I see no problems at all with the spine of our newspaper. I've no doubt at all that Len Downie, Don Graham,[3] and Bo Jones[4] want me to be pushing as hard as I can based on verifiable facts, whether or not we come under attack. I have from time to time taken a fair amount of heat from the Bush administration. I did from the Clinton administration, too. I would say that the Bush administration is more aggressive at vilifying reporters for their stories than any other that I've covered, but it's not a difference of kind, it's a difference of degree. I used to have very tough conversations with Jamie Rubin at the State Department under Madeleine Albright. He was very protective of his boss and quite aggressive in trying to stamp out or deter or make you regret stories that he didn't like, and we understood each other.

I'm working on another story on the Department of Defense. I'm not going to give you all of this, but I'll read you a line from an e-mail I just got from Bryan Whitman, the number two spokesman at the Department of Defense, in partial response to my questions. He says he's worried about my line of inquiry and he says, "It would be unfortunate if we have to get into another one of these situations where we are compelled to discredit a story in a very public way."

I confess I'm tempted, but I'm just not engaging on that. I'm saying, "Well, here are my questions and you'll do what you have to do." I let my editors know that this is coming and they say, "Just don't get in a big fight about it." There's an extent to which these guys want to cast us as political opposition since there is no real effective political opposition. If we're skeptical, or if one of our stories stings them or interferes in some way with what they want to do, they respond by casting as political opposition our motivations and our purpose and our depiction of reality. We don't want to get cast that way. It's important for us to try to persuade whoever's persuadable that we're looking to tell the truth as best we can. So I just respond very matter-of-factly to an e-mail like this: "Well, here are the questions that I don't think you've answered yet and here's what I'm ready to run with and I'd be very happy if you'd tell me more." He said, "It looks like you're trying to prove a hypothesis here," and I wrote back, "One of my hypotheses is that right now you've been unwilling to say almost anything about this very important subject. I'd much rather disprove than prove that one, but you'll have to help me."

You're not going to tell us the subject of your report? This book isn't coming out until the fall of 2005.

It's another chapter of this Rumsfeld clandestine human intelligence organization. I'm always reluctant to talk about it in advance, but it has to do with their performance and behavior.

There's more to say about whether or not we're cowed. They sure come at us, but it just doesn't seem to bother the *Post*. Now, individual reporters have to make their own decisions about their comfort level. If you're a daily beat reporter and you depend on a set of sources for access, you're always making trade-offs in your own mind about what you have to do to maintain maximum access to information over the medium- and long-terms. There might be stories that would so irritate someone, for so little purpose, that writing them would reduce prospects for getting more important stories later. I think it's human nature to think that way. I tried to resist that when I was a beat reporter, and our best people seem to manage quite nicely with a constant string of stories that make it look as though the official sources would never want to talk to them again. Look at Dana Priest, who is covering intelligence for us. She has a story on the front page today describing an awful case of CIA prisoner abuse. She's broken story after story after story about secret satellite programs or military prisoner abuses. I think she's a very effective beat reporter because she pushes hard and calls it as she sees it. Officials talk to her even when they're angry because she's so effective at working around them and because they know that they can't influence what she writes except by talking to her. Freezing her out, even if they might prefer that sometimes, would hurt them more than it would hurt her.

Official sources aren't the only sources to a story, and I think people forget that sometimes.

First of all, official sources are not giving you very much of an inside view these days. The idea that by cozying up to the Bush administration you're going to get a lot of inside dope that the White House doesn't want to say in public briefings has been pretty thoroughly rebutted by experience. They don't play that way, so it's a false aspiration. The more important thing is you have to protect your own integrity as a reporter and as a news organization. As a newspaper, the *Washington Post* stands 100 percent behind its reporting and just doesn't bend. I've seen Len Downie and other editors in conversations with big shots in the government taking a lot of heat and just being matter of fact about insisting that the only thing that will change their minds is new evidence.

Dana Milbank wrote a story recently about Rumsfeld going to Capitol Hill that portrayed Rumsfeld as impatient and somewhat disdainful of questions, and not seeing any reason to hide it. This made the Defense Department very angry. The Pentagon's spokesman, Larry DiRita, asked to see Don Graham to complain about Dana Milbank. Graham, as I understand it, said, "If you want to complain, you ought to talk to the editor, Len Downie." DiRita had been down that road several times before and didn't like the result, so he said, "OK, never mind," and just dropped it. That's the way the *Post* institutionally responds, but how an individual reporter responds depends on the integrity and resourcefulness of that reporter. I tend to think that the good ones understand and make their official sources understand that they prefer for their sources to cooperate and grant interviews. That's always good for readers, as long as there are no conditions restricting other reporting. On the other hand, if the official sources make it clear that you are persona non grata and they throw you off the airplane or they disinvite you from a meeting or whatever else, then you just become a magnet for everybody inside the government who doesn't like what they are doing and wants to drop a dime on them. I always tell people in government that I'm going to play both sides of the fence. I'm going to talk to anyone I can. If they try to clamp down on me and make this all about me, then they're just going to put more information in my in-box.

What about the whole Judith Miller business? What's your take on, and reaction to, her reporting on WMDs?

I've been really careful not to get involved as a press critic. I don't want to be a critic of the work of my competitors, whether it's Judy or anybody else.

You could fill in anybody's name, what I'm looking at is the use of sources there. She has a pretty good record as a reporter, but something happened here and I'm interested in examining it because throughout the course of this interview you've been talking about how you respond and react to your sources and I think it's very instructive. But here's a case where something happened with the use of inside sources. That's why I'm discussing this with you, not to beat up on Judith Miller.

Her stories look different from my stories. She found different things than I found. I reported what I saw and made my reporting as transparent as I could so readers would know how I thought I knew something. I was on the early side in saying there are no WMDs here and the hunt is falling apart. Let's just be straight about it. In May 2003, a month after the war, I wrote that the hunt was failing—that the clues were no good and the hunters were frustrated, and that the first group of them was going home and they didn't understand what went wrong. My favorite story was "The Odyssey of Frustration." I took one of the search teams and reconstructed their entire effort. I chronicled every single place they'd been, what they thought they were going to find there, what they did find there, and what it meant to them. That's the one that started with the vacuum cleaners, where they were at what they thought was a special security organization site. They had their spectrometers[5] and their pathogen assay kits[6] and their protective gear and they were knocking down doors and breaking through locks and going by flashlight into darkened corridors, and they finally came to the darkest deepest corridor and a set of steel doors and they broke down the innermost vault and there it was: a big cache of vacuum cleaners. It really was one punchline after another. They seized a document in Arabic with drawings of laboratory glassware and they went off and had it analyzed and it was a high school science test. It was a description of Boyle's Law.[7] This was then appended to their report and the report was classified. Boyle's Law is now classified "Secret" Appendix A. So is the high school science test.

What interests me about a reporter like you is that you can work in a certain area or with certain information for so long that you have this epiphany moment and the whole landscape becomes clear to you and you can predict the future. Can you tell me what you're seeing in terms of how the administration is behaving and what's going on in the Middle East and what you see developing?

If I were a stock analyst, I would advise you to sell short every single thing I ever recommend. My record of predictions is very bad.

Why is that?

Well, everyone's is. The world resists prophecy. I went to Iraq for the first time in April just after the fall of Baghdad. I told my editor that I thought I was being really smart because I wanted to go look at the historic WMD facilities, just about all of which are within fifty miles of Baghdad. I said, "The search can't begin in earnest until the fighting is over and the United States controls Baghdad, so if I get there for the second half of the month, I should arrive just in time for the first finds of the biological and chemical weapons." I was always skeptical of the nuclear case, but I thought the BW and CW were probably going to be there.

What's important by the way about epiphany—you used that word—is that you can look at everything you are gathering and then say, "Wow, this is not the picture I was expecting." Either it is or it isn't, but it's often not. I think if you're not surprised frequently, then it's a sign of poor reporting. If you could already guess it all, then why buy the ticket?

> I have to disagree with you there. I think there are people who can look at patterns and trends and details and figure things out. I'm not asking you about the WMDs; I'm asking you if we are going to attack Iran, if there is going to be a draft, if the Israelis are going to get involved. You have long experience with the Middle East; you were the Jerusalem bureau chief for the *Washington Post* and you don't come at this analysis with nothing.

Here's what does and doesn't work for me and I would argue it's not just for me. Taking current trends and projecting them forward and guessing what's going to happen, whether there will be a war with Iran or whether there will be a deal between Israel and the Palestinians, my experience is that it seldom works even when I have private opinions that I think are fairly well founded. They're at least as likely to be wrong as they are to be right, and you don't know which ones are going to be right until afterward.

So road maps like the Project for the New American Century [PNAC][8] aren't informative?

The PNAC allows you to know what one set of people would like to do when looking only at that thing. What you don't know is whether that set of people, when looking at all of the factors and all the considerations that face them at the actual moment of decision, are still going to want to do that—whether they're going to win the debates and whether they're going to feel like they have enough maneuvering room with the public or with the international community, with allies, with money.

Do you think the public matters that much?

I think that it was a very high priority for President Bush to marshal public support for a war against Iraq. He did so.

On the back of 9/11.

Yes, on the back of 9/11 . . .

. . . which was a false premise.

. . . And on the back of erroneous claims about WMDs. Nevertheless, if the public wasn't important, then why did he bother? All I'm saying is you might know where a certain set of political figures would like to go, but it's just a whole lot more complicated to know what price they will be able or willing to pay and what they will be able to get away with. I think this supposition that you're talking about does work as a lead for things that are happening now, or recently happened, or are really just right now about to happen that we don't know about. I do a lot of what you could dignify as reporting by hypothesis, but really a much better term for it is the military term—SWAG. That means Scientific Wild-Assed Guess.

Let's just take this Rumsfeld secret army story. Say I know the following things: Rumsfeld was very frustrated with the speed of insertion of Special Forces into Afghanistan soon after 9/11. He wanted it faster. He's had titanic struggles with George Tenet. He doesn't like being dependent on anybody. Although there are legal reasons why previous secretaries of defense have not felt they could do this kind of secret human intelligence, Rumsfeld is not always so impressed with the lawyering that he encounters and sometimes says there's more than one way to look at it. We know that he's putting more time and attention into Special Operating Forces. We know that General Charles Holland, the immediate predecessor of the current chief of Special Operations Command [SOCOM], was skeptical of giving SOCOM intelligence missions, and he got eased out of the job. Based on knowing those things, I bet Rumsfeld is considering pushing toward developing this sort of capability himself. Let's see if that's true. So sometimes I can guess things that are already happening based on their penumbras.

You don't need to guess if they are already happening, right?

But nobody knew it. This was a scoop. It was not in the public record. Congress didn't know it, but it was happening and you could sort of guess it almost the way you discover the existence of a tenth planet—by the perturbations of the orbits of the other ones. You can know things that are around the boundaries of a secret without knowing the secret, and that gives you an opportunity to try and go prove the secret or to find out if it's true.

> **To me, this development is a perfectly logical outcome to a learning curve that they went through prewar. Look at what happened when they were trying to sell the war. They came up with all these different offices, including the Office of Special Plans, to strong-arm CIA analysts and Pentagon people who weren't going along with the program and to come up with intelligence—true or false, it didn't matter—to buttress their arguments for going to war. It was a rapid response to the problem that they had before they went into Iraq, which was to prove their claims so they could go to war.**

Let's say that's part of the motivation. It's possible and it's very logical. You're doing the same thing that I was doing as a reporter. The next step is, is it true? It sounds very plausible. It's a good guess. It might be happening, but even if somebody says it's happening, can you find it out, can you get to the details? In this case, I was able to.

> **I think that we need more people who do the kind of work that you do and who have the background and intellectual wattage to do it because I think it's a more complicated arena and it's just going to get more complicated.**

I don't think that an academic background, at least certainly not my academic background, is terribly helpful in a direct way.

> **I disagree. I think that's why you're good at analysis and can think critically.**

Well, I suppose I'd say experience analyzing complex materials and a degree of intellectual self-confidence allows a reporter to add up one and one and get two even if someone else is insisting the answer is something else. Part of what happens is you get spinners working so hard that they try to make you doubt things that are facts and not interpretations. At some point you can say, "I'm sorry, but this is no longer an arena for spin. Either what you said before this was true or it was not true and all the evidence I have shows that it was not true, so what am I missing here? If you can't give me any new facts, then I'm going to report that it was not true." You have to have a certain amount of intellectual self-confidence to combat the spin once you have enough reporting and facts to back up what you want to say.

Don't you think that's particularly critical now because you have an administration—the Clinton administration was very good at it, too, by the way—that seems to be engaged in a more extreme agenda? This administration is so good at echo chambering and presenting its messages, whether true or not, and trumping critical journalism that seeks to report on whether or not those messages are true.

What happens is that our reporting all gets thrown into a highly saturated media environment that is dominated by commentary, or ill-informed analysis masquerading as fact. At some level, in my job, I just have to relinquish control and say, "This stuff is going to go off and be used as people wish to use it." But when there are very specific factual claims that are made, then I very occasionally do step in and respond. Pentagon spokesman Larry DiRita wrote a letter to the editor of the *Dallas Morning News*—not to the *Washington Post*—saying that my story about the Rumsfeld clandestine spy arm was almost entirely false, and he scolded the *Dallas Morning News* for writing an editorial based on the story. I took the unusual step of writing a letter to the editor of the *Dallas Morning News*, saying that Larry hadn't found time to talk to me about the story and that I wanted to point out that Larry had not identified either in his letter or to me or to anyone else that I knew of any fact that was not correct in the story.

So you see what I'm saying, it becomes a very muddy information environment for good reporting because you have to deal with that kind of stuff while you're already competing against television punditry, which is impossible to compete against because TV is the mass–public consciousness medium.

I'm always aware that one story is not going to change everybody's mind. We depend on readers to go out and gather information and be open-minded and judge for themselves. There are open-minded readers and there are readers who are not open-minded who only want to confirm what they already believe or want to believe. We're not good at predicting which lines of inquiry are going to have an impact on the public debate, and we ultimately can't let ourselves care too much about that. I spent the year 2003 probing whether or not Iraq had WMDs. A lot of people said to me, "Why bother? George Bush got the war he wanted, and polls show that most Americans already believe that Iraq has those weapons and actually used them against US forces. So what's the point of unpacking the question now?" And I said, "The point is just whether it's true or not. We'll find out whether anybody cares or anybody believes what evidence turns up." In fact, the public consensus shifted to a belief that the prewar case was exaggerated, false, and to some extent dishonest. You couldn't predict where the public consensus was going to go. I think we have to just believe that truth has its own elemental value, whatever becomes of it in the public debate.

That was marvelous.

And pious, very pious.

BARTON GELLMAN is a special projects reporter on the national staff of the *Washington Post*, following tours as diplomatic correspondent, Jerusalem bureau chief, Pentagon correspondent, and DC Superior Court reporter. He shared the Pulitzer Prize for national reporting in 2002 and has been a jury-nominated finalist (for individual and team entries) three times. His work has also been honored by the Overseas Press Club, Society of Professional Journalists (Sigma Delta Chi), and American Society of Newspaper Editors.

Gellman graduated summa cum laude from the Woodrow Wilson School at Princeton University and earned a masters degree in politics at University College, Oxford, as a Rhodes Scholar. He is the author of *Contending with Kennan: Toward a Philosophy of American Power*, a study of the post–World War II "containment" doctrine and its architect, George F. Kennan.

NOTES

1. This *Washington Post* series included "Broad Effort Launched after 1998" (December 19, 2001), "Struggles inside the Government Defined Campaign" (December 20, 2001), and "A Strategy's Cautious Evolution" (January 20, 2002).

2. On February 5, 2003, Secretary of State Colin Powell made a presentation to the UN Security Council that had, he said, two purposes: "First, to support the core assessments made by [chief UN weapons inspector] Dr. Blix and [the head of the International Atomic Energy Agency] Dr. ElBaradei. As Dr. Blix reported to this council on January 27, quote, 'Iraq appears not to have come to a genuine acceptance, not even today, of the disarmament which was demanded of it,' unquote. . . . My second purpose today is to provide you with additional information, to share with you what the United States knows about Iraq's weapons of mass destruction as well as Iraq's involvement in terrorism, which is the subject of Resolution 1441 and other earlier resolutions." http://www.whitehouse.gov/news/releases/2003/02/20030205-1.html. Later reports showed that Powell's presentation contained errors.

3. Don Graham is chairman and CEO of the Washington Post Company.

4. Boisfeuillet "Bo" Jones Jr. is publisher and CEO of the *Washington Post*.

5. According to Barton Gellman, a spectrometer "is an instrument for identifying chemical elements."

6. According to Barton Gellman, a pathogen assay kit consists of "little test strips, like a home pregnancy kit, to identify biowar agents."

7. Boyle's Law: the volume of a sample of gas is inversely proportional to its pressure, if temperature remains constant.

8. The Project for a New American Century (PNAC) says on its Web site that it "intends, through issue briefs, research papers, advocacy journalism, conferences, and seminars, to explain what American world leadership entails." It is generally seen as a neoconservative take on the role the United States should play in the world. The PNAC says it is a nonprofit educational organization dedicated to the propositions "that American leadership is good both for America and the world; and that such leadership requires military strength, diplomatic energy and commitment to moral principle." http://www.newamericancentury.org/.

9

GUERRILLA AT THE
WASHINGTON POST

Courtesy of the *Washington Post*

WALTER PINCUS
Reporter,
National Security Affairs,
Washington Post
Interviewed March 2005

W alter Pincus is very familiar with the intelligence world. He's inter-
acted with it for a long time. Beyond that, if he were ever to put everything he knows and understands about the workings of the US government
into a book, journalists covering or contemplating covering government
would be remiss if they didn't read it and keep it around for easy reference.

Pincus commands a great deal of respect among his colleagues in
national security reporting. Somewhere along the line, though, he picked
up a reputation for being a curmudgeon, so when I called to ask him for
an interview, I was a bit surprised to hear the voice on the other line say,
"Sure, I'll talk to you. I'll talk to anybody."

At seventy-three, Walter's hair is completely white, but the word "elderly" doesn't come to mind when you meet him. He is a journalist still very much in the fray and in full possession of his professional powers. He has a no-nonsense demeanor and was, at times, brutally frank in his criticisms of the press and the government. He speaks, however, with undeniable authority and the voice of long experience.

We sat down to talk in the cafeteria in his building. A cappuccino machine hissed occasionally in the background as he spoke about how government moved into a PR mode a long time ago and how the press just can't get past it, how our Constitution's system of checks and balances has been short-circuited, and how the press is apathetic and isn't playing the independent role it is supposed to play in America's democracy. We discussed how important stories he had written had wound up in the back pages of the *Washington Post* instead of the front page and how this current administration defends itself brutally when attacked in the press. "They're very good at it," Pincus observed, "That's why I try to carry on guerrilla warfare, because you have to do it that way."

He began the interview talking about an ingenious way he'd figured out for doing some real reporting on al Qaeda right after the 9/11 disaster occurred. Shortly thereafter, he started talking about the prewar coverage. In the middle of that, he said something that took me so much by surprise that I almost let out an incredulous laugh. "It's my big issue here," he said. "We don't write about the poor anymore. Nobody writes about the poor. The poor don't exist because we are all well paid and we are all in the very class that's being helped." I had just met Pincus that day. I'd heard and read a lot of things about him, both good and bad. But sitting across from me at that moment was just a man, spontaneously revealing his compassion. The moment faded, but it's what I remember most about my encounter with Walter Pincus that day.

As I said earlier, our conversation began with him telling me about his great idea for getting accurate information on al Qaeda.

I have this odd role where they let me do what I want to do in the national security area. So when 9/11 happened, I got intrigued with al Qaeda.[1] The first thing I did was read the transcript of the Kenya bombing trial that was held in New York, which we had covered off and on but hadn't taken very seriously. This was the trial of four men, Wadih el-Hage, Mohamed Rashed Daoud al-'Owhali, Khalfan Khamis Mohamed, and Mohamed Sadeek Odeh, who were accused of using a car bomb to blow up the US

Embassy in Kenya in August 1998. Twelve Americans and more than two hundred Africans died, and four thousand people were injured. They were convicted on May 29, 2001.

I wrote a couple of pieces about al Qaeda based on the trial documents because it was literally the best material on the organization that stood up. Two members of al Qaeda had testified about the group's whole background. That became the thesis from which I began writing about al Qaeda and the intelligence on their organization. I wrote about how the US government knew of all these people and had actually foiled another bombing plot in Kenya a year before. The people who were organizing the bombing were American citizens because they had been married to Americans. They'd been brought before a grand jury, but they refused to testify and were let go. This reporting set the whole pattern for what I did after that.

What do you think of the reasons that were given for going to war in Iraq?

I think they were planning to go to war, and they just took the best thing they thought they could find. I think it fit into a basic approach that they had coming in. There was a group of people around George W. Bush who thought that they'd contributed to a mistake his father had made back in 1991 when George H. W. Bush failed to take out Saddam. They've been talking about it in think tanks ever since. You can go back and read all their rhetoric about how we had not successfully gotten involved in the Arab-Israeli conflict because we had no leverage, and one reason why we had no leverage was because the Palestinians were getting support from Saddam. So they created this notion of "the road to Jerusalem goes through Baghdad," which is total nonsense. Saddam Hussein was in a box. He was not harming anybody. The irony is that Saddam didn't even have the weapons that they claimed he had and that they used as a rationale for going to war.

How do you think the press did in terms of covering the reasons given for going to war?

There is no such thing as "the press." There are different newspapers, there are wire services, there's television, there's an extraordinary number of outlets, and the people working for them all do it differently. Even within the *Washington Post*, there are people who have disagreements about what is important. We have fought among ourselves for years.

So you have to look at this question another way. You have to consider the source of the information that the press was getting about why we were going to war. Each administration is smarter than its predecessors in shaping public opinion. When it comes to government, we moved into a PR society a long time ago. Now, it's the PR that counts, not the policy. They can make any policy seem to be the right thing or the wrong thing, depending on what information they put out. They understand how we in the media work much better than we understand how they in the government work.

In the beginning of August of 2002 the vice president made two speeches, and it became clear that we were going after Iraq. Essentially, there was no stopping this White House from going to war. President Bush's chief of staff, Andrew Card, made a really prescient statement: "You don't roll out a new product in the summer." He was referring to launching the PR campaign to sell the war. The war was the product and the administration was going to sell it to the American people starting in the fall. And when this administration starts a PR campaign, they totally dominate things. I did a whole article about it. Twice a day, Rumsfeld, Wolfowitz, Pentagon people, Condi, and even Powell[2] were talking about Iraq, and we were covering it. They just kept pounding away. It was a full-blown PR campaign.

They do it all the time now. What do you think Social Security is about? Medicare and Medicaid are much bigger, much more immediate problems, but there are no votes in that because they're programs for poor people. Bush has done his Medicare number for the older people who have money. Now he's taking care of the greedy; he's found tax cuts and a series of programs that only satisfy people who have disposable incomes, and that's the middle- and upper-middle class, and they all vote. This is what we really ought to be covering. It's my big issue here, we don't write about the poor anymore. Nobody writes about the poor. The poor don't exist because we are all well paid, and we are all in the very class that's being helped. So it doesn't hit us.

But getting back to the prewar PR campaign, there was a whole pattern, and I wrote about it. The *New York Times* came out with the aluminum tube story on Sunday [September 8, 2002],[3] and Condi and Cheney both went on the air that day and talked about the aluminum tubes and the mushroom cloud, which in the *Times* piece is attributed to an administration spokesman and which is exactly what came out of Condi's and Cheney's mouths that Sunday on TV. They both referred to the *Times* piece. Then days later, you had the Blair-Bush press conference at Camp

David. They talked about a report that they mistakenly said showed that Saddam was six months away from having a nuclear weapon. It was supposed to be an International Atomic Energy Agency [IAEA][4] report.

Bush and Blair were talking about a report that didn't exist.

They misstated it, yes.

They didn't misstate it; they referred to a nonexistent report.

They made it sound like something brand-new when it really wasn't.

Not only was it not new, but the most recent IAEA report on that issue said the opposite of what they were saying.

But they weren't talking about the IAEA report. They were talking about a study that was put out by the International Institute for Strategic Studies [IISS][5] in London, England. They misstated the report. They called it an IAEA report when in fact it wasn't. The IISS report came out at the same time.

What I found fascinating was, even though they misstated it, since they mentioned an IAEA report, Journalism 101 tells you to go dig up that report and find out what it says. Very few people in the press did that. And when the administration was called on it, they didn't say, "We were actually referring to an IISS report." They said, "Well, that was our analysis at the time."

They have no shame. This is the first administration I've ever seen that has absolutely no shame about making mistakes. They just forget it.

Shame or no shame, where is the press in all this? I'm really trying to figure out this prewar reporting problem.

The problem is that the administration is speaking to the media every day. Keep in mind, there is a White House briefing twice a day. There's a Pentagon briefing three times a week. There's a State Department briefing every day. There is more news put out than anybody could possibly print and so you're put into a position in which you can't keep saying, "But they didn't answer this thing." You become kind of a nag and the press is not uniform. So after one person does it, and then you do it once or twice, you forget it and go on to the next thing.

Why doesn't the press confront them more during press conferences?

Read the White House press conferences. It does occur. People say, you said, "X,Y before," and they give some bland answer and go on to something else.

So journalists haven't evolved enough to deal with the government's PR machine?

I don't think so. There's less chance now to have good coverage than ever. Here at the *Washington Post*, we keep rotating people out of very important jobs so they don't develop any history. They don't have enough time to develop sources and they're more dependent on the press office people than before, so the whole system plays into the hands of making the PR people important. The second trend is that by limiting expertise, you're requiring reporters to find sources other than themselves to deal with official messages, and so now they go to the growing number of think tanks that have sprung up all over Washington. What happens to me all the time is, if I have an enterprise story, a story that's unique, the editors will want, as it's terribly known here, "voices" in the story. They'll want other people to talk about it. So if you're an enterprise reporter, you're faced with this dilemma of going out and telling people what you found and asking them what they think of what you found. In the old days, you just wrote a story with the facts in it and then the next day people would comment one way or the other. That's changed now.

In my broader view, the biggest change in journalism is that reporting is now looked upon as the lowest level job on the journalism ladder. This is driven by the big chain newspapers—Gannett, Newhouse, and Knight Ridder. If you're a good reporter, you're like a bricklayer, and if you've got any gumption, what you want to do is become a manager. So if you're a good reporter on a small newspaper, you get to be the editor of the paper, and if you're really good, in Gannett, you get to be the publisher of that paper. Then you work your way up and maybe you can end up being an editor in Rochester or for *USA Today*. That is now the business. In the old days here at the *Washington Post*, we used to rotate editors. Somebody would be the national editor for a while and then go back to reporting, because reporting is the heart of it. It still is. One difference I have with Len Downie, Don Graham,[6] and all the *Washington Post* executives is that they don't leave people on their reporting beats long enough for them to become experts. The reporters are the foundation of your paper, not the editors.

Talk about the stories that you were writing about the WMD issue before the war.

I was lucky to have personally known the chief United Nations inspectors. I know Rolf Ekeus,[7] who did the first UN inspections, beginning in 1991. I've known Hans Blix[8] for forty years. When Blix came in to run the inspections in 2002, I talked to him in New York City a couple of times. He thought, like everybody else, that the Iraqis obviously had something. But Ekeus had always told me that what people didn't realize was how much material that his group, UNSCOM, destroyed back in the 1991 to 1995 period. After the UN inspectors were thrown out of Iraq in 1998, they did a report a year later that focused on what Saddam Hussein had been unable to prove had been destroyed. They had no evidence that weapons and stocks of material they and the Iraqis did not prove were destroyed actually still existed. Nonetheless, the missiles, bombs, and weapons materials that were listed in the 1999 UN report became a basis for saying that Saddam possessed them solely because there was no proof that they had been destroyed. Blix had run the International Atomic Energy Agency [IAEA] at one point, and when he came in to oversee the inspections in Iraq in 2002, one of the first things he mentioned was that he was going to look at the whole allegation about the Iraqis buying uranium oxide in Africa. He knew they had absolutely no reason to do that unless they were looking to enrich uranium, because they had their own sources and supply, so that was one of the key points. I wrote a story about that: "For Iraq Inspectors, 'Yellow Cake' and Other Quarries." It came out in November 2002, a couple of weeks before he began the inspections.

Was it a front-page story?

No. Almost none of them were.

Why?

You have to go ask the editor.

I'm going to ask you to speculate here.

Well, I won't. I've been through this so many times.

Well, you have to give me something on this because that's key reporting that you were doing at a very critical time.

It's the whole choice business, the way the paper is put together is a function of what the editors think and whoever's editing at that time.

Who was editing at that time?

It varies from day to day. In those days it was Len Downie and I guess Robert Kaiser, and then Steve Coll. They also had a different editor every weekend. But the editors are looking at a different pattern. They're looking at how to balance a page for the readers and all the rest of it. That's their concern.

The reason I'm pressing on this is obviously this was important reporting.

The most famous story in that regard happened back in March 2003, but before that, there was a buildup in the early stories. By the time January 2003 came along, the inspectors had been in and they'd been fed intelligence from the United States, and nothing had turned up. Blix began having doubts. Then Karen DeYoung [former assistant managing editor then covering foreign policy for the *Washington Post*] and I wrote the Colin Powell speech analysis, "Satellite Images, Communications Intercepts and Defectors' Briefings" [February 6, 2003], and raised some questions. A couple of days after Powell's speech, I wrote another piece, "Alleged al Qaeda Ties Questioned: Experts Scrutinize Details of Accusations against Iraqi Government," and raised specific questions about some of Powell's statements. For example, Powell implied that Palestinian terrorist Abu Musab al-Zarqawi[9] had a cell in Baghdad that coordinated people, money, and supplies and that it represented a potentially "more sinister nexus between Iraq and al Qaeda." I reported in the same article that an intelligence analyst had said that Zarqawi wasn't associated with al Qaeda, and that senior government officials said that the Iraqi government did not operate, control, or sponsor Zarqawi's group. Powell also implied that Saddam's government had a special relationship with an Islamic fundamentalist group called Ansar in Kurdish Iraq, but the former head of Ansar made it clear that his group didn't want ties to Saddam: "I am against Saddam Hussein. I want Iraq to change into an Islamic regime." The story ended up on page A21.

Then came the famous story. It happened on Saturday, March 15, 2003. I had written a piece about how the inspectors had been unable to find anything and that it was uncertain that there were any WMDs. Bob Woodward[10] had come in to the office that day. I was trying to get the piece in the paper, but on the weekend, there's almost nobody here, so it becomes a big deal to try to get something in the paper that they had not planned for earlier. Bob and I started talking, and he said that what I'd written was exactly what he'd been hearing, too. He then said he would write a new lead for it, and he wrote his version and I took some of the ideas and worked with them. But what was most important was that Bob talked to the national weekend editor and to whomever was the assistant managing editor running the paper that day and said, "Just get it in the paper." So he got it in the paper and it ran the next day, on Sunday.

The piece was "U.S. Lacks Specifics on Banned Arms," and the lead was "Despite the Bush administration's claims about Iraq's weapons of mass destruction, US intelligence agencies have been unable to give Congress or the Pentagon specific information about the amounts of banned weapons or where they are hidden, according to administration officials and members of Congress." In the piece I also mentioned that senior intelligence officials had said that the administration was withholding some of the best intelligence on suspected Iraqi weapons locations from UN inspectors in anticipation of war and that some of these officials were saying that the administration didn't want to help the inspectors because a weapons discovery could bolster the argument for continued inspections and undermine the administration's case for war.

In the wake of that piece, some people in the intelligence community and at the Pentagon called me about how they were not finding anything. Blix was telling me, "We're not finding anything." Then I was going back to my own intelligence people, and they were saying, "Well, it might not be there." Then I tied in the fact that we weren't saying the weapons existed based on the fact that we knew they existed, but based on the fact that nobody could prove that the ones they said they had back in 1991 didn't exist anymore. You had to prove a negative. Also during this period, Judy Miller of the *New York Times* and some other people were doing the Chalabi[11] number, and every time Chalabi's people came up with something, I would check it out and the CIA would knock it down. They firmly disbelieved what the Chalabi people and some other defectors were saying.

On what page did the famous story run?

Seventeen.

I don't understand that. I'm trying to understand that. That's why I'm asking you these questions.

Well, the piece came out four days before we went to war. The troops were over there, we had reporters embedded, everybody in the media had people embedded, and the press was looking forward to the war almost as much as the administration. They had made this commitment. Everybody was all excited, and we had five or seven people sitting in Kuwait waiting for the war to begin.

So it was costing the paper money not to go to war.

That is a cold way to put it, but the papers and television networks weren't getting anything out of sitting there waiting for the war to begin, and they didn't want to bring everybody back after all that because the war was expected at any time and a lot of time, effort, and money had been spent to get people over there to cover the war. It's just like the military.

What does that bode for us in terms of what we're doing?

You see what the answer is. You can't stop an administration determined to go to war once it has sold the press and the public on what they are going to do. In my mind, there's a whole history to all this ability to manipulate the media, and it started with Ronald Reagan's deputy chief of staff, Mike Deaver. Before Reagan's time, there used to be morning technical meetings at the White House where the television producers would be told where the president would appear that day so they could make plans. Then Deaver came in. He would hold the meeting at nine o'clock, and he would essentially say, "Today, the president is going to speak about crime. He's going to use some statistics from San Francisco and Chicago and he will appear at 12:22 PM and make a statement which will cover this, that, and the other thing." So instead of sending producers and technicians to the meeting, the networks started sending their correspondents who would then call back in and say, "This is what's going to happen." Then the correspondents would go out to San Francisco and Chicago and shoot film for the bit of time that the president appeared. They'd go on the air that night with the story, because all the networks want to put their White House correspondents on the air, because they draw the audience. From then on, there was a presidential story every day. There never used to be a daily presidential story in the *Washington Post* because the president wouldn't do that much every day. You look at it today and the president goes out and says the same thing about Social Security almost every day, and every day we write a story about it. And there's absolutely nothing new about it.

You've been in this business a long time and you're covering an area that is about the extreme activities that our nation engages in both

domestically and internationally. How do you do a good job of that these days?

You do your best. I spent part of last year looking into the 9/11 Commission. They put out their recommendations, which were drafted by their staff and agreed to by the commission. The recommendations were not the central part of what they were doing. The central part was a report reconstructing what had happened, which was very good.

I think the recommendations were terrible. I think that 9/11 Commission director Philip Zelikow's role was much too expansive, and although he worked at the National Security Council, he's essentially an academic who did not spend enough time looking at changes in intelligence coordination that had been made during the post-9/11 period. Zelikow's emphasis on how things would have been different if they'd done a long National Intelligence Estimate doesn't reflect an ideal view of how intelligence works and how it works with this president or would work with past or future presidents.

I believe this because of my experience with the Clintons. My wife is from Little Rock, so I knew the Clintons twenty years ago, and when Clinton came to Washington, he was the first president in my time who had no personal friend at the CIA. His view and Hillary's view of the agency were influenced by the post-Watergate findings of the Church committee:[12] "These guys are renegades, they're all conservatives, stay away from them." Clinton appointed James Woolsey as his first CIA director although he had never met Woolsey until the day he appointed him. Woolsey was suggested to Clinton by his new Defense Department team, Les Aspin, Bill Perry, and John Deutch.[13] They had worked with Woolsey in the past. After Clinton did meet Woolsey, he didn't like him, which is understandable. So they never got along.

President Clinton and I had an informal conversation about the agency at a social event in the summer of 1993. I had been told he was canceling morning briefings with Woolsey because he read the CIA's President's Daily Brief [PDB] and found there was often nothing new in it, so he didn't see any reason to have a briefing with the CIA director. I was thinking about writing about it and eventually did. Clinton didn't understand that the morning briefings were like an umbilical cord and that the questions raised at that morning briefing then became part of the agency's agenda for that day. Clinton had followed George H. W. Bush, a president who had been a former CIA director. The morning meetings during Bush's administration were great informal exchanges about people involved in operations, and everybody was familiar and friendly. At some point, Clinton used Vice President Gore and Gore's national security advisor, Leon Fuerth,[14] to ask questions and keep the agency happy. That morning meeting, depending on the president, is very important and it goes to 9/11, because how today's President Bush deals with the agency is key. George W. Bush is not a reader. He may or may not read the PDB, but he takes things in orally. That's how he absorbs things. He got along with Tenet, and Tenet was the same kind of person he is personality-wise, so the briefing became very important. In the pre-9/11 period, the Bush administration was focusing on preparing new plans for fighting the War on Terrorism. The PDB and Tenet's briefings only infrequently mentioned Osama bin Laden and the possibility of attacks on the US mainland, even though Tenet himself had begun in the Clinton administration to raise concerns about terrorism.

So I don't think Zelikow and the members of his staff working up the recommendations really understood how the CIA works with the president and their recommendations reflected that. Also, before writing the recommendations, they never studied what was done in the agency or in the community after 9/11. They said nothing had changed. In fact, it had changed enormously. For example, Tenet started holding a daily five o'clock meeting during which he would direct things to happen, both domestic and foreign over the next few days. Nobody from the commission ever asked to go to the meeting, even though they were invited. Once, when 9/11 commissioner Richard Ben-Veniste and Zelikow were interviewing Tenet, he brought them in to the meeting, and they stayed for ten or fifteen minutes and that was it. Meanwhile, the CIA and the FBI were doing all sorts of new things to break down old barriers. For example, helped by the PATRIOT Act,[15] they could share grand jury information without fear of losing criminal cases.

I say all this because the recommendations the commission came out with were just some irrational ideas to create a new bureaucracy. The president responded to the commission recommendations in July 2002 by saying, "We're going to think about it." House Speaker Dennis Hastert said, "We may have hearings next year." However, after the recommendations came out, John Kerry,[16] in one of the greatest mistakes of his life, announced that if they were put in a bill, he would sign it. Then Senator McCain and somebody else put them in a bill and suddenly you had this rush to do a bill that nobody had really thought out, that had not been examined at any hearings, and that had no serious consideration. The

Democrats fell in line and this made Bush act. He first put out an executive order and then Congress got into the act. The House passed a version with amendments on related terrorism issues such as a driver's license for noncitizens, while the Senate approved a vastly different version. What emerged was the Intelligence Reform and Terrorism Prevention Act[17] that was several hundred pages long. Meanwhile, the *New York Times* was writing about how important it was to move on intelligence reform and how the 9/11 families were in favor of it. The chairman and vice chairman of the 9/11 Commission, former New Jersey governor Thomas Kean and former representative Lee Hamilton of Indiana, were going around the country and saying things up on the Hill that were somewhat inaccurate because they hadn't studied the changes made in the intelligence community post-9/11 or read the details of the legislation on the Hill.

Hardly anybody read the bill. I had read the bill; I spent five months writing about it. The bill is an ambiguous mess. Even now, they're still trying to figure out what the hell it means. So you ask: Why doesn't anybody do things? Well, you try to do things, but if everybody else is doing something else, it doesn't make any difference.

I actually agreed to moderate a meeting of the Council on Foreign Relations with John McLaughlin in January 2005, and I said, "I'm just going to ask you about the Intelligence Reform Bill." McLaughlin, the deputy director of central intelligence, had to announce then and there that he'd never read the five-hundred-page bill, and he had to sit down and do that because he didn't want to be embarrassed in front of the council.

Then he read the bill. By the time he spoke to the council about it, he agreed that the thing made no sense. Yet everybody was for it; the press was for it, the *Times*—I can't forgive the *Times*, because I felt that they never wrote once about the substance of the bill that was going to cause confusion within the intelligence community. But they regularly covered every press conference that the families held because that moved people. Everybody just went on the theory that "we've got to change the intelligence community," and they were willing to do it with this bill that they knew nothing about.

What people don't understand is that the intelligence community runs as each president wants to run it. There's no firm, rigid structure, and it depends on the people he puts in charge of key agencies. It's the way government works. The reason, historically, that you have a Central Intelligence Agency is because the Pentagon intelligence people are serving a policymaking body with an emphasis on military matters, as it should be.

The Pentagon's intelligence is always skewed, as it probably should be, toward the military threat because that's who they are and that's what their expertise is in. The State Department is skewed toward the diplomats and diplomacy because that's where their skills are. The CIA was put together to be the president's intelligence agency and was to be policy-neutral.

What's developed over the years because the CIA gets beaten up (sometimes they deserve it) all the time, is that they started being perceived as just another player in the intelligence game, as if they had no connection to the White House and were just another biased group pushing intelligence that supports their own policy views. Biased for what? Biased for themselves, biased for—who knows? So now, the CIA has been cut loose and it's out there floating somewhere.

Is it being co-opted by the Pentagon's new Strategic Support Branch?[18]

Not really. The Strategic Support Branch is about the Pentagon's intelligence people trying to have more influence based on Rumsfeld and Cheney's influence. But you don't have to structure those kinds of things. Cheney and Rumsfeld have a tremendous amount of influence—like it or not, whether there's a structure or not—but only if the president wants it that way.

One of the things you suddenly learn that people have forgotten goes all the way back to the Nixon era. In Nixon's day, everybody was saying, "Oh, Haldeman and Ehrlichman[19] are shaping his mind. But Nixon was running the whole show. The lesson is: presidents run everything, and people do what presidents want done.

So basically we don't have much of a checks and balances anymore.

There are checks and balances, but you can only have checks and balances if you understand what you're dealing with and people in the separate branches of the government actively play the roles the Founding Fathers gave them. Now, however, the press creates myths about people and refuses to make an issue out of the fact that the checks and balances system is not working.

Are you pinning this whole thing on the press?

We're partly to blame. We've encouraged officials to make use of us. I go back to the theory that the press doesn't care that it is not playing the important independent role it is supposed to play in our democracy, at least not concerning many serious national issues. It is waiting for others to raise those issues.

Do you think there's a problem of ignorance and provincialism in the new generation of reporters?

I think that has been growing. I think it is attributable to this sense that we journalists are somehow outside of everything and should not be players. Also we're considered much smarter than we really are. And individually, we don't have much history. For the last fifteen or twenty years, Congress has been treated in the media like a joke. It's treated like a joke because sometimes it acts that way. But the point is, it is a very important functioning branch of government, and if you treat it like a joke, it will act like a joke, and you lose something that's really important. The *New York Times* did a piece, "Congress's Midnight Frenzy," about the total misuse of Congress on the Schiavo case, which is a good example of what I'm talking about. All we in the press care about is the horse race and the surface stuff. We don't care about what's really going on, and that's because we have no history of what's going on. The people who are covering it are frequently shifted and don't have any history, so they don't have a chance to learn to respect the institutions they cover. I recognize I am biased, because in the 1960s, I took leave from journalism twice for eighteen months at the beginning and end of the decade to run two investigations for Senator Fulbright's[20] Foreign Relations Committee. It had a major effect on my career and certainly made me see the role that Congress can play.

So you think we were sold a bill of goods in terms of the reasons given for going to war?

Sure. But there are a whole bunch of people who think Franklin Roosevelt sold the country a bill of goods to go into World War II.

Why did they want to go into Iraq, do you think?

I think, like everything in this government, different people had different views. I would say that Cheney wanted to undo what he thought was a mistake he made back in 1991. I think Paul Wolfowitz and the neocons[21] basically believed that the way to solve the Middle East problem was to build democracy in Iraq and then Israel would be safer living next to a democracy. Wolfowitz and others misjudged what they were getting the United States into.

Why didn't they say they wanted to build a democracy in Iraq?

Because they couldn't sell that.

They couldn't sell democracy to the American people.

Of course not. You could not and probably should not send American soldiers into another country to establish democracy if US security is not threatened immediately and directly.

They're selling it now.

No, no. Democracy, to go to war, to save Israel? I don't think that's true for a minute. It would never happen.

No, to bring democracy to the Middle East.

Who among the American public at large cares that much about the Middle East? They're dangerous people, and I would guess most Americans believe we should not be responsible for how they govern themselves.

Well, they have all that oil. You don't think the oil had anything to do with it?

I think people believed we had Saudi Arabia so locked up. At the time, Saddam's Iraq was going nowhere. It was, as the Clinton administration officials described it, "in a box," and though regime change became the policy in 1998, that did not mean doing it by invading the country with US troops.

There are a lot of people who have emotional ties to the Middle East. And oil is part of that. This country does not work on single reasons. It's always a multiplicity of ideas that come together to make a critical mass and they developed a critical mass of ideas. They convinced one person, President Bush, and he's the only one they had to convince. Then they put the machine to work to sell it to everybody else.

Do you think the whole Israeli-Palestinian issue is well covered by your paper and by the other mainstream outlets?

I've never covered it.

Not that you necessarily personally covered it, but do you think it's well covered?

A lot of these ideas depend on what your basic belief is.

You're talking about belief, but I'm talking about journalism.

There is no such thing as objective journalism. We all have different upbringings, experiences, educations, and outlooks, all of which color these things.

> **There's no such thing as objective journalism, but I do think that there is such a thing as factual information available and then I think there's competent critical analysis.**

I think when you put in "competent," then you're reflecting your own view of where these people come out. I used to always argue that the *Wall Street Journal* editorial page under Robert Bartley used to be the best thing to read to get the thoughtful, conservative point of view, because I think they used to do what an editorial page should do. They did a lot of independent reporting, they were very tough-minded, and you knew where they were coming from, so you learned something from them. We now live in this age where everybody in journalism is supposed to be neutral, but none of us really are.

> **Whether it's neutral or not, or objective or not, what I'm trying to say is that when I look at foreign reporting, I think a lot of important things aren't covered.**

We talk about Iraq having gone for nuclear weapons and we talk about Iran going for nuclear weapons. But how often do those stories mention that one possible reason for their pursuit of nuclear weapons is that Israel has nuclear weapons and is considered a threat?

> **That's an interesting issue because I think a lot of that reporting is missing.**

A lot of it? It took time for me to get a story in the paper about Israel having nuclear weapons. People in government here don't often mention it unless they are pushed.

> **Why?**

Because the Israelis don't mention it and our public officials don't mention it.

> **Why?**

Because Israel is an ally and we don't appear to care if they have nuclear weapons and they don't admit it, so therefore we're not going to embarrass them. Also, and it's what I learned in the 1960s from Senator Fulbright, we don't think automatically of the other person's issues, such as Iran seeing Israel's nuclear weapons as a threat. We think only about our own issues.

> **Based on your reporting and what you've discussed with all your sources, how big a threat is al Qaeda?**

There is a group of people who believe—and I've written about it in terms of Zarqawi—that the biggest mistake Osama bin Laden ever made was attacking the United States, because the purpose of the attack was to get Americans out of the Middle East and to show that we would pay a penalty if we were in the Middle East. And once we were out, bin Laden could overthrow the royal family, Zawahiri[22] could overthrow Egypt's Mubarak, and Zarqawi could overthrow Jordan's Abdullah. That's what they want to do. They don't want to take over the United States, they don't want America to collapse; they just wanted to get us the hell out of the Middle East. And in fact, we didn't get out, we came in with both feet, and now we're there permanently. And it's been a dispute between Zarqawi and bin Laden, and Zarqawi, I think, is winning. This flurry the other day over bin Laden saying to Zarqawi, "You ought to think of attacking the United States," is emblematic of this kind of self-involvement on the part of Americans. But the Zarqawi terrorist attitude is, "We want people getting killed all over the Middle East, Americans, Israelis, even Arabs." But when it comes to people here in the United States, we don't care as much when the targets are Arabs. All we care about is us, us, us.

What about this whole Homeland Security business?

I think it's just overdone. The one thing these terrorists know how to do is truck bombs. It's the easiest thing to do. People were scared to death that after 9/11 the terrorists were going to come back with a truck bomb in the Midwest. If that would have happened, this country would have gone absolutely crazy. But they never did. These terrorists are not as dumb or rabid as we make them out to be. I can give you an analogy for all this. I covered nuclear weapons in the cold war, and "first strike" was one of the dumbest ideas anybody could ever think of. First strike was to be a Soviet nuclear attack on the United States that would simultaneously knock out all our land-based intercontinental missiles, our strategic bombers, and strategic nuclear submarines so that we could not strike back. We ran twenty years of policy based on it and built ten thousand weapons. The Russians were never going to do it. Bob Kaiser and I once wrote a piece in the *Washington Post* in 1979 about first strike being so stupid. We said, "Here's a country that can't make elevators work and they're going to carry off the most complex attack in the history of man? Why are they going to do it?" And the answer you'd hear from foreign policy people was, "They're crazy."

So then, the Russians go and suddenly we're worried about the Chinese. And if you talked to Richard Perle, who's a friend of mine, or

Frank Gaffney [president of the Center for Security Policy], or any of the other conservatives, they would tell you, "The Chinese, you can't deal with them, because there are so many of them that they can take being attacked with a nuclear weapon. It doesn't matter to them. They're crazy, they're not like the Russians." And I said to Perle, "Well, Richard, you were saying the Russians were crazy on first strike."

We have a whole policy now: don't let the Europeans sell conventional arms to the Chinese. To what end? You think they can't build their own? The *New York Times* won a Pulitzer talking about the Chinese buying communication satellites from US companies and how we ought to stop it. And they stopped it. The Chinese were going to buy a satellite for military communications that was built by the same company that builds the CIA satellites, and part of the sales agreement was that they couldn't look inside the satellite. And the *New York Times* reporter was told that selling those satellites to the Chinese would somehow give them the capability to fight the United States. The logic here is absurd: if they don't get the satellite from us, what are they going to do, use smoke signals? It was the same thing with Wen Ho Lee.[23] The line for that one was that the Chinese had stolen US secrets relating to building small nuclear warheads. They had to steal it because they weren't smart enough to do it. So does that mean that when the Chinese somehow cross the border and come to the United States they become brilliant, but when they stay home, they're really stupid?

I think nonproliferation is one of the most oversold ideas. Anybody with the time, energy, and desire can build a nuclear weapon. Are we going to fight everybody whose leader somehow decides he wants nuclear weapons? Also, we don't care about some people having it. The Taiwanese have tried to build them; that may have been what Wen Ho Lee's activities were all about. Wen Ho Lee spent time briefly at the Taiwanese version of Los Alamos, and nobody wanted to talk about that. He may not have been acting with China in mind. He may have been doing it for the eventual benefit of the Taiwanese. That's what all the investigative people think, and I wrote about it once or twice and everybody went crazy.

So what are your sources telling you about Iran?

One of our reporters, Dafna Linzer, had a very clever idea for covering this story. In the Ford administration, when the shah was in power, Cheney, Rumsfeld, and Wolfowitz went to the shah, and told him, "You're going to run out of oil, you ought to build nuclear power facilities and we'll help you and we'll sell you all this equipment." Cheney was among those who made the "you're going to run out of oil" argument. Dafna has some of the documents, but it took time to get the story in the paper.

Why would that be a battle?

Well, the administration has recently totally changed its view. The Iranians still have only a twenty-year supply of oil, but Cheney said the other day, "They're sitting on this lake of oil, so why do they want to have nuclear power when they have all this oil?"

So what is the truth?

The truth is probably a little bit of both. Why shouldn't the Iranians have a nuclear weapon? They're surrounded by countries that have nuclear weapons: India, Pakistan, China, Russia, and Israel. They are as smart as the others. I don't know if they have a nuclear weapon, or if they plan to get one, but most of their people seem to want one, and we should not care as much as we do. Nuclear weapons haven't done anybody any good since we first used them on Japan. They are more diplomatic and political weapons than they are military weapons.

What do you think the future holds for Iraq?

I think the minute we leave, it will split up or its then leader or someone else will turn into Saddam Hussein Jr. Iraq is a noncountry. The Kurds[24] are going to break away, if they haven't broken away already.

Two weeks ago, you started having all this glorification of the Palestinian election which worked only because Yassir Arafat[25] died. But nothing's changed. The Israelis are increasing the size of their West Bank community, and the Palestinians are going to keep fighting. But they've got to solve it on their own terms; the United States can't do it for them.

Here's what to me is the most frightening thing. I have a piece in the paper today about the Predator drone. We have turned the Predator into a hunter-killer. It's no longer a reconnaissance drone. The reason it's a hunter-killer is because under the new defense strategy,[26] a paper that many in the media have ignored and that is Rumsfeld and Cheney's view of the world, the thesis seems to be that we have got to be ready to attack anywhere, anytime, and that we are going to enforce sovereignty over countries that can't enforce sovereignty in their own countries. It is the most arrogant policy going. If you go back and read Condi when she was up for confirmation, she said, "We're going to insist—insist—that democratically elected governments act democratically toward all their people."

And I called up the State Department and said, "What does 'insist' mean?" And the answer was: "Oh, you'll have to wait and see." What she's doing with China and other governments is all part of the pattern. These people really believe that they're carrying on a mission. They believe their own rhetoric, and they also believe that as the most powerful country in the world, the United States has the right to enforce militarily what can't be done through diplomacy. Colin Powell thought he was buying time by getting the United Nations inspectors back into Iraq. But Cheney told Blix at the beginning that the inspections weren't going to change the administration's war plans. Cheney's attitude was, "We're watching you and the first mistake you make, we're shutting down your operation." I asked Blix what would have happened if the inspectors had found weapons. He told me that the United States was going to invade whether or not weapons were found. So what were the inspectors there for? They were there to give Powell a little bit of cover and time to persuade Saddam Hussein to leave. We never described the inspection process as anything more than finding the weapons that we knew were there. The fact is, the Iraqis had accepted a monitoring machine that would have consisted of one or two hundred people on the ground in Iraq forever. The idea that Saddam could secretly break out of that is no different from when we sent on-site inspectors into Russia. There was never a chance of a Soviet first strike, particularly after we had inspectors inside that country, but nobody ever talked about that. They never talked about monitoring; they never talked about the origins of the weapons, because it didn't fit into what they wanted to do, which was to get rid of Saddam one way or the other.

Now, this administration, under this new Rumsfeld strategy, is going to threaten everybody. They're literally putting together a military force that can go anywhere, anytime, to fight in countries that don't exercise control over their own territory and that, in Rumsfeld's mind, can become a breeding ground for terrorists that threaten us. But of course, they won't go into Darfur.

I want to talk to you about the Homeland Security aspect of things. First of all, what do you think of the new director of national intelligence, John Negroponte?

I actually like John, I've known him for a long time, and since nobody knows what his job is, it's going to be interesting to watch as it develops. The fact that he's got National Security Agency director Lt. Gen. Michael Hayden as a deputy is very good.

The bigger picture is kind of interesting because you have 9/11 occur-ring, and in the foreign arena we go to Iraq, and then domestically, we're becoming this, I don't know, national security and surveillance state, what is it? These huge bureaucracies are being built. What are your people inside saying is going on?

Most of them are carrying on their lives and doing what they think they have to do. Most of the intelligence community is now involved with terrorism. It is the flavor of the month. The biggest noncovered event is that the FBI has now gone from doing crime and subversion to terrorism. Over half the FBI budget is now involved in counterterrorism, counterintelligence, and intelligence analysis, and one of the ironies is that John Negroponte controls that part of the bureau operation. Meanwhile, the FBI, which is as much or more at fault than the CIA and the intelligence community for 9/11, almost totally gets away without criticism. Nobody is looking at this. Where's the scandal? They've spent almost a billion dollars on a computer system that doesn't work and [former FBI director] Louis Freeh just marches off into the sunset.

I remember the first World Trade Center bombing. The FBI's confiden-tial informant, an Egyptian policeman, Ehmad Salem, was right in there with Ramzi Yousef and the bombers, and they were paying him a few hundred bucks a week. All of a sudden, a few months before the bombing, they let Salem go. They told him he was costing them too much money. Salem actually taped the phone conversation when his handler fired him. After the bombing, they had to pay Salem a ton of money to come back and help them track down the bombers.

The bureau gets away with absolute murder.

Where is the press in all this?

We're essentially nowhere. We get led from one thing to another. What has dominated headlines the last four days? The Schiavo[27] case is being covered as if the end of the world's coming. Americans get shot in Iraq and it's put on the inside page. Today and tomorrow, we're going to be back to Columbine Jr.[28] because of the shooting in Minnesota.[29] The Predator piece almost got knocked out of the paper because there were so many Schiavo stories.

What page was the Predator piece on?

The bottom of page three.

You're moving up in the world, Walter.

The media has become driven and led by television. That's why I go back to Deaver. Deaver got print to follow TV. The real end of the Deaver story is that at the end of the first year of Deaver's tenure, David Broder[30] wrote a column saying Ronald Reagan was the least involved president he had ever seen in his life. And the letters came in by the ton saying, "How can you say that? We see him every night doing this and doing that."

It creates a virtual reality, really.

Yes. After the first two or three press conferences with Reagan, we would do truth-squading articles on all the mistakes he made. And the letters came pouring in, "Why do you keep picking on him?" We hardly do that now. We did a little one after Powell's UN speech, and we do it occasionally when the president speaks, but for the most part, we've stopped doing that. By the time George W. Bush came in, Deaver's theory had become so implanted that Bush's problem is described as "not staying on message." Think for a minute what you're talking about. You're talking about his PR. You're a good president if you stay on your PR message. When Clinton came in, he used to go crazy because he was accused of doing too many things in one day. He was characterized in the press as not being able to stay focused. It's lunacy.

What does this mean if people are supposed to be informed and we're supposed to be the messengers?

Take what you just said, "We are supposed to be the messengers." The messengers of what? My argument is, we've become a common carrier. Freedom of the press is built on the idea that there is a multiplicity of things going on. Newspapers used to be run by political parties or people who wanted to shape opinions. There's a First Amendment not because you have to tell the truth, but because you have a right to put forward your point of view. The idea of true democracy is that the citizens ought to keep themselves informed by reading a number of publications and absorbing different points of view. But you have had this enormous consolidation so that most newspapers are now in monopoly situations in most cities. What used to be the pressure on electronic media to carry all points of view has been turned around because there are a limited number of daily print outlets. So the multiplicity is gone. Bloggers are not the answer for many reasons, the first one being that they are not mass media. They become mass media only when they're picked up by print, or radio, or television, which remain mass media. So the blogger influence is totally tied to getting mass media to go along with them.

I think one of the worst things going on right now is journalists going to universities, which is now the big pet thing. Universities take you even further away from the reality of what is going on in government than being in the newsroom does. Everybody has their own thing, but I've tried to get a foundation to put up money so journalists can go to work in government—state government, local government, it doesn't matter, but not in PR. Most people in government are working hard to do the right thing, and we don't know it. We journalists, however, just know the outside, and with the growth of public relations, we're further outside than we've ever been. The Council for Excellence in Government formed a group that David Broder chaired with a group of journalists and some other people to look at the idea of a journalist program in government, among other ideas. One of the old journalists said, "Oh, it's great because they could expose what they see." There's the total belief that government is really bad, and it's not.

I think there is a general sense of corruption and lying, cheating, and stealing because when that happens, and particularly when it happens on a huge scale, that hits the mass public consciousness.

But then we never cover what happens afterward. This is the running disagreement that I have had with Bob Woodward. In the old days when he was exposing things, he believed that his job was to expose and somebody else's job was to clean up. My view has always been that you stay with it. If you create the mess by showing the public what wrong thing is going on, you should keep pursuing it until the wrong is righted or the law changed. It was what I learned from working for Fulbright in the 1960s, where I actually participated in changing the law. You keep doing it. I did Iran-Contra for five years. If you did it, you have to stay with it because changing it is very important, and the function of change is important. That's not the prevailing belief right now.

Carl Bernstein was saying the same thing Woodward says. And I told him I thought it was a hell of a thing for someone who had brought down a president to say.

It creates a feeling in the public that government's continually corrupt and can't be changed.

Well, let's face it, in this particular environment right now, where the lies are whoppers . . .

Oh, yes, but there's been almost no old-fashioned scandal. Look at the problem with Halliburton.[31] Halliburton has been charged about eight different ways from Sunday about money and cheating and all the rest of it, but the stories on Halliburton are nowhere. Who is the head of Halliburton? Has he been called before some committee, has he done anything? Richard Perle gets caught with contracts and all the rest of it, and there's never a hearing because this Republican Congress doesn't investigate Republicans.

You don't call that corruption?

Yes, but nobody pays attention to it. And in many ways it is worse than old-fashioned corruption. The whole system of checks and balances created by the Constitution is being short-circuited.

Here's the thing: If you have a Congress that won't do anything because it's politically co-opted, if you have a Justice Department that's not going to do anything because it's politically co-opted, where do you go, The Hague?

My concern is that you don't have journalists looking into it. We all have investigative units, but many of them, including ours, do sociological projects. We exposed the land trust and the idea that people are getting tax deductions by having their private homes made historic sites. A big newspaper like this.

When you go after the big kahunas, it costs a lot of money and there's a lot of danger.

But we have a lot of money. The *New York Times* just did a big long investigation on railroad crossings for which they won a Pulitzer Prize. But meanwhile Congress, as an equal branch of government, is going down the drain and billions are being spent in Iraq with little oversight. The press could do more if it had its own agenda.

I think there's more to it than that.

I think people don't like it.

I think, too, this administration defends itself brutally when you go after it.

They're very good at it. That's why I try to carry on guerrilla warfare, because you have to do it that way.

WALTER PINCUS has been writing for the *Washington Post* since 1966. He currently reports on the intelligence community and its problems, intelligence reform, terrorism, and the war in Iraq. Throughout his tenure at the *Post*, Pincus has written on a variety of subjects, including nuclear weapons and arms control, political campaigns, the American hostages in Iran, the Iran-Contra affair, and investigations of Congress and the executive branch. In 1992 he cowrote stories on the Bush administration's review of presidential candidate Bill Clinton's passport files, which led to the appointment of an independent counsel. He also covered the case of confessed spy Aldrich H. Ames and its aftermath, as well as allegations of Chinese espionage at the nuclear laboratories.

Pincus has also been a part-time consultant for NBC and CBS, developing, writing, and producing documentaries and segments for their evening news programs and magazine shows. In 1992 he coproduced a two-hour CBS documentary, *Watergate: The Secret* (aired June 17, 1992), which was accompanied by articles in the *Washington Post* and *Newsweek*. The following year, on the thirtieth anniversary of John F. Kennedy's assassination, Pincus directed a combined research effort among the *Washington Post*, *Newsweek*, and CBS News that resulted in a series in the *Washington Post*, a major package of articles in *Newsweek*, and a two-hour CBS documentary, *The Kennedy Assassination* (aired November 19, 1993).

Pincus has won various awards for his work, including a Pulitzer for National Reporting in 2001, which he shared with four other *Post* reporters for stories about Osama bin Laden. He also won a George Polk Award in 1977 for his stories exposing the neutron warhead and a 1961 Page One Award for magazine reporting in the *Reporter*. In broadcasting, Pincus garnered an Emmy for writing one hour of the 1981 CBS News documentary series *Defense of the United States*.

He began his journalism career as a copyboy for the *New York Times* before being drafted into the US Army in 1955, where he served in the Counterintelligence Corps in Washington until 1957. He then worked for various newspapers, including the *Wall Street Journal*, until arriving at the *Washington Post* in 1966. Pincus left the *Post* in 1972 to become executive editor of the *New Republic*, where he covered the Watergate Senate hearings and trial. During that time, he also wrote op-ed pieces for the *Post*. He returned to the paper in 1975.

In the course of his career, Pincus took two eighteen-month sabbaticals to direct investigations for the Senate Foreign Relations Committee under Senator William Fulbright. The first investigation was in 1962, when he looked into foreign government lobbying. His investigation led to a revision of the Foreign Agents Registration Act. Pincus conducted a second investigation in 1969, examining US military and security commitments abroad and their effect on US foreign policy. This led to a series of limiting amendments on defense appropriations bills that culminated in the Hatfield-McGovern legislation to end the Vietnam War.

Pincus has taught a seminar in government oversight at Yale (1988) and Stanford (2003, 2004, 2005) universities and consults for the Washington Post Company (the *Post*'s parent company), exploring joint editorial projects with other media outlets in print, electronic journalism, and television.

He received a BA from Yale University in 1954 and a JD from Georgetown University Law Center in May 2001. Pincus is a member of the Council on Foreign Relations.

NOTES

1. An Arabic word meaning "the base," al Qaeda is an international terrorist group headed by a Saudi, Osama bin Laden, which aims to oppose non-Islamic governments with force and violence and seek retribution for force and violence used against Muslims.

2. Secretary of Defense Donald Rumsfeld, then deputy secretary of defense Paul Wolfowitz, then national security advisor "Condi" Condoleezza Rice, and then secretary of state Colin Powell.

3. The article, "Hussein Intensifies Quest for A-bomb Parts," was written on September 7 but came out on September 8, 2002. Written by *New York Times* reporters Judith Miller and Michael R. Godard, it said, "In the last 14 months, Iraq has sought to buy thousands of specially designed aluminum tubes, which American officials believe were intended as components of centrifuges to enrich uranium. . . . The diameter, thickness and other technical specifications of the aluminum tubes had persuaded American intelligence experts that they were meant for Iraq's nuclear program, officials said." On October 3, 2004, *New York Times* reporters David Barstow, William J. Broad, and Jeff Gerth wrote the article "Skewed Intelligence Data in March to War in Iraq," saying that Rice went on CNN on September 8, 2002 (the same day Miller and Godard's article came out), "aware that the government's foremost nuclear experts had concluded that the tubes were most likely not for nuclear weapons at all . . . but probably intended for small artillery rockets."

4. On its Web site, http://www.iaea.org/About/index.html, the International Atomic Energy Agency describes itself as "the world's center of cooperation in the nuclear field. It was set up as the world's 'Atoms for Peace' organization in 1957 within the United Nations family. The Agency works with its Member States and multiple partners worldwide to promote safe, secure and peaceful nuclear technologies." The IAEA is also considered the UN watchdog organization for monitoring nuclear proliferation.

5. On its Web site, the International Institute for Strategic Studies in London bills itself as "the world's leading authority on political military conflict" and is "the primary source of accurate, objective information on international strategic issues for politicians and diplomats, foreign affairs analysts, international business, economists, the military, defence commentators, journalists, academics and the informed public." http://www.iiss.org/.

6. Len Downie Jr. is executive editor of the *Washington Post*. Don Graham is chairman and CEO of the Washington Post Company.

7. Rolf Ekeus, a Swedish diplomat, is the former head of the UN's Iraq inspection team. He was in Iraq from 1991 to 1997.

8. Hans Blix was director general of the International Atomic Energy Agency from 1981 to 1987 and in 2000 was appointed as the head of the UN's Monitoring, Verification and Inspection Commission (UNMOVIC). He was put in charge of overseeing weapons inspections in Iraq in 2002.

9. A Palestinian born in Jordan, Abu Musab al-Zarqawi is believed to have links to al Qaeda and is believed to be, according to a BBC profile, "the main source of kidnappings, bomb attacks and assassination attempts in Iraq." The BBC's profile can be found at http://newsvote.bbc.co.uk/mpapps/pagetools/print/news.bbc.co.uk/2/hi/middle_east/3483089.stm.

10. *Washington Post* editor and staff writer Robert "Bob" Upshur Woodward has been one of the best-known journalists in the United States ever since the early 1970s when he and former *Washington Post* reporter Carl Bernstein uncovered the Watergate scandal, which involved members of President Nixon's Committee to Re-Elect the President burglarizing and attempting to wiretap Democratic Party headquarters located in a building complex in Washington called Watergate. Woodward and Bernstein's investigation eventually led to President Nixon's resignation.

11. A British-educated former banker, Ahmed Chalabi has been the leader of the anti-Saddam Iraqi National Congress. He received large sums of money from the US government for his activities and was a source of faulty prewar intelligence. In an e-mail to her *New York Times* colleague, war correspondent John Burns, Miller wrote that Chalabi had "provided most of the front-page exclusives on WMD to our paper."

12. Idaho senator Frank Church was in charge of the Senate Select Committee to Study Governmental Operations with Respect to Intelligence Activities, which investigated America's intelligence agencies post-Watergate. The committee arrived at this conclusion: "In its consideration of covert action, the Committee was struck by the basic tension—if not incompatibility—of covert operations and the demands of a constitutional system. Secrecy is essential to covert operations; secrecy can, however, become a source of power, a barrier to serious policy debate within the government, and a means of circumventing established checks and procedures of government. The Committee found that secrecy and compartmentalization contributed to a temptation on the part of the Executive to resort to covert operations in order to avoid bureaucratic, congressional and public debate." The committee released fourteen reports in 1975 and 1976. The Church Committee reports are posted on the Web site of the Assassination Archives and Research Center. http://www.aarclibrary.org/publib/church/contents.htm.

13. Les Aspin was an eleven-term congressman from Wisconsin and served briefly as secretary of defense in 1993–1994 in the Clinton administration. Aspin resigned in February 1994, citing personal reasons, and was replaced by his deputy secretary of defense, William J. Perry. Perry served as secretary of defense from February 1994 to January

1997. John Deutch served as CIA director under President Clinton from May 1995 to December 1996 and after his departure was embroiled in a controversy having to do with classified materials being kept at his home and on his computer.

14. According to his biography on George Washington University's Web site, http://home.gwu.edu/~esialsf/biography.html, Fuerth spent twelve years in the foreign service and "became a known resource for strategic intelligence (chemical, biological, radiological and nuclear weapons); arms control; Society and Warsaw pact affairs; and NATO," and "was responsible to Senator Gore for all aspects of national security, including international trade."

15. In the PATRIOT Act of 2001, its purpose is stated as "to deter and punish terrorist acts in the United States and around the world, to enhance law enforcement investigatory tools, and for other purposes." The act has been criticized for, among other things, curbing civil liberties and citizens' rights to privacy. The act can be read at http://www.epic.org/privacy/terrorism/hr3162.html.

16. Senator John Kerry from Massachusetts ran as the Democratic Party's candidate against George Bush in the 2004 election and lost.

17. The Intelligence Reform and Terrorism Prevention Act was passed in December 2004. The bill can be read at http://www.c-span.org/pdf/s2845confrept.pdf.

18. In his January 23, 2005, article "Secret Unit Expands Rumsfeld's Domain," Barton Gellman of the *Washington Post* wrote: "The Pentagon, expanding into the CIA's historic bailiwick, has created a new espionage arm and is reinterpreting US law to give Defense Secretary Donald H. Rumsfeld broad authority over clandestine operations abroad. . . . The previously undisclosed organization, called the Strategic Support Branch, arose from Rumsfeld's written order to end his 'near total dependence on CIA' for what is known as human intelligence. Designed to operate without detection and under the defense secretary's direct control, the Strategic Support Branch deploys small teams of case officers, linguists, interrogators and technical specialists alongside newly empowered operations forces."

19. H. R. Haldeman was President Nixon's chief of staff. John Ehrlichman was Nixon's assistant for domestic affairs.

20. During his tenure (1945–1974) as a senator, J. William Fulbright became one of the most influential members of the Senate. According to his biography on the State Department's Web site, http://exchanges.state.gov/education/fulbright/fulbbio.htm, Fulbright passed legislation establishing the Fulbright Program via legislation in 1946 and since then, "this program has had extraordinary impact around the world. There have been more than 250,000 Fulbright grantees and many of them have made significant contributions within their countries as well as to the overall goal of advancing mutual understanding." Fulbright was the longest-serving (1959–1974) chairman of the Senate Foreign Relations Committee in history.

21. Former deputy secretary of defense (now head of the World Bank) Paul Wolfowitz is viewed as a neoconservative or "neocon." An explanatory column titled "Neocon 101" in the *Christian Science Monitor* provides information on neoconservative thought: "Neocons believe that the United States should not be ashamed to use its unrivaled power—forcefully if necessary—to promote its values around the world. . . . Neoconservatives believe modern threats facing the US can no longer be reliably contained and therefore must be prevented, sometimes through preemptive military action. . . . Most neocons share unwavering support for Israel, which they see as crucial to US military suf-

ficiency in a volatile region. . . . The original neocons were a group of mostly Jewish liberal intellectuals who, in the 1960s and 70s, grew disenchanted with what they saw as the American left's social excesses and reluctance to spend adequately on defense." http://www.csmonitor.com/specials/neocon/neocon101.html.

22. According to a BBC profile, Ayman al-Zawahiri is "an eye surgeon who helped found the Egyptian Islamic Jihad militant group, is often referred to as Osama bin Laden's right hand man and the chief idealogue of al Qaeda," and some experts believe that he was "the operational brains behind" 9/11. The BBC profile can be found at http://news.bbc.co.uk/1/hi/world/middle_east/1560834.stm.

23. Dr. Wen Ho Lee is a Chinese American computer scientist who was working at the government's Los Alamos Nuclear Laboratories when he was arrested in 1999 and charged with stealing secrets about America's nuclear arsenal for China. He was released in August 2000 after accepting a plea bargain and pleading to one count of downloading classified data. The other fifty-eight counts of illegal downloading were dropped, and the judge presiding over his case apologized for keeping him in jail for nine months.

24. A *Washington Post* profile of the Kurds at http://www.washingtonpost.com/wp-srv/inatl/daily/feb99/kurdprofile.htm describes them as fifteen to twenty million "largely Sunni Muslims with their own language and culture living in the generally contiguous areas of Turkey, Iraq, Iran, Armenia and Syria" collectively called Kurdistan. The Kurds seek their own state and have clashed with the nations in which their territories lie, including Iraq. In 1988 the Iraqis launched a poison gas attack on the town of Hallabjah and killed five thousand people.

25. Yasir Arafat was cofounder and chairman of the Palestine Liberation Organization until his death in 2004.

26. On March 1, 2005, Defense Secretary Rumsfeld signed the National Defense Strategy. In his March 22, 2005, *Washington Post* article, "Predator to See More Combat," Pincus reports that "the strategy calls for denying sanctuary to enemies such as terrorist groups in ungoverned territories within otherwise sovereign countries anywhere in the world." Pincus quotes Rumsfeld as saying that "a key goal" of the strategy program "is developing the capability to surge military forces rapidly from strategic distances to deny adversaries sanctuary," which would require "a number of capabilities, including persistent surveillance and precision strikes."

27. Terri Schiavo was a Florida woman declared by doctors to be in a persistent vegetative state and was at the center of a legal and moral battle surrounding the removal of a feeding tube that was keeping her alive. Eventually the courts allowed her husband to have the tube removed against the wishes of Schiavo's parents.

28. This reference to Columbine has to do with a massacre that occurred on Tuesday, April 20, 1999, when two students attending Columbine High School in Littleton, Colorado—Eric Harris and Dylan Klebold—went on a shooting rampage and killed twelve students and a teacher before killing themselves. It was the second-deadliest attack on a school in US history.

29. On March 21, 2005, sixteen-year-old Jeffrey Weise, a student at Red Lake High School in Red Lake, Minnesota, shot and killed his grandfather and his grandfather's girlfriend before going to school and killing a school security guard, a teacher, five students, and, finally, himself.

30. David S. Broder, who is nationally known for his reporting on politics, is a columnist for the *Washington Post*.

31. Halliburton is "one of the world's largest providers of products and services to the oil and gas industries." http://www.halliburton.com/. It is the largest recipient of contracts awarded for postwar work in Afghanistan and Iraq, according to Center for Public Integrity reporters Andre Verloy and Daniel Politi in their August 18, 2004, article "Halliburton Contracts Balloon." Halliburton, "where Vice President Dick Cheney served as CEO from 1995 to 2000, has come under increased scrutiny because of allegations of overcharging on food service and fuel distribution contracts, poor management and close ties to the administration." http://www.publicintegrity.org/wow/report.aspx?aid=366 &sid=100.

SOUND BITE'S TRUTH

DAVID MARTIN
National Security
Correspondent,
CBS News
Interviewed March 2005

Kelly O'Meara

David Martin works in the now very defensive Defense Department, so getting to his office in the Pentagon isn't easy. First, there's a long walk across a huge parking lot, up some stairs, across a bridge, and to the building. There are cameras everywhere and the way is dotted with gate-keepers. Inside the building, more gatekeepers check your two forms of ID and call the person you came to see.

Martin is a tall, slender man with a chiseled jaw and a cropped, camera-ready haircut who looks like the network correspondent that he is. He could, however, just as easily pass for one of the myriad military officers around him. He introduced himself in a soft southern accent and led the way to his office. We crossed the expansive Pentagon courtyard, went down hallways, then back outside and across an alley, up stairs, around corners, and down more hallways. Finally, we found ourselves in front of his door. I was taken aback when he opened it. David's office is a small, narrow, windowless room that, amazingly enough, also doubles as a tiny TV studio. On the wall facing the door is the background you see behind him from time to time when he's on TV. There's a chair against that wall in which he can sit while a camera on a moveable metal arm that juts out in front of the chair records him. On the left side of the room, his cluttered desk looks like a counter that comes out of the wall.

As massive as the Pentagon is on the outside, inside it feels labyrinthine and hypercompartmentalized. There's an overwhelming sterility and inwardness to the place. It struck me that the reporting challenges Martin faces, particularly post-9/11, mirror these qualities. He has to keep secrets while exposing others, and he has to know which to do when, because lives could be at stake. He gets stories, he told us, by strategically wandering the halls and dropping in on people. He's been doing that for eighteen years now, and he freely admits that some might perceive from time to time that he is too close to the people he covers. He certainly knows them well enough to know what they're thinking and to get their secrets out of them. And like some of them, he has to avoid the pitfall of getting the facts right but the analysis wrong. "The lesson is that you can never be sure of what you think is the case," he said, "and you just need to be more disbelieving." To live in a constant state of intellectual uncertainty is a survival skill for a journalist covering national security issues. It requires a great deal of psychological fortitude, brains, and uncompromising honesty. Clearly, Martin has all of those. And while there's no doubt that living among his sources, especially for so long, is a very delicate situation journalistically speaking, he handles it well. Ever mindful of his situation, Martin subjects everything he presents to the public to a process of exacting scrutiny. Sometimes the process requires that he wrestle at length with just one word, even though ultimately it may not make one whit of difference. Such is the case with what he referred to at one point in his interview as the "goddamned sound bites."

"It's either the sound bite or the picture that registers with people," he said, "not the reporter's narration. I sometimes wonder why I sit here and worry about whether I should use 'would' or 'could' or 'might' or 'may' in my script, because that's not what registers." Martin talked about writing "circumstantial evidence" and "no smoking gun" in his reports on Defense

Secretary Rumsfeld and Vice President Cheney claiming that Saddam Hussein could imminently possess WMDs. But all the audience seemed to see and hear were Cheney's and Rumsfeld's sound bites, not the narration that disputed what they said. This, he pointed out, is how the sound bite can undermine a television reporter's efforts to convey the truth.

Even two people in Martin's office is a crowd, but we settled in and he started talking about the immediate aftermath of 9/11. He talked about the smoke and body bags in the courtyard we'd just crossed and how that led to Afghanistan. Sitting in that airless office at Ground Zero Washington and listening to David's words, I suddenly felt like I understood the place a little bit better. I also felt the weight of Martin's responsibilities toward the millions who watch the results of his work.

I have pulled a ball of string straight to your office because a number of people have said that national security reporting was the key area of reporting post-9/11 and before the war. So talk to me about what you were reporting right after 9/11.

The immediate aftermath was a whodunit. It became known pretty quickly that al Qaeda[1] was responsible, and then there was the whole issue of some of these guys having been on watchlists, or some guys not having been on watchlists who should have been on watchlists. Some of these people were known to the FBI and the CIA.

Then there was the whole issue of the response of the air defense system. That consumed us, along with just counting the bodies. It was days before we knew how many people were dead here in the Pentagon. The courtyard that we just walked through to get to my office for this interview had body bags in it. It was really like a war zone, and the place just stank of smoke. At the same time there was the issue of retaliation and what we were going to do. It was obvious that we were going to do something and we were going to do it soon and we were going to do it in Afghanistan. Then began the game that I've played in God knows how many crises, of monitoring movements; ship movements, troop movements, and so on, which was made more difficult this time by the fact that a lot of it was secret because the first people that were moving were special operations forces and they are harder to find out about.

We started bombing October 7. By then we had special operations forces in Kazakhstan where we had a secret base. There were more forces in Pakistan, a whole bunch on Oman, and guys on carriers. But the first units that went in were these Special Forces A-teams, just very small units, and it wasn't until January of 2002 that I actually found out how that played out and how many times they had tried to get in and were stopped by bad weather.

Of course, troops on the ground was a sensitive issue because they were out there in small numbers and not very well protected. There were lots of false reports about what was going on in terms of the search for Osama bin Laden. Jack Kelly for *USA Today* had this one story and the dateline was in Pakistan and he was saying special operations forces were already on the ground hunting for bin Laden and it just wasn't true. I spent my whole day checking into his story, and of course the implication from my bosses was that if I couldn't confirm it, I must not have good sources, so stuff like that can get pretty annoying. But in all these military operations things move so rapidly that yesterday's crisis is quickly forgotten and you're on to the next thing.

During the Afghanistan operation, we were doing live stuff all the time, including hourly updates, so it was really quite crazed until the Taliban[2] fell. But after eighteen years of covering this place, I knew who to go to, I knew who to talk to, they knew me, and they knew that if they told me stuff that I wasn't going to report anything that was going to get somebody killed. It was just a very intense time and it went on like that until December. December was when we had this abortive attempt to get bin Laden in Tora Bora.

What's happened to the whole bin Laden search from the Pentagon's perspective?

They're still working hard at it. God knows what they're doing. The hunt for bin Laden goes on, but he's just gone underground and the area that he can be in is so vast.

Our Pakistani friends aren't helping us that much?

I think they are, but . . .

You don't think they're caught between a rock and a hard place?

They obviously could do more, but they're probably doing as much as they can politically. I haven't heard too many people who really know what the Pakistanis are doing complain about them. There are some complaints about, "You can't do anything in the Pakistani military without it leaking" and who's loyal, and so on, but that's not a lack of will on the Pakistani government's part, that's just a reflection of that society, which is so split. Some people in their military intelligence services are more loyal to bin Laden than they are to their own government. You've just got to work with that. But since Tora Bora, I don't think we've had a real clue as to where bin Laden is. The Pakistan-Afghanistan border area is huge.

Is that a lack of good field intelligence, good human intelligence?

It's a lack of having an agent inside Osama bin Laden's inner cell, but that's not realistic. Think about it. The only way that you would get a guy into bin Laden's circle is if you turned him. You couldn't insert somebody into that, you'd have to turn them, and to turn somebody, you have to have access to that person. If you were going to turn bin Laden's number two man, Ayman al-Zawahiri, you'd have to get to him first. If you were to turn one of his bodyguards, you'd have to get to the bodyguard, and we just don't have physical access there.

I have no doubt that we're using as agents bona fide Muslims of Arab heritage who speak the language perfectly and all that, but bin Laden knows we're doing that, so just because you're a good Muslim doesn't mean that you can get in the inner circle.

Talk about the prewar era. From where you were sitting, when did you see the attention veer toward Iraq, and what were you reporting at the time?

Right away, at the first weekend meeting up at Camp David after 9/11, Deputy Defense Secretary Paul Wolfowitz, in particular, was saying, "We've got to hit them both." Then I think the president, or certainly somebody really authoritative, came out and said, "No, we've decided we're going after al Qaeda." That all happened, it seems to me, within two weeks of 9/11. So Iraq was forgotten until after the fall of the Taliban. Then, beginning in the spring of 2002, you started hearing about Iraq.

What was your first impression when you heard that?

What did I know then? I'm trying to remember when reports of 9/11 hijacker Muhammad Atta allegedly meeting with the Iraqi intelligence officer in Prague came on my radar. It had to have been known, or at least reported, in the fall of 2001. So I remember thinking, "If that's true, that's a pretty good smoking gun."

I don't think it was true.

I don't think it was true, either. But you didn't know that then, and if it had been true, it would not have been illogical to think that Saddam was connected to 9/11 and to go after him. There was a school of thought that said that bin Laden couldn't have pulled off 9/11 without a state sponsor because it was too sophisticated an operation. Almost from day one, Defense Secretary Rumsfeld was talking about going after governments that support terrorist groups. He was talking about the Taliban, but the same logic could have applied to Iraq if there had been proof of a link to al Qaeda. That, too, made sense at the time. Now we know that al Qaeda was much more sophisticated than we ever gave them credit for and that we were much more incompetent than we imagined we could have been.

Why would we connect Saddam Hussein to bin Laden, a guy he publicly hated?

It didn't make sense on the face of it, but he could have used it as a cover: "the enemy of my enemy is my friend." You can come up with all sorts of rationales. You could preach it flat or round, but the point was, was there evidence? The two pieces of evidence were the early-on belief that this was the kind of operation that only a state could have put together and the meeting with the Iraqi intelligence guy in Prague. On this whole intelligence business, I talked to lots of people, but I basically had two sources who saw all the intelligence and who would talk to me. Neither of them put much stock in that meeting in Prague. They said, "We have no confirmation of it. It's true that we got this report and it's true that the Iraqi intelligence chief was under surveillance, but we can't confirm it."

Did you report that at the time?

I think so, yes. I haven't had to go through what *New York Times* reporter Judy Miller went through with people dissecting each and every one of my stories, so I don't have as good a recall as I probably should have on all these stories. But the al Qaeda connection to Iraq and to 9/11 was never very strong. It was never very strong in the minds of people I was talking to, which obviously didn't include Vice President Dick Cheney. So to me, it was always WMD that was the reason you could use to go to war with Iraq. And that's the question for which I still don't have a good answer. The US government was wrong. US intelligence was just flat-out wrong. It wasn't a product of the administration telling the intelligence community the answer it wanted, because the intelligence community had given the Clinton administration the same answer. The National Intelligence Estimate of October 2002,[3] which was the basic document about the chemical, biological, and nuclear weapons in Iraq, had not changed in any substantive way from the intelligence that the Clinton administration was getting. The Clinton administration believed that Saddam had weapons, not that he was working on them but that he had large stockpiles of them.

> **Then why did Powell say in February 2001 that Saddam was contained and "unable to project conventional power against his neighbors" and that he wasn't a threat to the United States?**

The difference is 9/11. You can never prove this, but I think there had to be among the top ranks of the administration an attitude of "Never again on our watch."

> **I still don't understand how "never again on our watch" pointed to Iraq. We addressed it logically initially by going after al Qaeda in Afghanistan, but after that Iraq was a stretch. You were talking about intelligence failure, but I've spoken to other national security reporters who were talking to midlevel intelligence analysts who were telling them, "We don't have any hard evidence that this guy is connected to al Qaeda or that he has WMDs." And then there's this whole business of the Office of Special Plans[4] cherry-picking intelligence to help make the case for war.**

This is my personal opinion about the Office of Special Plans. It is bureaucratically impossible for a small office of three or four guys who on a personal level were distrusted and even detested by the rest of the intelligence community for being neocons to affect a National Intelligence Estimate. They had no role in it. That National Intelligence Estimate had nothing to do with the Office of Special Plans. That was the judgment of the bona fide, real intelligence community. The Office of Special Plans gave talking points to people like Cheney and to any senior official in the Pentagon who would be meeting with a senior official from another country, and those talking points were cherry-picked intelligence, but that's not what took this country to war. Read the Senate Intelligence Committee's report[5] and Charles Duelfer's [director of central intelligence special adviser for strategy regarding Iraq weapons of mass destruction programs] report[6] on the hunt for weapons of mass destruction. Duelfer knows the Iraqis and their weapons programs better than any other human being. Then you need to read the 9/11 Commission's report. Of course, these are all done now and they weren't available before the war, but what the Senate intelligence committee said was that the entire intelligence community fell victim to groupthink. Groupthink apparently is a recognized psychological term.[7] A

Yale social psychologist named Irving Janis actually coined it, and there are papers and monographs on it. The groupthink in this case was, "We know he had them. Everybody agrees he had them. He hasn't proven that he destroyed them all," which is true; he never did prove it. The groupthink also was, "He always was in violation of those UN resolutions and why on earth would he risk his reign and not cooperate with the UN unless he were really hiding these things?"

Where is the connection to 9/11?

The connection to 9/11 is the risk of chemical, biological, and nuclear weapons in the hands of terrorists. That was the rationale. You can buy it or not, but if you believe that Saddam Hussein really has chemical and biological weapons, and is working on a nuclear weapon, then Iraq is a logical target. Everybody who mattered in this government—and sure, you could find an intelligence officer or an analyst someplace who doubted it—but everybody who mattered in this administration and in the Clinton administration believed that.

So you don't think that the Project for a New American Century[8] and "Clean Break"[9] documents had anything to do with the decision-making process involved in getting us to Iraq?

"Clean Break" document, what's that?

"A Clean Break: A New Strategy for Securing the Realm" was a document that Richard Perle and David Wurmser and Douglas Feith had handed over to Benjamin Netanyahu when he was prime minister of Israel. The document outlined a plan to take control of other countries in the Middle East to make sure they had governments friendly to Israel. Netanyahu rejected it. The Project for a New American Century basically expresses the same idea about the need to control the Middle East. Does the whole neocon foreign policy theory have any coinage with you at all in terms of fitting in to a plan to get to Iraq?

Not really. I never saw any evidence that Richard Perle had any determining effect on US policy. He just wasn't in a position to do so. I have heard the people who made the decisions, and I'd tell you who except it was off the record, but they were the absolute key people, and what they talked about was the risk of having a state like Iraq and a dictator like Saddam Hussein who had a long track record of supporting terrorist groups, not necessarily al Qaeda, but all the Palestinian groups. At that time, he was paying $25,000 to the family of every suicide bomber in Palestine.

It's a long jump from paying suicide bombers in Palestine to being a threat to the United States.

Saddam has this track record of support for terrorist organizations. The evidence on an al Qaeda connection is not convincing and I never heard a decision maker other than Cheney sound like he found it convincing, but it's the old "You don't know what you don't know." So what is the risk of allowing him to sit there in Iraq with chemical and biological weapons while he's working on nuclear weapons? That's what the intelligence told Rumsfeld he was doing. A guy like Rumsfeld can't go and investigate it for himself, he's got to take the word of the intelligence community, which is spending all those billions and billions of dollars on satellites and analysts and everything else. They were telling him that this guy had those weapons of mass destruction. So the issue was risk, and the question was: What is the risk of allowing this guy to have those weapons and what is the possibility that he would give a weapon to a terrorist group?

I just want to reconfirm what you said; you said the CIA was basically telling him that he did have these weapons.

Yes, that's what the National Intelligence Estimate of October 2002 was telling the president. The NIE is a formal product of the entire intelligence community, the National Security Agency [NSA],[10] the Defense Intelligence Agency [DIA],[11] the Central Intelligence Agency [CIA],[12] and the National Reconnaissance Office [NRO].[13] Then you had George Tenet telling the president that making the case for WMDs in Iraq was "a slam dunk."

How could they have been so wrong?

Read that Senate Intelligence Committee report and Duelfer's report; they explain it to you. The most interesting thing is what Duelfer determined, which is the piece that made all the evidence fall together about weapons of mass destruction. Duelfer posed the question: "Why would Saddam Hussein be risking everything and defying the world if he wasn't hiding them?" The United States was saying in no uncertain terms that if he didn't get rid of those weapons there was going to be a regime change. The president said that in a way in which he could not possibly back down.

Yes, but there were people on the ground all over the place looking for those things and they couldn't find them.

Until you've been exposed to actually trying to find it, that always seems simple. It's like finding bin Laden in Tora Bora. When you go there, you see how hard it really is. The fact that the inspectors couldn't find them—and remember all the stuff that the Iraqis were doing to interfere with the work of the inspectors—that just made the case, "He is hiding something, he is hiding something."

So it's the motive issue that made them believe that then. They felt that his motive for not being forthcoming was that he was hiding them.

The motive went with this vast body of evidence that they had, like the failure to account for all the stuff that had supposedly been destroyed and the arithmetic on how many Scuds the Soviet Union had sold him when they were still allies and how many had been shot off in the Iran-Iraq war and how many were left.

What about the Israelis? They're right there, their butts are on the line, basically, so they're pretty vigilant. Were they helping with the intelligence? Certainly when they saw the Osirak nuclear reactor being built near Baghdad in 1981; they bombed it.

I don't know. I don't remember seeing any reference to any intelligence that came from the Israelis that put us over the top. A lot of the intelligence came from services for countries that were opposed to going to war. The defector who described these mobile biological weapons was in the hands of the Germans.

That was "Curveball."[14] **He was lying, too.**

The Germans told us he had passed a polygraph. But to get back to Duelfer for a minute, what he found was that Saddam did not want to admit to the Iranians that he didn't have any WMDs, because he was afraid of Iran. He was more afraid of Iran than he was of the United States. He couldn't believe that the United States would invade him. Why he couldn't believe that is beyond me, particularly after Bush went to the UN in September 2002 and made statements like "He's got to get rid of them or else." Presidents just don't make those statements and then back off of them. Bush would have had no credibility if he had done that. As it turns out, he suffered a different credibility problem because the intelligence turned out to be wrong.

Do you think Powell believed what he was saying when he did his UN presentation?

I think Powell is a really interesting case. He could not have gone out to the CIA the weekend before it had been announced to the world that he would be making this speech and take a look at the evidence and say, "Oh, Mr. President, we don't have it. We can't give a speech. I'm not going to the UN with this crap." I don't know that that happened, but just imagine that situation. It's unthinkable that at that point he could have gone out there, looked at the intelligence, and said, "Oh, never mind." But Powell didn't doubt that the Iraqis had WMDs. He was not against going to war. You can check with him, but I know this. His position was that we didn't have to be in such a hurry. We didn't have to go in March of 2003. "Let's go another extra mile on inspections and give Saddam another yard of rope to hang himself with and then we'll get a coalition and we'll do it. If we're going to do this, let's do it right." That was his position.

He lost that argument, but he was not against going to war. All he was against was the timing. And he's a soldier, so he saluted his commander in chief and he said, "OK, we'll do it this way." So he went to the UN, and I assume that his mind-set was, "We're committed to doing this, there's no way we can back out of my giving this speech, so I've got to make the best case from what they give me." Then the whole issue was, "How do we keep this speech from being polluted by the stuff that Douglas Feith[15] has been telling the vice president and that the vice president has been trying to put into this speech? So it was a constant paring down of some of the wilder charges like the connection between Saddam and 9/11.

But he had those visuals of those bogus mobile biological weapons vans.

The communications intercepts on those were real; they just were based on a false premise. All those intercepts were evidence that confirmed what everybody already thought they knew, "He's got them." They never went back and reexamined their initial assumptions about Saddam having weapons. They were always building around that, adding evidence and casting out some of the driftier stuff. So Powell went out there, and I think he was badly served by Tenet, because Tenet had the ability to find out more, for instance, on the mobile weapons lab. Again, in the Senate intelligence committee report there's a long chapter and verse on the access to Curveball, the defector who was providing information on the mobile lab. The CIA analyst never made a decent firsthand assessment of him. Powell has said since that some of the sourcing on the information that he was given was bad. Well, that's George Tenet's responsibility.

I think that's why George Tenet was sitting right behind Powell during the UN presentation. Powell was basically telling the world that the

information he was presenting came from "My CIA man Tenet who is sitting right behind me."

People have an unrealistic view of how much we really know. They've seen too many Tom Clancy movies where the satellite goes over and takes a picture of what's going on inside a tent. That just doesn't happen. In the first place, the satellite can go over the same place on the earth twice a day and you've got to be lucky to catch something happening. Then you've got to have a long historical observation of that place to know how what you're seeing now is different from what you've seen before. It's much more difficult than people realize. But that doesn't excuse anybody in the intelligence community from making the wrong judgment.

I'm an American who was reared in a foreign country and I can tell you one thing: often these agencies send their people to foreign countries and they stick out like sore thumbs. They can't speak the language, they've got the blond hair and the blue eyes, and they don't try to mix with the locals.

I know.

Don't you think that's a big hole in the information-gathering department?

We're terrible at understanding other countries, and I think it is just an American arrogance: "Hey, you've got to learn to speak like us and you'd be better off if you looked like us." I just think that ripples through the culture. If you're American, to get ahead in the world, there's no real need to speak Arabic.

How big a threat do you think al Qaeda is now according to your sources and to your reporting?

Al Qaeda would if it could, but I don't think it has the wherewithal to mount anything approximating 9/11.

I want to talk to you about that Rumsfeld memo and how you got it and what you thought when you got it.

We were doing a one-year anniversary piece on 9/11, so I was just trying to do a tick-tock of that day. We were going around interviewing Rumsfeld's security agents who had gone outside with him to where the airplane had gone into the side of the Pentagon. I was trying to get the time line right and I was talking to somebody and this person was very busy and said, "Oh, here are these notes. You can use these." And so I went away with the notes.

This person's purpose was to help me establish a time line, not to put me on to the fact that the administration had been talking about hitting Iraq from moment one. This person was just trying to give me the time line of when Tenet called with the information about the al Qaeda connection and what they knew about the last plane as it went down and the orders to shoot it down and all that. I took the notes back to my office and I sat there reading them, and I saw: "Judge whether good enough to hit SH [Saddam Hussein] at same time. Not only UBL [Usama bin Laden]." I also saw: "Go Massive. Sweep it all up. Things related and not." This was September 2002 and we were already doing stories about the push to war, and so to me, the genesis of it was right there in those notes.

So this supported the reasoning of "Find a way to connect 9/11 to Saddam because he supports terrorists and has WMDs"?

I put everything useful out of those notes in the stories that I did, but it wasn't that clear-cut. This was more of a conviction that we were going to hit Saddam Hussein. If what you're asking me is did I think, "Oh, now I see why they're ginning up all this false intelligence," my answer is no because I was like everybody else, I had no reason to doubt the intelligence. Those two guys I told you that I was talking to, both of them said, and I put this in numerous scripts, "We've got no smoking gun. We've got no smoking gun, we've got no smoking gun, but the circumstantial evidence is overwhelming." That was the tenor of my reporting all along; circumstantial evidence, circumstantial evidence, circumstantial evidence. I don't know if I got "no smoking gun" into every single script, but I got it into most. I don't view that as anything to absolve me for not having broken the code on the fact that the intelligence was faulty. The question I have and I'm sure every reporter has is, What could we have done? Could we have gotten that right? The government wasn't lying to us. Put some of the stuff that Cheney was saying aside, because that was for domestic consumption, that wasn't intelligence. What Cheney was saying might have had a lot to do with the widespread belief that Iraq had a role in 9/11. But it didn't have any effect on me. I'm sure I used some of the sound bites of Cheney saying these things, but it did not have an effect on my thinking. My thinking was based on the false assumption that forty billion dollars of intelligence buys you good information and it didn't.

Is that what your experience tells you, that all that fancy equipment isn't as useful as it is expensive?

Well, it's a mixed record. All that fancy equipment did not help us one bit on things like the Iranian revolution,[16] which we totally misjudged, but the shah of Iran misjudged that too. It did not give us meaningful predictions on the collapse of the Soviet Union. Gorbachev[17] was surprised by the collapse of the Soviet Union.

But when it came to things like the Soviet buildup outside Afghanistan in December of 1979, they were all over that. When it came to the buildup just north of Kuwait before the 1990 invasion of Kuwait, they were all over that. They didn't believe Saddam was going to invade, but they could have told you chapter and verse on what Iraqi tank brigades where lined up on the border across from Kuwait. But they did misjudge Saddam's intentions. And you're always wrong about intentions. When you change administrations, you change consumers of intelligence. The same intelligence hits a different group of people differently, and it hit this group of people after 9/11 when everything in their worldview had changed.

In 1999 Rumsfeld headed up a commission that was looking into the threat posed by ballistic missiles. It was a setup job by Newt Gingrich[18] to come up with a justification for ballistic missile defense. But the trouble was, we didn't have the intelligence to say that we were in imminent danger of North Korea launching an ICBM at us. So Rumsfeld wrote this report that he got everybody to sign off on, including physicist Richard Garwin,[19] who is arguably one of the smartest people in America and an unremitting opponent of ballistic missile defense. The report basically said that you don't know what you don't know, that you can't be sure about CIA estimates on how many years away Korea or Iran are from having nuclear weapons, that the chance of surprise is great, and that you can't bet the farm on anything because of the history of strategic surprise. Rumsfeld and Wolfowitz's example of strategic surprise is that in Cheney's confirmation hearings for secretary of defense, the word "Iraq" was never mentioned, and then of course, we wound up going to war with Iraq. Rumsfeld came in as secretary of defense believing in surprise and in the need to hedge your bets against surprise. Then he gets hit by the biggest surprise of all, 9/11.

To me, this is all just so psychologically coherent and understandable, and does not have to be nefarious in the least. It doesn't have to be neocons plotting to take over the world. On the other hand, I'm sure somebody could turn around and tell you that I've been brainwashed by the Pentagon, that I've taken on the values of the institution that I cover.

What matters to me about what you're saying is that you're accurately reflecting what these people were carrying around in their heads, because that's what they acted on.

I don't believe that guys like Bart Gellman and Walter Pincus[20] are telling you that "those sons of bitches at the intelligence agency were making this stuff up and they were just lying to us to take the country to war." I can't believe that.

That's not what they were saying. Bart is interesting because he sees himself basically as an accountability holder. He doesn't think it would have been possible to get a really clear picture of what was going on within the administration and the intelligence agencies before the war, but he does think it's important to keep working on bringing it into better focus afterward for purposes of accountability.

Yes, he comes down and shoots the wounded. I don't mean for that to sound disparaging, because nobody does it better. He is terrific at circling back and doing that, he really is.

What do you think of Walter Pincus?

Walter's great. Walter's the great contrarian. He believes that newspapers are in business to make trouble.

What about you?

I want to scare the hell out of them with what I know and with the consequences of misleading me. That's what I want to do.

Have they misled you at any time?

Deliberately? I've been lied to, told "black is white," once and that was in 1980. I still worked for *Newsweek*, and it was the day of the Iran rescue mission and there was a rumor going around that there was a rescue mission in progress. I called the director of the joint staff, a three-star admiral who worked directly for the chairman of the Joint Chiefs. And I said, "Hey, Thor, is there a rescue mission going on?" He said, "No." In the next room, he could listen to the communications from Desert One.[21] He just flat-out lied to me. The next day, he called me back and apologized. I told him, "If you knew you couldn't talk to me, why did you take the call? And he said, "I was afraid if I didn't take the call, you would think something was up." That's the only time I've been flat-out lied to. There's lots of time I've been given bad information, because bad information comes into this building. When we shot down that Iranian airliner, the original story was that we'd shot down an Iranian F-14. That was all wrong, but that was what was being reported to this building. Nobody was lying to me; it was just garbage in, garbage out.

What about secrecy; do you think there's more secrecy here now? Is it harder to report from here?

I have a hard time answering that question because the longer you do this kind of reporting, the better you get at figuring out how to get the secrets. So if I'm still getting the secrets that I need to know about what's going on, are they at the same time getting better, or am I just getting smarter about how to find them out? I don't have a good take on that.

It is relatively easy to find out information up to stuff that is classified secret. Top secret and above gets a little harder. But most of the top-secret stuff you wouldn't report if you knew it anyway. You don't want to get people hurt and you don't want to compromise national security.

Walter says the government is getting a lot better at keeping secrets from the press. He says their PR spinning and manipulation machine has evolved much faster than the reporters.

That is a totally different issue from secrecy. The government has gotten so good at staying on message.

Is it just staying on message though?

Well, message is spin.

Isn't there some lying going on?

Spin, spin, spin.

What is spin?

Spin is telling the truth without being honest. The reason there is spin is because there's no percentage in putting out factually inaccurate information. You get hammered if you do that. Look at what happened to Bush when he put the inaccurate statement about the Nigerian uranium into his State of the Union address. So instead of lying outright, you put out truthful information that supports your side of the story. That's what spin is. You're not being honest, because that's not the whole situation and you know it's not the whole situation, but it's the truth. It's factually correct and that is what they have gotten so very good at. The people that come into government are smart. They work ungodly hours and it depends on the administration whether they're disciplined or not. This administration is disciplined. So this administration is very good at spin, and I have said before in public that, most days, they have our lunch. That's where we're losing.

How can we fix that?

How do we get better? I have a somewhat different view from Walter's "They're evolving faster than we are." I think in lots of cases, young, inexperienced reporters do the best work because they don't have access. What they lack is judgment, but that's why you have the Ben Bradlees[22] of this world. They also have no respect for the system because it hasn't been stroking them for ten, fifteen, twenty years. They go in and they look at these people who are running the government and who are the same age as their parents who they know are full of crap, and they have no trouble dealing with them.

It was so much easier when you thought the government was lying all the time. If you came of age during Vietnam and Watergate,[23] they were lying all the time, so it was really easy to go for people's throats. Now it's become much more subtle, because government has learned that if you tell a lie, you're going to get hammered. Even if you get away with it in the short run, you're going to end up with a scandal on the scale of Iran-Contra,[24] and half the government is going to have to hire lawyers to defend themselves against perjury. So you just have to have reporters who have not been in the forest for fifteen, twenty years.

The more times you have people come in with a fresh eye, the better. The *Washington Post* used to send guys—Bart Gellman was one of them, Fred Hiatt was another—who looked like they were old enough to drive, but probably not old enough to drink. They would come in and you would watch them learn. It would take them about three or four months to figure out how the Pentagon works and where to go for information, and then they were just spectacular. They wrote great, great stories. They had no particular experience covering national security, but they knew news. I think expertise on a lot of things is overrated. I know military hardware better than most reporters and I know how the Joint Staff works, and I don't know what difference that makes. What makes the difference around here is in my personal dealings with people. I know them, they know me. I've known some people around here for ten years or more. You meet a guy as a captain and one day he's a colonel and the next day he's a gen-eral and you're still here and he's gone up and you've dealt with these guys over the years and you know them. There are guys I use as single sources because I know they've never been wrong, never even remotely hyped anything, so if they tell me something, I go with it. There are other people who are always sort of in the neighborhood on information and I know that I've got to check their stuff out. There are people who have dealt with me who trust me and there are other people who have had bad experiences dealing with me and they don't trust me. Over the years, I've developed this network of relations, and that is an obvious benefit. But at the same time that you're developing that network of relationships, you're losing the ability to see things with a fresh eye, so it's a trade-off.

Talk about the postconquest period and what your sources and your reporting are telling you about that.

Right now, I think everybody is feeling pretty good about the way things are going since the elections. The elections turned out to be a much bigger deal and a much more positive development, and I think the feeling is that we definitely turned a corner and that we have a long way to go. The average insurgency lasts nine years.

Do we have the money for that?

We've got the money. Do we have the people? I don't know. They just raised the recruiting age for reserves to thirty-nine years. It increases the pool of recruits to something like fifty million people. The demographics of recruiting are just enormous. You change the percentage of women in the military by 1 percent and it opens up a huge pool of people. They'll always figure out enough incentives. They're going to start giving out $300,000 loans to buy your first home. It used to be just a college education. Now it's a college education and your first home. They really are pretty smart about recruiting because they've been doing it for a long time. This is the first time they've ever had to recruit in the midst of a war, but I think the combination of throwing money at the problem and the fact that sometime by the end of this year or the beginning of next we'll be able to start withdrawing some troops will solve the recruiting problem.

Are we going into Iran or Syria?

No, no. I was looking at the secretary of defense's schedule one day and on it was "lunch with Robert Novak."[25] A day or two later, on January 28, 2005, Novak wrote a column that began with "'We are not going to war with Iran,' a senior defense official told me this week." I don't know that Rumsfeld told him that, but I assume that he did and that's what everybody tells me. We do not have the resources to go to war with Iran. One of the squishy points in all the arguments about why Iraq, why not North Korea, why not Iran, which arguably pose greater threats, is that we didn't have military options with those guys. North Korea would be a disaster. And Iran, I forget how many more people it has than Iraq, but it's basically twice as big.

The Persians aren't the Iraqis, either.

Yes. We had a military option for Iraq. If the intelligence had been the same but we hadn't had a military option, we wouldn't have gone to war in Iraq. But we did have a military option and we'd even exercised it once before in 1990 and it worked like a charm.

Yes, but what about our long-term presence there?

I don't think we want to have a long-term military presence in Iraq.

Well, we've built those four huge bases, haven't we?

We built huge bases, but a lot of that stuff you can disassemble. When I went to the US air base in Balad, I said, "Holy shit, we're in for the duration," because they've got these big warehouses going up, but apparently they are modular warehouses and you can take them all down or you can just give them to the Iraqis for their military. But look, we've been in the Persian Gulf for a while.

Yes, but this is a different presence.

I don't think we intend to do that.

For how long do you think we'll be there? What do your sources say?

There's no plan, so there's nothing a source could tell you. There's no secret document to leak that would tell you. I don't even think there's a secret document for the next troop rotation or a secret plan yet for the beginning of troop withdrawals. They're really taking it slow.

Do you think it was a good idea that we did this? Some people are telling us, "We just increased the terrorism. We created a magnet for terrorists."

That's the beauty of being a reporter, you don't have to make those judgments.

You're getting paid a ton of money; you should be an analyst to some extent.

It is not for me to tell anybody out there whether we're doing the right or the wrong thing.

That's not what I'm asking you. I'm asking if you think that our presence there has created more terrorism or not.

I am sure it has. Rumsfeld has had this same argument with himself in that memo in which he asked, "Is it the case that the harder we work the behinder we get? Are we creating them faster than we're killing them?" I don't know how you measure that. When is a terrorist a terrorist? When he hates the United States and wants to bring it down or when he crosses the line and does something in furtherance of the terrorist plot?

That's not what we're talking about. We're talking about people who become radicalized enough to pick up a gun or pick up a bomb and go after our boys over there.

I'm sure we are radicalizing a hell of a lot of people, but I don't know how you make the judgment about whether or not we've created more terrorism over there. I guess a lot of it depends on how Iraq turns out. If Iraq were to become a failed state like Afghanistan, just another haven for the Zarqawis of this world, then we clearly would have failed. But this is not knowable yet. You just don't know what path Iraq is on.

Walter Pincus said this morning, "When we're out of there, it breaks apart into pieces. It's gone. Iraq will no longer *exist*."

Charles Duelfer has a great line. He says, "Now you know why Saddam Hussein was so ruthless. The place is tough to rule."

Like Tito in Yugoslavia.

Yes. You've got to keep all those factions together, and I don't know if they'll make it or not or if it'll fall apart once we're out of there.

I want to know what you think about people who criticize television coverage of the prewar and the current situation.

What's the criticism?

That, before the war, the administration's feet weren't held to the fire enough, that the tough questions weren't asked, that there was an

atmosphere of fear, and people were afraid to hold the administration's feet to the fire about why we were going to Iraq.

I certainly don't buy the atmosphere of fear. I think all those other criticisms are fair enough. Obviously we didn't hold their feet to the fire because we didn't expose the fact that the intelligence was a house of cards. We didn't report anything that made them go back and say, "Oh, shit," but was it realistic to expect us to have been able to do that? I don't know, I don't know. Even today there are very few people who have come forward and said, "Hey, I was telling them that this intelligence was a house of cards and was all wrong."

There was one guy, Greg Thielmann, who was acting director of the Office of Strategic Proliferation and Military Affairs, which was responsible for analyzing the Iraqi weapons threat. *60 Minutes* did a profile of him in February 2004, in which he said, "The main problem was that the senior administration officials have what I call faith-based intelligence. They knew what they wanted the intelligence to show. They were really blind and deaf to any kind of countervailing information the intelligence community would produce. I would assign blame to the intelligence community and most of the blame to the senior administration officials." What he's saying is credible because the analysts in the State Department's Bureau of Intelligence and Research scrubbed Powell's UN speech and took a lot of stuff out of the early drafts. While analyzing the speech, they were raising questions about some of the intelligence. But finally, in the end, they said, "Well, I guess we can live with this."

What about CNN's correspondent Christiane Amanpour, who was talking about CNN censoring itself before the war and about the atmosphere of fear and how Fox influenced everybody else's reporting.

In television, I think the problem—and I think the administration understands this perfectly and was able to use this to their advantage—is that you have to use those goddamned sound bites. You write a story in which the script says, "circumstantial evidence, but no smoking gun," but then your sound bite is Rumsfeld or Cheney saying, "Saddam Hussein has . . ."

. . . and, "You don't want the smoking gun to be a mushroom cloud."

Yes, and I think that's what sticks. It's either the sound bite or the picture that registers with people, not the reporter's narration. I sometimes wonder why I sit here and worry about whether I should use "would" or "could" or "might" or "may" in my script, because that's not what registers. During the first Gulf War, we got those first videos of all those bombs going down the airshaft, and every script I wrote, I'd try to put in that something like only 9 percent of the bombs that were dropped in the first Gulf War were precision guided, but all the bombs in the pictures were precision guided.

Nobody hears 9 percent. "It looks like 100 percent to me."

Everybody who works in television has had this experience where the picture tells the story and people just don't pay any attention to what's being said underneath those pictures. I don't know how many times people say to me, "Hey, I just saw you in Bosnia or Kosovo," and of course, I haven't left Washington.

Ted Koppel told us the same story. Ted said, "At the beginning of every *Nightline* I say, 'This is Ted Koppel from Washington,' at the end of every *Nightline*, 'this is Ted Koppel from Washington,'" and he said, "Let me see, how many shows do I do a year?" and he did the math and then he said, "And then I go out into the streets of Washington and people come up to me and go, 'Ted, what are you doing here?'"

It is so true. But you understand it. When people are watching, particularly the evening news, they're fixing dinner, worrying about their kids' homework, and doing a hundred different things. Very few people sit down and watch the evening news. We do, because it's our job. If one word different from what I've reported comes out of ABC, my phone will start ringing. But that's just not how it works in the real world.

But what about the part of your job that's about keeping the electorate informed? Are you engaging in exercises of futility here?

No. What I think you do, really, is keep the conversation going. You do a story and somebody says, "That's a crock, I'll tell the truth," and that person writes a story. Then Woodward comes along and he writes a book and then the guys from this administration will start writing their memoirs. I know what you're going to say, "That doesn't help you in the next election," but it's just the process where you build this historical record.

Here's where it troubles me. The run-up to the war troubles me because when you're going to send people to die, when you're going to spend billions of dollars, I think the people who are going to make the sacrifices should be very clear about why you've decided to do it.

What I find fascinating about all these interviews I've done, and everybody I've spoken to is supercompetent, is that there's no clear consensus on why we went to war.

It's pretty clear to me why we went to war. Well, OK, I guess that just depends on where you sit and from where you've observed these events.

But doesn't that also have to do with the messages that were sent out from the leadership?

That they deliberately tried to confuse the issue?

I don't know. I'm asking you what you think.

They had to get Congress to go along with this thing. They tried to make the strongest case possible, and in some cases, particularly the 9/11 connection, there's no question that they overreached. But Congress wasn't getting its information from sound bites; it was getting its information from the classified version of the National Intelligence Estimate. Now, why does a senator vote the way he does? Is it because of what he reads in a classified intelligence estimate or is it because of what his constituents, who have been listening to those sound bites, are telling him to do?

Also, the reasons for going to war, you have to admit, they morphed a bit. They went from WMDs and connections to al Qaeda to we have to bring democracy to Iraq.

No, no, no.

It was Operation Iraqi Freedom, wasn't it?

Yes.

We were bringing democracy to Iraq.

That was part of it, but nobody before the war started backed off the claim on WMDs. You know that line from Wolfowitz, "WMD was the one we could all agree on." You could certainly get an agreement on WMDs because of what the intelligence community was saying, but I don't think you could get an agreement to go to war to bring democracy to a country with the cultural history of Iraq.

How accurately do you think we're going to cover and perceive the situation now in Iraq?

I think the government has become much more conservative in, and less confident of, some of its judgments. Look at this refusal to put a good number on the number of insurgents. We know we don't really know. Nobody will go out there and make bloodcurdling statements about "We're going to get Zarqawi any day now" because they've learned the hard way.

We spoke to NPR's Deborah Amos,[26] and she was saying it's a nationalist insurgency.

People think that because the Zarqawi crowd is a minority and the foreign fighters are a minority.

She was saying that the ratio of foreign fighters to Iraqis was ten to one.

I think most people in this building would agree with that. Some people think that when bin Laden named Zarqawi the emir of Iraq, he made a huge mistake, because there you've got bin Laden the Saudi and Zarqawi the Jordanian agreeing that Zarqawi is the emir of Iraq. I think that pissed a lot of people off. There was a story in the *Washington Post* in March 2005 entitled "A Gruesome Find, With a Difference," about these bodies that had been found and they were foreigners and followers of Zarqawi and they'd all been executed. But if it's a nationalist insurgency, which I think is true, they will be harder to defeat. You never defeat them; they die on the vine.

The Vietnamese didn't die on the vine.

I don't know my history well enough to know, but Vietnam is the guerrilla war that's in all our minds. But if you were to look at all the guerrilla wars that have gone on, you'll find that most of them failed. Most of the insurgencies fail.

I remember a history professor just lighting into me one night because I said something equivocal about the war, like what I said to you about how psychologically this is all very coherent to me, and she said, "All you have to do is read history to know that this wasn't going to work." I've got one of these books on the Middle East, David Fromkin's *A Peace to End All Peace*,[27] and the arrogance with which the West drew the boundaries of all those countries and then the beating that the British took in Iraq makes you wonder, but the people who are reading the National Intelligence Estimates are not reading David Fromkin.

I want to ask you about the US death toll. I read somewhere that it is actually much higher than the current figure because a lot of people are dying in the hospital afterward. Is that true?

No. If you're alive when you reach the field hospital, you've got a 99 percent chance of living. I do a lot of stories out of Walter Reed, and they can tell you every single soldier who has died upon arriving at Walter Reed because there were so few of them. So there's no hidden death toll. You can argue about the wounded and whether accidents should count. I think they should because if you weren't running around Iraq in an armored Humvee, you probably wouldn't have that accident, and that would increase the wounded count, but the numbers of the wounded include a lot of people who will get a Purple Heart but will not have any disability. We tend to focus on the soldiers who have terrible disabilities. There are over eleven thousand wounded, and people get the impression that every one of those soldiers has lost an arm or a leg, but that's not true, although we just finished doing a story yesterday about blast effect causing brain injuries. More than fifteen hundred young people dead is just obscene.

Well, it's war, David.

I know, I know, and that's why war should be a last resort.

I think if you consider the Iraqi civilian casualties, it's a very small number. Let's understand that philosophically we agree that every life is superprecious, but the Iraqis have paid the bigger price by far.

There are people who make the argument that we could keep losing people at the rate we are losing them and it would be ten years before we equal 9/11.

What a calculation.

That's from the people who believe our way of life was at stake and all that sort of stuff.

For some reason it doesn't feel like before the war that the press was engaging in the groupthink of "This should be the last thing that happens, the last thing we want to do is go to war." Some people have told us that the press—certainly television—was looking forward to the war because it's exciting and a ratings booster.

I don't buy that. I don't buy that for a second.

Peter Arnett told us that and Walter Pincus talked about it, too.

I don't know what goes on in the executive suites of CBS News, but anything that even remotely approaches that never came my way. You spend one hell of a lot of money covering a war. In today's environment, I would think that, if anything, the bias would be the other way, "don't make us send all that equipment and all those technicians and all those people over there." I don't know enough about the CBS budget, but I think war is probably a loss leader.

I think everybody should go around with the thought that war is the last resort after everything else has failed. You can argue that the administration had that belief. There was this whole question of whether anybody ever called Saddam an imminent threat, and Rumsfeld had people go back and read every word he had spoken, and he said, "I never used the word imminent." And he didn't. Apparently, under international law, "imminent" has a specific connotation. But Rumsfeld did say, "immediate," and to me, much less anybody who's listening to a TV with only half an ear, there's no effective difference between "immediate" and "imminent."

Here we are in the spin zone again.

If you believed that he had WMDs, and you believed that he would give them to a terrorist group—al Qaeda or somebody else—and that he wasn't going to do business with the UN and he wasn't going to give them up, maybe it was the last resort. The line about "This was not a war of necessity, this was a war of choice" only got traction when we found out there weren't any WMDs there. It's the old problem of hindsight. Everything looks so obvious now.

I really don't know how to answer the question of whether or not the press did a good job of informing the American people in the aftermath of 9/11 and the buildup to the war in Iraq. We did a good job in that we accurately reflected what government was thinking and saying, but government was wrong.

Is that all that your job is, to reflect what government is thinking and saying?

No, you have to try to get at the underlying truths, but the underlying truth in this case was not very different from what was being said.

What do you mean? They said there were WMDs and there weren't.

I'm talking about the underlying truth of what the intelligence community was really thinking and what they were saying to each other. To go beyond that, you'd have to say that you would expect the press to go to Iraq and conduct it's own investigation of whether or not Iraq had weapons of mass destruction and to prove one way or another, and that just is not practical.

What is critical reporting? You can't just say, "This is a crock." You have to say, "This is a crock *because . . .*" We did not have the information to refute the government's or the intelligence community's claims about WMDs. We couldn't prove the negative. I think the record on skepticism on 9/11, on the al Qaeda connection with Saddam, is pretty decent. I'm saying that based on zero research.

It's interesting that a *Washington Post* poll[28] showed that a lot of people still believe Saddam is directly connected to 9/11.

That goes back to the sound bite. What do you do to cancel out the sound bite? You don't use them. But the dynamics of television drive you to use sound bites, and it's not unreasonable to put the nation's leaders in your stories. The question is, when you put them in your stories and they say something that is factually wrong or, exaggerated, do you call them on it? I think we kept the right amount of skepticism about the al Qaeda connection.

It didn't get any traction.

It didn't get any traction because Cheney, the vice president of the United States, has a very judicious way of saying some pretty bloodcurdling things. He's very, very smart, and whenever he talked about the al Qaeda connection and the meeting in Prague,[29] he always said it in a way that gave him just enough wiggle room, "It's still under investigation and we want to know if that meeting took place," and so on. That's a subtlety and it creates an impression about the possibility of a connection that stays with people. I remember in the immediate aftermath of the first Gulf War when the Arabs in the south and the Kurds[30] in the north were all rising up and it looked like Saddam was going to fall, somebody asked Cheney at a press conference, "Is Saddam Hussein going to fall?" And he responded with the cleverest sound bite I've ever heard, "Saddam Hussein's days are numbered."

You don't think, though, that it was a calculated thing to constantly mention this potential connection albeit in a subtly qualified way?

I guess you'd have to go see how times he volunteered it and how many times it was in response to a question. I don't know the answer to that.

He went around and did all those speeches at the veterans' organizations saying the same thing over and over about Saddam's WMD potential.

I can't remember what he said in those, and that would matter. Look, they were marshaling every argument they had to go to war. They clearly overstated. They overstated with Bush in the State of the Union on the uranium from Niger.[31]

But you think that they genuinely believed that he was part of this terrorism nexus?

They genuinely believed that he had weapons of mass destruction. All it takes is a vial to kill X thousand people. They genuinely believed that he was a supporter of terrorist organizations, not necessarily al Qaeda, but terrorist organizations, and they genuinely believed that there were terrorist organizations out there that would do anything, would stop at nothing, to destroy the United States. I think those are all true. Even today. No, he didn't have weapons of mass destruction. But his connection to these terrorist groups, these Palestinian groups, is clear.

But the connection with Palestinian terrorists is a different issue because that's about going after the Israelis because of the way they've dealt with the Palestinians.

But then it comes down to Rumsfeld's question of risk. How much risk are you willing to accept?

Do you genuinely believe that Saddam was a threat to the United States?

Yes, I do.

Because of his connection to these pro-Palestinian terrorists? I think that's a very specious road to walk down because support for the Palestinians against the Israelis is common in that entire region. The Saudis are paying off suicide bombers, too. Lots of people are paying off the jihadis against the Israelis, and that's been going on for a long time, that's nothing new, and that's nothing that really threatens the United States. Do you agree?

I agree that support of Palestinians doesn't get you to a threat to the United States. You had things like the fact that one of the people still wanted for the first World Trade Center bombing was in Iraq. You had the fact that Zarqawi was in Iraq.

By that logic, we should go to Sudan.
We did, remember?

Well, not to the extent that we have in Iraq.
The Clinton administration did in its own wimpy way.

Following your logic of going into countries that have anti-US terrorists, it would have made sense to attack Saudi Arabia, too.
No.

Why not? They were funding those guys.
In your mind, was going into Iraq any different from when Clinton ordered the firing of those cruise missiles in Sudan and said it wasn't in retaliation for the embassy bombings but that it was a preemptive strike against a terrorist attack with chemical weapons? The Clinton administration was the one that put out all the evidence about these Iraqi scientists that had gone down to Sudan and met with bin Laden.

One strike is different from a whole war.
That's what I'm asking you, is it?

Sure, because you're not using huge resources and large numbers of lives.
You're killing people.

Come on, David. We go all over the world doing covert ops that kill people all the time. That is different from marshaling thousands of troops and rearranging a society. There's a big difference between a war and some little constabulary operation or a covert operation. You know that.
I think that to take even a small military action you need the same level of proof that you have a threat that can't be dealt with by any other means. You can't say, "Well, I don't know if he's making chemical weapons in that plant, but hey, it's just a few cruise missiles, come on, let's do it."

Look at what the Israelis did to Saddam's reactor. They saw he was building it and they went out and bombed it. They didn't invade Iraq. Covert operations and wars are two separate things. The volume is so much different and also the impact on the entire society is so different so you can't say that, no.

I might still want to say it. I'm thinking. I don't know.

Remember those guys in the woods of Afghanistan who we sent that Predator drone out after because we thought that one of them was bin Laden? The Predator drone went in and killed him and a few other people. Turns out the intelligence was wrong. The guy wasn't bin Laden. Now there's a vast difference between killing a few people on bad intelligence and killing thousands upon thousands on bad intelligence. It sounds heartless to say, but it's true. In the Iraq war, it's the civilians who are dying en masse, not the fighters on either side.

Well, we lambasted the Clinton administration for the Sudan incident because the intelligence didn't stand up, and they deserved it.

Absolutely.

And we've lambasted the Bush administration because the intelligence didn't stand up, and they deserved it.

Yes, but the difference here is in the scale.

Obviously I can't argue scale, but you can't act on any level without being sure of your information and that it's your only option.

We do it all the time.

You're talking about tactical decisions in war, and they had guys looking at that video that the Predator was seeing for a long time. We still don't know who the guy was. Some say he was a rag-picker and other people say he was a sheikh. Who knows? Somebody probably does know.

I want to talk about something Walter said about there being a chronic atmosphere of distrust between the press and government that affects the way the press views information being presented to it by the government.

There is an atmosphere of distrust? I thought the problem was that there was not enough distrust.

There is distrust. What you're referring to is what the press is often criticized for, which is stenography, just quoting sources unquestioningly. You can distrust an official source and still be a stenographer.

The "press" covers so many sins. Is Sy Hersh the press? He's not a stenographer.

No, he's not, but he is the press.

He's not always right.

Nobody is.

Right. And I think news coverage is an accretion of all that sort of stuff, both right and wrong. I'm sure you've read Michael Massing's article in the *New York Review of Books*, critiquing Judy Miller and the *New York Times'* coverage. But he also pointed out who had been raising doubts and it was principally, as I remember, Knight Ridder. Knight Ridder deserves more credit than it's gotten.

When did the first wave of materiel and people start heading to the Middle East for this war?

They did it surreptitiously for a while, so it's hard to nail it down. They went there certainly before the agreement calling for Iraq to disarm was passed in November 2002. Even after that, it was all done under the guise of exercises and regularly scheduled deployments. By the time that they went public with the buildup, when they started putting in the combat troops and the combat planes and that stuff, the infrastructure was already there.

So this business with the inspectors was really "Who gives a damn whether the WMDs are there or not?"

No, because that stuff you can call off. You haven't visibly committed yourself, so you can just say, "Hey, the exercise is over."

Even after you've spent so much budget getting there?

Well, after we got to around January of 2003, Rumsfeld was saying publicly that even if Saddam were to come out and reveal all his weapons, we'd still have to go in to verify, so there was a point of no return before we actually went to war. I guess it was a question of whether we could have just gone in with somebody's permission as opposed to doing what we did. I don't know why this is so different from what other people are telling you. Certainly people aren't telling you that they were making up all the WMD stuff.

> **Some people are telling me that they think the administration purposely lied to the American public to go to Iraq, and the reasons for going to war that they've cited include things like oil, revenge for the assassination attempt on George H. W. Bush, an overall plan to control the Middle East, and so on.**

I don't know how you can know people's motivations. The fact that they tried to kill his father,[32] how do you factor that in? If they had succeeded in killing his father, maybe, but why would you commit that much American treasure just because they thought about or tried to kill his father? I suppose somebody else could see it and say, "That explains it all." But remember what he said when Bob Woodward asked him if he had gone to his father for advice about going into Iraq. He said, "He is the wrong father to appeal to for advice. The wrong father to go to, in terms of strength. There's a higher Father that I appeal to."

> **He did mention it in public once.**

He did, and he got hammered for it, and he didn't say it anymore.

> **You don't think there's a follow-the-money story in here, too, do you?**

Halliburton?[33] No. I really don't. The Army Corps of Engineers made those decisions. I've subscribed to the fact that Halliburton did some overcharging, but I don't think they got the contract because of the Cheney connection. I think the Cheney connection certainly didn't hurt, but the Army Corps of Engineers was looking around for somebody who had the wherewithal to do such a huge job, and they had to keep it secret at the time because this was still before we had committed ourselves publicly to going to war. So they couldn't put it out for a competitive bid, they had to do sole source.

> **Did you ever report that?**

I've maybe done four or five stories on Halliburton and most of them were about the overcharges, but I can't remember if I did a story on why they got the contract in the first place. The other thing is, on television, you've only got those twenty-two minutes and thirty seconds.

> **And you've got about one minute to do your thing.**

You also have to choose what's more important that day: the fact that Halliburton got this no-bid contract or whatever happened in the war. I make a choice and the *CBS Evening News* editor makes a choice, and that's what we do. Newspapers just have to choose between page 1 and page A16, but all the stories will be in there, so it's easier to prove in print that you had all the bases covered than it is in television. By the same token, I can pull out a script and say, "See, see, 'no smoking gun,' I said it; I said it there, and I said it there, and I said it there," but I would not sit here and try to tell you that I was skeptical enough of the evidence because obviously I wasn't, because the evidence was wrong. Having said that, people don't go to war for irrational reasons.

People don't go to war for irrational reasons?

In a democracy? This thing gets thought through at so many levels and then has to be blessed by Congress and every damned thing else.

Well, we had the domino theory for Vietnam and it seemed rational, but it wasn't.

Well, this seemed rational, too, right?

All these distorted perceptions of the world that cause so many deaths—this is like Alice in Wonderland or something.

The lesson is that you can never be sure of what you think is the case and you just need to be more disbelieving. Everybody does. The CIA does.

I have to say, though, that I think that maybe we could raise our percentage of accuracy a little more if we did something about our provincialism. Not only in terms of the types of people that we send out to countries but also our society in general, our educational system. If we're going to be the nine-hundred-pound gorilla on the planet, we really should know the planet, shouldn't we?

I agree with that. I don't know how many testimonies I've listened to from heads of intelligence agencies telling Congress they didn't have enough translators, and I've never done a story on the lack of translators, which in retrospect, is a big deal. But no amount of cultural sensitivity or cultural awareness would have allowed a reporter to go to the Iraq of Saddam Hussein and get any access to that society.

I don't know if I agree with you.

You might be able to go live with the marsh Arabs like the British explorer Wilfred Thesiger, but I don't think a reporter could go into the heart of Iraq, no matter what his language skills, without being under constant surveillance and harassment and bringing repercussions against anybody he talked to under Saddam.

That's a long discussion, but I do feel that we need more reporters who have the gift of going native.

Or how about just being able to read some of the local newspapers from the foreign country they're covering? We have a guy in-house who reads all the Pakistani press. He sends out a weekly memo that gives a compendium of everything that's been reported, which is good in one way, but in another way, you're right back to where you started, because everything's been reported, like, "Osama is here, Osama is there, Musharraf is allowing the US military to conduct crossborder operations, Musharraf isn't allowing . . ." You take it in and tell yourself, "At least I know what they're talking about over there," but it doesn't give you a meaningful lead to a story.

Thank you very much for the interview. We are going to disconnect you now.

Have I hung myself high enough?

DAVID MARTIN has been CBS News's national security correspondent, covering the Pentagon and the State Department since 1993. In that capacity, he has reported virtually every major defense, intelligence, and international affairs story for the *CBS Evening News with Dan Rather*, as well as for other broadcasts, including *60 Minutes* and *48 Hours*. He also contributed to *60 Minutes II*.

During the invasion of Afghanistan and the war in Iraq, Martin's in-depth knowledge of how the State Department, intelligence community, and military operate, both on the battlefield and in Washington, positioned him as the "big picture" reporter for CBS News. Utilizing his own sources and reports from CBS News correspondents in the region and around the world, as well as in Washington, he explained and assessed the military's strategies and operations for viewers.

Martin broke several significant stories before and during the Iraq war. He was the first to report, on the opening night of the war, that the United States was launching a strike on a palace bunker in southern

Baghdad in an attempt to take out Saddam Hussein. Martin also broke the story of the military's "shock and awe" strategy for its initial strike on Baghdad. During a trip to Iraq in May 2003, he was the first journalist to visit and report on Dora Farms, where Saddam was said by the CIA to have been hiding on the opening night of the war.

Martin has received two Alfred I. duPont–Columbia University Awards (2002 and 2004) for his body of work, most of which has appeared on the *CBS Evening News with Dan Rather* and *60 Minutes II*. Regarding the first citation, the award committee said that his "consistently excellent reporting on the beat of national security hit its peak this year . . . break[ing] news on a wide range of defense and security stories with details that only experience and doggedness can ferret out. This is exemplary reporting that repeatedly breaks through the barriers of official statements." In awarding the second DuPont, the committee said, "David Martin's reports on the Pentagon, the military build-up to the Iraq war and on the war itself demonstrate his exceptional grasp of national security issues. Teamed with his longtime producer, Mary Walsh, Martin consistently breaks new information with clear reporting on the Pentagon's goals. He exemplifies the role of a journalist: to measure what we are being told against what we find out."

Martin joined CBS News as its Pentagon correspondent in 1983. His duties were later expanded to include the State Department and intelligence beats. Before that, he covered defense and intelligence matters for *Newsweek* magazine from its Washington bureau (1977–1983). Martin was a reporter with the Associated Press in Washington (1973–1977), covering the FBI and CIA. He also was a member of the AP special assignment team (1977).

Martin began his journalism career as a researcher for CBS News in New York in 1969. He then became a news writer with the AP broadcast wire (1971–1972) and a fellow at the Washington Journalism Center (1973).

Martin is the author of two books, *Wilderness of Mirrors* (New York: Harper & Row, 1980), an account of the secret wars between the CIA and KGB, and *Best Laid Plans: The Inside Story of America's War against Terrorism* (New York: Harper & Row, 1988).

He was born on July 28 in Washington, DC. He graduated from Yale University in 1965 with a bachelor's degree in English. During the Vietnam War, Martin served as an officer aboard a US Navy destroyer. Martin and his wife, Dr. Elinor Martin, live in Chevy Chase, Maryland. They have four children.

NOTES

1. An Arabic word meaning "the base," al Qaeda is an international terrorist group headed by a Saudi, Osama bin Laden, which aims to oppose non-Islamic governments with force and violence and seek retribution for force and violence used against Muslims.

2. The Taliban (which means "those who study the book [Koran]" in Pushtu) was a very conservative Islamic movement that ruled most of Afghanistan from 1996 to 2001. According to the Internet encyclopedia Wikipedia, the Taliban restored order after civil war broke out following the demise of the Soviet-backed Democratic Republic of Afghanistan. They "eliminated payments that warlords demanded from business people . . . reduced factional fighting . . . and brought social benefits by imposing a set of norms on a chaotic society." Their rules included bans on "all forms of TV, imagery and music" and on women working or visiting hospitals for medical treatment (because contact with male doctors was not allowed). After September 11, the United States, supported by a coalition of countries, initiated military action against the Taliban for "harboring al Qaeda." http://en.wikipedia.org/wiki/Taliban.

3. The US Intelligence Community's Web site's definition of National Intelligence Estimates is "These reports are the DCI's [Director of Central Intelligence] most authoritative written judgements concerning national security issues. They deal with capabilities, vulnerabilities, and probable courses of action of foreign nations and key developments relevant to the vital interests of the United States. NIEs are produced at the national level by the NIC [National Intelligence Council, made up of senior intelligence analysts and outside experts] and are issued by the DCI with the approval of the NFIB [National Foreign Intelligence Board, a senior Intelligence Community advisory body]. NIEs are designed to identify trends of significance to national security and, when relevant, differences of views among the principal intelligence officers of the US government. Presidential Summaries of NIEs are prepared for the President, Vice President, and other key executive officers." http://www.intelligence.gov/0-glossary.shtml.

4. According to Julian Borger of the UK's *Guardian* newspaper, the Office of Special Plans "was set up by the defence secretary, Donald Rumsfeld, to second-guess CIA information and operated under the patronage of hardline conservatives in the top rungs of the administration, the Pentagon and at the White House, including Vice President Dick Cheney. The ideologically driven network functioned like a shadow government, much of it off the official payroll and beyond congressional oversight." "The Spies Who Pushed for War," *Guardian*, July 17, 2003.

5. The report is titled "Report on the U.S. Intelligence Community's Prewar Intelligence Assessments on Iraq." It was compiled by the US Senate Select Intelligence Committee and released on July 9, 2004. Pat Roberts of Kansas chaired the committee and John D. Rockefeller IV from West Virginia was vice chairman.

6. The report is titled "Comprehensive Report of the Special Advisor to the DCI on Iraq's WMD" and is dated September 30, 2004.

7. According to Wikipedia, "Groupthink is a term coined by psychologist Irving Janis in 1972 to describe a process by which a group can make bad or irrational decisions. . . . Janis' definition of the term was 'a mode of thinking that people engage in when they are deeply involved in a cohesive in-group, when the members' strivings for unanimity override their motivation to realistically appraise alternative courses of action.'" http://en.wikipedia.org/wiki/Groupthink.

8. The Project for a New American Century (PNAC) says on its Web site that it "intends, through issue briefs, research papers, advocacy journalism, conferences, and seminars, to explain what American world leadership entails." It is generally seen as a neoconservative take on the role the United States should play in the world. PNAC says it is a nonprofit educational organization dedicated to the propositions "that American leadership is good both for America and the world; and that such leadership requires military strength, diplomatic energy and commitment to moral principle." http://www .newamericancentury.org/.

9. "A Clean Break" can be viewed at http://www.informationclearinghouse.info/ article1438.htm.

10. The National Security Agency/Central Security Service "is America's cryptologic organization. It coordinates, directs, and performs highly specialized activities to protect US information systems and produce foreign intelligence information. . . . It is also one of the most important centers of foreign language analysis and research within the government." http://www.nsa.gov/about/.

11. The Defense Intelligence Agency's mission is to "provide timely, objective and cogent military intelligence to warfighters, defense planners and defense and national security policymakers." http://www.dia.mil/.

12. The Central Intelligence Agency "is an independent agency, responsible for providing national security intelligence to senior US policymakers. The Director of Central Intelligence serves as the principal advisor to the President and the National Security Council on all matters of foreign intelligence related to national security." http://www.cia.gov/.

13. The National Reconnaissance Office "designs, builds and operates the nation's reconnaissance satellites." http://www.nro.gov/.

14. In a July, 11, 2004, *Los Angeles Times* article, reporter Bob Drogin wrote: "The only American who met a now-discredited Iraqi defector codenamed 'Curveball' repeatedly warned the CIA before the war that the Baghdad engineer appeared to be an alcoholic and that his dramatic claims that Saddam Hussein had built a secret fleet of mobile germ weapons factories were not reliable. In response, the deputy director of the CIA's Iraqi weapons of mass destruction task force . . . suggested in a February 4, 2003, e-mail that such doubts were not welcome at the intelligence agency. 'As I said last night, let's keep in mind the fact that this war's going to happen regardless of what Curveball said or didn't say, and the powers that be probably aren't terribly interested in whether Curveball knows what he's talking about,' the CIA official wrote."

15. Before becoming undersecretary of defense for policy, Douglas J. Feith was an adviser to the Israeli government and a participant in the "Study Group on a New Israeli Strategy Toward 2000" that formulated the "Clean Break" document. He was also part of "The Project for a New American Century." As undersecretary of defense, he helped set up the secretive Office of Special Plans, whose purpose, according to national security reporter James Bamford, was "to conduct advance war planning for Iraq, and one of its most important responsibilities was 'media strategies.'" James Bamford, *A Pretext for War* (New York: Doubleday, 2004), pp. 307, 308. In September 2004 an analyst in his office, Lawrence Franklin, came under investigation for passing on a draft presidential directive on Iran to the pro-Israel lobby AIPAC (American Israel Public Affairs Committee). In January 26, 2005, the Department of Defense announced Feith's resignation, saying he was leaving for "personal and family reasons."

16. The Iranian Revolution "was the 1979 revolution that transformed Iran from an autocratic pro-West monarchy under Shah Mohammed Reza Pahlavi to an Islamic, theocratic democracy under the rule of Ayatollah Khomeini. The revolution was divided into two stages: the first saw an alliance of liberal, leftist, and religious groups oust the Shah; the second stage, often named the Islamic Revolution, saw the ayatollahs come to power." http://en.wikipedia.org/wiki/Iranian_revolution.

17. Mikhail Sergeyevich Gorbachev led the Soviet Union from 1985 to 1991. "His attempts at reform led to the end of the Cold War, but also inadvertently caused the end of the political supremacy of the Communist Party of the Soviet Union and the dissolution of the Soviet Union." http://en.wikipedia.org/wiki/Mikhail_ Gorbachev.

18. Newton Leroy Gingrich was Speaker of the House from 1995 to 1999 and is best known as the architect of the Contract with America, a list of Republican campaign promises that included tax cuts, a balanced budget law, and welfare reform. The contract is said to have helped the Republicans gain control of the House for the first time in forty years. In 1997 the House of Representatives reprimanded and fined Gingrich for using tax-exempt foundations for political purposes and then lying about it. He resigned as Speaker the following year. He is currently a senior fellow at the American Enterprise Institute, where he focuses on healthcare, information technology, the military, and politics.

19. Richard Garwin helped build America's hydrogen bomb. He is senior fellow and the director of science and technology at the Council on Foreign Relations. Garwin was a member of the Rumsfeld Commission that put out a report in 1998 titled "Report of the Commission to Assess the Ballistic Missile Threat to the United States."

20. Barton Gellman and Walter Pincus report for the *Washington Post*. See chapters 8 and 9 in this book.

21. Desert One became synonymous with a mission that was launched on April 24, 1980, to rescue fifty-three hostages being held in the American Embassy in Tehran. The mission ended in disaster with the deaths of five air force men and three marines and the loss of eight aircraft in a remote part of Iran.

22. Benjamin Crowninshield Bradlee is currently vice president at large for the *Washington Post*. As managing editor of the *Post*, he oversaw Bob Woodward and Carl Bernstein's reporting on the Watergate scandal.

23. In 1972 *Washington Post* journalists Bob Woodward and Carl Bernstein, with the help of a confidential source named "Deep Throat" (then FBI deputy director Mark Felt) connected a break-in at the Democratic National Committee headquarters located in the Watergate hotel and office complex in Washington, DC, to high-ranking sources in the Nixon administration and the Committee to Re-Elect the President. Their investigation eventually led to President Nixon's resignation in 1974.

24. The Iran-Contra affair was a "secret arrangement in the 1980s to provide funds [outside of congressional oversight] to the Nicaraguan Contra rebels from profits gained by selling arms to Iran. Iran/Contra was the product of two separate initiatives during the Reagan administration. The first was a commitment to aid the Contras who were conducting a war against the [Left-leaning] Sandinista government of Nicaragua. The second was to placate 'moderates' within the Iranian government in order to secure the release of American hostages held by pro-Iranian groups in Lebanon and influence Iranian foreign policy in a pro-Western direction." http://www.factmonster.com/ce6/history/A0825447.html.

25. Robert Novak is a syndicated columnist who participates in two CNN public affairs programs, *Crossfire* and *The Capital Gang*.

26. See chapter 19 in this book.

27. David Fromkin, *A Peace to End All Peace: The Fall of the Ottoman Empire and the Creation of the Modern Middle East* (New York: Owl Books, 2001).

28. The *Washington Post* poll question and answer can be found at http://www.washingtonpost.com/ac3/ContentServer?pagename=polls&nextstep=displayQuestion&interactive=n&pollid=2004169&pripollid=&varname=q25a&privarname=&questCategoryType=n&questCategory=Variables.questCategory&keyword=Variables.keyword&pollDateRange=Variable. The poll was conducted June 17–20, 2004.

29. Members of the Bush administration made a series of claims about al Qaeda links to Saddam Hussein, including one allegation that 9/11 hijacker Muhammad Atta met in Prague, Czech Republic, with an Iraqi intelligence officer. In a March 2, 2004, article, "Doubts Cast on Efforts to Link Saddam, al Qaeda," examining a series of these claims, Knight Ridder reporters Warren Strobel, Jonathan Landay, and John Walcott write that this particular claim was "contradicted by FBI evidence that Atta was taking flight training in Florida at the time. The Iraqi, Ahmed Khalil Ibrahim Samir al-Ani, is now in U.S. custody and has told interrogators he never met Atta." See chapters 12 and 13 in this book.

30. A *Washington Post* profile of the Kurds at http://www.washingtonpost.com/wp-srv/inatl/daily/feb99/kurdprofile.htm describes them as fifteen to twenty million "largely Sunni Muslims with their own language and culture living in the generally contiguous areas of Turkey, Iraq, Iran, Armenia and Syria" collectively called Kurdistan. The Kurds seek their own state and have clashed with the nations in which their territories lie, including Iraq. In 1988 the Iraqis launched a poison gas attack on the town of Hallabjah and killed five thousand people.

31. In his State of the Union address on January 28, 2003, President Bush said, "The British government has learned that Saddam Hussein recently sought significant quantities of uranium from Africa," allegedly from Niger. This turned out to be false.

32. Allegations that Saddam Hussein had ordered Iraqi intelligence to assassinate President George H. W. Bush in April 1993 during Bush's visit to Kuwait to commemorate the victory of the first Gulf War eventually led President Clinton to order an attack on Mukhabarat, Iraqi intelligence headquarters, which resulted in the deaths of eight civilians when some of the missiles landed on nearby homes. In a November 1, 1993, *New Yorker* article, "Case Not Closed," reporter Seymour Hersh wrote, "But my own investigations have uncovered circumstantial evidence, at least as compelling as the Administration's, that suggests that the American government's case against Iraq—as it has been outlined in public, anyway—is seriously flawed."

33. Halliburton is "one of the world's largest providers of products and services to the oil and gas industries." http://www.halliburton.com/. It is the largest recipient of contracts awarded for postwar work in Afghanistan and Iraq, according to Center for Public Integrity reporters Andre Verloy and Daniel Politi in their August 18, 2004, article "Halliburton Contracts Balloon." They also reported that Halliburton, "where Vice President Dick Cheney served as CEO from 1995 to 2000, has come under increased scrutiny because of allegations of overcharging on food service and fuel distribution contracts, poor management and close ties to the administration." http://www.publicintegrity.org/wow/report.aspx?aid=366&sid=100.

II

DANGEROUS NONSENSE AND THE NUREMBERG RULE

Emme Bruges/James Bamford

JAMES BAMFORD
Author and
National Security/
Intelligence Reporter
Interviewed February 2005

I f I had to identify the most rare breed of journalist, I'd point to Jim Bamford. He has covered the intelligence community for a quarter of a century and is a recognized intelligence expert. He has done spectacular work in both print and television and won numerous awards. But here's what separates him from everybody else: Bamford is the quintessential independent journalist. Indeed, he views his independence as a big part of his public value and is fiercely uncompromising about maintaining it.

His great gift for investigative journalism revealed itself at the very outset of his career. Twenty-three years ago, he began his signature work,

BAMFORD **DANGEROUS NONSENSE**   289

The Puzzle Palace: A Report on NSA, America's Most Secret Agency. Bamford was new to journalism and faced the enormous task of developing sources that would allow him to unveil the inside workings of the ultrasecretive National Security Agency. Not only did he accomplish his goal but, as *Washingtonian* magazine put it, the book is "a monument to investigative journalism." The *New York Times Book Review* observed, "Mr. Bamford has uncovered everything except the combination to the director's safe." Many reporters spend a professional lifetime acquiring the level of skill Bamford exhibited his first time out as an author.

I met him at his home, a quiet, immaculate place decorated with an elegant simplicity achieved by someone with a sharp eye for aesthetics. In the headshots on his latest book's dust jacket, Bamford has thinning white hair, a mustache, eyebrows arched in a V-shape, and an intense look in his eyes. Even though he's smiling slightly, all signs in the photo point to a serious, distinguished-looking older man. He greeted me at his door in blue jeans, a trim man of average height who moved and sounded like a much younger man. We spent five hours talking about the subject of this book, and as you'll see, he held nothing back.

Bamford minces no words when he talks about the Bush administration, particularly Vice President Cheney, "lying to push their agenda" to go to war in Iraq or about former CIA director George Tenet, who he says knew but failed to tell the American people that the intelligence was not good enough to make a case for war. He was equally critical of the press and often used the word "nonsense" to describe what he disapproved of: "All the talk fests like *Meet the Press*, *Late Edition*, and *Face the Nation*, had all the administration talking heads on, including Rice, Rumsfeld, and Cheney, and what they did was point to the headline and say, 'Look what the *New York Times* reported today about mushroom clouds.' They leaked this nonsense to the *New York Times*, the *New York Times* put it on the front page, and then they went on TV and pointed to the *New York Times* article as proof that their statements were credible."

Bamford is also contemptuous of colleagues who remain in a compliant mainstream press—particularly TV—that refuses to take hard looks and ask hard questions. His response to those who say that they do the best they can within the system is harsh: "If you're there, then you're part of the problem and you can't blow it off by saying, 'Well, I don't have any other choice.' You have lots of choices. If you're part of the problem, and all you're saying is, 'Well, I want to keep my $500,000 a year salary,' then accept the blame. You can't just say, 'Well, there's not much else I can do about it.' That's like the Nuremberg rule; 'I got my orders, I had to do it, I couldn't do anything about it.' It's even more extreme in this case, because nobody's getting orders. They can do it or they can leave."

Those who would dismiss Bamford for being too critical should keep in mind that throughout his career he has held himself to formidable professional standards. Beyond that, underneath all his hard-boiled analysis is a fundamentally humanitarian purpose:

> How many people are going to be attacking us if we change our foreign policy in the Middle East? What if we became known as the country that's trying to save the world by putting a large amount of money that's actually a small percentage of what we're spending on the Middle East, say fifty billion dollars, toward AIDS? First of all, you're going to have a lot of people liking you around the world, especially in the third world and some of the major AIDS areas like India, China, and Southeast Asia. How many terrorists do you think will be blowing us up then? What will they be blowing us up for? Are there any people who would hate us for doing the right thing?

With ultimately positive aims in mind, Bamford began the interview with a scathing assessment of the post-9/11, prewar press coverage.

With few exceptions, both print and television provided very poor coverage. Knight Ridder did a really good job. Walter Pincus at the *Washington Post* did a very good job. But the problem was, these people were fighting an entrenched mind-set that was accepting the Bush administration's rationales for going to war when they should have been doubting. That's why Walter Pincus's stories questioning the validity of some of the information that the administration was giving out ended up on page seventeen and Judy Miller's very unsubstantiated and extremely poor reporting[1] for the *New York Times* wound up on the front page. The editors at these places were pretty much just going along with the administration. It seemed like their biggest concern at the time was getting their reporters on a tank so they could ride through the desert instead of assigning them to question people as to why we were going into the war in the first place. I think we should have had far fewer reporters riding through the desert pointing out sand dunes and a lot more back here pulling Richard Perle and Paul Wolfowitz and Donald Rumsfeld[2] on to the stage and asking questions.

You can't blame individual reporters because the editors set the agenda. If Walter Pincus's editor puts Pincus's reports on the front page, it would encourage a lot of other reporters to start digging. If he puts Pincus's reports on the back pages, then the message that gets across is "You want to get on the front page, don't question the administration, just get some general to tell you how devastated we're going to be when Iraq attacks us." That's the way the reporting went. The editors set the agenda and the reporters fell in line with the way the wind blew with the editors. That's the way it's always been and the way it's been going. If Judy Miller's reports had been put on the back page, it would have been a lot more encouraging for other reporters to start digging deeper. I think the television press was the same way; all they wanted to do was to rush over there and embed reporters in every single little unit to get virtually the same information. The real question was "Why are we going into war?" not "How many miles is it to Baghdad?" ABC put Ted Koppel on that tank in Iraq; he should have been back here in Washington questioning Wolfowitz. Koppel had the credibility and the authority to ask serious questions of these people.

I've been covering intelligence for a long time. I talked to a lot of people in the intelligence community during the prewar period and I didn't get any sense at all that there was any imminent danger from Iraq, at least for the foreseeable three, four, or five years. The people I was talking to were saying, "We have very few indications at all and they aren't very credible that Saddam has a large stockpile of anything serious, especially nuclear weapons."

You need two things if you want to present a danger to the United States: a warhead filled with germs, chemicals, or nuclear fissionable material and a delivery system. Although warheads are somewhat difficult to find through technical means such as satellites, delivery systems are extremely easy to see. A three-stage missile, which is what you're going to need to attack the United States, can be seen from space the minute you start building it. Then, because you have to test it, the United States would have years to deal with the problem. So there was no imminent threat and that was the key thing. We had UN inspectors acting as spies for us over there and they were going everywhere. Anywhere the CIA had a question, the inspectors could go in and take a look. I think it was the most unique situation in history, where we had a target country and more spies there on the ground than anywhere else in the world. Saddam wasn't restricting them from going into the palaces or anyplace. So it was illogical to order the spies out and send the soldiers in. If Saddam were going to attack us, wouldn't it be nice to have the spies in there when he started launching the missiles? You want the spies in there as long as possible. And since they were UN inspectors, they weren't costing the United States anything. Now it's costing us four and a half billion a month.

I wrote three op-ed pieces in August, September, and October 2002 for *USA Today* saying, "This is crazy" and that the people I had talked to in the Energy Department had said that all the stuff about centrifuges was nonsense and that the tubes that had been found weren't the same kind of tubes needed for nuclear or chemical warheads.

The reports that were generating all the fear about Iraq were coming from the front page of the *New York Times*, and that newspaper carries an awful lot of weight. Knight Ridder did what you are supposed to do. In the old days when I was doing daily journalism, I always thought that what you should do is go on the opposite side. If the administration says "white," we should see if there's any black there. The *New York Times* wasn't doing that. They were going out and trying to find more white to help the administration. It was as if the administration was conducting an orchestra and the people in the orchestra were the press. The administration said, "They're about to attack us, we're under a threat," and started this ball rolling. Congress was going the same way and the press should have stepped on the brake and they didn't. They never took their foot off the accelerator as far as I'm concerned.

> **People have said to me, "You have to report what the official source says. If the president says Saddam can reconstitute his weapons of mass destruction in six months, or if Secretary of State Powell presents the administration's case for war at the UN, you have to report that. And besides, we had no hard proof that those weapons of mass destruction did not exist."**

Obviously you've got to report what the administration says, but that doesn't mean that that's where your job ends. It really wasn't that hard to counter a lot of those things. The Niger claims[3] were nonsense. Then CIA director George Tenet was saying that the Niger stuff was nonsense. If anybody in the press had talked to anybody in the CIA, they would have reported that this was nonsense. Yet one of the key things that pushed a lot of people over to the administration's side was the believability of that. Bush mentioned it in his State of the Union address, and there wasn't much questioning of it until about two months later when IAEA [International Atomic Energy Agency][4] director Mohamed ElBaradei came out in the United Nations and said, "We don't find any evidence of that." ElBaradei didn't have access to any classified US information; he talked to the same people the press could have talked to. There were a lot of instances like that.

People have to develop sources within the intelligence community if they want to report on national security. You can't just go through the front office and get press releases. Richard Nixon would have completed his eight years if all Woodward and Bernstein[5] had done was go to the White House press office. You've got to develop sources and get people to talk to you, but very few people do. The CIA on the working level was reporting upward that they thought this was a lot nonsense.

Look at the Senate Intelligence Committee report from July 2004 where they said the CIA had "overstated and mischaracterized" the intelligence on the existence of WMDs. The committee said that the ultimate document on which they based this assessment was the National Intelligence Estimate or NIE.[6] The NIE is a document that was put together in a hurry and that backed what the administration was saying. It wasn't based on any real reporting from the CIA's analysts. Their reporting was saying the opposite, that Saddam was interested in palaces of mass luxury, not weapons of mass destruction, that he hadn't been exhibiting any animosity toward the United States in any great way, and that he hadn't been threatening to do anything.

I've always had a lot of respect for the CIA, especially at the working level. The working people have one goal and that is to produce the best possible estimate on what they're looking at. They're not really interested in politics and they're there throughout many administrations. That's the whole reason that President Harry Truman [1945–1953] set it up in the first place, to be a Central Intelligence Agency, not a political organization. His original picks for director were very apolitical—generals and admirals. The problem the Bush administration had with the CIA's working people was that they were coming up with information contradicting what the administration wanted the picture to be.

If you want a perfect example of the administration—Vice President Cheney in this case—lying to push their agenda, it's when he was talking about this meeting in Prague between the 9/11 hijacker Muhammad Atta and one of Saddam's people. Cheney was trying to link 9/11 to Saddam. He kept bringing up this meeting in Prague. This was after both the CIA and the FBI had conclusively said that there was no evidence that this meeting ever took place. Now when the two agencies that are supposed to be the nation's premier intelligence agencies look into this and tell you it didn't happen and you go out and tell the public something different, the agencies are not in a position to hold press conferences and say, "The vice president is wrong on this." The most they can do is leak it to a few people. So even though he knew that his spies and FBI agents were contradicting what he was saying, Cheney went out and said it. To me, that's a lie. That's a basic lie.

The administration wanted Iraq to look like it was a very threatening, dangerous place connected to al Qaeda and ready to attack us. The CIA was not reporting that. The CIA was reporting almost the opposite. Some of the key people who really wanted the threat story to get out were Defense Secretary Rumsfeld and his henchmen, then undersecretary of defense for policy Douglas Feith and then deputy secretary of defense Paul Wolfowitz. To counter the mild information that was coming out of the CIA, they set up this little unit called the Policy Counterterrorism Evaluation Group, which was a handful of people led by Cheney's Middle East adviser, David Wurmser, one of the neocons[7] who has been associated with Feith for a long time. They've wanted a war in the Middle East since the midnineties, and they wanted this war in Iraq. The Policy Counterterrorism Group cherry-picked information that the CIA was not paying any attention to or discarding, like the false Niger report claiming that Saddam had tried to buy uranium from Niger in the 1990s. Then the administration would go public with the information and give the impression that it was true. That was the really dangerous part, the attempt to slant the intelligence for political reasons.

Why did Wurmser and Feith want to go to war against Iraq?

It's part of the neoconservative ideology. Their goal is to rearrange the pieces of the Middle East. One of their principal concerns is Israel. Back in 1996, Feith, Wurmser, and former Defense Policy Board chairman Richard Perle, who are the architects of the Iraq war, were part of a small group of people who created this document called "A Clean Break: A New Strategy for Securing the Realm."[8] It was a foreign policy plan for Israel that Richard Perle gave to Benjamin Netanyahu, who had just become the prime minister of Israel. The "Clean Break" report recommended that Israel go in to Iraq, remove Saddam Hussein, put somebody in there who would basically be a puppet, and then go into Syria, Iran, and the other countries that they were worried about.

The idea was that the United States would back them in every way. They even had a pretext in there about how they were going to do it to help the United States get rid of Syria's drug dealing and counterfeiting infrastructure in Lebanon. But they were out of power, and nobody paid any attention to them. Two years later in 1998, eighteen top neocons, including Wolfowitz, Perle, and Rumsfeld, signed a letter to Clinton saying that he was endangering the United States if he didn't attack Iraq.

Then they finally got into power in January of 2001. As soon as the Bush administration came into office, Wurmser wrote a paper urging the United States and Israel to launch a war in the Middle East and attack Baghdad, Damascus, and Tehran. He wrote it at the American Enterprise Institute.[9] One of the other things Wurmser wrote at that time was that "crises are opportunities."

Then September 11 happens. Feith gets Wurmser and puts him in charge of running this little unit to start cherry-picking intelligence information on Iraq that would make a case for going to war. On the very afternoon of September 11, while he's at the Pentagon and the Pentagon's still in flames, Rumsfeld is telling his aides that the CIA and the National Security Agency [NSA][10] have given him information indicating that it's likely Osama bin Laden was responsible but that he wanted "best info fast; judge whether good enough to hit S.H. [Saddam Hussein] at same time. Not only UBL [Usama bin Laden]."[11] Then at the first meeting at Camp David after 9/11, everybody's talking about Afghanistan and Osama bin Laden, and Wolfowitz is talking about going into Iraq.

The first person to report on Rumsfeld's comments was David Martin of CBS News. He reported the story on September 4, 2002.

After September 11, the administration promoted this flag-waving mentality and said that we shouldn't question them. It gave them leeway to make things worse than they were, which is what they've done. In recent testimony, CIA director Porter Goss said, "We're creating more terrorism now than ever before by this war in Iraq." So the idea that patriotism is about going along with the administration, instead of trying to give the public the truth of what's being said, is ridiculous. These people in the Bush administration were lying through their teeth.

A lot of the press was reporting this. Every time Cheney came out and talked about this meeting in Prague that supposedly took place, a lot of news accounts would say that sources at the CIA and the FBI said it never did. But do you think the people in Middle America are going to read something in the fourth paragraph of a story in the *Washington Post* or are they going to listen to the headline that comes from a report on Cheney's address before the American Legion?

There may have been a lot of press putting out the truth and reporting that the meeting in Prague never occurred, but that information didn't get any traction. It seems that as long as our leaders are the only people who have continuous, instant, whenever-they-want access to mainstream or mass–public consciousness media, any spin or lie they want to put out will trump the truth every time.

Exactly, they've got the bully pulpit.

In your book, you talk about how they literally created an administration and a bureaucracy for formulating and perpetuating these messages over and over.

It was like an assembly line. They had to counter the CIA, at least until after October 2002, when then CIA director George Tenet joined the administration's parade. You could see almost to the day when Tenet flipped. Up until October 2002, he was bucking the White House on Niger. He said, "The president can't put this stuff about Niger in his Cincinnati address or his first address about Iraq to the country because we don't give it any credibility." Tenet personally forced the National Security Council [NSC][12] to drop it from the president's address. It was a battle, and if you look at Tenet's background, you'd see that the last thing he wanted to do was have a bureaucratic fight. He doesn't like that. He likes going to the White House every morning, getting patted on the back, and being a team member.

But he fought them and he won. They took it out of the Cincinnati address. After that, he never took up the challenge again. From then on, he was on the team, and the ultimate example of that was the State of the Union address. Imagine this: The State of the Union address is being prepared. We're about to go into a war based on intelligence information and the director of the CIA doesn't even bother to read the address before it's given. He doesn't try to object to anything, not even when they put Niger back in the speech.

Tenet had two choices after winning that first battle in October, because he could see which way the train was going. He could get onboard or he could object again. If he had refused to go along a second time, he could have gone on *Meet the Press* and said, "Look, I tried to tell them that I didn't believe this because our analysts were saying that they didn't believe a lot of these things." I think Tenet more than any other person could have made a difference. Nobody else in the administration was in his position. His agency was the only one that really did know what was going on, and he chose being a team player over letting the

American people know what was really going on. So in terms of the responsibility for going to war on all this bad intelligence, Tenet has to take a lot of the blame. After he got out, he got his little rewards: a Presidential Medal of Freedom and a five-million-dollar book contract. He's never said a word since then to the press or to the public, to which he owes a tremendous amount of explanation as to why he did this. He's not saying a word publicly, even when he gets these twenty- or fifty-thousand-dollar speaking gigs. He excludes the press from his talks. I've never seen a case where somebody has gone out on speaking engagements and deliberately excluded the press and said, "Part of the contract for me giving this talk is that there's no press allowed in here."

Do you think his book is going to be a mea culpa?

No, it's going to be a "I did everything right." The point is, whatever he's going to say, he's trying to make money on it instead of apologizing to the public for his screwups. If you want to find out what the government did, you're going to have to give him thirty dollars for his book. It's almost impossible to sink much lower than that.

Is there no accountability to the public here? If you're a key public official, like the head of the CIA, and you allow this big lie to be perpetrated, and it's a lie that allows other public officials to spend billions of the public's money and send the nation's citizens to death in a war started on false pretenses, is there no accountability?

Apparently not. His only accountability would be through congressional hearings, and most of the times he's gone up there in the postwar period he's been behind closed doors talking to various commissions. So the only way we're going to hear or see his own words about what happened is if we pay him for his speech or his book when it comes out.

Do you think that former secretary of state Powell is somewhat in the same position? He said in February 2001, well before 9/11, "Saddam has not developed any significant capability with respect to weapons of mass destruction."

Exactly, he said that as soon as the administration came into office. He was saying, "He's kept in a box, we're not worried about him." We occupied half the country at that point. We had daily overflights and embargoes on the country.

The only difference between Powell and Tenet was that Powell had the intelligence that was given to him by the CIA. Tenet was telling President Bush that the CIA had a "slam dunk" case proving there were WMDs in Iraq. I feel a little bit sorrier for Powell because he was depending on Tenet. Tenet could have made a difference.

> **Yes, but if Tenet is coming to Powell initially and saying, "There's nothing here," and then later Tenet is saying, "slam dunk," don't you think that Powell, as a thinking man, would have taken a harder look at Tenet and the intelligence?**

I agree 100 percent. Powell would be a hero now if he had resigned in protest. It would have been a perfect time to resign after he presented the case for WMDs at the UN. Virtually everything he said in that UN address before the Security Council was false.

I talked with people very close to him. He did know a lot of it was false. When he went to do the address, the neocons in Cheney's office had come up with this script that he was supposed to read, and the script had stuff in there about the meetings in Prague. That was too much even for Powell and he refused to say that. He threw out the first script. He threw out virtually all the alleged links between al Qaeda and Saddam except for the one with Zarqawi,[13] but still he bought all the stuff about the mobile biological weapons van.[14] Powell bought a lot of what he said from Tenet. That's why he insisted that Tenet sit right behind him at the UN council because he wanted people to know that the information had come from Tenet.

> **Are you suggesting that Tenet knowingly duped Powell about the mobile biological weapons van?**

No, I'm saying that, by then, Tenet had become a sycophant and was just saying "yes, yes, yes" to whatever information the administration wanted him to use.

> **Who came up with those visuals Powell used?**

The CIA put the visuals together. There were three groups working together to help Powell put together the UN presentation: the CIA, Cheney's office, and the White House. They all had an interest in making it as dramatic as possible. Most of the information that went into the script came from Cheney's office. Cheney's chief of staff, I. Lewis "Scooter" Libby, wrote it. Libby was key in this whole thing because he was shuttling information between Wurmser's little unit at the Pentagon and Cheney's office. Libby and Wurmser played a major role, because every time Cheney gave a speech, he'd be emphasizing all this nonsense that Wurmser and Libby had arranged for him to get.

Libby is an attorney. He's always been part of the far right neoconservative establishment. The same way Karl Rove is Bush's brain; he's Cheney's brain. When I was doing interviews with people close to Colin Powell, they were very angry at the situation that Powell was in and they put a lot of blame on Scooter Libby and these other people because they were shoving the information down Powell's throat. You can't really have that much sympathy for Colin Powell because he went through so many red lights during this whole thing. He slowed down a little bit because he didn't put everything in the UN presentation that they wanted him to, but still, the half he left in there was bad information. That's where I'm a little sympathetic with him because he was at the CIA, he was trying to just limit it to the hard information, but Tenet was not being cautious at all.

It doesn't make any sense to me that a guy who is a general . . .

Not only a general, he was chairman of the Joint Chiefs of Staff . . .

For a guy like that to go and give a speech to the UN without really making sure that everything he says is nailed down makes no sense to me whatsoever.

I agree. You'd have to be in Powell's mind, but the point is afterward, regardless of what went through his mind at the time, he should have said or done something. He was taking everything and making it sound as bad as he possibly could.

There were the intercepts that came from the National Security Agency [NSA].[15] I interviewed the director of the NSA, Lt. Gen. Michael Hayden, who is now going to be the number two person at the CIA. He said there was a lot of ambiguity in this stuff. You didn't hear any ambiguity when Colin Powell was talking about it. The headlines afterward sounded as if the NSA intercept was the smoking gun. It wasn't anywhere near a smoking gun. There was a lot of ambiguity, but that ambiguity wasn't conveyed to the American public or to the world in Powell's UN presentation.

The most dramatic example was that biological weapons van, for which Powell had all kinds of graphics. He mentioned three or four sources that provided information on the van, but none were very credible and each one started falling away soon afterward. One guy turned out to be a fabricator who the CIA had known about for years. At that point, the only honorable thing for the secretary of state of the United States to do would have been to resign since he had just told the world a lie that was one of the key factors in getting the United States into a war and in trying to get everybody else into the same war.

> **But what happened here? Who's accountable for this? Also, I'm not suggesting that you should give the press a pass, but if you have this environment of patriotism and then you have this White House operation creating the Policy Counterterrorism Evaluation Group, creating the Office of Special Plans and the White House Iraq Group, all of which are creating this giant juggernaut to get us to Iraq and get the public to go along with it, how could the press possibly penetrate this wall of patriotism and political machination to get to the truth before the war?**

I think the only way would have been for the editorial management of these news organizations to reward digging up information that countered what the administration was saying. Take Judy Miller and those reports she wrote based on her interviews with defectors. I've covered the intelligence community for twenty-five years. I almost never depend on what defectors say. During the cold war,[16] you could get a Russian defector to say anything because their whole idea was to come to the United States and make it look like they knew more than they really did because they were depending on the CIA or whichever agency they'd gone to for help. If they came out and said, "The Soviet Union isn't that bad," what was the CIA or any other agency going to give them for that kind of information? So the Iraqi defectors would say, "Yes, I know they're building chemical weapons." The intelligence community usually discarded almost everything from these defectors.

What happened with Judith Miller?

She bought into this stuff. First of all, she started using as sources people who should have been targets. She started dealing with the neoconservative crowd. Some of her sources were people like James Woolsey, the former CIA director. He was a prowar cheerleader. He was promoting this war more than anybody else at the very beginning. Now, how credible a source is he going to be? And she should have identified him. He wasn't some confidential analyst working for the CIA; he's a former CIA director.

Woolsey is at the apex of the neoconservatives. Nobody's really written about Woolsey's role here, but it's significant. He was on TV all the time, just like Richard Perle. All these people are on shows all the time as if they're credible people. This is really amazing to me. A couple of things amaze me: one was the sloppy job the press did before the war and the other thing is how the press treats these people as if they're credible sources without ever asking them any hard questions. Perle was on *Nightline* a couple of weeks ago. The show was called "Iraq—Why Stay?" and it was a town hall meeting. Perle was sitting next to Koppel, and Koppel didn't ask Perle one hard question like "What did you do to get us into this thing?"

Why is that?

It's the same mentality as before; this is the establishment and we're not going to question the establishment. That's the whole problem with the "mushroom cloud" thing. I've written for the *New York Times*. I did a cover story on Iran-Contra for the magazine. You call up and you say you're from the *New York Times* and you can go anywhere. I was the only reporter to get into the National Security Council during Iran-Contra. It wasn't because of my name; it was because I was writing for the *New York Times Magazine*. I got the only exclusive interview with the National Security advisor at the time, Frank Carlucci.

Judy Miller got in and saw Condoleezza Rice.[17] Condi talked to her about the nuclear threats—the centrifuges and all that—on background, which is why Miller identified Rice only as "a senior administration official." It was during that backgrounder that Rice told Miller, "We don't want the smoking gun to be a mushroom cloud." I'm sure some White House speechwriter came up with that beautiful little sound bite.

The following Sunday, the front-page headline was "U.S. Says Hussein Intensifies Quest for A-Bomb Parts" [September 8, 2002]. The average person sitting at home was probably thinking, "This madman is about to throw an H-bomb at us." That same day, all the talk fests like *Meet the Press, Late Edition,* and *Face the Nation* had all the administration talking heads on, including Rice, Rumsfeld, and Cheney, and what they did was point to the headline and say, "Look what the *New York Times* reported today about mushroom clouds." They leaked this nonsense to the *New York Times*, the *New York Times* put it on the front page, and then they went on TV and pointed to the *New York Times* article as proof that their statements were credible.

That's part of the echo chamber.

Yes. They were getting this information from people like Ahmed Chalabi[18] who wanted us to go into this war for his own political reasons.

Chalabi wanted to be president of Iraq, and the neocons have wanted to go into Iraq for a long time. Bush hates Saddam because he thought he was going to kill his father.[19] Going to war had nothing to do with a possible WMD attack.

I was talking about warheads being difficult to see from space, and delivery systems being easy to see, and it being clear that the Iraqis had no delivery systems. Besides trying to come up with bogus proof of a nuclear threat, senior officials at the CIA who were part of Tenet's group—including the head of the National Intelligence Council [NIC], Robert Hutchings, whose people came up with the nonsense National Intelligence Estimate—told Congress that the Iraqis had developed sophisticated unmanned aerial vehicles that they could load with germs and launch against the United States. They reported that the Iraqis were going to put the drones in ships, sail them along the East Coast of the United States, and fly them off the ships.

How close do you think they would get to US shores without the United States seeing these ships carrying drones coming at them? Intelligence figured out later that the drones were made for observation, not for delivery of chemical or biological agents.

There seem to have been a lot of people involved who knew that this was BS.

In my book *A Pretext for War*,[20] I quote a number of people at the CIA. One middle-level analyst at the CIA who worked in the unit that was supposed to be looking for WMDs in Iraq told me that her boss came out, gathered together all fifty members of the unit, and said, "If Bush wants to go to war, it's your job to give him a reason to do so." And she said, "That was disgusting. I just about walked out at that point." But that was the mentality among those close to Tenet.

Nobody wanted to step out of his/her box and go public and say, "Look, here's what's going on?"

These are people who work for the CIA. They had a lot to lose. Most of them talked to me after the war. Getting these people to talk is very difficult. Before the war, the people who did talk to me weren't so concerned. They were saying, "A lot of what the administration is saying is nonsense, but it's just a bluff. They're just trying to bully Iraq into letting in all the inspectors. Once the inspectors get in there, they'll be able to go out and find all this stuff. We're not really going to war."

This was in December 2002. I thought, "It's pretty good if the Bush administration can do that," although contrary to public belief, it was the United States that forced the inspectors out in the first place because we wanted to go in there and bomb.

The United States had turned the UN inspectors into American spies when they were in Iraq. The inspectors had been out since 1998 and we wanted them back in, and Bush accomplished that through some really tough "We're going to blow your head off" Clint Eastwood dialogue. So they went back in, and a lot of people in the intelligence community that I was talking to thought it was a very good move. They thought that that was where it was going to end.

Didn't the Israelis have any idea about Saddam's weapons capabilities?

The Israelis were the key people outside the administration pushing for the United States to invade Iraq. After questions started coming out about the issue of weapons of mass destruction, the Israeli government did a study looking into whether or not Iraq had WMDs, and they didn't have any real information confirming they existed, so they were ginning up the rhetoric, too.

Was the Israeli branch of the Office of Special Plans in Sharon's office doing that?

That's right. They were constantly going back and forth with Feith. Feith is as close as you can possibly get to the Israelis. His law firm does business mostly in Israel and his partner, Marc Zell, is a leader of the settlement movement in Israel.

Didn't someone in his office get into trouble recently for allegedly passing secret documents on US policy toward Iran to the American Israel Public Affairs Committee,[21] which passed them on to the Israeli government?

Yes, Larry Franklin from his office is a key target of the FBI's investigation.

They've questioned a number of people in his office, and now Feith is the first neocon to say, "I'm leaving."[22] He's a protégé of Richard Perle. If you look at his background, this guy is an extreme right-wing pro-Israeli fanatic.

These neocons were basically born in the Reagan administration. They started under Senator Henry "Scoop" Jackson,[23] but Reagan was the first president to really take advantage of them and put them all in his administration. They didn't like George W. Bush's father because they thought he would be tough on Israel and he was. He was the toughest president since Eisenhower,[24] I would say. George H. W. Bush was very angry about the settlements because it's against US policy for the Israelis to build settlements. It's against UN resolutions too. So when Bush came in to office, Perle, Feith, and all the others left. Not only did they leave, but when Bush started becoming somewhat aggressive—and you have to take this in context, what I mean by "aggressive" is that Bush wanted to force Israel to stop building settlements—the neocons were so angry that Feith actually formed a committee to fight him, saying that he was anti-Israel and taking out a full-page ad in the *New York Times* attacking Bush. Feith also began running anti-Bush op-ed pieces in the *Jerusalem Post.*

Bush was saying, "If you don't stop building settlements, we're going to cut off your loan guarantees." That didn't mean that he was going to cut off their money; it just meant that he was going to cut off the second signature on their loan guarantees so that it would make it a little more difficult for them to get loans from various places.

So that's Feith. He's the number three person in the Pentagon and one of the architects of the war, and he's due to leave the Pentagon this summer.

I think we went to war because it's been this neocon agenda and they're running the government right now. George W. Bush brought in the neocons because he wanted to follow Ronald Reagan's blueprint instead of his father's, because his father only had one term and Reagan had two. So he brought back all the neocons from the Reagan years. They were called the "Vulcans," and they brought in a lot of money and political support from the Jewish community and pro-Israeli groups.

George W. Bush isn't a classic neocon. The classic neocons have always had an ideological agenda. Chalabi has been their designated pick for leading Iraq since the late eighties. They were all sort of ring knockers, old school boys—Chalabi, Wolfowitz, and Perle. All along they've been writing letters advising Israel and the US government to get rid of Saddam. But Saddam has never been a threat to the United States.

So all this is being done on Israel's behalf?

The original plan, "A Clean Break: A New Strategy for Securing the Realm,"[25] wasn't done for the Clinton administration. They weren't advising the current sitting US government; they were advising the current sitting Israeli government. They weren't telling Netanyahu to go in there and attack Iraq to make the United States safe; they were saying,

"Go in there to make Israel safe." It's right there in "A Clean Break," which is only three pages long.

Are you saying that the US government has been manipulated into putting all these American resources and lives into Iraq for Israel?

That's a key factor. I'm not saying that's the only factor. Two mind-sets congealed on January 30, 2001, at the first National Security Council meeting. The first mind-set is the neocon mind-set, which is what created this government in the first place. You've got Wolfowitz, Perle, Feith, Rumsfeld, Cheney, Scooter Libby—all key neocons with a long-standing agenda to attack Iraq—coming together to basically run the foreign policy of the United States. Cheney was sort of a token outsider who was pretty much marginalized.

Then you have Bush coming in with a different agenda. He hated Iraq for a different reason. The overwhelming reason for Bush was that he got a report from the FBI a number of years before he became president that said Saddam Hussein was going to kill his entire family. The report (and I'm not giving credibility to the report because Seymour Hersh has reported on it and raised a lot of questions), which is publicly available, said that Saddam had this plan to send a suicide car bomber into Kuwait to hit Bush family members who had arrived to commemorate the first Gulf War victory over Iraq.

Everyone in George W.'s family—his father, mother, two brothers and their wives—was there except for George W. himself. They were all going to be on this stage when the car bomber was supposed to blow it up and kill the entire family.

Yes, but you understand that for a guy to assume the presidency and the first order of business in his mind is to go and seek revenge for what he perceives could have happened to his family by taking the money and military resources of the nation to go and wreak his vengeance sounds extreme.

I think that's a key psychological factor for George W. Bush. I never thought oil had much to do with it. If you look at the neocon agenda, it has nothing to do with controlling world oil; it has to do with Israel. If you look at their past writings, they're always about Israel. That's the key common denominator. You seldom hear them talk about oil. Maybe it was a factor.

To understand this, you have to look at that very first National Security Council meeting Bush held on January 30, 2001, ten days after he got elected. This was all written about in the book *The Price of Loyalty*[26] that

Ron Suskind wrote about former treasury secretary Paul O'Neill. O'Neill said there were only two items on the agenda for that meeting where everybody came together for the first time. One was easing up on Israel, backing away from the Oslo Accords[27] and letting Israeli prime minister Ariel Sharon do what he wanted with the Palestinians. A lot of that was Bush because Bush only traveled outside the country twice before he was president. He traveled to China to see his father when George H. W. Bush was ambassador over there, and then the only other place he ever went to was Israel. He got some free trip to Israel when he was governor and he met Ariel Sharon. Paul O'Neill quotes Bush in that National Security Council meeting saying, "Has anybody ever met Ariel Sharon? I have." And then the president said, "We're going to ease up on Ariel Sharon." This is also part of this Christian fundamentalism that Bush believes in, where all Jews have to go back to Israel where they're going to be annihilated in the End Days except for one hundred and fifty thousand who actually accept Christ or some crazy thing like that.

So the Bush administration's agenda was to ease up on Israel and let them do whatever they wanted. Colin Powell objected to that in the National Security Council meeting, but Bush overrode him. The second part of the agenda was, "How are we going to get Saddam?" They had Tenet come in there with all these maps of Iraq and point out bombing targets.

Tenet's the only guy from the Clinton administration who stayed on with the Bush administration. He'd always been buddying up to the Bushes. His idea was to stay in power, and to stay in power is to be a team player. That's George Tenet in a nutshell. When they renamed the CIA headquarters the Bush Intelligence Center, he had this enormous party celebrating it and made all these great comments about George Bush's father even though George H. W. Bush was director of the CIA for less than a year and it was almost a do-nothing job for him.

You're giving me this big-picture context that I would say most journalists don't have.

They won't write about it. Mainstream journalism will not talk about "Clean Break." They're afraid of offending a special interest group. How are you going to tell what's going on in the government if you're afraid of offending a special interest group? I've just never believed in that.

What are the implications for this country if that's the case?

You can see the implications. The press were a bunch of lemmings during this entire prewar, WMD thing. They let the administration get away without any kind of real scrutiny.

The quality of the journalists is as good as it's ever been in terms of education and capabilities, but they've got to do what their editors are emphasizing. If you turn these people loose, they'll do very good work, just like Woodward and Bernstein, but they aren't being told to do that. Their editors don't come out and say, "Do this or do that," but it's what's implied. Prewar, Walter Pincus—and he's about as good an intelligence writer as there ever has been—really was digging and Knight Ridder was digging, but their reports were not going on the front pages of any newspapers. They were going on the back pages, or middle of the back, or page seventeen.

Pincus was well aware of what that was implying.

Yes, but he's a professional; he was going to keep doing it. Walter Pincus has been there since the early seventies doing all this work. He's got sources that nobody else has and they were essentially telling him, "Look, there is not a lot of evidence of a Saddam/al Qaeda connection or that these aluminum tubes are parts of nuclear centrifuges for enriching uranium." And it's hard to get this information, because you've got to go out there and get these sources, and they don't want to tell you, and then you're afraid you're going to overuse them, and then you're afraid they're going to get into trouble. There are a lot of things you've got to think about when you're doing the national security investigative stuff. You've got to worry about getting people in trouble because they're saying the opposite thing the administration wants them to say. So you go to all that trouble, and people do risk a lot by talking to you, and then it ends up behind the sports section. So what incentive is that for me to go out and do that again and tell these people to talk to me again? It's much easier to go get Condoleezza Rice to tell me about mushroom clouds or get some lunatic defector from Chalabi's group to tell me about H-bombs buried under hospitals or whatever, because then I'm guaranteed a front-page story, and my ultimate goal is to advance my career and I'm not going to do it by writing back-of-the-paper stories. The same thing goes for television, too.

So you're saying either advance your career or tell the truth, but you can't do both?

Walter Pincus had a choice, and he decided that telling the truth was far more important than being on page one. I'm using him as an example, but there were others. It's very risky for places like Knight Ridder to do it because they're syndicated. The *Washington Post* has a huge constituency in the Washington area that expects this kind of reporting from them. Knight Ridder has to have articles in Midwestern newspapers and Colorado and all these other places that don't have this liberal East Coast bias, so there's a bit of risk there that their papers may think that they're unpatriotic or something because they're writing all this stuff.

Did you get any flak for your book *A Pretext for War*?

Not from the administration because by the time it came out the tide had already begun to turn on the whole WMD issue. It came out in June 2004, and by then a lot of the information regarding the bogus biochemical van and the other stuff was already out there. I broke a lot of ground in terms of putting it all together into a big picture, plus there were a lot of quotes in there that I got from middle-level people in the CIA saying, "We were told that the president wants this war so it's our job to give him a reason for going to war."

Now there's been talk about Iran.

It's déjà vu all over again. If you look at the pattern and how they do this, it's almost this Orwellian psychology. In George Orwell's book *1984*, you have this "hate hour" every day. You have this guy, whoever he happens to be, and everyday at noon or whatever time, you go in and sit there for an hour and you hate this person. The whole idea is that you're always at war. In *1984* it was always East Asia or Eurasia; it didn't make any difference. It's the same thing that seems to be going on with Iran and Syria to some degree. First you start off by demonizing these people as subhuman, as enormous threats to the United States. Then you connect them with evil events so that you have this bombing that takes place in Lebanon, and that same day, even though there's absolutely zero evidence of who did it, the Bush administration immediately announces, "The president of Syria directly ordered this thing."

Why is that being reported without a shred of evidence?

The administration doesn't need that because all they have to do is imply it. Again, they've got the bully pulpit, and the key thing that Bush did was that very day or the next day he pulled the US ambassador out of Syria. So in the public's mind, these two events take place—the former president of Lebanon gets blown up and the United States pulls its ambassador from Syria while pointing a finger at Syria. You do that and—they did the same thing with Iraq—you build an impression in the public's mind that Syria's a threat, they're bad people and they're really evil, yet, just like we didn't prove WMD, we haven't proved that there's any link between this bombing and the government of Syria.

There are all kinds of factions in the Middle East that hate people. The only connection to Syria would be if this were state-sponsored terrorism, but there wasn't any evidence of that. Nevertheless, the administration is generating this fear and hatred of Syria among Americans with this sort of "hate hour" tactic. It's the same thing with Iran. Iran poses no threat to the United States in the near or far future. When have Syria or Iran ever threatened the United States? We're threatening them. Where is the balance of power in the Middle East? Israel is the country that has up to two hundred nuclear weapons, and we're complaining because Iran may have violated its agreement with the International Atomic Energy Agency [IAEA]. Israel hasn't even signed the IAEA agreement. We're complaining because the UN inspectors might not be getting full access to everything in Iran. Well, Israel won't let any inspectors in there. Talk about a double standard. People in the Middle East see this. They see this double standard constantly, where we've got our American colony, Israel, and it's armed with all these nuclear weapons, hasn't signed the nonproliferation agreement, and isn't letting any inspectors in. Also, Israel is an aggressive country. They've already attacked Iraq; they sent bombers over there to blow up Iraq's nuclear reactor. They're occupying an Arab country, Palestine, and they've initiated numerous aggressive actions against their neighbors, including invading Lebanon back in 1982. Yet when was the last time you read anything in the newspapers or heard the administration say anything about Israel not complying with these international accords?

Is Israel a touchy subject to the press?

It's enormously touchy. You can't talk about Israel in the press without somebody going crazy and accusing you of anti-Semitism or some other nonsense, so people are extremely worried about writing about it because they're afraid of being accused of being an anti-Semite or unpatriotic. The problem is that the press treats Israel in the same way that the administration does. There's a double standard there.

Isn't that because Israel is protecting our interests over there?

What interests? They're the cause of all the problems.

> **That's where we get to the oil, Jim. Why would we want to go and take over the Middle East if it weren't because we want their resources? What's the point?**

Again, the other argument, the nonoil argument is that if Israel is your client state, your colony, America's presence in the Middle East, or whatever you want to call it, you want to create . . .

> **. . . the conditions for its survival.**

It's what Israel has been pushing for years. You've got to look at the blueprint. The blueprint is "Clean Break." It was written by the people who created this war. The whole object is to roll back the Arab countries in the Middle East, roll back the governments of those countries. The key interest of the people running this administration is to create at the minimum a neutral Middle East, and at best a friendly Middle East. You could pick a thousand quotes on this out of the stuff they've written.

> **How do invasion, occupation, and aggression accomplish that?**

You're talking to the wrong person. I'm saying it doesn't. I'm not the one who led this war. You've got to ask those guys how it does. I'm saying it doesn't, and apparently the director of the Central Intelligence Agency agrees with me because he just came out and said that we're creating more terrorists than ever before. If this was supposed to end terrorism, we're doing the opposite.

> **Do you think we're going to go to war against Syria and Iran?**

I think the only thing holding us back right now is the fact that we can't afford to do it, both in terms of dollars and troops. We don't even have enough troops in Iraq. There was a *60 Minutes* program about a month ago, and talk about sending every last person you can lay your hands on, there was a little gray-haired woman, I think she was fifty-five years old, and she hadn't served on active duty for fifteen years but she hadn't resigned her commission yet, and the small print in her contract said she could be recalled, so there she was she was, four foot eight with a helmet on. And she was saying, "I'm on my way to Iraq. I don't want to go there, but I have no choice." That's what we've come to. They lowered the educational level. If you got drunk with a recruiter at one time and actually signed a piece of paper, you're on your way to Iraq. There are no second thoughts allowed. They're using everybody they can get their hands on.

Cheney invited Israel to attack Iran.

Exactly. Israel's already shown a proclivity for attacking its neighbors; it attacked Iraq, it attacked Lebanon, and it sent planes into Syria in the last year or so. Cheney would love to have Israel do it, not that that would fool anybody. An attack by Israel on Iran is an attack by the United States on Iran, especially after the encouragement. Israel is wisely doing what it always does; it would rather have the United States be the heavy in this. I don't know of any Israelis killed in the Iraq war. It's all been Americans and coalition troops.

How do you think the press is covering the postwar era?

The tide has turned. All of a sudden there's no requirement for backing the administration. We've already had a number of reports come out showing that all this WMD stuff is nonsense, so there's no reason to back the administration on any of that any more.

I think now the press sees a lot of parallels with Vietnam. They saw how Vietnam turned out. I think the reporting, at least compared to the prewar reporting, is certainly a lot better, a lot more honest, and they're digging up information. You see reports all the time about generals who are saying that we don't have enough troops over there. They're getting quotes that they should have gotten before the war, because there were a lot of people who had doubts before the war, but the press never got to them.

There seems to be a pattern. The pattern seems to be: unquestioning prewar coverage of the reasons for going to war, then "bang-bang" war coverage, and then, after the war has been going on for a while and/or postwar, the coverage starts getting more critical. How do you change that?

You've got to have management in the news organizations that want to do real journalism. You're always going to have your standard everyday reporters who just rewrite press releases. But then you've got to have a cadre of reporters who are experienced in going out and getting the other side of the story. If the administration says "white," you go out and get black, or if they say "black," you go out and find white. Whether or not your story actually makes it in to the paper depends on how credible the information is, but the point is you've got to assign people to start doing that, and most of the press or news organizations don't do that. Look at the resources of the television networks, for example, in terms of the money and people. ABC has *World News Tonight*. When you take the commercials out, you have twenty-two minutes left. Then you have to take out more minutes for Peter to say things and you've got to have the silly little kicker at the end about tortoise races in Phoenix or something, so when you get down to the hard-core news, you're talking maybe fifteen minutes a day at the most in a twenty-four-hour day.

Then you have *Nightline*. I've always loved *Nightline*; I still think it's a really good show. I've always liked Ted Koppel. I think he's one of the best journalists in the country. *Nightline* is twenty-two minutes of news every night, five days a week. So if you add twenty-two minutes from *Nightline* and fifteen minutes from *ABC World News*, you've got less than forty-five minutes of news a day. Then you've got all these other resources like *Good Morning America* and the magazine shows, and they're maybe five hours a week. And what do they do? They're focused on "there was a murder in 1983 . . ."

They're focused on Michael Jackson's penis right now.

Last night, *20/20* had a whole hour of Diane Sawyer interviewing Petra Nemcova, this supermodel who survived the tsunami.

But you understand the editorial stance. The editorial stance has got to be, "The people paying for the news are the advertisers." They don't want to hang their ads on some hard investigative show that's going to upset and/or anger the audience, the government, or some powers that be. They want to hang their advertising on inoffensive entertainment.

I know; it is the whole nature of this thing. *Primetime* and *20/20* are in a race with *Dateline*, so they're appealing to the lowest common denominator, the people who don't want to sit there and watch an exposé or analysis of the impact of Rumsfeld's actions. You get a much broader cross section of people who want to see the latest on Michael Jackson or some model.

Why is that still the case? On 9/11 two planes went into the Twin Towers because of external things going on that lots of people weren't aware of. Why aren't they more interested now in knowing what their leaders are doing and what's going on in the world?

I think part of it is the nature of this country. The two coasts are blue states, and then there's the big red area in the center. The difference between here and Europe is that in Europe you go one hundred and fifty miles in any direction and you've got a different culture, different history, different language, different food, different everything. And they've been affected by wars. They've had their cities blown up by neighbors, so they've got to be more sophisticated. They know that things that happen in other places affect them because they've got all these different people all around them, people who may want to attack them or may want to be friends. In Middle America, you go one hundred miles or a thousand miles in any direction and you've got the same mind-set, the same food, the same culture, and the same history. Nobody's ever attacked us except for the Japanese at Pearl Harbor, and Hawaii wasn't a state at the time. Also, the country is surrounded by huge oceans on two sides and very friendly countries on the other sides, so there's no incentive to think beyond who is playing for the Red Sox next week. Most Americans don't see foreign policy as having much impact on their lives. It's too complicated, I think, for a lot of them to think about very deeply, and that's why a lot of these people just latch on to the sort of right-wing bumper sticker mentality and say things like, "They're terrorists and they're out to get us and they don't like our freedoms." The terrorists aren't blowing up Stockholm, are they? I've read a lot of bin Laden's writings, and he hasn't said anything about our Supreme Court. It's our foreign policy in the Middle East that he's upset about. If Iraq was occupying the southeastern part of the United States and had a virtual colony within the United States that was very aggressive and had nuclear weapons, how would Americans respond? Those are the things people can't put in context. They think of the Middle East as a collection of little individual third world countries instead of realizing that it's a Muslim community, it's an entire region, so if you affect one part of the region, you're affecting people in other parts of the region. It's sort of like the United States.

> **It's fascinating to me that Americans don't seem to think about what it would be like if another country just came in and said, "Hey, we want your land or we want your homes or your resources, and we're going to come here now, and this is our place, so do what we want or move." They never try and step in the shoes of the other side. Yet laws of physics and nature tell you that for every action there's an equal and opposite reaction. How can you not think that if you go to the Middle East and exert your power and attack people that something isn't going to happen to you?**

Exactly. The evidence has always been there. All you have to do is go back to the first World Trade Center bombing and look at the people behind it and the motivations. I wrote about it in my book. I was astonished that none of this stuff had really come out before, but the bombers who blew

up the World Trade Center the first time, Ramzi Yousef, for example, who
was the mastermind, he's the nephew of Khalid Sheikh Mohammed.[28]
They're very close. They were secular, basically. When he was in the
Philippines, Khalid Sheikh Mohammed wore a tuxedo and chased women.
Ramzi Yousef, who is actually very intelligent—read the interviews he's
given—is an engineer. They laid out their reasons for bombing the Trade
Center in two letters that they left after the bombing. The FBI got the letters, and they sent one to one of the newspapers. I think the paper para-
phrased a few quotes from it, but that's about it. It was a one-day story
back then. But the letters laid out exactly why they did it, and it all had to
do with US foreign policy in the Middle East, particularly with respect to
Israel. And they said, "We're going to come back," and they did come
back. Ramzi Yousef got caught, but Khalid Sheikh Mohammed was the
mastermind behind 9/11. So if you're looking for the reasons, the reasons
are right there. You don't have to make something up about "They hate our
freedoms." But you can say that to hide the real reasons.

**Covering these missives that are left behind by the perpetrators seems
to be a political act in the world of journalism.**

Yes, exactly.

**Instead of saying, "Look, here's what they said, here's the letter," and
boom, you show the letter, only small fragments of it are quoted or
shown.**

I haven't seen anybody do that. I haven't seen anybody connect these dots.

**"We don't want to give the terrorists any airtime or space in the paper
for their propaganda" is the usual explanation.**

If you don't understand your enemy, you're never going to defeat him.

**I remember after 9/11 there were all these terrorism experts on TV. And
I kept thinking to myself, I wonder how many of them have actually
met and spoken to a terrorist?**

You can't walk ten feet in Washington without bumping into a terrorism
expert. A terrorism expert is anybody who can pronounce the word, I
think. At ABC, people would call me up all the time and say, "I'm a terrorism expert, I'd like to tell you how the terrorists are working." I think
that if you license beauticians you should really license terrorism experts
because they can cause far more damage—and they do. Most of them rep-

resent some special interest and are pushing an agenda. You don't have to be Albert Einstein to understand why somebody's attacking you. All you have to do is look at what they've said in the past.

If you just read all of bin Laden's writings, and you get rid of all the flowery references to the Koran, he's got three basic points of contention. He's always had three basic points: US involvement in the entire Middle East, which has grown from having people in Saudi Arabia to Americans being all over the place and threatening countries in the Middle East; US support for Israel as an aggressive and potentially threatening country to Arabs and particularly Palestinians; and the US embargo on the average people in Iraq.

What do you think about the election in Iraq?

It's hard to say how it's going to play out. I worry about the United States doing something covert or some other kind of manipulating to get Allawi[29] in there somewhere down the line. In about a year or so, I hope that it's not going to come out that whoever's in there is in there because of something the United States did.

You don't think we spent billions of dollars over there to tolerate somebody inimical to our interests being in power, do you?

No. It's exactly the point. It already looks bad because it looks like the person who is going to be prime minister, Ibrahim al-Jaafari,[30] is quite religious, very close to Iran, and his group, the Dawa Party, has been linked to a number of anti-American terrorist actions in the past, so I think they're very afraid. They originally wanted Chalabi in there, but Chalabi made such a mess.

How viable was Chalabi? He was outside of the country for all those years.

He has been the darling of the neocons and part of their agenda from the very beginning. Chalabi has been one of them since the late eighties, and he was working them as much as he possibly could to get there. The neocons all thought the Iranians would love Chalabi because he's smart. He's highly educated; he has a PhD from MIT. The only problems are that he's got a history of being a crook—he's been charged with bank fraud in Jordan—and he has no real connection to the people. He left Iraq when he was twelve years old.

Originally, the neocons figured the United States would go into Iraq, take over the country, and then fly Chalabi over there with his little band of cohorts, the Iraqi National Congress group, and they'd be paraded around town through cheering crowds. None of that came true.

How did they get it so wrong?

You've got to look at their background. These people are my contemporaries. We all go back to the Vietnam War period, and we were all eligible for the draft at the same time. I got number one on the very first draft lottery. Luckily, I'd already volunteered to go into the military just a couple of years before. I saw the draft coming so I volunteered, but I would have been on the first boat or plane over to Vietnam after the draft lottery if I hadn't. But these are the same people who were in favor of the war and who never served in the war. Cheney is famously quoted as saying he had better things to do. George Bush was all in favor of it, but he had no intention of ever going over and serving. So they spent their entire time in these K Street think tanks writing these papers that had no connection whatsoever with reality.

But how do people like that get into power?

I already explained it. The neoconservatives have had a following of people in this country who are pretty much single-issue people—particularly the pro-Israel group and the very wealthy—who donated a lot of money. When Reagan brought in the neocons, he won the pro-Israel group's support by a larger margin than almost any other president in a very long time. In terms of that one vote, he got an extra ten points or so, which was quite a bit of movement. The Democrats always get the majority of the pro-Israel vote, so it's not as though they were beating the Democrats, but Reagan got a larger plurality than any Republican had received before. And when you're talking about an election that usually comes down to a few points, that's an important factor. It's an important factor in certain key states, like Florida.

This is a political reality. There are certain interest groups that are more important than others. The pro-Israel interest group traditionally has a lot of political power that can bring a lot of people into your Democrat or Republican camp, and they give lots of money. That's why there's such an appeal to that group. Whoever gets a good percentage of that group has a better chance of winning the election.

Yes, but that group is traditionally pro-Democrat.

Right. It's 60 or 70 percent Democrat, but if you're a Republican and you can win ten extra points from this group and take those ten points away from the Democrats, then you're that much more ahead. Winning an election is about winning greater majorities from various groups. A Republican is never going to win more than 50 percent from the pro-Israel group because it goes to the Democrats, but there is a certain percentage of people in that group who are on the fence, and they're up for grabs.

Their number one issue is always Israel. That's the key issue. If you're going to be friendlier to Israel and tougher on the Arab states, then you're going to win a lot of those percentages, which is what the neocons did.

That trumps everything else that could happen domestically.

Yes, in this one group, and to win this group, you have to change your foreign policy. To get this group, you've got to alter the way the United States acts in the most volatile part of the world. That affects far more than giving price supports to the dairy industry or something.

George H. W. Bush lost that pro-Israel percentage. He didn't necessarily lose the entire election just because of that, but it was a key factor. George W. Bush reversed his father's position on the Middle East. Instead of being hard on Israel, he's easy on Israel. Instead of being sympathetic to the Palestinian cause, he's basically saying, "The hell with the Palestinians. We're going to go along with Ariel Sharon." And to demonstrate that he was going to do this, he brought in the super-hardliners, the neocons, and that sent the right message to the pro-Israel fencesitters. Again, the only problem with that is that when you get elected, it's not a question of giving a few extra dollars to dairy farmers, it's a question of changing the entire Middle East policy because you brought in the fanatics to help deliver the votes you needed.

Interest groups have always had swing votes in elections, and there are all kinds of them. The term "interest group" itself is not a pejorative term. Black people are an interest group, so are Catholics and the middle class. But what you do for them does not affect foreign policy.

Traditionally, there are two groups in the United States that politicians go after for votes that alter US foreign policy around the world to a detrimental effect, I think. One group is the Cuban Americans in Miami. It's beyond belief that we still have an embargo on Cuba. The cold war has been over for a decade. Any sensible person would say, "Who cares about Cuba at this point in terms of national security?" Russia's pulled out. It's just an island in the Caribbean, and it's only because of politicians pandering to this small group of anti–Castro Cuban Americans that the embargo still exists.

They give a lot of money.

And they have an awful lot of political power in a very important swing state. It's the same thing with the pro-Israel voters, and they aren't all Jewish. That's why I use the term "pro-Israel." There are fundamentalist Christians, like Jerry Falwell's group,[31] who are pro-Israel. When you pander to these groups, you're affecting the foreign policy of the United States. It's literally a handful of people in a country of two hundred and ninety million Americans who have, for the last thirty years, largely determined our policy in Cuba and the Middle East.

Cuba is Cuba, and it's not going to affect us one way or the other in terms of our national security. With the Middle East, you get buildings blown up if you do the wrong thing. I think the average voter doesn't think in these concepts, but you've got to think in terms of how special interest groups affect our foreign policy. There's no political benefit to being anti-Israel and pro-Palestinian, and the only time that you can get any realistic policies toward Cuba, like lifting the embargo and normalizing relations, would be after a president's been elected a second time when the risk isn't so great.

With respect to his policies on Israel, Bush is even more pro-Israel in his second term. He's a true believer. He's basically a sycophant to Ariel Sharon and a born-again fundamentalist. So in our president, you have the combination of hatred for Saddam Hussein and love for Ariel Sharon. You can read former treasury secretary Paul O'Neill's account of Bush's idol worship of Ariel Sharon in Ron Suskind's book *The Price of Loyalty*. Bush's entire second-term cabinet subscribes to this gung-ho ideology that promotes the use of preemptive war to take over the Middle East.

Where is Congress as the balance of power?

That's a good question. Congress was so afraid to vote against the White House. It was this whole flag-waving thing, feeling they would look unpatriotic if they voted against the war in Iraq. It was much easier to come out and join the crowd by saying, "Oh, yeah, there's enormous danger, the CIA's saying it." And they were. Tenet was saying it. Colin Powell was saying it. So it was an easy decision for a congressman. There were six Republicans who voted against the war: Ron Paul of Texas, James A. Leach of Iowa, John N. Hostettler of Indiana, Constance A. Morella of Maryland, Amory Houghton of New York, and John J. Duncan

Jr. of Tennessee. Talk about profiles in courage. There are only four of them left today.[32]

Bush says the goal is Victorian colonialism. Back in the Victorian days, the whole idea was, "We've got to civilize the world, civilize our brown brothers." He thinks America's manifest destiny is to bring civilization to these backward little countries. Now, instead of Queen Victoria bringing civilization, you've got King George bringing democracy.

But we're only interested in doing it in the Middle East and Cuba. Where else in the world are we talking about bringing democracy? Where in Africa? Or Asia? We're not going into Burma are we?

You've got to have a real understanding of what's going on from other people's points of view rather than your own little pejorative point of view. You've just got to understand what it is for the people in the Middle East to look at the United States and what we've done over there and what we continue to do over there. They didn't invade the United States. We invaded an independent country in the Middle East that wasn't threatening the United States at all. At the same time, we're supporting their enemy over there, which is Israel. I don't know of any Arab country that's threatening Israel at this point. Israel has two hundred nuclear weapons. Israel is the only country I know that's been threatening to go into Iran and wipe out a number of locations. It would be suicide for any country to do that to Israel, and it is just such a bizarre situation that we're supposedly going over there to protect Israel when no country has any intention of attacking them.

The American public hears this rhetoric all the time about how these countries are threatening the United States. When was the last time you actually ever heard Iran threaten to attack the United States? Or Syria? Syria's been helping the United States in the War on Terrorism.

Just recently, Bush was having a problem because the rhetoric that he was putting out against Iran wasn't compatible with the fact that the Iranians were cooperating with the United States on the War on Terrorism by handing over some terrorists they'd arrested. These sides of the story often don't get much play.

One key problem with programs like *Nightline* and others is the guests they bring on to talk about stories like this one. Far to the right people like Richard Perle are on there constantly, and the only counterweights to guests like Perle that are brought on are people from the middle and middle-right. When was the last time you saw Howard Zinn[33] on these programs? Now Howard Zinn is on the opposite side of the spectrum, and he'd be a fair balance for someone like Richard Perle, but instead, they'll bring Perle on with somebody like Democratic senator Joe Biden, the ranking minority member of the Senate Foreign Relations Committee. Biden wants to be president in four years, so he's not willing to say anything radical. So you have these people from the far right and right of center saying radical things on the show with people who are slightly right of center, so you never have a real right-left balance.

> It would be nice, too, to actually have someone on who does not have an axe to grind on either side but who is knowledgeable. There are plenty of those people around. And as for reporting, I definitely think that in the areas of foreign affairs and national security, we need a bigger cadre of more sophisticated people.

Definitely.

> But because of the entertainment value system that is creeping in more and more and basically taking over the news, it's actually going in the opposite direction. As you were pointing out, they're hardly giving any time to hard news these days.

PBS has a minimal budget and they do *Frontline* once a week. They repeat some of the shows and it's not a full year; it's just a season.

> But they're not in the ratings game.

No, but you'd think that the networks would be able to have one documentary a week. You've got *Nightline*, but it's a talking head show. One problem with *Frontline* is that they were buying into most of this WMD stuff before the war, too; their reporting was not very good.

> That surprises me.

It was the Judy Miller stuff. All they were doing was "Saddam's this huge danger" constantly, right up until the war. It was "Saddam this, Saddam that," and they were interviewing all the neocons. Afterward, they started interviewing a few other people, but leading up to the war it was neocon mania.

> You can kill the truth by doing official source journalism.

I know. First Judy Miller did the reports, and then she was on the shows as a talking head saying, "Yeah, they're definitely dangerous. We've got to be watchful because they may attack us at any time."

I don't think you need to spend much time working as a reporter to understand that official sources are going to lie to you from time to time and that the more sensitive the story, the greater the likelihood that they will lie to you. It's almost a basic principle of journalism.

When I was starting out and nobody had ever heard of me and I was writing *The Puzzle Palace*,[34] a book about this big intelligence agency, I was as low as you could get. I started on my own with no background and no experience, and I had to really dig hard to get the sources. But when you get up to the network level as an investigative producer or whatever the equivalent is for newspapers, it's very easy to succumb to what I call "silver platter journalism." They come to you all the time with a silver platter saying, "Here's a story. I'll give you the sources, these people will talk to you." It happens all the time, and I never went along with that when I was at ABC. But there were people who did go along with it.

That's where the *New York Times* has gotten into the worst trouble twice. It's the only two times they've ever had to do a mea culpa. The first time was on Wen Ho Lee, the government scientist at Los Alamos who was charged with spying for the Chinese. The right-wing from Congress put together a silver platter package for a reporter from the *New York Times*, and it had this whistle-blower and congressional staffers who were willing to talk about Wen Ho Lee being a metaphor for the administration's selling out to China. And they were coming out with all this stuff, which turned out to be 90 percent nonsense.

If I had been in news management at the time I would have said, "Let's take the opposite side of this story, because if it turns out that we can't find a valid opposite side, then fine, but at least let's look." The *Washington Post* did that, and they kept coming up with the opposite side and ended up being right, and they deserve a lot of kudos for it. The *New York Times* came out for the first time in my memory with this huge full-page mea culpa where they went back and relooked at all the sources and they said, "We made a big mistake." Four years later, they had to do the same thing because of Judith Miller.

Both times they came out with these mea culpas, and in neither case was there really any disciplinary action taken. And on the second one, the one on WMDs in Iraq, they never even mentioned Judy Miller's name. They did her a courtesy. They mentioned her stories and they said, "a reporter."

On the other hand, I think that the editorial side of the *New York Times* has been brilliant all along. I think the editorial page has been the best of any in the entire country. The actual worst, setting aside the *Wall Street Journal*, was the *Washington Post*. If you look at the *Washington Post* editorials from the time Bush took office, the editorial page was pushing for a war with Iraq from the very beginning. Take a look at the editorial on January 30, 2001, the same day that Bush had his National Security Council meeting for the first time. I think on that very day they said something like, "Bush was tough on Iraq during his campaign, let's just see if he puts his money where his mouth is." They were the last ones off the ship as it was sinking, and even now they're reluctant to admit that they screwed up so badly. But the *Washington Post*'s reporting was far better than the *New York Times*', even though the *Washington Post* did marginalize some of Walter Pincus's really good reporting.

If you were to give the press a grade card in terms of its track record of informing the American public about the critical issues, what grade would you give it?

It would get a D before the war and maybe a B now. The problem is, we needed the B before the war, not after the war. If we had had one-tenth of the investigative reporters focusing on the lies coming out of the White House about Iraq that were focused on the Clinton administration and Monica Lewinsky,[35] we might not have gone to war.

It's changed so much since I first went into journalism. I look at Fox—and I worked with a lot of those people, like Brit Hume,[36] when I was at ABC—and it's just so embarrassing. Talk about jingo TV. I think they have to go through inspection every day to make sure their little lapel flag pins are on straight before they're sent out in the field.

A big problem with the press during the lead-up to the war was that all the networks hired these retired generals as consultants, and every five minutes they were trotting out General So and So and asking, "Now, General, what do you think about this?" And he'd come out and say, "Well, we're going to beat Saddam and the way we're going to do it is we're going to move our troops . . ." They all kept saying "we." Who is "we?" CNN? They should have been saying "the United States" or "the military."

So you got this feeling that we were all part of this, that we were all cheerleaders at this football game. Where was the opposite side? Where was somebody saying, "What are we doing this for?" Instead of just talking about this as if it's a football game, why don't we talk about what we are doing over there? What's the purpose of it? What are we going to do when the war is over? What about the insurgents afterward, how many people are going hate us after the war?" They had nobody asking questions like that. All you had were these generals yanked out of mothballs and put on the air as if they were impartial CNN correspondents.

Why do you think they didn't bother to put in a counterweighing voice?

It would be looked upon as unpatriotic. Again, it's this jingoistic move: you've got to support the country, we're going to war, and to have anybody say anything negative would be bad. Well, that's slanting the news, because these generals were not impartial and were talking about strategy, not about why we were going over there, and that was what they should have been talking about. None of these generals ever said anything critical.

So what you're saying is that the current operating paradigm for mainstream journalism does not allow for the best possible journalism, particularly in times of crisis.

That's what I've been saying, yes, exactly. I think there are people out there who are far smarter than I and more experienced in terms of reporting, but the difference is that I'm independent so I can write what I want and take risks. You can't do that if you want to keep your job at a network or a big news organization. The problem is that you've got an infrastructure there that is worried about losing viewers or readers and worried about being accused of being unpatriotic and, as a result, they're putting pressure on the people writing the stories. Subtle and not so subtle benefits come to the people who are keeping with the status quo, not to the people who are trying to prove that the president was involved in Watergate or something.

Tom Yellin (Peter Jennings's executive producer for his documentaries) and Ted Koppel said that they do what they can within the framework they're operating in, which in their case is network television.

I wasn't willing to accept that, which is why I'm writing books. People have to take responsibility. You can't just say, "Well, I do what I can."

There is this system out there. It needs journalists. Journalists go in and they push the envelope as far as they can, and they're trying to make a living. You have been able to be a successful enterprising journalist. Basically, you're an independent entrepreneur. There are not a lot of people who can do what you've done.

I know, but the blame has to go someplace, and I would put the blame on the people who are in the management positions.

But the companies that own the news operations squeeze them to make money.

Then get out. If you're there, then you're part of the problem, and you can't blow it off by saying, "Well, I don't have any other choice." You have lots of choices. If you're part of the problem, and all you're saying is, "Well, I want to keep my $500,000-a-year salary," then accept the blame. You can't just say, "Well, there's not much else I can do about it." That's like the Nuremberg rule;[37] "I got my orders, I had to do it, I couldn't do anything about it." It's even more extreme in this case, because nobody's getting orders. They can do it or they can leave.

It's hard to leave that check.

Exactly, it's hard to leave the check. That's what you should say and not "I do what I can." Really, where is the hard investigative reporting on anything?

That costs a lot of money.

I know it does. I spent a lot of that money when I was at ABC. I know how much it costs, but I'm saying that if your goal is just to make money and not rock the boat, then you should accept part of the blame for it and not say, "I did what I can."

I think the goal is to both make money and do the best you can.

I know that's what they said. I'm saying fine, I don't buy it . . .

. . . And here's a big box of blame for you.

Yes. You have a choice. Stay there and keep making your money-producing reports on Jesus and UFOs or do a hard-hitting report examining why we are in Iraq. You've got choices. People make choices. I chose not to do that, but people do make those choices. I just don't think it's a viable excuse to say, "Well, we do what we can."

Sometimes, too, when you present controversial or politically incorrect information to the public, it just blows up in your face; it's not appreciated, you're sued, you're vilified, and/or you're marginalized.

I was in law school during the Watergate period, which was very interesting. I was learning about law and the Constitution at the same time that the president was going down for lying and abusing government. That was one of the reasons I went into investigative writing, to uncover bad things going on in government. The first book I wrote was *The Puzzle Palace*, and the government twice threatened me with prosecution under the espionage statute.

It was the first book ever written on the National Security Agency [NSA]. I'd spent three years working on the book, and the NSA just didn't want it coming out. One of the things I did was submit a lot of Freedom of Information Act [FOIA] requests. Even though the NSA is excluded from the FOIA, I was able to get a lot of stuff. I got some good stuff from the Justice Department, including documents having to do with this very secret investigation of the NSA. Turns out there was illegal spying that went on and the Justice Department took a long time, but after about nine months they released to me this thick report. It was actually an investigation of the NSA that was classified above top secret. Justice released it and the NSA found out and they went crazy. They asked the Justice Department to try to get it back from me.

This was in the last days of President Carter's administration [1977–1981]. Attorney General Benjamin Civiletti was the one who signed off on releasing it to me. Bobby Inman was the director of the NSA at the time, and he was saying, "This is top secret, it should never have been released." Civiletti said, "What are you talking about, I released it, why should I get it back?" and he paid no attention to Inman.

Then the Reagan administration came in and William French Smith became the attorney general and Bobby Inman went back to him. Now you've got a far-right administration in power, and French Smith said, "OK, we'll try to get it back from him." He assigned one of his deputies at the time to be in charge of it, a guy named Ken Starr.[38] So they went after me, and the first thing they did was call me up and say, "This is the Justice Department, we'd like to have a meeting with you to discuss something very important." I knew this was not going to be good. I got a lawyer in Washington, Mark Lynch, who was with the ACLU and was very, very good. We met with some Justice Department people in Mark Lynch's office, and they said, "The Carter administration made a mistake in declassifying the document, it's been reclassified top secret now, and we want you to give it back." They went through this whole explanation, which was really good because I learned a lot more than I knew before. I was getting a lot out of this and I had no intention of giving back the document. So I said, "We've got to have another meeting, I haven't decided yet."

The ball was in my court. I had to fly down from Boston where I was living and where my publisher was, so I said, "The next meeting should be in Boston." So they all flew up to Boston the next time and we met in my publisher's conference room. My publisher, Houghton Mifflin, agreed not to have anything to do with this, because I was afraid that they were going to make a deal behind my back. David Kahn went through something similar when he wrote the *The Codebreakers*,[39] and his publisher did cave in.

I met with them in the conference room, and this time it was two attorneys from the Justice Department, the NSA's general counsel, and the NSA's head of policy, and they started off really aggressive right away: "How many copies have you made of the document? Who's seen those copies? Who have you given copies to?" I said, "I'm not answering any of those questions." Mark Lynch was back in Washington. He couldn't come up for the meeting, so I said, "You're going to have to call Mark Lynch and run these questions by him before you even ask me." They called Mark Lynch right then and there. I could hear the conversation, and it was not going very well. They started bringing up the espionage statute. There is a part of the espionage statute that says if you come into possession of classified documents and refuse to give them back to their proper custodian, you could be charged under the statute, and that's what they were talking about with me. So Mark said, "Why don't you put the phone down and go wait outside the conference room and I'll talk to Bamford on the phone alone." So I got on the phone and he said, " Look, they're getting way over your head, they could have a warrant for your arrest in their pocket or a summons or a subpoena, so my advice is put the phone back down, go outside and tell them that I want to talk to them again, and as they go in the room, you just disappear." So I did that and Mark said, "You guys are getting over your heads, you're talking espionage statute. I'm not there, and Bamford, he's just dealing with a document that the Justice Department gave to him."

They waited there a while for me to come back, and I never showed up. They were really pissed off. Then they started sending me letters saying, "You are currently in possession of classified documents and we demand their return." And there was another little thing. There was another law called the "Executive Order on Secrecy." It's an executive order that has the effect of law and it dates back to before Reagan, and it says that once a document has been declassified, it can't be reclassified, which is exactly what they were trying to do. So we kept sending this letter back saying, "Go back and read the Executive Order on Secrecy." And they'd send a letter back, "Regardless of that, the document has been reclassified as top secret"—it was actually higher, it was top secret umbra—"and we demand that Bamford give it back." Then President Reagan changed the executive order to say that once a document has been declassified it can be reclassified, but in law there's a thing called the ex post facto principle; you can't create a law and then prosecute somebody who did the act when it wasn't against the law, so they couldn't apply it in my case, and I was home free. They finally went away because I didn't do anything wrong. So that got a lot of attention, and one of the funniest ironies is that the person who wrote the first story about that on me for any newspaper was Judy Miller.

There's a whole generation of reporters who have grown up in the current era of compliant journalism as opposed to the Ben Bradlee, Woodward and Bernstein, and Sy Hersh go-out-and-rock-the-boat era. Maybe the pendulum will swing back. Actually, it is starting to swing back, but it's just too bad that this time the stakes are a lot more serious than they were during the Vietnam War. The Vietnam War was never going to trigger a possible nuclear war or a war where terrorists were going to blow things up in the United States. Other than the fifty-five thousand or so who died in Vietnam, there wasn't any detrimental action taken within the United States. Now there's the potential of terrorists who can get very deadly weapons or make deadly plans and come over to the United States and wreak havoc. During Vietnam you had a small regional war where a lot of people were being killed, but it didn't have the prospect of expanding into an enormous regional conflict that would end up being a nuclear conflict, or having the war come back to the United States.

Do you think there will be more devastation here in the United States as a result of what's going on?

I think that there's far too much fearmongering going on and that the talk is far worse than the reality. Terrorism itself is just so overused. This administration uses it as a vehicle to drive fear into people, and the fear drives the war. The average number of Americans who died in international terrorist incidents was nine a year for a decade leading up to September 11. After that, it's been even less. You have one spike there of three thousand people, which was terrible. But if you look at it from a cost/benefit ratio of keeping people safe in the United States and you amortize three thousand people over a ten-year period, you're talking about a very small number of people. Every single year, just from colon cancer alone, fifty thousand people die.

That's qualitatively different in terms of the specters that it raises.

What I'm talking about is how much money we're putting toward terrorism, which is creating more terrorism.

And then you have the other changes here, like the PATRIOT Act.

That's why I'm saying there's an overreaction to the terrorism. My simple solution to this whole thing has three steps. One, change our Middle East policy starting with Israel, which should be treated as a country and not as anything other than a country, not as the fifty-first US state or anything else. We imposed sanctions on South Africa when they were doing terrible things during apartheid and they changed; they did away with apartheid. The United States has never been able to get Israel to stop building settlements. Even if Israel pulls out of Gaza, which would be to their advantage, they're going to continue building settlements in the West Bank. The United States has to change its foreign policy toward Israel, which for thirty years has been a policy of the carrot, just giving more and more carrots—money, constantly money—without any stick. There's absolutely never been a stick used with Israel, and I think you've got to start changing that. If they want to build more settlements in the occupied territories in violation of both US and UN foreign policy, then there should be a price for it. Number one, they shouldn't get any more money from the United States, and number two, the United States should impose sanctions until they stop doing what they shouldn't be doing. If an Arab country attacks them, then fine, we'll come in and help defend them. I'm talking in a fantasy world here, it will never happen, but sanctions would do two things. They would help create a climate within Israel to force the government to do what's right, which is to pull out of the occupied territories, and they would show the Arab world, the Europeans, and the rest of the world that we're not just being this sycophantic country to Ariel Sharon. That would be a major factor within the Middle East in terms of changing their attitude toward the United States, and it would also save the United States four billion dollars a year.

The same thing goes for the war in Iraq. You've got to end it. I think the best way to end it is to pull everybody out. We didn't do that in Vietnam, and instead of ten thousand people being killed, more than fifty thousand were killed. I think the only thing keeping the Europeans from entering Iraq as peacekeepers is the United States. The United States is doing two things there. One, it's attracting more and more terrorism within Iraq. I'm using the administration's word, "terrorism," but these so-called terrorists are resistance people fighting to expel the invaders, basically. So you decrease the amount of violence in Iraq if you start pulling everybody out, and number two, I think the Europeans will agree to go in there as peacekeepers, as UN "blue hats," once the United States leaves.

Then you could take a large chunk of the money that we save from pulling out of Iraq and not giving to Israel, and you start another euphemistic war. Instead of the war on terror, you'd have a war that actually saved people, the kind of war that we never ever get involved in, a war on AIDS for one thing. It kills three million people a year and it's growing. It's growing in areas of the world where it could largely affect foreign policy. You get a country devastated by AIDS, and it's opened up to being taken over by terrorists. A lot of countries in Africa are like that.

We've had this "let's get a man on the moon by the end of the century" type of attitude, but we never get involved in a war on AIDS. How many people are going to be attacking us if we change our foreign policy in the Middle East? What if we became known as the country that's trying to save the world by putting a large amount of money that's actually a small percentage of what we're spending on the Middle East, say fifty billion dollars, toward AIDS? First of all, you're going to have a lot of people liking you around the world, especially in the third world and some of the major AIDS areas like India, China, and Southeast Asia. How many terrorists do you think will be blowing us up then? What will they be blowing us up for? Are there any people who would hate us for doing the right thing?

JAMES BAMFORD has written extensively on national security and intelligence issues and is the author of three national best-sellers. His most recent book, *A Pretext for War: 9/11, Iraq, and the Abuse of America's Intelligence Agencies* (New York: Doubleday, 2004; Doubleday/Anchor 2005), was listed by the *Washington Post* as one of the Best of 2004 and in a cover review said, "Bamford does a superb job of laying out and tying together threads of the Sept. 11 intelligence failures and their ongoing aftermath." Before that, he wrote *Body of Secrets: Anatomy of the Ultrasecret NSA: From the Cold War to the Dawn of a New Century* (New York: Doubleday, 2001; Doubleday/Anchor, 2002), which was a sequel to his first national best-seller, *The Puzzle Palace: A Report on NSA, America's Most Secret Agency.* A cover review in the *New York Times Book Review* called *Body of Secrets* "an extraordinary work of investigative journalism." The book has been published in other countries, including the United Kingdom, Australia, Germany, Italy, Japan, China, and Korea, and was awarded the Investigative Reporters and Editors Gold Medal, the highest award given by the professional association of investigative reporters. Bamford's first book, *The Puzzle Palace* (Boston: Houghton Mifflin, 1982; Viking Penguin, 1983) was awarded the Investigative Reporters and Editors Book-of-the-Year Award. *Washingtonian* magazine called it "a monument to investigative journalism." There are various foreign editions of the book, which has been reprinted more than forty times.

Bamford has also written in-depth investigative articles for many national magazines, including cover stories for the *New York Times Magazine*, the *Washington Post Magazine*, and the *Los Angeles Times Magazine*. He has written scores of intelligence-related op-ed pieces and book reviews for the *New York Times*, the *Washington Post*, the *Los Angeles Times*, and *USA Today*, where he served on the newspaper's board of contributors. In addition, he has been quoted extensively in the *New York Times*, the *Washington Post*, the *Los Angeles Times*, *Time*, *Newsweek*, the *Sunday Times* (London), the *Observer* (London), and other publications.

In 2002 Bamford was Distinguished Visiting Professor of National Security at the University of California at Berkeley's Goldman School of Public Policy. From 1989 to 1998, he was Washington investigative producer for ABC News *World News Tonight with Peter Jennings*. The topics he covered ranged from locating spies in cold war–Europe to finding terrorists in the Middle East to tracking down fugitives in China. Bamford also covered the White House during the investigations into the Clinton administration. He received numerous television reporting awards, including the Overseas Press Club Award for Excellence and the Society of Professional Journalists Deadline Award for Best Investigative Reporting in Television.

An intelligence expert, Bamford has testified as an expert witness on intelligence issues before committees of both the Senate and the House of Representatives as well as the European Parliament in Brussels and the International Criminal Tribunal for the former Yugoslavia. He has been a lecturer for the Central Intelligence Agency's Senior Intelligence Fellows Program, the National Security Agency's National Cryptologic School, the Defense Intelligence Agency's Joint Military Intelligence College, and the Pentagon's National Defense University. He has also served as a consultant to the US State and Justice Departments and has appeared as an intelligence expert dozens of times on every major American television program, including ABC's *Nightline, ABC World News Tonight, NBC Nightly News, CBS Evening News, PBS News Hour* with Jim Lehrer, and Fox News. Bamford has appeared on many overseas television networks, including those in the United Kingdom, France, Germany, Japan, and Australia.

Bamford received a BA in 1972 from Suffolk University in Boston and a JD from Suffolk University Law School in 1975. Prior to that, he served in the US Navy for three years.

NOTES

1. The *New York Times'* Judith Miller wrote articles like "Illicit Arms Kept till Eve of War, an Iraqi Scientist Is Said to Assert" (April 21, 2003) and "U.S. Says Hussein Intensifies Quest for A-Bomb Parts" (September 8, 2002), which turned out to be false. In an e-mail she wrote to her colleague, *New York Times* war correspondent John Burns, she admitted that the discredited Ahmed Chalabi "has provided most of the front page exclusives on WMD to our paper." Although he didn't specifically mention Miller's reporting, *New York Times* public editor Daniel Okrent issued this mea culpa on May 26, 2004: "Editors at several levels who should have been challenging reporters and pressing for more skepticism were perhaps too intent on rushing scoops into the paper. Accounts of Iraqi defectors were not always weighed against their strong desire to have Saddam Hussein ousted. Articles based on dire claims about Iraq tended to get prominent display, while follow-up articles that called the original ones into question were sometimes buried. In some cases, there was no follow-up at all."

2. Richard Perle is the former chairman of the Defense Policy Board, which Seymour Hersh describes in his March 17, 2003, *New Yorker* article "Lunch with the Chairman," as a "Defense Department advisory group composed primarily of highly respected former government officials, retired military officers and academics. . . . The board meets several times a year at the Pentagon to review and assess the country's strategic defense policies." Perle has been reported to have been influential in crafting the Bush administration's policy toward Iraq. Paul Wolfowitz was named head of the World Bank in March 2005, but prior to that he served as deputy secretary of defense in the Bush administration. Donald Rumsfeld serves as secretary of defense in the Bush administration.

3. In his State of the Union address on January 28, 2003, President Bush said, "The British government has learned that Saddam Hussein recently sought significant quantities of uranium from Africa," allegedly from Niger.

4. On its Web site, http://www.iaea.org/About/index.html, the International Atomic Energy Agency describes itself as "the world's center of cooperation in the nuclear field. It was set up as the world's 'Atoms for Peace' organization in 1957 within the United Nations family. The Agency works with its Member States and multiple partners worldwide to promote safe, secure and peaceful nuclear technologies." The IAEA is also considered the UN watchdog organization for monitoring nuclear proliferation.

5. In 1972 *Washington Post* journalists Bob Woodward and Carl Bernstein, with the help of a confidential source named "Deep Throat" (then FBI deputy director Mark Felt), connected a break-in at the Democratic National Committee to high-ranking sources in the Nixon administration and the Committee to Re-Elect the President. Their investigation eventually led to President Nixon's resignation in 1974.

6. The US Intelligence Community's Web site's definition of National Intelligence Estimates is: "These reports are the DCI's [Director of Central Intelligence] most authoritative written judgements concerning national security issues. They deal with capabilities, vulnerabilities, and probable courses of action of foreign nations and key developments relevant to the vital interests of the United States. NIEs are produced at the national level by the NIC [National Intelligence Council, made up of senior intelligence analysts and outside experts] and are issued by the DCI with the approval of the NFIB [National Foreign Intelligence Board, a senior Intelligence Community advisory body]. NIEs are designed to identify trends of significance to national security and, when relevant, differences of views among the principal intelligence officers of the US government. Presidential Summaries of NIEs are prepared for the President, Vice President, and other key executive officers." http://www.intelligence.gov/0-glossary.shtml.

7. An explanatory column titled "Neocon 101" in the *Christian Science Monitor* provides information on neoconservative thought: "Neocons believe that the United States should not be ashamed to use its unrivaled power—forcefully if necessary—to promote its values around the world. . . . Neoconservatives believe modern threats facing the US can no longer be reliably contained and therefore must be prevented, sometimes through preemptive military action. . . . Most neocons share unwavering support for Israel, which they see as crucial to US military sufficiency in a volatile region. . . . The original neocons were a group of mostly Jewish liberal intellectuals who, in the 1960s and 70s, grew disenchanted with what they saw as the American left's social excesses and reluctance to spend adequately on defense." http://www.csmonitor.com/specials/neocon/neocon101.html.

8. The document can be viewed at http://www.informationclearinghouse.info/article1438.htm.

9. The American Enterprise Institute for Public Policy is generally viewed as a conservative think tank. Its Web site is http://www.aei.org/about/contentID.20038142213000031/default.asp.

10. The National Security Agency/Central Security Service "is America's cryptologic organization. It coordinates, directs, and performs highly specialized activities to protect US information systems and produce foreign intelligence information. . . . It is also one of the most important centers of foreign language analysis and research within the government." http://www.nsa.gov/about/.

11. On September 4, 2002, CBS News national security correspondent David Martin reported that an "aide" who was with Secretary of Defense Rumsfeld in the National Military Command Center on September 11, 2001, had written down this quote from Rumsfeld. Martin discusses the notes in chapter 10 of this book.

12. On its Web site, http://www.whitehouse.gov/nsc/, the National Security Council is defined as "the President's principal forum for considering national security and foreign policy matters with his senior national security advisors and cabinet officials. . . . The function of the Council has been to assist the President on national and security policies. The Council also serves as the President's principal arm for coordinating these policies among various government agencies."

13. A Palestinian born in Jordan, Abu Musab al-Zarqawi is believed to have links to al Qaeda and is believed to be, according to a BBC profile, "the main source of kidnappings, bomb attacks and assassination attempts in Iraq." The BBC's profile can be found at http://newsvote.bbc.co.uk/mpapps/pagetools/print/news.bbc.co.uk/2/hi/middle_east/3483089.stm.

14. In his February 5, 2003, presentation to the UN Security Council, Powell said, "We have firsthand descriptions of weapons factories on wheels and on rails. The trucks and train cars are easily moved and are designed to evade detection by inspectors. In a matter of months, they can produce a quantity of biological poison equal to the entire amount that Iraq claimed to have produced in the years prior to the Gulf War. Although Iraq's mobile production program began in the mid-1990s, UN inspectors at the time only had vague hints of such programs. Confirmation came later, in the year 2000. The source was an eyewitness, an Iraqi chemical engineer who supervised one of these facilities."

15. The National Security Agency/Central Security Service "is America's cryptologic organization. It coordinates, directs, and performs highly specialized activities to protect US information systems and produce foreign intelligence information. . . . It is also one of the most important centers of foreign language analysis and research within the government." http://www.nsa.gov/about/.

16. According to the online encyclopedia Wikipedia, the cold war was "the open yet restricted rivalry that developed after World War II between the United States and its allies (roughly speaking NATO [North Atlantic Treaty Organization] members) and the Soviet Union and its allies (roughly speaking, Warsaw Pact members). The struggle was called the *Cold War* because it did not actually lead to direct fighting between the superpowers (a "hot" war) on a wide scale. The Cold War was waged by means of economic pressure, selective aid, diplomatic maneuvers, propaganda, assassinations, low-intensity military operations and full-scale war from 1947 until the collapse of the Soviet Union in 1991." http://en.wikipedia.org/wiki/ Cold_War.

17. At the time she was speaking to Judith Miller of the *New York Times* about Hussein's WMD potential, Condoleezza "Condi" Rice was national security advisor. She became secretary of state for the Bush administration in November 2004.

18. A British-educated former banker, Ahmed Chalabi has been the leader of the anti-Saddam Iraqi National Congress. He received large sums of money from the US government for his activities and was a source of faulty prewar intelligence. Although he has no industry experience, he is currently acting oil minister for the new Iraqi government.

19. Allegations that Saddam Hussein had ordered Iraqi intelligence to assassinate President George H. W. Bush in April 1993 during Bush's visit to Kuwait to commemorate the victory of the first Gulf War eventually led President Clinton to order an attack on Mukhabarat, Iraqi intelligence headquarters, which resulted in the deaths of eight civilians when some of the missiles landed on nearby homes. In a November 1, 1993, *New Yorker* article titled "Case Not Closed," reporter Seymour Hersh wrote about the alleged assassination plot, "But my own investigations have uncovered circumstantial evidence, at least as compelling as the Administration's, that suggests that the American government's case against Iraq—as it has been outlined in public, anyway—is seriously flawed."

20. James Bamford, *A Pretext for War: 9/11, Iraq, and the Abuse of America's Intelligence Agencies* (New York: Doubleday, 2004).

21. The American Israel Public Affairs Committee (AIPAC) is a pro-Israel lobby.

22. In September 2004 Lawrence Franklin, an analyst in Douglas Feith's office,

came under investigation for allegedly passing on a draft presidential directive on Iran to the pro-Israel lobbying group AIPAC (American Israel Public Affairs Committee). In January 26, 2005, the Department of Defense announced Feith's resignation, saying he was leaving for "personal and family reasons."

23. Democratic senator Henry Jackson from the state of Washington served in Congress for almost forty-three years, beginning as a congressman in 1940. For more information, go to http://www.hmjackson.org/bio.html.

24. Dwight D. Eisenhower was the thirty-fourth president of the United States and served from 1953 to 1961.

25. "A Clean Break: A Strategy for Securing the Realm" can be viewed at http://www.informationclearinghouse.info/article1438.htm.

26. Ronald Suskind, *The Price of Loyalty: George W. Bush, the White House and the Education of Paul O'Neill* (New York: Simon & Schuster, 2004).

27. The 1993 Oslo Accords, officially known as the Declaration of Principles on Interim Self-Government Arrangements, was a series of agreements between Israel and the Palestinian Liberation Organization that called for the "withdrawal of Israeli forces from the Gaza strip and the West Bank and the Palestinian right to self-government within those areas through the creation of the Palestinian Authority." http://en.wikipedia.org/wiki/Oslo_Accords. In the May/June 2005 issue of the Council on Foreign Relations *Foreign Affairs* publication, Amos Perlmutter (professor of political science at American University) said that the Oslo Accords were "for all intents and purposes dead," citing Palestinian suicide bombers and a "wave of fundamentalist terrorism" as reasons for the demise of the accords.

28. A BBC profile describes Khalid Sheikh Mohammed as "the self-proclaimed head of al Qaeda's military committee" who is believed to have masterminded 9/11 and been linked to various other terrorist acts, including the kidnapping of US journalist Daniel Pearl. The BBC profile can be found at http://news.bbc.co.uk/2/hi/south_asia/2811855.stm.

29. Former Baathist and interim Iraqi prime minister Iyad Allawi is, the BBC reports in "Who's Who in Iraq: Iyad Allawi" (May 28, 2004), "one of a U.S.-backed clique of secular Iraqi opposition figures who lived in exile until the fall of Saddam Hussein's regime in April 2003." A secular Shia Muslim, Allawi is head of the Iraqi National Accord Party in the Iraqi National Assembly.

30. Ibrahim al-Jaafari, who is a Shiite Muslim, was elected prime minister of Iraq in April 2005. For more information on Jaafari, see chapter 20 in this book.

31. Falwell's "group" is the Moral Majority Coalition. For more information, the group's Web site is http://www.moralmajority.us/.

32. Constance A. Morella of Maryland was not reelected, and Amory Houghton of New York retired.

33. Howard Zinn is professor emeritus of political science at Boston University. The Internet encyclopedia Wikipedia describes him as "an influential American historian and political scientist, whose political philosophy incorporates ideas from Marxism, anarchism, socialism and social democracy." http://en.wikipedia.org/wiki/Howard_Zinn. Zinn has authored more than a dozen books, the most popular being *A People's History of the United States*.

34. James Bamford, *The Puzzle Palace: A Report on America's Most Secret Agency* (Boston: Houghton Mifflin, 1982).

35. Monica Lewinsky was an intern at the White House with whom President Bill Clinton initially denied having sexual relations. He said this in a televised statement on January 26, 1998. Later, in August 1998, Clinton admitted he'd had an inappropriate relationship with Lewinsky. Less than one month later, after conducting an investigation into the matter, independent counsel Kenneth Starr delivered a report to Congress outlining a case for impeaching Clinton on eleven grounds, including lying under oath to a federal grand jury, obstructing justice, and witness tampering. The House approved impeaching the president for lying under oath to a federal grand jury and obstruction of justice. On February 12, 1999, the Senate voted to acquit the president on both charges.

36. Fox correspondent Brit Hume is currently Fox News's Washington, DC, managing editor and anchors *Special Report with Brit Hume*. He came to Fox after twenty-three years at ABC.

37. According to the online encyclopedia Wikipedia, the Nuremberg Trials "is the general name for two sets of trials of Nazis involved in World War II and the Holocaust (genocidal ethnic cleansing program targeting various groups, particularly Jews). The trials were held in the German city of Nuremberg from 1945 to 1949. . . . The first and most famous of these trials was the Trial of the Major War Criminals before the International Military Tribunal." http://en.wikipedia.org/wiki/Nuremberg_Trials. Bamford is referring to those on trial defending themselves by saying that they were just following orders.

38. Republican attorney Kenneth Starr was the US independent counsel in charge of investigating possible misconduct on the part of President Clinton in the Whitewater real estate scandal as well as investigating grounds for impeaching him for, among other things, lying under oath to a federal jury and obstructing justice during the Monica Lewinsky scandal.

39. David Kahn, *Codebreakers: The Story of Secret Writing* (New York: MacMillan, 1967).

12

BURROWER-IN-CHIEF

Chuck Kennedy/KRT

JOHN WALCOTT
Washington Bureau Chief,
Knight Ridder
Interviewed March 2005

More often than any other journalist or news organization, Knight Ridder was mentioned by those in this book as the best source for post-9/11 reporting. The person most responsible for setting this platinum standard of journalism is John Walcott. Long after the Twin Towers had collapsed, Walcott and his crack team of reporters were virtually alone in their pursuit of what the real intelligence analysts were saying about the White House's case against Saddam. As I write this, they are once again out in front of everybody else in the US press with yet another major discovery. A British intelligence memo shows that Bush had decided to invade Iraq earlier than he had claimed the decision was made. Also, the administration had "arranged the intelligence about Iraq to support what it knew was a weak case for war." Cumulatively, Knight Ridder's reporting damns the Bush administration in devastating detail. The thing is, for now, Knight Ridder isn't on the radar where Team Walcott's work would really count: Washington and New York. Nonetheless, Walcott persists.

John is in his fifties and looks mild-mannered enough in his wire-rimmed glasses and blue oxford shirt. But with his brains and the telephone on his desk, he rocks the boat hard. Before the war, what he and his team did that others didn't was search for the truth where it could actually be found: "We . . . burrow[ed] down into all of the bureaucracies to the people who were not just reading the cables but writing them; not just reading the analysis but writing it; and not just reading the reports but making them. . . . The answers that started coming back from people inside the government were: 'No way, there's no evidence of it,' and even more interestingly, 'a lot of the things the administration and its allies are talking about are not true.'"

Talking to Walcott, one is reminded that there is a real art to certain types of reporting. For example, how do you definitively answer the question of whether or not Saddam has WMDs if it is impossible for you to go to Iraq and do a complete physical inventory yourself? It takes a combination of imagination, high-end analytical and investigative skills, and a solid base of background information to formulate the right questions and then answer them. Walcott is a master at this.

Besides his obvious zeal for journalistic excellence, Walcott felt an acute need to look hard at the rationales for going to war for another reason: "Unlike a lot of our competitors who write for the people who send other people to war, we write for the people who get sent to war, and for their mothers and fathers and their sisters and brothers and their sons and daughters. We don't publish in Washington and New York. We write for Columbus, Georgia, and Fort Campbell, Kentucky, and Fort Hood, Texas, and Shaw Air Force Base, South Carolina, where the people who get sent to war live and where they leave their families behind." He has definitely done his job on that score, but his reporting would have been of more help to the "people who get sent to war" if it reached the "people who send other people to war." Knight Ridder's absence in the cities monopolized by the *Washington Post* and the *New York Times* is an incalculable public loss. I would like to think that if John Walcott and his team were ever packaged into a television news show, what passes for news on all the networks right now would be forced to change or sink into oblivion. The contrast would be that stark and compelling.

In this interview, Walcott reveals the inner workings of how he and his team do what they do, providing a fascinating window into how the very best journalism is achieved. First, he set up three tracks.

It was clear to everyone within days of 9/11 that the administration was already beginning to turn its attention to Iraq, so the reporting we did from the very start was on three tracks. There was a terrorist track that had to do with al Qaeda[1] and what was known about that. There was an Afghan war track, where we formed a fairly extensive team of people from all over Knight Ridder to go to Afghanistan and cover combat operations while some of us here tried to learn what we could about al Qaeda as documents were uncovered. So there was a terrorism track, an Afghanistan track, and almost from the beginning, an Iraq track. Literally the day after 9/11, people either close to or in the administration began talking about Iraq. As 2001 turned into 2002, it became clear that the president had made the fundamental decision to overthrow Saddam Hussein. Warren Strobel and I wrote a story about it on February 13, 2002, "Bush Has Decided to Overthrow Hussein." The lead was: "President Bush has decided to oust Iraqi leader Saddam Hussein from power and ordered the CIA, the Pentagon and other agencies to devise a combination of military, diplomatic and covert steps to achieve that goal, senior US officials said Tuesday."

What were your colleagues reporting at the time?

Nothing of that sort, and there's been a big semantic debate about when the decision to invade Iraq was made, because the decision to overthrow Saddam was not necessarily a decision to invade the country. But it's becoming clearer that the decision was made a good deal earlier than the administration let on. A British memo that recently was leaked to the *Sunday Times* of London reported that the president had decided to invade Iraq before the end of July 2002. Warren Strobel[2] and I wrote a story ["'Downing Street' Memo Indicates Bush Made Intelligence Fit Iraq Policy," May 5, 2005] about it a few days after it appeared in Britain because it not only says that the decision was made much earlier than the administration has said it was, but it also reports that the administration arranged the intelligence about Iraq to support what it knew was a weak case for war:

> A highly classified British memo, leaked in the midst of Britain's just-concluded election campaign, indicates that President Bush decided to overthrow Iraqi

President Saddam Hussein by summer 2002 and was determined to ensure that U.S. intelligence data supported his policy.

The document, which summarizes a July 23, 2002, meeting of British Prime Minister Tony Blair with his top security advisers, reports on a visit to Washington by the head of Britain's MI-6 intelligence service. The visit took place while the Bush administration was still declaring to the American public that no decision had been made to go to war.

"There was a perceptible shift in attitude. Military action was now seen as inevitable," the MI-6 chief said at the meeting, according to the memo. "Bush wanted to remove Saddam through military action, justified by the conjunction of terrorism and WMD, weapons of mass destruction."

The memo said that "the intelligence and facts were being fixed around the policy."

Once you begin making plans, ordering up troops, and making commitments, it gets harder and harder to stop the train. In fact, the train develops a timetable of its own. You can't get forces in motion and leave them in limbo for long periods of time. It's something of a mystery why all of this came to a head when it did, in March of 2003, but I think the best explanation is that's simply when things reached a point of no return and holding them up any further would have been impossible militarily, logistically, and politically. But as the British memo indicates, the fundamental decision to use military force to overthrow Saddam was made very early and everything else flowed from that.

A couple of things flowed from the decision to overthrow Saddam. One was that it was reasonable to assume that getting rid of Saddam Hussein was going to require military action. The United States did not have the covert means to overthrow him. We knew perfectly well that the CIA had no operations of any note inside Iraq. They had, for a long time, been relying almost entirely on exiles and defectors, so they didn't have the wherewithal to mount an internal coup against Hussein. The political situation inside Iraq was such that there was no one to work with. Saddam had killed everyone who even looked at him cross-eyed. So trying to find an opposition to support was a nonstarter, as was the idea that he would leave voluntarily. There was no prospect of that.

At the time that you were first reporting that the Bush administration was saying that he had to go, were you getting any sense of why they felt he had to go?

There clearly was a fear that Saddam and al Qaeda would make common cause and that the next World Trade Center attack would include biological, chemical or radiological, or even nuclear weapons. Warren Strobel and I reported that in the February 13, 2002, story, "Bush Has Decided to Overthrow Hussein." The president feared another attack and, I'm afraid, feared being held accountable for such a terrible thing. No administration wants something like that to happen on its watch. That's sensible enough. As time went on, the administration was talking about Saddam more and more frequently, and the decision to invade Iraq was being more and more clearly articulated.

This prompted two basic questions. One had to do with the war in Afghanistan, which was unfinished at best: What were the implications of subordinating the war against al Qaeda, the group that did attack the United States and kill three thousand people, to a new war?

Second, a decision to go to war, even a war against a third-rate power such as Iraq, is the most serious decision any president can make, and we wanted to know: What was the case for war? Why was it essential? We thought that our readers would be particularly interested in the answers to these questions because, unlike a lot of our competitors who write for the people who send other people to war, we write for the people who get sent to war, and for their mothers and fathers and their sisters and brothers and their sons and daughters. We don't publish in Washington and New York. We write for Columbus, Georgia, and Fort Campbell, Kentucky, and Fort Hood, Texas, and Shaw Air Force Base, South Carolina, where the people who get sent to war live and where they leave their families behind.

But why wouldn't that be important coverage for everyone?

You'd think it would be. But the other news organizations are going to have to answer for themselves. To me, it's self-evident. Any time a country proposes a step that dramatic, one that may cost lives, one that asks our young men and women to go and kill someone else's young men and women, that should receive the toughest scrutiny. It doesn't get more serious than that. It does not. We know that not only from going to Arlington Cemetery but from going to Walter Reed Hospital. This is serious stuff. We felt that it was our duty to examine as critically as we could the case for war as the administration made it. We felt that we had to ask the questions about whether the case stood up. We felt a real responsibility to do that.

There were, from the outset, some very troubling things about what the administration was saying. They were troubling at a commonsense level. The first one was the notion that Saddam and al Qaeda were going to make common cause. Blind acceptance of this idea had red flags all over it from the very start. It simply didn't make sense. A secular regime run by a guy with two Cognac-swilling sons is not a likely ally of a Wahhabi[3] extremist. In fact, one of Osama's goals is to establish a new caliphate in the Arab world and to sweep away apostate rulers such as Saddam Hussein, Egypt's Hosni Mubarak, the Saudis, King Abdullah of Jordan, and the rest of them. So the idea that Saddam would do anything to strengthen a mortal enemy raised a lot of questions in our minds. I think that the basic fact of Saddam's secularism, despite his putting on Islamic trappings rather late in his career, and Osama's theocratic agenda were perfectly plain for anyone to see, even somebody who wasn't deeply versed in Wahhabism or the nature of Saddam's regime. I think it was fairly obvious. So to me, the question of why these two would get together, what was the likelihood of their getting together, was pretty obvious and bore looking into.

The minute we started looking into it, the answers that started coming back from people inside the government were: "No way, there's no evidence of it," and even more interestingly, "a lot of the things the administration and its allies are talking about are not true." These people were also growing more and more alarmed by two things: First, this fixation with Iraq was beginning to detract from the war against Osama, which to this day is still unfinished. Second, intelligence information was being misused to assemble the case for war.

This started coming out in the summer of 2002. I'll give you two concrete examples of the misuse of intelligence information. The first one was the allegation that was very frequently made that Saddam had a hijacking training facility at a place called Salman Pak. That one was being bandied about a lot both by people in the administration and by members or allies of the Iraqi National Congress. When we called folks in the government who were knowledgeable about that and asked, the answer that came back was that the intelligence indicated that Salman Pak was a counterhijacking training facility and that there was no evidence that foreign terrorists had visited the facility. There were no passport records and no overhead photography. Now, American intelligence on this was, to put it mildly, limited because of the CIA's and other agencies' inability or unwillingness to take the risks necessary to penetrate Iraq. So you didn't necessarily want to bet the farm on what intelligence sources said. But it was interesting that there was no evidence to support the allegation that Iraq had set up an international terrorist training camp to teach people how to hijack airplanes. The evidence did suggest that what they were doing was teaching their own people how to foil hijackings, which was even more interesting because, who were they afraid might hijack their planes? Probably people like bin Laden.

A second example of the misuse of intelligence information occurred when the administration argued at one point that the Iraqi ambassador to Turkey, who was a former director general of the Iraqi intelligence services, had gone to Afghanistan in 1998 after the Clinton administration bombed some al Qaeda camps in retaliation for US embassy bombings in Africa. They said that this gentleman had offered sanctuary in Iraq to Osama and to bin Laden's second-in-command, Ayman al-Zawahiri. They also said that he had met with Taliban[4] leader Mullah Omar. So we asked our sources about that. It turns out that there was a record showing that the guy had gone and met with Mullah Omar and bin Laden and made such an offer. But the administration never mentioned bin Laden's answer. Bin Laden not only said no, but he turned to one of his people later on and said, "We're not going to Iraq because if we go there it will be his agenda and not our agenda." So not only had he declined the offer, but he also had made it clear that he didn't share Saddam's agenda. He preferred to stay in Afghanistan, even at the risk of getting bombed, to pursue his own agenda rather than subordinating it to Saddam's secular agenda. The administration simply left out the second part of the story. We reported this on October 8, 2002, in "Some in Bush Administration Have Misgivings about Iraq Policy." The crux of that story, though, was that a growing number of military officers, intelligence professionals, and diplomats were having misgivings about the White House's rush to war:

> These officials charge that administration hawks have exaggerated evidence of the threat Iraqi leader Saddam Hussein poses—including distorting his links to the al-Qaeda terrorist network—have overstated the amount of international support for attacking Iraq, and have downplayed the potential repercussions of a new war in the Middle East. They charge that the administration squelches dissenting views and that intelligence analysts are under intense pressure to produce reports supporting the White House's argument that Saddam poses such an immediate threat to the United States that pre-emptive military action is necessary. "Analysts at the working level in the intelligence community are feeling very strong pressure from the Pentagon to cook the books," said one official, speaking on condition of anonymity. A dozen other officials echoed his views in interviews with Knight Ridder. No one who was interviewed disagreed. They cited recent suggestions by Defense Secretary Donald H. Rumsfeld and National Security Advisor Condoleezza Rice that Saddam and Osama bin Laden's al-Qaeda network are working together.

The story was ignored here in Washington. We don't have a paper here. Our nearest paper is in Philadelphia. I think the administration felt, probably correctly, that it could afford to ignore us, and that, in fact, the wisest course was to ignore us, because no one else was reporting this. It was a perfectly sensible political decision on their part, and that's pretty well how it went for a year and a half. But the important thing, I think, is that almost all of the reporting we did was prompted by allegations that we knew were dubious or that simply didn't make any sense.

I'll give you another example from the famous Powell speech to the United Nations.[5] Just off the top of my head, two things stuck out. First, there was the notion that the Iraqis had been photographed backing trucks up to secret facilities to go hide stuff. The Iraqis know to the minute when American satellites are overhead because the Soviets taught them long ago how to figure it out. So why, if they were trying to hide something, would they back up trucks in broad daylight when they knew a satellite was passing overhead? It doesn't make any sense. Second, knowing that virtually all of their communications had been compromised, why would Iraqi officers get on the telephone and talk about hiding stuff? It's almost as if they wanted us to believe they had WMDs; as if they were trying to fool us into believing they had them. They might have wanted us to think that because their only hope of heading off an invasion would have been to make us believe that they had this stuff and were ready to use it.

Why do you think we went to war?

I think there was a genuine fear in the administration that Iraq somehow was going to link up and provide some material support to al Qaeda. I think there were a lot of officials who believed that Iraq had WMDs. The Iraqis had been lying, and their track record with the UN inspectors was not a very encouraging one. It was a logical enough thing to worry about. But worrying about something and having enough evidence to send people to war are two different things in my mind.

What about the conflicts between the intelligence agencies and the White House?

I assume Jon Landay[6] has talked to you in some detail about how this first burst into full view during the controversy over the aluminum tubes. The administration said Saddam was trying to procure them for his nuclear weapons program, while others said that the tubes were for launching artillery rockets. The State Department intelligence bureau and the

Energy Department—which is the repository of most of the expertise on technical matters such as this—disagreed with the administration and registered their dissents in the National Intelligence Estimate report.[7] The dissents were ignored. We found that this pattern was repeated over and over again. In fact, it was worse than that because officials who dissented tended to be punished, exiled, banished, not listened to, and not invited to meetings.

What other examples can you give that you reported on about that pattern?

I'm trying to go back. The best single report of that is the one that Jon Landay did on the comparison between the public version of the National Intelligence Estimate on Iraq and the classified version, in which they stripped all the caveats, all the dissents, and all the cautionary notes out of the public version. They ran up every red flag and produced a report that the Silberman-Robb WMD Commission[8] says is one of the many things that was, in its words, "dead wrong."

Landay wrote up a whole laundry list of differences between the public and classified versions of the NIE in his February 9, 2004, article, "Doubts, Dissent Stripped from Public Iraq Assessments":

> For example, the public version declared that "most analysts assess Iraq is reconstituting its nuclear weapons program" and says, "if left unchecked, it probably will have a nuclear weapon this decade." But it fails to mention the dissenting view offered in the top-secret version by the State Department's intelligence arm, the Bureau of Intelligence and Research, known as the INR. That view said, in part, "the activities we have detected do not, however, add up to a compelling case that Iraq is currently pursuing what INR would consider to be an integrated and comprehensive approach to acquire nuclear weapons. Iraq may be doing so, but INR considers the available evidence inadequate to support such a judgment."
>
> What the comparison showed is that while the top-secret version delivered to Bush, his top lieutenants and Congress were heavily qualified with caveats about some of its most important conclusions about Iraq's illicit weapons programs, the caveats were omitted from the public version. The caveats included the phrases, "we judge that," "we assess that" and "we lack specific information on many key aspects of Iraq's WMD programs." These phrases, according to current and former intelligence officials, long have been used in intelligence reports to stress an absence of hard information and underscore that judgments are extrapolations or estimates.
>
> Among the most striking differences between the versions were those over Iraq's development of small, unmanned aircraft, also known as unmanned aerial vehicles [UAVs]. The public version said that Iraq's UAVs "especially if used

for delivery of chemical and biological warfare [CBW] agents—could threaten Iraq's neighbors, U.S. forces in the Persian Gulf, and the United States if brought close to, or into, the U.S. Homeland." The classified version showed there was major disagreement on the issue from the agency with the greatest expertise on such aircraft, the Air Force. The Air Force "does not agree that Iraq is developing UAVs primarily intended to be delivery platforms for chemical and biological warfare [CBW] agents," it said. "The small size of Iraq's new UAV strongly suggests a primary role of reconnaissance, although CBW delivery is an inherent capability."

The public version contained the alarming warning that Iraq was capable of quickly developing biological warfare agents that could be delivered by "bombs, missiles, aerial sprayers, and covert operatives, including potentially against the U.S. Homeland." No such warning that Iraq's biological weapons would be delivered to the United States appeared in the classified version."

Deleted from the public version was a line in the classified report that cast doubt on whether Saddam was prepared to support terrorist attacks on the United States, a danger that Bush and his top aides raised repeatedly in making their case for war. "Baghdad for now appears to be drawing a line short of con- ducting terrorist attacks with conventional or CBW [Chemical Biological Weapons] against the United States, fearing that exposure of Iraqi involvement would provide Washington with a stronger case for making war," the top-secret report said. Also missing from the public report were judgments that Iraq would attempt "clandestine attacks" on the United States only if an American invasion threatened the survival of Saddam's regime or "possibly for revenge."

Landay concluded that "as a result, the public was given a far more definitive assessment of Iraq's plans and capabilities than President Bush and other U.S. decision-makers received from their intelligence agencies. The stark differences between the public version and the then top-secret version of the October 2002 National Intelligence Estimate raise new questions about the accuracy of the public case made for a war that's claimed the lives of more than five hundred U.S. service members and thousands of Iraqis."

One of the assessments mentioned in the new report from the presi- dential commission assigned to look into intelligence failures that came out today, March 30, 2005, was that they were recommending more interagency discussions, more devil's advocate exchanges among the intelligence agencies about the intelligence.

The opposite was true during the prewar phase. Dissenters were punished.

What, then, do the administration's prewar activities in the intelligence area amount to?

They took the nation to war using a lot of bogus information. The other thing I should mention in the bogus information category is Mr. Ahmed Chalabi and the Iraqi National Congress [INC].[9] Why anyone would take at face value information from a group that was thoroughly distrusted by the intelligence professionals—not only at the CIA but also at the DIA and the Department of State—and that had a clear interest in encouraging an American attack, is beyond me. I just can't understand why that kind of information was accepted so uncritically.

Do you think there was an orchestrated deception campaign?

Yes, I wrote about this in a June 1, 2003, article, "Doubt on War Felt at Top Levels." The INC delivered the same bogus information to the news media and the Defense Department. So when the *New York Times* and other publications did what looked like homework and called the Defense Department and were told, "Oh yes, we've heard that too, we think that's authoritative," reporters thought they had two sources. In fact, they had only Chalabi, as their source and as the Defense Department's source. Hearing the same information from two different directions is no guarantee that it came from two different sources.

There's a second issue here, which is the nature of your sources. There's a mistaken notion in a lot of journalism, but especially in Washington, that the value of a source is directly proportional to his or her rank. I think that the relationship is more often the inverse for two reasons: The first one is that in any bureaucracy, whether it's a company, a newspaper, a television network, or a government, information flows from the bottom up. Not from the top down. There are many, many more people at the bottom of the pyramid collecting information, sorting it and passing it up, than there are at the top. The people at the top almost universally rely on their subordinates for information. They don't have time to read everything that people at lower ranks with more specialized jobs read. Often they don't have the same expertise. They don't speak the language. They haven't spent time in the culture. They're simply not as expert; that's not their job. The second reason is the obvious one, which is that the higher you go in any hierarchy, the more political people become and the more what they tell you is prepackaged or spun. So if you confine yourself to reporting on people you go to cocktail parties with, and whose names you like to drop to impress other people, you are exposing yourself to a much greater risk of being spun by people who are, first of all, more skilled at spin, and second, whose job it is to spin you.

What we did was burrow down into all of the bureaucracies to the people who were not just reading the cables but writing them; not just reading the analysis but writing it; and not just reading the reports but making them. That's where we found a real cognitive dissonance between what was being said and believed at the middle levels and what we were hearing at the top levels. Now I don't want to go too far with that because there were also people at very high levels in this administration who shared the doubts of the people below them.

One of the most fascinating things that I've discovered doing this book is that among this nation's top messengers there really is no consensus about why we went to war.

Yes, and I don't have an answer for you on that one. You've heard all the speculation, and I don't know what the real answer is. The one thing I will say is that I do believe there was a genuinely deep, deep fear that another attack was coming and that somehow Saddam would seize an opportunity with al Qaeda to strike back at the United States in some much more dramatic way. There was a very deep-seated fear of that.

Why was he so much on the radar for that when he was pretty much contained?

He was contained, but it was reasonable to think that he was trying to keep his weapons programs alive. He was a thoroughly bad actor on the international scene and at home.

Yes, but he wasn't particularly effective.

He was never particularly effective and, second, he had no particular track record of international terrorism. The now-deceased Palestinian terrorist Abu Nidal provides an instructive example. Abu Nidal was a terrible problem when he was based in Libya. When he relocated to Iraq, he ceased being a problem because the Iraqis sat on him and wouldn't let him do anything. The same is true of a much lesser known fellow named Abu Ibrahim, who was a Palestinian bomb maker. Once he was in Saddam's clutches, Saddam pretty well sat on him. So there was not a big record of Iraq being a big exporter of terrorism.

I don't know there was any record.

No, there really wasn't. There is the one contentious incident of Saddam allegedly trying to assassinate the president's father in Kuwait.[10] There are questions about that. Once again, there's dissent within the intelligence community about that, but if it were my father, I might be inclined to take it a little more seriously, too.

Well, you might be inclined to look into it to see exactly who it was.

I think the president said at one point, "He tried to kill my dad."

What was he basing that on?

That he was a thoroughly bad guy. He was a terrible person.

He was a friend to the United States in the past, though.

No, he was the enemy of our enemy. He was never America's friend.

He was the guy who we were dealing with and we certainly helped him.

In that case, I think you could make a case and probably still can today that Iran was a much greater threat to American interests and American lives than Iraq was and had claimed more of them through its surrogates in Lebanon and elsewhere.

I think you're right about that.

And that Iran was an active exporter of terrorism, as opposed to Iraq, which was less so.

Absolutely. The Europeans have a lot of direct personal experience with Iran, particularly the French.

Yes, they do.

What I found fascinating with the prewar coverage was we went to Afghanistan looking for Osama and al Qaeda, which made sense, and then all of a sudden we were going to Iraq, and no one seemed to question the leap of logic there when it happened.

A lot of it rests on Ramzi Yousef.[11] The administration sent Jim Woolsey[12] to Wales to interview the South Wales Constabulary to try to prove that Yousef was an Iraqi and to forge a link between him and Iraq. He came up empty on the connection between Yousef and Iraq. Clearly there was an effort to find every potential link, but my impression is that when that effort fell short, they began stretching the truth, as in the case of the Iraqi ambassador to Turkey.

The other thing that I find interesting is why, if you have this fear that he's going to be involved in terrorism, why don't you just tell the public? Why don't you just give that as the reason for going to war? Because it seems like the WMDs and the connection to al Qaeda were pretexts.

I don't know. I can't say that. I'm not sure anyone can say that they're pretexts.

Why?

I think it's entirely likely that the vice president, his chief of staff, the president, and others honestly were convinced that Saddam had these weapons squirreled away and was likely to give them to somebody to use against Americans, either at home or somewhere else in the world. Now, was that an uncritical belief? Was that belief accepted too readily? Clearly it was, because now we have stacks and stacks of reports saying that that was not the case and that no evidence has been found to support that allegation. But did they believe it at the time? Yes, I think they probably did.

So that basically means then that there is a crisis within our intelligence services.

I think there are two crises. First of all, it is tragic that our intelligence services did not have enough reliable information to provide an antidote to the unreliable information that was being spooned up by others in their own self-interest. I think that's highly unfortunate. I also think that the report looking into intelligence failures released on March 31, 2005, by the Commission on the Intelligence Capabilities of the United States Regarding Weapons of Mass Destruction, as well as other reports, suggests that the same is true of the intelligence on North Korea. If anything, North Korea is an even harder target than Iraq was. In Iran, we've had two networks of agents taken down. We've never really been able to penetrate the high levels of the Iranian government or its nuclear program. So there's a problem there.

The second problem is the relationship between the intelligence community and policymakers and the ability of policymakers to skew intelligence reports, to be selective about what they choose to believe and to use carrots and sticks to get intelligence community members to tell them what they want to hear. The tendency to please the boss is powerful in any institution. We've seen a lot of private businesses, including newspapers, fall victim to that syndrome, so it's not unique to this administration or to government. But when you are dealing with something as serious as going to war, it becomes a serious issue when policymakers are deciding that they'll ignore this department and they'll ignore that opinion, and that they'll create their own intelligence office to tell them the kinds of things they want to hear.

They were looking for reasons to go to war, and they knew they had to make a public case for it. In a democratic society and in the world community, they made every effort to collect allies for this venture using the same kinds of information. They needed to put together a campaign that suggested that risking thousands of lives was not just justified but necessary.

So they ignore the institutions that are supposed to provide them with this service and they actually create ad hoc groups and offices to come up with what they want to hear.

Correct. Is there something wrong here? There are two things wrong here. First of all, the deep distrust that a lot of people in this administration had for the intelligence community is pretty well founded. The intelligence community did not perform well in Iraq. It isn't performing well in Iran, isn't performing well in North Korea, missed the Indian nuclear test, and missed the sale of Chinese Silkworm missiles the size of boxcars to Saudi Arabia. Not a great track record. They had all sorts of problems: counter-intelligence problems, intelligence collection problems, and analytical problems. So that distrust is not crazy in any way, shape, or form. The CIA long ago became bureaucratized and risk-averse, partly in the wake of the Church and Pike Commission reports.[13] Almost all of its agents were operating out of embassies. There were very few so-called NOCS or nonofficial cover agents.

So the idea of trying to be more aggressive and setting up your own operation to bypass this very troubled agency is there from the start. And it's compounded in Afghanistan where the Department of Defense is frustrated once again at the absence of an on-the-ground network there and has to build one from scratch after 9/11. Rumsfeld is on the record as being impatient waiting for the CIA and having to depend on it, so that heightens the notion that some officials held: "If we want to do this right, we've got to do it ourselves, and we can't wait for them." So that's not crazy. The problem—and maybe the irony—here is that a lot of the people who believe this had as their scripture the "B team" exercise of the 1970s,[14] Paul Wolfowitz chief among them. He's a very smart guy and a much more complicated fellow than the caricature would have it.

I wish our press would do a better job of telling us who these people are.

It's hard to get anybody to read things like that. Believe me, Paul is a very complicated person, and you're starting to see it a little bit now as he talks about this World Bank job.[15] He talks about his experience as US ambassador in Indonesia, when he was assistant secretary of state for East Asian and Pacific affairs and when he really tangled with the Reagan administration about Marcos.[16] The president's inclination was to stick with Marcos, and Paul and a few others argued, "No, we should be pressuring the guy to leave." That's not the side of Paul you ever hear about, but it's true.

Anyway, the "B team" exercise crystallized a lot of the belief that you couldn't really fully trust the agency and that you ought routinely to second-guess them. The trouble, in my judgment, is that this B team didn't set up another B team to second-guess themselves.

Did they want to be second-guessed?

Nobody likes to be second-guessed.

Well, no, but you do when you are considering such an extreme activity as war.

I would want to be a little more careful, for example, with the information from defectors and exile groups, not just the INC but the Kurdish[17] groups and walk-ins like "Curveball."[18]

With respect to Curveball, it's been a given for a long time that you can't trust a defector because he wants asylum and is going to blow as much smoke as he can to get the best deal.

That's somewhere in the first week of case officer training, absolutely, but it's also human nature to believe what you want to believe and to filter out what you don't want to believe. What you have to do in government, and in intelligence work as in journalism, is to set up procedures that don't allow you to do that. And they didn't.

I was asking one big reporter about the weapons of mass destruction story and this reporter said, "Look, the only thing we could do was report what the administration was saying," and "how are we going to confirm this story, we can't go and do a needle-in-the-haystack tour of Iraq and do a physical inventory." When I was talking to Jon Landay, he said that he went through this whole analytical process of trying to figure out how to find out if the statement was true or not and he asked himself, "If Saddam had these WMDs, what facilities would he have, and so on, and what could be easily seen," and he investigated that.

Look, I can't emphasize strongly enough the fact that an awful lot of the things the administration alleged didn't make sense and raised big questions: Saddam was going to put a biological weapons facility in his own basement? A Kurdish defector had complete access to Iraq's most secret weapons programs?

How does this nonsense become real?

I can't answer that. All I can say is that it didn't become real here. And it doesn't make any sense to me that it was treated as real elsewhere. Why would you believe that Saddam would have given a Kurd access to his most sensitive facilities? Why would you believe he would put a biological weapons facility in his own basement?

Reading your prewar reporting, which is all about raising these questions, I'm surprised that nobody ever called you from various places, the State Department or the Pentagon, for example. Another reporter I spoke to said the Pentagon absolutely believed that Saddam had weapons of mass destruction.

No, they didn't. It depends on who you ask. If you ask about Undersecretary of Defense for Policy Doug Feith,[19] he believed it. Donald Rumsfeld believed it. Paul Wolfowitz believed it. Remember what I told you. You have to talk to the lower-echelon people who were most expert and actually handled the information in the first instance.

I'm just telling you this reporter has been in the Pentagon for almost two decades. And this reporter's sources were saying, "We believe it."

You didn't have to go very far to find people who had doubts. Having said that, no one ever told us absolutely that he didn't have them. It took two years of going through the place with a fine-toothed comb to be able to say with some certainty that he didn't have them. So no one ever told us he didn't have them, but what they did tell us was, "This piece of information has been twisted, this piece of information got left out, this doesn't make any sense, this contradicts what they're saying." That's the most that people could say. But going back to where I started, if what you're talking about is making a decision to go to war, those dissents, questions, and loopholes become pretty important. So the contrast between people at the most expert levels across the government saying, "We're not so sure," and people at the top level saying, "We're absolutely sure," was really striking.

The other thing is that the leadership of the country has instant and continuous access to the mass consciousness media, to television, so if they want to send out a message that is quite different from that of their experts, they can.

That's right, sure.

So Knight Ridder, and I say this with all due respect, was, in a sense, reporting the experts' messages from inside a paper bag.

That's correct. I don't disagree with that at all. It wasn't just television; it was the most powerful print institutions in the country or in the world that were reporting mostly what the leadership was saying.

Yes, but TV is what really matters with the public.

Yes, but TV get its lead from reading the *New York Times*.

Sometimes.

Very often. What I'm suggesting is that the likelihood of a major television network taking a reporting tack very different from that of the *Times* is nil.

It's less than nil, because even what they would take from the *New York Times* would be dry-cleaned. That's the nature of their business.

Sure. So if you were setting out to influence public opinion, how would you do it?

You have to go on TV.

Yes, but if you were going to set the tone, to establish that it's a given that he has all this stuff and that he's a great danger to us . . .

You just send that message over and over and over.

They're very good at this "message discipline," as they call it. The repetition was very effective. So effective, in fact, that we still have a healthy percentage of people—not all of them Fox News viewers—who still believe that Saddam had weapons of mass destruction and somehow was involved in 9/11.

This is the most troubling aspect to me. Fox, let's face it, only has 1.8 million viewers. That's pretty small. We have more than 295 million people in this country. How can so many of these people still believe this?

Because the most powerful institutions in our country, both in media and government, said it was so. It's a pretty potent alliance.

Did you come under any pressure from the administration?

Oh, Lord, we sure did. It was the usual. It works in a couple of ways. Again, it's carrots and sticks. You don't get phone calls returned, you get taken off the call lists, you can't travel with Rumsfeld or Cheney, you get berated, and there are the usual phone calls.

You got a few of those?

I got a few a day.

What did they say to you?

They made accusations: "The story was inaccurate," "You're looking for trouble here"—the usual stuff. It's all the normal Washington game.

But no active campaign to silence you.

It was an active campaign to discredit us with other reporters, but I'll tell you in all honesty that if we had been the *New York Times* on the Pentagon Papers[20] or the *Washington Post* on Watergate[21] we would have gotten a lot more heat. Although we're bigger than either of those organizations by quite a lot in terms of the number of readers, our national reach, and our presence in a lot of key electoral states, we're under the radar most of the time.

Well, you don't have a presence in this town.

No, we don't, but the Internet is changing that. By the way, I don't think the *New York Times* did a terribly good job on the prewar reporting, but they do a very good job on any number of other things. It's one of the best papers in the country.

I spoke to Walter Pincus at the *Washington Post*. Walter was interesting because he was talking about how all his reports asking the pertinent prewar questions were ending up on page seventeen. Who makes the decisions on your papers for what gets on the front page?

Each paper makes its own decisions. The important thing is that there was never any second-guessing, much less pressure, from above my head about any of the prewar reporting. Never once did anyone at corporate, from Tony Ridder on down, do anything but encourage us to keep doing what we were doing or express anything other than pride in what we were doing, even though they came under pressure.

I don't think the president ever called them and I don't think the vice president ever called them, but friends in local Republican parties and local activists came at them. I'm sure they were attacked in blogs when they ran stuff that Republicans didn't like. But never once did any of that roll back. At that level, we had nothing but support.

The bottom line is very simple: we could not have done what we did throughout this entire period without the support of my boss, Clark Hoyt, who is the Washington editor, and the total support of his boss, Jerry Ceppos, the vice president for news, and his boss, Tony Ridder.

I'm very interested in the fact that your reporters here, Jon Landay and Warren Strobel, are still pursuing the prewar story.

Sure, because there are still some unanswered questions. You've asked a lot of them that I can't answer.

I want to move on to Iraq and to ask you what your sources are telling you about what's going on there and what the potential is there for democracy, because now the message from the White House is that democracy is on the move.

I think it's premature to say that. I don't think we know what the outcome is going to be. Our reporters there say that it is not clear whether a functioning democracy can take root there or whether the old religious, ethnic, and tribal divisions will reassert themselves and make a functioning democracy impossible. I think that the possibilities range all the way from some democratic success that brings Sunnis[22] into the picture, all the way to the worst-case scenario, which is civil war and Iraq as a new Afghanistan, but with oil and in the heart of the Middle East.

Yes, but don't you think that the newly elected prime minister, Ibrahim al-Jafaari, is going to move toward a theocratic government?

I don't think you can take anything as a given. I'm not sure about that, but I do believe that Ayatollah Sistani is not an Iranian ayatollah or a Khomeini.[23] We'll see. Historically, in Najaf,[24] the center of Shiism,[25] a more moderate brand of Shiite theology was practiced than what is practiced in Iran. Thanks in large part to our friend Saddam, Qom[26] and the Iranians hijacked Shiism and put their own much more radical brand on it. I'm not sure that this Iranian brand, the one we are most familiar with and afraid of, is going to take root in Iraq, because historically there have been pretty serious divisions. One of our reporters, Soraya Sarhaddi Nelson, wrote about that pretty intelligently. She is of Iranian extraction from a Shiite background and understands it better than a lot of folks do. She wrote a pretty interesting piece about the distinction between Najaf and Qom and Iraqi and Iranian Shiism.[27] I don't think you can prejudge the nature of Iraq's future government because, as a nation, it does have a secular tradition, not a theological one, even within most of the Shiite community. And when it comes to women's rights, it has a tradition of relative liberalism.

Yes, but that was thanks to Saddam.

It was.

The question is: did that take root enough for it to translate into the new government?

We don't know. But are there going to be a lot of Iraqi women eager to put on burkas? We'll see. It is unfinished business, and it could go in two extreme ways. It could degenerate into a Lebanon-style civil war. It already has a lot of the characteristics of Lebanon, starting with a down-trodden Shiite majority that's been disenfranchised for years and now has a lot of scores to settle. Or it could be the place where some forms of democracy, pluralism, and political tolerance begin to take root in the Arab world. So there are a couple of big questions. One is: How will the Shia handle power now that they have it? The other one is: What do the Kurds really want? And if what the Kurds really want is all the oil revenue from Kirkuk[28] because they have a few scores to settle with the Shia, then you've got formulas for trouble. But it's too early to know, and none of our reporters out there pretends to have a crystal ball that can show you what Iraq's going to look like five months from now, much less five years from now.

I just want to go back to the prewar era for a second. One reporter told me that he thought that the reason we went to war was predetermined even before Bush came into office and that this was clear from the "Clean Break" document[29] and from the Project for a New American Century.[30]

That's not a plan to go to war, but there are a number of very sensible reasons for thinking that way. First, the continued reliance on Saudi Arabia doesn't look like a very good bet. We're coming very quickly to a generational change in that country. The "Sudairi seven," the seven members of the royal family, are all elderly, and the next generation is much larger, on the order of two thousand princes, and much more diverse. They range from very pro-Western and English-educated to Osama types. So the stability of Saudi Arabia can't be taken for granted in terms of it continuing to provide military bases for the United States, which were very important during and after the first Gulf War, and in terms of it being a reliable provider of oil and a regulator of the global oil market. It was sensible to look around for other ways to secure America's economic and military interests in that part of the world. For reasons we talked about before, Iraq looked like a pretty decent candidate. It had a highly unpopular tyrannical minority regime that was hated by 80 percent of the country's people. That's not a bad place to start. It has a tradition of secular rule, again, thanks to Saddam. There was no highly organized radical Islamic movement, no Iraqi Islamic Jihad, and no Iraqi Muslim Brotherhood[31] to speak of.

You also have to look at going into Iraq in terms of resolving the Israeli-Palestinian crisis. When Arafat was still alive, you didn't have the hopes that the new PLO chairman, Mahmoud Abbas, and company have raised in terms of discussing peace with Israel. That picture looked pretty bleak with Arafat in power. So if you could knock out another one of the props underneath Palestinian radicalism—it's not the only one, but there aren't too many left—by getting Iraq under control and willing to sign a peace treaty with Israel, you might finally be able to bring the Palestinians around to accepting the fact that they've got to make a deal.

The plan was to install Ahmed Chalabi.[32] And the idea of having American military bases in Iraq constraining the ability of both the Iranians on one side and the Syrians on the other to misbehave and having a friendly government headed by Chalabi in Baghdad willing to allow these bases seemed like a good one. Remember, another part of Chalabi's sales pitch was that he would sign a peace treaty with Israel. So if you believe he could deliver on that, what would the effect be on the Palestinians if an Iraqi government did a complete 180 and did what the Egyptians first did and signed a formal peace treaty with Israel? That looks pretty attractive.

As a journalist who's been in that region and had experience in that region, what is your response to that?

Analytically, it's a pipe dream. I'm afraid that Iraq may not be nearly as fertile soil for democracy as it might appear to be, because of the ethnic divisions. I have to admit that, as I sort of "B team" myself, a Lebanese-style civil war weighs very heavily in my thinking, maybe too heavily, because they're two completely different countries with two completely different histories. But I see Sunnis and disenfranchised Shia and Kurds, and I tend to see Lebanon, which may be a mistake, but there it is.

You can call what we're trying to install there a democracy, you can call it all kinds of things, but the underlying social and cultural structure is really tribal, so that's an issue.

Yes, it is in Lebanon, too. I ask myself: What is the effect of American action bringing this about as opposed to internal uprising? Could that backfire not just in Iraq but throughout the Muslim world, and wouldn't it benefit Osama more than anybody else? Wouldn't it also benefit the Iranians?

How is your coverage differing right now from that of your competitors?

It's nowhere near as different as it was in the prewar phase, and I guess the best and most self-serving way to put that is to say that I think a lot of the other coverage is much better on Iran and North Korea than it was on Iraq.

Well, maybe it's easier to cover.

Nah, it's always hard. It's always hard dealing with this stuff.

JOHN WALCOTT is Washington bureau chief for Knight Ridder, the nation's second-largest newspaper company. Knight Ridder's Newspaper Division publishes thirty-one daily papers, including the *Detroit Free Press*, the *Kansas City Star*, the *Miami Herald*, the *Philadelphia Inquirer*, and the *San Jose Mercury News*, with a total readership of 8.7 million on weekdays and 12.6 million on Sundays. Knight Ridder Digital is the founder and operator of the Real Cities network of Web sites in more than 110 US markets.

The Knight Ridder Washington Bureau has a staff of thirty editors and reporters in Washington and also oversees Knight Ridder's nine foreign bureaus in Baghdad, Beijing, Berlin, Jerusalem, Mexico City, Moscow, Nairobi, Rio de Janeiro, and Tokyo.

Mr. Walcott previously was foreign editor and national editor of *U.S. News & World Report*, national security correspondent at the *Wall Street Journal*, and chief diplomatic correspondent, national political correspondent, and economics correspondent at *Newsweek* magazine. He started his career in journalism at the *Ridgewood (NJ) News* and the *Bergen Record* in Hackensack, New Jersey.

His work has won the Edward Weintal Prize for Diplomatic Reporting from Georgetown University, the Edwin M. Hood Award for Diplomatic Correspondence and the Freedom of the Press Award from the National Press Club, the National Headliner Award, the James K. Batten Prize for Journalism Excellence, and several Overseas Press Club awards.

With CBS News Pentagon correspondent David C. Martin, he is the coauthor of *Best Laid Plans: The Inside Story of America's War against Terrorism*, published in 1987 by Harper & Row.

In addition, Mr. Walcott is an adjunct professor in the Edmund A. Walsh School of Foreign Service at Georgetown University. He served as senior counselor to the Federal Advisory Commission on Gender-Integrated Training and Related Military Issues in the Office of the Secretary of Defense and as the United States representative to the United Nations Roundtable on a New World Information and Communication Order. He also is a member of the board of advisers of SmartBrief, Inc., a Washington-based information services company.

He is a graduate of Williams College in Massachusetts and an alumnus of the Georgetown Leadership Seminar and of Knight Ridder's Executive Leadership Program.

NOTES

1. An Arabic word meaning "the base," al Qaeda is an international terrorist group headed by a Saudi, Osama bin Laden, which aims to oppose non-Islamic governments with force and violence and seek retribution for force and violence used against Muslims.

2. Warren Strobel covers foreign affairs and the State Department for Knight Ridder.

3. According to the BBC's Middle East analyst, Roger Hardy (in his September 30, 2001, article "Analysis: Inside Wahhabi Islam"), Muhammed Ibn Abdul-Wahhab founded Wahhabism, an Islamic revivalist movement, in the eighteenth century because he "felt that the local practice of Islam had lost is original purity." The Internet encyclopedia Wikipedia describes Wahhabism as a "fundamentalist, puritanical form of Islam, which is often considered as having deviated from Sunni Islam. A major instance of this change is their anthropomorphic beliefs about God." Wahhabism is "the major sect of the government and society of Saudi Arabia." http://en.wikipedia.org/wiki/Wahhabism.

4. The Taliban (which means "those who study the book [Koran]" in Pushtu) was a very conservative Islamic movement that ruled most of Afghanistan from 1996 to 2001. According to the Internet encyclopedia Wikipedia, the Taliban restored order after civil war broke out following the demise of the Soviet-backed Democratic Republic of

Afghanistan. They "eliminated payments that warlords demanded from business people ... reduced factional fighting ... and brought social benefits by imposing a set of norms on a chaotic society." Their rules included bans on "all forms of TV, imagery and music" and on women working or visiting hospitals for medical treatment (because contact with male doctors was not allowed). After September 11, the United States, supported by a coalition of countries, initiated military action against the Taliban for "harboring al Qaeda." http://en.wikipedia.org/wiki/Taliban.

5. On February 5, 2003, Secretary of State Colin Powell made a presentation to the UN Security Council that had, he said, two purposes: "First, to support the core assessments made by [chief UN weapons inspector] Dr. Blix and [the head of the International Atomic Energy Agency] Dr. ElBaradei. As Dr. Blix reported to this council on January 27, quote, 'Iraq appears not to have come to a genuine acceptance, not even today, of the disarmament which was demanded of it,' unquote. . . . My second purpose today is to provide you with additional information, to share with you what the United States knows about Iraq's weapons of mass destruction as well as Iraq's involvement in terrorism, which is the subject of Resolution 1441 and other earlier resolutions." http://www.white house.gov/news/releases/2003/02/20030205-1.html. Later reports showed that Powell's presentation contained errors.

6. Jonathan S. Landay is Knight Ridder's national security and intelligence correspondent. See chapter 13 in this book.

7. Released on October 1, 2002, the report was titled "National Intelligence Estimate: Iraq's Continuing Programs for Weapons of Mass Destruction." Compiled in a record three weeks, it was a key report for deciding what the US government's policy toward Iraq would be.

8. In February 2004, this Commission on the Intelligence Capabilities of the United States Regarding Weapons of Mass Destruction was formed by an executive order signed by President Bush. The commission submitted its report to the president on March 31, 2005. The report can be read at http://www.wmd.gov/report/index.html. Regarding the intelligence failure with respect to Saddam's WMDs, the report says that it "was in large part the result of analytical shortcomings; intelligence analysts were too wedded to their assumptions about Saddam's intentions." The introduction also mentions that there was a failure on the part of the agencies to collect good intelligence for analysis, and that much of what was collected was "worthless or misleading." The commission was cochaired by former Virginia governor and senator Charles S. Robb and Judge Laurence H. Silberman, a senior circuit judge on the US Court of Appeals for the District of Columbia.

9. According to the Center for Media and Democracy's *Source Watch*, the Iraqi National Congress [INC] was "created at the behest of the U.S. government to foment the overthrow of Iraqi dictator Saddam Hussein." Led by Ahmed Chalabi (currently acting oil minister for the new Iraqi government), the INC received millions from the US government for its activities and was a source of faulty prewar intelligence. http://www.source watch.org/index.php?title=Iraqi_National_Congress.

10. Allegations that Saddam Hussein had ordered Iraqi intelligence to assassinate President George H. W. Bush in April 1993 during Bush's visit to Kuwait to commemorate the victory of the first Gulf War eventually led President Clinton to order an attack on Mukhabarat, Iraqi intelligence headquarters, which resulted in the deaths of eight civilians when some of the missiles landed on nearby homes. In a November 1, 1992, *New Yorker* article titled "Case Not Closed," reporter Seymour Hersh wrote about the alleged assassi-

nation plot, "But my own investigations have uncovered circumstantial evidence, at least as compelling as the Administration's, that suggests that the American government's case against Iraq—as it has been outlined in public, anyway—is seriously flawed."

11. Ramzi Yousef is believed to be one of the masterminds behind the first attack on the World Trade Center.

12. James Woolsey served as director of the Central Intelligence Agency under President Bill Clinton.

13. Idaho senator Frank Church was in charge of the Senate Select Committee to Study Governmental Operations with Respect to Intelligence Activities, which investigated America's intelligence agencies post-Watergate. The committee released fourteen reports in 1975 and 1976 and arrived at this conclusion: "In its consideration of covert action, the Committee was struck by the basic tension—if not incompatibility—of covert operations and the demands of a constitutional system. Secrecy is essential to covert operations; secrecy can, however, become a source of power, a barrier to serious policy debate within the government, and a means of circumventing established checks and procedures of government. The Committee found that secrecy and compartmentalization contributed to a temptation on the part of the Executive to resort to covert operations in order to avoid bureaucratic, congressional and public debate." The Church Committee reports are posted on the Web site of the Assassination Archives and Research Center at http://www.aarc library.org/publib/church/contents.htm. According to Richard A. Best Jr., the Library of Congress's congressional research service specialist in national defense, foreign affairs, defense, and trade division, in 1976 Congressman Otis G. Pike chaired a House Select Committee on Intelligence that "conducted a wide-ranging survey of intelligence activities." Among the Pike Commission's recommendations was that except during wartime, covert actions should not include assassination attempts. Best's summary of the Pike Commission and its recommendations is on pp. 27–29 at http://www.fas.org/irp/crs/ RL32500.pdf.

14. In May 1976, then CIA director George H. W. Bush created a "Team B" to perform a competitive assessment of a 1975 CIA National Intelligence Estimate [NIE] on Soviet Strategic Objectives. Lawrence J. Korb, a senior fellow at the Center for American Progress, writes: "The NIE did not endorse a worst-case scenario of Soviet capabilities." Paul Wolfowitz was one of the outside experts on Team B, which eventually concluded that intelligence analysts had underestimated the Soviet threat. "Ultimately," Korb writes, "the Team B analysis was deemed a gross exaggeration and completely inaccurate." Korb's August 1, 2004, column on Team B, "It's Time to Bench 'Team B,'" is at http:// www.americanprogress.org/site/pp.asp?c=biJRJ8OVF &b=140711.

15. Former deputy secretary of defense Paul Wolfowitz is the World Bank's tenth president. He was selected in March 2005 and has been serving since June 1, 2005.

16. Ferdinand Marcos was the tenth president of the Philippines. He served for twenty-one years, from 1965 to 1986.

17. A *Washington Post* profile of the Kurds at http://www.washingtonpost.com/ wp-srv/inatl/daily/feb99/kurdprofile.htm describes them as fifteen to twenty million "largely Sunni Muslims with their own language and culture living in the generally contiguous areas of Turkey, Iraq, Iran, Armenia and Syria" collectively called Kurdistan. The Kurds seek their own state and have clashed with the nations in which their territories lie, including Iraq. In 1988 the Iraqis launched a poison gas attack on the town of Hallabjah and killed five thousand people.

18. In a July 11, 2004, *Los Angeles Times* article, reporter Bob Drogin wrote: "The only American who met a now-discredited Iraqi defector codenamed 'Curveball' repeatedly warned the CIA before the war that the Baghdad engineer appeared to be an alcoholic and that his dramatic claims that Saddam Hussein had built a secret fleet of mobile germ weapons factories were not reliable. In response, the deputy director of the CIA's Iraqi weapons of mass destruction task force . . . suggested in a February 4, 2003, e-mail that such doubts were not welcome at the intelligence agency. 'As I said last night, let's keep in mind the fact that this war's going to happen regardless of what Curveball said or didn't say, and the powers that be probably aren't terribly interested in whether Curveball knows what he's talking about,' the CIA official wrote."

19. Before becoming undersecretary of defense for policy, Douglas J. Feith was an adviser to the Israeli government and a participant in the "Study Group on a New Israeli Strategy Toward 2000" that formulated the "Clean Break" document. He was also part of the Project for a New American Century. As undersecretary of defense, he helped set up the secretive Office of Special Plans whose purpose, according to national security reporter James Bamford, was "to conduct advance war planning for Iraq, and one of its most important responsibilities was 'media strategies.'" In September 2004, an analyst in his office, Lawrence Franklin, came under investigation for allegedly passing on a draft presidential directive on Iran to the pro-Israel lobby AIPAC (American Israel Public Affairs Committee). In January 26, 2005, the Department of Defense announced Feith's resignation, saying he was leaving for "personal and family reasons."

20. The online encyclopedia Wikipedia describes the Pentagon Papers as "a 7,000-page top-secret United States Department of Defense history of the United States involvement in Vietnam from 1945 to 1971. The Pentagon Papers were leaked in 1971 by Department of Defense worker Daniel Ellsberg. . . . The document revealed, among other things, that the government had planned to go to Vietnam even when President Lyndon Johnson was promising not to, and that there was no plan to end the war." http://en.wikipedia.org/wiki/Pentagon_Papers.

21. In 1972 *Washington Post* journalists Bob Woodward and Carl Bernstein, with the help of a confidential source named "Deep Throat" (then FBI deputy director Mark Felt), connected a break-in at the Democratic National Committee headquarters located in the Watergate hotel and office complex in Washington, DC, to high-ranking sources in the Nixon administration and the Committee to Re-Elect the President. Their investigation eventually led to President Nixon's resignation in 1974.

22. Sunni Islam is the largest denomination of Islam in the Middle East, but Sunnis are in the minority in Iraq. Sunnis adhere to Sunna, the "model behavior which the Muslim community should follow, which consists of the words and deeds of the prophet Muhammad. According to traditional Sunni theory, the idea already existed in Muhammad's own lifetime that one should consult and follow the Prophet when there was some doubt about a religious or legal matter." http://au.encarta.msn.com/encyclopedia_761565794/Sunni.html.

23. Grand Ayatollah Ali Husaini Sistani was born in Iran and now lives in Najaf, Iraq. A very traditional Shiite cleric and the Shiites' top spiritual leader, he is considered one of the most influential religious figures in the Middle East. In chapter 20 of this book, Knight Ridder's foreign correspondent, Hannah Allam, said that before he was elected, Iraqi prime minister Ibrahim al-Jafaari told her: "We're not going to set up a theocracy, but at the same time we'll probably see a more conservative government and a more prominent role for

Islam. . . . People are turning to religion and they reflected that by voting for a list that was backed by the most revered Ayatollah Sistani." Allam says that for Prime Minister al-Jafaari, "that's a mandate." Sistani's Web site is http://www.sistani.org/. The Ayatollah Rouhollah Mousavi Khomeini became absolute ruler of Iran in April 1979 following the deposing of the Shah Mohammed Reza Pahlavi of Iran in January 1979. Khomeini's theocratic government gave complete political control to clergymen.

24. Najaf is one of the holiest cities in Iraq for Shiites and the center of Shiite political power.

25. Shiism is "a collective term for several distinct Muslim sects that make up some 10 percent of the Muslim world—the rest being chiefly Sunni. Sunnis and Shiites differ from each other in many ways. They disagree over ritual law and diverge most in ethos, theology and how they conceive legitimate authority." http://au.encarta.msn.com/encyclopedia_761570168/Shiism.html.

26. One of the holiest cities in Iran for Shiites, Qom is the site of the country's largest seminary and theological center.

27. In her April 13, 2003, article posted on the Monterey Herald Web site, "Saddam's Fall Could Lead to Religious Upheaval in Iran," Soraya Sahaddi Nelson writes about the differences between the Iraqi and Iranian Shiites. http://www.montereyherald.com/mld/montereyherald/news/special_packages/iraq/archive/5613556.htm?template=contentModules/printstory.jsp.

28. Kirkuk is a city in the Kurdish area of Iraq. It is one of Iraq's most important oil-producing areas.

29. "A Clean Break: A Strategy for Securing the Realm" is described by National Security reporter James Bamford in chapter 11 of this book as "a foreign policy plan that [then adviser to the Israeli government] Richard Perle gave to Netanyahu, who had just become prime minister of Israel. The 'Clean Break' report recommended that Israel go into Iraq, remove Saddam Hussein, put somebody in there who would basically be a puppet, and then go to Syria, Iran, and all the other countries that they were worried about." The document can be viewed at http://www.informationclearinghouse.info/article1438.htm.

30. The Project for a New American Century (PNAC) says on its Web site that it "intends, through issue briefs, research papers, advocacy journalism, conferences, and seminars, to explain what American world leadership entails." It is generally seen as a neoconservative take on the role the United States should play in the world. PNAC says it is a nonprofit educational organization dedicated to the propositions "that American leadership is good both for America and the world; and that such leadership requires military strength, diplomatic energy and commitment to moral principle." http://www.newamericancentury.org/.

31. According to the online encyclopedia Wikipedia, Islamic Jihad "is a militant Islamist group based in the Syrian capital, Damascus. . . . It first came to prominence with the April 1983 US Embassy bombing in Beirut. Several groups in other Arab countries also go by the name Islamic Jihad, notably the Egyptian Islamic Jihad and the Palestinian Islamic Jihad. . . . The name is also occasionally used by the Lebanese militant group Hezbollah. Islamic Jihad has used teenagers as suicide bombers." http://en.wikipedia.org/wiki/Islamic_Jihad. The Muslim Brotherhood rejects secularism and advocates a return to the precepts of the Koran. In a September 11, 2004, *Washington Post* article, "In Search of Friends among Foes," reporters John Mintz and Douglas Farah write, "The

Brotherhood . . . is a sprawling and secretive society with followers in more than 70 countries. It is dedicated to creating an Islamic civilization that harks back to the caliphates of the 7th and 8th centuries, one that would segregate women from public life and scorn nonbelievers. In some nations—Egypt, Algeria, Syria, Sudan—the Brotherhood has fomented Islamic revolution. In the Palestinian territories, the Brotherhood created the Islamic Resistance Movement, or HAMAS, which became known for its suicide bombings of Israelis. Yet it is also a sophisticated and diverse organization that appeals to many Muslims worldwide and sometime advocates peaceful persuasion, not violent revolt. Some of its supporters went on to help found al Qaeda, while others launched one of the largest college student groups in the United States. . . . They run hundreds of mosques and dozens of businesses engaging in ventures such as real estate development and banking." http://www.washingtonpost.com/ac2/wp-dyn/A12823-2004 Sep10?language=printer.

32. A British-educated former banker, Ahmed Chalabi has been the leader of the anti-Saddam Iraqi National Congress, which was formed with US government backing for the purpose of overthrowing Saddam Hussein. He received large sums of money from the US government for his activities and was a source of faulty prewar intelligence. Although he has no industry experience, he is currently acting oil minister for the new Iraqi government.

13

"THE VICE PRESIDENT IS LYING"

AND OTHER THINGS THE DEEP THROATS SAID

WARREN P. STROBEL
Senior Correspondent
for Foreign Affairs,
Knight Ridder

JONATHAN S. LANDAY
National Security and
Intelligence Correspondent,
Knight Ridder
Interviewed March 2005

One of these days, America is going to wake up and realize that Jonathan Landay and Warren Strobel are *the* heavy mettle rock stars of post-9/11 reporting. They were in the zone right from the beginning:

"The most surprising thing to us was we had the field to ourselves for so long in terms of writing stuff that was critical or questioning the administration's case for war," says Strobel. According to Landay, when the going got tough, the tough started feeling a little insecure: "There were times when we were deeply concerned that maybe we really had gotten it wrong and maybe everyone else was right. But that's the kind of stuff that got us going." They persisted with a full chorus of Deep Throats in various parts of the government singing in their ears.

Landay tackled the WMD issue by figuring out what it would take to have one. "It requires quite a bit of physical infrastructure. You need thousands of high-speed spinning machines called centrifuges if you are going to go the uranium enrichment route, which was the way the Iraqis were going. . . ." Then, Vice President Cheney made this statement in August 2002: "It is believed that the Iraqis have reconstituted their nuclear program and some of us believe that they may have a nuclear weapon soon." That grabbed Landay's attention: "I went, '*what?*' From what I was able to learn through just educating myself about the kind of infrastructure required to build a weapon and knowing that the UN had destroyed what the Iraqis had had, this just seemed to me to be really weird and wrong. So I started making phone calls. I talked to somebody who follows this issue, not a senior official, but a working stiff who follows this issue, and this person's words to me were, 'The vice president is lying.'"

Singly, jointly, and/or sometimes paired up with their boss, John Walcott, Strobel and Landay documented over and over again instances where key information provided by the administration as it made its case for war was either withheld, spun via sin of omission, distorted, or outright false. "We started seeing this pattern emerging, where they would make definitive statements about things that were actually being disputed within the intelligence community and tell us just partially what they knew about different subjects," says Landay. "It wasn't just some of their own experts; there were some very senior people who had serious problems with the case that was being made. Serious problems. *That* was the story."

I talked to Landay and Strobel for about two hours. Jonathan is more gregarious, while Warren is quiet and thoughtful. As a team, they seem like perfect foils for each other. Clearly, they were stoked about what they were doing.

So just how far are they willing to take their investigation? Landay talks about what was going on in his head while he was writing a stunning article listing the critical differences between the public and classi-

fied versions of the National Intelligence Estimate [NIE] report. "I struggled with this story for months from the point of view of the use of the
kind of information they were putting out. There's a law that prohibits the
American government from propagandizing its own people. It's a law that
was passed long before the age of the Internet and twenty-four-hour television and instant communications, and trying to prove that any law was
broken by the creation of these two different versions of the NIE was
incredibly difficult and I couldn't do it, but it wasn't for lack of trying. . . .
The fact is, that as far as this government goes and as far as our business
goes, there's been no accountability whatsoever." The news flash for
those who might have reason to worry about being held accountable is
that Landay and Strobel aren't letting go: "We're backtracking. We're still
going back to the prewar issues."

First, we discussed that troublesome NIE report.

Strobel: Congress was saying, "OK, where's the National Intelligence
Estimate?"[1] Florida's Senator Bob Graham, the former chairman of the
Senate Intelligence Committee, was making a big brouhaha about there
not being an NIE. Bush didn't want to do one. The administration only
did it under duress. It came out that following October, and it was put
together in about three weeks. Generally, the process is, an NIE is done
and then a decision is made as to what the policy is going to be, whether
it's going to be war, or diplomacy, or sanctions, or whatever, but the NIE
comes first. In this case, they did it the other way around. The decision
was made that one way or the other, they were going to take out Saddam.
That was in January of 2002. John Walcott [Knight Ridder's Washington
bureau chief] and I reported that. And look at the July 23, 2002, memo on
US-British prewar discussions that was leaked in London on May 5,
2005. It makes clear that they had decided on war by July 2002, if not
before. It quotes the head of MI-6 [British foreign intelligence service],
who had just returned from Washington, as saying: "The intelligence and
facts were being fixed around the policy."

Landay: The NIE is usually the product of a considerable amount of
work and digging into all of the intelligence. This one was put together in
a rush. People I've talked to say they've never seen such a badly put-
together analysis. It just broke all the rules on how an NIE should be put
together and how it should read.

Then, at the same time that they were giving policymakers the classified version of the NIE that had all these caveats as well as a dissent by

the State Department's Bureau of Intelligence and Research and the Air Force on the NIE's judgment that Saddam had unmanned aerial vehicles that could be used to deploy biological and chemical weapons, they produced a public version of the NIE with all that stuff taken out. In fact, stuff was actually added to the public version of the NIE that wasn't in the classified version. The public version warned that Iraq could quickly develop biological agents that could be delivered by "bombs, missiles, aerial sprayers and covert operatives, including potentially against the US homeland." The classified version contained no such warning about a potential Iraqi biological warfare attack on the US homeland.

Is there any kind of law being broken by doing this?

Landay: I struggled with this story for months from the point of view of the use of the kind of information they were putting out. There's a law that prohibits the American government from propagandizing its own people. It's a law that was passed long before the age of the Internet and twenty-four-hour television and instant communications, and trying to prove that any law was broken by the creation of these two different versions of the NIE was incredibly difficult and I couldn't do it, but it wasn't for lack of trying. There are laws that make it a crime for a public official to willfully or knowingly mislead or lie to Congress. It's a high crime under the Constitution's impeachment clause to manipulate or deliberately misuse national security intelligence data. And under federal criminal law, it's a felony to "defraud the United States or any agency thereof, in any manner or for any purpose."

Strobel: We looked at one other law that might have been broken, which is a law that says if Congress gives you money, you cannot turn around and use that money to lobby the US government. We found evidence that Ahmed Chalabi's Iraqi National Congress [INC],[2] which had provided false and exaggerated intelligence to the administration for making the case for war, may have broken that law. But the INC was not charged with anything.

Landay: In February 2004 we wrote an article, "Officials: U.S. Still Paying Millions to Group That Provided False Iraqi Intelligence," about how the Iraqi National Congress was still getting money from Congress. The lead was "The Department of Defense is continuing to pay millions of dollars for information from the former Iraqi opposition group that produced some of the exaggerated and fabricated intelligence President Bush used to argue his case for war." Two weeks after our story came out they turned off the money.

Talk about the prewar reporting. Talk about what you were doing. I'm sure you're aware of what your colleagues at the *Washington Post* were doing. Who were you talking to and what were they telling you? And what were you seeing your colleagues do?

Strobel: The most surprising thing to us was we had the field to ourselves for so long in terms of writing stuff that was critical or questioning the administration's case for war. Nobody else was doing it until the Niger story about how the statement Bush had made in his January 2003 State of the Union speech about Saddam trying to buy uranium from Africa turned out to be false. Then, it began to dawn on people that they were never going to find WMDs in Iraq. For months and months before the war and even right after the war, there was almost nobody reporting on this stuff.

I don't know why that was. I keep coming back to the psychosis induced by 9/11 and everybody believing we were going to be hit again and everybody wanting to be patriotic and believe what the president said. I think that's a lot of it. The other thing is that we had a lot of sources in the bowels of government, and they were telling us a different story, and we chose to believe them rather than the administration's public statements. They were, in many cases, skilled people who either knew the Middle East region, or knew intelligence, or knew WMD issues, and they were saying that the case the administration was making was not true or that they had real problems with the intelligence that they were seeing, and that it didn't add up to the case for war that the administration was making. They were credible people.

Landay: The way I got into it was to familiarize myself with what it takes to have a WMD program. I decided to familiarize myself with what Iraq had had, and I did that through open sources, particularly the UNSCOM [UN weapons inspectors] reporting on what they found and what they destroyed. In particular, I focused on the question: What kind of physical infrastructure do you need to build a nuclear weapon? It requires quite a bit of physical infrastructure. You need thousands of high-speed spinning machines called centrifuges if you are going to go the uranium enrichment route, which was the way the Iraqis were going, because it is very, very difficult to get the spent fuel you need from which to extract plutonium, which is the other way to go. They had tried that route. They had tried them all. They had tried everything.

So the question was, did they have the infrastructure? They had it at one time, and it had been destroyed. The UN inspectors destroyed it. My next question was, with the spy planes and spy satellites overhead and the

UN inspectors on the ground in the country—at least until 1998—with all this containment going on, how could they have been able to re-create this infrastructure without anybody knowing? As I was familiarizing myself with this stuff, Vice President Cheney, on August 28, 2002, made a speech to the Veterans of Foreign Wars. This was really the beginning of their public spin campaign in which he said, "It is believed that the Iraqis have reconstituted their nuclear program and some of us believe that they may have a nuclear weapon soon." And I went, *"what?"* From what I was able to learn through just educating myself about the kind of infrastructure required to build a weapon and knowing that the UN had destroyed what the Iraqis had had, this just seemed to me to be really weird and wrong.

So I started making phone calls. I talked to somebody who follows this issue, not a senior official, but a working stiff who follows this issue, and this person's words to me were, "The vice president is lying." That led me to write my first story, "Lack of Hard Evidence of Iraqi Weapons Worries Top U.S. Officials." It ran on September 6, 2002, and it set us off on this whole thing. We had made phone calls and got to a bunch of midlevel and very senior people, and the lead was: "Senior U.S. officials with access to top-secret intelligence on Iraq say they have detected no alarming increase in the threat that Saddam Hussein poses to American security and Middle East stability."

So this got us rolling, and then our boss, John Walcott, called us together and said, "This is a really important story. They're putting together a case for war and as journalists we have an obligation to question, or at least to look into what the administration is telling the American people and whether or not it's right. As Knight Ridder journalists, we have an even greater obligation because three of our papers serve the military bases where most of the ground troops will be coming from if they're going to go to war. So we have a special obligation to the people who read our papers in those areas to explain to them why their loved ones are being sent into harm's way."

When you guys started reporting this, did you get any phone calls from your colleagues or anyone in the government?

Landay: Not at first, no. We were laboring in the wilderness basically. Then we did a story that really got us further down the road we were on. The story was the result of a conference we had with our boss where we talked about what questions needed to be answered before we decided to invade Iraq. What would be the impact of the war? What do Americans need to know? Warren, our White House correspondent, Ron Hutcheson, and I worked on it, and we put together a fairly big story about how it could affect the economy, how it could affect relations with other countries, how it could affect other situations in the world, and so on. "Unresolved Issues Shadow Iraq Conflict" came out on September 30, 2002, and the lead was "War plans are on President Bush's desk. Troops and arms are moving toward the Persian Gulf. Resolutions authorizing Bush to use military force against Iraqi leader Saddam Hussein are before Congress and the United Nations."

After that story ran, our boss got an e-mail saying, "You're asking the right questions, keep on." Karen Kwiatkowski, a retired air force lieutenant colonel who was working in Undersecretary of Defense Douglas Feith's office at the Pentagon, contacted Warren and said, "You're absolutely right, that's exactly what we're asking, too." It was through Kwiatkowski that we started hearing about the Office of Special Plans, a top-secret, highly compartmentalized cell broken away from the rest of the Pentagon policy shop to develop anti-Saddam and postinvasion policies.

Strobel: Kwiatkowski was not an expert on WMDs or terrorism or anything, but she and others started telling us a lot of disturbing stuff about that office and things that were going on there that made us believe even more deeply that the administration was ginning up false intelligence and doing all sorts of out-of-bounds things.

Landay: She was telling us how they'd taken this Near East and South Asia [NESA] bureau, which is where all the policy analysts are, and they had walled off the guys who dealt with the Northern Gulf and Iraq into a whole separate unit. They had put them in a separate office and just surrounded it with secrecy. She would hear watercooler conversations and hall conversations about what they were doing in terms of shutting out the State Department and being told not to pay attention to what the State Department was saying and not to share information with their State Department colleagues and not to pay any attention to what intelligence analysts were saying about the possible impact of an American invasion.

What were they mandated to do?

Strobel: To prepare for war and make the case for war. They had their own intelligence stream.

Landay: They walled off this special unit and filled it with true believers. The people who were brought in to work there were people who came from a very set political point of view. Whereas the case for war was supposed to be made based on professional intelligence analysis, this was the political analysis unit of the Pentagon.

> **You had the Office of Special Plans [OSP],[3] which Rumsfeld set up and put then defense undersecretary Douglas Feith in charge, which was involved in cherry-picking intelligence that would help make the case for war. In his book *Pretext for War*,[4] Jim Bamford wrote that the OSP had a mirror office in Prime Minister Sharon's office in Israel.**

Landay: We worked that one hard and we couldn't confirm that. My friend Julian Borger of the *Guardian* reported that, and he said his sources were "a senior military officer who had recently left the Pentagon, and a former CIA official and Middle East specialist." We were never able to confirm it, but one of the things that Karen told us was that they allowed Israeli civilian officials and military officers to bypass all of the formal security procedures when they'd come into the Pentagon.

Strobel: She also told us that during her first week in the office, she was told during one of these watercooler conversations: "Don't say anything pro-Palestinian around here or anything sympathetic or even neutral."

> **What about the Policy Counterterrorism Evaluation Group that was being run by vice presidential adviser David Wurmser?**

Landay: Their job was to look for links between Saddam and al Qaeda and to review the issue of state sponsorship of terrorist groups. In the process, they came up with this so-called link analysis that they did, which basically said that if you had used the same phone booth that an al Qaeda operative had used, or if you had used or stood at the urinal next to Osama bin Laden's at some point, you were probably an al Qaeda operative.

Strobel: It was a kind of "six degrees of separation" exercise.

Landay: Exactly, and the memo that came out of that exercise was subsequently leaked to the *Weekly Standard* and they wrote a piece about it titled "Case Closed: The U.S. Government's Secret Memo Detailing Cooperation between Saddam Hussein and Osama bin Laden." Both the Department of Defense and the CIA disowned the memo as a legitimate analysis.

Strobel: While we're on this topic of terrorism, you asked us at the beginning how we got started on this, and there was another thing that really got me. I'd been in Iraq four times before the war during Saddam's time and I spent, like John, a lot of time covering terrorism. I did not believe, and I knew that all the experts that I knew did not believe, that Saddam had any interest in being allied with a fanatical Sunni like bin Laden. Saddam was a secularist who believed in control, and his security services were good at one thing and one thing only: eliminating opposition to Saddam both at home and in various capitals around the world.

Landay: Plus, Saddam was a target; he was the kind of regime leader that al Qaeda wanted to get rid of. We started looking into that too and came up with a bunch of stuff that went into a story about how the administration's case for proving that Saddam and al Qaeda were cooperating was even weaker than their case on WMDs. "Doubts Cast about Effort to Link Saddam, Al Qaida" came out on March 2, 2004, and the lead was "The Bush administration's claim that Iraqi leader Saddam Hussein had ties to Al Qaida—one of the administration's central arguments for a pre-emptive war—appears to have been based on less solid intelligence than the administration's claim that Iraq had hidden stocks of chemical and biological weapons."

Nobody was calling you after that one, either?

Landay: No. I don't think people really cared as long as it wasn't being read in Washington. As long as it wasn't having an impact here politically, then we could write what we wanted. If it had been in the *New York Times* or the *Washington Post*, then you would have seen a whole different reaction.

It sounds like you guys were reporting in a paper bag.

Landay: Well, I spent five years living in the Balkans and reporting on the conflict there, and I was eventually expelled from Serbia for writing a story that said that two years after the Yugoslav army had said that they'd pulled out of Bosnia, they were still in there helping the Bosnian Serbs. Until I wrote that story, Serbia's president at the time, Slobodan Milošević, was content to have me write anything. Whatever I was doing was fine because it wasn't being read where it counted, which was in Belgrade, inside Serbia. The Serbian people couldn't read my stuff, so as long as it wasn't having an impact where it counted, I was OK. I got the feeling that the same thing was happening here. Oftentimes Warren and I would look at each other and we'd say, "Are we right about this? We're the only ones writing this stuff."

There were times when we were deeply concerned that maybe we really had gotten it wrong and maybe everyone else was right. But that's kind of stuff that got us going. Then two more things happened that really firmed it up for us and convinced us that we were on to something. The first was the aluminum tubes. I remember distinctly the president going to the UN on September 12, 2002, and saying, "Iraq has made several attempts to buy high-strength aluminum tubes used to enrich uranium for a nuclear weapon." Then, a couple of days later, in a televised address to the nation, he said the same thing. Unequivocally. "These tubes are for their nuclear program." The week after that, the CIA submitted a routine report that it has to submit every six months on worldwide proliferation trends. It's a congressionally mandated report that is unclassified. They happened to deliver it the week after the president gave his public address. I opened it up and started reading it, and it was saying all the same stuff about Iraq until it got to the aluminum tubes part, in which it said, "There is a dispute between analysts as to what the purpose of these tubes were." I looked at that and I said, "Wait a minute, the president just told the world unequivocally that these are for the nuclear program, and I'm reading in this report to Congress that some intelligence analysts believe that they're for ground-to-ground rockets." I made a few phone calls and I wrote a story. I got somebody in the American centrifuge program who had studied the data, and he said, "These are not for centrifuges, you can't use these for centrifuges," and I knew right there that President Bush had withheld information from the American people. So first we had Cheney making assertions that were not supported by the intelligence and then we had the president withholding information from the American people.

There were other red flags. At some point the president said, "We know that a senior Iraqi intelligence official met with Osama bin Ladin in Khandahar in 1998 after the East Africa Embassy bombings and offered to provide al Qaeda refuge in Iraq." That was all he said. Now the logical question that one asks after a statement like that is, "What did Osama say?" They didn't tell us that. We found out that Osama actually said, "No way, because it won't be our agenda, it will be Saddam's agenda." But again that information was withheld from the American public.

Strobel: That happened over and over and over again.

Meanwhile, Judy Miller's reporting came out in the *New York Times* about how Saddam had tried to buy aluminum tubes for his nuclear program.

Landay: That was before the CIA report came out. The *New York Times* story on the aluminum tubes came out on a Sunday, September 8, 2002, and the same day, Cheney and Condi[5] go on the Sunday talk shows and say, "Well, we can't talk about what the intelligence says, but look at what the *New York Times* reported." It's pretty obvious what happened there. It's what happened with most of the *New York Times* reporting, which is that they were fed stuff to bolster the administration's case. They were used.

Strobel: What happened here in terms of the journalism is that the *New York Times* and others were fed stuff to make the administration's case, and they would present that at the top of their stories and then they would do their due diligence by burying a few question marks in paragraphs seventeen, eighteen, or nineteen, whereas we and a very few others critiqued the administration's comments instead of just reporting what they said, and we made that the lead. Then we'd put in a few paragraphs saying what the administration said. We put our focus on the questions because we're not just stenographers and this was a question of war and peace and lives and troops and everything else, and we felt that the way we should handle it was to put our emphasis on the critique.

Landay: But this was after we started seeing this pattern emerging, where they would make definitive statements about things that were actually being disputed within the intelligence community and tell us just partially what they knew about different subjects.

Other journalists have said to me when I asked them how we missed the WMD story that it was because there was no way to check it out and that they couldn't physically go and look all over Iraq for WMDs. What's your response to that?

Landay: My response to that is that one of the things that we were very aware of, and that everybody was aware of because it was no secret, was the huge disputes over policy within the administration between the State Department and the CIA on one side, and the vice president's office and the Pentagon on the other side. And you say to yourself, "Wait a minute, if they are fighting about policy on Iraq, there must be something fueling those feuds." And the logical conclusion is that maybe some of the stuff that they're dealing with in terms of the intelligence isn't as cut and dry and black and white as they'd like us to think, and that there are different interpretations of the intelligence. If that's the case, then there are going to be people in the government who've seen this and have really serious reservations about what our elected officials are saying about the information they have on Iraq, and if that's the case, maybe they're going to talk to me about it because they're so angry or so concerned because the most profound decision a leader can make is the decision to go to war. It is so, so profound, so important, that this may be the one time that they're so bothered that they'll be willing to talk about it. So that's my response to that.

Strobel: It's also important to point out, I think, that we never wrote that there were no WMDs. I was as surprised as the next guy that they actually found nothing. I always thought they'd find something, but we were questioning what they were saying.

Landay: We were just saying: The evidence to substantiate what they're saying isn't there. We're not saying there are no WMDs. We're just saying they're telling us things that they don't have, that they have a pretty weak case on.

Strobel: And that some of their own experts disagree.

Landay: It wasn't just some of their own experts; there were some very senior people who had serious problems with the case that was being made. Serious problems. *That* was the story. The other thing I would say is, how many times after briefings were held on the Hill did you have senators come out and say, "Well, I haven't seen anything different. They haven't shown me anything new that raises my concern level." Do you need somebody to shove your face into this stuff and say, "See what they are saying? These are the people who are seeing the intelligence. Isn't there something wrong here?"

I have also been told that the Pentagon absolutely believed that there were WMDs there . . .

Landay: So what?

I talked to a reporter who has been at the Pentagon for a very long time and has impeccable sources, and this reporter said that there was no reason to believe that they were wrong or to dispute them.

Strobel: I think a lot of people around Rumsfeld certainly believed there were WMDs. I think a lot of Defense Intelligence Agency [DIA] analysts believed there were WMDs.

Landay: I'm not so sure about DIA because there was dissent in DIA, we know that. And we know they set up the Office of Special Plans and then stuck this seal on it where no one was allowed to talk to the State Department and no one could share paper with them or read their paper, so you have to say, "Wait a minute, they're closing themselves off to alternative points of view, so certainly they're going to believe what it is that they're seeing, because some of the stuff they were seeing was stuff that no one else was seeing." Why? Because it wasn't going to the CIA or the State Department.

They were seeing stuff from Chalabi's Iraqi National Congress [INC][6] group that the CIA and the State Department weren't getting. There's a letter that the INC wrote to the Senate Appropriations Committee in 2002 after the Appropriations Committee staff asked why the State Department was paying for an Iraqi exile group's intelligence gathering-program. The INC wrote back saying, "Here's all the value you're getting for your money," and in the cover letter it said, "Our stuff is going directly to William Luti[7] in Rumfeld's office and to John Hannah[8] in Cheney's office." Luti and Hannah categorically denied that they were getting the material, yet there it was in black and white that this material was going directly into their offices.

So the INC was sending its intelligence to the Office of Special Plans and then somehow Judy Miller at the *New York Times* was getting the same information.

Strobel: Karen Kwiatkowski and others also said that staff members in Doug Feith's office would give talking points based on this bogus intelligence to all their conservative columnist friends, like . . .

Landay: Let's not name any names. We were told, and not by Karen, they were passing out position papers to influential journalists and columnists.

Where was Secretary of State Powell in all this?

Strobel: I think Powell and his people tried to slow this down. They tried to get more troops so that when the war did happen, things might have turned out differently afterward.

Landay: It was Powell who won the battle over going to the UN and trying to get a UN resolution to legitimize the use of force. He met with the president and was able to prevail on that issue, even though there were very senior people in the government who didn't believe we needed to go to the UN, didn't believe we needed a coalition. So he played the role of a diplomat. But ultimately, Powell has been a soldier his whole life. He's been taking orders from his military and civilian superiors and that's what he did; that was his job, even as secretary of state. I think that in his mind, that's the way it worked.

Why do you think we went to war?

Strobel: That's the sixty-four-million-dollar question, isn't it? I think it was a combination of reasons. I think a lot of it was that people like Cheney really got it stuck somewhere in their minds after 9/11 that there was going to be another attack and that Saddam had links to terrorists and WMDs. I really think he believed that. I think he believed that we had to do this even though the evidence was to the contrary. He didn't look at the evidence. So that's one reason.

I also think a lot of it goes back to George H. W. Bush and people like Deputy Defense Secretary Paul Wolfowitz and others who felt like they had made a mistake in not taking out Saddam the first time. And they wanted to finish that job. There's also the whole neocon thing about establishing democracy in the Middle East: "Let's get rid of Saddam, we'll start a democracy in Iraq and that'll spread throughout the region." Finally, there's George W. Bush's "He tried to kill my Poppy"[9] rationale.

Landay: I think it was a confluence of different interests. Different constituencies within the administration supported the war for different reasons. For instance, there was the school of thought that the United States has this unparalleled opportunity following the collapse of the Soviet Union and the end of the cold war[10] that left us as the world's biggest military, political, and economic power to shape the world in a way that's favorable to our interests. That ties in with people who believe that we should be supporting democracies everywhere. What is the only democracy in the Middle East? Israel. How do you make the Middle East safe for Israel? You spread democracy. And to spread democracy, you've got to use your power to shape the region.

I also think there was the idea that because we had the power that we had, and because there was this view after 9/11 that our attention was going to be directed predominantly toward this arc of instability that goes from Bosnia and Kosovo, through Turkey and the Muslim world, and then to central Asia and all the way to Xinjiang in China, that the United States needed to be able to project its power anywhere in that arc. We could not do it from our bases in Saudi Arabia, because it was too far away. We needed bases closer in. So Iraq was of great interest for several reasons. Mr. Chalabi had already said that he would give bases to American troops in Iraq if he became prime minister. We needed to get out of Saudi Arabia because our presence there was fueling al Qaeda, which was threatening the continuation of the Saudi monarchy and stability in Saudi Arabia. So by going into Iraq, the United States could shore up the Saudi regime by pulling its troops out of Saudi Arabia and it would be better able to project its power into the arc of instability because it would have bases right in the center of it. Finally, there's this charge that it had to do with oil, that we want to be able to control the source of 55 percent of the world's oil production. I like to turn it the other way around. I don't think it was a question of being able to control the oil in the Persian Gulf. I think it was a question of not allowing anyone else to control the oil. In other words, if the oil flows freely, more oil flows onto the market, lowering the price. You want to be in a position to ensure free passage of oil from the Persian Gulf through the Strait of Hormuz out into the Indian Ocean to the rest of the world. You don't want Saddam to be in a position to interfere with that. If you have your forces in that region, you are in a position to prevent Iran from closing the Strait of Hormuz and you are also in a position to ensure that nobody controls the gulf's oil and that the free market prevails.

Do you know what the Iraqis think?

Landay: Sure, I spent a lot of time there. They think we went there to grab their oil.

Strobel: And establish military bases.

I've spoken to a number of journalists for this book, and there's no consensus on why we went to war. What does that mean?

Landay: You'll have to talk to the administration about the effectiveness of their public relations campaign. But it doesn't matter anymore, does it? We're there.

What are the implications of that?

Landay: You see the implications everywhere. Go to Europe and talk to people about their attitude toward the United States. China and other countries see that and say, "The Americans believe that they now have the ability and the power to interfere wherever they want and will." Look at the Iranian nuclear program. If there wasn't one there before, there sure as hell is going to be one there now.

The impression all this gives is that the executive branch has all the power. If the DIA, the CIA, and all the intelligence agencies that were supposed to come up with a good NIE upon which we base our reasons for going to war are essentially put aside by an ad hoc intelligence operation, what does that mean?

Strobel: And where was Congress in all this? That's what really bothers me.

Landay: This was post-9/11, people were still operating in that highly charged political atmosphere, and I think most people really did believe that this cartoon character who ran Iraq really had weapons of mass destruction. Plus, look at the polls even today. Seventy percent of the Republicans believe that he was working with al Qaeda.

Do you think that by virtue of the fact that our leaders—Bush, Cheney, Condoleezza Rice, Rumsfeld—can all go out there and send out the same message about mushrooms clouds, by virtue of the fact that they have constant, anytime access to the mass media, that they can trump just about any journalistic effort they don't like?

Strobel: I think trump is too strong a word. I think we did have some impact but it's very hard.

Landay: It depends on who your audience is. If we had been writing this stuff for the *New York Times* and the *Washington Post*, who knows what impact it would have had on this administration's ability to go to war.

Then what does it say about the journalism of our major papers?

Landay: Without naming any particular paper, the fact is that as far as this government goes and as far as our business goes, there's been *no accountability whatsoever. No one's been held accountable,* neither in the government nor in our industry, for what went on. There was this bandwagon effect among the press that just regurgitated the administration's case for war. If there hadn't been that bandwagon effect, would it have been so easy for this administration to take us into war? I don't know. I can't go backward; I can't turn the clock. But I think certainly that bandwagon effect made it easier for them to do it.

Any administration can have its wish list, its goals, but it can't accomplish those goals in this country, in this democracy, without two things: the support of Congress and the permission of the American people. What I'm saying is, the fact that the press jumped on the WMD and al Qaeda/Saddam connection bandwagon made it easier for the administration to accomplish its goals.

There were politicians on the Hill who voted against the resolution to go into Iraq. There were people who said, "We're not satisfied with this, sorry." We were writing about that, but you had the 9/11 effect, you had obsequious, gutless, feckless politicians who weren't interested in whether or not the administration's case was valid. The fact is that they only cared about being on the right train at the right time.

You cannot divorce what happened from the atmosphere of the day. Also, two things were happening: first, in every single speech and interview they gave, the top members of the administration would inject a couple of lines about 9/11, al Qaeda, and Saddam, over and over and over, and they'd say, "If the terrorists get their hands on a WMD, God knows what could happen the next time, it could be millions of people." Over and over and over and over and over, you had that coming from our topmost officials.

Strobel: Cheney went the furthest on that.

Landay: Second, you had a coterie of people outside the government, fellow travelers, talking heads, who were going on CNN every night, Fox News every night, MSNBC every night, on the op-ed pages of the *Washington Post*, the *New York Times*, the *Wall Street Journal*, who were saying the same thing. Beating the gong. Beating the drum. It began on September 12, 2001. It's my recollection that Mr. James Woolsey, the former head of the CIA, began suggesting right then and there that this operation was too big not to have had state sponsorship and that if he had to point to a particular state, the only state that would really have an interest in doing this is Iraq. So you had that going on, too.

Strobel: It's disgusting, but it wasn't just Woolsey; look at Richard Clarke's book *Against All Enemies: Inside America's War on Terror*.[11] Clarke writes about how in the days immediately after 9/11 he realized that Bush and his aides were going to use the attacks to go after Iraq.

Landay: You had Rumsfeld talking about "It's time to hit Saddam," which brings me back to—and this is very, very important—another key reason we invaded Iraq. We had to show the world in some way or another that we weren't going to just sit here and let people attack us: "We're going to show you what we'll do if you dare do this to us." So we went into Afghanistan, but that wasn't enough. Why? Because they were pushovers. They were just a bunch of turbaned guerrillas wearing sandals. To really send this message home, we had to go after one of the members of the axis of evil.[12] I think that was a huge consideration.

Strobel: I agree with you absolutely. In fact, Doug Feith said almost as much at one point.

Landay: But getting back to attacking Iraq because of Saddam's WMDs, don't forget, none of our leaders ever said Saddam actually had a weapon;

they said things like, "He's trying to reconstitute his arsenal, he may soon have one, he's still interested in developing . . ." I agree with Warren that some of these guys really did believe that Saddam had this stuff, but only because they *chose* to believe that and because they chose to believe it; they read what they wanted to read in the intelligence, some of which was really wrong.

That's like blowing smoke into your own left ear.

Strobel: Yes, that's exactly what that is.

Landay: Don't forget, Wolfowitz was a member of Team B, which was an intelligence analysis unit that George H. W. Bush set up in 1976 when he was CIA director to do intelligence estimates relating to Soviet aims and capabilities. You've got to go back to that experience. Team B was brought in to dispute the CIA's analysis of the Soviet Union. They came out saying that the Soviet Union was a huge military power and that it was a giant threat and an expansionist power, and they were completely and totally wrong. Successful intelligence analysis depends on how you go into that process. The reason why these guys were all terrible intelligence analysts was because they brought a viewpoint into the process. If you come in with a viewpoint and a goal, you breach the first rule of intelligence analysis, which is don't come into the process with any prejudice or bias. Because if you do have this prejudice, you are going to look for anything in the intelligence that substantiates your point of view, and that's what happened with Team B in 1976 and with the neocons in the Pentagon before the war. That's why the cherry-picking was done.

So you don't think there was a plan from day one and that 9/11 created the opportunity for speeding up that plan?

Landay: There may have been.

Strobel: Maybe not in the minds of President Bush or Rumsfeld, but I think that was in the minds of some of the others.

Landay: There very well may have been, but you need to create the public support and the congressional support for it.

9/11 was the Vaseline for that.

Landay: That may well be, but the fact is that these guys had no faith at all in the CIA and to some extent they were justified. The CIA missed the Indian nuclear test, they missed the North Korean launch of their multistage weapon—they knew there was going to be a launch, but they had no idea that it was going to be a multistage missile—and they missed the collapse of the Soviet Union. They missed the extent of Saddam's nuclear weapons program before the first Gulf War.

Go back and read the Rumsfeld Commission's July 15, 1998, "Report to Assess the Ballistic Missile Threat to the United States" on missile proliferation.[13] You can read between the lines the commission's distrust of the CIA's ability to forecast and analyze.

Why are our intelligence services so poor?

Strobel: There are a bunch of reasons, but in fairness to the intelligence services, we never hear about their successes, we only hear about their failures. Part of it has to do with the fact that after the cold war, and again during the Clinton administration, their budget was severely cut back.

Read our story today: "Old Problems Dog New Intelligence Gathering, Panel Concludes" [March 29, 2005]. Here's the lead: "A presidential commission that's investigating U.S. intelligence failures in Iraq has concluded that many of the same weaknesses that plagued American efforts to investigate Saddam Hussein's regime are preventing the United States from collecting accurate intelligence on Iran's and North Korea's nuclear programs."

So the more things change, the more they stay the same. The commission was also saying that the intelligence services should seek a diversity of opinions and do more devil's advocacy thinking.

Landay: For quite a few years, the CIA has had a special red team that does nothing but do this kind of thinking outside of the box. But before the Iraq war, the administration did not want diversity of opinion. They only wanted to hear from people who supported their case.

What are you digging into now, postinvasion?

Landay: We're backtracking. We're still going back to the prewar issues. Part of our story yesterday was about this guy "Curveball," an Iraqi exile who showed up at a German refugee camp in 1998 and somehow came to the attention of German intelligence. He's a chemical engineer who started giving them information about a program the Iraqis had for developing mobile biological warfare facilities. The detail with which he was imparting this stuff was just incredible. He was drawing diagrams and what have you, and the Germans brought him to the attention of the

United States. For some people, Curveball was the golden egg. They thought he was it; his information was the clincher, particularly since the UNSCOM inspectors had at one time postulated themselves that this was what Saddam had done, even though they couldn't find these facilities. Then there were a couple of other defectors who were making statements that appeared to corroborate what Curveball was saying. There were some problems though. The first thing was that the Germans said Curveball didn't want to meet the Americans and that they couldn't let them meet him. That should have been a red flag right there. The second red flag was that both the Germans and the Americans say Curveball is the brother of a very senior Iraqi National Council official. The INC denies this. I just got an angry e-mail from their spokesman, Zaab Sethna, about it.

It's been determined that Curveball's defection to Germany was not engineered by the INC, but the fact is that the INC is on the CIA and State Department blacklists and that the head of the INC, Ahmed Chalabi, has at least one burn notice that the CIA put on him back in 1995 or 1996 for giving them bad information. So why would the CIA suddenly start believing a guy who has connections to the INC? Third, the Germans were apparently telling the Americans that they were having problems handling the guy. Eventually, it became known that he was an alcoholic. The Germans did agree to send to the DIA the texts of his debriefs with the German intelligence agency, but they sent them over in German, even though the briefs had been done in English and Arabic. So Curveball was initially talking in English and Arabic, then his comments were being translated into German and given to the DIA, who were then retranslating them back into English. As someone said to me the other day, the DIA's people were being no more than paper pushers, office clerks.

There was no attempt to bring this issue up to a very high political level and to say, "You've got to get the Germans to let us talk to this guy." There were other red flags, like how he got to Germany and how he financed his trip. It wasn't apparent how he had made it to Germany. He came out with mounds of trivia, stuff that was just useless, and he stretched the interrogation out. I think there were ninety-eight transcripts of interviews with him. Typically, this is a sign that a defector is looking for a deal. You don't want to give up the information all at once; you want to stretch it out so you can get the house and the new personality, and a stipend. This was going on, but it didn't raise any red flags.

The fact that the Americans didn't get to debrief this guy was one of the biggest no-nos. It became known via the Senate Select Committee on

Intelligence's [SSCI] report,[14] that there was one DIA analyst who was giving the CIA's Directorate of Operations technical advice on proliferation and weapons of mass destruction, who did actually get to meet Curveball in 2000. And the DIA analyst was saying, "I have some real problems with this guy. He knew he was going to meet me, and yet the night before he got blasted." So the analyst was warning the CIA that he had serious problems with Curveball's information and these warnings *went on right up to the day before Powell gave his speech at the UN.* He sent an e-mail saying, "We should not make this the backbone of our biological weapons case against Saddam because I've got some serious problems with this. There are some unanswered questions about this man and his reliability." We found out that nobody told Powell what the analyst was saying as his UN speech was being prepared. Powell didn't even know that the Americans had never debriefed Curveball themselves and that they were relying on German-to-English translations of German translations of English and Arabic.

Strobel: The mobile biological weapons presentation was one of the most dramatic parts of Powell's presentation. I was sitting in the UN that day and it was just *WOW.*

Landay: Curveball's case was bolstered by the claims of another defector, a Major Harith, who was produced by the INC and was determined by the DIA to have been a fabricator. Yet, when his material was brought up at the preparation session for Powell's speech, nobody said, "Oh, we've got a flag on this guy. There's a fabricator notice appended to all of his material in the intelligence community's archives."

Why didn't they raise the red flag there?

Strobel: They weren't looking for red flags. The Curveball thing was so good that they just wanted to believe it.

Landay: I agree with Warren. Look, you've got political masters who are saying, "You've got to find this stuff," and the intelligence analysts are saying, "But we don't have it," and suddenly you've got this claim that's corroborated by more than one source. As a journalist, I'd say, "Let's go with it, let's write the story." And they did. But the question is: if Powell had known that no one in US intelligence had ever debriefed Curveball, would he have ever gone public with this material?

Yes, but why does Powell have to do that kind of vetting himself?

Landay: That's right. In fact, a former very, very, very senior intelligence official said to me the other day, "It should never have gotten up to Tenet's level. It should have never made it off the desks of the analysts."

Tenet, there's another one. What happened there?

Landay: I don't know; it's hard to say. I think that until a certain point, he tried his best to be the objective, neutral intelligence analyst. Somewhere along the line, that changed.

The NIE report basically said that all these intelligence analysts came before them and told them that they hadn't been subjected to any pressure to ginger up the intelligence.

Landay: That's not what the minority report said. Go read "11 Rockefeller Minority Report. Additional Views of Vice Chairman John D. Rockefeller IV, Senator Carl Levin and Senator Richard Durbin."[15]

Strobel: The way that the NIE report presents the issue of pressure is a false way to look at it. The analysts were saying over and over, "There's no pressure, there's no pressure," but what they meant is that they didn't put a gun to their heads and say, "Change that report or it's your job." But they created this environment that John was just talking about where they made it clear what answer they wanted, they made it clear how important it was, and they made it clear that it was important for people to come up with the stuff they wanted.

Landay: The vice president made multiple visits to the CIA. He went out to the National Security Agency [NSA],[16] too, because he wanted to see raw intelligence. That's really unusual, and as the report says, Cheney was asking the same questions over and over again, "Are you sure? Maybe you should do that again. Maybe you should take another look at that." If you're an intelligence analyst and the vice president of the United States is saying, "But couldn't you read it this way?" what are you going to say, "No sir"?

Strobel: You see what they did to people like Joe Wilson and Valerie Plame[17] and other people that we could mention who were retaliated against for publicly contradicting the information the administration was touting to sell the war. I just think this whole administration, Bush, Condi, and everyone else, are control freaks, and if anybody steps out of line on any issue, they are reprimanded or worse.

By the way, are you looking at all at the role of TV? It just struck me sitting here that the print press has a lot to answer for, but where was the broadcast media in all this? Nowhere. One thing you have to understand about this administration is that more than any administration in history they try and go around the print press and use TV to get their message across.

It makes absolute sense because TV is the mass consciousness medium.

Strobel: Look at Condi Rice's first two months in office. She gave interviews to Reuters, Agence France Presse, the *Washington Post*, the *Los Angeles Times*, and the *Washington Times*, and I would have to count, but I guess she gave about one hundred television interviews. One hundred!

That's how they sold the war, too—via television.

In terms of sending out your message to the masses, TV is the way to go.

Landay: So that's why our stuff wasn't being noticed.

You really need to have a broadcast presence. But believe me, if from today to tomorrow you were to have a broadcast presence, you would start feeling much more heat for your reporting, you have no idea.

Landay: I *don't* have any idea. What I was going to say when you asked me about television was that I can't tell you anything about it because I stopped watching network news years and years ago when I came to realize that they rarely put any kind of hard news on that breaks ground or is controversial, unless it's already been in a newspaper. Why? Because they don't want to jeopardize the income from their sponsors.

They're a business.

Landay: That's right, and they lost the ethic surrounding their responsibility to inform the American people in return for the privilege of using the airwaves and being able to interact with the American public, and that has diluted and weakened our democracy. I do know that they didn't report on any of the administration's questionable evidence for going to war until we had the controversy over the sixteen words in Bush's January 2003 State of the Union address: "The British government has learned that Saddam Hussein recently sought significant quantities of uranium from Africa." That's when they finally realized that the Niger thing was dicey, and then everybody jumped on the bandwagon and started revisiting the aluminum tubes, which was stuff we had already done.

WARREN P. STROBEL, forty-two, is senior correspondent for foreign affairs for Knight Ridder newspapers. He joined Knight Ridder's Washington bureau in February 2001. Strobel is the cowinner of the 2004 Raymond Clapper Memorial Award, a National Headliner Award, and a 2004 James K. Batten Excellence Award for reporting on intelligence problems and planning failures prior to the Iraq war. His and colleague Jonathan Landay's skeptical prewar coverage of the administration's claims about Iraq has received widespread acclaim, including in the *New York Review of Books*.

Before coming to Knight Ridder, Strobel was a senior editor at *U.S. News & World Report* magazine, covering national security and intelligence. He began his reporting career at the the *Washington Times*, where he was White House correspondent from 1995 to 1998 and chief diplomatic correspondent. From 1994 to 1995, Mr. Strobel was a Jennings Randolph Peace Fellow at the US Institute of Peace. At the institute, he conducted research for a book on how the news media impacts American foreign policy and public opinion. The book, *Late-Breaking Foreign Policy*, was published in 1997. Mr. Strobel was also a coinvestigator on an institute grant to study how the Internet is used as a tool by those seeking nonviolent change in Burma. He coauthored the resulting paper, "Networking Dissent."

Prior to being selected as a fellow, Mr. Strobel spent nine years with the *Times*. From 1989 to 1994, he covered American foreign policy under secretaries of state James A. Baker, Lawrence Eagleburger, and Warren Christopher. In this post and his others, he has reported from ninety-two countries and has been on assignment to the Middle East, Sudan, the Balkans, the former Soviet Union, and Vietnam.

From 1986 until 1989, Mr. Strobel was national security correspondent and reported on US-Soviet arms control negotiations, the Reagan administration's Strategic Defense Initiative (Star Wars), and military and civilian space programs. In 1989 he wrote an award-winning story on how incorrect launch codes had been inserted into nuclear-tipped Minuteman III ICBMs, revealing that, unbeknownst to anyone, they could not have been launched if needed for an entire year.

Mr. Strobel has lectured at the National Defense University, the US Army War College, Quantico Marine Base, the US Naval Academy, Harvard University, George Washington University, American University, the University of Quebec at Montreal, and elsewhere. He has appeared on C-SPAN, CNN, and Fox TV. His commentaries have appeared in the *Washington Post*, the *Christian Science Monitor*, *Newsday*, and the *For-*

eign Service Journal. In July 1998 he served as a member of a joint International Republican Institute–National Democratic Institute team observing national elections in Cambodia. He is a 2005 graduate of the Georgetown Leadership Seminar.

Mr. Strobel received a bachelor of journalism degree from the University of Missouri-Columbia in December 1984. He was editor-in-chief of the student newspapers both at Missouri and at St. Mary's College of Maryland. The son of a US naval officer, Mr. Strobel was born in Japan and has lived in Okinawa, the Philippines, and England. He lives near Annapolis, Maryland, with his wife, the former Lisa Jane Mayr, and has two sons, Mitchell, seventeen, and Adam, thirteen.

JONATHAN S. LANDAY, national security and intelligence correspondent, has written about foreign affairs and US defense, intelligence, and foreign policies for twenty years. From 1985 to 1994, he covered South Asia and the Balkans for United Press International and then for the *Christian Science Monitor*. He moved to Washington in December 1994 to cover defense and foreign affairs for the *Christian Science Monitor* and joined Knight Ridder in October 1999. He speaks frequently on military-media relations and national security matters. In 2005 he was part of a team that won a National Headliners Award for "How the Bush Administration Went to War in Iraq." He also won a 2005 Award of Distinction from the Medill School of Journalism at Northwestern University for "Iraqi Exiles Fed Exaggerated Tips to News Media," and shared with Warren Strobel the Washington Press Club Foundation's 2004 Raymond Clapper Memorial Award for their reporting on the use of faulty intelligence in Iraq war planning.

NOTES

1. The US Intelligence Community's Web site's definition of National Intelligence Estimates is: "These reports are the DCI's [Director of Central Intelligence] most authoritative written judgements concerning national security issues. They deal with capabilities, vulnerabilities, and probable courses of action of foreign nations and key developments relevant to the vital interests of the United States. NIEs are produced at the national level by the NIC [National Intelligence Council, made up of senior intelligence analysts and outside experts] and are issued by the DCI with the approval of the NFIB [National Foreign Intelligence Board, a senior Intelligence Community advisory body]. NIEs are designed to identify trends of significance to national security and, when relevant, differ-

ences of views among the principal intelligence officers of the US government. Presidential Summaries of NIEs are prepared for the President, Vice President, and other key executive officers." http://www.intelligence.gov/0-glossary.shtml.

2. A British-educated former banker, Ahmed Chalabi has been the leader of the anti-Saddam Iraqi National Congress, which was formed with US government backing for the purpose of overthrowing Saddam Hussein. Chalabi received large sums of money from the US government for his activities and was a source of faulty prewar intelligence. Although he has no industry experience, he is currently acting oil minister for the new Iraqi government

3. According to Julian Borger of the UK's *Guardian* newspaper, the Office of Special Plans "was set up by the defence secretary, Donald Rumsfeld, to second-guess CIA information and operated under the patronage of hardline conservatives in the top rungs of the administration, the Pentagon and at the White House, including Vice President Dick Cheney. The ideologically driven network functioned like a shadow government, much of it off the official payroll and beyond congressional oversight." "The Spies Who Pushed for War," *Guardian*, July 17, 2003.

4. James Bamford, *A Pretext for War: 9/11, Iraq, and the Abuse of America's Intelligence Agencies* (New York: Doubleday, 2004). See chapter 11 in this book.

5. Then national security advisor to President Bush, Condoleezza Rice.

6. According to the Center for Media and Democracy's *Source Watch*, the Iraqi National Congress [INC] was "created at the behest of the US government to foment the overthrow of Iraqi dictator Saddam Hussein." Led by Ahmed Chalabi (currently acting oil minister for the new Iraqi government), the INC received millions from the US government for its activities and was a source of faulty prewar intelligence. http://www.source watch.org/index.php?title=Iraqi_National_Congress.

7. William J. Luti, undersecretary of defense for Near Eastern and South Asian affairs, was among those working in the Office of Special Plans.

8. John Hannah is a senior national security aide on Vice President Cheney's staff.

9. Allegations that Saddam Hussein had ordered Iraqi intelligence to assassinate President George H. W. Bush in April 1993 during Bush's visit to Kuwait to commemorate the victory of the first Gulf War eventually led President Clinton to order an attack on Mukhabarat, Iraqi intelligence headquarters, which resulted in the deaths of eight civilians when some of the missiles landed on nearby homes. In a November 1, 1992, *New Yorker* article, "Case Not Closed," reporter Seymour Hersh wrote about the alleged assassination plot, "But my own investigations have uncovered circumstantial evidence, at least as compelling as the Administration's, that suggests that the American government's case against Iraq—as it has been outlined in public, anyway—is seriously flawed."

10. According to the online encyclopedia Wikipedia, the cold war was "the open yet restricted rivalry that developed after World War II between the United States and its allies (roughly speaking NATO [North Atlantic Treaty Organization] members) and the Soviet Union and its allies (roughly speaking, Warsaw Pact members). The struggle was called the cold war because it did not actually lead to direct fighting between the superpowers (a "hot" war) on a wide scale. The Cold War was waged by means of economic pressure, selective aid, diplomatic maneuvers, propaganda, assassinations, low-intensity military operations and full-scale war from 1947 until the collapse of the Soviet Union in 1991." http://en.wikipedia.org/wiki/Cold_War.

11. Richard Clarke was President Clinton's national coordinator for security, infra-

structure protection, and counterterrorism in May 1998 and continued in that position under George W. Bush. In his book *Against All Enemies: Inside America's War on Terror*, he writes a scathing indictment of the way the Bush administration handled the war on terror.

12. In his January 29, 2002, State of the Union address, President Bush defined the axis of evil. He mentioned North Korea, Iran, and Iraq as "regimes that sponsor terror" and said, "regimes like these, and their terrorist allies, constitute an axis of evil."

13. The 1998 report of the Commission to Assess the Ballistic Missile Threat to the United States can be viewed at http://www.fas.org/irp/threat/missile/rumsfeld/.

14. The SSCI report is the Report of the Select Committee on Intelligence on the US Intelligence Community's Prewar Intelligence Assessments on Iraq, Senate Report 108-301 (Washington, DC: US Government Printing Office, July 9, 2004). The report can be viewed at http://intelligence.senate.gov/iraqreport2.pdf.

15. The additional views can be viewed at http://durbin.senate.gov/sitepages/addSSCI_report.htm.

16. The National Security Agency/Central Security Service "is America's crypto-logic organization. It coordinates, directs, and performs highly specialized activities to protect US information systems and produce foreign intelligence information. . . . It is also one of the most important centers of foreign language analysis and research within the government." http://www.nsa.gov/about/.

17. Ambassador Joe Wilson, a career foreign service officer and former chargé d'af-faires in Baghdad (1990), was asked by the CIA in February 2002 to travel to Niger to investigate claims of a sale of uranium yellowcake to Iraq in the late 1990s. Wilson found no evidence of this. On January 28, 2003, President Bush said, "The British government has learned that Saddam Hussein recently sought significant quantities of uranium from Africa," referring to Niger, which the CIA had already dismissed as false based on Wilson's investigation. Wilson criticized the president's Niger claims, and shortly there-after, an anonymous source told columnist Robert Novak that Wilson's wife, Valerie Plame, was a covert CIA operative. Novak reported this, even though disclosing the iden-tity of a covert CIA operator can be a federal offense. Wilson and his wife were seen by many as victims of a White House revenge campaign.

THE MIDDLE EAST

HISTORY AND CONTEXT

14

BLOGGER HITS THE HUNDREDTH-MONKEY PHASE

Courtesy of Juan Cole

JUAN COLE
Blogger and Historian.
Areas of Expertise:
the Middle East,
Muslim Radicalism,
and the War on Terrorism
Interviewed April 2005

The United States has, of course, been involved in the Middle East for a long time, but much more intensely in the last two decades. Even so, for many Americans—including journalists and policymakers—the region remains as enigmatic and inexplicable as ever. The level of interest in the region has risen along with the deaths of Americans connected to US Middle East policy, so the fact that it took Professor Juan Cole almost fifteen years to get on the public's radar is not as astonishing as it is unfortunate.

As far back as the first Gulf War, he was trying to get attention: "I tried to get op-eds published during the Gulf War and signally failed. No one had ever heard of me and I couldn't get past the slush pile and my being an academic specialist in the Middle East really got me nowhere with editors and journalists."

Fast-forward to 9/11. That night, Professor Cole, who teaches at the University of Michigan in Ann Arbor, appeared on his local ABC television affiliate and fingered al Qaeda as the culprit. How did he know so soon? "Al Qaeda had grown up on the terrain that I knew," says Cole. "I knew Egypt, I knew Pakistan, and I had been following the modern fundamentalist movements."

At that point, his e-mail in-box was flooded with questions from colleagues in the academic world asking him what happened and why. Cole's blog, "Informed Comment," at www.juancole.com, was born months later to handle this limited traffic more efficiently. But like the ripples from a stone thrown into a pond, "Informed Comment" started gaining a wider and wider readership. And no wonder. The blog's name is an understatement. The information it contains is pure gold. It's all there: the insight, the analysis, the history, the context.

Cole's academic credentials and experience are too vast to list here, but there is one line in his bio that I think is key to understanding why his blog is so superior contentwise: "Cole commands Arabic, Persian, and Urdu and reads some Turkish, knows both Middle Eastern and South Asian Islam, and lived in a number of places in the Muslim world for extended periods of time."

"Informed Comment" really started taking off after the Iraq war in the spring of 2003 when the Shiite Muslims began emerging as the dominant group in Iraq. People in America's political and journalism establishments started looking around for Shiite experts and finally discovered Cole: "I . . . had been studying them for thirty years, admittedly from a distance and historically, but nevertheless, I knew who the major players were, who their fathers were, and who their great-grandfathers were, and I could put them in some kind of historical and political context."

The blog hit the hundredth-monkey phase[1] about fourteen months later, when American forces began battling the followers of Shiite religious leader Muqtada al-Sadr. "A lot of people started coming to my site because . . . that was a marines versus Shiite conflict. Families of soldiers as well as policymakers, journalists, and the general public started visiting my site in large numbers." By then, he was getting a million pageviews a month. Needless to say, Professor Cole no longer has any trouble finding outlets for his op-ed pieces.

I interviewed him on the phone. He sounds as professorial as he looks in his photo. Obviously accustomed to presenting information in a well-ordered way, Cole speaks in a straight line. He doesn't meander. But the real pleasure in interviewing him, as in visiting his Web site, has everything to do with the information he imparts. Cole had me glued to the phone during our interview. Everything he said—from his comments on the fundamental flaw in the way American press reports are structured, to his assessment of why the United States went to war in Iraq, to his analysis of the Bush administration's intentions and much more—built a view that was stunning in its clarity and logic. First, he talked about the birth of his blog.

I set my blog, "Informed Comment," up in the spring of 2002, and it was a direct result of 9/11. In the wake of September 11, I was often approached by colleagues on e-mail lists who were concerned with the Middle East to explain what had happened and why. Al Qaeda had grown up on the terrain that I knew. I knew Egypt, I knew Pakistan, and I had been following the modern fundamentalist movements, so I would answer their questions on e mail. But e mail, in those days at least, was inconvenient in the sense that once you sent it, it was inconvenient to try to find it again when people would ask for a copy. So when Weblogging came along, I thought it was a nice place to publicly archive some of my messages on the War on Terrorism. I teach a course on war in the Middle East, and al Qaeda was always the last section that I did. I had done some research on al Qaeda, and knowing Arabic, I had access to sources that a lot of people didn't so that was another reason why I started the Weblog.

When 9/11 occurred, al Qaeda was not well known. Even whether al Qaeda was behind the attack was controversial for a while. I was sure that it was. In fact, I called it on September 11 itself that evening on the local ABC news affiliate.

I had been following al Qaeda. Organizations have modus operandi and you could tell. In the midnineties, Ramzi Yousef, who had been involved in the first World Trade Center bombing, was in the Philippines hiding out. He had been working on some plans there in an apartment and a fire broke out in his kitchen. He ran downstairs and the firemen came up, saw suspicious notations, and called the police who confiscated his papers. It turns out that he had lots of plans for attacks, including hijacking a plane and flying it into CIA headquarters, hijacking a number of planes in Southeast Asia, and assassinating the pope. So this idea of hijacking a plane and ramming into a building was known to be something that al Qaeda was thinking very seriously about. People who were seriously following al Qaeda knew this. The National Security Council staff,[2] for instance, knew that al Qaeda was behind 9/11 the day that it happened.

Talk about the press's prewar coverage and what you were putting on your Weblog and what the differences or similarities may have been.

I said at my Weblog before the Iraq war that I felt the administration was underestimating the strength of Arab nationalism. In the spring of 2002, Vice President Dick Cheney took a tour of the Middle East to make initial inquiries about putting together a coalition against Saddam Hussein and was roundly rebuffed everywhere he went. Hosni Mubarak of Egypt told him this would be a good way to create a thousand bin Ladens, and King Abdullah II of Jordan told him that he would throw the entire eastern part of the Arab world into flames. The Saudis and others seemed to have been similarly pessimistic. Cheney's trip was a huge fiasco in so many ways. It wasn't, I think, covered by the Western press very much. Certainly the full extent of the disaster was not reported, but it seemed clear to me that there would be no coalition for an invasion of Iraq and that the Arab world viewed aggression on a fellow Arab country as contravening the Arab league charter and that they wouldn't join in.

The wire services reported that Mubarak and others had said these things. I heard the executive editor of the *Weekly Standard*, Fred Barnes, on a talking head show saying that you couldn't pay attention to what the Arab leaders said in public and that behind the scenes they were assuring Cheney that they were all onboard. This was something that somebody on Cheney's staff told Fred Barnes. It wasn't true, but Barnes believed it. Later, he admitted that he had been wrong. So I think there was an assumption that Arab political discourse is somehow insincere and that you can't pay attention to these people, which is frankly a form of prejudice.

I was in contact with Middle Easterners who explained to me that the reason Hosni Mubarak had been willing to join the coalition during the Gulf War in 1990–1991 was that Saddam had contravened the Arab league charter by invading a fellow Arab country, Kuwait,[3] and so all they were doing in that situation was helping to restore the status quo before the invasion, but the Egyptians would not have been onboard for an American invasion of Iraq at that time, and they weren't this time, either. As it turns out, the Egyptians gave the United States airspace and engaged in some behind-the-scenes facilitation of the Iraq war, but they wouldn't politically commit to it. So I think you have to know something about Arab nationalism and about the way the Arab league works to understand these things, and, quite frankly, most of our journalists don't know Arabic, haven't spent very much time in the Arab world, don't have good sources there, and don't understand the premises from which people are arguing.

I think this is a huge problem, and I think what I'm saying is borne out by the exceptions to it, because there are some journalists who do excellent work in the Middle East and they know Arabic. I think everybody agrees that Anthony Shadid[4] at the *Washington Post* has done outstanding reporting on the Iraq war and it's because he can talk to Iraqis in their own language. Shadid had the enterprise to go and ask the ayatollah in Najaf what he thought, because he knew that Najaf was a center of moral authority for Iraqi Shiites. A lot of the journalists who arrived in Iraq in April of 2003 didn't have a clue as to what the Shiite religious hierarchy looked like and what it stood for, and since the journalists are informing the rest of us, this aspect of the story was underplayed until much later. The American press—and to some extent the American government is the same way—is so afraid of someone becoming overly attached to their subject and losing their objectivity that they insist on a kind of generalism and an attitude that essentially amounts to ignorance as a safeguard against bias. But ignorance can produce its own bias.

Do you also think that part of the problem is that American journalists view Arab sources as less important than American sources and that what they say should not be taken as seriously or as being more true than American sources?

I don't know the answer to that question. A University of Maryland study that was done on press reporting[5] on the Iraq war suggests that the inverted pyramid form of American journalism may well be part of the problem. What they mean by an inverted pyramid is that you're supposed to put the most important thing first in an article, and then the second most important thing second, and so forth. Then you would put background information at the very end. This way of writing is not followed everywhere. The French press tends not to follow it. One thing that this inverted pyramid structure does is give the US government, and particularly the president, pride of place because if the president says anything about a subject this morning, then surely that goes first in the article as opposed to what a low-ranking Iraqi official said. So when Bush came out in June of 2003 and said there was no guerrilla war, his line took precedence in any US article on the situation in Iraq over that of an Iraqi official on the ground in Baghdad who could see that there plainly was a guerrilla war going on around him.

Moreover, they know about the inverted pyramid at the White House. Take, for instance, the Abu Ghraib story on torture of Iraqi prisoners.[6] It broke on a Wednesday night on *60 Minutes II*. On Thursday morning, the Bush people put out a statement from the president condemning torture and so the way the story broke was, "President condemns torture at Abu Ghraib."

Let's talk about the reasons for going to war. What was your reaction to the WMD rationale for going to war, what were you putting on your blog back then, and who was picking up your information and using it?

First of all, it should be said forthrightly that before the Iraq war, my blog was not a phenomenon, so it had limited readership. I don't think I got more than five hundred hits a day, and so what I was saying was not widely followed. I am not a weapons inspector or an intelligence analyst, so I didn't have any special sources for this, but I was extremely skeptical of the argument that Iraq posed a threat to the United States. I said this repeatedly in e-mail, in radio interviews, and here on our own campus. I also wrote a piece on the pros and cons of going to war. It just didn't make sense to me logically. First of all, the administration kept talking about weapons of mass destruction, but they seemed mainly to be talking about chemical weapons. Military figures don't view chemical weapons as weapons of mass destruction; they view them as battlefield weapons. And it was not clear to me how you would deliver these chemical weapons to the United States from Iraq. The Aum Shinrikyo cult[7] in Japan attempted to poison large numbers of people in the Tokyo subway in 1995 with sarin gas, and they were only able to kill twelve people because of the way the urban air patterns worked to disperse the gas. Indeed, if, God forbid, somebody let loose something toxic in Times Square, the city is a heat pump that keeps pushing hot air into the atmosphere, so it would send the stuff into the stratosphere pretty quickly. So it just didn't make sense to me. Also, there wasn't any obvious way that you could deliver mustard gas from Iraq to the United States.

As for the nuclear threat, I think we all knew that Iraq did not have a nuclear bomb, and even the most alarmist of the reports suggested that it was at least five years away. Then there were people like Imad Khadduri[8] who was a nuclear scientist and ex-patriate from Iraq living in Canada. Khadduri was giving press interviews in which he was saying that there was no nuclear program, that it all had been dismantled after 1991.

On the other hand, there were other people like Khidhir Hamza[9] who was working for the American Enterprise Institute[10] promoting the war and who maintained that there must be a large and important nuclear program, although he admitted that he hadn't been in the country for fifteen years. So there were two different stories coming from the former Iraqi nuclear scientists about that program. It seems to me that the US mass media were, at the very least, gullible and weren't doing their jobs because every time Khidhir Hamza said something, they should have been bringing in Imad Khadduri to contradict him and they weren't doing that. Khadduri and Scott Ritter and other skeptics got little press time or were marginalized, and people like Khidhir Hamza were brought on television every night.

Why do you think that is?

I think there was a prejudice toward believing that Iraq was dangerous, and I think the tone for that was set by the Bush administration, by Vice President Dick Cheney, President Bush, National Security Advisor Condoleezza Rice, and others who kept saying these things. The rest of us were at their mercy in a way, because intelligence is secret; it's not shared with the public and the sources of the intelligence were not identified. So when Dick Cheney went on television and said, "I was briefed by our intelligence agencies [which cost the American public thirty billion dollars a year] and I was told that Iraq has a nuclear program of some sophistication," then what could a historian in the Midwest say to that?

Why do you think we went to war?

It was overdetermined; that is to say, there were many reasons for doing that. The US government is always a disparate coalition of forces, so everybody in the government had their own reasons for wanting to go, but they were all actively working toward the same goal.

What were the prevailing reasons that really got the ball rolling?

First of all, the United States is a superpower and it is interested in the architecture of international security. Petroleum plays a large role in that, and the United States consumes an enormous amount of petroleum. Its economy depends on free access to it. Two-thirds of the world's proven petroleum reserves are in the Persian Gulf, and the Persian Gulf was a mess from an American security point of view. The Iranians were open enemies of the United States and couldn't be trusted. Saddam Hussein was an open enemy of the United States and couldn't be trusted. The other countries in the Persian Gulf region that are tiny, Kuwait, Bahrain, Qatar, and so forth—even Saudi Arabia is not that populous—couldn't form any kind of counterweight to the others. So if you were looking at that and you were in the Pentagon or the State Department, it didn't look good. The United States had put various forms of sanctions on both Iran and Iraq, but the Europeans weren't happy with them and they could have collapsed at any time. Then, both countries were constantly getting petroleum money with which they could buy sophisticated weapons, which could eventually lead to them posing an actual threat to US security. Moreover, they dominated the Persian Gulf region from which the oil was flowing. So I think people like Dick Cheney were interested in this war to improve the security infrastructure for the United States as a superpower. It's not about owning Iraqi petroleum, by the way, but it's about removing obstacles to maintain free access to it.

Why do you think that oil was never officially mentioned as a reason for going to war?

There was no interruption at that time of the oil supplies, so it would have been a hard argument to make. Suppose the concern was that the sanctions on Saddam Hussein were slipping and that the Europeans were increasingly unwilling to keep those sanctions active. Saddam could therefore actually start receiving billions every year from state-owned petroleum operations, and he might then turn around and use that to build himself up into a regional superpower and threaten the United States' access to Persian Gulf petroleum. Suppose this concern was on a five- to ten-year-out basis. The administration couldn't go to the American public and say, "This might happen in ten years, so we have to go now." The bureaucratic impulse is to solve the problem that you see coming, but the political conundrum would be to make the United States public, especially Congress, sufficiently alarmed to agree to go to war based on a problem that looked like it was going to occur fairly far in the future.

Yes, but it's supposed to be illegal to go to war on false pretenses.

The particular form of reasoning that I'm suggesting is not false; there really was a problem of security in the Persian Gulf region. The question is whether war was the best way to resolve that problem. I can't prove that any of the Bush administration people were lying, that they knew, for instance, that there was no nuclear program and that they insisted there was one anyway. Certainly the CIA and other agencies were coming up with sources that alleged these things, including biological weapons programs. The allegations weren't completely implausible because such programs had existed in the late 1980s. But I do think that there was a bias toward war and a bias toward believing those sources. Some sources, like "Curveball," turned out to be drunken liars. Ahmed Chalabi provided false information. I think we can all agree that there was a reckless disregard for getting at the truth, but I can't prove that the Bush administration actively lied.

Talk about the effects of the invasion on Iraq and the surrounding area.

The invasion has destabilized the Eastern reaches of the Arab world, including the Gulf region. The Iraqi regime was an odious regime, but you could, if you were in Baghdad and you weren't involved in politics, send your kid off to school in the morning and be pretty sure that he or she would come back in the evening with no problem. That's over with now. There's no security in Iraq, and something like a failed state has been produced, which has no army to speak of. There's a guerrilla war going on that is not winding down and won't wind down for some time, if it ever does, and so there are communal tensions. There are Sunni-Shiite tensions between Jordan and the Iraqi Shiites, and between Saudi Arabia and the Shiites in Iraq. The Iraqi situation may well have been the background of the bombing in Beirut that killed Lebanese prime minister Rafic Hariri and threw that country into turmoil.

The group that claimed responsibility for that bombing was headed by a man named Ahmad Abu Adas who is a Palestinian from a Palestinian refugee camp in Lebanon. Abu Adas left Lebanon and lived in Saudi Arabia for some time. He also lived in Syria and traveled to Iraq in the past two years, and he seemed to have hooked up with Abu Musab al-Zarqawi's[11] terrorist group and developed al Qaeda ties. He may have been involved in the guerrilla war in Iraq against the Americans. Groups like Zarqawi's see the Saudi royal family as a lackey of the United States and want to overthrow it. Rafic Hariri was an expatriate from Lebanon who adopted Saudi citizenship and made his career and his billions in Saudi Arabia. He had been, in the 1980s, the Saudi kings' envoy to Lebanon, which was seen as a kind of outpost of Saudi influence in the eastern Mediterranean. The royal family in Saudi Arabia is hard to get at, so a radical Islamic group that really hated them and wanted to strike at them could go after a softer target like Hariri. This theory of the assassination is not nailed down and is disputed—some people say Syria is behind Hariri's killing—but it is at least one plausible scenario and one that has emerged in the public. So the instability in Iraq, the rise of a kind of new Islamist international to fight the Americans and the pro-American forces in the Middle East from Iraq, may well be destabilizing places like Lebanon.

> **What about the elections? How legitimate do you think they were? President Bush is talking about democracy being on the march in the Middle East. What's your assessment?**

The Iraqi elections were a mixture of the sublime and the ridiculous. One has to admire the courage of the Iraqi public, the Shiites and the Kurds, in coming out to vote. They knew they were risking their lives. Over fifty people were killed in attacks that day, so it was a significant risk. So again, one has to admire that courage and determination. The ridiculous part of it is that the candidates could not reveal their names in the run-up to the election because they would be killed. There were assassination attempts on the candidates. There was, therefore, no real electoral campaign. What could be done was that the broad lists of political party coalitions that had been put together could campaign in a vague way to convey what they stood for. So the major coalition of Shiite parties campaigned as the party of Grand Ayatollah Sistani.[12] He's widely respected and they used his picture widely. But this is a little bit shady. It would be like the Christian Democrats in Germany plastering the pope's picture everywhere. It would be tacky. In fact, Allawi, the interim prime minister and secularist, complained bitterly about it. So it was an anonymous election. People didn't know for whom exactly they were voting. I wonder myself if it's fair to call it an election at all. It had more the form of a referendum, a referendum on which large party coalitions were going to be nominated for parliament. An election should be between known candidates, so it certainly wasn't a model for anybody else, and the idea that the Lebanese were inspired by this process is silly. The Lebanese have been having lively parliamentary elections since the French mandate period in the 1930s, so I think that kind of master narrative that the administration put out is overblown. But the elections in Iraq did advance the political process there, and they have produced a parliament that may form a government that would have the confidence of some 80 percent of the people, which is not an insignificant achievement.

> **Some people are saying they think that there's effectively a civil war going on in Iraq. Do you buy that?**

I lived in Lebanon during the civil war there,[13] so I don't think this looks like a civil war. It's a guerrilla war. And all the violence notwithstanding, the dispute, so far, has been limited. The Shiites insist that they are not angry with the Sunni Arab community in general, only with specific people who were involved in the Baath Party.[14] It's the Baathists who killed them during Saddam's reign, not the Sunnis. So far, their behavior has supported that. They haven't engaged in large-scale reprisals against the Sunni Arabs in general and, in fact, even when they've been provoked by car bombings on holy days and at Shiite shrines, they have declined to reply with violence toward the Sunni Arab community in general. So I don't characterize the situation as a civil war and nor do I think that a civil war of the sort we saw in Lebanon is possible in Iraq as long as US troops and especially the US Air Force are there.

What outcome do you think the Americans are looking for?

I think that there's probably a dispute in the American political establishment about what the ideal outcome would be. There are forces and personalities who insist that we're on the verge of outright winning in Iraq.

The Bush administration has been very clear about their goal. They want to do to Iraq what was done to Japan and Germany, which is to transform a former enemy into an ally and moreover a forward base against other enemies. These advocates of a forward policy think that they can subdue the insurgency, install a pro-American government in Iraq, build bases, and then use Iraq as a springboard to further adventures in the Middle East, particularly the overthrow of the Syrian and Iranian regimes.

It's a fantasy and a very dangerous one. First of all, I think the guerrilla war will go on for some time, and the likelihood that the Iraqi public is ever going to put up with permanent US bases seems very low to me. There's a key contradiction in the US policy that Gen. Wesley Clark pointed out to me. He said that for the United States to have a good outcome in Iraq, which is to say to see a stable country emerge, it needs the cooperation of Iran and Syria, and you can't hope for their cooperation at the same time that you make it known that you're gunning for them.

Do you think the US government suffers from provincialism or arrogance?

It's certainly arrogance if nothing else. The United States is now militarily the only superpower and can do as it pleases, and no one can oppose it, at least in a conventional way. So ambitious elites, such as the ones in the Bush administration who want to reshape the world, can do so at will and the rest of the international community has nothing to say about it. Moreover, they can easily defeat their enemies in a conventional war. So they are very tempted to use their power to achieve policy aims. Now what Iraq should have taught them is that people have unconventional ways of subverting such plans and using guerrilla tactics to tie down a big army. Pundit Max Boot has said, "It's 1942 and it looked very dark then but if we just stay the course, we'll win." They think that it's World War II and it's 1942 and so they have every reason to want to stick to their policies, even in the face of evidence that they're not working.

Germany and Japan certainly are not the Middle East in so many ways. The big difference is that, in the wake of World War II, Germany and Japan had enemies that they worried about aside from the United States. The Germans worried very much about the Russians and, of course, part of Germany was occupied by the Soviet Union. The Japanese were very worried by both the Soviet Union and China. So I think to a very large extent, the acquiescence of the Japanese and Germans to an American-dominated order had to do with their fear of their neighbors. I don't think any similar factor is operating in Iraq. The Iraqi Shiia majority is not afraid of Iran and the Iraqis don't think they need protecting from their neighbors, so there's no reason for them to want or need the United States to protect them. It's a very different dynamic.

I think the arrogance of the administration and their misunderstanding of the particular historical and geopolitical moment causes them to have these grandiose dreams of reshaping the Middle East. And while it certainly is the case that they can invade Iraq and overthrow Saddam, shaping the region in a way that's amenable to the Bush administration is a different order of business, and in that they have not succeeded.

I'm a historian and not a prophet and so I cannot say exactly where this is going, but I think the triumphalist master narrative of the Bush administration that democracy is on the march and a pro-American sentiment is brewing can be shown to be false. Lebanon was interpreted by the American right as a Cedar Revolution,[15] as a sign of prodemocracy yearnings, but they tended to discount the very large and important counterdemonstrations held by the Shiite fundamentalist group Hezbollah.[16] What it really showed was that Lebanon is deeply divided, and were it to become more divided, there could be a return to civil war. So what I see in Lebanon is instability. Likewise in Egypt, many of the same groups that are demanding open elections most loudly are denouncing the United

States most loudly as well, so the idea that more democracy will equal pro-Americanism is simply not true, and the idea that instability will lead to democracy may well not be true, either.

The guerrilla war in Iraq is being prosecuted primarily by Sunni Arab activists who are diverse in their background. Some of them are Baath army and military intelligence. Some of them are radical fundamentalists. Some of them are Baath military that went over to Islamism and so form an intermediary group that's able to coordinate between the two. I would say that the biggest myth that we heard during the first year and a half of the guerrilla war was that it was mainly the work of foreigners. That is obviously not true; it's mainly an Iraqi guerrilla war. In the Sunni holy city of Fallujah,[17] only 6 percent of the fighters captured were foreigners, and of the 10,500 Iraqis in US custody in Iraq who were caught in the course of guerrilla actions, relatively few of them are foreigners. So I think there were reasons for which the Bush administration and the Iraqis wanted to give the impression that these were foreign spoilers with possible al Qaeda links who were behind most of the incidents. That is not true. It's mainly an Iraqi operation.

You say "guerrilla war" instead of "insurgency." Is that a conscious thing?

Yes, I don't tend to use the word insurgency. An insurgency implies a rebellion against legitimate authority.

How strong do you think the guerrilla movement is?

The chairman of the Joint Chiefs of Staff, Gen. Richard Myers, admitted last month that once these guerrilla wars begin, especially those based on ethnic grievances, they tend to go on for a decade or so. It seems to me that if you're looking for a historical analogy for Iraq now, it would be Lebanon, where the war went on from 1975 to 1989, or Sri Lanka[18] or northern Ireland.[19] I don't think there is any evidence that the guerrilla war is lightening up or petering out. The number of attacks per day is around sixty. This is less than the eighty of last fall, but last fall the United States was actively pursuing a fight against Fallujah, which increased the number of attacks. At the moment, the United States seems not to be engaged in any large-scale military action, so sixty a day is much more than it was in late 2003. I can remember elation when the number of attacks fell to only seventeen per day in the fall of 2003 and people were saying that after Saddam had been captured it was a tipping point and the guerrilla war was winding down. Now it's spring of 2005, and we're at sixty attacks a day. So I just think that there's a theme of the winding down of the guerrilla war that the press keeps recycling at every opportunity and that there's no reality to it. In fact, the evidence is that Sunni Arab public opinion is more in favor of attacking Americans now than it was a year ago. The Kurdish city of Mosul, with a population of over a million, did not turn actively hostile to the United States until the second campaign against Fallujah, during which four thousand Iraqi police resigned and the city and its region became unstable. The second Fallujah campaign appears to have decisively alienated the Sunni Arab population, even those who were fence-sitters for much of 2003 and 2004.

Who in the press do you think has done a good job of covering this and who hasn't?

I'm not in close enough personal contact with journalists or haven't followed their work in a systematic enough way to talk about that sort of thing. I've already mentioned that Anthony Shadid does a wonderful job. I think Alissa Rubin of the *Los Angeles Times* is very good. I think pretty much everybody who has been reporting for Knight Ridder has done a very good job gathering reports from the ground and subjecting US official pronouncements to a fair amount of searching criticism.

I depend very heavily on the journalists in the field. A lot of them are reporting under difficult situations. But they're reporting a particular corner of the story and can't even see the whole country's story. I don't mean to put down journalists at all, especially those who are risking their lives and getting us the story from the ground, but I think that there are a lot of editorial writers and commentators in the United States who tend to follow the line coming out of Washington, DC, whatever it may be, and those I'm very critical of.

What stories do you think are being underreported postinvasion?

Everything is being underreported now. We have no idea what's going on in Iraq. It's very difficult for reporters to move around and most are stuck in downtown Baghdad. A lot of the reporters just can't get out to the field, so we don't have any idea what's going on in a place like Ramadi.[20] We'll hear shadowy stories coming out of the US military about a firefight here or a car bombing there, but what are the political forces in Ramadi? How are they arrayed? We don't know. We don't even know the specific makeup of the elected parliament. If this were a European election, you would know all about the two hundred and seventy-five members of the new parliament right after the election was over. You would know their leanings, their education, and where they were coming from politically. We don't know that information about the newly elected members of the Iraqi parliament. We don't even know what subblocks there are among the deputies and how they're operating with one another. And now that parliament has excluded journalists from its deliberations, we know even less. So I would maintain that we're information-poor about Iraq and we don't have a good database for coming to conclusions about what is really going on there.

I think it's because of the poor security situation. If people could go out to Ramadi, they would. I think that's clear. There is another issue, which is that there are constraints on what can be reported in the United States and to some extent in Europe. First of all, our press is a capitalist press; it is a private enterprise for the most part and it has to make a profit. If it's television, it has to generate advertising dollars and viewers, and if it's newspaper, it has to generate circulation and advertising. There are lots of things that viewers and readers won't sit still for, like a long detailed disquisition on the members of parliament in Iraq and their various maneuverings. You probably couldn't get that in a major newspaper or on TV.

Today, at my Weblog, I did an analysis drawn mainly from the Iraqi press of the maneuverings behind the election of the Sunni Arab Speaker of the House, Hajim al-Hassani, and of what I thought the political implications of that event really were.[21] I think that you'd find it to be a completely different take from what the US press is reporting with regard to the details about who voted, how many voted, what the popular reaction was, and so on, as well as with regard to the conclusions that I draw from the event, which are much more pessimistic. The general lead of the stories in the American and British presses was that this was the breaking of a logjam, this was a step forward, this was Shiites reaching out to Sunnis. I don't think any of those things is true.

The candidate who emerged, emerged because of rancor between the Shiite deputies and many of the Sunni Arabs who had been elected to parliament. About a dozen of the Sunnis had either served in Saddam's parliament or had other family or personal links to the Baath Party. There are only seventeen Sunni Arabs sitting in parliament. There should have been at least sixty, by the proportion of population, but the Sunni Arabs sat out the election for the most part. Three of the Sunni Arabs in parliament ran on the Shiite ticket and they were not acceptable to the Sunni party as potential candidates for Speaker of the House. The Speaker of the House has to be a Sunni, so there were really only two people in parliament who were acceptable to all parties: Hajim al-Hassani and Ghazi al-Yawir. Al-Yawir didn't want the job. His refusal tells me that there are a great many problems between the Shiites and the Sunni Arabs, especially the Sunni Arab elite. The type of person among the Sunni Arabs who is likely to get elected to parliament is likely to have been a member of the Baath Party or to have had family links to it, and the Shiites are extremely unforgiving of that.

Although some groups and individuals have called for a national reconciliation commission, nothing has happened. Imagine the situation in South Africa if none of the whites who had served in the apartheid party were allowed to hold high positions in politics in South Africa. It would cause enormous difficulties. That's the kind of situation you have in Iraq now, so I don't see this as a positive step at all.

Do you think Prime Minister al-Jafaari is going to push for a theocracy?

It depends on how you define a theocracy. That's a more complicated subject than most Americans realize. Certainly the United Iraqi Alliance, the coalition of Shiite religious parties that won the election, wants Sharia law, or Muslim religious law, to be the law of the land in Iraq. They want to get rid of civil law, especially with regard to personal status matters like marriage, divorce, alimony, and inheritance. I think there's a very high likelihood that the Iraqis will move to such a system, which also exists in some other Middle Eastern countries. Personal status law based on religious strictures is common in Lebanon, Israel, Egypt, and Pakistan, so whether you consider that theocratic or not is the question. Certainly if the system is applied in Iraq in the way that it is applied in countries like Saudi Arabia, women would lose their full rights as citizens. Under this kind of system they would get half of the inheritance that men do and their testimony in court would be worth half that of men, which would make it almost impossible to convict a rapist. If that's theocracy, that's certainly the direction in which Iraq is headed. If you mean by theocracy the kind of clerical rule that you have in Iran, then no, I don't think Iraq is headed in that direction.

Do you think al-Jafaari's government is acceptable to the Americans?

Jafaari would not have been announced as the candidate if the Americans hadn't green-lighted it. He's minimally acceptable to Washington. The leader of the United Iraqi Alliance, Abdul Aziz al-Hakim, who is also the leader of an expatriate Tehran-based party called the Supreme Council for

Islamic Revolution in Iraq and who did very well in the elections in the southern provinces, might well have been the logical candidate for prime minister, but I think the Americans let it be known that they didn't want him.

What about Allawi and Chalabi?

Allawi[22] lost. The United States did its best to give Allawi a platform and all the advantages of incumbency. He ran in these elections and his party got 14 percent, mainly from the middle and upper-middle classes from Baghdad and Basra. These are more secular-leaning voters. But 14 percent in this parliament gets you nothing, so Allawi has lost big time.

Allawi is very much about power, and last Tuesday he walked out of parliament in anger because his candidate for Speaker of the House had been rejected for having Baath Party ties. Of course, in his youth, Allawi himself had Baath Party ties, so the religious Shiites are sending the message that "We're not in a forgiving mood and the Allawi-type people are just not going to amount to anything in the new Iraq." The Kurds and some of the Shiites would very much like to have a government of national unity and they would like to bring Allawi into the government if they possibly could, but not if the price is prohibitively high from their point of view. Allawi himself has no leverage to make these things happen anymore, so I'd say his next big chance to amount to anything in Iraqi politics won't come until the next parliamentary elections, which probably won't be for at least a year.

Ahmed Chalabi[23] ran on the winning party ticket, United Iraqi Alliance, and has many friends inside that alliance. He's also on very good terms with the Kurds. Chalabi was appointed one of three deputy premiers in the new government and continues to be an important power broker, once again proving himself an astonishing survivor.

So being connected to the Americans is not necessarily a negative thing.

Chalabi, whether he meant to or not, distanced himself from the Americans. He had a big public fight with them, so I don't think he's seen as close to the Americans anymore. They tried to arrest him. They accused him of spying for Iran. There may be people in Washington who are still pro-Chalabi, like Richard Perle,[24] for example, but Perle's out of power. If you say "Chalabi" in Iraq right now, people don't think of him as an American agent. They might think that about Allawi, but not about Chalabi.

Does the Israeli-Palestinian situation have any bearing at all on the current situation in Iraq?

No, the Middle East is very much every tub on its own bottom. There are things that travel across national borders, but the word that was coming out of the Washington Institute for Near East Policy and other think tanks before the war about how the roots to peace in Jerusalem ran through Baghdad turned out very clearly not to be true.

What issues do you think that Americans really don't grasp and need to about the Middle East?

That's a difficult question for me to answer because it would require knowing what Americans think about the Middle East. One thing I could say is that there is very clearly a misunderstanding among Americans about Middle Easterners in general. Most Middle Easterners are not Muslim fundamentalists. Opinion polling in the Middle East shows that most Middle Easterners have very high regard for democracy, and so the thing that keeps being said about people in the Middle East hating Americans because of their values is simply not true. There are value differences on issues of sexual morality and homosexuality. Middle Easterners in general have a profile somewhat like that of the religious right in this country. The religious right's concerns about the culture wars, about the influence of Hollywood, sexual promiscuity, and homosexuality, are generally the same views that are held by most people in the Middle East and for the same reasons. Just as Alabama and Arkansas are kind of under siege from Hollywood and Washington with regard to policymaking on these issues, Hollywood and Washington have a big impact on Algeria and Afghanistan. So there is that kind of values difference, but the fight is really not over whether democracy is a good thing or not. Everybody agrees that Middle Easterners want more of it.

Do you think that culturally the Middle East would lend itself to the kind of democracy that we have here?

Parliamentary governance is a pretty flexible form of government and is practiced by people of various cultures all over the world. The Middle Eastern nations are not in some way peculiar or different from parliamentary countries like India, for instance. India is more culturally distant from Europe than it is from Morocco or Egypt. I'm a historian so I see these questions as having to do with genealogy, history, and how things have developed in the modern world. It's now forgotten that many countries in the Middle East had parliamentary regimes in the 1920s, 1930s, and 1940s and engaged in fairly lively parliamentary politics after they escaped European dominance. This was true of Iraq and it was true of Egypt. They weren't perfect elections; landlords played a disproportionate role in them, but then that was true of nineteenth-century Britain as well. What really ended those experiments in parliamentary governance in my view is the cold war.[24] The United States overthrew the elected government of Iran in 1953 and imposed a monarchical dictatorship. Now the Americans are saying that what they really want is a parliamentary government in Iran. Well, they had that in 1953, but it was a government that was nationalistic in character and wanted to nationalize the oil companies, and the United States got rid of it in favor of a dictatorship that destabilized the country and helped to bring about the Islamic republic. Likewise, the United States interfered heavy-handedly in the Lebanese elections of 1957, which began the first Lebanese civil war and a process of destabilization in that country. It is widely alleged that the United States had something to do with the Baath coup of 1968[26] in Iraq. So I think the evidence is that the jockeying between the Soviet Union and the United States drove a lot of the politics in the region in an authoritarian direction. The Arab-Israeli conflict had something to do with that as well. But there's nothing inevitable about it.

Obviously the United States hasn't always played that role of promoting democracy and has undermined or overthrown democratically elected governments like the government of Allende in Chile[27] and the government of Mossadegh[28] in Iran. It's a great power and it plays great power politics. The Bush administration espouses rhetoric supporting democratization, but its record in that regard is still mixed. It's true that they overthrew Saddam, who was a horrible dictator, but it is also not yet clear that they will support genuine democratization in a number of other countries. They haven't complained—at least openly—about Tunisia, where there is more or less a president-for-life and an authoritarian government, or a whole range of close US allies. And they haven't done anything about the West Bank and Gaza where people are living under dire conditions and haven't had an opportunity to elect the Israeli military governor that rules over them. So it's still unclear.

Given Bush's fondness for Sharon, what do you think the chances of that are going to be?

So far, I would say there's a certain amount of hypocrisy in this regard. I don't want to come to too abrupt a decision on the matter of how sincere they are in democratization, but there are real questions here.

I want to talk about terrorism for a minute because on your blog you talked about the history of how terrorism got a big push from the United States after the Soviets left Afghanistan. Could you connect the dots up to Iraq?

When the Soviets invaded Afghanistan late in 1979, the Carter administration was still in office. Initially, President Carter's national security advisor, Zbigniew Brzezinski, was the one who came up with the idea of fighting the Soviets with a guerrilla insurgency funded by the United States. Ultimately, the United States came to depend upon the most hardline of the Islamic fundamentalist groups based in Pakistan, who were also refugees from Soviet-dominated Afghanistan. Then the Reagan administration took up the plan, but where Carter was giving it sixty million dollars a year, Reagan, by the mideighties, was giving it half a billion dollars a year. The money was funneled to the Pakistani Inter-Services Intelligence [ISI], which is their military intelligence. The ISI, in turn, gave it out to these hard-line fundamentalist groups, some of them very unsavory characters. Although the CIA says it is proud that it kept all the money from going to the most unsavory among them, I think the most unsavory got at least a fifth of it. Moreover, the Reagan administration put pressure on the Saudis to match that money and we didn't have any control over where the Saudi money went. In fact, the Saudi intelligence minister at the time, Prince Turki al-Faisal, looked around for a fund-raiser to help with this holy war against the Soviets and found a dedicated young man from a wealthy family named Osama bin Laden. So to any extent that the Reagan administration leaned on the Saudis to help with this and then the Saudis chose Osama to be their fund-raiser, there was a sense in which the Reagan administration created Osama bin Laden for the purposes of embarrassing the Soviets and pushing them out. The Soviets were forced out by late 1988 and the war wound down, but these guerrillas, who had been created with all this very big money—you're talking a billion dollars a year—and who were involved in opium growing and drug smuggling, looked around for other targets. They decided that they were very upset about the first Palestinian uprising, or intifada, and the way that the Israelis were cracking down on the Palestinians. They were upset about the military government's cancellation of elections in Algeria in 1992 when the Islamists had won there. They were upset about Chechnya[29] and the way that Russian president Boris Yeltsin used a scorched-earth policy against the Chechen rebels. They were upset about Kashmir, where the Indian government was repressing an autonomous movement among Kashmiri

Muslims. They looked around the world and they said, "Look, we had this problem of the Soviet atheist-communists coming into our Muslim Afghanistan and we solved that problem by organizing and using guerrilla tactics to push them back out. We should use the same tactics now to address all these other problems that we see." So they did. They went after the Algerian government and the Egyptian government and the Saudi government, but they couldn't make any headway. They finally decided that the reason they couldn't overthrow, say, Hosni Mubarak in Egypt was because the United States was giving him two billion dollars a year and military support. So Ayman al-Zawahiri, an old Muslim Brotherhood type who founded a splinter group called al-Jahad al-Islami and who ultimately joined up with bin Laden to form al Qaeda, put forward the notion of "hitting the far enemy before hitting the near enemy," and that meant attacking the United States on its own soil. That's the origin of September 11. So there's a direct line from the Reagan jihad against the Soviets to the attacks on New York and the Pentagon on September 11.

Assess the terrorist threat to the United States now. Do you think it warrants all the things that are being done in this country to thwart potential future attacks?

It doesn't warrant everything that's being done. It certainly doesn't warrant gutting the US Constitution or some of the more draconian measures that have been put into the so-called PATRIOT Act I and PATRIOT Act II.[30] It doesn't require four hundred billion dollars a year in Pentagon spending. It seems to me a kind of police work now. I don't think there are more than about twenty-five thousand hard-core jihadis out there and there are very, very few in the United States. You'll note that September 11 had to be planned and carried out from Europe and Afghanistan. They didn't have a base in the United States. So to find these people and keep them from doing harm, you need intelligence work on the ground, you need to cooperate with Moroccan authorities and Yemeni authorities, and it's not something that lends itself to conventional warfare. In fact, the conventional warfare that was waged in Iraq has essentially opened four million Sunni Arabs to being wooed by radical Islamists in a way that they weren't under Saddam, and it could well blow back on us big time.

In what way?

We just destroyed the city of Fallujah. We're killing Sunni Arabs every day who are involved in the guerrilla war against the United States presence. Many Sunni Arabs in Iraq had been secular-minded members of the Baath Party and supporters of a secular socialist Arab-nationalist government. Now that the Baath Party has been discredited and shown to be weak, a lot of Iraqi Sunni Arabs are turning to radical Islam as their ideology. The Zarqawi group, which has now linked up with al Qaeda, has an orange and black symbol, and there have been instances in Haifa Street in Baghdad or Samara where crowds of people have shown up with stockings over their faces wearing this black and orange insignia on their clothing. You never want to see al Qaeda insignia on crowds so that it emerges as a kind of political party. This is not something that could have, or would have, happened in Iraq three years ago. So those four million Sunni Arabs in Iraq are being brutalized by the US presence, and some of them are turning to radical Islam as a result. Some of them have already started talking about hitting the United States on its own soil in revenge for things like Fallujah.

What happened to Osama?

When President Bush is asked why he can't find Osama bin Laden, he replies, "It's because he's in hiding." Bush is putting three hundred billion dollars at the very least into the Iraq adventure, but he hasn't put anything like that into finding bin Laden or destroying al Qaeda. So if you follow the money and you think about where the US energies are going, I take away the lesson that Bush isn't interested in al Qaeda very much and is very interested in Iraq.

He's not interested in al Qaeda but he's very interested in Iraq for what?

I think I mentioned the architecture of oil security has a great deal to do with Iraq.

Do you think that the Project for a New American Century is basically the road map?

I think that one of the factions of the Bush administration that wanted this Iraq war was certainly the Project for a New American Century [PNAC][31] people, many of whom are neoconservatives. These include WASPs [White Anglo-Saxon Protestants] like John Bolton[32] who are involved in the PNAC. They wanted an Iraq war in large part to bolster the Israeli right of the Likud Party, to remove any conventional threat from Likud Party militarism in the region, and to allow the Likud Party to have a forward policy in the West Bank so they could grab as much Palestinian land as possible. I think that's behind a lot of their enthusiasm for the Iraq war. It was also a way of breaking Iraq's legs and making it not a threat. Moreover, some of them seem to have thought that an American puppet regime in Iraq would announce a separate peace treaty with Israel and would reopen the oil pipeline from Kirkuk[33] to Haifa. All of these ideas were fantasies. The Iraqi public is as angry at Israel's treatment of the Palestinians as all the other Arab publics are. No Iraqi government is just going to break with the Arab League in that regard, and the only consensus, by the way, is that the Arab League would like to make complete peace with Israel, if only the Israelis would go back to 1967 borders.

Do most Arabs really think that Israel does want peace with Palestine?

No, nor is there any evidence that the Sharon government wants peace with the Palestinians. Basically, Ariel Sharon has spent the last fifteen years campaigning against the peace process. They had a peace process starting in 1992, when Israeli prime minister Yitzhak Rabin and PLO chairman Yasir Arafat signed the Oslo Agreement. The Oslo Agreement envisaged that the Israelis would withdraw from, at the very least, most of the West Bank and Gaza, and they didn't. In fact, Israeli settlements doubled in the 1990s, and the Palestinians felt very betrayed and ultimately went into rebellion. No one in the American political or intellectual establishment will ever admit that the Israelis were the ones who did not abide by the Oslo Accords and that moreover there was a series of time lines for Israeli withdrawal from various parts of the West Bank that they did not meet. Then when Yitzhak Rabin was assassinated, his enemies, Benjamin Netanyahu and Ariel Sharon, successively came into power and both of them were dead set against Oslo. They did not agree that one should trade land for peace and did not ever want to see a Palestinian state, so the Israeli right destroyed the Oslo process, the far right killed Rabin for attempting it, and the political right scuttled the whole thing. So, objectively speaking, it's hard to see in what way the Likud governments in particular have demonstrated a desire for peace.

Do you think the American press adequately covers this?

No, absolutely not.

Why not?

I couldn't tell you that; I'm not an insider with the press. What is very clear is that the US press is extremely biased on this issue. Anyone who has lived and traveled in the rest of the world finds the American press reporting on the Israeli-Palestinian conflict to be a form of pro-Israeli editorializing rather than anything else. I think there's a very strong pro-Israeli community in the United States that is not without resources and puts pressure on the US media in this regard. I think there are threats of boycotting advertisers and denunciations for anti-Semitism and so forth that come from especially pro-Likud community organizations. I think that, on the other hand, the legacy of the cold war is important and that during the cold war local conflicts were reworked into great power conflicts and that, on the whole, the Israelis were supported by the United States especially from 1967 on and that many of the Arabs therefore became close to the Soviet Union to offset the American-Israeli alliance. Egypt, Syria, and the Palestinians all developed close relationships with Moscow and that created an image of the Arabs as enemies of the United States. It wasn't forgiven that they became close to Moscow, and so the Palestinians in American opinion polls are among the most reviled and hated groups in the United States. The Palestinians have, I think, also made a big mistake in resorting to terrorism as a tactic. When a Palestinian group blows up a cafeteria at Hebrew University or a pizzeria in Jerusalem or a bus in Haifa, they're killing ordinary innocent people— children, women, and Israeli Arabs in the mix. This has very much damaged them with regard to public opinion in the United States.

I think the Palestinians are obviously in a very weak position. They face an enormously powerful enemy in the Israeli right, many of whom openly speak of ethnically cleansing the Palestinians. The Israeli air force can fly more missions in the same amount of time than the US Air Force can. Israel is a nuclear power, so it is a tremendously wealthy and powerful country in Middle Eastern terms. The Palestinians are weak; they are seeing their land being gobbled up by the Israelis, they're losing access to land that they once owned, they're losing access to resources, including water, and some of the anger that then develops into these terrorist attacks is coming from Israeli aggressiveness toward them. But they have all along had other options besides terror.

Political engagement of various sorts would have been far more constructive. Terror is a tool of anticolonialism, and we saw it used effectively in Algeria, but it's not always an effective tool. I think it's particularly poorly suited to the Palestinian-Israeli conflict. The Algerian guerrillas were trying to make the French leave. If you blew the French up enough, you really could make them leave and go back to France from

Algeria in 1959, 1960, and 1962. But the Israelis are not going anywhere. That's the only country they've got and blowing them up is not going to cause them to leave, so what exactly is it going to accomplish?

What about Iran, its nuclear potential, and the United States?

I don't think there's any mystery why the Iranians might like to have nuclear weapons; they have powerful enemies in the region that have them. On the other hand, the Iranian regime is in a posture of enmity with the United States, denounces the United States, and has in the past made a lot of trouble for the United States. Iran was probably intimately involved in blowing up three hundred marines in Beirut in 1983, in blowing up the American Embassy there, and in kidnapping the CIA's station chief in Beirut. So there's a long history of violent conflict between the United States and Iran on the margins in displaced places like Lebanon, and the United States is concerned that a country that seems to dislike it so much might have this very powerful weapon.

In international politics, evenhandedness is rare. I think that the Iranians genuinely do want a nuclear weapon, and the evidence that I've seen is that they are trying to get one, so the real question is whether that can be prevented and how. The Europeans are hoping to forestall it with diplomacy, and the Bush administration initially rejected that stance and it looked very much as though the United States was going to take military action. But now the Bush administration has backed off and is saying that it will give European diplomacy an opportunity to work. I think the developments in Iraq have made it very difficult for Washington to take a military stance toward Iran. The Shiite religious parties that won the recent elections in Iraq have warm relations with Tehran and their rank and file would object vehemently to a US bombing of Iran. Also, the guerrilla war in Iraq is tying down the US military so it would not have the capability to respond to Iran militarily on the ground. I think the reason for which Bush has now adopted the European line of diplomacy is that he has no military options that are any good because of the geopolitical situation after the Iraqi elections.

I think the guerrilla war in Iraq will go on for a long time. On the other hand, I don't think the guerrillas can win, so I expect there to be trouble for a while. The Sunni Arabs are only 20 percent of the population, and not all of them support the guerrillas. They cannot defeat the vast majority of the country. But they can make life miserable for years to come.

I want to ask a couple more questions about your blog. When did your blog hit the hundredth-monkey phase? When did you really began to feel that all of a sudden you had a lot more attention?

It began to take off during and immediately after the Iraq war in the spring of 2003, especially after the war. When the smoke cleared and Saddam had been overthrown, the first thing that happened was that the Shiite Muslims emerged into view and they were engaged in a pilgrimage to Karbala[34] and flagellation and they really were going to be a very important factor in the new Iraq. They were the majority and the US political and journalistic establishment by and large didn't know much about them. I, on the other hand, had been studying them for thirty years, admittedly from a distance and historically, but nevertheless, I knew who the major players were, who their fathers were, and who their great-grandfathers were, and I could put them in some kind of historical and political context. So it was in late April and through May that I started being called for television appearances and I started getting notices from journalists that they were reading the Weblog for background. It grew from there all through the summer of 2003 and into the fall. In the fall, some prominent political bloggers linked to my site. Josh Marshall at "Talking Points Memo" very kindly put me on his blog roll. I think he gets a half a million hits a day, so that's a good address and his support has been invaluable. "Riverbend," an Iraqi blogger who is a young Sunni Arab woman who is very much against the war, also linked to my site. So that kind of crosslinking in the Web world produces big results. I went from five hundred hits a day during the war to six thousand by the fall of 2003. Then, during the fighting in the fall of 2004 between Muqtada al-Sadr and the Americans, a lot of people started coming to my site because I am a Shiite expert and that was a marines versus Shiites conflict. Families of soldiers as well as policymakers, journalists, and the general public started visiting my site in large numbers. By April, May 2004, I was getting a million page views a month.

How influential do you think blogs are and where are they headed?

They're still not a mainstream medium. A relatively small proportion of Americans reads them. On the other hand, measuring these things is awfully difficult because, for instance, nowadays it's very easy to e-mail a Weblog entry to a friend and from there it gets passed on. That kind of e-mail circulation of the blog entries is impossible to track, but on the whole, the evidence is that it's a niche market at the moment. When I say they're a niche market, I'm not saying that they're without effect. But the way things work, if you look at the Dan Rather goof about those memos, you can get a million bloggers on the right really upset about this. There are eight million bloggers. And those one million bloggers, because of people e-mailing things around and checking into major blogs and so forth, can have a big impact. Perhaps the analogy for it is when the networks decided to cancel *Star Trek*. The trekkies all got together and got a third season for the show because they were really, really interested in having that show and they mounted a public relations campaign and managed to change the executives' minds. It wasn't that there were that many trekkies; it was just that they were a niche that made itself heard. I think that's the way that blogging is having its major influence right now.

I see blogs as an extension of other kinds of media. Think about the Christian Coalition back in the 1980s when fundamentalist Baptist Jerry Falwell first got it going. They didn't have blogging or the Internet; they did telephone and telegraph campaigns. They would get out letter writers and put all this pressure on Congress to adopt certain policies. We shouldn't discount the power that the old media—the telephone, the mail system, and faxes—had. The Internet is really a kind of extension of those mediums of communication. I think they change the dynamic somewhat and they're not unimportant, but it's not as if they've changed the face of politics all of a sudden. The same kinds of politics are going on, but these new media are giving certain people access that they didn't have before. Someone like me couldn't have a voice in the old system very easily. I tried to get op-eds published during the Gulf War and signally failed. No one had ever heard of me and I couldn't get past the slush pile and my being an academic specialist in the Middle East really got me nowhere with editors and journalists. The gatekeepers really had a different set of criteria for who got in the gate, and so my blog allowed me to display my ability to contextualize and explain Middle Eastern politics in a way that the journalists and the editors could see. It created a way for me to get out of the slush pile. Once the editors and journalists were reading me, then they would invite me to write op-eds, which I've discovered is much the better way to do it.

JUAN COLE is professor of modern Middle East and South Asian history at the History Department of the University of Michigan. He has written extensively about modern Islamic movements in Egypt, the Persian Gulf, and South Asia. Since September 11, 2001, he has given numerous media and press interviews on the War on Terrorism and the Iraq war. His current research focuses on two contemporary phenomena: Shiite Islam in Iraq and Iran and the "jihadi," or "sacred-war," strain of Muslim radicalism, including al Qaeda, the Taliban, and other groups. Cole commands Arabic, Persian, and Urdu and reads some Turkish. He knows both Middle Eastern and South Asian Islam, and has lived in a number of places in the Muslim world for extended periods of time. His most recent book is *Sacred Space and Holy War* (London: I. B. Tauris, 2002), a volume that collects some of his work on the history of the Shiite branch of Islam in modern Iraq, Iran, and the Gulf. He treated Shiism in his coedited book *Shi'ism and Social Protest* (New Haven: Yale University Press, 1986) and his first monograph, "Roots of North Indian Shi'ism in Iran and Iraq" (1989). His interest in Iranian religion is further evident in his work on Baha'i studies, which led to his book *Modernity and the Millennium: The Genesis of the Baha'i Faith in the Nineteenth-Century Middle East* (New York: Columbia University Press, 1998). Professor Cole has also written a good deal about modern Egypt, including *Colonialism and Revolution in the Middle East: Social and Cultural Origins of Egypt's 'Urabi Movement* (Princeton, NJ: Princeton University Press, 1993). His concern with comparative history and Islamics is evident in a book he edited, *Comparing Muslim Societies* (Ann Arbor: University of Michigan Press, 1992).

NOTES

1. According to the online encyclopedia Wikipedia, "The story of the 'Hundredth Monkey' apparently originated with [botanist, zoologist, biologist, anthropologist, ethnologist, and author] Lyall Watson in his 1979 book *Lifetide*. In it he claimed to describe the observations of scientists studying macaques (a type of monkey) on the Japanese Island of Koshima in 1952. Some of these monkeys learned to wash sweet potatoes, and gradually this behavior spread through the younger generation of monkeys—in the usual fashion, through observation and repetition. However, according to Watson, the researchers noted that once a critical number of monkeys are reached—the so-called hundredth monkey—this previously learned behavior instantly spread across the water to monkeys on nearby islands. . . . In 1985 Elaine Myers reexamined the original published research . . . [and] found [that] the original research reports by the Japan Monkey Center . . . differ from Watson's story in significant ways." http://en/wikipedia.org/wiki/Hundredth_Monkey.

The Hundredth Monkey phenomenon did not occur when the original research was conducted and Watson's claims were debunked by Myers, but the term is still used to describe the moment when critical mass is reached. I am using the term as a means of expressing how Juan Cole's "Informed Consent" blog achieved exponential growth—from five hundred hits a day in 2003 to his current (2005) level of one million page views a week—in a relatively short period via the virtual Internet medium.

2. On its Web site, http://www.whitehouse.gov/nsc/, the National Security Council is defined as "the President's principal forum for considering national security and foreign policy matters with his senior national security advisors and cabinet officials. . . . The function of the Council has been to assist the President on national and security policies. The Council also serves as the President's principal arm for coordinating these policies among various government agencies."

3. Saddam Hussein attacked Kuwait after claiming that the Kuwaitis were over-producing oil and thereby destroying Iraq's economy and that they were also stealing oil via slant drilling into Iraq's Rumaila oil field.

4. See chapter 15 in this book.

5. Susan Moeller's "Media Coverage of Weapons of Mass Destruction" (March 9, 2004) is available from the Center for International and Security Studies (CISSM) at the University of Maryland and can be viewed at http://www.cissm.umd.edu.

6. At the Abu Ghraib prison in Iraq, American soldiers from a US military intelligence unit, US military police, and some civilian contractors abused and tortured their prisoners. Shocking photos of their activities were released, showing naked prisoners being forced into humiliating sexual and other poses, while their captors were pictured with them giving "thumbs-up" signs and, in at least one case, holding a leash with a prisoner on the other end.

7. The Aum Shinrikyo cult is a Japan-based group that mixes Hindu and Buddhist beliefs. For more information, see Wikipedia online at http://en.wikipedia.org/wiki/Aum _Shinrikyo.

8. Imad Khadduri worked for the Iraqi Atomic Energy Commission (IAEC) from 1968 to 1998. In April 1993 he wrote an article, "The Mirage of Iraqi Weapons of Mass Destruction," which can be seen at http://www.globalresearch.ca/articles/KHA304A.html.

9. In a report that he wrote for the *Bulletin of the Atomic Scientists* 54, no. 5 (September/October 1998), Khidhir Hamza described the roles he played in Iraq's nuclear program: "I was chief of the fuel division in the 1970s, head of the theoretical division of the enrichment program in the 1980s, scientific advisor to the chairman of the Iraqi Atomic Energy Commission [IAEC] in the mid-1980s, and—for a brief period in 1987—director of weaponization."

10. The American Enterprise Institute for Public Policy is a think tank that is generally viewed as conservative. The institute's Web site is http://www.aei.org/about/content ID.20038142213000031/default.asp.

11. A Palestinian born in Jordan, Abu Musab al-Zarqawi is believed to have links to al Qaeda and is believed to be, according to a BBC profile, "the main source of kidnappings, bomb attacks and assassination attempts in Iraq." The BBC's profile can be found at http://newsvote.bbc.co.uk/mpapps/pagetools/print/news.bbc.co.uk/2/hi/middle_east/3483089.stm.

12. Grand Ayatollah Ali Husaini Sistani was born in Iran and now lives in Najaf, Iraq. A very traditional Shiite cleric and the Shiites' top spiritual leader, he is considered one of the most influential religious figures in the Middle East. In chapter 20 in this book, Knight Ridder foreign correspondent Hannah Allam said that before he was elected, Iraqi

prime minister Ibrahim al-Jafaari told her: "We're not going to set up a theocracy, but at the same time we'll probably see a more conservative government and a more prominent role for Islam. . . . People are turning to religion and they reflected that by voting for a list that was backed by the most revered Ayatollah Sistani." Allam says that for Prime Minister al-Jafaari, "that's a mandate." Sistani's Web site is http://www.sistani.org/.

13. "The Lebanese Civil war (1975–1990) had its origin in the conflicts and political compromises of Lebanon's colonial [French colony] period and was exacerbated by the nation's changing demographic trends, Christian and Muslim inter-religious strife, and proximity to Syria and Israel. After the Civil War itself ended in 1976, civil strife continued, with the focus of the fighting primarily in South Lebanon, occupied first by the Palestinian Liberation Organization and then by Israel. Events and political movements that contributed to Lebanon's violent implosion include, among others, the departure of European colonial powers, the emergence of Arab Nationalism, Arab Socialism in the context of the Cold War, the Arab-Israeli conflict, Baathism, the Iranian Revolution, Palestinian terrorism, Black September in Jordan, Islamic fundamentalism and the Iran-Iraq War." http://en.wikipedia.org/wiki/Lebanese_Civil_War.

14. The Baath Party, of which Saddam Hussein was a member, follows a secular ideology that advocates pan-Arabic unity, Arab socialism, nationalism, and militarism. http://en.wikipedia.org/wiki/Ba'ath_Party.

15. The cedar tree is Lebanon's national symbol, and what the "American Right" is referring to as the "Cedar Revolution" has to do with a series of demonstrations in Lebanon calling for Syria to withdraw its troops from the country in the wake of Lebanese prime minister Rafik Hariri's assassination in February 2005.

16. In chapter 15 in this book, the *Washington Post*'s Anthony Shadid described Hezbollah as a "movement that came out of the Israeli invasion of Lebanon in 1982 with Iranian backing. . . . It's probably one of the most efficient, effective, noncorrupt movements in the Middle East and provides everything from dental clinics to hospitals to schools to nurseries to orphanages. It set out to serve Shiites in southern Lebanon and southern Beirut living in communities that traditionally were most discriminated against, the poorest and most disenfranchised. They also entered Parliament as a political party. And they had their military arm, which fought the Israelis in southern Lebanon and forced them to withdraw."

17. In November 2004 US forces launched a major assault against Fallujah, which was targeted as a rebel stronghold. The Iraqi city, known as "the City of Mosques," is a Sunni stronghold and has a population of several hundred thousand.

18. The ethnic conflict in Sri Lanka has been going on since the country gained its independence from the British in 1948 and is between Buddhists, who are the governing majority, and the Hindu Tamil (Tigers) minority.

19. After the Government of Ireland Act of 1920 split Ireland into separate political units—the Catholic south and the Protestant north—the south cut all ties to Britain and declared itself the independent Republic of Ireland in 1949. Centuries of religious animosity on top of this political division have resulted in an ongoing cycle of violence between the two populations.

20. Ramadi, a city one hundred kilometers west of Baghdad and the capital of Al Anbar province, has been a focal point of resistance to the American occupation. It is considered to be the southwest point of Iraq's Sunni triangle. http://en.wikipedia.org/wiki/Ramadi.

21. See "Speaker of Parliament Elected amid Rancor" (April 4, 2005) at http://www
.juancole.com/2005/04/speaker-of-parliament-elected-amid.html.

22. Former Baathist and interim Iraqi prime minister Iyad Allawi is, the BBC reports
in "Who's Who in Iraq: Iyad Allawi" (May 28, 2004), "one of a U.S.-backed clique of secular Iraqi opposition figures who lived in exile until the fall of Saddam Hussein's regime
in April 2003." A secular Shia Muslim, Allawi is head of the Iraqi National Accord Party
in the Iraqi National Assembly.

23. A British-educated former banker, Ahmed Chalabi has been the leader of the
anti-Saddam Iraqi National Congress, which was formed with US government backing for
the purpose of overthrowing Saddam Hussein. Chalabi received large sums of money
from the US government for his activities and was a source of faulty prewar intelligence.
Although he has no industry experience, he is currently acting oil minister for the new
Iraqi government

24. Richard Perle is the former chairman of the Defense Policy Board, which Seymour Hersh describes in his March 17, 2003, *New Yorker* article "Lunch with the
Chairman" as a "Defense Department advisory group composed primarily of highly
respected former government officials, retired military officers and academics. . . . The
board meets several times a year at the Pentagon to review and assess the country's
strategic defense policies." Perle has been reported to have been influential in crafting the
Bush administration's policy toward Iraq.

25. According to the online encyclopedia Wikipedia, the cold war was "the open yet
restricted rivalry that developed after World War II between the United States and its allies
(roughly speaking NATO [North Atlantic Treaty Organization] members) and the Soviet
Union and its allies (roughly speaking, Warsaw Pact members). The struggle was called
the cold war because it did not actually lead to direct fighting between the superpowers (a
"hot" war) on a wide scale. The Cold War was waged by means of economic pressure,
selective aid, diplomatic maneuvers, propaganda, assassinations, low-intensity military
operations and full-scale war from 1947 until the collapse of the Soviet Union in 1991."
http://en.wikipedia.org/wiki/Cold_War.

26. The 1968 Baath coup was bloodless and put Baathist general Ahmad Hassan al-Bakr
in power. Al-Bakr appointed his cousin, Saddam Hussein, as vice president. Hussein gradually usurped more and more of his uncle's power before formally taking over in 1979.

27. Salvador Allende Gossens was the democratically elected (in 1970) Marxist president of Chile until his death during a military coup (1973), which the United States
helped foment. Allende was replaced by Gen. Augusto Pinochet, who remained in power
until 1990 and escaped punishment for his actions, which left thousands dead.

28. Iranian prime minister Dr. Mohammed Mossadegh was removed from power in
1953 and replaced by Mohammed Reza Pahlavi (the shah of Iran) via a largely CIA-engi-
neered coup after Mossadegh nationalized the British-owned Anglo-Iranian Oil Company
when the firm refused to change the terms of its oil concession deal with the Iranian government and pay higher royalties.

29. Chechnya is a Muslim region in the northern Caucasus that declared its independence in 1991 following the collapse of the Soviet Union but is still seeking its independence from Russia, which considers it a republic of the Russian Federation. In 1994
Russian president Boris Yeltsin sent troops in to retake Chechnya, and since then, Russia
has been engaged in a guerrilla war with Chechnyan separatists, which president Vladimir
Putin now considers part of the War on Terrorism.

30. In the PATRIOT Act of 2001, its purpose is stated as "to deter and punish terrorist acts in the United States and around the world, to enhance law enforcement investigatory tools, and for other purposes." This act gave the government new powers to wiretap telephones, spy on US citizens without judicial review, conduct secret searches, and look into the reading habits of library users. PATRIOT Act II, called the Domestic Security Enhancement Act of 2003, would add more than one hundred new provisions. The PATRIOT Act of 2001 can be read at http://www.epic.org/privacy/terrorism/hr3162.html. The draft version of PATRIOT Act II can be read at http://www.publicintegrity.org/docs/PatriotAct/story_01_020703_doc_1.pdf.

31. The Project for a New American Century (PNAC) says on its Web site that it "intends, through issue briefs, research papers, advocacy journalism, conferences, and seminars, to explain what American world leadership entails." It is generally seen as a neoconservative take on the role the United States should play in the world. PNAC says it is a nonprofit educational organization dedicated to the propositions "that American leadership is good both for America and the world; and that such leadership requires military strength, diplomatic energy and commitment to moral principle." http://www.newamericancentury.org/.

32. John R. Bolton, former undersecretary for arms control and national security, was nominated by President Bush as ambassador to the United Nations in March 2005. Opponents to his nomination have referred to him as being abrasive and undiplomatic. At a 1994 Citizens for Global Solutions forum, Bolton, who is a neoconservative member of the Project for a New American Century, said, "There is no such thing as the United Nations. There is only the international community, which can only be led by the only remaining superpower, which is the United States." He has also said, "The UN can be a useful instrument in the conduct of American foreign policy."

33. Kirkuk is the largest city in one of Iraq's most important oil-producing areas, with oil pipelines running into the coastal cities of Tripoli in Lebanon and Yamurtalik in Turkey.

34. Karbala is one of the most holy cities in Islam, particularly for the Shiites.

15

DEMOCRACY
AND ISLAM
THE DREAMS AND NIGHTMARES

Bill O'Leary/Washington Post

ANTHONY SHADID
Islamic Affairs Correspondent,
Washington Post
Interviewed April 2005

S hadid had just returned from the Middle East when I called him at home for a phone interview. We had to reschedule on the spot. Something more important had just come up. Young Miss Shadid had walked into the room and wanted her daddy's attention. I hung up thinking about the serious personal sacrifices Anthony makes to do his job.

Attention to human relationships and the emotional temperatures of events is a hallmark of Shadid's reporting. He knows that greater truths can often be found not just in what people say but in how they feel, and that emotions are a legitimate part of an accurate record: "Being fair doesn't mean being bland. I think we can still bring passion and emotion and fear and pride to our coverage. I think we can give voice to these things while

427

still being fair and credible." Indeed, Shadid's reporting achieves a level of lyricism and literary elegance that is rare in journalism. In a war characterized by dehumanization—from the utterly perverse Abu Ghraib prison scandal to the Pentagon's insulting refusal to record the deaths of Iraqi citizens, including US-trained security forces—Shadid puts names and faces to the human tragedy unfolding in Iraq. He tells, for example, the gut-wrenching story of Salem: Sabah, Salem's son, was accused of informing for the Americans and helping them with an operation that resulted in the death of four members of his village. Tribal law dictated that Salem kill his son. If he refused, the villagers would kill Salem's entire family. Sabah was shot to death by his father and his brother.

Perhaps it is because he is of Lebanese descent that Shadid cares so much. Perhaps it is just a function of who he is as a person. Ultimately, it doesn't matter why. I think his journalism is simply more compelling, more real, and more true on more levels.

But there is far more to Shadid's reporting than heart. His mastery of history and context also sets him apart. His book *Legacy of the Prophet: Despots, Democrats and the New Politics of Islam* is a must-read primer for understanding the multidimensional interactions between Islam and democracy in the Middle East. "What was fascinating to me in researching *Legacy of the Prophet*," he says,

> is that by its very nature, change in the Arab world is going to empower Islamists. So this idea that the US government has, that change equals democracy and democracy equals secularism, is not the case. So what we may see in Syria or Egypt is the strengthening of a very religious current in the politics of those nations. That could very well be the main consequence of democratization. . . . As Americans, when we hear these promises about how we're going to bring democracy to the region, it sounds idealistic, it sounds like it springs from our own traditions of liberty and democracy and equality. But from my own experience, I can say that when a lot of people in the third world and the Arab world hear this, it is rife with suggestions of centuries-old colonialism and their attitude toward it is, "Who are you to tell us how to live our lives?"

As for Iraq, he sees a physically and psychologically battered nation that hangs somewhere between a dream and a nightmare: "I think it's very possible that in ten years Iraq will be a somewhat stable country with a relatively well-functioning democracy that may be an example for the entire region. I think it's just as likely that Iraq will descend further into violence, chaos, and civil war and will be even more miserable than it is right now. Perhaps it will be something in between."

As Shadid was talking to me about why the Iraqis think the United States is in their country, I heard a little voice in the background say, "I love you, daddy." "I love you, too, sweetheart," are the last words on Shadid's transcript. His first words are a thumbnail sketch of the history of the US involvement in Iraq. Here again, he presents hard facts and hard feelings.

If we're talking about the current situation in Iraq, I'd begin a sketch of the history of US involvement in Iraq with the Iran-Iraq war and how it affected Iraqi society as well as what it said about US-Iraqi relations and how Iraqis perceived those relations. During that war, there was a certain level of US engagement with the Iraqi government and support for Saddam Hussein. Toward the end of the war, it was pretty clear that the US government had decided to back Iraq against Iran in the hopes that Iraq would emerge with at least a tactical victory. That did happen in the end. I think a lot of people in Iraq perceived the US support as being for Saddam himself, and that started what became a very ambivalent relationship between the Iraqi population and the United States.

The Gulf War followed, and US troops expelled Iraqi troops from Kuwait.[1] That same year, in 1991, there was a Shiite uprising against Saddam in Iraq, along with an uprising in the north among the Kurds.[2] It was another decisive moment in US-Iraqi relations, because many Shiites involved in that rebellion thought that the United States was going to back them and the United States did not. That cast a long shadow over the evolution of Shiite attitudes toward the United States. Following Saddam's invasion of Kuwait and throughout the 1990s, the United Nations imposed sanctions on Iraq, which eviscerated Iraqi society. The middle class was basically wiped out. This had a profound psychic impact on Iraqi society, turning what was once a country with the GDP of Greece and a standard of living that was comparable to some of Europe's poorer countries into one of the most miserable places in the Middle East. The recent US invasion followed after the allegations that Saddam had weapons of mass destruction. He was toppled on April 9, 2003, and that marked the chapter that we're still seeing being written. What country emerges from the occupation, strife, and aftermath of the Baath Party[3] and Saddam Hussein is still undetermined.

For a lot of people in the West, the easiest way to understand Iraqi politics is to see it through the sectarian and ethnic lenses. The Shiites and Sunnis are both Islamic sects. Most Shiites and Sunnis are Arabs. Then there is the ethnic divide between Arabs and Kurds. The clear majority of the country is Arab, but there is a very sizable Kurdish minority, mainly in northern Iraq. In this tapestry of sects and ethnicities, you also have small communities of Assyrians, Chaldeans, Sabians, and Armenians. It is quite a diverse country.

What's happened in Iraq over the past few years is that this somewhat superficial Western perception of Iraqi politics has, particularly since the invasion, conformed more and more to reality. It's almost as if we saw it that way and in the end it became that way. I think that one of the great legacies of the occupation will be this hardening of sectarian and ethnic lines in Iraqi politics.

The way this hardening of the lines has spilled out into the insurgency is that, especially among Sunnis, there's a sense of disenfranchisement, a feeling that they've lost their stake in the government. This has propelled the insurgency forward. There's a lot of talk about foreign fighters playing a big role in the insurgency. I think their role is minimal, even though they are responsible for spectacular acts of carnage. What we are really dealing with is a homegrown insurgency that will continue as long as US troops are in the country. We've seen the insurgency take many shapes at the same time, and there are different currents within it. Some groups sanction horrific attacks on civilians, and some say they should only attack American soldiers. I think the hardening of lines that we're seeing among the different sectarian and ethnic communities is a dangerous trend that seriously reduces any incentives for reconciliation.

After the election, I remarked to some friends that I felt more optimistic and more pessimistic than I ever had. I felt more optimistic because I saw the empowerment of Iraqis who were exercising their rights. It struck me that I felt more enthusiasm, more jubilation in the streets on the day of the vote than I had on the day of Saddam's fall in Baghdad on April 9, 2003. My sense was that here you had an example of Iraqis feeling like they were actually taking their fate into their own hands, rather than having foreigners do the job for them. Iraqis often say that they couldn't overthrow Saddam themselves. There was a sense of jubilation that Saddam was gone, but also a sense of shame that foreigners had to do it. You didn't have that on election day. You had this real jubilation, and it was surprising to me to see it unfold. But I was also more pessimistic than I had ever been too, because the election had empowered some factions that are not necessarily interested in reconciliation but in settling scores and empowering one community at the expense of the others, or at least claiming the spoils of the government for one community. I think we're seeing that play out now.

The Shiite Islamist parties, and the Supreme Council[4] in particular, read Iraqi politics through a very specific sectarian lens. Over the past three years, each group or party's political style differed, depending on where it had stood under Saddam. If you were in exile, it was one way; if you were in Iraq, it was another way. This hardening of sectarian and ethnic lines that I mentioned before is in part an import from exiled parties who returned after Saddam's fall. That's how they operated abroad. That's how they operated in opposition. Figures, groups, and factions that remained in Iraq, I think, are less that way, even if they despised Saddam. The most senior Shiite cleric in Iraq, Grand Ayatollah Ali Sistani, is one example. Even Muqtada al-Sadr, the young militant Shiite cleric who inherited the movement of his late father, a revered ayatollah, might fit in this category. They speak much more about reconciliation, about national politics and national identity. So what made me more pessimistic than ever was that these exile groups that saw things only on a sectarian basis and were determined to settle scores from their time in exile were actually the ones who were going to be making the key decisions on the fate of Iraq.

All this raises the question: Where does that leave the Americans? Over the last couple of years, the Iraqis' perceptions of American troops has run the gamut. I was there during the war, and there was almost awe of American power when they saw them wage the war and topple in three weeks a government that had been in power since 1968. What ensued immediately after that was looting and chaos and anarchy that did far more damage to Baghdad than the entire war itself, and there was resentment that the American troops did nothing to stop it. In a way, people were mystified by America's inability. As time went on, there was another sense that the Americans were bringing more fighting to Iraq by attracting these foreigners to come do battle there. There was also a sense that if the Americans left, there would be civil war. Sentiments contradicted and conflicted.

In time, the question becomes: How do you bring legitimacy as long as the Americans are there? That's a difficult one. The best thing about being a journalist is that you don't have to offer answers; you only have to understand the way it is. But it's really difficult to see how it's all going to pan out. I think it's very possible that in ten years Iraq will be a somewhat stable country with a relatively well-functioning democracy that may be an example for the entire region. I think it's just as likely that Iraq will descend further into violence, chaos, and civil war and will be even more miserable than it is right now. Perhaps it will be something in between.

I noticed on election day that the US government narrative of what was happening in Iraq was, "Here's the culmination of our efforts in the country. We're having an election and we're going to empower a democratic state that makes a democracy of Iraq." That may be true. What I saw in the streets that day in Iraq, though, was people primarily exercising rights that had been long denied to them, and that in itself was empowering. It wasn't a question of who they were voting for, what system they envisioned, or which candidate they were voting for. A lot of that was irrelevant. They probably didn't even know what the platforms were, but they were exercising a right that they had been denied, and by exercising that right, they believed that they were going to make a better future for themselves. The American narrative of creating a democracy and the Iraqi sense of exercising rights don't necessarily conflict, but they remain different narratives. There may be a lot of overlap between them. But I think each had a different sense of what the elections meant, and I'm not sure that we as journalists always conveyed that.

But isn't that only a momentary empowerment if the ultimate result is this continued horrendous bloodbath?

Definitely, and I think that there's a sense of that within Iraq right now. Time and again, you hear people say, "There was such a momentum created by the election." I went in expecting it not to happen, to be honest. I'll admit, too, that I expected the violence to be so overwhelming that day that it would be a mixed bag. It really wasn't a mixed bag. The day itself was actually a triumph. I did not expect that at all. So I was surprised. The most enjoyable part about being a journalist is when you are surprised by what you see. But, in the end, I think the result was much more amorphous. There was indeed, early on, a sense that the vote created a new dynamic: "We have momentum now, we can try to bring about change." But the ensuing violence has been horrific and the carnage has been unbelievable and there's very much an acknowledgment within Iraq at this point that the momentum has slowed and it's fading, that the election is perhaps less of a landmark and more a moment of empowerment, and that unless it's capitalized on, it won't have a big impact on the country as the months go on.

A second thing I want to mention is this question of identity or of legitimacy, because I think it's profoundly important. What Saddam was so successful at during those years of dictatorship and tyranny was destroying any semblance of civic identity, political empowerment, or legitimacy outside of his party, and that's what evolved into his own individual rule. What you saw after Saddam was gone were groups and communities asking themselves: "Now that he's gone, what do identity, politics, and citizenship mean? What constitutes legitimacy? Who are we?"

I once wrote this line in a story: "What creates legitimacy? Is it guns, God, law or tribal traditions?" After the fall of Saddam, you saw this really remarkable resurgence of tribal authority filling the void of lawlessness and chaos and the sense of "We don't know who's in charge." I think it has receded a little bit. What we've seen in its place is guys with guns and a lot of places where the law of the gun prevails. Sectarian identity has surged, as has religious affiliation. And, in general, that search for legitimacy continues.

People have their own little personal militias.

That's right. We are limited in what we see and what we understand, but I was in southern Iraq a few weeks ago and I was so struck by the fact that in this vast part of the country, which in some ways is the wealthiest part of Iraq because of the oil there, the Americans weren't there. There are British troops in Basra,[5] but it's a vast swath of territory where nobody's really sure exactly what's going on. And what I saw was that one certain militia could have taken over one of those southern cities in a week and we as journalists would probably have no idea. So are militias a temporary way to maintain stability so that a state can be built? Or are they, in fact, the abortion of a state? Are we seeing what the future's going to be—rule by militias among certain territories that they can defend? I don't know the answer to that.

Tell me about your new book, *Night Draws Near: Iraq's People in the Shadow of America's War*.[6]

I spent a couple of years in Iraq, and during the war I met several families and individuals. We became friends and I stayed with them through the war's aftermath. The book is, on one hand, about the war and its aftermath and, on the other hand, about these people and their lives and how they were shaped and reshaped by war and this brutal interregnum between war and peace that we've seen until now.

I was struck by so many things—particularly, as I already mentioned to you, how the perceptions of the Americans changed as time went on, the hardening of ethnic and sectarian lines in the country, and the lack of identity at one level and the attempt to create a new identity on another. To me, this question of legitimacy is the cornerstone of understanding

Iraq. Unfortunately, legitimacy is far easier to deny than to bestow. The fundamental question of legitimacy is: Does this government or this individual have a right to be in power? That's a huge question, and it's a question that hasn't been answered yet because what confers that right to rule hasn't been clearly established. The Shiites, who have taken part in the American project, would say, "The elections have confirmed our right to rule." Now Sunnis, who are opposed to the American presence, would say, "You can never achieve that right as long as the American military is present in this country, as long as there is an occupation." Some more religious figures would say, "This is all irrelevant. The question of the right to rule comes from God. It's a religious question and the clergy are endowed with the right to decide who rules. So it can go on and on. This is such a fascinating question because it's so difficult to answer.

What do you know about the new prime minister, Ibrahim al-Jafaari?

He's one of these people who came from exile. To me, who he is, is less important than where he came of age as a politician. That he came of age in exile has a very big imprint on his politics. Jafaari was the first president of the Iraqi Governing Council that Paul Bremer[7] established in 2003. Bremer had set up this rotating presidency system and Jafaari was the first of the rotating presidents and he had the position for about one month. I think he came across to a lot of Iraqis as a benevolent figure. He was soft-spoken. He was such a contrast to Saddam because he was engaging, personable, and seemed like a decent person. I think he gained a lot of popularity from his short stint as president of the council. On the other hand, he's not seen as very forceful. I think there are some people who speculate that the Shiite Supreme Council or certain factions within the Shiite alliance that Jafaari represents could see him more as a figure-head or somebody who'd be a little more pliable if they tried to enforce their agenda. I think a lot of people were embarrassed by how long it took to create this government and how long it's taken Jafaari to create a cabinet, which is still not complete. There is some Sunni Arab representation in his cabinet, but not the kind of Sunni Arab representation that he would need to be able to say that politics are going to be different than they have been for the past year. Again, that goes back to the question of legitimacy. It's interesting, I was in Najaf [a Shiite holy city], talking to the clergy a few weeks ago, and they felt that this government that had been created had international legitimacy because, in the eyes of the rest of the world, it was an elected government. They also felt that it had national legitimacy because, in the eyes of the people who took part in the election, it is what they voted for. What they felt it didn't have was regional legitimacy because other predominantly Sunni Arab countries in the region don't see this as a successful project yet. The same thing goes for Sunni Arabs within Iraq. They don't see themselves as invested in this process because it is still an American process.

Do you think that the Sunnis feel that way because, looking nakedly at it, they lost power? Why would they want to legitimize a process that robbed them of their power?

I go back and forth on that. There's definitely a constituency that feels exactly like that. They're mad that they've lost power and they're bitter. But I also think that there is a large constituency within the community that really does want to take part in a democratic process but that sees this particular election from a nationalist and antioccupation perspective and cannot stomach it as long as the Americans are seen as pulling the strings.

You wrote an article, "Preaching the Rule of Law in a Tribal Land,"[8] about the challenges that the mayor of Basra, Mohammed Musabah, was facing. Talk about his exchanges with the people who came in to his office, because I think they're emblematic of what people are thinking, where their priorities are, and what the problems of governing them are.

As a preface to answering the question, I want to mention that in Iraqi Arabic, people will use the word *shafafia*, which means "transparency," or *tadudiya*, which means "pluralism." They say these phrases in a joking way, like, "Listen to this new kind of language that they're always talking about now, but nobody's sure what it means." So it's a bit of a joke when you refer to *shafafia*. When I met with the governor of Basra, I found out that these words actually mean a lot to him. He sees transparency as essential for the future of Iraq. He believes in the rule of law. He wants to get rid of the power of tribes because he's worried about police being more loyal to parties than they are to the government, and he believes that the only way he can change this is through the rule of law. He wants his administration to represent law, a law that is supreme in the land, and everyone has to answer to that law. So he gets into these very fundamental questions of how to organize a society. He let me spend a day with him, and it was fascinating, because that rule of law concept was tested at almost every turn by the people who walked into his office: "Fine, you represent the law, but how do you ensure that that law is supreme? Are you going to give us money? Are you going to arrest the people who don't like you?" At every turn, he was facing this question. The most dramatic illustration of that was when four tribal heads came in. They could not settle a dispute among themselves about the appropriate compensation for the death of one of their tribal members who was killed at a wedding party. And they were insisting, "You have to throw several families out of the city, they have to go into exile," and the governor was looking at them with his eyes wide because how was he going to bring this dispute under the umbrella of the rule of law, which he is supposed to represent? Then he just delayed it and said, "Come back next Thursday and we'll try to figure it out." It was interesting to watch, because you had this idealistic mayor saying, "it's the rule of law, it's the rule of law," and then at the end you could almost see what his epitaph might be: "Well, at least he tried to make the rule of law supreme." So whether it will work or not is a question.

> **I may be wrong, but now that the Shiites are not only the majority of the country in terms of population but also the elected ruling majority, it seems like the rule of law is going to be based on Sharia, or Islamic law, which means when these tribal members come in and say, "Hey, my family member was killed," Sharia has one way of taking care of it and secular law has another way of taking care of it.**

You're probably thinking of tribal law, and that would be different from Sharia. That's really tradition. Arab tribal tradition, Bedouin tradition, predated Islamic law by centuries and centuries. In Islamic law, Sharia is mainly personal status law. It's not something that we would necessarily endorse in the West. Women are unequal under personal status law—laws regulating divorce, marriage, and inheritance. There's a different Sharia for Sunnis and a different Sharia for Shiites with respect to inheritance, for example. What a Shiite woman is entitled to inherit is different from what a Sunni woman is entitled to.

But Sharia is so many different things and there are so many different interpretations, and importantly, the rule of law and the rule of Sharia are not necessarily mutually exclusive. It's still the rule of law—however that law is conceived—and it's not impossible that a majority of people in southern Iraq might want Sharia as their law. That's where it runs up against this American notion of what we're trying to create over there, the difference between a secular vision and what exists on the ground. I don't think that that has ever been reconciled. The American perception is that democracy and secularism are the same thing, and they are not. There can be an intersection between Islam and democracy, or there should be, or there may be. There hasn't necessarily been an intersection at this point, but my sense is that that has to be reconciled as part of a democratic future.

I'm not sure what an Islamic democracy would look like. I'm not sure what a secular democracy in the Arab world would look like. I don't think we've seen either necessarily at this point. When we think of secular democracy, we often think of an American or European example.

But how many secular people are there in the Middle East?

There's a current. It's less so than it was thirty or forty years ago. I don't know what the numbers would be, but it's definitely a current. The secular voice is not to be dismissed, and Iraq, of course, used to be one of the most secular countries in the region.

I find, ironically, that Iran seems to be trying very hard to create a kind of democracy that the Americans would find acceptable. Am I wrong?

I think there's definitely an attempt to reconcile Islamic democracy in Iran—probably more so than in the past—and there's been some success and some failure. It's not an unreconstructed Islamic dictatorship. There is a certain element of democratic choice in that government. In my first book, *Legacy of the Prophet: Despots, Democrats, and the New Politics of Islam*,[9] I explored how those two things intersected: Islam and democracy or, more specifically, political Islam. I saw very clear trends of where it was headed, but I don't think we've seen the result yet.

I think there was a thread that went through your book in terms of all the attempts to set up Islamic governments. It always came down to the power of the person in charge and that person's tribe or that person's belief being imposed on everybody else. That's what it seemed like to me, with the exception of Iran where Khatami seems to be trying to reconcile the secular with Islamism and to bring Islam into the twenty-first century, but it seems like everybody else is just trying to shoehorn the society into their particular paradigm. That's what I saw. Tell me if I'm wrong.

I think that's true. I think that traditionally that has definitely been the case. But I think there are some counterexamples going on now. Just the idea that you can have competing ideologies and that all those ideologies are acceptable is a huge breakthrough. I think some groups within the Muslim Brotherhood[10] do that, as do the Turkish Islamists. Lebanon's Hezbollah says it believes that—there's a question whether they do or not—so you're starting to see some counterexamples to an exclusivist political Islam. But you're exactly right; the biggest threat is the attitude of "We represent one ideology and only this one ideology is true." That's what you saw in the wake of the Iranian revolution and in earlier Islamic movements, this attitude of "We represent Islam. If you're against us, you're against Islam and therefore you're illegitimate."

> **The other thing that I found interesting in your book were the discussions about Hezbollah and HAMAS, because these are organizations that are essentially doing what the state doesn't do, which is providing all these social services. But they also have these brutal military arms, and I'm wondering if their power and money don't derive also from their military activities, which in turn allows them to pay for all the social welfare activities.**

I think HAMAS's money often comes from sources in the Gulf—from the Saudis, the Emirates, and elsewhere. It's not money that's going to kill Israelis necessarily; it's money that's also going to help Palestinians, an issue which to most Arabs remains a very nationalist and patriotic thing to do. Hezbollah is a movement that came out of the Israeli invasion of Lebanon in 1982 with Iranian backing. It was, in its original conception, dedicated to forcing foreigners out of Lebanon, and it left a trail of destruction in its wake, like the bombings of the American embassy and the marine barracks. But then every movement evolves, and Hezbollah developed its political arm and social arms along with its military arm. In the 1990s, we saw the real coming of age of its social welfare network. This has time and again proved to be the essential tactic of Islamic movements in the Muslim world to curry support in countries like Turkey, Lebanon, Egypt, Palestine, and Jordan. All these countries have seen Islamic movements fill the void left by governments that inadequately serve their people, and Hezbollah was one of those groups. There are a lot of different reasons why the governments of these nations aren't successful. They're authoritarian and they don't derive their legitimacy through popular support, so it doesn't matter if they serve the needs of the people. They're financially strapped because they're military-heavy and don't have the resources to serve all the needs of the society. Hezbollah filled that void and filled it very successfully. It's probably one of the most efficient, effective, noncorrupt movements in the Middle East and provides everything from dental clinics to hospitals to schools to nurseries to orphanages. It set out to serve Shiites in southern Lebanon and southern Beirut living in communities that traditionally were the most discriminated against, the poorest and the most disenfranchised. They also entered into parliament as a political party. And they had their military arm, which fought the Israelis in southern Lebanon and forced them to withdraw. These three components were essential to making Hezbollah what it is today, and each of them is emphasized to different degrees. In much of the Arab world, Hezbollah is seen as heroic for fighting the Israelis and for winning by forcing them to withdraw from southern Lebanon. In Lebanon, Hezbollah is primarily a political actor. It takes part in parliament and represents a huge constituency, the Shiites, who are the plurality in the country. To a lesser degree, it is also seen as a social welfare group, although I think most Lebanese would see that as part of their political program.

I think in the eyes of the West, Hezbollah is still seen mainly as a terrorist group because of its history. In the 1980s, it orchestrated some of the most spectacular acts of terrorism of the century. Obviously, the Americans have a long memory over what happened. I think sometimes we in the West see movements like Hezbollah as static; what they did in the 1980s determines what we think they are today. It actually does determine to a certain degree what they are today, but it's not the whole picture anymore. There's definitely been a remarkable evolution of these groups and of Hezbollah in particular. As I was saying, in the eyes of the Arab world, in the eyes of most Lebanese, they are a far different group than we saw twenty or thirty years ago.

Sheikh Hassan Nasrallah, who is the head of Hezbollah, is probably one of the most dynamic figures in the Middle East today. He took over the movement when he was in his early thirties. His son was killed by Israelis, which delivered him an amazing amount of support. Again, the movement is seen as incorruptible and they are remarkably efficient. Hezbollah recruits rigorously among all elements of the society. Obviously there is clerical representation within the movement, but they're very often technocrats. It's a movement that went through the crucible of fighting a guerrilla war, and I think you see that dynamism in a lot of guerrilla groups or opposition movements that come out of that. They're very fit, very well honed for doing what they need to do.

Could you talk about the US view of Islam and what Islam really does represent over there?

My thing about reporting on the region and even writing the book *Legacy of the Prophet* was to convey that there is no one Islam and that the biggest disservice we make to understanding the region is to say that there is an essential quality to Islam. Islamic politics differ from country to country. If you looked at an Islamic movement in Egypt, it's a movement that is primarily there to serve the crushing needs of a population that's underserved by its own government. If you look in Palestine, it is political Islam tailored to a situation under occupation. I should note here that when I say political Islam, I'm not talking about Islam as a set of beliefs that orders a person's life as a religion. It is Islam as a political philosophy. In Lebanon, political Islam was the vehicle for empowerment of the Shiite community. In Turkey, a way to create a new identity. In each of these places, political Islam proves incredibly adaptive at shaping itself to the circumstances on the ground. That's what makes it so successful. And if you're contrasting those perceptions to what American perceptions or Western perceptions are, it is that the West often sees Islam as somehow monolithic, and it's not. And that's where the biggest mistakes are made.

> **You also wrote that you thought that the United States views Islam as a menacing force "driven by faith and radicalized by persecution."**

Yes, definitely. I think Islam has been conflated with terrorism to a certain degree—or militancy at the very least—and that has created a certain image that has entered the mainstream here.

> **I had an interesting experience with a French investigative journalist who is being protected by the French government because he has a fatwa[11] on his head for exposing an al Qaeda cell in London and France. I wanted to invite him to come here and go undercover in the New York area. He is a devout Muslim, and when I was proposing the project to him, all he kept saying to me was, "I'll do it, but I must not be humiliated. I will not have the American authorities rob me of my dignity when I come into the country." So here was this guy with humongous cojones, just absolutely fearless, and humiliation was his main problem. That's profound. I see the American presence in Iraq and hear some of the things that war correspondents have described to me, and it just hits me in the face and I think we're breeding feelings of "We don't give a damn what you're bringing here, we don't want you here."**

I think there's truth to that. As Americans, when we hear these promises about how we're going to bring democracy to the region, it sounds idealistic; it sounds like it springs from our own traditions of liberty and democracy and equality. But from my own experience, I can say that when a lot of people in the third world and the Arab world hear this, it is rife with suggestions of centuries-old colonialism and their attitude toward it is, "Who are you to tell us how to live our lives?" It is a relationship that's based on one side being more powerful than the other and that power is intensely felt by the other side. It colors everything that follows. My sense is that it's almost like these two ideologies, philosophies, cultures, and approaches can't exist in the same space sometimes.

Well, that brings me back to the question of why we are there.

That's a good question. I wish I knew the answer. I think there are a lot of reasons why we're there, but what's the main reason? What will history say was the reason? I don't know. I wonder.

What are the "a lot of reasons" why you think we're there?

I think it depends on whose actions we're trying to explain. I think some people actually did believe that there was a prospect of weapons of mass destruction. Some people were incredibly offended by Saddam's tyranny and were benevolent in their hopes of freeing Iraq. Some people worried about Iraq posing a threat to Israel, and others were interested in Iraq replacing Saudi Arabia as the strategic military linchpin of US policy in the region. Oil was a huge issue for others. I think all these things came together and made it very attractive to a lot of people. Which of those reasons was the main one? I don't know. What I do think is overstated is this American desire to create a democratic state in Iraq. I think at this point the only way that the US presence in Iraq can be called a success is by doing that, but I don't think it was the driving force behind it in the beginning by any means.

What happens if the democratic process goes through and a leader comes in and all of a sudden he decides he wants a full-blown theocracy? You don't think the United States is going to respond to that?

They say they're not. I'll be curious to see. It would be hard to see them overthrow another government in Iraq, so I don't know. I'm sure they'd try to figure it out. There are ways of doing it. You can push the Kurds to be very hard-line in their demands on the role of Islam in the constitution or federalism and you could push Allawi's people to be very hard-line in their negotiations. There are ways to blunt religious Shiite aspirations without a sledgehammer.

During the elections, the Americans were very much in the shadows because they knew that if their hand ever showed in the deliberations over creating the government, that government would be deprived of legitimacy. They are much more mature now than they were a year ago, or under Bremer and the Coalition Provisional Authority [CPA].[12] The CPA was not successful at all, and I think it would be hard to measure any kind of success under Bremer. But these people know what they're talking about, and I think they were relatively successful in keeping their hand hidden if it was there.

The Iraqis are trying to get this government on its feet, but the violence keeps injecting itself. Doesn't that rob the government of its power and legitimacy?

I think it does. At almost every turn in Iraq since the war, you've seen this burst of optimism followed by a lot of gloom. You saw it when Saddam fell. There was fear about what an occupation would represent, but there was also jubilation that Saddam was gone. That was followed by weeks of looting, which scarred the city. There was the creation of the Governing Council by Bremer later that year. Again there was optimism and then it was followed by the most high-profile attacks—the bombing of the UN building, the bombing of the Jordanian embassy, and the assassination of Mohammed Bakir Hakim, a Shiite Muslim leader. Then there was the appointment of Allawi's[13] government and Bremer's departure in 2004—another moment of optimism that was again followed by some of the worst violence yet, and that culminated with the second American attack on Fallujah. Then there was the election and the creation of a new government where you saw the same optimism, and that's been followed by violence and, again, gloom and pessimism. I think you're right; it does discredit the project. I think it is one of the biggest dangers to this government's success. The other huge challenge is just improving people's lives there. We're still dealing with a country where the electricity is out half the day. It's going to be worse this summer than it was last summer.

Where are all those billions that we sent over there?

A lot of it is going to security and there's a lot of incompetence, too.

Your mayor in Basra has a twenty-three-thousand-dollar operating budget for a city of 1.3 million people.

Wasn't that unbelievable? I could not believe it when he told me that. There is a lot of corruption. His explanation is corruption and inattention from the central government. It's hard to tell what's really at work; I've never actually reported on it.

Do you think our presence in Iraq has created more terrorism?

It depends on how you define terrorism. Has our presence there created an insurgency that's not going to end as long as the Americans are there? Most definitely. Is this insurgency working on a logic where the violence has to continually be more spectacular to generate attention? Definitely. So those two trends to me are really troubling because the insurgents are very well read and they listen to how they are covered and how they're perceived, and they heard all this talk about the insurgency fading in the weeks after the election and the violence we've seen in the past week or two is the result. It works under the logic of violence, and the logic of violence dictates continual escalation to continue to create that spectacle. We're locked into that kind of process right now, and it will continue as long as the Americans are in Iraq. The Americans believe that the alternative is worse. Maybe, I don't know, but it is clear that as long as they are there you are going to see the violence.

It breaks my heart for the Iraqi civilians who are basically ignored in the press here.

Yes. We're failing on our part as journalists by not capturing what this is doing to the society.

Is that because you can't get out?

I think that's part of it. I think part of it is, do you write about one person when twenty have died or do you try to capture the scope of the actual carnage. I think it's a reporter's tendency, when you have so many people dying, to write it as a spot news story. We haven't yet appreciated that most readers don't want to read a story that way; they want to read about human lives. I think we have to rethink how we do news so that it's done in the most compelling way, while still doing justice to the story. There's not a clear answer on how to do that right now. When I was covering the war, my whole thing was, "This war itself is not going to be interesting. Obviously the Americans are going to win. You go to the news conferences and it's just propaganda, so why spend all your time doing that?" I decided that the only way I was going to cover the war was to treat it as a backdrop for understanding how lives were shaped and reshaped by siege and conflict. In the end, it worked out OK. You could take that same approach to now, although it's much more complicated and difficult because during the war we just covered Baghdad, but now there's an obligation to cover the entire country.

Does the Israeli-Palestinian conflict figure into the picture of what's going on in Iraq?

Iraqis who were in Fallujah or were fighting with Muqtada al-Sadr see these American Apache helicopters in the air and of course they're going to connect them to images of Israel and Palestine. Where you see that really play out is in the rest of the Arab world. But I think these two occupations have been unfairly conflated to a certain degree.

They are such different occupations. The Americans aren't settling Iraqi land. They're not expropriating Iraqi land. They may take some land to create bases, but it's nothing along the lines of what's happening in the West Bank and Gaza, where you have tens of thousands of settlers. The Iraqi occupation is just not equivalent. Now, in terms of what's going to happen to resources and who is going to control those resources, those questions might be asked, but in terms of the very premise of what the occupation of Iraq represents, it is different.

As I said before, I don't think they are the same occupations, but many Arabs do, in fact, see them as the same occupation. You hear the word *ihtilal* in Arabic, and *ihtilal* means one very specific thing: Israelis fighting Palestinians on the West Bank. And they're using American-funded or American-built Apache helicopters to prosecute that conflict. Iraqis see these Apaches in Iraq, and they see American soldiers with the technology, and they see Israeli soldiers with the same technology. So while they are very different occupations, what you are saying is right, that one of the consequences of Arab satellite television is that people see the same images across the region and those images can be very inflammatory.

What was the Arab world's reaction to 9/11?

I once tried to make a comparison between the reaction of the Arab world to September 11 and the feelings of Bigger Thomas in *Native Son*[14] after he commits a murder. On a psychological level, there is a degree of brutalization in the Arab world, a degree of such searing resentment over the sense of being on the wrong side of justice for so long that it definitely colored the reaction to September 11. There was a reluctance to say this to a journalist who would put it in print, but it was often said in private that the Americans were finally experiencing what the Arabs had experienced for a long time. I think that was very difficult for us to understand in the West.

I think that people feel a little differently about the United States right now than they did right after September 11. The Israel-Palestine issue isn't inflamed to the degree it was at that time. The Americans are seen as an abject failure in the rest of the region, so Iraq isn't creating resentment as much as this reaction of "What on earth are they doing?" I don't want to overstate it, but I think there is some sense among the Lebanese and Egyptians and Palestinians that what Bush is promising in terms of democracy may create some change in their countries. Not that they've become enamored with the United States at this point, but I think there's a sense that American policy is a little bit different. How important or how inconsequential that becomes has definitely not been answered at this point.

But there is an element of thinking that the Americans are so intent on creating some kind of change in the region that you are actually going to see change. That Egypt's president Hosni Mubarak is going to have to do something to get the Americans off his back in Egypt. That Syria had to get out of Lebanon, otherwise they would have faced repercussions. That if the Palestinians—now I'm not saying I believe this, I'm just saying what I hear—feel that only the Americans can put enough pressure on Israel to give concessions and that there's a possibility, possibly remote, but there is a possibility, that that may happen. This is not what everybody is saying, this is not what most people are saying, this is what some people are saying, and it's interesting.

Americans are not loved in the region. Ninety-nine percent of the Egyptians dislike US policy and dislike the American government. Again, my biggest fear is to overstate these things. But I think there is a sentiment pronounced sometimes that there is a new dynamic in the region that wasn't there before and that the Americans are in part responsible for that.

I find that fascinating, particularly after having just read your book, which outlines the history of American involvement in the Middle East, which essentially has been about taking down more or less democratic governments.

That's exactly right, and this is what's so fascinating about this moment.

So how could they possibly believe that the Americans are there for altruistic purposes now?

Well, nobody imagined September 11, and we're still seeing its repercussions. I don't think the United States has any idea of what it's about to unleash, for good and bad. Did we have any idea of what we were going to unleash in Iraq? None. We inaugurated a Shiite revival, Sunni militancy, questions of identity, and the empowerment of the clergy. None of these things was ever foreseen. People can say they saw it coming, but they didn't see it coming.

I actually wrote a story before the war about how this question of religion was going to become very important after the war, but I had no idea that what I was seeing was the Shiite revival and the empowerment of Grand Ayatollah Sistani[15] and the clergy. Before the war, I didn't even know who Sistani was.

Just because the Americans are helping to create change doesn't mean that they can determine what shape that change takes or what consequences that change has. What was fascinating to me in researching *Legacy of the Prophet* is that, by its very nature, change in the Arab world is going to empower Islamists. So this idea that the US government has, that change equals democracy and democracy equals secularism, is not the case. So what we may see in Syria or Egypt is the strengthening of a very religious current in the politics of those nations. That could very well be the main consequence of democratization. Now this is not the democracy that Bush ever envisioned, and it's not a democracy that most Americans would necessarily want, but it is a certain form of democracy, and are the Americans going to allow that? Are they going to support it? Are they going to sanction it? That to me is the decisive question of the future of the region. It goes back to what we were talking about earlier: How do political Islam and democracy intersect? How does it work in Iraq? How might it work in Egypt? How might it work in Syria? How might it work in Saudi Arabia, where any democratic opening there will probably create a more radical government? I don't think these questions are necessarily being asked, but they are hugely important.

You don't think that democracy is just the next step to theocracy?

It wouldn't be hard to believe, but maybe not, though. I don't know. What I love about being a reporter is that almost every time I've made a prediction, I've been proved wrong. It's really amazing.

That's what Bart Gellman said to me, too.

It's just amazing. You get to see these consequences as they're unfolding and you get to try to understand them, but you're damned if you try to understand what's next.

Yes, but Anthony, you're not getting paid those big bucks just to say, "Ten people died today in a car bomb"; you're being paid to say, "Ten people died today in a car bomb and here's why, here's what's going on with the bigger picture."

Oh, yes, definitely to understand it, but not to predict. We have to understand it in the broadest perspective possible.

How good a job do you think the press does of covering the Middle East?

The *New York Review of Books* is my favorite on the Middle East right now. I think they're not afraid to question, not afraid to be critical, and I think their articles on Israel and Palestine and on Iraq are just first-rate.

Do you think there's a reluctance in the American press to really look at the Israeli-Palestinian issue?

I think there's a sense in journalism in general, and about that story in particular, that to be fair means to be bland. You're so conscious about representing both sides that, in the end, you don't say anything. I think it's a very direct consequence of that conflict and of the coverage of that conflict being so politicized. Every word you write about it is going to be interpreted in twenty thousand different ways. It has debilitated the journalism there. Being fair doesn't mean being bland. I think we can still bring passion and emotion and fear and pride to our coverage. I think we can give voice to these things while still being fair and credible.

Why do the Iraqis think that we are over there?

You'll hear often the more conspiratorial—"conspiratorial" is not fair, they're right—but you often hear that the reasons are oil, military bases, and control of the region. Some Iraqis think the Americans are there for altruistic reasons; that they want to create a democracy in the region. But I think the majority would say that the Americans are there for their own interests. These interests include a lot of different things: military bases, oil, economy, resources, and protecting Israel. There are all these different things, but I think the great majority of Iraqis think that it's a self-interested project.

I find it interesting that when I ask foreign correspondents and people who cover stuff over there why the Iraqis think we're there, the first thing they say is oil, and here, oil is hardly ever mentioned as a reason.

You hear it in almost every conversation, "They're here for our oil." There's a deep kind of suspicion in Iraq about oil. The Brits were there for a significant number of years and, I think, controlled the oil for a while, too, so I think there's just this attitude that you can't trust a foreigner. I hear that phrase time and again, "You can't trust a foreigner." I think there's reason not to trust the foreigner in the history of the Arab world, because the Arabs often have been manipulated and deceived. I think Iraqis are very aware of their history. They're very conscious of what's happened in the past, and there's no reason to think that it's going to be different in the future.

ANTHONY SHADID is the Islamic affairs correspondent for the *Washington Post*. Since September 11, 2001, he has reported from Egypt, Lebanon, Iraq, the Persian Gulf, Europe, Afghanistan, Pakistan, Israel, and Palestine, where he was wounded in the back while covering fighting in the West Bank. In March 2003, weeks before the US invasion, he traveled to Iraq, his third visit to the country. He remained in Baghdad during the invasion, the fall of Saddam Hussein, and the war's aftermath. He left in the spring of 2004, then returned later that year.

Before the *Post*, Shadid worked for the *Boston Globe* in Washington, covering diplomacy and the State Department. He began his career at the Associated Press in Milwaukee, New York, Los Angeles, and Cairo, where he worked as a Middle East correspondent from 1995 to 1999. He is a native of Oklahoma City, where his grandparents emigrated from Lebanon, and a graduate of the University of Wisconsin–Madison.

Shadid was awarded the Pulitzer Prize for International Reporting in 2004 for his dispatches from Iraq. That year, he was also the recipient of the American Society of Newspaper Editors' Award for deadline writing and the Overseas Press Club's Hal Boyle Award for best newspaper or wire service reporting from abroad. In 2003 Shadid was awarded the George Polk Award for foreign reporting for a series of dispatches from the Middle East while at the *Globe*. In 1997 Shadid was awarded a citation by the Overseas Press Club for his work on "Islam's Challenge." The four-part series, published by the AP in December 1996, formed the basis of his book *Legacy of the Prophet: Despots, Democrats, and the New Politics of Islam*, published by Westview Press in December 2000. His second book, *Night Draws Near: Iraq's People in the Shadow of America's War*, will be published in September 2005 by Henry Holt.

NOTES

1. Hussein attacked Kuwait in 1990 after claiming that the Kuwaitis were overproducing oil and thereby destroying Iraq's economy and that they were stealing oil via slant drilling into Iraq's Rumaila oil field.

2. A *Washington Post* profile of the Kurds at http://www.washingtonpost.com/ wp-srv/inatl/daily/feb99/kurdprofile.htm describes them as fifteen to twenty million "largely Sunni Muslims with their own language and culture living in the generally contiguous areas of Turkey, Iraq, Iran, Armenia and Syria" collectively called Kurdistan. The Kurds seek their own state and have clashed with the nations in which their territories lie, including Iraq. In 1988 the Iraqis launched a poison gas attack on the town of Hallabjah and killed five thousand people.

3. The Baath Party, of which Saddam Hussein was a member, follows a secular ideology that advocates pan-Arabic unity, Arab socialism, nationalism, and militarism. http://en.wikipedia.org/wiki/Ba'ath_Party.

4. The Supreme Council for Islamic Revolution in Iraq (SCIRI) is a Shiite group that was formed in Iran in 1982 to oppose Iraqi aggression against Iran. After Saddam's fall, SCIRI led the Shiite coalition that dominated Iraq's elections. SCIRI's military arm, a militia known before as the Badr Brigade but now calling itself the Badr Organization, has unprecedented authority. Although the Badr Organization claims it is now operating as a political group, many accuse it of kidnapping and killing Sunnis, particularly clerics, in sectarian violence.

5. Basra is a city of almost one million inhabitants where oil is refined and exported.

6. Anthony Shadid, *Night Draws Near: Iraq's People in the Shadow of America's War* (New York: Henry Holt, 2005).

7. Paul Bremer was named presidential envoy to Iraq on May 6, 2003. As head of the Coalition Provisional Authority in Iraq, he was the administrator for the US-led occupation government until the handover of political power to the Iraqis in June 2004. The Coalition Provisional Authority appointed the Iraqi Governing Council, the provisional government of Iraq, which was made up of a group of Iraqi political, religious, and tribal leaders.

8. Anthony Shadid, "Preaching the Rule of Law in a Tribal Land: An Iraqi Governor's Challenge: Making Democracy Work," *Washington Post*, April 16, 2005.

9. Anthony Shadid, *Legacy of the Prophet: Despots, Democrats, and the New Politics of Islam* (Boulder, CO: Westview, 2001).

10. The Muslim Brotherhood rejects secularism and advocates a return to the precepts of the Koran. In a September 11, 2004, *Washington Post* article, "In Search of Friends among Foes," reporters John Mintz and Douglas Farah write: "The Brotherhood . . . is a sprawling and secretive society with followers in more than 70 countries. It is dedicated to creating an Islamic civilization that harks back to the caliphates of the 7th and 8th centuries, one that would segregate women from public life and scorn nonbelievers. In some nations—Egypt, Algeria, Syria, Sudan—the Brotherhood has fomented Islamic revolution. In the Palestinian territories, the Brotherhood created the Islamic Resistance Movement, or HAMAS, which became known for its suicide bombings of Israelis. Yet it is also a sophisticated and diverse organization that appeals to many Muslims worldwide and sometime advocates peaceful persuasion, not violent revolt. Some of its supporters went on to help found al Qaeda, while others launched one of the largest college student groups in the United States. . . . They run hundreds of mosques and dozens of businesses engaging in ventures such as real estate development and banking." http://www .washingtonpost.com/ac2/wp-dyn/A12823-2004Sep10?language=printer.

11. A fatwa is an Islamic religious edict or proclamation; in this case one that targeted the journalist for death for exposing an al Qaeda cell.

12. The Coalition Provisional Authority, headed by Paul Bremer (who was appointed by President Bush), took over being in charge of reconstructing Iraq from the Office of Reconstruction and Humanitarian Assistance and was dissolved in June 2004.

13. Former Baathist and interim Iraqi prime minister Iyad Allawi is, the BBC reports in "Who's Who in Iraq: Iyad Allawi" (May 28, 2004), "one of a U.S.-backed clique of secular Iraqi opposition figures who lived in exile until the fall of Saddam Hussein's regime in April 2003." A secular Shia Muslim, Allawi is head of the Iraqi National Accord Party in the Iraqi National Assembly.

14. Bigger Thomas, the main character in James Baldwin's *Native Son*, is a poor, uneducated young black man who accidentally kills a white woman, his first act of asserting power against the whites who have brutalized and oppressed him. The book's title implies that Bigger's story is common to American culture and that he is, indeed, a "native son."

15. Grand Ayatollah Ali Husaini Sistani was born in Iran and now lives in Najaf, Iraq. A very traditional Shiite cleric and the Shiites' top spiritual leader, he is considered one of the most influential religious figures in the Middle East. In chapter 20 in this book, Knight Ridder's foreign correspondent Hannah Allam says that before he was elected, Iraq's prime minister Ibrahim al-Jafaari told her: "We're not going to set up a theocracy, but at the same time we'll probably see a more conservative government and a more prominent role for Islam. . . . People are turning to religion and they reflected that by voting for a list that was backed by the most revered Ayatollah Sistani." Allam says that for Prime Minister al-Jafaari, "that's a mandate." Sistani's Web site is http://www.sistani.org/.

THE WAR
CORRESPONDENTS

"IT'S MINE, THE WHOLE GODDAMNED STORY IS MINE!"

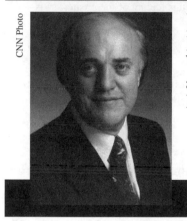

PETER ARNETT
International/
War Correspondent
and Author
Interviewed February 2005

Now seventy years old, Peter Arnett is still the baddest bad boy of American journalism. For decades now, he has been a lightning rod for criticism in all kinds of circles, including the one inhabited by other eminent journalists. But after spending five hours interviewing him, I can definitely say that the last thing Arnett cares about is winning popularity contests. What he really cares about is good journalism, and in that department, most, if not all, of his critics have to take a backseat. No other war correspondent of his or subsequent generations has achieved "Mr. Peter's" international news icon status. His career stats are spectacular: Covered thirty-five wars. Spent thirteen years in Vietnam and filed more

than three thousand stories. Spent twenty years at the Associated Press
and eighteen years at CNN. Won fifty-seven major journalism awards,
including a Pulitzer. Wrote his autobiography, a *New York Times* "Book
of the Year."

Arnett has had more than his share of defining moments, but the
mother of all moments occurred during the first Gulf War.

> I remember the day everyone had left except for the last two CNN staffers. It
> was day three and a rocket hit the al Rasheed hotel near where they were sitting
> and they said, "We're out of here." So they left and I stood in the foyer—the al
> Rasheed has this huge foyer about a block long, all marble and polished wood.
> There was one guy behind the desk, and I had this feeling of the greatest satis-
> faction and I figured "It's mine, the whole goddamned story is mine." You fan-
> tasize in your dreams about covering a war by yourself; it can't happen. But
> there I was covering it by myself.

And then, during the second Gulf War, in a coincidence almost too bizarre
to believe, he relived his once-in-a-lifetime experience: "When the
second war came and I'm on the roof of the information ministry and running around and I was by myself again with NBC, I thought, "This is
crazy." In fact, I just said, "This is ludicrous." I really felt it."

As a journalist and a man, Arnett is entirely self-made. He came from
practically nowhere—Invercargill, New Zealand. From there, he put on
his thousand-league boots and went to Asia, where he eventually wound
up in Vietnam. While he's not physically imposing, there's a real tough-
ness to him. As a journalist, he has always been, I'm sure, as mercenary
as necessary to get his story or beat the competition. He also has the gift
of being able to go native wherever he is. He has a very healthy ego, but
he'll be the first to tell you exactly what he's done wrong and when, as
well as what he really thinks.

Every extraordinary person I've ever met has possessed a distinct
combination of extreme characteristics. In Peter's case, I picked up on
two. First of all, he is extraordinarily energetic. He's seventy but acts and
moves like a person at least two decades younger. Second, he's fearless.
He refers to risking his life as "playing the odds." "I don't mind playing
the odds," he says. "I do it all the time. It's not a noble act to undergo a
degree of risk."

We talked in his New York apartment, which was filled with beautiful
antiques and artifacts from Asia. As each hour went by, I realized that I
was talking to a journalist who was literally the tribe's memory for the
Vietnam War and subsequent US military engagements. He began the

interview talking about General Westmoreland, who commanded the US troops in Vietnam. Arnett, who is an American now but was a citizen of New Zealand at the time, roundly criticized Westmoreland during the war. Westmoreland didn't like him, either.

Westmoreland would say about journalists like me, "They're not American, how can we trust them?" Years later in a conversation with him I said, "You never gave me an interview, General." He said, "You weren't an American, so I couldn't really associate with you." And I said, "But New Zealand had ten thousand troops there." He replied by saying, "Well, maybe that's why. I didn't trust them, either."

I kept in touch over the years with Westmoreland at Vietnam assessment conferences. I covered his abortive run for governor of South Carolina. I saw him a couple of years ago at his retirement home in Charleston, South Carolina. He's suffering from Parkinson's. We came to our peace a long time ago. In the end, I found that I had more in common with him than differences. I don't think any other journalist has bothered with him.

But about the coverage, in the early to mid-1960s, the lines of controversy were already developing. The Kennedy administration was saying, "We are in Vietnam to save democracy. We are in Vietnam to prevent Communist expansion and what we're doing is necessary." We in the press didn't argue with that. We were saying, "What you're doing is not working." They didn't like that. The Pentagon didn't like it. The Pentagon was under fire directly as a consequence of our field reports. When a military action in the delta or the field went terribly wrong, the Pentagon was responsible in the end because their advisers hadn't done an adequate job. When advisers like Lt. Col. John Paul Vann began complaining publicly, it became much more than a tempest in a teacup.

It was epitomized by an exchange I had with Adm. Harry Felt, who was the commander-in-chief of US forces in the Pacific in late 1962, early 1963. He was giving a press conference in Saigon and I was asking him some critical questions and he turned to me and said, "Arnett, why don't you get on the team?" That epitomized it: Why aren't you guys on the team. That was the thinking: We're all in this together so why are you taking potshots at the United States? We're all in this together and we've got to get through this. It was a little like the War on Terrorism today. Officials would ask the media, "What are you bitching about? This is in our national interest to do what we have to do." Our view as journalists

was, "Hey that's fine, but you're not doing it right. It's not working." Officials didn't like the criticism and they didn't act on any of it. The other
attitude toward the press was, "In World War II everyone was on the team,
what's wrong with you guys?"

Another issue was their message management back in the States. Up
to the mid-1960s the attitude was, "This is a patriotic war, we're all in this
against the Commies. Our boys are dying." You heard this message
echoed when Rumsfeld went on *Meet the Press* on Sunday, February 2,
2005, and answered Tim Russert's question about setting a timetable for
withdrawing our troops by saying, "The courage of our troops and the sacrifice of those that have fallen and were wounded is important," and that
when the troops can leave is "not knowable." That's what Defense Secretary Robert McNamara said in 1966. He said, "We've lost a lot of people"
to justify continuing the war. Rumsfeld said, "Our country has invested a
lot of lives, a lot of heartbreak." He essentially used the same words. Of
course, Rumsfeld says a lot of things to justify his criticized policies.

**What did you say to Admiral Felt when he asked you why you weren't
on the team?**

His attitude didn't matter one iota to me or to the other reporters at the
Associated Press [AP] or to the rest of the media in Saigon. We had
reality in front of us every day. The story was right there, either on the
streets of Saigon with the political story or with the advisers in the field
or with the Vietnamese military and civilians who we knew. It was also
with the American troops after they arrived. We were talking to them, we
were in the field with them, and we were riding in their helicopters. We
went into action with them in the paddy fields and the jungles. We were
reporting the real story. We also had a lot of superb photographers. They
had the pictures and we had the stories, so who was going to successfully
mess with us? To mess with us was to mess with the truth. So our view
was, "What the hell's Washington saying? We're seeing it all; we're going
out and risking our lives to get the real story."

I'd be in as many as six different war locations every week. I had
bylines from all over the country. We'd go anywhere, anytime, as far as we
could reach. Routinely. It was this willingness to cover all the stories that
saved us and our reputations because whatever President Lyndon Johnson
or Henry Kissinger (his national security advisor at the time) said, in the
end, when the Pentagon was assessing anything about the United States,
they had to ultimately acknowledge that we were there on the ground. The

thing about our stories that was most effective was that the AP had three thousand member newspapers around the country, and on any given day, the AP reports would mention twenty or thirty GIs from different parts of the country and every hometown paper would put those stories in. Our reporting was everywhere. I was one of the primary AP reporters, and some of my stories were played really big across the country. That triggered an unstoppable momentum of attention, something like the media frenzy you sometimes see caused by cable news today.

I wrote in my book *Live from the Battlefield*[1] about occasions when Lyndon Johnson was calling publishers and calling in the AP president and complaining that the momentum was too great and that the AP was challenging his view of the war and to stop it. AP's president, Wes Gallagher, would then ask the president, "What has he written that's not right?" "Well, generally the attitude . . ." "What do you mean the attitude, what has he written that's not right?" "Well, the attitude . . ." "What do you mean 'the attitude'? Give me a few examples of incorrect reporting. The guy's written eight hundred stories in the last six months; show me the inaccurate ones." They couldn't.

You were well supported by your bosses here in the United States.

They did support us, but my boss, Wes Gallagher, did warn me sometimes, "Peter, don't ever make a mistake. You make one mistake and you're finished because you are so divisive." I had few differences with my bosses. But one changed my life. That was the case where Kevin Buckley came into my life. He'd been writing for *Newsweek* in Saigon, and I'd see him occasionally, but there was no big social interchange between reporters because we were all too busy. Then the United States invaded the famous "parrot's beak" area in Cambodia in late 1970 during President Nixon's term. The action was controversial because it widened the war. I was with a US armored unit that went to this town called Snuol. During the battle, Snuol was blown apart. Unlike Vietnamese towns, this one was prosperous, with jewelry stores and other shops. The US soldiers thoroughly looted it. The AP actually killed the story. So I leaked that to Kevin Buckley and he did a whole page on it for *Newsweek*, and then the president of the AP had to apologize. It didn't ruin my relations with Gallagher, AP's president. He's a wonderful man and when I came back from Vietnam he promoted me and was good to me, but when he left the AP, I was out.

Why did they kill the story?

The murderous Kent State incident had happened when campuses across the country were rioting and protesting the Cambodian invasion. At Kent State, several students were killed by National Guardsmen while protesting the bombing of Cambodia. The editors of the AP deemed the situation so inflammatory that they wanted to keep down any reporting from Vietnam that could inflame it. They felt that my story dealing with GIs looting and killing civilians in Cambodia was too inflammatory. It was the first time US soldiers had been in Cambodia, and they just went crazy. It was the first time they'd ever seen anything worth looting. There was nothing in Vietnam worth looting. But in this Cambodian rubber plantation town, there were motor scooters, there was jewelry, and all sorts of things. It was a prosperous little community because it hadn't previously been in the war. The US soldiers were invading a country that was comparatively prosperous, and so they were loading motorcycles on their tanks. I wrote the story. There was a UPI [United Press International] man with me at the scene, Leon Daniels, a competitive and excellent journalist. We wrote basically identical stories because we had seen the same things. The AP killed my story and killed the pictures and messaged me: "We have to be aware of inflammatory information. We have to be more careful of what we report from the field." The UPI ran Leon's story. The *Washington Post* used his story as an editorial saying, "We're publishing this as an editorial today, we don't need any further commentary," because it was American soldiers just going wild and the *Post* was essentially saying, "What the fuck are we doing there? Let's get the hell out. What is this?"

I didn't leak the story to *Newsweek* for personal aggrandizement. I thought it was really important to note that, after all these years, the AP had actually killed a story. They hadn't done it before. It damaged my career with the AP, but I think it was worth it in the end to stand clear and say, "What are we doing interfering with the story? It was a really a significant development in the war, that US troops were running wild." We needed to report it. There was the other angle, too. The US High Command had been warning the South Vietnamese military for years to get along with the locals, to stop looting their villages, so that they would have a chance to win their hearts and minds. But here our troops were doing it.

It's just like Abu Ghraib or the prison abuse stories in Iraq. What the hell are our soldiers doing? We can't allow things like that to happen. If you have people who do it, get them out of the service. I mean, what the hell is going on? In Vietnam, they did move against the soldiers involved in the My Lai massacre.[2] The military in Vietnam were, I think, more aware of the Geneva conventions than they ever have been in Iraq.

Talking a little about the nature of the coverage, up to 1965, we were expected to refer to the Vietcong[3] as terrorists. It was just standard procedure. You could say "Vietcong" or "Vietcong terrorists." There was never an attempt or a willingness to qualify the Vietcong in terms of being efficient or able or loyal or idealistic fighters. The Vietcong were like the World Trade Center bombers; they were terrorists. Now the World Trade Center bombers, I think, were just plain terrorists. What did they represent? Nihilism. Total destruction. They weren't working for any particular government. What is their ideology? Destruction of the status quo and returning the world to the Middle Ages. Bin Laden, what does he represent? Himself. So I think you could argue that it's hard to put the destruction of the World Trade Center in a politically heroic light. But the Vietcong [VC] had inherited this nationalist war against French colonialism. There were historical precedents for the war. But US officials at the time were interested in portraying the VC in the worst light. So when David Halberstam wrote pieces for the *New York Times Magazine* early in the war talking about the Vietcong's military prowess, his assessments were not popular in official circles. And when one of our reporters, John Wheeler, in early 1965 attributed qualities of bravery and military cunning to the Vietcong, he was admonished in a teleprinter message from our headquarters in New York: "What are you doing? How can you endow these terrorists with those qualities?" I would frequently write long assessments of the war's progress for the AP that were at odds with the optimistic views of US officials. The US High Command would complain, "You do these assessments of the war and you don't have General Westmoreland's view." I said, "To hell with it, I know more than he does. I go to more places than he does." And they said, "That's unacceptable!"

Certainly by the mid- to late 1960s, my assessments were getting wide usage. I was earning the trust of my editors with the many war stories I was writing. You could see that the war was quickly changing as US units were committed to fight in Vietnam in 1965. Some units were quickly bloodied. A brigade from the First Cavalry Division fought a brutal battle in the Ia Drang Valley. Two hundred and forty-seven Americans were killed there. You could hardly say they were killed by terrorists.

The Pentagon started conceding that the North Vietnamese were not terrorists, that they had full-fledged regiments and divisions that had fought the French at Dien Bien Phu[4] and beaten the pants off them. So then you got a more realistic view coming through. In the end, the reverses were so obvious in Vietnam. There were lots of positive stories about bravery on the part of the GIs, but you couldn't put them in any kind of positive light in terms of effectiveness. It's like today in Iraq. US soldiers are sometimes performing bravely and their commitment is recognized, but that doesn't change the overall disastrous nature of the situation. During Vietnam, the Pentagon, however unhappy it felt about the coverage, never did interfere to any great degree in our reporting. Secretary of State Dean Rusk is on record saying, "We could have introduced censorship, but then that would have brought in so many other factors and we didn't want to do it. Maybe we should have, but we didn't."

By early 1965, the United States was desperately searching for ways to use the South Vietnamese with greater effectiveness against the Vietcong. At that point, the South Vietnamese were losing eight or nine hundred men a week. It was a bloodbath. They were being overrun and overrun. But the US military had various tricks up their sleeves that we had fun writing about. One was a device attached to a helicopter that they called a "people-sniffer" that could detect ammonia from urine as it flew over the jungle. The resultant bombing killed a lot of cattle and pigs in addition to the bad guys. Then they started experimenting with nonlethal gas, and we followed up on that story. Horst Faas, the great AP war photographer, took pictures of South Vietnamese soldiers wearing gas masks during a military operation. He came back from the field and said, "They've used it, this gas, what a story." We could not get any comment from the military authorities. People I knew in the military said, "It's secret." So we ran the story anyway, and the international press jumped on it and played it up: "U.S. gassing Vietnamese." But it was a nonlethal, souped-up riot gas. They were basically pumping it into caves and tunnels and, as people ran out, they'd mow them down. After my story came out, the Pentagon raked me over the coals. In later Pentagon studies, that story was used as an example of my ill reporting. Even though they assessed my reporting overall as very good, they looked at this report as "Peter Arnett overdid it with that story." They felt it was a story that was hyped in a way that was detrimental to the US effort. My feeling and the AP's feeling was that it wasn't hyped, that the use of such weaponry was controversial. It was actually one of the stories that won me the Pulitzer Prize in 1966. The Pentagon didn't publicly address the gas issue, but eventually they stopped using it. By 1971 the United States had signed the international agreement not to use any riot control agents or other gases in war.

I did another controversial story that same year after one of our local photographers told us he'd learned that a big action was going to happen the next day about thirty-five miles south of Saigon and that many people would die. His English wasn't good, and when we got it translated we learned he'd been down to the Mekong Delta town called My Tho and his Vietnamese military contacts had told him, "Oh, we're going out tomorrow and a lot of us are going to die." As we queried him, it came out that they were actually going to be part of a movie being made for the United States Information Agency [USIA].[5]

So I went down there the next day thinking, "This is great." The traffic was blocked way down Route 1, the main road south, so I walked along a few hundred meters and I heard all this shooting and saw smoke in the air. I walked into a field where there were about two hundred Vietnamese shooting into the ground, and American civilians were running around with movie equipment. So I asked, "What are you guys doing?" They told me they were making a movie to promote the idea that the South Vietnamese forces were really effective. So they had fake Vietcong and guys running around setting the whole thing up.

I said to the senior producer, "This is a dangerous goddamned area," and he says, "Don't worry, we've got three battalions out there so the VC won't get into the act." I wrote a tongue-in-cheek piece that said they were doing a movie about the great South Vietnamese fighting forces when in fact the South Vietnamese hadn't been capable of fighting a real battle. This was a game of let's pretend. My story was well used, and the resultant dustup killed the project. That angered Carl Rowan, the liberal columnist, who was then the USIA director. Up to his death he was pissed off at me. He was the most liberal guy, but he felt that that was the biggest blemish on his record.

> **Bill Moyers, who's a big proponent of a free press and being able to report all kinds of things that are hard to report these days, particularly on this current war situation, was working for Johnson at the time, and he was not happy with what you were reporting.**

He was specifically angry at Morley Safer and me in the early years of the American war. Morley Safer, a Canadian who was a correspondent for CBS, covered a story with the US Marines that created controversy. Soon after the marines had got to Danang, they'd gone to secure the outer area of the Danang airport where there was a troublesome little village called Cam Ne. So they went in and Morley Safer went along and they burned all the houses down with their Zippo lighters. Morley did a passionate story, "Oh, the women and children . . ." He pulled out all the stops, masterfully using TV's powers of emotive reporting. I could never write a story like that. We couldn't do it on a wire service. The effectiveness of my stories was in the fact that there was no emotion; it was all just the hard-driving boom, boom, boom, boom of war. I envied Morley his skills. About a decade ago, *60 Minutes* revealed a couple of documents in which Moyers had specifically said back then, "We can't trust Arnett and Safer because neither of them are American." Moyers was a young, born-again Christian who worked with and believed in everything President Johnson said. But that was a long time ago. Moyers has since well proved his dedication to a free media.

Johnson did attempt to influence publishers and the AP. In 1965 he had the FBI run an investigation on me, John Chancellor, and one of the best-known liberal columnists at the time—Joseph Kraft. This came out in congressional testimony in 1973. He was looking for any kind of dirt. John Chancellor at that point covered the White House for NBC. It was just Lyndon Johnson's paranoia. But that was relatively benign. In another country, we could have been shot in the back or something. I was out in the field alone all the time, so it would have been easy to wipe me out, but I never figured the US government was in the business of assassination.

So we had the gas story and the USIA story. Then came the first military story that angered the Pentagon. It was called "Supply Column 21" and it happened in August 1965. The marines had launched what they called "Operation Starlight," invading a peninsula south of the then-small US base of Chu Lai so that it could be expanded. Eventually, it became a huge base.

There were no reporters around when this operation was launched. On that particular day, they had faked out a big press contingent in Danang by inviting them to go north with Gen. Lew Walt on an inspection tour of Hue. When we learned about the operation, I hitchhiked on a military transport to Danang and then a pal of mine flew me down from Danang to Chu Lai. Tim Page, the photographer, had arrived, too. We got on a chopper and flew over the peninsula area and saw fires and smoke. The chopper was carrying several drums of gasoline and a crewman had told us, "We're looking for someone to give it to. We know there's resupply needed." So they saw these armored vehicles sitting there and they said, "Let's go down and dump it." We landed and started rolling the drums off the chopper, and suddenly out of the woods came these

American marines, bandaged and dirty and carrying wounded. They threw the wounded onto the chopper and took off for a medical assistance hospital, and we stayed on the ground.

What had happened was that the vehicles were part of a resupply column with water, rations, and ammo that had landed from a freighter. They'd gotten lost in the swamps the previous night. The VC attacked and blew up three-quarters of their vehicles and killed about twenty Americans. As we moved through, we saw bodies lying in the mud and all these survivors hiding in one vehicle. I took pictures and wrote notes. Late that afternoon, reinforcements came in, and I departed and wrote the story that night. It was well used because I had taken pictures and had interviews with the soldiers who talked about hand-to-hand fighting with the VC. The story was also prominent in *Newsweek*; they used the double fold with all my pictures. The *New York Times* put it on page one. It was a story about the first big setback for the marines in Vietnam. There was no doubt about it, the VC had outmaneuvered them, and it showed how armored vehicles were worthless there. It also showed that the VC were capable of ingenuity that resulted in all these dead Americans.

The Marine Corps was very unhappy with the story and Gen. Wallace Greene put out a denial. They repeated the denial at a Saigon briefing a few days later. I happened to be there, and I said, "C'mon you guys . . ." "No, no we deny it." None of the press corps bought the denial. They said, "Peter was there, he's got all the pictures, we know it's true." No one doubted what I'd written or photographed.

Later that year, the AP invited General Greene to its board of directors' meeting. The AP had put together a slide show of that whole operation and Greene saw it and said, "You know, I didn't know that." Who was he kidding? My story and Morley Safer's piece convinced the marines the press had it in for them. So I was not popular with the marines, but I still kept going there. I wrote many stories that emphasized the marines' bravery and ability, particularly during the long siege of Khe Sanh in 1968.[6] I have nothing to apologize for.

At another level, I had very good relations with some army division commanders because many of the stories I wrote turned out to be morale-building accounts of soldiers in action. I covered GIs launching patrols, going into swamps, and demonstrating bravery and ability. I wrote what I saw, and I saw a lot commendable behavior. So like Iraq today, there's a lot of good stuff happening, but the overall picture is disastrous. There were a lot of decent American officials and soldiers in Vietnam, but the whole strategy was flawed. It wasn't going to get anywhere, and the United States wasn't in a position to fight the VC to the end. Fortunately, in Iraq, everyone realizes that the war is not for the United States to win, that acceptable victory can come only with the Iraqi armed forces. It took years for everyone to realize they couldn't win in Vietnam. Everyone's waiting for the Iraqis to say, "We're ready to bear the burden," so the United States can get the hell out of there.

What is a foreign correspondent's mission?

Telling the truth is the mission of all reporters, foreign or domestic. It is being absolutely realistic about the endeavors, first of all, of our own government, and then of endeavors that all governments engage in or support. If you're an American or you work for the American media, you're looking at what your own government is doing and who it is supporting. The mainstream media should be the eyes and ears of the public in a democracy, and it should demand accountability of all officials at home and abroad.

Wars have been fought since the beginning of human time and have been written about either in legend or as eyewitness accounts. Wars shape our history, and the most dramatic accounts of conflict shape our literature. So a reporter goes to war knowing the great tradition he is following and, if he has taken the trouble to read, is well aware that violence comes with the territory. Expecting blood on your boots does not make the reality any less easy to take, but you're there for a purpose, to write the story of war with the same skills and balance that you would any other story. Actually, writing the story every evening of war is a cathartic experience. You feel you are fulfilling your mission and passing on to your public what you believe they need to know about what is going on. The World Trade Center attack was a severe test for the media. Three thousand people died in the most traumatic of disasters. You have to keep your head when you cover that kind of tragedy.

Plenty of people have said to me, "How can you cover death and destruction for so many years?" Well, look at the World Trade Center. I was here in New York City at the time. I'd come in from Istanbul the previous night. I saw the morning events on television and was down there in the afternoon. The point is, what is worse than that? It was the most frightening sight of all the things I've seen. Looking at mass death, my feeling then was, "How do you tell the story?" I was freelancing then, so I did a few radio broadcasts for Radio America and an overseas company just to talk about it. Being a journalist and being in a position to describe such events is a cathartic thing. If I'm driving and there's a car wreck and I go by and there's blood on the road and a car's mangled, I feel "What a waste." If I were a regular beat reporter I'd stop the car, go and write about it, and say, "Maybe my story will have people driving smarter the next goddamned time." That's why you do it. I covered most of the wars of the past fifty years. I kept sharpening my reactive reflexes every time.

Toward the end of my career with the AP, they were reluctant to use me on big war stories. I think they didn't want to have me killed somewhere. And they had a whole team of younger reporters. They wanted to bring them up to speed without me hogging the story. I don't hesitate to admit that I wanted to be the best in anything journalistic and that at the AP I learned by writing all those stories how to achieve that. Of course, joining CNN was a whole other deal because I was going into a new medium and a new way of presenting information, a new way of covering war.

You said covering the Gulf War for CNN was the most controversial thing you've done.

Which one?

Peter, you've been in trouble so many times you can't even remember.

I was talking to my ex-wife Nina some time ago, and she said to me, "Peter, that second war in Iraq, you blew it, you ruined your career." I said, "No, I didn't. Nina, even you in Saigon in 1965 were telling me I shouldn't criticize Westmoreland. Over the years I've been told I shouldn't do this, I shouldn't do that, and now you're saying that because I shouldn't have talked to Iraqi television, I'm ruined. Come on, people have been saying I shouldn't all my life."

Why did you apologize for appearing on Iraqi television?

Initially, NBC put out a statement of support saying, "Peter Arnett can say what he likes. We don't feel his interview was that terribly outrageous and we're going to stick with him." I'd had an arrangement with *National Geographic Explorer* that was providing news documentaries for MSNBC. They had a half-hour program on Sunday evenings and were seeking to boost it up a bit. I'd done several documentary-style stories on the Afghanistan war, long pieces for high-definition television. I produced them on the road, an hour a week, it was fun, and I had a good team with me. *Explorer* got in touch in 2002 to do some documentaries about me in the field. They wanted me to go to Iraq because it was in the news at the time and I was experienced there. They sent three cameras with me and I was filmed talking to people and getting around Baghdad, and then I'd be interviewed regularly. I was aware of what National Geographic was all about. You can show breasts from Africa, but don't get political, don't get controversial. After my return to the United States, the war bells started tolling and conflict was approaching and they called me in and said, "We want to follow three families before, during, and after the war. Would you be willing to go?" And I said yes.

They gave me the same team that I had gone in with earlier, including the producer, Charles Poe, a very competent, persuasive young man. I met with them and I said, "Look guys, we're going to be there through the war and I'm willing to go, but no reporting. I don't mind doing some commentary but I've given up action reporting. The younger guys can have it, I don't want to do it." "OK, of course you don't want to do it. Understood. No reporting." "But I'll be happy to do all the interviews with you and so on." "OK, fine." So just before we go, they call me down and say, "MSNBC wants to talk to you." I go see MSNBC and they want to give me radios and cameras and I say, "No, no reporting." "Please." "No, I'm not going to compete with CNN and Fox and your own people to cover the war. I've done it, I've set the standard or whatever I've done, and there's no way I can top what I did before. I'm not going to do it. But if you want me to do some commentary, OK." "Well, OK."

I gave that message to *National Geographic Explorer* just before I set out. I said to them, "You don't want me to do any reporting, I'm too controversial. Let's do the limited arrangement we have, following these three families through the war." It was a great idea, and it would have been great if it had worked out.

We get over there, and Charles Poe says, "Do you mind if we do an assessment of things every few days? We'll follow you around and do an angle of the story and send it off, because I'd love to use it for MSNBC." "But we're doing something for a Sunday evening hour, right?" "Well, would you do this in addition to that?" "OK, I'll do it." Charles was very persuasive. So we'd go and visit some hospital or follow up an interesting angle and we'd do these five-minute pieces that MSNBC would run. As tensions grew in Baghdad with the beginning of the war imminent, there was some nervousness on the part of the American media. They all started peeling off—CBS, ABC, and then finally NBC. I reminded Charles, "I'm not going to do any reporting." When NBC left, leaving only CNN on the ground, the bureau left behind two live cameras. One of them was on top of the information ministry. It was just sitting there, running. The Iraqis were so unsophisticated they didn't even notice. I didn't think they were aware of it, but if they were, somebody had been paid off to let the cameras run. So you could see them looking over the city and feeding live pictures into NBC headquarters from Baghdad twenty-four hours a day.

My team and I had moved to the Palestine Hotel. Poe placed a concealed camera in one of our rooms. It was focused directly on the presidential palace area just across the Tigris River from us. We figured the palace would be the first US bombing target.

So I was doing some commentary for MSNBC, and when the war began, Charles prevailed upon me and I agreed to do a live report. My one report led to another and then a flood of reports from early morning on the *Today Show* with Katie Couric and Matt Lauer to late at night on NBC and MSNBC. The world was in a state of war hysteria. MSNBC's ratings went up several times in the first few days.

It was old home week for me. Here I was back covering a war pretty much exclusively again. I was just talking about what was going on. I was standing on top of the information ministry, and let's face it, I was enjoying it. The information ministry was bombed one morning and everything was blown off the roof. So I stood there and all around me was this chaos, and I would just say, "Yes, Katie, this is going on . . ." I was having a ball. Meanwhile, I knew a lot of colleagues from Europe who had stayed, and I was giving them interviews all the time. I was having fun talking about journalism and what it was like to be there. Many of the reporters said, "We're here simply because you were here in the first war."

Iraqi officials had been watching me, and those who had given me access to Iraq's deputy prime minister, Tarik Aziz, several times came to me one evening and said, "Look, we've got Iraqi satellite television here, how about saying a few words?" And I thought, "I'll do it, fuck it." After all, I wasn't bound by the old rules of the mainstream media, and I didn't have any contract with MSNBC. I was just helping them out. My contract was with National Geographic to do a documentary on three Iraqi families.

When I gave the interview, NBC's reaction was professional. The top executives figured I had the right to do pretty much anything I wanted to. But they expressed concern about the reaction of Fox cable. "Otherwise," they told me, "you're clear to keep reporting." This was Sunday morning. That afternoon, I learned that Fox did a whole hour-long broadcast attacking me. All day they were kicking me to pieces. There were various ideological reasons for the attack, but also I think they saw this as an opportunity to level the playing field. Fox had no one in Baghdad. I was helping MSNBC boost its ratings.

NBC called me and said, "Look, we're going to announce that we're not using you. It's just too hot." They got thirty thousand e-mails from viewers and affiliates. NBC said, "The problem is not public relations; our affiliates don't want to use you. If our affiliates won't use you, they won't use the *Today Show*; it's that serious now." Later I said I was "shocked and awed" by NBC's decision. In fact, it was worse, because I wasn't the only one affected. I felt bad for my *National Geographic Explorer* team and my family, which has been bouncing around in the wake of my professional controversies for forty years. I composed myself and I said to NBC, "Look, I want to personally bow out," because I felt that I had a pretty good on-air relationship with Brokaw[7] and Katie. It had really been a bold and exciting ten days. And they asked, "What are you going to say?" I said, "I'm sorry that this happened."

When I was waiting to go on the *Today Show*, Katie was interviewing the wife of a serviceman who had been killed in Nasariya, and the woman was crying and saying, "I'm pregnant and I'm going to have a baby in two months, but I know my husband died for a great cause." It was just the most soul-wrenching interview. So when Matt Lauer[8] came out and said, "I have to announce that we're not going to use any of Peter Arnett's material anymore, he did an interview with Iraqi television," I knew what I had to say. It was with that woman's face in my mind that I said, "I'm sorry I did it, I'm sorry I made everyone so unhappy." I was sorry for that particular moment. I wasn't in a position to sell anyone my side of the story by saying, "I was here to help you guys out. You guys didn't pay me." I was ready to apologize. It wasn't easy, but I got through it and I think it cut back the controversy. The reaction of my foreign colleagues was totally supportive. I was deluged with job offers.

> **You're saying that you apologized for the distress, not really for what you said. In your interview with Iraqi TV, you were basically saying what the Pentagon was saying, that they had met with greater Iraqi resistance than they had expected.**

I know that, but it was the whole idea of giving an interview to Iraqi television, the enemy television. It was impossible for me in that *Today Show* appearance to explain, "Look, I'm a commentator, I'll talk to anyone and I thought I had every right to talk to Iraqi television." Everyone thought I was working for NBC, on staff. And this war was very different from others the United States had fought. It was more like a coup d'état. Before the war started, US officials had offered Saddam and his family the opportunity to leave and to seek sanctuary in any other country that would take them. The Pentagon promised to rehire any Iraqi army officers and men who refused to fight against the invading US force. The US Air Force was dropping cell phones behind the lines and inviting Iraqis to call in any interesting information. The celebrity Iraqi information minister "Baghdad Bob" al-Sahaf was released twelve hours after the United States picked him up. He resettled in Dubai to become a star on Arab TV. Al-Sahaf arranged the Iraqi TV interview I did.

Why was it impossible for you to say that?

It's the *Today Show*; you've got a minute and a half. Two days later, I gave it all to the *LA Times*, and they wrote a piece saying all that. I didn't feel that the apology was such a terrible thing and I would still apologize. I think it was a gray area. I felt that I was right in doing it under those circumstances, because I was appearing on a mainstream media operation, if not really working for it. I thought, "I'm going to get out of this real fast."

It was an exit strategy.

It was an exit strategy.

The reason why I'm interested in this has more to do with assessing this new environment where reporters are attacking reporters.

A *Time* magazine writer had a column about media and the war the following week in which he opened by writing, "A reporter does a broadcast which endangers the lives of many American soldiers. Another reporter makes a statement that embarrasses people. Who gets fired? The reporter who embarrasses people." He was talking about Geraldo Rivera and me. I think I was more a victim of the media wars than the cultural wars.

What sparked that incident anyway? Who called whom and complained about this?

The AP's Cairo bureau picked up the broadcast and taped it. Ironically enough, few saw the original Iraqi satellite show. My old wire service compadres saw it and thought it was a news story. The AP picked up the broadcast and ran it word for word. Then the *New York Times* ran the whole thing word for word, "Peter Arnett criticizes . . ." That's a story. Peter Arnett criticizes the war effort. That part shocked me, and I said,

"Jesus, what's happening?" I didn't realize that I was being projected into a huge controversy. Some people wrote, "Poor Peter Arnett, he was looking for a comeback and he didn't make it." I wasn't looking for a comeback. I'm seventy years old. Come on. I literally didn't want to come back. I'm not kidding you here. Peter Arnett lost a chance at his comeback? What the hell?

What a difference between the first Gulf War and this one. In the first Gulf War, the conservative right wing led by the antimedia group Accuracy in Media[9] mobilized its constituency, and CNN got thirty-five thousand letter cards from around the country criticizing me in Baghdad. This was before the era of e-mails. Although there was enormous pressure from the White House and from some senators, Ted Turner was an independent and didn't give in to it. CNN had no affiliates. We lost some advertising, but our ratings went up enormously. We were exclusive. We had the story to ourselves and were not going to give it up. But if CNN had received thirty-five thousand cards in one day, what would they have thought? Would they allowed me to stay in Baghdad?

In the decade that followed, you had Fox cable, a voice that was able to generate all these bloody e-mails and excite people in the affiliates, and I was just swept away by Fox's ability to do that. Now they do it to anyone who has the misfortune to come into their sights. Look at Bob Kerrey[10] two years ago when the revelations about the so-called atrocity incidents in Vietnam came out. Where has that controversy gone? One member of his team said Kerrey executed twelve civilians. All the others swore he hadn't. I wrote a piece for *USA Today*[11] about that, but the point is, look how the right-wing media can mobilize public opinion against its targets. Geraldo worked for Fox during the war. If he had worked for NBC and had done what he had done in Iraq,[12] he would be gone. There's no doubt about it. Gone.

I'm not saying that I have not been criticized in the past, I have. President George H. W. Bush never got over my coverage of the first Gulf War, and in both his books,[13] he complains about me bitterly.

What stuck in his craw most?

It was the baby milk plant story four days into the first Gulf War. I quoted Iraqi officials saying that the United States bombed a baby milk plant and that the administration had said it was a germ-warfare testing facility. I was criticized for quoting Iraqi officials asserting the baby milk claim. In his books, Bush claims he has information proving otherwise. But when

Hussein Kamel, who was Saddam's son-in-law and the man in charge of all defense industries, defected in 1995, CNN interviewed him and asked in one question, "Come on, tell us what was in the baby milk plant." He replied, "Baby milk."

I just want to add a couple of reflections here. The media is an easy target in America's comfortable society where most people say they don't trust us. The truth is the first casualty not only in war but when solid citizens feel they have earned their right to the good life and don't like being reminded that nasty things happen around the world, or that their political leaders don't always make the right decisions and don't always tell the truth. Look how long it took for the US public to accept that the Vietnam War was a waste of men and money. The Vietnam press corps had, by the middle of the war, figured out that *the* story was that the war was not going well. By the time of the Tet offensive,[14] most journalists—even Walter Cronkite, who had supported the war up to that time—said, "This is not working, forget it." There were some arguments later about the Tet offensive.

It was a lousy war and we had a lot of friends die, but we can sleep comfortably knowing that we tried to do our best to tell the story. Out of that, it's said, came the impetus to challenge Nixon over the Watergate affair,[15] to do investigative journalism. But there was a taint about the Vietnam coverage. I've said it a few times that even though I was well used in American media, the editors would rather I had been more positive. But it was the reporting from a losing war. Defeat. Who wants to be part of it? Vietnam was a national disappointment.

But then what is a reporter's job?

A reporter's job is to report the facts and hope he keeps his job while doing it. What was very interesting to me after the first Gulf War was that even though some saw me as against the war and therefore opposing the United States while I was covering it, the fact that the war was won made me something of a minor celebrity. I've got a picture of me winning an award—Father of the Year, 1992—with cowinner Colin Powell, who was chairman of the Joint Chiefs of Staff back then. I was at parties with prominent officials. I was on the lecture circuit with President Bush when his wife, Barbara, was promoting a book. Bush could not resist sniping at me, saying, "Peter Arnett has just come down from Haiti and he just can't help supporting Clinton's policies there. He was wrong in Iraq and he's wrong in Haiti, ha ha ha." It was bizarre. It was all associated with victory, victory. That was the difference from Vietnam.

The point is, even though I was controversial, it was a winning war and everyone felt great about it. *Vanity Fair* magazine had me posing with my girlfriend as one of the twelve most newsworthy people of the year. I was in a swimsuit with a loose white dressing gown and I had this blonde girlfriend, the all-American beauty, posing in front of the Washington Hilton. And there was Gen. Norman Schwarzkopf on the next page, and then President Bush. I was one of the twelve top guys.

I've got the sense now that the media has pulled in its horns since the War on Terrorism began. Probably 85 percent of American media power exists in New York City, where you have the networks, the newspapers, and correspondents from all over the country that are here covering the UN and the rest of it. When the World Trade Center towers came down, every journalist either saw them with their own eyes, or were covered in dust covering it, or watched it on television. It had the same effect that the Tet offensive had in Saigon. Tet just traumatized the reporters in Saigon, many of whom never went out in the field. When Tet came and rockets were landing in their neighborhood, they panicked and started writing more negative stories.

I tried to be realistic right through the Tet offensive. I said, "The Communists are here, they did this, but they're out now." But my colleagues were, "Oh, my God . . ." Walter Cronkite was saying, "Oh, my God, it's over!" The World Trade Center disaster had the same impact: "God, we're under attack. This is the most terrible thing." Why? Because it happened in our own backyard and the ripple effect of all that is to some degree still being felt. It was very easy for the networks and the newspapers to say, "We're under attack. We've got to get on the ball with the government. This is a national emergency."

I can understand it. It was an attack. But it was that ripple effect. When you hear about the "9/11 effect," it is true. Now, the reasons for going to war against Saddam in Iraq were so transparently obvious. President George W. Bush himself said earlier in 2002, "This guy tried to kill my dad."[16] That's what he said. That's why he went to war. It was for revenge. With a side helping of oil. Why not go in and make sure it's our cap on the wells? I and others kept saying this all through 2002. Weapons of mass destruction? The UN was saying there were none there.

The Bush administration also asserted that even if Saddam had no WMDs, he would have gone on to produce them in the future. They essentially said, "He had these plans and he was already making alliances with neighbors and they were going to let him do it, so we've got to stop him now." In fact, my investigation since the war suggests Saddam was pretty much out of the picture. He had not been known to have visited one military unit between the first Gulf War and the second. This was a man who, his aides say, was so disenchanted by what had gone on with the economic sanctions and the feuds within his family, that in the last three years of his life in power he was writing romantic novels and drawing up plans for palaces and mosques. One of his novels is reportedly going to be published by his daughter Raghad in Amman, Jordan. He wrote and supervised a fifty-four-part television series of his early life that didn't make it to air. He was cavorting with new girlfriends. The guy was out of it in the end. His sons were fighting over the spoils. In fact, in the piece I did for *Playboy*,[17] I reported that his sons had expressed no desire for regional or international dominance. They wanted the money. They wanted the power. Neither of them seems to have given a damn about weapons of mass destruction. It was their dad who had squandered the nation's wealth and power on such weapons.

Ahmed Chalabi,[18] and those who defected relatively recently, apparently didn't tell the Pentagon that the vaunted Republican Guards had so deteriorated that they were not a capable force and that the regular army units were not being paid. The whole Iraqi military had deteriorated. That's why the war was such a walkover. Most of these units did not fire a shot as US forces invaded. I've been told that several of the senior commanding officers told their men after the United States invaded, "OK, guys, go home. Don't surrender; just go home to your houses and sit there." The Pentagon had often told them in reports and leaflets, "We'll rehire you once Saddam's gone." It was the classic coup d'état, "We'll take the top off and . . ." So they just went home.

How did the press get so snookered?

Because there was no way of denying what the Iraqi exiles were saying, which was that WMDs existed. No one had said that Saddam hadn't visited any military units, because the Iraqi government trapped itself, to some degree, with its secrecy. No one ever saw how deteriorated the military units were. No one knew that his sons, Uday and Qusay, were fighting like crazy. There were odd little rumors, but no one knew that Saddam was writing romantic historic novels and not planning the next world war.

How come no one knew? What kind of intelligence operations did we have over there?

The CIA admitted it had no agent in Iraq in the last decade. Not one. All they had were exiles coming out. It was just an indifferent effort. I don't think the Clinton administration gave a damn. Clinton's secretary of state, Madeleine Albright, essentially said, "Look, we figured Saddam was contained." They didn't care.

> **Colin Powell (then secretary of state for the Bush administration) had said in February 2001 and May 2001 that Saddam was contained and so did Condoleezza Rice (then national security advisor) in July 2001.[19]**

That's right, so therefore why the rush to war by Bush? I think the media agrees that it didn't look into it. When Judith Miller does a piece for the *New York Times* saying there are weapons of mass destruction all over, what are you going to do? How do you say there's not? Now you did have the former UN weapons inspector, Scott Ritter, who said, "There's nothing there." But he didn't have anything to back up his claim. He said, "I've been there, there's nothing," but that's not good enough.

There was also a rush to war by the media. You had Eason Jordan, who was then running all of CNN's coverage. He announced in Houston at one of these big cable meetings that "this will be CNN's war, and we're investing five million in it." The networks talked of it as being "their" war. When I went to Afghanistan, I met a *New York Times* reporter and I said to him, "You guys are doing so well," and he said, "We had a meeting and we were told, 'This will be the *New York Times'* war." They looked at it in terms of "our war." They wanted the war to happen. I told you that NBC had these cameras all over Baghdad. They wanted the war. The media was not challenging it. They wanted to cover the war, they wanted the drama, the ratings.

> **So it was good for business.**

Great for business, great to have a great story, and they were all onboard because of 9/11. Part of it was revenge. Let me tell you, if they'd played it right, if rather than firing all the Iraqi military Paul Bremer had said, "OK, we're going to reconstitute ten divisions and we're going to have these Sunnis here," there wouldn't be an insurgency. There'd be trouble, but you wouldn't have more than seventeen hundred Americans dead. Because in the end, when Saddam was kicked out, when he ran away, most people in Iraq—even his supporters—basically said, "Saddam's an asshole anyway, the hell with him, let's move on." I was talking to them. I met and I know dozens of them. I went to their houses and they were saying, "All we want is to get a job and start all over again." These were senior Baathists.[20] They didn't have the fight in them; they knew Saddam was gone along with Uday and Qusay. These are the people Bremer and the others let go. Could you imagine if the US officials had been more insightful, more realistic? If they'd had elections six months after the war, with an Iraqi government and no insurgency, who would have remembered about the WMDs? My personal view is that if the war hadn't happened, Saddam would have been out of it sooner rather than later and his sons would have been struggling. There would have been a collapse, then power grabs and chaos, but it wouldn't have been the disaster we've had in the past two years.

What about Iran now?

I don't think the administration is in any position to attack Iran in any way, shape, or form. They have, in fact, stated as much. Condoleezza Rice was in Europe the other day [February 4, 2005], and she said, "We're not planning any military operations against Iran." They're going for the European solution. She's right now making a speech in Paris that apparently will say, "We've got to work together." The moment you get onboard with Europe, you're getting on to negotiations with Iran. They realize that there's no way they can continue to show indifference and affront the Europeans. They need them. That's one factor; you've got to work with the Europeans. The other factor is that militarily the best you could do is a series of air strikes on Iran that could not complete the job and that would just add to the flames of anti-Americanism in Europe and elsewhere around the world. There's no convincing case being put forward that Iran has these nuclear plants that are that dangerous. There is a way out, and that's negotiations and inspections, which were not used well before the Iraq war. We know why Bush didn't want the inspectors to complete the job. He wanted to invade Iraq. The Bush administration was just desperate to prevent the inspections from being successful.

But it's illegal to attack a nation for no reason, unprovoked.

The Bush administration didn't accept that. They said that you could launch preemptive strikes. In this particular administration, they legalize everything, including torture. So I think that the preemptive strategy is debatable and arguable and of course Democrats have said they don't believe in it. But if you're president of the United States, you can clearly get away with a hell of a lot. The United States went into Vietnam in the same way. There was no consensus from the UN to do it. The only consensus war was the Korean War, which the UN backed. They didn't back Vietnam.

Was the Gulf of Tonkin[21] incident real in your mind?

Part of it was, part of it wasn't. The first part was real, the second was made up, that is historical fact now. What was not said was that the United States caused the initial incident by going into North Vietnamese waters and landing South Vietnamese saboteurs. That's why they had the incident.

So was that a provocation on the part of the United States to create the war?

Yes. Lyndon Johnson used it; we know that.

What about the first Gulf War and the reasons for going there?

There was an international consensus, including the UN and most of the Arab world. The first Gulf War was kosher.

A lot of people talk about Peter Arnett being the only TV correspondent in Baghdad during the first Gulf War, and they speculate that CNN made a deal with the Iraqi government. Would you set the record straight on that?

We had a very smart producer, Robert Wiener, who was sent to Baghdad a few weeks after the invasion of Kuwait, and like all producers, he sought access. Some of what he did was in the movie *Live from Baghdad*. He waited on the Iraqi officials running the media and persuaded them to cooperate. The reason he was successful was that CNN was the only international television organization in existence. They could look at CNN in the foreign ministry and the information ministry. They could see the reports. So when they had a demonstration in the streets opposing American policy, there it was, on CNN. When they gave an interview, it was on CNN. So they knew what was there, and CNN knew that they knew and relied on the balance issue from outside. So you get Saddam's deputy prime minister, Tariq Aziz, and he gives an interview. You don't have the correspondent saying, "I talked to Tariq Aziz and he says that right's on their side, but he's a goddamned liar and fascist." They let President Bush say, "Tariq Aziz is a liar and a fascist." So we had this arrangement that was very effective. The Iraqis could get their viewpoint across on CNN with their live press conferences and interviews with Saddam Hussein. They got very familiar with CNN's operations and they realized,

"This is something, we know what's going on." ABC's Peter Jennings came in to interview Saddam and I think Dan Rather did, too, and the Iraqis didn't even see the broadcast. But they could see CNN's broadcasts. So they became comfortable with it, and they could see that CNN was having an effect internationally. As the war approached, Wiener talked them into letting us stay and he got visas for eighteen or twenty people and they prepared to cover the war. It wasn't a matter of money; the Iraqis didn't need the money. They had so much money. They could see that CNN would be a very influential opportunity for them.

What happened to the other networks?

The other networks weren't smart enough to get the inside track. CNN discovered the Iraqis had a hard-line communication link between Baghdad and Amman. It was part of a military link and could withstand bombing. CNN paid $4,000 to $5,000 a month for it, and it was worth every penny the night the war began, when we had the only communications link with the outside world. The other networks didn't even think about it. The other networks were doing two minutes of coverage a day. Network news was covering the whole American buildup. The last thing they gave a damn about was Baghdad, and when the opportunity came, they took off real fast. They didn't want to stay and didn't stay during this last Gulf War, either. CNN called me up from my post in Jerusalem to bolster the Baghdad coverage. Everyone eventually left, but I stayed and for ten days I covered the war with a satellite phone. Then five very brave CNN engineers brought in a live uplink truck across the desert and we began covering the war live with pictures.

Why did I stay? I figured out I could cover the story and I knew it was one hell of a story. I remember the day everyone had left except for the last two CNN staffers. It was day three and a rocket hit the al Rasheed hotel near where they were sitting and they said, "We're out of here." So they left and I stood in the foyer—the al Rasheed has this huge foyer about a block long, all marble and polished wood. There was one guy behind the desk, and I had this feeling of the greatest satisfaction and I figured, "It's mine, the whole goddamned story is mine." You fantasize in your dreams about covering a war by yourself; it can't happen. But there I was covering it by myself. When the second war came and I'm on the roof of the information ministry and running around and I was by myself again with NBC, I thought, "This is crazy." In fact, I just said, "This is ludicrous." I really felt it.

What does that tell you about the press?

I'm not going to be criticizing because I can't blame people for worrying about their lives. But the thing is, it was no effort to me. Now you would say, "Arnett throws caution to the winds," because as I said, on top of the information ministry there'd been bombing and I was there covering it, and the sirens were going, but I had an Iraqi cameraman there focusing on me. I just figured the odds were probably good. Maybe not good, but I don't mind playing the odds. I do it all the time. It's not a noble act to undergo a degree of risk.

Are you an adrenaline junkie, Peter?

I don't quite know what that means, adrenaline junkie.

Do you need a high level of stimulation in terms of being in physical danger; is that when you feel most alive?

I feel most alive when I'm on a Caribbean beach with a pretty girl and a rum daiquiri, and it doesn't happen enough these days. I'm living in Baghdad now, where there are no beaches, no pretty girls, and no rum. I live there only because it is where I can research and write magazine articles and books about Saddam and Iraq.

Do you live in the Green Zone?

No, I've got a house down in the business district. I'm accredited to the US mission, but I don't go out with US forces very much, and I try to spend as much time as possible with the Iraqis. I want to tell their story.

What's your assessment of the coverage of the Iraq war?

I think the media is doing as well as can be expected. A reporter can die or get kidnapped any moment he/she is outside the house or protected area. I have a sense that the terrorists or insurgents aren't trying specifically to kill journalists but will sweep them up if they see them and ransom them off. Some malcontent who thinks that all Americans or foreigners are shit can shoot you, too. Or you can be done in accidentally by a car bombing or a roadside firefight. The reporters take their chances and it's very dangerous. Rockets come in the Green Zone. The other day, two diplomats were killed. Rockets can hit the Palestine Hotel, too, where many journalists live. You're relying on your Iraqi staff 95 percent of the time. Some of them are good, some of them aren't, but they're doing the best they can.

It's clear what's going on as we talk today. The insurgency is rising. The United States hasn't found the key to it. The Shiites are a very powerful force that could be a destructive force if they create a theocracy. The next struggle will be political along with the insurgency. These are troubled times, and I think that that is coming out in the stories. Beyond that, I think the issues are not so difficult as they were in Vietnam where you had the nationalist struggle against the Communist struggle. The issue was the fate of South Vietnam under the Communists. Would it benefit Russia and China or not? That's not that kind of argument in Iraq's case. The question is: Are the Shiites going to dominate? Of course. The story is: To what degree are they going to dominate?

Do you think there's going to be a civil war when we pull out?

There is one now, the Sunnis against the Shiites and the Kurds. It is a civil war in fact. What you have is a strong Kurdish army and the strong Kurdish identity[22] that for the time being is unified, which is a positive thing. Then you have the Shiites, who are the majority in Iraq. Both the Kurds and the Shiites can live with the United States. The Shiites would want the United States to leave eventually, but they're not that desperate about it. Then you have the Sunnis, who are a minority (20 percent of the population) and were in power when Saddam ruled. They are pissed off and feel aggrieved. They've lost power and weren't given an opportunity to get it back, and it's confusing for them. That could be behind the dynamic that determines whether all this leads to a prolonged civil war. The Kurds would like to be independent; their leaders have said it. But realistically, they're not going to get it because to declare independence you have to be recognized by the United States and who's going to recognize them? I don't think anyone wants to. An independent Kurdistan would mean breakaway parts of Turkey, Iran, and Syria, and that's not going to happen.

This insurgency, who is it made up of? What groups?

You have some genuine terrorist elements. There's Abu Musab al-Zarqawi, who was initially operating out of a protected enclave in the Kurdish area next to Iran. He is a Jordanian-born terrorist with ties to al Qaeda. There's the growth of an Iraqi-based Sunni rebellion that came out of misrule by US forces in Fallujah. Very early on, the Third Infantry killed eighteen Iraqis because they were surging toward an American checkpoint. The US soldiers panicked and killed them. There were a lot of incidents like that. There were six hundred thousand Iraqi military and security people that Paul Bremer had fired who didn't have jobs. Al-Zarqawi simply used them to infiltrate the insurgency, even though he had nothing to do with Saddam. Zarqawi has a very limited operation, but he's very effective. He has efficient operatives. Even when Fallujah was nominally in insurgent hands, he didn't control Fallujah, but he operated out of there. The insurgency is a disparate group of like-minded people: criminals, nationalists, extremists, plus outside fighters. There've been quite a few coming in. The outside fighters are going into Iraq as they went in to Afghanistan in the 1980s. In those days, the Russian invasion attracted Muslims from all over the Islamic world. It's happening in Iraq. What no one has quite known is the numbers, but they're killing Egyptians, Moroccans—all sorts of people have been dying in various actions taken by the government and US forces. The future is uncertain because clearly the United States wants to get the hell out of there. There's an anxiety there that is obvious. They're looking for an excuse. Bush said in an interview three weeks ago, "If we're asked to leave, we'll leave." He also said, "We don't expect to be asked, but if the new government wants us to leave, we'll leave." It's sort of the equivalent to his "bring 'em on" statement, but it's a mess, a big mess.

It's an insurgency with no headquarters. They don't even specify their politics. There's no evident political party and no international recognition or recognizable international backing. There's nothing. What is it? It hasn't grown yet. It's still an incipient thing. So the best a reporter can do is go out with the marines or the Third Brigade and look at yet another house that's been blown away and talk to Iraqis who say, "We don't have any power or water." There's nothing much to it. What you have are fanatics who are amazing. The amazing part about it to me is the willingness of so many to participate in suicide attacks. Where the hell do all these people come from, as many as ten a day, to blow themselves up? That, I don't think, is discoverable. You cannot reach the insurgents to get their story.

People who we've spoken to say that there was a lot more censorship and controlling and manufacturing of information post-Vietnam, during the first Gulf War and the Iraq war. Is that true?

To get embedded with a unit you have to sign an eight-page closely typed document in which you agree to have all your material looked at and all your pictures approved. That's standard procedure. Eight pages. It started at one; now it's up to eight. On the other hand, that did not stop NBC from airing during the Fallujah battle a really incriminating video of an Amer-

ican marine shooting a wounded prisoner. Overall, they are not in a position to control information. It's failing simply because the insurgents have
their own camera people who get out stories to Al Jazeera and Al Arabiya,[23] and if they have it, everyone gets to use it. So media control is not
succeeding. The greatest containing factor is just the danger of being
there. Vietnam was never as dangerous as this. Saigon was never as dangerous as Baghdad. Saigon life was active; restaurants were open. Early
in the war, there were car bombs, but not many. You could move around,
even during the Tet offensive. You were never concerned about being kidnapped in Saigon. Baghdad is the most dangerous place since Beirut, and
Beirut set new low standards for living. In 1985 Terry Anderson and
others were kidnapped.[24] Women journalists were raped and brutalized,
and they all left Beirut. I think that if the United States starts pulling out,
all the journalists are going to go. I think the journalists are there simply
because the US forces are there. If the United States leaves, you're going
to have Iraqi reporters covering it, sort of like in Somalia. But as I said
earlier, the headlines are the story. The car bombs continue. The kidnappings continue. The political situation is uncertain. What is there left to
hide? If you're with an American unit, you're limited to interviewing a GI
because you're required to have escorts. The truth is, in Iraq, most GIs are
gung ho. They're professionals. The national guardsmen are gung ho
because they're from little hometowns and they're all together there, and
even though a lot of Americans are dying, most aren't dying. This is what
you have in Iraq. You have 130,000 soldiers and 1,833 [as of August 6,
2005] have died. In Vietnam you had 550,000 soldiers and 30,000 died.
So if you had four times the number of GIs in Iraq you'd have, say, 7,332
dead as compared to 60,000 in Vietnam. So relatively speaking, there's
not a lot of danger. There is, but there's not. There's not that many dying.
The United States has a lot of firepower, so the average GI says, "Fuck it,
I'm going to get any guy who gets me." The dangerous part is driving
along these goddamned roads, and they know it. But once you're at the
destination, morale is pretty good.

One of the biggest impact attacks was the suicide bomber who got
into the mess tent at a US camp south of Mosul[25] and killed people. That
was a big morale killer. But around Camp Victory at the airport in
Baghdad, you can get beer and walk around, and there are even a few
clubs. In Camp Victory, the biggest trading item is Viagra. One-third of
the people there are women. The other day there was a big mud fight down
in Basra. The woman was disciplined for showing her tits, so what the hell

have we got here? Don't tell me in that mud fight that morale is low; they're having a ball. In Vietnam, you had units that didn't fight, but in Iraq, when units get unhappy, they simply write home or tell their wives and it goes on the Internet. There's a different level of communication. In Vietnam, the AP or the *New York Times* was the conduit and then television did a little, not a lot, because they had to ship their film back to New York. They usually used wire service copy with wire service pictures, and then had a report from their own correspondents a couple of times a week. Now you've got the Internet and e-mails, so how the hell can the military hide anything? They haven't. So to that degree, I don't think the military has succeeded in containing the story. Even though they try with their eight pages of conditions, it ain't working. You had the case where Defense Secretary Rumsfeld went to Iraq and this soldier, Spc. Thomas Wilson, got up and asked, "Why do we soldiers have to dig through local landfills for pieces of scrap metal . . . to uparmor our vehicles?" That could never happen in Vietnam. No GI would have got up and asked that question of Defense Secretary McNamara. They didn't. I covered every McNamara press conference. But in that southern area in Basra, a reporter put this guy up to it. It couldn't have happened in Vietnam. No soldier would have listened to a reporter trying to put him up. No reporter would have told a soldier to do that. But in this current communications environment, the guy who asked the question is famous. So anyone will ask anything. It's a different environment. The danger is, I think, that if you— not just the media, anyone—decide that the war is not worthwhile, there are many who are willing to put you down and threaten you for being treasonous. When I was reporting in Vietnam and I was called a pro-Communist, other than President Johnson who put the FBI on to me, there was no suggestion that I was treasonous and working for the other side. It didn't come through as clear as what could happen today. In those days, being a Communist was important. What are you now if you're a critical reporter in Baghdad? An insurgent? A supporter of suicide bombing? It's very hard, so what they do is this patriotism thing. If you do anything that is negative, you're unpatriotic. Even though you may have been right to do it, it's still unpatriotic because it's perceived as hurting the cause.

Do you think it's a more sinister environment now in terms of that than it was before?

Yes, I think it's dangerous. There are people out there who get angry if you don't go along with the program. I had two or three instances around

Washington, DC, where men came up to me and basically threatened me and said, "You're a damned fascist." But they were blowhards. After the first Gulf War, Dave Halberstam[26] said to me, "Don't go on the lecture circuit because you'll get shot." I think I could have been shot after this last Gulf War, I was so identified with being antipatriotic, anti-American.

I got an insight into this whole feeling the other night. I love buying DVDs of old movies. You can get ten movies for six bucks and I got one called *Stage Door Canteen*, which I played while trying to sleep the other night. It's set in New York City during World War II and there are all these entertainers in the film, like Jerry Colono and Gracie Fields, and the atmosphere is superpatriotic. Gracie Fields sings a song, "Marching into Berlin," and there's a romance between a GI and one of the stage door canteen darlings. Again, everything is superpatriotic and flag-waving. And I realized, "Geez, in World War II you were either onboard or you were out." To some degree, that's been, and still is, the feeling here. It's like recovering this superpatriotic attitude, which the Bush administration is playing into, although it's increasingly difficult now because Saddam didn't play out as a Hitler. Saddam was a dangerous man, and he was brutal, but the equivalent of the Holocaust with the weapons of mass destruction didn't happen. Without the WMDs, doesn't Saddam just look more like a tired old man?

What about Osama? What happened to him? He was the big bogeyman, wasn't he?

He is still a big bogeyman. The United States did not really try to get him. The Northern Alliance[27] fought the Afghanistan war. The Tajiks from northern Afghanistan fought the Afghanistan war. They're the ones who took Kabul. They're the ones who did the fighting. They're the ones, unfortunately, who were sent in to Tora Bora to trap Osama, and they missed him. The United States didn't really go to war in Afghanistan. They have lost some people, and we're all sorry to hear that, but the point is they didn't fight the fight to get Osama, not like they went after Saddam in Iraq. Bin Laden does remain the most charismatic figure in the Arab world now. He represents anti-Americanism; there's no doubt about it. Bin Laden, in a sense, is taking over from Yasir Arafat. One of the tragedies of the war in Iraq is that it is helping him. There are experts who say that Iraq is the next Afghanistan in the sense of being a recruiting ground for terrorists. I think that's pretty clear and that Syria and Iran aren't doing much to stop them from going in.

Do you think the press did a good job covering the prewar period?

No, they didn't do a good job covering prewar. You talked about Judith Miller's correspondence, which is being widely criticized, and the willingness of not only the *New York Times* but also the rest of the media to go along. I talked earlier about the great buildup and CNN saying, "It's going to be our war" and the millions spent on production values and how they wanted to be part of the big game. They covered it like a Super Bowl. There was no questioning. How much questioning was there of the war effort?

You implied that Fox has this huge sway not only over its own audience but over the other networks.

It's very effective in going after anyone whose political views or sense of patriotism offends them. I'm not speaking just personally; I mean across the board, you name it. Fox is brilliant in that it took tabloid newspaper journalism that Murdoch had mastered with the *Sun* in Britain, the *New York Post* here, and newspapers in Australia, and turned it into television. Read the opinion columnists that write for the *New York Post* these days. Andrea Peyser does the most outrageous columns; she called Christiane Amanpour a "war slut." Fox correspondents make such statements routinely. They're opinionated and they influence the media, there's no doubt about it.

You're saying that they influence ABC and CBS and NBC.

Yes, sure. Frank Rich, who writes commentaries on culture for the *New York Times*, does great stuff on Fox. He calls Fox the "state television company."

Tom Curley, the president and CEO of the Associated Press, said that he felt that Fox was a good thing because it's another voice and that what they did was very smart.

What does he mean another voice? What's a voice? CNN is not a voice; CNN is simply a vehicle for news. What does he mean another voice? That's what gets me.

He's saying that they are serving an audience that heretofore has not been served.

They're giving right-wing judgments on the news, on the world, on anything that's going down culturally, politically, or anything else. Sure they have the right to do so. But they say, "We report, you decide." Come on.

Are you saying that it's used as an attack arm?

It's an attack arm for the ideologically involved. It's an attack arm for the neoconservative movement. Rush Limbaugh does on radio what Fox does on television. You can say that Rush Limbaugh caters to an audience of twenty million bigots out there who want to hear him. Fox appeals to fewer. That's it. And it appeals to the administration because it uncritically presents their viewpoint.

What is your assessment of this current generation of journalists working for the mainstream?

The new generation comes in with an enormous amount of journalistic history to consider as they develop their careers. When I was a kid, Ernie Pyle[28] and the British reporters who covered World War II were totally heroic in my mind because they covered a war to save mankind. Some died doing it, further ennobling them. This new generation of journalists is aware of Ernie Pyle and other great World War II reporters as icons of American journalism. But now they have the Morley Safers, the David Halberstams, the Dan Rathers, the Sy Hershes, and others, all of whom have been controversial for one reason or another. Our careers of challenging government are weighed against the other earlier models of journalism, the patriotic models that are uncritically supportive of government policies. Looking back on my career, I've often wondered what it would have been like if I'd been ten years younger and was a reporter in World War II, where there was only one side to cover—your side. As I looked into the history of World War II, I discovered there were some reporters at the AP and elsewhere who had problems. One AP reporter announced the end of the war twenty-four hours before Eisenhower wanted it, and he was fired and was looked upon as having betrayed his profession. What did he do? He reported the end of the war accurately, but twenty-four hours before the deadline. He was my kind of guy. There were others who had problems but, overall, it was a great patriotic war with heroic journalists, as opposed to the wars in Vietnam and Central America, where the media was criticized a lot. Somehow, media demanding accountability of a country when that country was engaged in questionable international activities was ultimately seen as unsupportive and wrong. So I don't think it's easy for young journalists coming in to pick a model. What model are they going to pick? Where are they going? I often talk to journalism institutions, and students often ask, "Where do we go, how do I become a reporter?" I find that my career is admired by some who feel that it would be great getting out there and stirring up controversy. But I'm sure there are just as many who feel, "What he's done, would we want to be there in his shoes?"

My sense is that in one particular area of journalism, photography, the influence of Vietnam has been very deep. You have a new generation of young photographers who go hell-bent into photography and who are right in the thick of the action, but they're limited by the willingness of their proprietors and bosses to use the pictures. Journalist and writer Pete Hamill had a great piece on Eddie Adams's death in which he said Eddie's picture of Saigon police chief Lt. Col. Nguyen Ngoc Loan assassinating a Vietcong agent in the streets of Saigon during the Tet offensive probably wouldn't be taken today.[29] He said that the photographers probably wouldn't be allowed to get that close and, if they did, they probably wouldn't take it because it's not the kind of picture that the newspapers and magazines want. He was suggesting that photography has changed, but I think in terms of bravery and getting close to the story, it's remarkable that there are so many out there. In terms of American reporters, I think that American media bosses and bureau chiefs are unwilling to allow their reporters to get into too dangerous areas. The fact that they didn't stay in Iraq during both wars is an indication. I think it's primarily the dangers of the story, rather than upsetting the government. Bush encouraged journalists to leave both wars, but Rumsfeld said, "I know that some guys always stay so, OK." Europeans, on the other hand, stayed in Baghdad in large numbers. Quite a large amount of American reportage is gained from non-Americans now, whether they're Europeans or, in the case of Iraq, Iraqis. Much more material comes from non-Americans than before. But mainstream print media—the *New York Times* and the *Washington Post*—have competent reporters over there. Television is doing its best, but let's face it, Iraq is the toughest story of recent years to cover.

What do you think of the controversy surrounding the reporting of Judith Miller of the *New York Times*?

Certainly she's getting a lot of attention over her reporting on WMDs and other issues. Did you see that piece on her in the *Times* on Sunday, February 6, 2005? The title was "Talking on the Air and Out of Turn" and it was written by Daniel Okrent, the paper's ombudsman. He complained that while appearing on *Hardball* [January 30, 2005], Judith Miller said that the Bush administration had been "reaching out" to Ahmed Chalabi to "offer him expressions of cooperation" and that, "according to one report, he was even offered a chance to be an interior minister in the new government." Okrent wrote that that particular information had never appeared in the *New York Times* before, during, or after that interview. He had some scathing remarks about the propriety of a *Times* reporter peddling information not deemed worthy enough for the paper. It was a pretty tough attack.

Judith Miller has been a high-profile *New York Times* correspondent for years. She has been regarded by many as an expert on the Middle East, Iraq in particular, so anything she wrote about the region was seen as probably reliable. The whole business of what WMDs did Saddam have, what he didn't have, what he was doing, what he wasn't doing, is really at issue now in terms of the Bush administration's avowed reasons for going to war and the intelligence information that was used to back that policy. Judith Miller's reports that appeared in the *Times* before the war pretty much backed up what the Bush administration was claiming. So along with the intelligence community, she has been getting intense scrutiny about the content and origin of her reports. She is also, however, bearing the burden that should be borne by the whole US media. During 2002 how many media voices were raised in the United States challenging White House assessments that Saddam was a madman with weapons of mass destruction that he might have used against the United States? The media went along with those assessments even after UN weapons inspectors began dispelling that possibility after conducting intensive searches of believed weapons sites. Even after the inspectors suggested that Iraq had, in fact, destroyed its weapons stockpiles—and this was before the bombs fell—the media still went along with the White House.

Saddam's secretive governing style and iron control of the Baghdad media during his three decades of power allowed all manner of rumors true and false to circulate outside the country. We now know that prominent Iraqi exiles most intent on ousting Saddam's government peddled masses of information to the US government that was false. I can only presume that Judith Miller relied on those sources, as did US authorities.

What do you think of the reporting out of Iraq?

I've already indicated that Iraq is the most dangerous important news story to cover, as difficult as any in modern times. The task is made tougher by the controversial nature of the conflict, the question of its international legality, and the WMD and terrorist issues that quickly evaporated only to be replaced by concerns about the nature of the new Iraqi government. Trying each day to track the direction in which Iraq is heading is an impossible task for the media to achieve with the security situation remaining as dangerous as it is, yet the press is still expected to do it. Consequently, Baghdad reporters have been in the line of fire from the political Left and the Right, just as they have literally been in the field. The physical constraints and the political sensitivity of the coverage in these post-9/11 times means that the reporting on Iraq falls short of the ideal. I'm not saying this to disparage the bravery or abilities of the many reporters based there. I live there myself, but I've got no illusions that I'd be doing a better job if I were with the mainstream media.

Because of the terrible security situation, the media is more likely to cover and give emphasis to the official story. They'll cover press conferences, embed with US forces on military stories, and interview Iraqi politicians who are under the necessary protection of US security forces. They're more likely to cover those stories than the reality of a tumultuous Iraq outside the Green Zone. That was evident to me during the January 2005 elections when Iraqis voted freely for the first time in half a century. I'm a fan of Peter Jennings, and I watched his coverage from the United States. I noticed that much of ABC's coverage, like the coverage on the other networks, was from the US military vantage point. I understood why, because in a war zone like Iraq, to stray far from security is to invite personal disaster. But such dependence on the military can give a false impression. Praising the voters of Baghdad's impoverished Sadr City from the perspective of a US Army tank might raise questions of favoritism to a fair-minded person. For visiting reporters, quickly traveling around Iraq requires depending on US military transportation, and I noticed the extremely high profile given to interviews with US generals on all the US networks during the elections. The coverage gave the impression of an election that measured up to our standards of democracy and that had put Iraq on a clear course to victory. It was an impression that the Bush administration greatly desired. In fact, the elections were but one hurdle on a very long obstacle course whose end is not yet in sight.

Pulitzer Prize–winning correspondent **PETER ARNETT** has spent a lifetime covering wars and international crises for major American news organizations, most recently 2003's Gulf War and its bloody aftermath. Arnett is best known for his live television coverage from Baghdad during the first Gulf War in 1991. His coverage is credited with making CNN a household name.

Arnett was born in New Zealand and began his career on The *Southland Times* newspaper in Invercargill. He later worked on daily newspapers in Sydney, Australia, and Bangkok, Thailand, before joining the Associated Press (AP) in 1961. Arnett spent thirteen years covering the Vietnam War for the AP, filing more than three thousand news stories during that time. Writer-historian David Halberstam has described Arnett as "the best reporter of the whole Vietnam War."

Arnett joined the fledgling CNN in 1981 after a twenty-year career with the AP. Over the next eighteen years, Arnett and his CNN TV crews covered wars and civil disturbances in scores of countries in Latin America, the Middle East, central Asia, and Africa. After leaving CNN in 1999, Arnett worked for ForeignTV.com interviewing international political figures such as Yasir Arafat, Queen Noor, and Benazar Bhutto. He also worked with Camera Planet TV in New York for a series of documentaries on the War on Terrorism in Afghanistan. For HDTV-Denver, he did a series that included reporting trips to Israel and Iraq. Arnett was on assignment in Baghdad for *National Geographic Explorer* when the second Gulf War broke out in March 2003. He volunteered to help out the NBC TV network and MSNBC in daily news coverage after the network's crew left Baghdad at the beginning of the war. That coverage came to an end after Arnett gave a controversial interview to Iraqi TV. However, he continued to cover the war for the *London Daily Mirror* newspaper and several Arab, European, and Asian TV networks. Arnett currently resides in Baghdad and is writing a book about Saddam Hussein and his family in the final years before the second Gulf War. A chapter from the upcoming book about Saddam's son Uday appeared in the April 2005 issue of *Playboy* magazine.

Arnett has received fifty-seven major journalism awards for his reporting, including a Pulitzer and many other awards for his Vietnam coverage. His critically acclaimed autobiography, *Live from the Battlefield*, was published in 1991 and named "Book of the Year" by the *New York Times*. Arnett has received honorary doctorate degrees from universities in the United States and Brazil. He is an American citizen and has homes in Virginia and New York City.

NOTES

1. Peter Arnett, *Live from the Battlefield: From Vietnam to Baghdad: 35 Years in the World's War Zones* (New York: Simon & Schuster, 1994).

2. The massacre at My Lai of five hundred unarmed men, women, and children by US soldiers occurred in South Vietnam on March 16, 1968. Lt. William Calley initiated the massacre. Army photographer Ronald Haeberle was there and took photos of the dead.

3. The People's Liberation Armed Forces, or Vietcong, was established by North Vietnamese Communists to fight the anti-Communist Republic of Vietnam in the south.

4. "The Battle of Dien Bien Phu occurred in 1954 between Viet Minh forces and French airborne and Foreign Legion forces. . . . The battle . . . became the last battle between the French and the Vietnamese in the first Indochina War, which had begun in 1946." http://www.nationmaster.com/encyclopedia/Battle-of-Dien-Bien-Phu.

5. The United States Information Agency (USIA) describes itself as "an independent foreign affairs agency within the executive branch of the US government. USIA explains and supports American foreign policy and promotes US national interests through a wide range of overseas information programs." The USIA was folded into the State Department in 1999.

6. Beginning January 21, 1968, some twenty thousand North Vietnamese Army troops (NVA) laid siege to the remote marine base at Khe Sanh as a diversionary tactic to draw attention away from troop buildups taking place all over Vietnam for a large-scale effort that would be launched later, including the Tet offensive. The siege lasted for seventy-seven days, was one of the most brutal battles of the war, and was prominently featured on television every day. In the end, thousands of NVA were killed and wounded while two hundred and fifty Americans lost their lives. Tactically, Khe Sanh was a failure for the NVA, but strategically, it served its diversionary purpose.

7. Tom Brokaw, former NBC News anchorman, retired in December 2004.

8. Matt Lauer is Katie Couric's cohost on NBC's *Today Show*.

9. On its Web site, http://www.aim.org/static/21_0_7_0_C, Accuracy in Media defines its mission as "a nonprofit, grassroots citizens [*sic*] watchdog of the news media that critiques botched and bungled news stories and sets the record straight on important issues that have received slanted coverage."

10. Former senator Bob Kerrey, who served in Vietnam as a Navy SEAL, admitted that his SEAL team unit had unintentionally killed civilians during a raid on a Vietnamese village in 1969. Kerrey said that his unit was looking for a pro-Communist political leader and that they opened fire after hearing enemy fire. Gerhard Klann, a member of the unit, disputed Kerrey's account, saying that no enemy fire was heard and that the civilians were put in a group and fired upon.

11. Peter Arnett's op-ed piece in *USA Today* is titled "Brutal Fate for Those in War's Way" (May 3, 2001).

12. During a live broadcast as an embedded reporter for Fox News during the Iraq war (2003), correspondent Geraldo Rivera drew a map in the sand that the Pentagon felt revealed potentially damaging strategic information. When the Pentagon announced two days later that they were forcing him out of Iraq, Rivera announced that he'd be reporting on the war from Kuwait from then on. http://en.wikipedia.org/wiki/Geraldo_Rivera.

13. George Bush and Brent Scowcroft, *A World Transformed* (New York: Knopf, 1998); George Bush, *All the Best, George Bush: My Life in Letters and Other Writings* (New York: Scribner, 1999).

14. A turning point in the Vietnam War, the Tet (lunar New Year) offensive was a coordinated surprise attack by the Vietcong and North Vietnamese army on hundreds of towns, villages, and cities throughout Vietnam, including Saigon and Hue. TV footage of

Vietcong entering the American Embassy in Saigon became emblematic of the disparity between the optimistic reports of the war's progress that the US military was presenting to the American public and the reality on the ground. Although the Communist forces were defeated during Tet, it turned American public opinion against the war, which eventually led to a US withdrawal from Vietnam.

15. In 1972 *Washington Post* journalists Bob Woodward and Carl Bernstein, with the help of a confidential source named "Deep Throat" (then FBI deputy director Mark Felt), connected a break-in at the Democratic National Committee headquarters located in the Watergate hotel and office complex in Washington, DC, to high-ranking sources in the Nixon administration and the Committee to Re-Elect the President. Their investigation eventually led to President Nixon's resignation in 1974.

16. Allegations that Saddam Hussein had ordered Iraqi intelligence to assassinate President George H. W. Bush in April 1993 during his visit to Kuwait to commemorate the victory of the first Gulf War eventually led President Clinton to order an attack on Mukhabarat, Iraqi intelligence headquarters, which resulted in the deaths of eight civilians when some of the missiles launched landed on nearby homes. In a November 1, 1993, *New Yorker* article, "Case Not Closed," reporter Seymour Hersh wrote about the alleged assassination plot, "But my own investigations have uncovered circumstantial evidence, at least as compelling as the Administration's, that suggests that the American government's case against Iraq—as it has been outlined in public, anyway—is seriously flawed."

17. Peter Arnett, "Blood and Betrayal," *Playboy*, April 2005.

18. A British-educated former banker, Ahmed Chalabi has been the leader of the anti-Saddam Iraqi National Congress. He received large sums of money from the US government for his activities and was a source of faulty prewar intelligence. In an e-mail to her *New York Times* colleague, war correspondent John Burns, Miller wrote that Chalabi had "provided most of the front-page exclusives on WMD to our paper." Chalabi is currently acting oil minister for the Iraqi government.

19. In a September 22, 2003, article titled "The Big Lie," UK journalist John Pilger reported in the *Mirror*: "In Cairo, on February 24, 2001, Powell said, 'He [Saddam Hussein] has not developed any significant capability with respect to weapons of mass destruction. He is unable to project conventional power against his neighbors.' On May 25, 2001, Powell went further and said that Saddam Hussein had not been able to 'build his military back up or to develop weapons of mass destruction' for 'the last 10 years.' America, he said, had been successful in keeping him 'in a box.' . . . Two months later, Condoleezza Rice also described a weak, divided and militarily defenseless Iraq. 'Saddam does not control the northern part of the country,' she said. 'We are able to keep his arms from him. His military forces have not been rebuilt.'"

20. The Baath Party, of which Saddam Hussein was a member, follows a secular ideology that advocates pan-Arabic unity, Arab socialism, nationalism, and militarism. http://en.wikipedia.org/wiki/Ba'ath_Party.

21. In a July 27, 1997, article for Fairness and Accuracy in Reporting, "Thirty Year Anniversary: Gulf of Tonkin Lie Launched Vietnam War," Norman Solomon wrote: "The official story was that North Vietnamese torpedo boats launched an 'unprovoked attack' against a U.S. destroyer 'on routine patrol' in the Tonkin Gulf on August 2 [1964]—and that North Vietnamese PT boats followed up with a 'deliberate attack' on a pair of U.S. ships two days later. The truth was different. Rather than being on routine patrol on August 2, the U.S. destroyer *Maddox* was actually engaged in aggressive intelligence-

gathering maneuvers—in sync with coordinated attacks on North Vietnam by the South Vietnamese navy and the Laotian air force." President Johnson ordered US bombers to retaliate, and the Gulf of Tonkin Resolution essentially declaring war on North Vietnam passed through Congress easily. http://www.fair.org/index.php?page=2261.

22. A *Washington Post* profile of the Kurds at http://www.washingtonpost.com/wp-srv/inatl/daily/feb99/kurdprofile.htm describes them as fifteen to twenty million "largely Sunni Muslims with their own language and culture living in the generally contiguous areas of Turkey, Iraq, Iran, Armenia and Syria" collectively called Kurdistan. The Kurds seek their own state and have clashed with the nations in which their territories lie, including Iraq.

23. Founded in 1996 and based in Qatar, Al Jazeera is the largest Arabic news channel in the Middle East and provides twenty-four-hour news coverage. Al Arabiya is a twenty-four-hour news channel based in Dubai Media City.

24. Journalist Terry Anderson was Middle East correspondent for the Associated Press when Shiite Hezbollah partisans kidnapped him in Beirut (March 16, 1985) as part of an effort to drive the United States out of Lebanon. Iran supported Hezbollah in retaliation for Israel's use of US weapons and aid in strikes against Druze and Muslim targets in Lebanon. Anderson spent almost seven years in captivity and was released in December 1991. Several other Americans were held at the same time as Anderson. http://en.wikipedia.org/wiki/Terry_Anderson.

25. On December 21, 2004, a twenty-year-old Saudi suicide bomber named Ahmed Said Ahmed al-Ghamdi blew himself up in a US military mess tent in the northern city of Mosul, killing twenty-two people.

26. Journalist and author David Halberstam covered the Vietnam War for the *New York Times*.

27. During the Afghanistan war, the Northern Alliance was "made up of an ethnically and religiously disparate group of rebel movements united only in their desire to topple the ruling Taliban. Made up of mainly non-Pashtun ethnic groups, it relie[d] on a core of some 15,000 Tajik and Uzbek troops." http://news.bbc.co.uk/1/hi/world/south_asia/1552994.stm.

28. Ernest Taylor Pyle was a war correspondent during World War II who wrote from the perspective of the common soldier.

29. Pete Hamill, "Remembering Eddie Adams," *Digital Journalist*, October 2004. http://www.digitaljournalist.org/issue0410/hamill.html.

17

"WHAT DO YOU MEAN YOU'RE TELLING THEM To KILL ME?"

JON ALPERT
Independent Journalist
and War Correspondent
Interviewed May 2004

His close-cropped hair is gray now that he's in his midfifties, but Jon Alpert still looks and sounds like the lean, fearless "run and gun" reporter/cameraman that he has been known as. For thirteen years, he covered the world's hot spots for NBC. In this interview, he talks about covering the first Gulf War. From start to finish, it reads like a tense thriller. It is also a Kafkaesque account of an independent journalist's worst nightmare.

Once on the ground in Iraq, Alpert and his team realized that the only way they were going to do any real reporting was to break the rules: "You could not pan your camera. You had to inform your babysitter—everybody was assigned his own personal censor—exactly what shot you were going to do, when you turned the camera on, and when you turned the camera off. You could not shoot from a moving vehicle, you could not shoot government buildings, you couldn't shoot anybody in the army, you couldn't shoot any religious institutions, you couldn't shoot any schools —you couldn't do anything."

Ironically, neither the Americans nor the Iraqis wanted the truth to get out. "It was really a conspiracy with Saddam Hussein and the American government both trying to keep the press from seeing the same thing. The Americans didn't want us to see it because they wanted the American public to think that nobody was getting hurt. Saddam didn't want anybody to see it because he was pretending that he could take anything that the United States would give him." But Alpert and his team came up with all sorts of ingenious ways to get forbidden footage, including irrefutable evidence that the US military's smart bombs were veering off course and hitting civilians.

Eventually John and his team headed home with damning videotapes hidden in John's socks. They began crossing the desert on their way to the Jordanian border. Suddenly, they were stopped by a group of armed men. "One guy has a gun. He grabs me and puts the gun to my temple and he starts yelling and screaming and pulling the trigger. . . . I'm thinking I'm going to die, but I'm happy that my translator, Khaduri, is fighting for me. He's yelling at the guy. All of a sudden, Khaduri's not yelling any more. He's just standing there. I'm going, 'Khaduri, what'd you tell them?' He says, 'I'm telling them to kill you.'"

That particular moment was actually less absurd and unreal than what happened to Alpert upon his return to the United States. A hard lesson in what's wrong and what's missing in American television journalism is revealed in the second part of this courageous reporter's story. "The people in the United States are so profoundly ignorant about what's happening in the rest of the world that it's a very, very dangerous situation," says Alpert. "Now, if you want to know what's happening with some bachelor who twenty girls are trying to date, you're going to know everything you want to know about what he does in the morning, when he shaves himself, and what type of perfume he prefers on women, but does anybody have the slightest idea what's going on in Mexico right now, which touches on the United States? We don't. The press has done an astonishingly bad job of helping America understand the world."

With his wife, Keiko Tsuno, and their production team, Alpert has worked and often struggled to help America understand the world through programs produced at their Downtown Community Television Center (DCTV) in New York City. On its Web site, DCTV is described as "the most honored independent nonprofit media center in the nation," with programs that "reach over one hundred million viewers a year." I interviewed Alpert at his DCTV offices, which are located in a converted firehouse. First, he explained how a guy like him winds up heading for places that others are fleeing.

My team and I had been working for NBC News for thirteen years, initially with *Nightly News* but then primarily with the *Today Show* after that, and we had covered many different conflicts. We did a lot of coverage from Central America. We went to the Philippines when they had the insurrection with Marcos and covered guerrilla warfare there, and we covered the Vietnam-China border war. We had covered almost a dozen wars. As the conflict began brewing in the Middle East, I raised my hand and said, "I want to go." This seemed to be a war that could be covered from a safe distance. If you remember, there were a lot of reporters who became war correspondents, but they were based in Saudi Arabia, really, really far away from the conflict. Everybody was lining up to be a war correspondent. NBC told me to sit down.

I was watching all the coverage on TV and the generals would come on and they would have their press briefings every single day. Then the war actually started, and most of the American correspondents were evacuated from Iraq. Peter Arnett most famously stayed behind and everybody else either left voluntarily or was kicked out. This created a vacuum, the type of vacuum that I had used in the past to get an assignment to go. So again I was saying, "I can get into Iraq, I can get into Iraq." Of course I didn't know whether I could get into Iraq, but historically I had been able to get in under those circumstances. NBC, because they were uncovered, said, "OK, moron, if you want to go, go ahead."

I sent a buddy of mine to the Iraqi Embassy in Amman, Jordan, with a stack of tapes with all the wars that my team and I had covered and told him to ring their bell every two hours starting at six o'clock in the morning and drive them crazy until they agreed to look at the tapes. They did agree to look at the tapes, and he called me after three or four days and said, "OK, you will get your visa. It'll take about ten days, but start packing your stuff and get ready to come." I notified NBC News, and they said, "That's great, have a nice time covering the war."

That afternoon I got a phone call from Ramsey Clark. I had never talked to Ramsey Clark before. I had some vague idea who he was. In fact, he had been attorney general of the United States under President Lyndon Johnson. Ramsey Clark informed me that he was actually on his way to Iraq the next day and that he was being let in. He had intended to take a camera crew with him, but his cameraman had just been assigned a Coca-Cola commercial and was going to make enough money to put his daughter through college and had quit on Clark the day before Clark was leaving for Iraq, so would I like to go? I called up NBC and said, "I don't have to wait ten days. I can get in tomorrow." They said, "That's even better. Just make sure that you have a separation between you and Ramsey Clark, that you're not part of his agenda, that he's doing whatever he wants to do, and that you're doing your thing." So I went up and met with Ramsey and I said, "We need to maintain complete separation. I'm working for NBC News." He said, "That's fine, I just want somebody in there who will see what's going on. There aren't many cameras in Iraq, and people in America especially need to know."

So my team and I are waiting at the airport to board the flight when NBC's vice president of news, Don Brown, somehow finds me and orders me not to go to Iraq. I said, "Why in the world?" He says, "Because we just don't want you to go. First of all, our correspondent who has fled Baghdad says that you are stealing his visa and that there are a limited number of visas. Once NBC gets a visa and you're getting the NBC visa, we won't be able to get anybody else in. We want to have him and we don't want you and you can't go." I think the biggest factor that was going on here was that Don Brown used to be in charge of the Miami bureau for NBC News, and they were responsible for Central America. His correspondents didn't do as good a job as my team and I did. They never went up in the mountains. They didn't eat dirt. They didn't get bit by the flies. They didn't get shot at. We kicked their butt, story after story after story, and he didn't like it. Brown's bosses would say, "Hey, we're paying your correspondents all this money, how come this jerk Alpert is going down there and scooping up all these stories?" He had been rising up in the corporation, and he certainly remembered that we had made him look bad and this was an interesting opportunity for him to get back at us and he certainly was taking it. So I said, "OK, Don, who do you want in the country?" He says, "I want Tom Aspell, he's our reporter. I don't want you." I said, "OK, if I can get Tom into the country, can I go?" He says, "Oh, you can't do that. Don't even play." So I said, "Ramsey, the plane's leaving in thirty minutes. I have a problem. I can't go unless we get Tom

Aspell in the country." So Ramsey makes a couple of phone calls and the Iraqi officials tell him that anybody who enters the country as part of his caravan can get in. So I call back Don Brown. I mean, they're announcing our flight. I said, "Don, I can get him in the country. I can get twenty NBC people in the country, just line 'em up, we can get them all in." He says, "That's unacceptable and I order you not to go." So I said, "Wait a minute, what's going on here? You can't keep me from going, OK? I feel that it's my duty as a reporter to go. There's Peter Arnett's eyes in Baghdad and, as sharp as those eyes might be, they're not enough. It's my duty, beyond being a reporter; it's my duty as an American. My country's at war, and I'm not sure we know exactly what's going on there and I think that people in the United States need to know, so I'm going and you can't stop me." All of a sudden I was independent again and the problem was that all I had with me were NBC clothes. I had to get duct tape and tape over the NBC letters on my shirt. So I had something that said "news" on it, and you could see NBC's peacock logo, but you didn't see "NBC." I didn't have anything else to wear.

We arrived in Iraq unaffiliated, but I had said to Don Brown, "I hope that if we do good reporting and we have something that the American people could benefit from seeing that you'll broadcast it, and that whatever feud or reasons you have for trying to keep me from going won't stand in the way of letting the American people see important news." He said, "Well, I don't think you're going to get anything."

In the beginning, we thought he was going to be right. The Iraqis had the most severe press restrictions and censorship that I had ever experienced. You were presented with a two- or three-page document that listed all the prohibitions. You could not pan your camera. You had to inform your baby-sitter—everybody was assigned their own personal censor—exactly what shot you were going to do, when you turned the camera on, and when you turned the camera off. You could not shoot from a moving vehicle, you could not shoot government buildings, you couldn't shoot anybody in the army, you couldn't shoot any religious institutions, you couldn't shoot any schools—you couldn't do anything. We said, "My goodness, if we follow these rules, we don't have a prayer at showing anybody what's going on here in Iraq."

I don't know if people remember that the news that was coming from the war came from military press briefings. A general would get up and he would have a TV set behind him and would show the image from a plane's point of view of a target, sort of like a computer game, and you would see the bomb or the missile leave and precisely hit its target. It would always hit. I remember watching one of these news conferences and a reporter said, "General, we've seen these videotapes now for about a week, and we've never seen a single instance of a plane missing its target. Has a plane ever missed its target?" And he replied, "Absolutely not. We've had 100 percent accuracy." That particular statement set off alarms—ding, ding, ding—because I had been to so many wars, and there really isn't such a thing as a perfect war. There's no such thing as a bloodless war. Things go wrong. Things miss their target. It's inevitable. I wondered whether something like that was happening in Baghdad, whether these precision-guided bombs and missiles might inadvertently have gone off into a suburban neighborhood, might have hit a school, might have hit a hospital. Nobody knew, and with the Iraqi press restrictions, nobody would ever know. So I decided my team and I had to beat these press restrictions.

It took us three or four days to finally figure it out. I'm not sure I want to give away our secrets, but we had lots of tricks. We had coughing codes and all sorts of ways of shooting with the camera under our armpits. We had multiple cameras. We were using little tiny hi-eight cameras that the Iraqis had never seen before. Newspeople considered them to be toys and hadn't brought them into Iraq. Well, this was our war weapon.

The Iraqis knew we were tricking them. They could feel it. But they didn't know how, and it was driving them nuts. Every afternoon, they would send up the really big, tough censors to our room. They wanted to watch the tapes, because anything that was fed out of Iraq had to be seen from front to back by a censor. And we would come up with all these cocka-mamie excuses, "Oh, the batteries are dead. We're charging the batteries. Come back." Then something would happen, all the power would disappear, and we'd say, "Gee, we couldn't charge it." We had lots of extra batteries, but we just didn't tell them. If you stalled them long enough, there would always be another air raid, and they would all go down into the shelter in the basement and we wouldn't. We'd run out to the garden to film or we'd stand next to the window. So if you waited long enough, you could always get rid of the censors because they would go hide in the air raid shelter. After a week, we had irrefutable documentary evidence that all the smart bombs weren't so smart. We had evidence that this was not a bloodless war and that, in fact, people were dying. We had evidence that it wasn't just soldiers who were dying, that it was civilians, it was mothers, it was fathers; the average Iraqi was getting clobbered by some of the weaponry.

We were able to visit suburban neighborhoods in Baghdad and in Basra[1] that had been leveled by American weaponry. We talked to people whose fathers and neighbors had been killed. We saw the bodies. We had stuff that people needed to see because it becomes really dangerous if people in the United States think that we can wage a bloodless war where there are no casualties and people don't get hurt, because then you don't think twice and you figure, "Well, we just snap our fingers and all the bad things go away and nobody suffers." But people were really suffering.

The minders did not want us to see this death and destruction. Saddam Hussein and the American government were both trying to keep the press from seeing the same thing. The Americans didn't want us to see it because they wanted the American public to think that nobody was getting hurt. Saddam didn't want anybody to see it because he was pretending that he could take anything that the United States would give him. He was sort of "Ha, ha! Didn't hurt. Can't hurt me at all." So ironically, we had to overcome not only our government's attempts to present a certain point of view but also the Iraqis. And we did.

So we had these videotapes and we had to figure out how in the world we were going to get them back to the United States. We couldn't send them by satellite because the censor sat there and watched the images being transmitted. This was the difficulty that Peter Arnett had to contend with. He had to be very, very careful about what he was showing and what he was doing, and he couldn't break the rules like we were breaking them. He could challenge the censors and he could fight with them, but ultimately, they were going to filter the footage that he was sending out. If he was going to send something out that would ultimately get him kicked out of the country, then he would lose his bird's nest seat. We didn't intend to stay there for the whole war. First of all, we didn't have a way to send things out every day. Peter Arnett had a daily feed to the United States. We had nobody.

Peter Arnett's good. Everybody has certain talents. One of Peter's talents is that he's like a barnacle that attaches itself to the bottom of the boat and you just can't get it off. He knows how to do it. He did it in Vietnam and he did it in Iraq. Is Peter Arnett the world's best television reporter in terms of his ability to paint word pictures of what goes on during a war? Maybe there are other people who could do things better, but there isn't anybody better at digging in when everybody else gets kicked out. He does it with tenacity and he does it with courage. I saw him standing out there in the garden literally digging the heels of his shoes into the ground as the missiles were coming over and the Iraqis were trying to get him in the basement going, "Mr. Peter, Mr. Peter, come to shelter, Mr. Peter," and him going, "I'm standing here and the missiles . . ."

Meanwhile, we did not have the opportunity to send out our footage. First of all, NBC didn't want it. Remember that when we were getting on the airplane, Don Brown had said, "You're on your own, buddy," so we didn't have anybody to receive it.

We had to figure out how to get this footage of what was really happening in Iraq back to the United States and on the air. Arnett loaned me his satellite phone, and I called Steve Friedman, one of my buddies at NBC News. I described in elliptical terms the material that I had so that the Iraqis couldn't figure it out.

Steve was the executive producer of NBC *Nightly News* at that time. He had been the executive producer of the *Today Show*, and I had worked with him for many, many years. He's a very honest newsperson. He's also a friend. And he said, "We'll get it on the air. Just bring it back." So the challenge was, how are we going to get this stuff back to the United States?

We had four good tapes, and I put all four in my sock. We created a whole system of decoy tapes with labels and stuff like that so that if we were ever stopped we could hand over the fake tapes and I'd still have the real ones in my sock.

So we get ready to leave Baghdad. Now my team—producer Maryanne Deleo and our translator and coreporter Khaduri al-Kasey—and I were leaving, again, with Ramsey Clark. We set out on the highway to Jordan. Five minutes after we leave the hotel, the Americans bomb the bridge down the road and knock it out, so there's no way that we can take the highway. We start riding through the desert, winding our way around, hoping that we can eventually come back to the highway. I start seeing things that get me really excited, things that looked like military-industrial complexes that everybody was talking about. So I get up from the sunroof and I'm filming, and they're yelling, "John, sit down! Stop it!" And I'm saying, "But this is really interesting!" Then out from the middle of nowhere, I see these Iraqis sitting there with a big antiaircraft gun. I film them as we go by.

We come over a hill into this little town called Heet. I'd never had an experience like this before; it was like going back into biblical times. As soon as we came over the top of the hill, centuries rolled backward and old men in white robes were riding around on donkeys. I'm filming this, and we come to a bridge that has been knocked out by American air fire, so now we're crossing something that looks like oil cans that have been lashed together.

The problem with going through the desert in this circuitous route is that we begin to run out of gas. We had enough gas to go in a straight line to Jordan, but not enough to do this and the needle was moving toward empty. All of a sudden, at the end of the road, almost like a mirage, is a gas station. It was like seeing a McDonald's in the middle of the desert. We're going, "We're saved! We're saved!" and we drive up to it. It's closed. I get out and I figure, I'll shoot this because I might have to put this travelogue into the story, this adventure of trying to get out of the country and sneak these tapes back to America, and how we were stranded in the desert for a week because we had no gas. As I'm panning from the sign of "gas station" to the abandoned pumps, three cars come racing up. Actually, it was a car, a pickup truck, and a garbage truck. These guys had been following us the whole time and seen moron me filming. They come pouring out of their vehicles, yelling and screaming. One guy has a gun. He grabs me and puts the gun to my temple and starts yelling and screaming and pulling the trigger. He was trying to kill me. Luckily, the bullet jammed. The magazine that went into the handle of the gun must have been put in crooked or something. So he's pulling the trigger and the gun's not going off. The more it's malfunctioning, the more frustrated and angry he's getting. He's trying to do this, but he's jamming the thing more. He's screaming and pulling the trigger and everybody's yelling.

I'm thinking I'm going to die. I'm thinking I'm going to die, but I'm happy that my translator, Khaduri, is fighting for me. He's yelling at the guy. All of a sudden, Khaduri's not yelling any more. He's just standing there. I'm going, "Khaduri, what'd you tell them?" He says, "I'm telling them to kill you." And I said, "What do you mean you're telling them to kill me?" He says, "I'm telling him to kill you because he's going to get in a lot of trouble if he does. I'm telling him that you're a famous reporter, that we have official permission to leave, and that he's going to be in a lot of trouble, but to go ahead and kill you." Khaduri's argument didn't work on the guy because he kept on trying to pull the trigger. Then his friend calmed him down. The whole thing went on for maybe two or three minutes, but it seemed like an eternity. Finally, they took the gun away from him, packed us all into this little car, and drove us to the local police station.

Meanwhile, I have the tapes in my sock. I didn't want them to make me strip or do anything because they'd find the tapes in my sock. I'd also been filming all these things that I knew I was not supposed to be filming.

Normally when you're in a situation like this, you give them your camera, attempt to replay your tape and show them that you're not doing anything that they wouldn't like, and hope that you can talk your way back into the car and get the hell out of there. I couldn't let them look at my tape. Luckily, they had never seen one of these little cameras before. If this thing had happened now, when people know about little cameras, we'd have been in a lot of trouble.

In Iraq, sometimes when they torture you, one of the things they like to do is beat you on the soles of your feet with a bamboo stick. While about fifteen people were grilling us, there was one guy who never said anything. He was just looking at me and hitting his palm with a bamboo stick. I'm thinking, "Holy cow. First, he's going to take my shoes and socks off. He's going to find the tapes there and then he's just going to beat the hell out of us." I thought we were never going to get out of there.

Eventually, they sent over some lieutenant who managed to call Baghdad. It took about six hours for somebody in Baghdad to confirm that we were indeed invited guests and that they should treat us with respect. At this particular point, they invited us over for dinner and they couldn't have been nicer. I just sat there going, "Listen, thank them very much, get in the car, ask them to fill the gas tank up, and let's get the hell out of here." Which is what they did, and we managed to get back to Jordan. From there we flew to New York.

We arrived in New York with our four tapes and went directly to NBC. NBC looked at them and said, "This is amazing. Nobody in the United States knows that this is happening and this will be our lead story tomorrow night on NBC News." They said, "Go home, start to edit and get ready." So we edit all night long. We're about ready to start calling up everybody and tell them to watch the show when I get a phone call from Steve Friedman telling me there's bad news. He says, "You're about to get a telephone call from Michael Gartner, the president of NBC News, and he is going to do two things. He is going to cancel the broadcast of this tape and he's going to fire you." I said, "You know what, he can't do this over the telephone. He's got to look me in the eye." So Steve said, "Great, come on up." Gartner had no trouble looking me in the eye. When I asked him why he wasn't going to broadcast the tape, he said, "Because I'm sick and tired of you running around with the Ramsey Clarks of this world. I'm sick and tired that every time you go to the third world you make trouble for us. I won't broadcast this tape and you will never work at NBC again. There's the door." So there we were standing in front of 30 Rockefeller

Plaza with our little tapes in our hand. By this time we had edited the story into the three-minute broadcast that NBC had said they wanted.

So we were thinking, "What in the world are we going to do with this?" I remembered that CBS used to call every time I had a story on NBC News. Every time we scooped them, CBS would call and curse me out and say, "John, you're a moron, you're wasting your time with NBC. You should be working with us, don't ever work with them again. The next time you have a story, call us." So I call up CBS and I say, "Listen, I'm just back from Iraq and I have something, would you like to see it?" And they said, "Sure, come on over." So we went up to CBS and we showed the tape to Tom Bettag, the executive producer of their evening news program. He said, "This is astonishing. We have to broadcast it; we'll show it tomorrow. Go home, we'll send a producer down to see you. NBC never should have passed on this, and in the future, when you have all your scoops on CBS, they'll be kicking themselves in the butt for having made this mistake." We had certainly gotten all our teeth kicked in, but CBS had put them back and we went home thinking, "Great, we're finally going to get this story on the air."

I'm sitting around waiting the next morning for the CBS producer to show up and he doesn't show up. So around noon I'm getting worried and I call and they say, "Oh, you haven't heard? Two o'clock in the morning, Tom Bettag was fired."

I can't say for sure why he was fired. The coincidence certainly seems somewhat alarming that both networks for some reason had gotten cold feet and decided not to run the story. Why would somebody call and fire the head of the CBS evening news program at two o'clock in the morning? Tom maintains that it's got nothing to do with trying to keep the story off the air.

I don't specifically know otherwise. The only other thing that I do know is that there certainly was a concerted effort to control the press and keep stories like this from going on the air.

I can tell you about two other stories, one that concerns me and one that concerns a friend of mine. During the first Gulf War, the government came up with this pool system. Reporters were put into pools, and they thought that they were going to be taken into battle to see the action, when in fact they were diverted, sometimes hundreds of miles away. It was fairly brilliant of the government to do this. The people who were getting the best stories—certainly in the beginning of the war—were people who were working outside the pools. CBS and ABC both did stories from outside the pool that showed us things that nobody would have ever seen otherwise.

I had a friend who was working for a large weekly newsmagazine. I can't tell you my friend's name because he wants to keep working. He allows me to tell his story but doesn't allow me to use his name. He refused to go into those pools and was operating independently along the Saudi border. He actually received the first surrender of Iraqi soldiers during the war. He was wandering around in the desert when a bunch of Iraqis came over a sand dune and he was the only American around, so they surrendered to him. I don't remember what his other stories were, but he was getting all these herograms from his editor, "You're just doing a great job. Keep at it. You're the best." Then all of a sudden he got a message that he should go back to his hotel and not leave his room until he joined one of the government pools. He didn't understand this because he'd been operating outside the pools and been doing such a good job and they were telling him that.

What had happened was that the congressional liaison from the Pentagon had contacted the large media conglomerate that owned his newsmagazine and said, "You know that bill, that communication bill that's going through Congress? If you would like that bill to emerge in any form that you would find favorable, you tell your reporter to get in his hotel room and not to come out unless he's in a pool." Those were orders that were given to my friend. I'd like to tell you my friend's name, but he's still working in the media and he has kids to feed. And just so the audience knows, this bill that was going through Congress, if the law were written one way, it meant millions and billions of dollars for the mass communication companies, and if it were written another way, it meant they would lose millions and billions of dollars. There was direct pressure applied to these big companies to toe the line during the first Gulf War, and what happened to my friend is proof of that.

I can also tell a story about myself. After we got fired from NBC, after we tried to show the tape at CBS and the executive producer at CBS News was fired, there was no way that anybody in the United States was going to show our tape. The handwriting was on the wall that something bad is going to happen to you. It was the curse of our tape. So the tape was shown in Japan and Europe, and it's possible that if you were watching TV in Europe at this time, you might have seen this report. We won the Italian Peace Prize—whatever that is. I got to meet the president of Italy.

So our reports from Iraq got some distribution and attention in Europe. I was invited to the Amsterdam film festival to show them. While I was there, I was on a panel with Professor Philip Taylor from Leeds College. He was doing a scholarly study about the control and manipulation of the media by the American government. As part of his study, he had managed to get himself invited to a psy-ops convention. These are the psychological operatives who have the job of controlling and manipulating the media. They work for the US government, for the armed forces. He got into their convention down in Florida. They were sitting around one night celebrating and congratulating themselves for the tremendous job that they had done leading the press around during the war. He began complimenting them, too, and they were toasting each other and they said, "Yeah, we did a fantastic job. Ninety-nine percent." And he says, "Oh, yeah? What's the missing 1 percent?" They said, "That bastard Alpert." So what's interesting—and I certainly wasn't aware of what was going on and the specifics behind the scenes—was that the government was aware of what we were doing and had obviously thought that they weren't successful. I thought they were completely successful. Our reports were silenced.

The press completely fell down on its job during the first Gulf War. It's a shame. It's a scandal. They accepted this pool arrangement. They took all the information that the government was giving them at face value, and they presented it to the American people. They flag-waved in a way that I think ultimately damages our democracy. Everything was shown in red, white, and blue with heroic music. They made going to war seem wonderful, something like a harmless video game, when in fact it's a moment of horror. It's a moment of horror not only for our country but also for the people who are on the receiving end.

I think there was a degree of shame in the American press with the way in which they had been manipulated and used by the government during the first Gulf War. Not all reporters are fools, and there was a push within the reportorial community to gain better access to the Iraq war and not be so manipulated. There was some criticism of embedding, but it provided a far better opportunity for people to see what was going on. There were moments of extraordinary coverage during the Iraq war. If we step back and look, did they still do the flag waving, did they still have the heroic music? Yes, they did. But there were more instances where you were actually seeing what was going on, seeing the dead bodies, the fires, and what was really happening.

Why is it that CNN alone got to stay in Baghdad during the first Gulf War?

CNN, when they were starting, did something brilliant. They went to countries all over the world, and they executed treaties with the foreign ministry or the communications ministry. In exchange for getting access to the country, they would donate a number of satellite dishes to the country so that all the officials could see CNN. They would also invite these communications ministers to come to the United States to sign the agreement. Imagine if you were the communications minister of Laos, and you don't get out of Laos, and you get invited to Atlanta, Georgia, to sign this big deal, and you come back with satellite dishes for all the big shots in your country. CNN had ingratiated themselves with the elite of many countries around the world through this very intelligent strategy. So CNN had an advantage over other networks because they were being watched.

For the leadership of Iraq, it was an opportunity to have a window on the world and to see how they were being perceived. Could they have watched CNN with their satellite dishes and booted Peter Arnett out at the same time? Yes, but I think that Peter Arnett had convinced them that he would report objectively. I think that they had trouble with some of his reports, people on all sides might have had trouble, but I think Peter was doing his best to be honest and the Iraqis accepted that. But again, this is his talent. There are some boxers who can go in the ring against somebody who is ten times bigger than they and still be standing at the twelfth round. That's Peter Arnett's talent. He's able to be in the middle of all this fury and, somehow or other, he's standing at the end.

After the first Gulf War, you got an interview with Saddam Hussein. Was that aired anywhere?

It aired in certain places. I don't want people to think that there's a black cloud that's been following us around because for many years we were the only independent organization that got reports on the commercial networks. We had a spectacular thirteen-year run at NBC. I feel very privileged to have been part of that. Whenever the bell was ringing someplace in the world, we could be on the first plane out. We didn't have to clear a lot of this with any gatekeepers at NBC. We had a tremendous amount of autonomy, so much so that our biggest problem was jealousy from fellow reporters. They all envied the opportunities that we had during this period of time. I don't know whether I was too naive to perceive this, but there's a difference in war coverage. When the United States is engaged in a proxy war, when we were arming and financing the contras in Nicaragua[2] or when we are helping some group in some other part of the world, if

American soldiers aren't on the ground, you can make a report that might be critical of the American government and not get the death penalty, figuratively speaking. It's not fatal, because American troops aren't involved. That's the big difference. Once American soldiers hit the battlefield, you can look at the coverage in the American press and, whether it's because of pressure from the government or misplaced patriotism, the rules change. I don't want to be seen as a critic, but when your report contradicts what the American government is saying, it's the death penalty. And we got the death penalty. When we said, "The United States is doing something in El Salvador that they shouldn't be doing," they didn't like it, and they tried to keep those reports off the air, but they didn't try to make us walk the plank. But there's no room for forgiveness in a situation when American troops are actually involved in combat.

This not only tells me, this tells everybody who is reporting, that they better be darn careful because consequences are going to be paid if you see the American government doing something wrong and you feel the American people need to know. You can get your head handed to you. It's interesting. If I were a critical reporter in Iraq under Saddam Hussein, I'd be dead in two seconds. The way my government responds to people like me is very benign compared to the majority of countries. In the majority of countries, I'd be looking up at six feet of dirt right now. I love my country as a result of the freedoms that we have. But I was always taught that we need to be vigilant and that we need to defend our freedoms, and I always felt that I was doing something very, very patriotic with our reports, and I'll continue to do so. The problem is that it's more difficult now for us to get people to see them.

When the Iraq war was starting, we were trying to figure out what we could do that would be useful. We had lost our broadcast platform since the first Gulf War. It had been almost impossible for us to get programs on the commercial news channels. And we thought, "Why don't we have American and Iraqi youth speak to each other before the war? Let them get to know each other, because whenever you have a war you tend to demonize the other side." Maybe if the Americans and the Iraqis could talk to each other, it would be useful." If you've been to as many wars as I have, you would like to have people talk instead of fight. So it was with that objective—to promote a conversation—that we went over to Iraq and set up this satellite dialogue between American youth and Iraqi youth. It was a nice program. The fascinating part about it is that it changed the minds of so many people who saw it. But this was another case in which it was almost impossible to get the program on TV in the United States.

It was taken to PBS, CBS—everyplace. *On the Media*, which is a program on National Public Radio, actually did a story about the spectacular un-success we had in getting this program on the air, because they had watched it and thought it was good. PBS rejected it because it dealt with youth and for some reason the rules about youth programming were very specific and it was rejected for that reason. Sometimes you don't get an answer. Sometimes they just don't call you back. I'd be happy to have anybody look at that program and the follow-up program that we did after the war. If the programs are boring, if they are uninformative, if you would rather watch the hockey game or the soccer game or something like that, I can understand that, but most people who have seen these programs find them compelling. The programs ultimately wound up on satellite TV, on Link Television, which goes into a lot of people's homes, but not a lot of people watch it.

Given your experience as a journalist and a cameraman/reporter, do you think what you have been experiencing is because American soldiers are involved in this conflict?

The United States is basically a very patriotic country. When our soldiers are on the battlefield and could get killed, we want to support them. The general public wants to believe the government, and that's how they start out. If the government is telling the people the truth and if the cause that we are engaged in is a just cause, people want that. We don't want to think that we're doing something wrong and that we're killing people who don't need to be killed. We don't want to think that we're being sent off on a fool's errand. So there is a natural prejudice against anybody who is coming and saying, "By the way, you had better pay attention to this because I don't think the government is telling you the truth" or "Maybe some people haven't thought through very clearly what mission you're on and you might have been sent on a fool's errand." So it's very difficult. You're really walking up a very steep hill when you start out trying to tell the truth sometimes.

Also, if I were a general, maybe it's not in my best interest to have reporters walking around the battlefield and seeing what happens in a war. War is ugly. It's just really hard to put a pretty face on it. You have to sell a war by telling people that at the end of this ugly, nasty road is something worthwhile. It's the same reason why they don't let people into a sausage factory. When you're eating the sausage, it looks good and tastes good, but if you ever saw how they were made, you'd never eat another sausage again. If you see what goes on in a war, you're not going to want to go to war. You're not going to want to have your country wage war, you're going to do everything you can to avoid it. I've seen all these wars, so I have a prejudice for peace in general because I've seen the horror of wars. But once a general commits to war, he doesn't want anything in his way. We get in the way when we're out there saying, "By the way, yes, 99 percent of the bombs hit their target, but you happened to have missed over here and you hit a school and there are twenty dead school children." They don't want anybody to know that. I believe that in many cases, the United States military is making an extraordinary effort to be accurate with their weaponry. They're not trying to kill civilians. But it's a war and it happens and it's our job as reporters to report the totality of what happens. We should put it in perspective. I've always thought that our reports were balanced and that people need to see them. But there are people who try to keep the audience from seeing these things, and we've paid the consequence of that.

As I sit here right now, I'm confessing to you that we are embedded with the American military in this war. From the moment the Arkansas National Guard received notice of their activation on up through their training and deployment in Iraq, we have been filming them. We have had unfiltered access. Part of this is because the primary filmmakers come from Arkansas. They understand the people they're filming, and the people they're filming understand them. There is a great deal of trust. We are reporting exactly what happens to this unit. Some of it is quite traumatic. I don't know what's going to happen when this stuff goes on the air and people say, "Oh, my goodness, what in the world are these guys doing?" But up to this particular moment, the military has treated us the way we want to be treated as reporters. They've let us do our job, and we've made sure we haven't gotten in the way. When you're embedded, the one thing you're not allowed to do is compromise the security of the unit. You can't reveal where they are. You have to very careful about that. Those are the rules. On the government side, they're not supposed to tell you that you can't film things. The only thing you're not allowed to do is reveal a death before the family gets notified. We've been very, very careful to follow the rules, and they've followed the rules on their side.

What about coverage of the Iraqi side? Do you think there's been good coverage of that?

The coverage of the war has primarily been how it affects America, how it affects American troops, and what's happening to the American troops.

So there is a preponderance of that. But there has been more reporting on the consequences for Iraqis during this war than during the previous Gulf War. Everybody should know how dangerous it is to do that reporting. We were there right after the invasion was over, and there was an almost anarchistic situation in the country. There was an absence of law and order, an absence of protection. One of our cars was carjacked. We were covering Iraqi athletes and what had happened to them under Saddam and his son Uday, and how nobody could make any mistakes and how barbaric Saddam and Uday were. The fact that these guys aren't in power is wonderful. They were torturing their own athletes. If you were on the Iraqi national soccer team and you'd lost a game and you were flying back into the country, Uday would be waiting at the airport to take you to a camp and torture you for three days. It was incredible.

We were doing this report when our driver asked if he could go out and get lunch. So he goes out and gets lunch and we're done filming the soccer team. We're standing around wondering, "Where the hell is this guy?" Three hours later he comes back on foot. His car was carjacked. Two days later, one of my coreporters was driving through Baghdad. He was five blocks away from the Palestine Sheraton Hotel complex, which is where all the reporters were staying. The car in front of him stopped at an intersection, and four guys came out—boom, boom, boom, boom— each one of them had a gun. They killed a guy in the car in front of him, yanked the guy out of the car, and drove off in his car. If my colleague had arrived at the intersection three seconds earlier, he'd be dead. Reporters are being targeted now. The people who are working the streets in Iraq right now to bring you the news of what's happening to the Iraqi people are doing so with extraordinary courage in a very, very dangerous situation. I've ordered our reporters not to do that type of coverage because it's too dangerous. It's a suicide mission right now. So what's going to happen is you will begin to get less and less information about what's going on with the Iraqi people. It's just too dangerous.

I covered the first Gulf War and the Iraq war, and I don't think the press coverage has really helped the American people understand what they need to know. We are the world's lone superpower. We can be a blessing to the world or we can be a bully. Our government at this particular moment is projecting its force in areas of the world far, far away from us here in New York City, and it is imperative that the American people know what happens when we push here and when we push there. If they think that we can push over here and the flowers start sprouting up and that there aren't any consequences in waging war, this world becomes a very dangerous place, because we're going to start waging war everywhere. If you've seen war, you know how horrible it is. It's just not pretty and you don't want it to happen. So right now, the press has a tremendous responsibility to try and help the American people understand what's going on everywhere and especially in Iraq. Have we done a great job? We haven't. We really need to do better. We need to do better for the sake of our own democracy, but also for the safety of the world.

If you look at television in the United States, it's almost as if we've red-lined much of the world and we never do any reporting on those areas. When was the last time anybody in the United States saw anything about Latin America? Maybe there were five programs about Latin America on American television last year. When was there anything on Southeast Asia? When was there anything about what's going on in Indonesia? All of a sudden we became aware that there were Islamic fundamentalists in the Philippines. What's going on in the Philippines? The people in the United States are so profoundly ignorant about what's happening in the rest of the world that it's a very, very dangerous situation. Now if you want to know what's happening with some bachelor who twenty girls are trying to date, you're going to know everything you want to know about what he does in the morning, when he shaves himself, and what type of perfume he prefers on women. But does anybody have the slightest idea what's going on in Mexico right now, which touches on the United States? We don't. The press has done an astonishingly bad job of helping America understand the world.

People who think that the press is doing a great job will point to the emergence of the twenty-four-hours-a-day news networks. These didn't exist fifteen years ago. That's good. That's a development that can help inform people in the United States. So there are things that have happened in recent history that have improved the opportunity for people to learn through the press, specifically through television. But at the same time, there is this incessant need and drive for profitability within almost every media organization that can get in the way of providing the reporting that would be most useful.

I'll tell you a story from MSNBC. I went there with some projects that I wanted them to consider and was in the process of getting this project rejected. I happened to be sitting in the office of one of their producers there. Now we have these scandals of the moment on which television focuses an extraordinary amount of attention. There was the most famous one, the O. J. Simpson[3] case. The one going on at the moment that I was in the producer's office was called "Nannygate." This was, I think, a British nanny who shook the baby that she was taking care of too hard and the baby died. This was getting around-the-clock coverage. Well, this particular producer had decided that he was going to put on something else. He put on an economic report the previous day that was just astonishing in terms of the unemployment statistics. I don't really know the details, but it was a very significant but boring report about what was going on with the American economy. I was in the office when the head of NBC News called him up and began screaming at him. We have to bleep all the words, but he said, "What in the blankety-blank are you doing putting this crap on the air? I told you, put that nanny on the air and you keep her on the air and you don't put anything else on except the nanny!" The guy was a little bit embarrassed because the yelling on the other end of the phone was so loud and so filled with dirty words.

The TV networks have minute-by-minute ratings, and the news president was watching the ratings go up with nannygate, nannygate, nannygate. All of a sudden, the economic story came on and the viewers dropped. That's when he called the producer and scolded him. So there's tremendous pressure to hold your audience, to hold your ratings. People like to be titillated. Let's not pretend that people at home aren't sitting and watching some of this junk.

> **So what do you do? Here we are the nine-hundred-pound gorilla on the planet and we have a press that for many reasons can't really do a proper job of informing. What ideas do you have for creating a more vibrant, viable press and informing the American people?**

I like to think that the programs that we make are entertaining and informative at the same time. The record seems to bear that out. The shows that we manage to get on television have all been critically acclaimed and have gotten high ratings at the same time. We're working primarily with HBO now, and our programs score. So I think it can be done. But we really need a little more courage on the part of the people who are running the news organizations. The difficulty is that if you're doing your job as a reporter, you're quite often kicking people in the shins. If you kick people in the shins enough, they're going to kick you back. If you kick the government in the shins, it kicks back really hard. There are so many ways in which large corporations can have their bottom line change as a result of government regulations. The media is a regulated industry. The government may not totally control the media, but it sure has a good grip on certain sensitive parts. The guys who run these media companies aren't stupid. They behave accordingly.

You've defined the problem, but what's the solution? Now that we're in the mass-consciousness media era, to have any impact you've got to reach a large audience, otherwise you're just reporting out of a paper bag.

I'll tell you what we're doing here at Downtown Community Television Center. We're providing the resources and training to build a generation of new reporters who don't come from privileged backgrounds, who come from the poor parts of New York City, who are people of color. They're people who have never had access to the media before, and they come here and get training. We're training a hundred and twenty at-risk high school students. We're training a group of disabled producers. You want to talk about a group that gets really biffed around or ignored by the press, it's the disabled—the largest minority in the United States. We're training them. We're thinking of starting a TV high school next year. We have built a bus with a TV wall on the side of it that we drive around the United States so we can directly reach people. Is this broadcasting? It's not; it's narrowcasting. Is it labor intensive? It is. It is frustrating sometimes. But do we reach people directly? It enables us to do so. We're trying. The tightrope wire from here to the people is stretched out, and we're doing our best to walk across it. We've fallen down very dramatically a couple of times, but we keep climbing back up and we keep trying. I'm not trying to say that we're saintly or we're wonderful. There are other people who are doing the same thing, who are trying to do honest reporting and to give access to the media to other people who have been disenfranchised. I think that our freedoms need to be constantly defended, and that's what we're doing. That's what we were brought up to do. When you're brought up in the United States, you're in a free country and you defend your freedom. We're doing it.

JON ALPERT has distinguished himself as an award-winning journalist, educator, and community activist. He has received eleven National Emmy Awards for news and documentary programs and founded the premier not-for-profit media education center in the United States, the Downtown Community Television Center (DCTV), in lower Manhattan.

In 1971, just one year out of college, Alpert and his wife, Keiko Tsuno, started the media center. It began as a grassroots effort. Alpert bought a used mail truck for five dollars, installed TV sets in the side, and began showing his videotapes on street corners in Chinatown. At first nobody watched, but soon his tapes about local issues from community board elections to the Chinatown street fairs began to attract small crowds. Soon thereafter, DCTV was born as a neighborhood center where members of the community could come to learn the emerging art of video at affordable prices. Alpert's vision for DCTV was not just a center where one could view documentaries but as a place that would put the power of the media directly in the hands of its viewers.

Students and citizens alike were soon coming to DCTV to take classes, borrow equipment, and make their own videotapes about issues that concerned them. Alpert, too, was busy making innovative documentaries about hot news spots all over the world. Between 1974 and 1979 he coproduced five one-hour documentaries for public television. The earliest, titled *Cuba: The People,* presented the first American television coverage inside Cuba in ten years. The *New York Times* selected Alpert's work as one of the best television productions in the country that year. His 1977 award-winning piece on Vietnam called *Vietnam: Picking Up the Pieces* marked the first time an American TV crew had filmed in Vietnam since the war. All the while, Alpert fostered the continued growth of his cutting-edge media center in Chinatown. In 1976 he won one of three duPont-Columbia Citations and a Christopher Award for his work *Chinatown: Immigrants in America.*

Alpert began contributing to NBC in 1979 with his coverage of the Vietnam-China border wars. Over the next dozen years his investigative reporting, editing, and camera work earned an impressive string of awards and scoops. He interviewed and helped repatriate the last known American POW, Bobby Garwood. He was the only reporter to gain entry into "reeducation" camps for former South Vietnamese officials. During the hostage crisis in Iran, he was the last reporter to gain entry into the embassy where the American hostages were being held, and he broke the news of the conflict between Iran and Iraq. When Fidel Castro came to address the United Nations, Alpert and his team were the only non-Cubans allowed access to the Cuban leader. Alpert was in China during the Tiananmen Square massacre and, by posing as a tourist, reported from parts of the county off-limits to other reporters. Alpert's reports on the first Gulf War were awarded the Italian Peace Prize by the president of Italy. He is the only reporter to have interviewed Saddam Hussein after the war. Alpert's work with NBC garnered seven National Emmy Awards, five Monitor Awards, the Clio Award, and the Gabriel Award. Alpert remains the only Emmy-winning reporter to be honored in both the editing and the camera work categories.

In recent years, Alpert has worked with HBO to produce a series of investigative documentaries. His *Lock-up: The Prisoners of Rikers Island* won critical acclaim and the highest ratings of any HBO documentary. In 1995 *High on Crack Street—Lost Lives in Lowell* was hailed as the best antidrug documentary ever made and won Alpert his third duPont-Columbia Award.

Alpert remains committed to DCTV and its mission of promoting strength and diversity in the media by empowering independent producers whose artistic or cultural roots are based in the community. In 2001 DCTV celebrated its thirtieth anniversary and continues to serve as a model of success for media centers across the country. With Alpert acting as codirector, DCTV trains over two thousand students each year and loans video equipment to more than four hundred community organizations. DCTV's programs for minority youth have transformed former dropouts into student video champions winning an array of festival awards and honors. The New York City mayor's office called DCTV's programs "the best in the City."

Alpert continues to push the envelope with state-of-the-art media education at DCTV. In the past two years, he has overseen the completion of America's first Cyberstudio, which can transmit live programs into millions of homes via cable, direct satellite, and the Internet This is matched by Alpert's most recent accomplishment, the DCTV Cybercar, an ordinary coach bus that was converted into a fully mobile television production studio with an exterior video wall and full broadcasting capabilities. Alpert's early love of mobile, democratic media out of a mail truck in Chinatown has now been transformed into a first-rate media tool of the twenty-first century.

NOTES

1. Basra is the second-largest city in Iraq and is about 340 miles south of Baghdad.

2. The Iran-Contra affair was a "secret arrangement in the 1980s to provide funds [outside of congressional oversight] to the Nicaraguan Contra rebels from profits gained by selling arms to Iran. Iran/Contra was the product of two separate initiatives during the Reagan administration. The first was a commitment to aid the Contras who were conducting a war against the [Left-leaning] Sandinista government of Nicaragua. The second was to placate 'moderates' within the Iranian government in order to secure the release of American hostages held by pro-Iranian groups in Lebanon and influence Iranian foreign policy in a pro-Western direction." http://www.factmonster.com/ce6/ history/A0825447.html.

3. Football great Orenthal James Simpson was tried for murdering his wife, Nicole Brown Simpson, and her friend, Ronald Goldman, who were stabbed to death on July 12, 1994. Simpson was acquitted in 1995 of criminal charges, but both victims' families won judgments amounting to $33.5 million in damages against him in civil court in 1997.

18

"WE'RE NOT MOTHER TERESAS IN FLAK JACKETS"

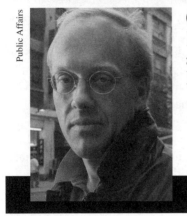

Public Affairs

CHRIS HEDGES
Foreign/War Correspondent
and Author
Interviewed May 2004

C hris Hedges thinks that, above all, war correspondents should speak for the victims. When he does, it is devastating. During his interview, he talked about the horrors he had seen and heard in a calm voice that conveyed restrained rage. His words landed on my chest like a lead weight. Some may find this entire interview difficult to read. The truth in it is almost unbearable.

Hedges doesn't look like a guy who spent fifteen years subjecting himself to all kinds of physical and psychological duress to cover wars. He definitely doesn't look like a guy who speaks Arabic. Or a guy who would shave his head, put on a uniform, and pass himself off as a US military officer to get past checkpoints during the first Gulf War. Meeting him, you realize that his strength isn't a matter of muscles and marrow but mind and spirit. Hedges is definitely a spiritual man. It's not just because he's the son of a Protestant minister or has a master of divinity from Harvard University. It's because what he says, does, and writes show that he's constantly striving to live a well-examined and conscionable life. Telling what he knows to be true is a big part of that, and Chris is fierce and unsparing in his criticism of the war coverage, American society, and America's presence in the Middle East.

> If we really reported war as it is, people would be so disgusted and appalled they wouldn't be able to watch. War is packaged and sanitized the same way the poisons of tobacco or liquor are packaged and sanitized. We see enough of the titillation and excitement to hold our interest, but we never actually see what wounds do to bodies. We never have to watch a kid with his stomach blown out or his legs blown off spending twenty minutes dying on the sand. That's what war is.
>
> I don't think Americans yet have a clear view of how hated we are not only in Iraq but also throughout the Middle East and increasingly throughout the globe. I don't think they have a clear understanding that in many ways we deserve to be hated. . . . We are a very ignorant, hedonistic society. Unfortunately, we wield a great deal of power. We wield it blindly and we are a danger to others and we are now a danger to ourselves.

While delivering a commencement speech in Illinois, Hedges was nearly mobbed by an angry crowd that viewed him as heretically unpatriotic for speaking about their nation this way. He, however, sees himself in a diametrically opposite light: "The fact is that the role of a patriot is in many ways to be a dissident. It's to be self-critical to make the country a better place."

Although Hedges seeks the higher moral ground, he admits that he and his ilk are by no means saints: "I think that there are many motives that go into creating a good war correspondent, some of which are very dark . . . such as an addiction to war, a sense of empowerment, and all that kind of stuff. Those are all very real. We're not Mother Teresas in flak jackets." What drove him to put his life on the line for all those years, he says, is a "deep distrust of authority [and] a sense of outrage at injustice and abuse."

The day we spoke, the *New York Times* had issued an apology for its prewar coverage. Chris's first comments were about the paper's willingness to criticize its own performance.

Today, the *New York Times* ran an editor's note[1] that said that the prewar coverage failed to ask the kinds of critical questions that should have been asked and gave too much prominence to charges that have turned out be fabrications; that there was a tendency to believe the most salacious stories about what was happening in Iraq and a failure to question the veracity of those stories and give the proper display to critics of those stories and to highlight holes that were punched in those stories.

I think it was courageous and overdue. It was long overdue, but I think the paper has to own up to its failure to examine the kinds of stories that it was being fed. It was a terrible failing, not only on the part of the *New York Times* but also on the part of most of the American press.

Some journalists have said to us that they think the press did as good a job as could be expected before the war.

As somebody who was on the investigative unit after 9/11 and who covered al Qaeda, as someone who spent seven years of my life in the Middle East and who speaks Arabic, I found the coverage shameful and appalling. I'm surprised that in retrospect anyone would defend it. During that time, there was this kind of blind euphoria and patriotic zeal and fear, which often happens in wartime. Remember, the attacks happened in New York, and that affected many of the media organizations based there. That led to a really unquestioning attitude on the part of the press toward the information that was being handed to it by ideologues who we now know cooked the information. So it disturbs me that people would defend it. I think that self-criticism is extremely important so that we are aware of the errors we make, and we work hard not to make them again.

How does that happen? Isn't part of being a professional journalist not getting caught up in any waves of patriotism or fear?

There are two types of journalists. There are the journalists who hang out in Washington and "do lunch." They are dependent on high-level sources for their stories. They're dependent on leaks. Then there are those of us who, as in my case, spend almost twenty years abroad in the field. We are often at war not only with officials in Washington but also with our own bureaus in Washington. So this is an old story. It goes back to Vietnam and before, where you have policymakers spinning out a story or a version of events about what's happening in a foreign country that makes them and the administration they work for look favorable. Then you have those of us in the field. For instance, I was in Sarajevo during the war.[2] Those of us reporters in the field were saying, "The Dayton Peace Plan is not going to re-create a multiethnic Bosnia. It is a partition plan."[3] And we butt heads.

We butt heads with the officials, and we butt heads with the reporters who over time in Washington become too close to these officials and lack any kind of critical distance. Those two currents have always been strong within American journalism, and that tension has always been there.

Is there something that's not being reported now that you desperately wish would get out in terms of what's going on in Iraq?

I don't think Americans yet have a clear view of how hated we are not only in Iraq but throughout the Middle East and increasingly throughout the globe. I don't think they have a clear understanding that in many ways we deserve to be hated. We don't yet see what we're doing through the eyes of the other. I think that good reporters have to step outside of their own circle, their own nation, their own society, and report on how others view us, especially the United States, being at this point the occupying power. This takes time. It took time for the French in Algeria to finally understand what was happening in Algeria.[4] It took time for us to understand what happened in Vietnam. What is happening in Iraq is a classic colonial occupation where we rule by force and we maintain control by force. We do it in an extremely brutal and bloody manner, and I think Americans don't yet understand how horrific the violence is from our end.

That brings me to that speech you gave at Rockford College.

I gave a commencement talk at Rockford College in Rockford, Illinois, on May 17, 2003. This was not long after President Bush had landed on the aircraft carrier in his flight uniform under the banner saying, "Mission Accomplished." I used the commencement address to criticize what was happening in Iraq. I talked about how isolated we were becoming. I talked about how we had folded in on ourselves as a nation and built a kind of alliance, a troika against terror with Russian president Vladimir Putin and Israeli prime minister Ariel Sharon, men who do not shrink from carrying out gratuitous and senseless acts of violence in Chechnya and Palestine. I talked about how certainly the Muslim world, one-fifth of the world's population, most of whom are not Arab, now see us through the prism of Palestine, Chechnya,[5] and Iraq. I said that the violence was not over but was, in fact, just beginning; that what we were seeing was a war of liberation, but it was a war of liberation by Iraqis against American occupation.

This deeply angered the crowd. Very shortly into the speech, people stood and began to boo and jeer. My microphone was cut off twice. Two or three students tried to climb onto the platform to push me away from

the podium. They were escorted off. If one of those students had succeeded, there's no doubt that several hundred people in this crowd of
about a thousand would have cheered and applauded. I was removed from
the ceremony while it was in process by campus security and police and
put on a bus to Chicago before the graduation ceremony ended. The reaction of the crowd was so virulent because I wasn't just challenging a
viewpoint (which, of course, I was), I was challenging their right to that
kind of emotional euphoria that comes with victory, the sense of victory,
with identifying with American power. The tension between me and the
crowd was one where I was bursting their bubble, in a sense. Or attempting to burst their emotional bubble. That's why people reacted so emo-
tionally. There were people standing in the crowd weeping, singing "God
Bless America." They also were chanting, "Send him to France" (there
are worse fates). The experience drove home to me the degree to which
large numbers of Americans had become infected with this disease of
nationalism and blind patriotism, which ultimately is about self-exalta-
tion, and how deeply entrenched it had become within my own society.
Now this is not something new, I've seen this in other war zones, but it's
deeply disturbing and unsettling when it's your own country.

You can't blame the blind support for the war simply on the press or
on the Bush administration. The American people were complicit. The
press, the coverage of the war, and the buildup to the war, was almost
exclusively focused on the power of our weaponry and the might of our
military. Not only were the graphics quite consciously designed to look
like a video game, but the message was that not only are our weapons
powerful, but we as a people are powerful. People watched this, and they
felt empowered through this relationship between our military and our
cruise missiles and all the military hardware that we have and the sophistication of it. We ate it up. Unfortunately, the worst elements of the press
fed it to us, but we wanted it. So I think that there was a deep complicity
on the part of the American public in the war, and the press realized very
quickly that this was something that appealed to the basest elements of
American society, perpetuating that sort of myth of war, of glory, of
decency, of heroism, of might. That mythic narrative of war is something
that always boosts ratings and sells newspapers. It's how William Randolph Hearst built his empire at the turn of the century, by creating a war
where there was no need for one.[6]

If we really reported war as it is, people would be so disgusted and
appalled they wouldn't be able to watch. War is packaged and sanitized

the same way the poisons of tobacco or liquor are packaged and sanitized. We see enough of the titillation and excitement to hold our interest, but we never actually see what wounds do to bodies. We never have to watch a kid with his stomach blown out or his legs blown off spending twenty minutes dying on the sand. That's what war is. The only people who ever see war are the people who go there, and that's been true in every conflict I've been in. Even in Sarajevo, when these huge shells would come in to a crowd and leave bodies eviscerated and pools of blood and children screaming in agony, the pictures that were sent back were horrific but didn't come close to matching the horror of the experience. And that's always true in war. In a sense, the censorship of the real images of war and the real tragedy of war leads to the perpetuation of the myth. It's very hard for us to get a sense of what war is like because it's not shown.

How were you regarded by your editors at the *New York Times*? They must have had mixed feelings about you.

I was a headache. After I gave this commencement talk, I had a letter of reprimand from my newspaper. I didn't become a reporter to work for the *New York Times*. I went to Latin America in the early 1980s as a freelance journalist because I thought it was as close as my generation was going to come to fighting fascism. This was the age of Pinochet and the dirty war in Argentina and the death squads in El Salvador. That doesn't mean that I would ever lie on behalf of the victims or of the organizations such as the FMLN[7] that were fighting the government—I would not. But that kind of passion or activism creates in the world of American journalism a great deal of tension. It's not as easily accepted as perhaps it might be in Europe.

American journalism is a different animal from European journalism, from, let's say, *Le Monde* or the *Guardian* in England. It purports to be objective. Of course, this is ridiculous. There's that old joke we used to say about this foreign affairs magazine, but I think it applies to American journalism: Some people say Mexico looks north, some people say Mexico looks south, some people say Mexico looks north and south. By the third paragraph you have no idea what's going on, but it has included all viewpoints. That very much is the disease of American journalism, where they end up canceling out the truth by giving so much space to people who are lying through their teeth. It's a little easier when you're abroad to take more leeway or latitude. For instance, there were things that I could write or say about Slobodan Milošević[8] that I could never say about George Bush. Slobodan Milošević's press machine wouldn't come after me the way the White House or the State Department would. So, while I was overseas, I had a lot more latitude to be critical within my reporting. Since I've come back, I've been completely consistent as to who I am, but of course, now I have problems with my own government and my own editors. I haven't changed my approach nor will I. If it comes to a point where in order to remain a journalist I'm muzzling myself, what's the point? There's no point. That's not why I took the kinds of personal risks that I took in war zones. I'm not interested in it. So I will keep my voice, and if an institution becomes too uncomfortable with it, then it's time for us to divorce.

I have had terrible problems with administrations in the past as a foreign correspondent. I had terrible problems with the Clinton administration in Bosnia. They could lie as rapidly, I'm afraid, as this administration.

After the Dayton Peace Accords were signed, the warlords and war criminals were running the country. Especially on the local level, the warlords who had engaged in terrible atrocities were still in control. The Clinton administration did not want this as an election issue. So they spun out this lie that free and fair elections could be held and that it was going to be a multiethnic state, and it was a big success. Now, the *Washington Post* had pulled their reporter out, so I was pretty much alone. And I was hammering home the point that we didn't have peace in Bosnia, what we had was the absence of war. And they went after me. They went after me, I think, in a way that was often not honest. For instance, I wrote a story on corruption, and Jamie Rubin, who was the spokesperson of the State Department, got deeply involved in this.

I wrote stuff on the Kosovo Liberation Army, and I felt that the kinds of accusations they were making were unfounded and untrue. I spoke at one point about how money had been invested by USAID[9] and the Swiss Embassy and some other bank run by gangsters in Bosnia and these guys had taken the money and fled. The State Department held a press conference and said, "It's not true that we lost the money," and then when my editors called, they explained, "It's not true, because we could still get it back." It was that kind of stuff that was just really dirty. So when one spends as long as I have outside the United States reporting on stories that are often at variance with the line given out of Washington, one comes away with the feeling that every government lies and no government, no matter what their political stripe, is an exception, and I think that's probably a pretty accurate statement.

During the Persian Gulf War in 1991, the press were put into a very restricted pool system—one hundred and eighty, I think, journalists, total. It was a smaller version of the system of embedding that took place in this war, where the journalists didn't have access to their own vehicles. They were completely dependent on the military for logistics; they only could go places that the military took them to and only saw what the military wanted them to see. I did not participate in the pool system. I had an advantage in that I speak Arabic so I could get out into villages and negotiate. I also shaved off all my hair, got a uniform, and decorated my jeep with orange flashes to make it look like a military vehicle. I would actually get up to the checkpoints and the MPs would call me "sir." I lived out in the desert and moved from unit to unit. I went into Kuwait on my own, and as my stories came back—I was writing for the *New York Times* and they're very high profile—the administration, particularly Vice President Dick Cheney, got angrier and angrier and angrier. There were only a handful of journalists doing this kind of reporting. Some good French reporters were doing it, actually. Toward the end of the war, the US military drew up a list of fourteen of us who they wanted expelled. Unfortunately for them, they couldn't find me because I was sleeping in homes, mostly of Bedouins. I moved around. I filed by cell phone. When the war started, I went into Kuwait City with a US Marine Corps unit that I was with. So it was a constant battle.

I was at one point picked up by MPs, held, and had my press credentials taken from me, but I didn't need my press credentials. I didn't use them. I had a long conversation with my newspaper and told them, "I came here to be a reporter, and if I can't be a reporter, I'm going home. I'm not going to sit in a hotel and write pool reports. I'm not going off on a dog and pony show in a press bus run by the military. It's not what I do. It's not what I've ever done, and I'm not going to begin now." I expected that there would be a pretty good chance of my being expelled and I also expected that it would destroy my career at the *New York Times*. I was a new reporter. I had just been hired, and institutions like this don't always deal with controversy very well. Being a conformist within any bureaucracy or institution is a good way to advance yourself, and being a nonconformist is a good way to remain on the fringes of that organization. But I just have other motives. I'm not a careerist. I'm not trying to rise within an institution; it's not why I do this. Obviously I would have found that experience of being fired from the *New York Times* extremely unpleasant, but it was a risk I was willing to take.

The *New York Times* covered the fact that I was picked up by the MPs in the bottom of a story, and the *Washington Post* wrote a feature story in which I was the lead. I think the difference was that the *Times* story was a news story, and the *Post* story was a feature story about press problems, so they used my experience as a sort of anecdotal lead to describe the pressure that was being put on the press.

My experience with the MPs is a classic example of how censorship is misused. I was up on something called a tap line road, which runs along the northern part of Saudi Arabia. When the US troops were deployed there, all the Saudi shop owners tripled their prices, and it really angered the troops. I am pretty sure that's the story I was doing when I was picked up. They wanted that story covered up because they knew it wouldn't play well back in the United States that the Saudis, our great allies who we'd come to assist, were gouging our soldiers. It was a fairly innocuous story. But when you have that kind of iron control, censorship always goes beyond military necessity. I agree that there is a need in a war for minimal censorship in terms of troop size and armaments and where they are and that kind of stuff. That basic stuff is acceptable. Nothing else is.

When the Iraqi forces before the attack on Kuwait made a probe into Hafji, this border town, I happened to be with a Marine Corps unit. We got into Hafji, and it was very clear what was happening. There were no Saudi troops in Hafji. The Saudi defenders of the town had fled. All of them. Saudi soldiers were climbing on fire trucks and speeding out of Hafji as fast as they could. And they called the marines in to push the Iraqi forces back.

This was an operation that was being carried out largely by the Marine Corps and a Qatari tank battalion who all turned out to be Pakistani mercenaries. Back in Riyadh and Dhahran, they were giving press conferences talking about the gallant Saudis defending their homeland. They organized press buses up to the edge of Hafji so that you would have the backdrop of the concussions of the explosions and the smoke, and people were there doing stand-ups talking about or characterizing a battle that was completely fictitious about Saudi troops defending their town.

There wasn't a Saudi soldier in Hafji. I got into Hafji with a couple of French photographers, and it was very clear what was happening. We were roughed up by Saudi military police, and got the story out. Once we published what was happening, they had to change their tune, and they said, "Oh, it was a combined operation," which wasn't true. So that's the kind of example of when you have that ironclad censorship, you are allowed to create a fictitious narrative and then use the press to spin it out.

Unless you have independent reporters who defy that kind of control, the whole picture and image of the war is fantasy.

In wartime there is a hunger on the part of the public—that looks at war now as sort of reality TV—for a hero. In the Gulf War, we turned Norman Schwarzkopf, a surly, alcoholic, unpleasant human being, into a General Grant, or our big warrior. This was a man who detested the press. But the press fell all over themselves for twenty minutes in the helicopter with the great man and the questions were fawning and it was just disgusting. But it was that urge or need to create the hero. We need the hero. At the moment that Jessica Lynch[10] appeared, things were not going as we had been told they would go. Convoys were being attacked. There were fuel shortages. There was more resistance than the Americans expected. So there was a thirst on the part of the public and the press for a hero, and the people who spin out the military propaganda were only too happy to oblige. It was highly embarrassing, but not in any way unique. We need to create heroes, and the most effective medium that we have to create heroes is the press. That's what the press does in war and has done in war since the creation of modern war correspondents in the Crimean War.[11] There's nothing new about that. It fits a pattern. In wartime the press is always part of the problem, always has been and probably always will be.

At the end of the Gulf War, there were a large numbers of Iraqis fleeing Kuwait City in a huge convoy on a highway running north out of the city. They were attacked from the air, and for about seven miles, there were just destroyed vehicles. We nicknamed it "The Highway of Death." I drove up that road shortly after the attack in which there were charred bodies half hanging out the windows of the cabins of the trucks, and you could see where cars had veered off into the desert to try and escape the explosions. It was a horrible carnage, one that shook up the Bush administration, because the images were so horrific. On the other hand, that is what war is like. The poor Iraqi soldiers who were stuck in those trenches and were buried alive under the sand also suffered a terrible, terrible fate. Those images were not broadcast, but the highway of death was. It was the first glimpse, perhaps, that Americans had of what our weapons were doing on the other end. That's, of course, the problem with the war in Iraq. We reveled in the power of the weapons, and we were never shown what those weapons did so that somehow the consequences of these machines of death were sanitized. That, I think, is always dangerous.

The broadcast coverage of this current war and the Gulf War can be summed up in one word, which is "cheerleading." Everybody, especially in the electronic media, wanted to do their bit for Uncle Sam. It was just nauseating to watch. It used every stupid cliché I have ever heard about war. There was no context to the images. You would get an embedded reporter, for instance, and they would get near a firefight, and you would see some smoke in the distance and maybe hear the rattle of some gunfire and they would speak about it as if they were sports commentators: "I see two tanks coming up here and . . . oh, look over there," but you don't learn anything about the war. It's this gee-whiz-bang kind of stuff, but you probably know less, although we have the technology to transmit images in real time, than you did before we could do that. As a matter of fact, I'm sure you know less because in the Vietnam conflict or in El Salvador where I was, TV crews would actually go out and report a story and produce it and send it back. That reporting has vanished now, and it's been replaced by this running commentary by people who are essentially giving a verbal description of what we're seeing on the screen. The reporting doesn't seem to go beyond that. So I found the reporting atrocious in this war. Most of these embedded reporters had never been in a war zone, so they were frightened. War is frightening. There was a feeling that they were going to protect the military who were protecting them. That's a very natural feeling and I've felt it. But it's very corrosive to honest journalism; you do your bit for the unit, and the unit does its bit for you. You could see it in the way they would talk and say "we." "We're going up the road to Baghdad." There was such a heavy identification with the military units that the press was traveling with that essentially they became propagandists for those units.

The situation now is that Iraq is so dangerous that if you are an American reporter who looks like me, it's very risky to go out on the streets of Baghdad or Fallujah. So unfortunately, what these reporters do is gravitate to the press briefing rooms inside the Green Zone and just serve as a conduit for government propaganda. That's not reporting. That's called stenography. It's called being a stenographer for people in power. It has nothing to do with reporting, and if I were in a situation like that, I would leave. I don't do that stuff. I think that some of these journalists are going to have to examine their conscience when it's over. Unfortunately, a lot of them don't stop and ask the questions.

The former president and CEO of the Associated Press Lou Boccardi said about the Gulf conflict: "I can say it was the most covered war in history." What do you think about that?

How do you want me to respond to it? What do you want me to say? I'd rather just let him say it and he can live with himself.

Why do you think we went to war in Iraq?

We went to war in Iraq because a group of very limited, neoconservative people who know nothing about the Middle East and how the world works thought that we'd have a cakewalk into a big pond of oil and be able to run it.

Are there other real bottom-line issues in the Middle East that the press isn't covering properly and that makes it dangerous for us?

The American press does not cover the Palestinian and Israeli conflict well. Most Americans have no concept of the suffering of the Palestinian people. If you take a list of the restrictions put on South African blacks during the apartheid regime and you make a list of the restrictions the Palestinians have under Israeli occupation, there's almost no difference. Yet there's no empathy for what they're undergoing, or understanding, and it's the hugest hole in American journalism and one that I think deeply distorts our understanding of the roots of rage within the Middle East against us. Remember that when Palestinian refugee camps in Gaza like Khan Younis are attacked from the air, they are attacked with F-16 or Apache helicopters, with American weapons. Remember that the Israelis get three billion dollars a year from us and another ten billion dollars in loan guarantees. If we took away just the loan guarantees, they would never be able to continue this occupation. We are complicit in what's happening, and our press is very, very bad about explaining to us what's happening. I think the European press is much better.

There are cultural and historical reasons why Americans are bad at covering the Muslim and Arab world. We haven't had the kinds of ties with that world that, for instance, the British and the French have. American journalists don't have the linguistic skills; they don't speak Arabic. Culturally, we tend to see the prism of the Middle East through this very strong Israeli lobby that exists. I think it's always dangerous when you go into a country or a region and you don't understand the culture, you don't understand the religion, and you don't speak the language, because it's incomprehensible to you and, unfortunately, the easy way out as a journalist is just to certify it as incomprehensible. I think that's what we've done with the Palestinians and, perhaps, with many Muslims in the Muslim world. We don't understand the historical antecedents that have created the distortions and anger and violence. We think they come from another moral universe, and of course they do not. For years since 1967, the Palestinians were under a horrendous occupation, and they pleaded and cajoled and begged through the United Nations and everywhere else for people to look. It was as if they were trapped behind a large glass partition. We all walked by, we couldn't hear their voices, we never looked—they were invisible. After decades of abuse and indignities and humiliation, they burst through the glass with the blood streaming down their faces in a rage, and we panicked and we just wanted to get rid of them. I think that that inability to understand what they're going through and what they have gone through—and I'm not defending the suicide bombers, these are horrific crimes—but until we understand what created their rage, and the process by which these people were pushed to this extreme, to a point where the only way they felt they could affirm themselves as human beings is through death, until we begin to understand that process, we're not going to solve the problem. We are not going to make the Iraqi resistance go away by bombing Fallujah.[12] Nor are the Israelis going to make the opposition go away by dropping iron fragmentation bombs or tank shells on a refugee camp. What you're only doing is fueling the conflict and empowering the extremists. That's what the Israelis have been doing for years in the occupied territories and it's what we are doing now in Iraq. With the decline of American journalism, especially broadcast journalism, where it's all become entertainment, where foreign bureaus have been closed and where there are fewer and fewer newspapers—my own paper being one of the exceptions—that seriously attempt to cover foreign news, Americans have less and less information. We have completely folded inward. We are a very ignorant, hedonistic society. Unfortunately, we wield a great deal of power. We wield it blindly and we are a danger to others and we are now a danger to ourselves.

In the summer of 2001, I was very frustrated, having spent so much time in the Middle East and so much time in Gaza and the West Bank. I took vacation time and I went to Khan Younis, a Gaza refugee camp. I stayed there for eight days, and I wrote every day what happened in that camp. Now that camp is surrounded in a kind of horseshoe shape by Israeli settlements, and they come right up to the fence. The first afternoon I was there I heard an Israeli army jeep through a loudspeaker in Arabic going, "Ta-al, ta-al," which means "come" in Arabic. Then the Israeli soldiers started cursing at some Palestinian boys playing soccer: "Ibn sharmuta" [son of a whore], horrible words like this. The boys started to throw stones. They were ten-, eleven-year-old boys. The jeep, which was armored, was behind an electric fence. So the boys were throwing stones past an electric fence toward a jeep—if the stones even made it that far—that was armored. The soldiers got out of the jeep and started firing live rounds at the children. I was in shock. I had been in places like Sarajevo where kids were killed by snipers, or in El Salvador, but I had never seen soldiers entice children like mice into a trap and shoot them for sport. I went back every afternoon, and the same thing happened.

I went to every funeral of those children who were killed, or I visited them in the hospital if they were wounded. In the story I wrote about Khan Younis, I had their names, when they were wounded, where they were wounded, or if they were killed. The Israelis went berserk. So did the Israeli supporters in the United States, but there was nothing they could do because the reporting was ironclad. So what they did, of course, was character defamation. They went after me personally. I would appear to speak at universities, and the campus would have to hire extra security. People would be picketing me outside. No one was allowed to bring electronic recording devices in or out of the room and no one was allowed to leave or enter the room while I spoke, that's how bad the tension was. It's more an example of how ignorant we are about what's happening. The anger, the response was so visceral and so deep; it puzzled me as to why. Over time I felt that the response was so passionate because it wasn't just that I was reporting a very unpleasant truth of the occupation, it's that I was taking away that trump card that some Israelis supporters use, which is victimhood. Because in Gaza, the victims are Palestinian; they are not Israeli.

My report was the cover story of *Harper's Magazine* on October 1, 2001, and the title was "A Gaza Diary—Israeli-Palestinian Conflict." The reaction to it was quite strong. People were very, very angry and made statements about me as a person and as a journalist that were untrue and were meant to defame my integrity and my character.

You wrote that "the national myth often implodes with a startling ferocity after the lies and absurdities surrounding it become too hard to sustain." Could you talk about when that happened in Vietnam and if it's happening now?

I think it's important to remember that, despite what the press tells you, the press is almost always reactive. The press will wave the flag as long as everyone else waves the flag. When people stop waving the flag, the press will stop waving the flag. That's what happened in Vietnam. When enough body bags came home and enough lies were exposed, and the American public began to question the enterprise of the war, then the press was free to question the enterprise of the war. Journalists such as I. F. Stone who had questioned that enterprise before that had occurred were ostracized not only by those in power but by their own, that is, the press. What will happen in Iraq is that the coverage will get a lot better once Americans start asking—and I think they are beginning to ask—the kinds of questions that the press should have asked before this thing began.

Talk about Abu Ghraib[13] **and what it means from both sides.**

The exposure of the abuses in Abu Ghraib is a window into the reality of war. The abuses are not exceptional; that is normal behavior in war. What we do in war is we turn other people into objects, first literally and then physically, in terms of corpses, objects to either gratify or destroy or both. That perversion of war—war always turns the moral order upside down— was played out in the prison of Abu Ghraib. It was played out in the camps that were set up in Bosnia, it was played out in the torture centers in El Salvador, it was played out in the French interrogation centers in Algeria, and it was played out when American atrocities were committed in Vietnam. That's what always happens in war. There is a kind of pornographic element to war, because pornography does what war does, which is turn women into objects. There's always a huge rise in pornography in war zones as the violence rises, because they're part of the same phenomena. So what happened in Abu Ghraib is what war does to you. It's how war perverts and distorts you. That's what war is. That's the face of war.

If you owned a network, how would you report this war?

I would give camcorders to Iraqi Muslim journalists and send them into Fallujah and let Americans watch what Americans are doing from the other end.

What do you think about Al Jazeera?[14]

I know Al Jazeera from my time in the Middle East, and I've always thought they were very good. I can't comment on how they are covering right now because I don't watch it, but especially with the Israeli-Palestinian conflict where I used to see it every day, I had a great deal of respect for them.

Tell the story of your friend John Wheeler.

Jack Wheeler graduated with Gen. Wesley Clark [former Supreme Allied Commander of NATO] from West Point, class of 1966—the class that took the most casualties of any West Point class in Vietnam. It also had the highest attrition rate of any class. People did their four years and got out of the army as fast as they could. Jack was a very thoughtful, moral man. When asked what he did in Vietnam, he said, "I was a witness to the decimation of my class," in particular, his close friend, who was the head of the honor society at West Point. Now the honor system at West Point is quite strict and severe. One is not allowed to lie. One is expected to act with a great deal of personal integrity. But, of course, that's at variance with how anybody rises within a bureaucracy, including the army.

So who was leading the army during the Vietnam War? It was General Westmoreland, who was lying every single day. Jack's argument was, if lying is the way that you achieve success within the military, then let's tell that to the plebes, or the incoming students at West Point, so they know. He has a point. That stress of personal integrity and personal responsibility at West Point is something that I respect, and the tragedy is that you lose it because of ambition, because you want to rise within the institution. What will make you, if not a successful soldier, certainly a successful and a moral human being, is to hang on to that honor system and that integrity, even at the cost of your career. I think that's what Jack understood. In large part, that's why he left the military.

Do you think that's applicable to journalism?

Yes, I think journalists who lack integrity and who feed people what they want to hear—and let's face it that's essentially what the networks and the cable shows do now—are not journalists; they're propagandists. Or they're celebrities. Most of these people we see, like former NBC news anchorman Tom Brokaw, they're not journalists. They are celebrities with a lot of makeup on pretending to be journalists with sort of deep voices, and they still have all their hair.

CBS's Dan Rather was saying things like "I'm an American first, where do I line up?" That's not patriotism. That's blind allegiance to the state. It's that line from Orwell, "My country right or wrong," which is the moral equivalent of "My mother drunk or sober." The fact is that the role of a patriot is in many ways to be a dissident. It's to be self-critical to make the country a better place. It's not to rush out with the crowd and start chanting at the balcony of the president or anywhere else. We are not cheerleaders. If we want to be popular, we'd better go do another profession (I'm not sure what we do is a profession) or another trade. I find that kind of hunger to be accepted as part of the mainstream in time of war very common in the press and very dangerous. You need critical distance to have integrity. Unfortunately, there were very, very few people who had that kind of distance.

> **You were talking about modern war being different from past wars because now civilians are targeted. Has reporting caught up with that, and is there censorship involved in that?**

When you report a war where your country is not actively involved, for instance, when I reported the war in Bosnia, it was easy for me to go into a town and say, "Here is the number of civilian dead. Here is the number of houses that have been burned." This is the story of how the troops came into the town. Here's what they did." When your own country is at war, you immediately go into the same situation and search for that mythic narrative. Who's the hometown hero? What are the horrible, perfidious, evil deeds that the enemy committed against our people? Where are the people who are liberated who were thrilled to see our troops? Where are pictures of our troops giving candy to children and engaging in kind, compassionate, humanitarian acts that reflect well on us as a people? In the war in Bosnia, if a Muslim went into a town that had just been liberated from Serbs, that's what they did. I'm not picking on Muslims or Serbs, because we do it, too. So we go in with a stage set, and we are just are looking for all the characters to put against the backdrop of the scenery. We re-create over and over and over this mythic narrative that is false but that makes us feel good as a people and that everybody back home wants to read and hear. It's war as boy's adventure. That has been a phenomenon for decades. It's not going to go away. Unfortunately, it's completely untrue, and you get huge distortions in the coverage because of that yearning and need to create yet another story that fulfills that myth of the heroic ideal.

I think that the only way to understand war is to see it through the eyes of the victims. As long as you have images of violence—the Bible calls it "the lust of the eye" and warns believers against it—that eroticism of violence, that fascination with violence, overpowers the message. It's like trying to make a movie against pornography and showing erotic love scenes. The best way to understand war is to eschew those images of violence and focus on what war does to the victims, because they are the majority in war. A constant hammering home of the cost of war upon the innocents, and even upon the young soldiers, I think, begins to drive home the fact that this is not a glorious and great enterprise. It begins to expose the essence of war, which is death and destruction, and it begins to puncture holes in that notion of the mythic ideal. That's very hard to do when you're traveling with a tank unit in a Humvee on the way to Baghdad and coverage consists of shell bursts and sand dunes. It requires real reporting, and that's hard and difficult work. Within the broadcast media, it's almost nonexistent. Within the print media, there are just fewer and fewer of us who have the institutions willing to back us in order to do it.

Any time a nation enters war, it should enter with a deep sense of tragedy. If you enter war and you're euphoric, then something is deeply wrong with you as an individual and a country. Any people that feels a legitimate threat, and I think of those who were in Sarajevo—I was in Sarajevo during the siege—understood the horror and tragedy of the war. But they also understood that if they did not fight the Serb forces that were surrounding the city, they would be annihilated. When there is a clear and credible threat to your own survival or the survival of your nation, you will fight, even if the images of war are gruesome and horrible. The problem is that, when we sanitize those images and we create this notion that war is a video arcade game, war becomes easy to wage, because we no longer understand the tragedy of war and the cost of war. That's precisely what happened in Iraq.

The American people are saying—you hear this all the time—9/11, that was our big tragedy, that's what we're responding to.

Every war is justified by the warmakers by the initial death of innocents who may not have anything in common with us other than the fact that they are part of our race, our nationality, or ethnic group. Now sometimes, as in the case of what happened in Sarajevo, those accounts of the deaths of innocents are murky. In the case of 9/11, they were innocents. But what happens is that you create this kind of invisible crowd of the dead, and you use death to sanctify the war, and to question the enterprise of the war is to dishonor the memory of the dead. It's a kind of sacrilege against the dead. This is a very good technique for keeping at bay any kind of criticism of the war. But it's also very dangerous because we no longer ask questions, because even to pose questions becomes a betrayal of those who have died. So when we had the attacks on 9/11, we suddenly had this mass—their pictures were all over the subway stations in New York—and any kind of questioning of the enterprise against Afghanistan, against

Iraq, became a kind of defiling of the memory of those who had been killed. Yes, we did suffer a horrible tragedy and a crime against humanity, but it was manipulated and used—as these things often are by the war-makers—to carry out a war that should have never been fought.

What, to your mind, is a journalist? What does a journalist do?

Giving people what they want is not journalism; it's propaganda. It's advertising. If our role is to give people what they want, there's no need for us to be around. There's no shortage of public relations firms that can do a much better job of it. I think it's the role of a journalist to give people what they may not want but what they need, to ask the kinds of questions they may not want to ask but they should ask, to give the kind of information that is uncomfortable and unsettling but allows people to open their eyes to the veil that's been pulled over them. That's the role of a great journalist. It's to allow people to step out of their own shoes and step into the shoes of another and see themselves from the perspective of the other. With that perspective comes not only a greater clarity of the situation that you're in but also empathy. You can't build relations with the other if there is no empathy or understanding for the other. The only way we are going to get that understanding is through journalism. Good journalists or good reporters are those who go and report and understand cultural traditions, religious traditions, speak the language, and allow us to have a kind of reflection of ourselves.

Do you think there's a problem of provincialism among our media elite who may not speak foreign languages, who may not be culturally sensitive?

America is a very provincial country. We're not required to speak any other languages because we can get by with English. We are very isolated, even when we travel abroad. When I lived in Cairo, I'd hang around with ex-pats, and all the Americans would hang around with each other and usually just complain about Cairo or Egypt although, of course, they were all living like the Raj. So I think that that kind of isolation is very much part of our national characteristic and one that gives us a greater propensity to be cut off from the rest of the world, which is why we need a vigorous and strong press to break that kind of barrier. It's especially important when we're engaged in operations such as we are in the Middle East.

We need a press that has the cultural and linguistic ability to report from the other side and to fairly present not only their perspective but what they're undergoing, perhaps even at our hands. The numbers of those in the press that have that ability are fewer and fewer. You can probably, unfortunately, count them on one or two hands. With that, of course, comes the inability to bring to a story cultural sensitivity and linguistic ability and cultural history, and that means that we gravitate toward the familiar; people who are like us, like well-educated Iraqis who studied at MIT—as in the case of Ahmed Chalabi. Or we gravitate toward people who are like us to explain the situation, and that gives us a very distorted view of what's happening.

Is there an image in your head or an event that just won't go away?

Five years covering the war in El Salvador alone produces a lifetime of images. My problem is that I have so many images that some days can be very difficult. I carry a lot within me, and there are times when it just seems too much to bear. There's a lot there.

What is it like to be a war correspondent?

Reporters and photographers in a war zone work really hard—night and day. Just the logistics of getting a story are staggering. By the time you actually get to the village, you're exhausted. Physically getting ahold of the story is extremely difficult and tiring. You don't have much of a life—that *is* your life. I used to tell my translator in Bosnia that I knew I'd really aged when my most fervent dream was to get into a bed alone and just sleep.

It's a rough life. You're stressed out. You're in danger, you're working all the time, and you are so exhausted. My eyes were just black under here. In El Salvador, I had a nervous twitch.

When I began as a war correspondent, it was still telexes. Then it was computers and then it was satellite phones. In Vietnam, you had dead time. You could send out film and go off drinking. You can't do that now. The editors are calling you all night long. You have a shorter and shorter leash. I talk to colleagues of mine who were in Vietnam; they'd send off their story and go out to dinner. We never had that luxury because we were hooked up all night long. People would call me on the satellite phone at eleven at night to start editing my story, and it was brutal. I think it was probably better journalism in terms of accuracy but it was a harder lifestyle.

What's the best psychological and emotional construct for a great journalist?

Someone who hates authority. Passionately. Somebody who is angry, gets angry, and through that combination of anger and deep sense of injustice is willing to take tremendous risks to try and expose what's happening to innocents and the atrocities that are being committed. I think that we're impossible people. We're difficult people. I wouldn't want to have somebody like me work for them.

I think the psychological and emotional makeup of a good war reporter is somebody who thrives on a very high-octane, adrenaline-driven lifestyle. Someone who has a deep distrust of authority. Someone who has a sense of outrage at injustice and abuse and through that combination of love of excitement and anger and feeling that wrongs must be righted and that we have a small role to play in righting those wrongs will take tremendous risks to report abuses that are being committed against innocent human beings. For instance, I think most of the reporters who were in Sarajevo during the war took the risks that they took—remember, forty-five were killed and many were wounded, including my photographer who was wounded shortly after I arrived—because they believed that what was happening in Sarajevo under the siege of the Serbs was a crime. A crime that should be stopped. And they were right. We were appalled that the rest of the world sat for three and a half years and watched it happen and did nothing.

I think that there are many motives that go into creating a good war correspondent, some of which are very dark and which I tried to chronicle in my book, such as an addiction to war, a sense of empowerment, and all that kind of stuff. Those are all very real. We're not Mother Teresas in flak jackets, yet I think also there is a sense of idealism, and that idealism plays a large part in especially those of us who kept going back into war zone after war zone. That anger was very, very real, and that anger saw us do things that were very dangerous.

Are you going back?

No.

You done?

Yes. My thrill now is doing laundry and making my daughter take a bath.

CHRIS HEDGES has been a foreign correspondent for fifteen years. He joined the staff of the *New York Times* in 1990 and previously worked for the *Dallas Morning News*, the *Christian Science Monitor*, and National Public Radio. He holds a BA in English literature from Colgate University and a master of divinity from Harvard University. He is a lecturer in the Council of the Humanities and Ferris Professor of Journalism at Princeton University. Hedges was a member of the *New York Times* team that won the 2002 Pulitzer Prize for Explanatory Reporting for the paper's coverage of global terrorism, and he received the 2002 Amnesty International Global Award for Human Rights Journalism. He is the author of *War Is a Force That Gives Us Meaning*, which was a finalist for the National Book Critics Circle Award. In 2003 Hedges published a second book titled *What Every Person Should Know about War*. His third book, *Losing Moses on the Freeway: The Ten Commandments in America*, was released in May 2005.

NOTES

1. *New York Times* public editor Daniel Okrent issued this mea culpa on May 26, 2004: "Editors at several levels who should have been challenging reporters and pressing for more skepticism were perhaps too intent on rushing scoops into the paper. Accounts of Iraqi defectors were not always weighed against their strong desire to have Saddam Hussein ousted. Articles based on dire claims about Iraq tended to get prominent display, while follow-up articles that called the original ones into question were sometimes buried. In some cases, there was no follow-up at all."

2. Sarajevo is the capital of Bosnia and Herzegovina and the site of a long siege that began on April 6, 1992, when the city was surrounded by Bosnian Serb paramilitary forces who, after the Bosnian government declared its independence from Yugoslavia, wanted to secede from the newly independent Bosnia. The siege lasted for more than three years. An estimated twelve thousand people were killed. A cease-fire was arranged in 1995 after international forces intervened. The Dayton Peace Agreement was signed later that year.

3. The Dayton Peace Agreement was initialed at Wright Patterson Air Force Base in Dayton, Ohio, on November 21, 1995, and signed in Paris in December 1995. It is known as the Dayton Peace Accords and ended the war in what was formerly Yugoslavia. "The Dayton Agreement recognized a second tier of government in Bosnia and Herzegovina, comprised of two entities—a joint Bosniak/Croat Federation of Bosnia and Herzegovina, and the Bosnian Serb Republika Srpska (RS)—each presiding over roughly one-half the territory. The Federation and RS governments are charged with overseeing internal functions. . . . Inter-entity borders . . . were postulated as part of the political agreement that was based on ethnic division and are used to determine the extents of political jurisdictions within entities." http://en.wikipedia.org/wiki/Political_divisions_of _Bosnia_and_Herzegovina. For more on the terms of the accord, see http://www.state .gov/www/regions/eur/bosnia/bosagree.html.

4. France declared Algeria a part of France in 1848, after which European settlers created a colonial society and confiscated Muslim land and denied them political rights. The Algerians organized nationalist independence movements after World War I. In 1954 the Front de Liberation Nationale, or FLN, proclaimed a war of liberation and launched terrorist attacks against the French in both Algeria and France. General Charles de Gaulle proclaimed Algeria's independence in 1962.

5. Chechnya is a Muslim region in the northern Caucasus that declared its independence in 1991 following the collapse of the Soviet Union but is still seeking its independence from Russia, which still considers it a republic of the Russian Federation. In 1994 Russian president Boris Yeltsin sent troops in to retake Chechnya, and since then, Russia has been engaged in a guerrilla war with Chechnyan separatists, which President Vladimir Putin now considers part of the War on Terrorism.

6. William Randolph Hearst was the son of a millionaire miner and rancher who built a media empire that at its height consisted of twenty-eight major newspapers, eighteen magazines, and several radio stations and movie companies. He sensationalized journalism by introducing banner headlines and lavish illustrations and is believed by many to have initiated the Spanish-American War of 1898 to encourage newspaper sales. When an explosion sank the US battleship *Maine* (that had gone to Cuba to protect Americans during the conflict between the Spanish and Cubans) and killed hundreds of sailors in Havana Harbor on February 15, 1898, Hearst's paper's headline was: "War? Sure!" When his illustrator, Frederic Remington, requested to return from Havana, Hearst said, "Please remain. You furnish the pictures, I'll furnish the war." Hearst was known to fake pictures and stories to sell papers. http://www.zpub.com/sf/history/Willh.html.

7. FMLN, or Frente Farabundo Martí Para La Liberación Nacional, was a Marxist coalition guerrilla movement in El Salvador that emerged in 1980 and became a major political party drawing supporters from former radicals and more moderate leftists.

8. Slobodan Milošević is the former president of Serbia who is now being tried at The Hague for committing war crimes in Kosovo and Croatia, and for committing genocide in Bosnia.

9. USAID (US Agency for International Development) "has been the principal US agency to extend assistance to countries recovering from disaster, trying to escape poverty, and engaging in democratic reforms." USAID "has always had the twofold purpose of furthering America's foreign policy interest in expanding democracy and free markets while improving the lives of citizens in the developing world. Spending less than one-half of 1 percent of the federal budget, USAID works around the world to achieve these goals." http://www.usaid.gov/about_usaid/.

10. In April 2003, nineteen-year-old Pvt. Jessica Lynch was captured when her company took a wrong turn and was ambushed near Nassiriya, Iraq. Nine of her fellow soldiers were killed. She was taken to a hospital by Iraqi soldiers, where she was held for eight days with a broken thigh, broken arm, and dislocated ankle. The Pentagon falsely claimed to the press that she had stab and bullet wounds and had been slapped in her hospital bed. They released footage of a daring raid on the hospital to rescue Lynch and talked about "brave souls putting their lives on the line to make it happen." Lynch had been treated well at the hospital, and there were no soldiers there when her rescuers arrived with cameras rolling to take her away. In his May 15, 2003, article for the UK's *Guardian*, John Kampfner described Lynch's rescue as "one of the most stunning pieces of news management yet conceived."

11. The Crimean War (1854–1856) was fought between the Russians on one side and the British, French, and the Ottoman Empire on the other. The roots of the war's causes lay in the rivalry and strategic conflicts between the British and the Russians for control of places like Afghanistan and the Balkans. Crimea is a peninsula in the Black Sea.

12. In November 2004 US forces launched a major assault against Fallujah, which was targeted as a rebel stronghold. The Iraqi city, known as "the City of Mosques" and a Sunni stronghold, has a population of several hundred thousand.

13. At the Abu Ghraib prison in Iraq, American soldiers from a US military intelligence unit, US military police, and some civilian contractors abused and tortured their prisoners. Shocking photos of their activities were released, showing naked prisoners being forced into humiliating sexual and other poses, while their captors were pictured with them giving "thumbs-up" signs and, in at least one case, holding a leash with a prisoner on the other end.

14. Founded in 1996 and based in Qatar, Al Jazeera is the largest Arabic news channel in the Middle East and provides twenty-four-hour news coverage.

19

MARHABA KEEFIK!

"TWO AMERICAN SOLDIERS DIED TODAY"

ABC Archives

DEBORAH AMOS
Foreign Correspondent,
National Public Radio
Interviewed March 2005

Nothing about Deborah Amos's clear, strong voice on NPR would suggest how warm she really is in person or the fact that she is actually quite petite. Amos is one of those high-energy people who obviously loves what she's doing and has accumulated the authority and expertise to do a superior job of it. She's been a Middle East correspondent for twenty years. It is clear from her radio work that she understands the social, cultural, and political complexities of the region and the nations comprising it. It is clear, too, that she cares deeply about the people there. Her reports are filled with Middle Eastern voices that just aren't heard anywhere else.

Before interviewing Amos, I went to NPR's Web site and listened to all of her archived shows. I was immediately drawn into another world. It was like taking the ultimate insider's tour of the Middle East through a series of priceless vignettes. Her reporting and analysis always seemed to go in unexpected directions. The voices she chose took me into their world and made me stand in their shoes.

Much of Amos's interview is an account of how cultural misunderstandings compounded by more cultural misunderstandings resulted in disasters and missed opportunities on a grand scale in Iraq. Early on, she became a firsthand witness to the country's transformation into a tragic theater of the absurd.

> I did a documentary in August 2003 about the roots of the insurgency. I was in Minneapolis, and the guy who agreed to run it, who was very nervous at the time, said, "You were two years ahead." . . . We went to Fallujah every day. We would go to people's houses and everybody let us come in because they thought that if they told us about what was going on that it would stop. And they would say, "the Americans stole our money, they dragged me out in the middle of the night and they put their boots on my head." For Muslims, the only thing that's supposed to touch the ground is your forehead in prayer. So these were terrible things that the Americans were doing. They were shaming parents in front of their children and looking at the wife and not waiting for her to put her scarf on. These are mistakes you'd have to make up, they were so unbelievable. . . .
>
> Then in May 2003, the Americans shot eighteen Iraqis in Fallujah. . . . Essentially, the Iraqis got shot because the Americans didn't have enough translators and didn't understand what they wanted. . . . I've always said that the insurgency in Iraq started out as the "You killed my uncle Mohammed and I am duty-bound by tribal culture to shoot you back."

One Westerner's efforts at positive communication with the Iraqis shows how even one small, absurd gesture could make a big difference: "I was in Basra, there was a twenty-two-year-old Scotsman who would go up in the turret and sing at the top of his lungs, and then he would yell out, 'Marhaba Keefik! Hello! How are you?' He knew enough Arabic to do that, and the whole posture was just so different in Basra than it was in Fallujah." There is a hopeful note in this anecdote. There is also a huge lesson.

Although far more cultured than the average American, Amos is definitely very American, which is why getting her to look through the eyes of Middle Easterners and report what she sees is a very instructive exercise. We jumped right into such an exercise when I asked her why the Iraqis think the United States invaded their country.

They have a variety of conspiracy theories that are close to reality and far from reality. You will always have the conversation that says the Americans are here for the oil no matter how many times you say, "But why would they spend $120 billion and allow so many Americans to be killed when they can just buy the oil?" It's hard for me to have that conversation because that's not the reason and I know it. Other people will say it was because of Saddam, other people will say that the Americans lied about the weapons of mass destruction, but it's very hard for Iraqis to figure out why, because once it was clear that there were no weapons of mass destruction, and if you are smart enough and know it wasn't for the oil, then you're kind of at a loss, because, why did we do this? Can it be that the Bush administration did it to bring democracy to Iraq? The Iraqis have a hard time getting their heads around that, that that could be possible, that Americans would do that. Remember, they see us like others in the Middle East do, as the Israeli-backing, Palestinian-bashing, Muslim-hating Westerners. So I think Iraqis have not really—the smart ones, I'm not talking about all the conspiracy theorist ones—the smart ones do have a hard time when you try to press them on why they think the Americans came to Iraq.

You can understand their perplexity, I think, just like you can understand, perhaps, the perplexity of people here . . .

I have it sometimes myself.

Because if you're going to invade a country to bring democracy to it, why bother with the WMD story, why don't you just say, "Look, we've decided to invade this nation to bring democracy to it."

Remember, it was Deputy Secretary of Defense Paul Wolfowitz who told *Vanity Fair* magazine that the WMD cause was the only one they could all agree on. There was a variety of thought before and after 9/11, and Wolfowitz was one of those who before 9/11 wanted to go after Saddam. He'd been wanting to since 1991. And there were others.

Remember, we helped put Saddam in there.

Not early on, but we certainly backed him during the Iran-Iraq War, and there's no doubt about that. I covered that war, and we certainly tilted toward Saddam, as did the Saudis, the Egyptians, and everybody else. He was the lesser of two evils against the Iranians, so yes, that's true.

There's a second stream of thought in Iraq that says Saddam became a bad boy, that the Americans put him in office and he didn't behave himself, so they removed their guy because he was annoying them. That is what you'll hear from people who are smarter than the "they did it for the oil" people. That theory moves up the intellectual chain.

Why was Saddam annoying the United States in their view?

Because, Iraqis will say, he invaded Kuwait and he was paying suicide bombers in Israel. He was paying ten thousand dollars per family, and he did it for a long time. So Iraqis will say that the Americans put him in and they took him out, because, once again, the Iraqis have a hard time wrapping their heads around this idea that we actually came to bring democracy. If you look at what's happening with the government now, all these people have said, "We came out, we risked our lives to vote, and these people can't compromise and have a government!" So the idea that Americans want it this way, that this is democracy, is more than they can take onboard.

What do you think of the prewar press coverage here?

I have to say that I was part of it. I covered Secretary of State Colin Powell at the United Nations,[1] and when that was over I thought, "Gosh, I guess they got Saddam." It was a very, very, very convincing performance. After that, I had very little doubt that we were going to go to war. That was pretty much my thinking; that this administration was hell-bent to do it, that there was a bit of a slowdown going to the United Nations, but that we were going to do it. I have to say that on the way into the war, I was, I wouldn't say prowar, but I was pro getting rid of Saddam. I've been a Middle East correspondent since 1982 and spent fourteen years in the Middle East and was in Iraq in the 1980s, and I knew firsthand how terrible this guy was. I was in Kurdistan[2] in 1991 and heard then for the first time about Anfal, Saddam's genocidal campaign to eliminate the Kurds, and I couldn't believe it. I couldn't believe what people were telling me. Kurds would just disappear. Kids were killed in front of their parents. It's sort of banal to go through the list of the kinds of stuff that this regime would get up to, but I heard it all after 1991, when you could go up to Kurdistan and finally talk to the Kurds.

In the 1980s, I always said to myself, "I'm never going back there until he's gone," which I thought meant forever. So I was as surprised as anybody when these guys got serious about taking him out. I suspended my disbelief about the reasons for going to war, I suppose, although I knew in the back of my mind that they didn't have a plan for the peace and I worried about it. I did a piece for *Nightline* before the war started, and that was essentially my reporting premise: Could they figure out how to manage the peace? I interviewed David Fromkin, who wrote the bible that everybody reads, *A Peace to End All Peace*,[3] and he essentially said, "No, they have no idea." That piece never ran. *Nightline* never ran it. Ted

Koppel was already out there embedded and it was Ted's show, and he was doing almost all the war coverage and I think that my piece was a little off the beaten track. It's not that they had problems with the coverage; it just got lost in the shuffle of war coverage.

I've talked to several people, national security reporter Jim Bamford among them, and Bamford isn't buying the democracy rationale. He says the plan for going to Iraq came straight out of the "Clean Break: A New Strategy for Securing the Realm"[4] document, which was a plan for taking control of the Middle East that Richard Perle, David Wurmser, and Doug Feith[5] initially tried to sell to Netanyahu when he was Israel's prime minister. He also mentioned the Project for a New American Century,[6] which talks about controlling the resources of the Middle East and controlling the region.

I do think that there are people in the administration who genuinely buy that. After 9/11 there were some people who thought that it was one policy option, because nobody had a clue how to combat al Qaeda and Islamic fundamentalism. I think you could say that up to this day they don't have a clue.

What they really don't understand is the soft-power part of dealing with Islamic rage and anger at us. They don't understand how to deal with it. They don't understand why there is so much rage, what makes people radical, whether or not we are in a clash of civilizations, whether Islam and democracy are compatible, why nineteen people would be swayed to get on an airplane, why there are Saudi *madrassas*[7] all over Pakistan, what Wahhabism[8] means—I could go through a long list of what they don't understand.

This administration, more than the Clinton administration, doesn't understand what we have looked like to the people in the Middle East. You get points in the Middle East for trying. Even if you don't succeed, you do get points for trying. Everybody knows that the Palestine-Israel conflict is tough and that Clinton put his reputation on the line to go to Camp David.[9]

Another critical point to understand is that something like 60 percent of the people in the Middle East are now under twenty-five. At the same time, you have a media revolution. Their information is no longer controlled by their governments. In Egypt, ten thousand people now have ATM cards. There are huge multiplex shopping centers all over Cairo. Egypt has joined the globalized world. However, the divide between the rich and the poor has become more apparent because people can see it in their daily lives and on Al Jazeera;[10] and they can see it at the local shopping center. This is all new to these people, the majority of whom are under twenty-five.

I'm actually describing the entire Middle East, because it's the same all over. Here are some more figures: the unemployment rate for people under twenty-five in Egypt is 70 percent. In Syria it is unofficially around 50 percent, and this is a primarily state-run economy where the government guarantees jobs to its citizens. One example: If you got your degree in engineering, you have to work for the government for five years. This was the first year the government said, "no deal" to these students, and there's not much of a private sector to suck them up. There's no place for them to go. So all of these things, an impossible job market, the globalized world, the media revolution in the Middle East and the rhetoric of the mosque—the only place that young people can gather—have combined to make people really angry.

There's a second part to this that is hard to understand. When you look at the people who got on the planes that flew into the Twin Towers, almost all of them were Muslims who lived in Europe. What is that about? A lot of people have been writing about this and trying to understand it since 9/11. How can it be that 9/11 hijacker Muhammad Atta, who was brilliant—he was a sociopath, but he was brilliant—somehow decided to join al Qaeda when he was in *Germany* and not when he was in Cairo?

I think that whatever it was that ended up in 9/11 for us is very, very complex. I do think that there are people within the administration who believe that pressing democracy is an answer. I don't think they all do. I talked to a professor last night who said, "It could just be that we are looking at parallel universes, that the Middle East has been ready for democracy, that there's a middle class out there, that people have been watching television and are now hooked into the global economy and information economy, and they want things." At the same time, the Bush administration stands up and says that it is because of their actions that these things are happening. It is true that there is some sort of democratic spring in the Middle East. The Bush administration can claim credit for it, but they had very little to do with it.

I think the United States doesn't put billions of dollars and American lives into a country unless it has some kind of deep interest there, and it often does have something to do with resources.

Yes, "No eternal friendships, only eternal interests," I believe is what Winston Churchill says.

Exactly. So I disagree with you that the oil is not of interest because there's a big oil pond over there and our national security is based on oil.

Yes, I agree with you, but all I am saying is that you don't need to invade a country to ensure that you have access to oil.

Sure you do, because they can choose whether they want to sell it to you.

No one has done that. As the Saudis say, "We can't drink it, we've got to sell it to someone," and the truth of the matter is that we do not get a majority of our oil from the Middle East. The problem is, all of our allies do. And in an interdependent world, if the Middle East cuts off the Japanese, that would be a problem for us.

I'm also looking at the Chinese, and oil is their cocaine right now and their need for it is only going to grow.

Yes, we are going to be competing with them. I agree with you.

How much does the Israeli-Palestinian conflict figure into the equation in Iraq?

Less than anyplace else in the Middle East, and for one interesting reason: the Iraqis hate the Palestinians almost as much as they hate the Kuwaitis.

Do they fear the Israelis at all?

I think that their thinking is not so evolved on that issue. They would not sign a peace treaty with Israel tomorrow as Ahmed Chalabi[11] had promised that the new Iraqi government would do, and as he has said for ten years, which is how he convinced the American Israel Public Affairs Committee, the pro-Israel lobby, to go along with all of this. There are parts of Iraq where Iraqis don't like Jews and will say it. They worry that the "Jews" are coming back to get their property [before the 1950s, Baghdad had a large population of Iraqi Jews]. Iraqis in Mosul and Basra don't talk like that. Those are two more sophisticated towns, and they don't have this "if anything bad is happening it must be the Jews mentality." But Saddam so favored Palestinians; they were kings at the university.

The Iraqis don't like Jordanians either for the same reason. They had bucks and they came in and flashed them around in the 1990s and so the Iraqis are less angry with the Israelis than other Arabs are simply because taking that stance is almost a rebellion against Saddam's policies. Fallujah, the restive town in the Sunni triangle, is a different story. Less than two weeks after the Israelis assassinated the HAMAS leader, blind sheikh

Ahmed Yassin on March 22, 2004, four American contractors were killed and two of them were hung on a bridge in Fallujah. There was graffiti in the town saying that the hangings of the four contractors was in revenge for the sheikh's assassination. I've also seen posters in Fallujah of Islamic Palestinian leaders. Fallujah is a much more Islamist town then Baghdad. Fallujah is a jihadists' town. Baghdad has always been more secular.

I want to go back to the prewar reporting. Were you aware of the brouhaha about an International Atomic Energy Agency [IAEA] report that Bush and Blair talked about in a press conference on September 7, 2002, which they claimed showed that Saddam could reconstitute his weapons program in six months and that, in fact, not only did that report did not exist but a genuine older report basically said just the opposite?

At the time I probably didn't question it. Looking back, we didn't know then what we know now about this administration. These guys are master spinners. I don't know if I've ever seen an administration as good as this at manipulating information. Look at the story that broke in the *New York Times* about fake news taking Jon Stewart one step better.[12] It's astonishing that even after it was in the *New York Times* they still said, "As long as it's true and is not propaganda as we see it, we will not stop doing this."

So they cite this IAEA report, and practically no one goes to look for it even though that's Journalism 101.

You are asking why didn't anybody do that? As the administration is spinning, the news business is in disarray. Before the war, I was working for ABC, and all they were doing was continuing to cut budgets and fire people. Everybody was on a big banana peel there, so nobody was doing much investigative stuff. Brian Ross, ABC's chief investigative correspondent, was doing some, but for the most part, there was no investigative reporting going on.

But that's something you can check literally by calling the IAEA and getting them to fax over the report. There seems to be a pattern that has repeated itself since Vietnam in that before a war, when the reasons for going to war are presented to the public, everybody falls in line, no questions asked.

It's just what the press does. I can't answer the question. I really can't. I won't dodge and say I wasn't covering prewar because I was, off and on. I was not assigned to it, it wasn't my beat, but you are right, I could have looked up the IAEA report and I didn't.

Do you speak Arabic?

Taxicab Arabic.

I'm interested in your analysis of what it is that our leadership and the American people don't understand about Iraq.

With respect to Iraq, I know postwar so much better than prewar. I did a documentary in August 2003 about the roots of the insurgency. I was in Minneapolis, and the guy who agreed to run it, who was very nervous at the time, said, "You were two years ahead." I knew that then because I could see it. You would have had to be blind not to see it. We went to Fallujah every day. We would go to people's houses and everybody let us come in because they thought that if they told us about what was going on that it would stop. And they would say, "the Americans stole our money, they dragged me out in the middle of the night and they put their boots on my head." For Muslims, the only thing that's supposed to touch the ground is your forehead in prayer. So these were terrible things that the Americans were doing. They were shaming parents in front of their children and looking at the wife and not waiting for her to put her scarf on. These are mistakes you'd have to make up, they were so unbelievable. Every day we would go to Fallujah and every day we'd hear more. And you could see by June 2003 that the insurgency was on its way.

I remember sitting in our little bed and breakfast in Baghdad and hearing reports of a shooting of US soldiers. It was very clear that it was a planned shooting. Two cars were involved. One came up to the American checkpoint, and the guys in the next car got out and shot the soldiers manning the checkpoint. So we decided the next day that we would go out and try to find out what happened, except halfway out the door we said to each other, "But where are we going to go?" And the BBC's Arabic guy was there, and he said, "I have an idea for you. Drive to Ramadi and go see the head of the Dulaym tribe because that province, Al Anbar [which includes the town of Fallujah], surrendered to the American army without a shot, and the only way that the army could have accomplished that is by working it out with the tribes, because it's a very tribal area. So go see what happened."

So we arrive at the Dulaym house and of course being tribal people they have to let us in, and then they have to give us lunch, and so this goes on all day and we find out that the Americans had killed twenty-four members of one family with six JDAMs [Joint Direct Attack Munition "smart" bombs] because they thought that Saddam Hussein was in the

Dulaym house. And I don't know what to do with that piece of information, because I don't understand it.

The Dulayms were pretty angry about this because nobody came to say, "Gee, we're sorry." I found out later—I didn't know it at the time—that this was a tribal family with wide connections in Iraq that had been working with the CIA to try to overthrow Saddam in the 1980s. So that's how the United States pissed off the major tribespeople in the Al Anbar province.

Then in May 2003, the Americans shot eighteen Iraqis in Fallujah. Essentially, the Iraqis got shot because the Americans didn't have enough translators and didn't understand what they wanted. What they were trying to tell the Americans was, "Get out of our school. We didn't have any fighting here, so what we always do when governments change is we go back to work and our kids go back to school. We don't know what people are doing in Baghdad, but here, after a coup, we go back to work. So get out of our school." But eighteen people died instead. I've always said that the insurgency in Iraq started out as the "You killed my uncle Mohammed and I am duty-bound by tribal culture to shoot you back."

And here's the thing. The Baathist loyalists,[13] the Mukhbarat [Saddam's secret police] guys, and the jihadists kicked off the insurgency, but only after they saw that the "they-shot-my-uncle-Mohammed" people got away with killing Americans and seemed to be pretty good at it. All of a sudden it was very clear to everybody: "There are not enough American troops here, so we can do it, too!" And so it grows. A lot of people had a lot of reasons to go after the Americans. There were the Islamists in Fallujah, and there were foreign fighters—not very many, but some, and there were local tribal guys. In the beginning, when Rumsfeld was calling them "dead-enders" and saying that they were on the other side of history, we were writing and saying, "No, no, no, no, that's not what's going on here. This is growing; it is not shrinking. And these American soldiers are making it worse by going into people's houses at three o'clock in the morning and doing all these things while trying to find out who these people are." The British kept saying, "don't do this."

You pointed out in one of your reports that the Brits were given cultural sensitivity training and language training and were told not to wear sunglasses when they were on patrol. Why don't the Americans do that?

They're just doing it now, two years in. You could argue that we're not a great colonial power. The Brits have had a lot of practice because they were in Ireland. They will tell you that themselves. I was in Basra with the

Brits in January 2005, and they were saying, "We just know how to do this." Now I'll tell you something about how the Iraqis see it. The Iraqis say, "The Brits know us better. They've been here twice." But when you are talking to the Iraqis one-on-one, they don't like the Brits, because the Brits are arrogant. The Brits think that Iraqis are lesser mortals. What they say about their one-on-one encounters with the Americans is, "They don't have a clue, they don't understand anything about us." But they love Americans more than Brits 'cause we're big puppy dogs and we don't make judgments like "Muslims are second-class citizens." We don't. One-on-one, the Iraqis will take an American any day of the week over a haughty Brit. But when it comes to policy and how to run a town, they will take a Brit over an American any day because what they see, and what I see, are nineteen-year-old US soldiers scared witless at places like check-points where Iraqi civilians die unnecessarily because of a lack of cultural sensitivity training and people being terrified because of this deployment.

When I was in Basra, there was a twenty-two-year-old Scotsman who would go up in the turret and sing at the top of his lungs, and then he would yell out, "Marhaba Keefik! Hello! How are you?" He knew enough Arabic to do that, and the whole posture was just so different in Basra than it was in Fallujah. We reported all of this, we saw it, and every time Rumsfeld called the insurgents dead-enders, it made my blood boil.

Did you ever have a chance to ask anyone in the administration if they heard your reports and why or if or how they didn't make an impact?

No, I've never done that. I go, I come back, and I say what I say on the radio. I don't go to Washington, I don't live in Washington, and I don't mix with those kinds of people. I do know that the Coalition Provisional Authority [CPA][14] people were not nice to us. They didn't like us.

They were pretty embattled, weren't they?

They were also taking names.

What do you mean they were taking names?

You would have access problems if you reported what they didn't like. I had a moment with Dan Senor, the senior adviser to the Coalition Provisional Authority. We, the press, were all in a gaggle, as they refer to it, and he would not make eye contact with me. No matter what question I asked, he simply wouldn't answer it, and I thought, "Oh, I forgot, I made his guy in Karbala look like an idiot on the radio this morning. That's why."

We had done a story about the CPA in Karbala. Karbala is Shiite Aya-tollah Ali Sistani's town, but the CPA continued to insist on appointing everyone on the town's city council. John Berry was the CPA coordinator there. He happened to speak Arabic, but I have no idea how much he knew about the local culture or Arab culture at all. But in my interview with him for a radio report[15] that I did, he hangs himself. He is so arrogant and out of touch that I really didn't have to do much. All of his sound bites played twice as long as I usually play them, because even my editor went, "Oh, my God, are you kidding me?" In the report, Berry talked about inter-viewing potential candidates to add to Karbala's US-appointed council. He said he was asking them all the same questions: "How did Iraq ever get into this pickle that you had this dictator run your country for thirty years? I asked people what their understanding of democracy was." The patron-izing way that Berry and the CPA had of choosing who was going to sit in local governance must have driven Iraqis out of their minds.

I had occasion last night to look at an old documentary about the Spanish-American War. I didn't know much about that war, but there is some hilarious stuff that shows up in the press about both the Philippine and the Cuban rebels. There were reports that mentioned Uncle Sam and the little monkey children in the Philippines and Cuba. We have this his-torical idea that we are special people who come and put our hands on you and bring our knowledge to the little children of the world. There are elements of that in the way the CPA treated Iraqis.

One day my translator, my driver, and I went out to Sadr City.[16] Young American army officers were trying to put together a city council, and they were going door to door. I give them "E" for effort. They really did a lot of work trying to pull Iraqis together and to get them to under-stand what the council was going to be. These were nineteen-year-old sol-diers doing this. Then at one point, in July 2003, I went to one of these meetings where they had to decide on who was going to be the council's secretary, president, and vice president. My translator, my driver, and I watched and listened, and we were embarrassed for our respective coun-trymen. We left and I never put it on the air because it was so painful to listen to. It was the way that the American soldiers were talking to the Iraqis—in that kind of "OK, children, settle down here, we have to have democracy." And it was the kind of Iraqis who were coming forward as candidates. There was a man who came up and said, "I'm an epileptic and I'm running because I need some help." It was such a mismatch. There were great intentions on both sides, but it was doomed to failure.

Somehow the translator and the driver and I knew that, and we could hardly even talk about it. We just rolled our eyes when it was over and were sad for where this democracy experiment was going.

How do you think this democracy experiment is now, eighteen months later?

Now it's getting interesting. I don't know what Iraqis will make of it because I'm reading how bitter they are that they risked their lives to vote and nothing is coming out of it. I was in Basra during the election in January, and you cannot deny that people wanted their voices to be heard. I will not deny that even a cynic like me got teary-eyed on that day. I saw what people went through and the calculations that they had to make to go vote because there was so much violence going on and they knew there was a possibility that they might die in the process.

You were reporting about how a husband and a wife would go vote at different times, just in case.

So their kids wouldn't be orphans. Unbelievable stuff.

But in this process, I question how much cultural consideration has been given to the Iraqis. Who are we to bring our democracy to these people?

We can't. That's not going to happen. Forget it. And the Bush administration has finally had to acknowledge—whether they will ever do it in public I don't know—that this ain't the democracy that they thought was coming to Iraq. It will be more religious than they want, it will deny women rights—which wasn't part of the deal—and it will be friendlier to Iran than they want.

We did this in Iran, remember?

Yes.

We brought in the shah. He was going to be the modern man, and what happened?

I know.

Khomeini.[17]

It's early days. I'm not willing to go there yet. I'm not willing to go there because of all the things that I said before about everybody being hooked up into the global world now, and because even Algeria taught the

Islamists to talk like democrats: to abandon the notion of one man, one vote, one time. I was in a conference last week in Maine, and my hero Juan Cole[18] was speaking. He's a blogger, he's brilliant, and he said, "A lot of reporters ask me what I think the goals are of SCIRI, the guys who won the last election, and I say to them, the Supreme Council for the Islamic Revolution in Iraq, I wonder what their goals are." But they have evolved, too. Ten years ago, you could find quotes from the Hakim [Abdul Aziz al-Hakim is the current leader of SCIRI] family that said, "one vote, one man, one time." Now their rhetoric has changed, they, too, have embraced the language of democracy. I don't know yet. I don't know.

Well, here's the thing: Iraq was one of the more secular countries when Saddam was in power, let's face it.

Yes, by comparison, there's no doubt about that.

And let's face it, Saddam was burying his enemies, but women were doing better there.

The women were, that is exactly right.

I grew up in Haiti under Papa Doc who was iron-fisted and murderous to his opponents, but you could safely walk down the streets of Port-au-Prince any time of the day or night.

Police states are safe. Every time I go to Damascus, I say to my husband, "Don't worry, I'm going to a police state, nothing's going to happen." Iraq, it's a problem. Damascus, it is not a problem.

Exactly. The democracies that the United States brings in always seem to produce the outcome that the United States wants.

In the case of Iraq, it won't. Here's where I am on the side of the Iraqis. What are the Americans thinking? What are they doing? Do they understand anything? Two months ago the administration tells everybody in Europe that Hezbollah[19] is a terrorist organization, and then they turn around and say, "Oh, it isn't now, it's OK."

Former NBC correspondent Ashleigh Banfield got into trouble trying to explain that Hezbollah, to a lot of people in the Middle East, is like the Red Cross and that, while they have an armed component, they also have this big social service component.

Yes, they do.

That's my point. Do we have enough reporters like you, who know the historical context, who understand the culture, who maybe can speak the language?

There are some.

Because plugging current facts into that kind of contextual, analytical reporting—which is what we really needed prewar—that's what you really need to cover Iraq.

That's why I went back to National Public Radio [NPR]. First of all, ABC wouldn't send me to Baghdad. They told me, without being explicit, "Boys only, thank you." That was so annoying to me that I called up Loren Jenkins [senior foreign editor for NPR] and asked him to send me to Baghdad. And he said, "When can you go? Welcome back."

I barely escaped the network cannibals.

You don't live in the Green Zone[20] do you?

No. The networks don't, either. Only Fox has moved into the Green Zone. The *Wall Street Journal* moved in because a car bomb went off right in front of their house. It's hard for me to be grumpy about who's in the Green Zone because I know why. If a car bomb went off in front of my house, it would be hard for me to continue living there. But they moved into the Green Zone, and now they all want to jump off the roof because it's so boring and sterile inside they can't stand it.

Peter Arnett told us that one-third of the people in the Green Zone are women and that the most popular product sold is Viagra.

Here's what I notice. On my way to Basra, there were T-shirts that you could buy, and I saw one that said, "Operation Iraqi Freedom, my grandmother served there." These T-shirts were for adults. This tells you a lot about the culture of this war. Viagra and "My grandmother served there" are two ends of a very peculiar deployment.

Go and read *Newsweek*'s Middle East regional editor, Christopher Dickey. He knows what's going on in Iraq and the Middle East. So does *Newsweek*'s Baghdad bureau chief, Rod Norland. The *Newsweek* people are good. Dexter Filkins of the *New York Times* has done a great job. There are people out there who know and have written some good stuff.

Why doesn't this kind of reporting penetrate the mass public consciousness?

It does. I'll tell you why I think so. I didn't think so for a long time. My husband [former NBC correspondent Rick Davis] and I go off to teach at a college once a year. We always go to little tiny colleges, and we do it as part of a program that is run out of the Woodrow Wilson Center at Princeton. We've been doing it for ten years. Last year [2004], we went to Moraga, California, to St. Mary's College. It was the biggest one we'd ever been to. It has around three thousand students, and it's run by an order of Catholic brothers whose focus is education. And there came a morning when we had breakfast with the brothers. They don't do a whole lot with the college, some of them teach, but mostly they go off and read stuff. And this brother said to me, "Here's why people don't understand anything that you're reporting from Iraq. In the Israeli-Palestinian conflict, everybody's picked their team by now, and you don't need to know a lot to read the paper in the morning. You like Jews, you don't like Jews, you're for the underdog, you're not for the underdog—there are a variety of reasons why you've chosen your team. So every time you read the paper, you think, 'Oh, those Palestinians have done it again, or oh, those Israelis,' and you engage. Whose team are you on in Iraq?" And I've been saying recently, that's right, you have to decide, "Am I for the Shias or the Sunnis?" And how many Americans know, first of all, that there are Shias and Sunnis and what side they should be on? That's what's gotten hard about Iraq, because now you have to judge.

Well, if you are for a democracy . . .

Then you've got to be for the Shias.

But you talked about it yourself, about people worrying about the tyranny of the majority.

Yes, that's a problem, because this is all quite new. But recently, I heard things that make me think now that the brother was wrong. I just gave a talk in Minnesota, and I was astonished by what people were asking. Astonished. They were six hundred public radio listeners. They understood the difference between Sunnis and Shias, and they wanted to know how religious the Shias were going to be, and they wanted to know if the Kurds and the Shias could sort it out over Kirkuk,[21] and they wanted to know how close they were to Iran. A boy of twelve raised his hand and said, "I read the *Onion* [an online farcical newspaper featuring world, national, and community news that posts this caveat: "The *Onion* is not intended for readers under eighteen years of age."], that's where I get my news, and the headline said that the Iraqi exit strategy was through Iran. Is that a joke?"

I said, "What do you think of the draft?" Then I said, "Here's the thing. We've run out of troops. The reason that's a joke is because there was a time when people in the administration did think that they could take a right turn into Iran and a left into Syria and be done with the whole region. But there isn't an army to do it; there isn't a military to do it."

Do you think this war has increased terrorism?

It's not that I think it; it's a documented fact. The CIA says so. People inside the administration say so.

How big is the insurgency now? How much of it is coming from outside and how much of it is homegrown?

I think the insurgency is primarily Iraqi. I think that all you have to do is look at the numbers of how many foreign "terrorists" they've caught, and it's 1 percent of all the prisoners that they have. Even military intelligence people there don't talk about the insurgency being a foreign phenomenon anymore. The foreign people who are coming in are, a lot of times, suicide bombers, so they do a lot of damage. But this is a nationalist uprising that has to be dealt with.

Who is going to deal with it?

The *Atlantic Monthly*'s Jim Fallows wrote one of those great guidelines for all of us about all the military people who are thinking about exit strategies and how the best of them are talking about the fact that Americans are incapable of dealing with the insurgency because you have to have a cultural understanding and you have to be able to speak the language to deal with it and we have neither, so we cannot deal with the insurgency because we do not know how.

So does that mean that five years out we are still going to be in the soup?

Yes, it could. If they can't figure this out, if this government can't put something together, if it can't bring in the Sunnis, then our troops won't be able to leave. You are asking neophyte Iraqi politicians to do some very, very, very complicated things, and there's no telling whether they can or not. But to go back to the administration and democracy, I think even back in June it was very clear that the "democracy" that the Bush administration wanted to bring to Iraq was simply not doable, no matter what pictures you see on television.

Why wasn't it clear when they came to power that they were planning the war?

Because ideology is a blinding thing. Journalists are part of the "reality-based" community; the administration's neocons are not.

They say they are creating reality.

One of my favorite quotes was in Rajiv Chandrasekaran's piece in the *Washington Post* where John Agresto, the Coalition Provisional Authority's guy in charge of reconstructing Iraq's educational system, said, "I am a neocon mugged by reality. We can't deny there were mistakes, things that didn't work out the way we wanted. We have to be honest with ourselves."[22] I think all of those people who work there understood very well what a disaster it was. These were people who wanted to bring "No Child Left Behind"[23] to Iraq. We can't even manage it here, let alone with Shias and Sunnis and Kurds. And the Iraqis said, "That's what Saddam did; he tested everybody so that's not going to go well here." We already did "No Child Left Behind." So you won't get any points for that. Also, the CPA wanted to put antiabortion language into the Iraqi constitution.

One of the things that many of us said is, "What you need to do is just give Iraqis money. You crushed the army, you destroyed the state—the state was the major employer—so just give them money." But the Americans running the CPA were ideologically against welfare. So you couldn't.

I always thought that money was the solution, but it was the problem. Maj. Gen. David Petraeus, who is in charge of rebuilding Iraq's security forces, would say, "Here's how we dealt with things in Mosul: If it didn't create jobs we didn't do it, because at the end of the day, what this is all about is jobs jobs jobs jobs jobs."

If you were to poll Iraqis today, based on your experience and reporting, what do you think they would say are their five top priorities?

Electricity, water, being able to take their kids to school safely, a job, and normalcy.

Are Iraqis missing the normalcy that was Saddam?

Yes. You bet. Even though every once in a while under Saddam you'd get swept up and you wouldn't know why, and if you were a Kurd, life was horrible, and if you were a Shiite in 1991,[24] it was diabolical, but you got along—people knew how to deal with the situation. Chaos is hard for two years. You can't imagine how hard it is. I see the strain on our translators who've been with us for two years and how much it has aged them.

Do you think Americans are getting a sense of what you just said coming through television?

Not at all, no. This is the Deborah Amos theory of why coverage is so bad. Even our editors—all of them—were having a tough time figuring out how to explain what is going on in Iraq. I see it more with the newscasts than in print. We have two very smart people who are running NPR's foreign desk. They've both been Middle East correspondents; they're tough, no bullshit, don't-try-to-trick-me journalists: Loren Jenkins and Doug Roberts. Doug speaks fluent Arabic. But it was easier to always do "Two US soldiers died today" for the newscasts than stories on the Sunnis and Shia, or the complications of the insurgency. The insurgency story was much harder: it was confusing, it raised the question, "What side am I supposed to be on, who are the good guys and who are the bad guys?" So from all of us, from Fox to NPR—I don't mean that as a political scale—the newscasts were always the same, "Two American soldiers died today."

The bigger story for Americans is that the Iraqis are mad at us, and we need to gauge just how mad they really are. But you have to balance this. This is why it's so difficult. Yesterday, everybody did the same report, which was that 70 percent of Iraqis say the future will be better. All the USAID people say to me, "When that number hits 50 or 40 percent, we better get out of there, because they are going to shoot all of us." We can stay as long as that number is up to 70 percent and as long as the Iraqis continue to say, "Let's just get through this, I didn't think it was going to take this long, we're not a model for anything, don't any of you try this, this is horrible, but now that we're in it, we'll persevere, and we'll come out the other end."

Do you think it was a neutral sign, good sign, or bad sign that the Sunnis really did not participate in this election?

I talked to people in Jordan—which is where you can meet tribal people —and to intellectuals who said it was a mistake.

Can that mistake be reversed?

I think it can. But I believe that there was more than one reason why the Bush administration held fast to the January 30 date for holding the elections. I think one of those reasons was that Bush wanted to claim that victory in the State of the Union address. And he did. I've listened to a UN adviser say off the record at the Council on Foreign Relations that "you could have gotten Shia religious leader Grand Ayatollah al-Sistani on board to hold talks with the Sunnis before holding the elections and that would have been better. You would have at least been seen as trying to bring the Shias and Sunnis together, even if the Sunnis said, 'We're out of here. We're not doing this.' You were going to have to talk it out with them either before or after the election, take your choice, but you couldn't get out of it." All the things that the Americans could have done before the election, they're having to do now, and the Iraqis are saying, "What is wrong with you people? When are we going to have a government?" So at the expense of losing precious public support in Iraq, you created a positive impression in the United States by rushing the elections so that you could talk about them being held in your State of the Union address.

All of these things cost. They're now having the discussion that they should have had before the elections. That's why it's been so tough to put this government together, because the Shias and the Kurds know the Sunnis have to be included, and the Kurds are having their own fight about Kirkuk to boot. They want guarantees that Kirkuk will be a Kurdish city.

How much longer do you think the Iraqis want us to stay?

They are up and down about that. Every Iraqi will tell you that they want us to leave tomorrow. That's an emotional response, and politicians must be mindful of that. I think that part of the reason for the high voter turnout was about Iraqis thinking that there are two ways to get the Americans out: you can shoot them out or you can vote them out. The majority of Iraqis believe that they can actually vote us out of there, which is one of the big things that brought them to the polls.

But can they?

They think so. Their politicians say that this is the better way. Grand Ayatollah al-Sistani's line is, "We're different from the Sunnis who are fighting the Americans via the insurgency; we will vote the Americans out of here." I think that if the security situation were good, al-Sistani would be agitating to get them out tomorrow. The problem is that we dissolved their army and their state and we can't leave until they can protect themselves and they know that, so they're in a real quandary. Now it is very possible that they will ask us to leave early.

They are in a quandary because the insurgency is a nationalist insurgency that is trying to get us out and they're creating insecurity with their violent attacks, and as long as there is insecurity, we'll stay, and as long as we stay, there will be an insurgency, so it seems to be a circular problem, doesn't it?

Yes. What's always been said about the Iraqi insurgency is that if the Shiites join in then we are out of there because there's no way that we can sustain the occupation if that happens. So far, the Shiites have not joined in.

Do you think the press is covering and analyzing this current situation well?

When you say the press, I would say yes. However, I am paid to read it all and so, over time, if you read it all, yes. But you have to read it all. That's a lot of work, and nobody has time to do that except for those of us who do it professionally.

Do you think television, which is the mass–public consciousness media, could do a better job?

No. No. It cannot. They are more reduced than we in radio are to "Two American soldiers died today" because they're a linear medium. The complexity of the Middle East doesn't lend itself to television. I was thinking today about how I would do it. How would I do on television what I do on radio? Somebody has to figure out a new format for explaining foreign news and these tough, complex situations to people, because the traditional way of doing it, presenting an entire story in two minutes if you're lucky, is out of the question.

But overall, I think television could have done a better job. I think they could have tried a little harder to get the other side.

Right now, you can't. That's the problem. It's too dangerous for Western television people to be on the streets. The camera makes them too obvious.

How much better is radio at telling these complex stories than TV?

It's easier to tell these stories on radio. We did an hour in September 2003 titled "Iraq: The War after the War" about the early missed opportunities and cultural misunderstandings that may have contributed to the ongoing insurgency. Nobody paid any attention. We were two years too early. Timing is everything with these subjects, it really is.

Another interesting aspect of this whole story is that old cultures like those in the Middle East have large populations living in medieval conditions, but then they have their elites who are among the most sophisticated elites in the world.

You bet. They are amazing.

And their peasantry is different from ours. We are largely a country of rich peasants in a sense.

Their peasants are really living in a different age. Anthony Shadid wrote a brilliant piece about a guy who was fighting in Fallujah, and you understood that this fighter was a nihilist. He had no ideology about anything. He was just a walking angry bomb. He was willing to risk his family. The story was horrific.[25] Anthony speaks Arabic. He sat with this guy in this room with no electricity and no water, and you think holy shit, how do you talk to this guy, how do you convince this guy that things are going to get better in Iraq? He doesn't have anything in his head.

The other thing is that we can't understand the suicide bombing mentality. But if you look at the cultural and spiritual paradigm of these people, it makes sense.

Yes, I know. I just finished Olivier Roy's book *Globalized Islam: The Search for a New Ummah*,[26] which is really good in describing that.

Part of the spiritual paradigm is essentially that death is really not death; it's moving on to some place better.

I had a revelatory moment in London when I went to see the Aztec exhibit. It's all about death, and the only way you could get to heaven was if you died in childbirth or battle. These people flayed other human beings and kept big pots of flayed skin. And if you died of old age, you had to wait around in purgatory or the equivalent for a long time. This was a warrior culture, so if your holy people convince you that battle gets you to heaven faster than any other way. . . . But I know plenty of Muslims who don't think like those suicide bombers.

Of course. Look at Osama, he's not getting on a plane and driving it into the World Trade Center.

Neither is Ayman al-Zawahiri.[27]

You did mention in one of your reports that support for Osama has grown in Iraq.

Yes, it's another way to express anti-Americanism.

Another thing you mentioned in passing in a report was that, after three wars in Iraq, the cancer rate in Basra is incredibly high.

That was what the oncologist at the hospital there told us.

High cancer rate from what?

It's interesting that you ask me that. I don't know from what and the doctor didn't say, and I didn't ask because it wasn't what I was doing that day. I came back, I put it in the story, and my editor said, "Oh, you just stepped in a controversial area, how do you want to handle that?" I said, "I'd like to leave it in there but I'm not going to raise the question of from what. Those are the doctor's numbers. He gets to say those numbers." That's fact. Whether it was from depleted uranium shells or not was not my business that day.

I was listening to the report, and all of a sudden it just jumped out at me right there toward the end.

I'd forgotten that was a big controversy, to tell you the truth.

DEBORAH AMOS covers Iraq and the Middle East for National Public Radio (NPR) News. Her reports can be heard on NPR's award-winning *Morning Edition*, *All Things Considered*, and *Weekend Edition*. She was also, until 2004, a correspondent with ABC News, a role she began in 1993.

Prior to joining ABC News, Amos spent sixteen years with NPR, where she was most recently London bureau chief. Previously, she was based in Amman, Jordan, as an NPR foreign correspondent. Amos won several awards, including an Alfred I. duPont–Columbia Award and a Breakthru Award, as well as widespread recognition for her coverage of the Gulf War in 1991. She spent 1991–1992 as a Nieman Fellow at Harvard University and is the author of *Lines in the Sand: Desert Storm and the Remaking of the Arab World* (Simon & Schuster, 1992).

Amos joined NPR in 1977, where she was first a director and then a producer for *All Things Considered* until 1979, after which she worked on documentaries until 1985. In 1982 she received the Prix Italia, the Ohio State Award, and a duPont-Columbia Award for "Father Cares: The Last of Jonestown." In 1984 she received a Robert F. Kennedy Journalism Award for "Refugees."

Amos began her career in 1972 after receiving a degree in broadcasting form the University of Florida at Gainesville. She is a member of the Council on Foreign Relations.

NOTES

1. On February 5, 2003, Secretary of State Colin Powell made a presentation to the UN Security Council that had, he said, two purposes: "First, to support the core assessments made by [chief UN weapons inspector] Dr. Blix and [the head of the International Atomic Energy Agency] Dr. ElBaradei. As Dr. Blix reported to this council on January 27, quote, 'Iraq appears not to have come to a genuine acceptance, not even today, of the disarmament which was demanded of it,' unquote. . . . My second purpose today is to provide you with additional information, to share with you what the United States knows about Iraq's weapons of mass destruction as well as Iraq's involvement in terrorism, which is the subject of Resolution 1441 and other earlier resolutions." http://www.whitehouse.gov/news/releases/2003/02/20030205-1.html. Later reports showed that Powell's presentation contained errors.

2. A *Washington Post* profile of the Kurds at http://www.washingtonpost.com/wp-srv/inatl/daily/feb99/kurdprofile.htm describes them as fifteen to twenty million "largely Sunni Muslims with their own language and culture living in the generally contiguous areas of Turkey, Iraq, Iran, Armenia and Syria" collectively called Kurdistan. The Kurds seek their own state and have clashed with the nations in which their territories lie, including Iraq. In 1988 Saddam launched a poison gas attack on the Kurdish town of Hallabjah and killed five thousand people.

3. David Fromkin, *A Peace to End All Peace: The Fall of the Ottoman Empire and the Creation of the Modern Middle East* (New York: Owl Books, 2001).

4. "A Clean Break: A Strategy for Securing the Realm" is described by National Security reporter James Bamford in chapter 11 of this book as "a foreign policy plan that [then adviser to the Israeli government] Richard Perle gave to Netanyahu, who had just become prime minister of Israel. The 'Clean Break' report recommended that Israel go into Iraq, remove Saddam Hussein, put somebody in there who would basically be a puppet, and then go to Syria, Iran, and all the other countries that they were worried about." The document can be viewed at http://www.informationclearinghouse.info/article1438.htm.

5. Richard Perle is the former chairman of the Defense Policy Board, which Seymour Hersh describes in his March 17, 2003, *New Yorker* article "Lunch with the Chairman" as a "Defense Department advisory group composed primarily of highly respected former government officials, retired military officers and academics. . . . The board meets several times a year at the Pentagon to review and assses the country's strategic defense policies." Perle has been reported to have been influential in crafting the Bush administration's policy toward Iraq. David Wurmser is principal deputy assistant to Vice President Cheney for national security affairs. Douglas Feith was undersecretary of defense for policy, but resigned. According to a September 4, 2004, *Washington Post* article, "Leak Inquiry Includes Iran Experts in the Administration," federal investigators were asking questions about Perle, Feith, and Wurmser in connection with sensitive US intelligence on Iran being given to the Israeli government.

6. The Project for a New American Century (PNAC) says on its Web site that it "intends, through issue briefs, research papers, advocacy journalism, conferences, and seminars, to explain what American world leadership entails." It is generally seen as a neoconservative take on the role the United States should play in the world. PNAC says it is a nonprofit educational organization dedicated to the propositions "that American leadership is good both for America and the world; and that such leadership requires military strength, diplomatic energy and commitment to moral principle." http://www.new americancentury.org/.

7. *Madrassas* are Islamic schools for Muslim children.

8. According to the BBC's Middle East analyst Roger Hardy (in a September 30, 2001, article, "Analysis: Inside Wahhabi Islam"), Muhammed Ibn Abdul-Wahhab founded Wahhabism, an Islamic revivalist movement, in the eighteenth century because he "felt that the local practice of Islam had lost its original purity." The Internet encyclopedia Wikipedia describes Wahhabism as a "fundamentalist, puritanical form of Islam, which is often considered as having deviated from Sunni Islam. A major instance of this change is their anthropomorphic beliefs about God." Wahhabism is "the major sect of the government and society of Saudi Arabia." http:// en.wikipedia.org/wiki/Wahhabism.

9. Camp David 2000 was a July 2000 meeting at the presidential retreat among President Clinton, Israeli prime minister Ehud Barak, and Palestinian Authority chairman Yasir Arafat to attempt a peace agreement between the Israelis and Palestinians. The talks failed.

10. Founded in 1996 and based in Qatar, Al Jazeera is the largest Arabic news channel in the Middle East and provides twenty-four-hour news coverage.

11. A British-educated former banker, Ahmed Chalabi has been the leader of the anti-Saddam Iraqi National Congress, which was formed with US government backing for the purpose of overthrowing Saddam Hussein. He received large sums of money from the US government for his activities and was a source of faulty prewar intelligence. Although he has no industry experience, he is currently acting oil minister for the new Iraqi government.

12. On February 19, 2005, *New York Times* columnist Frank Rich wrote "The White House Stages Its 'Daily Show'" about President Bush and White House spokesman Scott McClellan having friendly question-and-answer exchanges during press conferences with "Jeff Gannon," who turned out to be a man named James D. Guckert working ostensibly for "Talon News," a Web site staffed mostly by volunteer Republican activists. Guckert's nude photos on hotmilitarystuds.com and reports of his alleged activities as a gay prostitute also raised questions about his status as a real journalist. On March 14, 2005, Robert Pear of the *New York Times* wrote "U.S. Videos, for TV News, Come under Scrutiny." The lead was "Federal investigators are scrutinizing television segments in which the Bush administration paid people to pose as journalists praising the benefits of the new Medicare law, which would be offered to help elderly Americans with the costs of their prescription medicines."

13. The Baath Party, Saddam Hussein's party in Iraq, follows a secular ideology that advocates pan-Arabic unity, Arab socialism, nationalism, and militarism. http://en .wikipedia.org/wiki/Ba'ath_Party.

14. The Coalition Provisional Authority was the US caretaker administration in Iraq until the handover of political power to the Iraqis in June 2004. The Coalition Provisional Authority appointed the Iraqi Governing Council, the provisional government of Iraq, which was made up of a group of Iraqi political, religious, and tribal leaders.

15. Deborah Amos, "Karbala Debates Elections," *All Things Considered*, National Public Radio, February 25, 2004.

16. Baghdad's largest Shiite ghetto.

17. The Ayatollah Rouhollah Mousavi Khomeini became absolute ruler of Iran in April 1979 following the deposing of the Shah Mohammed Reza Pahlavi of Iran in January 1979. Khomeini's theocratic government gave complete political control to clergymen.

18. See chapter 14 in this book.

19. In chapter 15 in this book, the *Washington Post*'s Anthony Shadid described Hezbollah as a "movement that came out of the Israeli invasion of Lebanon in 1982 with Iranian backing. . . . It's probably one of the most efficient, effective, noncorrupt movements in the Middle East and provides everything from dental clinics to hospitals to schools to nurseries to orphanages. It set out to serve Shiites in southern Lebanon and southern Beirut living in communities that traditionally were most discriminated against, the poorest and most disenfranchised. They also entered Parliament as a political party. And they had their military arm, which fought the Israelis in southern Lebanon and forced them to withdraw."

20. The Green Zone, now called the International Zone, is the heavily guarded area of closed-off streets in central Baghdad where the US occupation authorities live and work. Coalition partners and US forces also live there, as do journalists. http://www .globalsecurity.org/military/world/iraq/baghdad-green-zone.htm.

21. Kirkuk is the largest city in one of Iraq's most important oil-producing areas, with oil pipelines running into the coastal cities of Tripoli in Lebanon and Yamurtalik in Turkey. Kirkuk is one of the centers of Kurdish identity. The Kurds are Sunni Muslims who want to have their own nation.

22. Rajiv Chandrasekaran, "An Educator Learns the Hard Way: Task of Rebuilding Universities Brings Frustration, Doubts and Danger," *Washington Post*, June 21, 2004.

23. On the US Department of Education Web site, Education Secretary Rod Page writes that No Child Left Behind was added to the reauthorized 1965 Elementary and Secondary Education Act in 2001 and "asks states to set standards for student performance and teacher quality. The law establishes accountability for results." http://www.ed.gov/ nclb/overview/intro/guide/guide_pg3.html.

24. On February 15, 2001, President George H. W. Bush called on the Iraqi military and people to overthrow Saddam Hussein. Shiites in the south responded with an uprising and turned to the American forces already there for help, which the US forces didn't provide. In response, Saddam Hussein's forces "leveled the historical centers of the Shiite towns, bombarded sacred Shiite shrines and executed thousands on the spot. By some estimates, 100,000 people died in reprisal killings between March and September [2001]. Many of these atrocities were committed in proximity to American troops, who were under orders not to intervene." Peter Galbraith, "The Ghosts of 1991," *Washington Post*, April 12, 2003.

25. Anthony Shadid, "After Fallujah, Son Is Gone, but Fervor Remains: Father Who Left Reluctantly Waits to Fight Another Day," *Washington Post*, December 1, 2004.

26. Olivier Roy, *Globalized Islam: The Search for a New Ummah* (New York: Columbia University Press, 2004). *Ummah* means "community" or "people."

27. According to a BBC profile, Ayman al-Zawahiri is "an eye surgeon who helped found the Egyptian Islamic Jihad militant group [and] is often referred to as Osama bin Laden's right hand man and the chief idealogue of al Qaeda." Some experts believe that he was "the operational brains behind" 9/11. The BBC profile can be found at http:// news.bbc.co.uk/1/hi/world/middle_east/1560834.stm.

20

"YOU HAVE TWO EARS AND ONE MOUTH, SO YOU SHOULD LISTEN TWICE AS MUCH AS YOU SPEAK"

Chuck Kennedy/KRT

HANNAH ALLAM
Baghdad Bureau Chief and
Foreign Correspondent,
Knight Ridder
Interviewed April 2005

Hannah Allam was in the United States taking a break from Baghdad when I spoke with her by phone. She'd been traveling around and, as she does in Iraq, was talking to people in the streets:

> It's been jarring to hear from people in Oklahoma, Texas, Washington, Maryland, and Virginia—all the places I've been in the past week or two. When I tell people I live in Baghdad, they say, "Oh, Baghdad, it's a good thing it's all better now." I've been appalled to hear that people really are buying the spin that this has been a successful campaign because US troops aren't being attacked as much anymore and the violence has decreased.
>
> At first I'd say to them, "What are you talking about? No, it's not." And

they'd look at me like I was a grumpy, cynical liar at worst, or unpatriotic at best. . . . I can't count how many times I've had to say in the past week, "Yes, you're right. . . . Americans aren't being killed at the same rate, but then again, they're in fortresses. But ordinary Iraqis certainly are dying everyday, and the Americans aren't releasing a civilian casualty count."

Allam is as deeply concerned about America's lack of interest in the fates of average Iraqi citizens as she is about the way they are portrayed in the press. "They've been dehumanized. And there are very clear-cut roles for them. In the newspaper and TV stories, it's like, 'OK, we've got to quote a cleric here and a woman there—it doesn't really matter who she is—a toothless mother of four, OK, she'll do.' This kind of coverage just doesn't do anything for the people who are on the other end of a two-thousand-pound bomb, or an occupation, or a raid in the middle of the night. I've sort of made it a mandate in my coverage to show the diversity and break out of what I call the 'central casting' roles."

As a young, twenty-something journalist of Middle Eastern descent who was reared in Oklahoma, Hannah knows she has her work cut out for her with respect to explaining what's going on in Iraq and the Middle East to the American public. The fact is, she does a spectacular job of it. So good, in fact, that journalists, particularly those covering the White House and the Pentagon, would be well advised to read Allam's articles on a regular basis and compare her reporting and analysis to what government officials are saying about Iraq. Her work would serve them well as a baseline reality check.

Hannah obtained one of the first and most extensive interviews with Iraqi and foreign insurgents. Her reporting on the insurgency sets the same standards of excellence as that of some of her much older and better-known colleagues. Her coverage of the political scene in Iraq is also superior. As a reporter, she does have the advantage of looking Middle Eastern and speaking Arabic: "I can get out and overhear conversations where Iraqis aren't tailoring what they're saying because a Westerner is around." In this interview, Allam provides the untailored view of Iraq. But language skills and looks are only part of the reason why she regularly gets the insider's perspective. Hannah never forgets her grandfather's advice: "You have two ears and one mouth, so you should listen twice as much as you speak." Of course, I was asking her to do the opposite. We had our conversation within a day or so of the two-year anniversary of the fall of Baghdad.

On the second-year anniversary of the fall of Baghdad, there was an anti-American demonstration organized by Shia cleric Muqtada al-Sadr who everyone thought was out of the picture, but lo and behold, here he is again. He's been adept at reorganizing and getting his militiamen out to fight American and Iraqi forces. Others joined Muqtada al-Sadr's people for the demonstration, including a few militant Sunnis who have allied with Muqtada in the past.

The Iraqis are frustrated. There's still a lack of basic services, and I think the demonstration just shows their frustration. When you do a person-on-the-street interview, a lot of times the first thing you hear is, "It's two years and what have the Americans done for us?" Of course, that's mainly in Baghdad, which is where I'm restricted to operating these days. Unless I want to embed with the US military or travel with the government, I do not have access to most of Iraq.

Iraq, to me, is the incredible shrinking country. I used to be able to say, "Let's go to Kurdistan[1] for the day." Or we would go to Najaf and Kufah[2] for Friday prayers, grab some kabobs, and drive back to Baghdad, no problem. Now if I want to go to Najaf, I have to arrange a huge conference between my editors on speakerphone in Washington, DC, and our security advisers in Iraq. We have to decide which route I take, if I take a flak jacket or not, if we have armed guards in the next car or not, if I present my fake Iraqi ID or my press ID, and if I say I'm Egyptian or American—it's just so involved that I can't really travel at all anymore.

Up until the beheadings and kidnappings began, we could still go out at night in Baghdad. There's still a French journalist unaccounted for, and I think two Romanians are being held. I haven't seen if they've been released or not. An American contractor was kidnapped a couple days ago. He was just in a video with two gunmen standing over him. As long as we keep getting those videos, I'm not allowed to go anywhere.

During the day in Baghdad I can move around more freely than some of my more Western-looking colleagues, but still, the second I whip out a notebook or start asking the wrong questions, I'm spotted as a foreigner. I speak conversational Arabic and I don't have an Iraqi accent, so definitely I'm spotted as a foreigner when I start interviewing. I live in this heavily fortified hotel, and there's one way in and one way out. Everyone knows there's foreign media staying there, so if someone wanted to get me, it wouldn't be too hard. They could just follow me and wait, and that would be it. So I don't take it for granted that I can move around freely. I'm extremely cautious, but the fact that I blend in and can walk the streets of Baghdad is an advantage. I can get out and overhear conversations where Iraqis aren't tailoring what they're saying because a Westerner is around.

What I hear is a lot of frustration, a lot of uncertainty, and not a lot of hope. There's definitely a feeling of anti-Americanism across the board. Even Kurds, who have been the most pro-American group in Iraq, are starting to express their frustration with the US presence. The Shia, who have gained the most from Saddam's overthrow, are very anti-American.

There was an initial euphoria after the fall of the regime. The country was under occupation, there were foreign tanks and troops going through neighborhoods and entering families' homes, but there was still an initial euphoria about getting rid of a dictator who had crushed dreams and families and religion for thirty years. That was quickly replaced by anti-Americanism. I think the reporting shows that there were a series of cultural and political missteps. For example, from the Sunni perspective, disbanding the army and the process of de-Baathification[3]—which really became a witch-hunt where top university professors, doctors, and a lot of members of Iraq's intelligentsia were purged from their positions—created a lot of resentment.

A lot of Baathists weren't pro-Saddam; they just had to join the party to get the PhDs and access to Western universities and exchange programs. Many were shocked when they were removed from their jobs, and they were saying, "Everyone knows we just toed the party line. We had to join. We never rose in rank to become senior leaders in Saddam's government." But when the Shia, especially exiles, came into power in Iraq, they went on a very vengeful campaign to purge the universities, the professional ranks, and the military officer corps of people they thought had blood on their hands just from being in the party. So suddenly there was this brain drain, and top doctors, top thinkers, philosophers, professors, and attorneys were either jobless or switched to menial jobs. I've met prominent engineers who are taxi drivers now. Most of them fled the country because they had some money saved up and they could get out. Now you'll find them in Amman or Dubai or Sweden or the Ukraine of all places—that seems to be a big spot for Iraqi exiles. So basically, the political exiles are back in power. They've come back from Iran and London and the United States. Their return has created a whole new class of exiles who had stayed under Saddam and who arguably know more about Iraq and Iraqis because they've been there for the past twenty, thirty years.

American policy supported de-Baathification. The head of the Coalition Provisional Authority, Paul Bremer,[4] ordered that the army be dissolved, leaving thousands and thousands of Iraqis jobless. Pretty soon, when there were no new jobs because reconstruction was stalled and available jobs were being farmed out to American companies, the best job around became attacking an American convoy for five hundred dollars. The jobless became easy prey for the insurgency.

One result of this is that Iraqis don't have a lot of faith in the new government. They say, "How can someone like Ahmed Chalabi[5] or anyone else who spent the better part of three decades outside the country come back and think they can rule us? They didn't suffer with us under Saddam."

Chalabi is still very much a player. There were charges related to a murder or kidnapping filed against him in Iraq, but they were dismissed. His party did well in the election. He's in the national assembly, and he's allied with the winning ticket, the United Iraqi Alliance, so he's still very much in power. I think some members of the top echelon of the new Iraq government are US citizens. Some of them spent a lot of time outside, particularly among the Shia. Ibrahim al-Jafaari, the new prime minister, has spent the past two or three decades in Iran and England. Ditto for the person whose name is coming up as interior minister. They all received money and training and refuge in Iran.

With respect to the new government, the big question is: Will Islam inspire the constitution or will it be the full foundation of the constitution? I've interviewed Jafaari for two years now, ever since he was a member of the governing council. I saw him just a few weeks ago. I had lunch at his home with a small group of reporters. It was before he had been named prime minister, but everyone knew he was going to get the job. We asked him what his plan was, and he said, "We're not going to set up a theocracy, but at the same time we'll probably see a more conservative government and a more prominent role for Islam. This is a time of crisis in Iraq. People are turning to religion, and they reflected that by voting for a list that was backed by the most revered Ayatollah Sistani."[6] So to Jafaari, that's a mandate.

Jafaari was the strategic choice. He's sort of timid and quiet and he's a scholar. When his name first came up as a prime minister candidate, those of us in the press corps along with ordinary Iraqis thought, "He'll never get it, he's too mild-mannered, he's too nice." He's a very likable, sweet person, but everyone thought that to fill Iyad Allawi's[7] shoes, the candidate for prime minister would have to be someone equally tough or at least tough-talking and kind of a strongman type. Al-Jafaari is as far as you can get from that. He's a very soft-spoken scholar who in just about every interview I've had with him will read me a poem he's written.

I think he was acceptable to the Americans because he is not as militant or close to Iran as, say, Abdel Aziz al-Hakim of the United Iraqi Alliance, who would like Iraq to be an Islamic state. When I talked off the record to people from the United Iraqi Alliance, they told me, "We're not really concerned about the prime ministership. We want to staff the constitutional committee. That's where the real power is. This prime minister is only going to last until elections in December or January, so we don't really care about him. We're putting our money on the lasting permanent constitution." I think drafting the constitution is going to be a long, drawn-out, contentious, tedious process. The Kurds, of course, have veto power, so I don't think the United Iraqi Alliance can create an Islamic republic in the constitution, because the Kurds are there with their veto.

It's interesting that the old leadership, the Sunnis, who are obviously a minority in terms of population, are now marginalized, and the Kurds, who were marginalized, are now in the ascendancy. Given the culture over there and how things work, how do people view this role reversal? What is their view of American democracy?

It has pitted groups against one another. Obviously, there are traditional rivalries among Sunnis and Shia, Arabs and Kurds, and secularists and Islamists. All of those divisions have become more pronounced since the elections, and they are playing out in places like Kirkuk, which historically was a Kurdish city until Saddam, through the process of Arabization, forced out thousands of Kurds and replaced them with Arabs. Now we're seeing the reverse of Arabization with the Kurds trying to sway the demographics in Kirkuk by pushing in thousands of Kurdish residents who really don't have any place to live. They're just camped out in a stadium there, but they'll vote as residents of Kirkuk. This has angered Arabs across the board. It's not just Sunnis who are upset about that. Shia are also growing frustrated with what they see as the Kurds being overrepresented in the new government. More Kurds were able to come out and vote because their region is safer and more conducive to elections, so they had a very high voter turnout in Kurdistan. Kurdistan really feels like an independent nation.

The Shia were also blaming the Kurds for holding up the process of forming the government by making too many demands. Indeed, the Kurds, who were oppressed for many years and who feel that this is their chance to grab power because who knows what the next elections or the constitution will bring, were asking for the moon and seeing what they could get.

So there is some resentment. There are these little eruptions of ethnic violence every day, and definitely on a weekly basis we would hear that a Kurdish council member was assassinated or a Sunni police chief was assassinated over in Kirkuk and its surrounding villages. Low-level ethnic violence has been going on for the past two years, but it's definitely more pronounced since the elections.

Some see the election as a good thing, and some don't. The supporters of the United Iraqi Alliance think it's good. They have a government that they feel is backed by their spiritual leader, Ayatollah Sistani, and whether they like the people on the list or not, they consider Sistani's word law. They voted for Sistani, essentially. He wasn't a candidate. He's not even an Iraqi citizen—he's Iranian—but the second that they saw his photo on campaign posters (which was a very big controversy), that sealed the election.

Why do the Iraqis think the United States invaded Iraq?

You hear everything from oil, to setting up a staging ground to protect Israel, to wanting to reshape the Middle East. The Iraqis were more generous in their view of the Americans two years ago, when they said, "Thank you for getting rid of Saddam; we'll take it from here." But that didn't happen. The Americans have stayed and stayed. Some Iraqis say, "Well, they had to because in the postinvasion chaos, had the Americans just left, it would have been even worse." But you also have Iraqis saying, "Look, maybe we would have had a civil war, maybe not, but it would have been an Iraqi provisional government, and Iraqis would be in charge of their country." They feel that the occupation authority was the wrong way to go, that an Iraqi provisional government should have been set up immediately, and that they should have skipped the stage where there was a US overseer for Iraq.

I don't know why they didn't do it that way, because the Iraqi advisers to the coalition all tell me that that's what they advised. Maybe the Americans thought that there was just too much money floating around and that there needed to be an occupation authority to make sure it was properly spent. They had made promises of reconstruction that they had to keep. Also, I don't think the Americans knew who to trust at that point, because as we can see from how ineffective and unpopular the governing council has turned out to be, when they finally did get around to choosing an appointed government, they didn't choose people with much constituency at all. I think these poor choices can be traced back to a lack of understanding about Iraq and a lack of human and other intelligence about Iraq. They relied too heavily on people who didn't have strong constituencies in Iraq or who had been out of touch with the country for so long that they had formed visions of Iraq and Iraqis that just didn't square with the reality.

Why do you think we went into Iraq?

I don't know. It's not something that has become clear in the first two years of occupation, but perhaps it will be clear down the line. Their stated reason was to bring democracy to Iraq, after charges of WMDs and Saddam's links to al Qaeda collapsed. What they've done is install a pro-Iranian government, and that would seem to be counterproductive to their vision of an American-style model of democracy for the Middle East.

The Middle East has been problematic for many administrations now, and they currently have fewer friends in the region than they had before. Saudia Arabia has become problematic. When you saw, for example, that the FBI had listed a number of the 9/11 hijackers as "possible Saudi nationals," it drew attention to the troubles brewing inside the kingdom. I think the United States wanted to create a friendly state in the region to set an example, maybe for Syria, which is now the last rogue Arab state.

The bottom line is that I'm not sure why the United States went in to Iraq, but I see the realities of what an occupation does to a country, and a people. I see the humiliation and emasculation of an entire country, and it's terrible and pitiful and sorrowful to watch. Now, two years into it, we've got a pro-Iranian government, arguably fewer rights for women, still a devastating lack of basic services, and a fledgling security force that is infiltrated, inept, poorly equipped, and poorly trained.

In one story, we were being told that the security force had grown to two hundred and ten thousand men.

Maybe two hundred and ten thousand guys who needed a paycheck signed up with little or no vetting or background checks and were shipped off to Jordan or wherever for a six-week training course and given a uniform or not—because there's a lack of supplies—and given body armor or not. Just the other week, we had a correspondent who came back and told me that she'd just talked to a group of Iraqi policemen and, as she put it, "It was eight Iraqi policemen, three flak vests, two guns, and, one bullet." That's really how it is. That's the force that President Bush on down are saying, "Oh, look, Iraqi forces now outnumber US troops there, so what a big success."

Since you've been back here in the United States from Baghdad and reading a few papers maybe, what's your assessment of the coverage of what's going on in Iraq?

It's been jarring to hear from people in Oklahoma, Texas, Washington, Maryland, and Virginia—all the places I've been in the past week or two.

When I tell people I live in Baghdad, they say, "Oh, Baghdad, it's a good thing it's all better now." I've been appalled to hear that people really are buying the spin that this has been a successful campaign because US troops aren't being attacked as much anymore and the violence has decreased, or that Iraqis feel that they had free and fair elections and that there's a new security force that's going to take over from our troops.

At first I'd say to them, "What are you talking about? No, it's not." And they'd look at me like I was a grumpy, cynical liar at worst, or unpatriotic at best. They'd look at me as if I were saying things that were anti-American, and they'd say, "How can you say things aren't going well? They had elections, a dictator is gone, there's a new security force, and there's an elected government." I just found there's no sense in arguing with them, so I'd say, "It might not be as rosy as all that." I can't count how many times I've had to say in the past week, "Yes, you're right, there haven't been any major attacks on US troops recently, but just a few weeks ago we had the single deadliest attack since the war began in Hillah. One hundred and twenty-five people were killed in a single suicide bombing. So you're right, Americans aren't being killed at the same rate, but then again, they're in fortresses. But ordinary Iraqis certainly are dying everyday, and the Americans aren't releasing a civilian casualty count."

I've been so surprised at the depth to which the administration's message has gotten out to Americans. I don't watch American TV or read a lot of American newspapers when I'm in Iraq, so I don't know where they're getting this information, but shopkeepers in Oklahoma and gas station attendants in Texas who I talked to truly believe that Iraq is better and safer and freer than two years ago. If you spend a week in Iraq, you'll know that's not the case.

Do you have any estimate of how many Iraqi civilians have died?

No, and I'm really skeptical of anyone who does because we've tried so hard to get them. We've gone through the Iraqi Ministry of Health and gotten some figures, but they are not being released anymore and it's difficult to say how reliable they are. A colleague of mine, an Egyptian American named Nancy Youssef who is reporting for the *Detroit Free Press*, did a story on the civilian death toll. She managed to get partial figures from the Iraqi Ministry of Health, so we at Knight Ridder ran a big story about it and the Ministry of Health promptly stopped giving out those figures. They probably thought they were going to get in trouble with the Americans. We've asked for those figures again and again, but now we see they're not going to be giving any figures.

They've even stopped releasing the noncivilian figures. They used to release figures on Iraqi security forces killed, but as of mid–last year, already six or seven hundred Iraqi policemen had been killed. So they stopped releasing those figures as well. It's really a massacre for those guys on the security force. They are killed by the dozens in gun battles and attacks on police stations. They're kidnapped from recruiting posts, ambushed, or assassinated one by one. They're really being mown down. But they're not in an American uniform so, even if we write those stories, they don't get a lot of play in the States.

Our stay in Iraq has been indefinitely extended because they're saying we have to wait until these security forces are up to a certain number and up to a certain speed, but based on what you're saying, how's that going to happen?

I don't know. Getting people to sign up isn't hard. Even though there are kidnappings, beheadings, and mass suicide bombings of Iraqi troops, there are still Iraqis lining up at recruiting stations because they need jobs. What's difficult is finding people who won't be bought out by the insurgents and who really are loyal to the cause, who respect human rights and who won't torture people. I've watched beatings during interrogations. I don't know why, but an Interior Ministry official allowed me to watch interrogations of some suspects they had rounded up. He was very proud of this all-Iraqi operation and told me, "You can come watch the interrogation." So I grabbed my translator, Huda, and she and I went together. One by one, these guys were brought in. They were blindfolded, pushed down to the floor, kicked, beaten, and sat on. Clearly, Geneva Conventions were being violated. If this had happened in Abu Ghraib, it would be a huge international story. But these were Iraqis doing this to other Iraqis. I wrote the story, and there wasn't even a blip.

What does the insurgency look like to you? What is it made up of and what is its purpose?

I think the foreign fighter element has gone down. They're small but effective, so they're still definitely a threat. The Zarqawi,[8] al Qaeda–type insurgents are still there and still operating, but they are behaving more strategically. I don't know that they're still working in conjunction with the homegrown insurgency as much, because there's been a split. Before the latest battle in Fallujah in November 2004, there were reports based on our interviews that there was evidence of foreign fighters working with the Iraqi insurgents. But the beheadings did it for a lot of Iraqi insurgents.

They said, "That's not our style; we don't do that to people. That is a foreign import. We are an antioccupation force; we're not in the business of kidnapping some Korean or American and beheading him on tape. That's not our MO." What they do is attack American convoys. For a while, there was even a resistance group that called itself the Real Iraqi Resistance, and they said they were going to go after foreign fighters as well as American targets. So there's a split there. It is a very fragmented insurgency. No one's quite sure who's doing what. Are they Islamist? Are they Baathist? Are they just nationalist? All these elements are working in the insurgency, which makes it hard to sort out. If I knew that they were just nationalists or Baathists, I could approach them and make inroads into talking to them. I couldn't trust them completely, but I could trust them more than I could the Islamic extremists.

These guys know the value of the press and getting their message out. We've had the most success reaching nationalist insurgents, but it's just a wild card with the foreign fighters, because they really stop at nothing. They're very ruthless. They think the media is part and parcel of the occupation and that the only reason we're there is because of the occupation and to cover US troops. In most Arab states, the media is an arm of the state, so the concept of an independent media is foreign to them, which is why a journalist is fair prey. So I'm not going to risk my life to go see what's on their minds if I don't even know who I'm dealing with.

The aim of the nationalists or Baathist remnants is to get rid of the American forces. They haven't articulated their game plan for after that. The Islamists obviously want a Taliban-like state or some sort of puritan Islamic government, but that would include, I'm sure, oppressing the Shia, whom they don't consider true Muslims. That would be a problem considering that 60 percent or more of the country is Shia. The Islamists attack Sistani all the time, calling him a polytheist because of the Shia doctrine. The Shias believe, of course, in the prophet Muhammad, but they also place a lot of weight on the twelve imams. The twelve imams are the successors to the prophet Muhammad. So the Shias pray to these saints as well as to Allah, and the Islamists consider them polytheists, so it's another problem that breeds sectarian violence.

All the insurgents are anti-American, but they differ on tactics and strategies. The Islamic extremists that we have spoken to say, "Yes, we're going to have to kill some civilians in the process, but they'll be martyrs and go to heaven, so they should thank us."

The nationalists say, "We try to minimize civilian fatalities." I spoke with one insurgent who said, "Look, we had this whole operation set up. We knew that this convoy was coming at a certain time, but when the time came to attack, there was a kid riding a bicycle near the convoy so we scrapped it at the last minute because we wanted to spare an Iraqi life." So the tactics differ, the postoccupation view differs, and unlike a lot of other insurgencies, there's no spokesman and no organized national liberation front.

The insurgency is not like Hezbollah or HAMAS with one goal and a centralized leadership.[9] There are angry Shia in anti-American militias. There are Kurds and Sunnis who are anti-American. There are Sunnis in Zarqawi's pro–al Qaeda network as well as in the homegrown resistance. They don't work together. The closest thing to them working together was the Shura Mujahadeen, the Resistance Council of Fallujah, where each group had a vote. This was when Fallujah was an absolutely insurgent-controlled city. That ended after the American forces retook Fallujah in November 2004.

The US military put the number of foreign fighters in the low hundreds but, as for the rest of the insurgency, I've even seen numbers as high as two hundred thousand, which, I think, is on the high side and would also include so-called part-timers or people who have not picked up arms yet but would be willing to if provoked. They're kind of waiting in the wings. If it ever came down to all-out jihad or some kind of huge attack or revolt, they would join.

Among the general population, I don't see as much support for the insurgency as I used to. I think that's because the lines have been blurred between antioccupation nationalists and ruthless Islamic extremists. People have said things to me like, "I used to support the mujahadeen, but when I saw that man beheaded on TV, that was it for me." Or "When I saw those four contractors' corpses mutilated in Fallujah, Islam doesn't teach us to disrespect and dismember a body, to treat a corpse that way. That's sickening. To us, that's brutal. It's savage. How can we be proud of a resistance that does that kind of thing?" For suicide bombers, there was what I call armchair support. Actually, it's sort of an armchair resistance; people would turn the other way when they knew that the Jamil family of New Baghdad had a son who suddenly disappeared and there would be a martyr's funeral for him because everybody knew what happened to him. They didn't report it to authorities. They would also look the other way when they saw somebody loading rocket-propelled grenade launchers in the back of their car. They looked away partly out of fear that if they turned someone in, they would be retaliated against, but also partly because they knew that these guys were out attacking Americans, and that was all right with them. But now, I don't see as much support on the streets for the insurgents.

The insurgents are deadly and scary, but just as bad are the criminal gangs that have popped up. It's just like Colombia. Kidnapping has become a business.

People over there must be so tired of the violence.

They are. They're sick. Their kids can't go to school. Their favorite shops have been blown up. Not too long ago at the Happiness Bakery in Baghdad, people were inside buying their bread and in came insurgents who sprayed the place, killing twelve people. And everyone asks: For what?

Why are they focusing on civilians?

I don't think they're focusing so much on civilians; they are focusing on Iraqi security forces and anywhere that there's an Iraqi patrol. People don't get near them. We used to stop in the street and ask Iraqi policemen for directions if we got lost. If we were following an explosion, we would stop and ask them where it was. But now we don't get near them because at any moment they could be blown up.

But why blow up the Happiness Bakery?

That was a strange one. That one, I think, could have been sectarian because it was a Shia-owned bakery. Sometimes we find things out later, like they were supplying bread to a US base and the foreman at the base told someone where the bread was coming from. Not too long ago, four cloth merchants were assassinated in broad daylight in a marketplace because they were supplying the camouflage for the Iraqi army uniforms.

What about the attack on the Abu Ghraib prison recently? What was that about?

It looked to me like they were practicing a large-scale ambush. One day, they'll get it right, and they will manage to penetrate an American position. They haven't done anything like that since they attacked the US military dining facility in Mosul where they killed twenty-two people. A suicide bomber wearing an Iraqi uniform infiltrated the facility, walked to the middle of the mess hall, and blew himself up. I remember Shia militants telling us that, to them, that was a great operation, a great success.

Even some politicians who are now in the National Assembly and who we called for quotes after that said that from their perspective it was a legitimate attack because no civilians died. They said it was an attack on a military installation, so it was a legitimate act of resistance. More Iraqis were supportive of that than, say, a suicide bombing at a mosque or something where kids died.

What's the general view of the reconstruction and how that's been handled and how it's proceeding?

The general view is that it has been slow, with few results. People are more confounded than anything. What you always hear is, "After the 1991 Gulf War, Saddam rebuilt in six months." On one hand, that's true. There was electricity again, he rebuilt everything, and all the new buildings were painted with an Iraqi flag to show that Iraqi architects had redesigned and rebuilt them. But they were all Band-aid fixes. A lot of that stuff fell apart later or was bombed this time. The Americans went in and found that it was really flimsy and had been hastily rebuilt for propaganda purposes. So they are having to go in and redo everything from the ground up. To their credit, they said, "We could have done the Band-aid fix and we didn't. We're going in and replacing the whole power grid." But it's taking so long because so many of their foreign contractors refuse to come to Iraq now, or they come and are killed or kidnapped.

Do they use the locals much?

In some cases yes, in some cases no. Every time I'm at Baghdad International Airport, I see foreign workers disembarking. One time, I saw a whole plane full of Filipino workers coming in. Another time, it was a whole plane full of Indian workers coming in to work on the bases and on reconstruction efforts. And I thought, "What does this look like to Iraqis who are jobless and demonstrating in the streets to get their jobs back?" Here we are importing labor in a country with at least forty and probably more like 60 percent unemployment. But the Americans say, "We've had too many inside-job attacks. A Filipino is not going to blow himself up in the middle of a mess hall."

What does all this look like to you down the road?

What I fear most is civil war. I think that because I see changes among our own Iraqi staff, which is very evenly Shia-Sunni. There used to be good-natured teasing from time to time, like, "How could you do that, you did it backward, what are you—Kurdish?" Now, there's a mean-spirited tone to it. After the elections, there was such a rift between our Shia and Sunni staff members that I had to have a talk with them. For example, we had a Shia woman on staff who would make a big show of kissing the TV screen every time Ibrahim al-Jafaari came on TV and saying, "Oh, look, look at our prime minister, we elected him." The Sunnis on our staff, who didn't vote and can't stand the thought of Ibrahim al-Jafaari being president after he spent so many years in Iran, would change the channel. Things would erupt into these little fights, and there was bickering all the time. During Aashura, the month of mourning for the Shia saint, Imam Hussein, they play this mourning music, so some of our Shia staff members were playing the music in the office. And a Sunni said, "He died three hundred years ago, quit crying." It's been so sad to see our own staff unravel this way. These are educated Iraqis, people who went to school, speak fluent English, and are solidly middle class. I can't imagine what's happening in the rest of the country, particularly in the poor neighborhoods where Sunnis and Shias are still living side by side.

Is there a sense among people in Iraq that we're there to establish a new base for continuing operations to move into other countries?

Yes, there is. They say, "What's next? Let's take bets, is it going to be Syria or Iran?" There were jokes going around when President Bush talked about Lebanon and said, "Syria has to get out of Lebanon because free elections can't be held under foreign occupation." Our Iraqi staff had a field day with that. It got to the point where I wrote a story about it because there were so many jokes going around. The headline was: "Latest Casualties in Iraq: Ethnic Jokes" [March 23, 2005].

Bush came out right after Lebanon's prime minister Hariri was assassinated and basically said that the Syrian government did it. What was everybody else's response over there to that statement?

Syrians aren't popular in Iraq right now. They're widely viewed as supporting and funding the insurgency and funneling fighters and weapons into Iraq, so it wasn't a leap for a lot of Iraqis to say, "It was the Syrians because they are behind every bad thing everywhere." Jordanians are unpopular, too. Iranians are extremely unpopular. And as jaded as this sounds, to Iraqis, the Hariri assassination was a small-potatoes operation. They're used to ones that take out a prominent ayatollah and a hundred other people at a time, so the Hariri assassination was just a garden-variety killing for them.

How does the Israeli-Palestinian conflict fit into this whole picture?

There's a very prominent piece of graffiti in Baghdad, it's on a main wall and it says, "Be patient Palestine, we haven't forgotten you, but Baghdad is bleeding right now." You see everything there: "Out USA," "Down USA," or "I hate you Bush," but that one has really stuck in my mind because Palestinians weren't the most popular people in Iraq, because Saddam offered them refuge and a lot of people say he gave them more privileges than ordinary Iraqis had. There was a special place called Haifa Club that was a compound for Palestinians, and they were given free education in the universities. Iraqis who had been frustrated over the preferential treatment of the Palestinians stormed into Haifa Club, evicted all the Palestinians, and took over their homes. They're still there today, living as squatters. So in one sense there wasn't a lot of sympathy for the Palestinians, but in the wider sense, the Iraqis say, "We're under occupation, just like Palestine." I've met insurgents who say, "I'm fighting because I don't want this to be another Palestine." And there are definitely Shia militants who say, "We're modeling ourselves after Hezbollah. We will only attack military targets and we'll open hospitals and schools"

Speaking of Hezbollah, I got e-mails from Iraqi friends in Iraq when the news came out this week about Hezbollah flying a drone over Israel. This was the second time they've done it, but it's the first time the Israeli government acknowledged that Hezbollah flew a spy aircraft over their land. So Iraqis were e-mailing me saying, "Way to go. We should learn from them," and that kind of thing.

How are the US soldiers viewed over there?

I divide it into pre-ABG and post-ABG—before Abu Ghraib and after Abu Ghraib. Pre–Abu Ghraib, they were considered a nuisance. They occasionally killed civilians, they were rude, they didn't ever have a translator with them and so there were communication problems, and they were just considered sort of brutish nuisances. After Abu Ghraib, they were considered savages out to rape, humiliate, and torture Iraqis. There was a profound change in how they were viewed. Any hearts and minds that were won before Abu Ghraib were lost after those pictures came out.

What's your assessment of the way the Middle East is covered here in the United States?

I think it's been ignored for so long that there's not a very clear understanding of the Middle East. There are a lot of assumptions and stereotypes that are repeated again and again in the press. There's no understanding of the diversity of the Middle East—of the fact that Morocco is not like Saudi Arabia or that Egypt is not like Iraq. There is a perception that all the women are covered up, that all the men are wife beaters, and that they wear turbans and are backward. In Iraq, they are very sophisticated and cosmopolitan, especially in Baghdad. I've sort of made it a mandate in my coverage to show the diversity and break out of what I call the "central casting" roles: the grieving widow, the turbaned cleric, the young militant with a mask on his face. That's what you see out of the Palestinian territories, out of Lebanon, out of wherever. You don't see the pediatrician who happens to be a woman, you don't see a lot of the diversity. I asked a young woman at Baghdad University who her fashion icon was—we were just talking girl-talk—and she said, "I really like Beyoncé."

There's no concept of those people. They have no place in our papers, it seems. So I really try to get their voices in. During the siege of Najaf, I was inside the shrine with some guerrillas during the US military's bombing campaign. They dropped a two-thousand-pound bomb on the compound the night I stayed there. Before going in, I, like everyone else, believed that it was just a bunch of terrorists holed up in there. When I went in, there were families in there. Two seven-year-old girls tagged after me and clung to my abaya, my robe, the whole night, scared to death. There were children in there. I think sometimes when we don't get access to these places we tend to lump them all together, when in reality it's all so much more nuanced and diverse.

They've been dehumanized. And there are very clear-cut roles for them. In the newspaper and TV stories, it's like, "OK, we've got to quote a cleric here and a woman there—it doesn't really matter who she is—a toothless mother of four, OK, she'll do." This kind of coverage just doesn't do anything for the people who are on the other end of a two-thousand-pound bomb, or an occupation, or a raid in the middle of the night.

For a long time, a lot of news organizations, including Knight Ridder, didn't have Middle East bureaus. They had long ago closed their Cairo or Beirut bureaus and focused on other places. Then 9/11 happened, and they realized that there were going to be a lot of changes—a lot of unrest and fragility—going on in the Middle East and that they didn't have anyone there who knew the place, had been there, and could cover it.

I think the Middle East, like a lot of other areas, has been the victim of parachute journalism: "OK, Colombia's over, let's move on to Baghdad."

Do you think also there are political pressures involved in covering Israel and Palestine?

Yes, I see that especially in reporters who've come from the Palestinian territories or Jerusalem, and it's just not the same story because the occupation in Iraq is new and the diversity of Iraq makes it all the more complicated. There are some who do it wonderfully. Anthony Shadid of the *Washington Post* is my hero. He has been so objective, so successful in his coverage, and it's because he always includes historical, social, and cultural context in his stories that are missing from so many stories out there. There's a lack of historical context, and Arabs are frozen in time and place and dealt with in just the current circumstances without any kind of look back at the colonialism, revolutions, and dictatorships that shaped those current circumstances. That's been the hardest thing to convey, how important history is, especially for Arabs. History is so important to them and there's so much of it that it really is daunting to come in and do a good job reporting. I knew nothing about Iraq when I came in, and I know just a little bit now after two years, because it's so steeped in history and religious significance. It's really, really hard to come into a place like that and find your feet.

How have you found your feet?

I talk to ordinary Iraqis. My grandfather in Oklahoma says, "You have two ears and one mouth, so you should listen twice as much as you speak." That's what I try to do. I just listen to them and ask them about their lives. Even our Iraqi staff members who are earning up to one hundred dollars a day—which is a fortune in Iraq—are still going home to no electricity. They're sleeping on the roof because it's so hot and they don't have air conditioning. They come in to work with dark circles under their eyes and I ask them, "Why do you look like a zombie?" And they say, "I was up all night fanning my child on the roof because I had to cover her in a blanket because I'm worried about shrapnel or stray bullets."

HANNAH ALLAM is Knight Ridder's Baghdad bureau chief and Iraq correspondent. In January 2006 she is slated to open a Knight Ridder bureau in Cairo and will serve as bureau chief there. Allam came to the Baghdad bureau in December 2003 after four years at the St. Paul Pioneer Press in Minnesota. In St. Paul, she covered courts, the suburbs, terrorism, and reaction to the war in Iraq. In the summer of 2003, she spent two months in Baghdad, where she obtained one of the first and most extensive interviews with Iraqi and foreign insurgents. Allam has lived in Saudi Arabia, Egypt, and the United Arab Emirates. She graduated from the University of Oklahoma in 1999 and interned at the *Washington Post*, the *Wichita (KS) Eagle*, and the *Star Tribune* in Minneapolis. She speaks French and conversational Arabic.

NOTES

1. Kurdistan is north of Baghdad. See the Global Security Web site for maps of Kurdistan: http://www.globalsecurity.org/military/world/war/kurdistan-maps.htm.

2. Najaf is one of the holiest cities in Iraq for Shiites and the center of Shiite political power. It is about eighty miles south of Baghdad. Kufah is near Najaf.

3. De-Baathification means rooting out former members of Saddam Hussein's Baath Party, who were generally more secular, better-educated Sunnis or those who wanted to get ahead or gain advantages by joining Hussein's party.

4. Paul Bremer was named presidential envoy to Iraq on May 6, 2003. As head of the Coalition Provisional Authority in Iraq, he was the administrator for the US-led occupation government until the handover of political power to the Iraqis in June 2004. The Coalition Provisional Authority appointed the Iraqi Governing Council, the provisional government of Iraq, which was made up of a group of Iraqi political, religious, and tribal leaders.

5. A British-educated former banker, Ahmed Chalabi has been the leader of the anti-Saddam Iraqi National Congress, which was formed with US government backing for the purpose of overthrowing Saddam Hussein. He received large sums of money from the US government for his activities and was a source of faulty prewar intelligence. Although he has no industry experience, he is currently acting oil minister for the new Iraqi government.

6. Grand Ayatollah Ali Husaini Sistani was born in Iran and now lives in Najaf, Iraq. A very traditional Shiite cleric and the Shiites' top spiritual leader, he is considered one of the most influential religious figures in the Middle East.

7. Former Baathist and interim Iraqi prime minister Iyad Allawi is, the BBC reports in "Who's Who in Iraq: Iyad Allawi" (May 28, 2004), "one of a US-backed clique of secular Iraqi opposition figures who lived in exile until the fall of Saddam Hussein's regime in April 2003." A secular Shia Muslim, Allawi is head of the Iraqi National Accord Party in the Iraqi National Assembly.

8. A Palestinian born in Jordan, Abu Musab al-Zarqawi is believed to have links to al Qaeda and is believed to be, according to a BBC profile, "the main source of kidnappings, bomb attacks and assassination attempts in Iraq." The BBC's profile can be found at http://newsvote.bbc.co.uk/mpapps/pagetools/print/news.bbc.co.uk/2/hi/middle_east/3483089.stm.

9. In chapter 15 in this book, the *Washington Post*'s Anthony Shadid described Hezbollah as a "movement that came out of the Israeli invasion of Lebanon in 1982 with Iranian backing. . . . It's probably one of the most efficient, effective, noncorrupt movements in the Middle East and provides everything from dental clinics to hospitals to schools to nurseries to orphanages. It set out to serve Shiites in southern Lebanon and

southern Beirut living in communities that traditionally were most discriminated against, the poorest and most disenfranchised. They also entered Parliament as a political party. And they had their military arm, which fought the Israelis in southern Lebanon and forced them to withdraw." In the Palestinian territories, the very traditional Islamic Resistance Movement, or HAMAS, became known for its suicide bombings of Israelis. "Yet it is also a sophisticated and diverse organization that appeals to many Muslims worldwide and sometimes advocates peaceful persuasion, not violent revolt. Some of its supporters went on to help found al Qaeda, while others launched one of the largest college student groups in the United States. . . . They run hundreds of mosques and dozens of businesses engaging in ventures such as real estate development and banking." http://www.washington post.com/ac2/wp-dyn/A12823-2004Sep10?language=printer.

2I

"OMAR, WHAT'S GOING ON?"

Chuck Kennedy/KRT

TOM LASSETER
Foreign Correspondent,
Knight Ridder
Interviewed March 2005

Tom Lasseter has the final chapter in this book for a specific reason: to leave you with a searing last impression. My purpose is not to torture anyone but to leave an indelible reminder of what is really going on in Iraq and to encourage long, hard thinking about what our nation is doing and what is at stake. There is a story among Tom's words that you'll recognize immediately as the one you will not be able to forget. Keep in mind, too, that the person telling the story is a journalist who is barely thirty years old.

Lasseter called me by phone from Baghdad. He speaks like the gen-

Xer that he is. From time to time, he'd say something that gave me the impression he has read a lot of good books. In his photo, he wears a goatee and looks like a young poet, but he actually expresses himself in a right-smack-between-the-eyes manner:

> Getting shot at sucks. It is no fun. Seeing people killed is awful and seeing dead bodies is awful and it is a bad deal to see that sort of stuff or experience that sort of stuff. That said, I think you have to be careful not to fall into the bullshit of "I am a dark knight who has seen things you would not understand." We're all here because we're journalists; we're here because we decided to be here and it's just part of the deal that it's a dangerous place. Bad things happen in Iraq, and if you come to Iraq and something bad happens to you, you might end up wishing that you hadn't come, but you did.

Lasseter talks about Iraq as a nation of people "coping with" post-traumatic stress syndrome. When asked about details on the political landscape or the insurgency, he would often preface his comments with "It depends on whom you are talking to." Tom is keenly aware that no matter what aspect of Iraq one is contemplating, things can shift as often and dramatically as the sands in a desert. "The best advice I've had about covering Iraq came from a Jordanian who said, "No matter what you write about Iraq, the opposite often will be true." This point was so critical to Tom that I promised him I would make sure that in the edited transcript I would retain this final comment: "I guarantee you that by the time this is printed, everything will be different. All that stuff I just said about Sunnis and Shias will be different in some powerful and dynamic way."

The one constant, however, is the violence. But that, too, has myriad sides, some of which are unfathomable even to the locals. "I have a translator I worked with for a while," says Tom, "and when we went out to some massive car bombing site, or something absurd or violent was happening in traffic, I would ask him, 'Omar, what's going on?' And he'd say, 'Iraq is a place of much mysteriousness.'" While risking his life to unravel Iraq's moveable mysteries, Lasseter has also picked up some very practical lessons: "I've learned that if I'm not embedded, that if I have to choose between body armor and tennis shoes, I'll take tennis shoes because sometimes running fast is what is important. . . . Tennis shoes, snugly tied, and I'll be all right."

The first question I asked him was one I asked virtually everyone in this book. Tom, like several of the war correspondents I interviewed, was reluctant to answer it. He was more willing to tell me how the Iraqis would respond.

Why do you think we went to war?

I try not to get into the domestic political side of the Iraq war mostly because Tom Lasseter's opinion about it doesn't really mean anything at all. I know I sound like I'm sidestepping the question, but I think that the US military is here now and the important thing is to concentrate on reporting on what's happening now in Iraq and what has been happening. The debate about the invasion, the debate about the intelligence, all that sort of stuff, as my friends in the US military would say, "That's out of my lane." I don't cover domestic politics or intelligence agencies.

Why do the Iraqis think we went to war?

Most Iraqis think that the United States military is in Iraq because the United States wants Iraq's oil. There are certainly deviations from that line of thought, but the overwhelming majority of Iraqis that I speak with—who are mostly Shias and Sunnis south of Kurdistan—think that the United States is here primarily as an occupation force interested in the country's natural resources. There are an awful lot of other conspiracy theories, but that's a common denominator in conversations with Iraqis from across the spectrum.

Why do the US soldiers think they're there?

That really depends on the soldier you're talking to. I've spent a whole lot of time with soldiers over the past two years and one is really different from the next. During the war proper in March and April 2003, a young first lieutenant walked up to me and took out of his back pocket a map of the world—I think it was from the *Atlantic Monthly*. It was a map of the world's oil reserves. He pointed to it and with this sort of conspiratorial wink said, "Why do you think we're here?" I've also spoken with plenty of soldiers who say that the United States is here because of September 11 and the attacks on the World Trade Center. It is, to their mind, part of the larger War on Terrorism, which began with 9/11. They very much see it as a continuation of that. I also speak with a lot of soldiers who say they're here because it's their job, because they're soldiers and soldiers go where they're sent and fight. They don't choose the wars; they fight them. The soldiers are an eclectic lot, and it just really depends on who you're talking to.

How do they view the country, the culture, and the people over there?

Again, it depends completely on the soldier that you're talking with. I've spent time with soldiers who volunteer to go to Arabic classes, spend time off from patrols doing online Arabic studies, and have books about the region and Iraq, as well as Arabic language books. I've also spent time with other soldiers who joke about "killing fucking hajjis." There's a wide spectrum; they are not a monolithic group. They're an interesting lot, who end up in the military for a lot of different reasons.

Last summer, I was up in Muqdadiyah, a town north of Baqubah, with some American troops. It was the preface to a raid, and everyone was just sitting around. Going up to Muqdadiyah, a bad IED [improvised explosive device] roadside bomb had hit the Humvee in front of the one that I was in, and two guys were pretty badly mangled. After that, there was a firefight. A day or two later, the guys were getting ready to go out on this raid. I looked over at this guy and he was reading *The Count of Monte Cristo*, I think. I was a little surprised. He told me that he was reading the world's great books through Amazon.com. He would order a bulk of them and work his way through them and then have Amazon ship more out to Muqdadiyah.

You're a fairly young guy. What's it like for you there? What are some of the things you've seen that you wish you didn't have to carry around in your head and how has it affected you?

There's an awful lot. I can't tell you how many car bombings I've covered. I don't go out to them anymore because of security. That's the one silver lining to having less mobility these days. I don't have to go out and see those things quite as often. They're just Dante-esque. It's really hard to describe what it's like to see, especially when you start to get into the dozens killed and seeing body parts all over the place. All that's really terrible stuff. Being in very angry crowds and just being surrounded by rage. In July and August last year, I covered the fighting between the US military and Shia cleric Muqtada al-Sadr's Mahdi militia in Sadr City and Najaf. I covered that as what the US military would call a "unilateral" or roving reporter covering both sides of the conflict. I spent a fair amount of time with the Muqtada militia, and it was a distinctly different experience from being embedded with US troops. It's very dangerous. There's a lot of shooting going on, but it's people shooting at each other while you're trying to avoid getting hit. When you're embedded, particularly in a rough area, it's people shooting at you. You are riding with the target. It is not a good thing to be in a Bradley Fighting Vehicle that people are shooting RPGs [rocket-propelled grenades] at. When you're not embedded, you have to be smart about negotiating the danger and you need to be fast and careful not to get caught in a crossfire. You face a much bigger risk of getting hit by a tank round or helicopter fire. They're different environments with different sets of risks.

Then there are the small things. On February 1, 2004, there were twin suicide bombings in the town of Irbil in northern Iraq that killed dozens and dozens of people. They were celebrating a Muslim holiday inside two buildings housing the offices of Kurdish political parties. They were terrible bombings. Later, I was at a hospital and there was a child there, a young boy, and we went in to interview him. His uncle was there, and he explained that the boy had been standing next to his parents at one moment and the next moment he woke up with parts of his parents on him and he'd been struck mute. The uncle was talking to the boy, trying to get him to say something. Suddenly, I saw the scene from outside myself: this reporter standing next to a bed with a boy who had woken up with his parents all over him who had been struck mute, and I looked down on the ground and I was standing in blood and I thought, "This is awful," and I said to the uncle, "Please, leave him alone, we're leaving right now." There's the large-scale gore and then there's moments like that boy or a mother just beating her face with her fists as hard as she can because she just lost a child or a husband. The big gore seems surreal in a way, but when you see the survivors, or the relatives of the survivors, and that grief, that stays with you.

What toll do you think this violence is taking on the country nationally and what is it doing to people's attitudes. What is the effect?

It affects everything. On a meta level, it affects the ability to put in electricity or work on sewage and all that sort of stuff. The insurgency here has affected everything; it has affected the psyche of the nation, and people talk about how the violence is different than during Saddam. Even Shias, who were terribly oppressed under Saddam, say that Saddam was a savage and brutal man and they're glad that he is gone and they wish all sorts of horrible violent fates on him, but that when he was in power, they could walk down the street and not worry about car bombs. It's the randomness of the violence that is so nerve-racking. Iraq is a nation that has, in a strange and really unfortunate way, learned to get used to the violence. It's become a part of life, a part of the world that you might be blown up and that there are stray bullets. People live their lives, they go to work, and they are very much afraid of their children or their families getting kidnapped. They worry in traffic that every time a US convoy goes by, the convoy is going to get involved in an attack or be hit by a car bomb and that they'll be part of the collateral damage, either from the insurgent attack or from the US response. An awful lot of people I meet seem to be coping with this national posttraumatic stress syndrome.

How do they sort this out? Who do they blame?

It depends on who you're talking to. These are generalizations, but Sunnis by and large will blame the American occupation before they blame the insurgents, but certainly they blame the insurgents as well. When you talk with Shias, oftentimes they'll blame the insurgents first and the American occupation second. It also just very much depends on what day of the week you're talking with somebody. They seem to blame everyone and everything one day, and then the next day they'll blame some really cryptic conspiracy by the Israelis to attack their brother's car shop or something. It's pretty wide ranging.

Does the Israeli-Palestinian issue influence what's going on in Iraq that much?

The perception of it is an issue with just about everyone in this part of the world that I've spoken with. It's just a constant lens through which the world is viewed. Politically, it seems like everything comes back to Israel, and those are just conversations based on my time here in Iraq and trips to Jordan, and some time in Cairo and Kuwait. I've not canvassed the whole region, and it's not something I've reported on, but it's hard to have a conversation about politics in this part of the world without Israel coming up.

In what context do they talk about Israel?

There's a real suspicion of and sense of conspiracy about Israel; that there's this unseen hand involved with politics across the region that in one way or another is connected with the mechanisms of Israeli intelligence services or that sort of thing.

Let's talk a little bit about the insurgents. You wrote about a raid on an insurgent training camp, and I noticed you didn't mention who was in charge of the camp. You mentioned that there were a few foreign fighters there. Give me a profile of who the insurgents are and talk about this shift from attacking US soldiers to attacking civilians and what that means.

Like so much of the rest of Iraq, the insurgency is diffuse and complicated and it depends on what day of the week it is. There seems to be a general agreement that the insurgency is comprised of Baathist loyalists, people who are loyal either to the Baath Party[1] or to Saddam Hussein. There are domestic radical Islamists, there are foreign radical Islamists, there are people who fight—and this is generally out west, particularly in the Al Anbar region—out of a sense of tribal revenge—they feel dishonored or disrespected by the US military and so they take up arms. There are people who fight out of a sense of nationalism; they think of themselves as protecting their country against a foreign occupier. And then there are mafia-like criminal gangs who have taken advantage of centuries-old smuggling routes for a very long time and they don't want to see those routes or their criminal enterprises messed with, so they fight. There is also, at the local neighborhood level, violence that's ascribed to the insurgency but that is actually just people fighting across sectarian lines: Shia militia in a neighborhood attacking Sunnis because Sunnis had attacked Shias and so on in a vicious circle.

It's a wide range of folks, which is part of what makes it difficult to fight. There's no RICO chart out there, no mafia don on top of it all who you could go take out to bring down the organization. There are so many different organizations and sometimes they change their names and sometimes a guy who fights for one organization one day might fight for another one the next day because his uncle is a part of it.

Some of the people whose stated common cause is fighting the Americans really don't agree about anything else. A Baathist fighter is not going to agree about anything with a foreign jihadi. The Baathist fighter typically is going to be secular and Western in his thoughts. He's going to be a guy who perhaps went through university, had a decent job under Saddam, and comes from a substantially different background and worldview than a guy who is coming over from Syria to fight jihad.

Is there a majority group?

That depends on who you talk to. The US military would say that the majority of them are disgruntled former Baathists and that the minority are foreign jihadis. A lot of the foreign jihadis bring to Iraq technical expertise and training that they got in camps in Afghanistan and become sort of Johnny Appleseed–like figures who teach the locals guerrilla fighting tactics that are a lot more sophisticated than the training a twenty-year-old kid in Ramadi [a town about seventy miles west of Baghdad] with an RPG would have. So they can be, as the US military calls it, force multipliers. But at the end of the day, these aren't people—the Baathists and jihadis—who agree on anything else.

Talk a little bit about the shift in the insurgency's focus from American soldiers to Iraqi civilians. Which part of the insurgency is doing this and why?

Again, I emphasize that this is a really diverse group of people and it's hard to read the tea leaves much, but looking at the numbers postelection, post–January 30, 2005, the number of US soldiers killed has dropped dramatically, and there's a corresponding rise in attacks on Iraqi civilians and Iraqi security forces. A lot of that violence goes along sectarian fault lines, again, a militia in a Sunni neighborhood fighting Shias, that sort of thing. One part of the insurgency that would be involved with that could be Sunni Baathists, who look at the political process and see that they're losing in a pretty big way. The Sunnis did not come out of the elections looking good at all. They did not vote much—some out of security concerns, and others because they were boycotting the elections. So that Baathist loyalist is going to be cornered even more than he was before. Then your Sunni jihadi is going to see the Shias, who have this ascendancy and power right now, as apostate. That hard-line jihadi Sunni really disagrees with a lot of Shia Islam and is going to see their rise to power in Iraq as a real threat. So both of those groups have a vested interest in attacking Shias and a vested interest in fomenting chaos, and a quick way to do that is stoking civil war.

Do you think this invasion has triggered a civil war?

I don't know. There are many in Iraq who would say there is a low-intensity civil war going on right now. Others say they don't think it will happen, and others think that it might one day happen but that the time is just not right, right now. I see it less through the lens of civil war and more—and perhaps this is a definition of civil war—as groups competing for the future of Iraq that have competing interests along several lines: ethnic lines, religious lines, and so on. Now, increasingly, especially at the local neighborhood level, you see a lot more sectarian disputes being solved with weapons and violence. It's certainly more that way now than it was in the summer of 2003 when there was more talking things through, more an attitude of "let's caucus, let's come to the table."

I think that for Sunnis inclined to fight, they take a look at the January 30 elections and they see a two-hundred-and-seventy-five-member national parliament where Sunni Arabs have about seventeen seats. They also see a large group of Shias in the United Iraqi Alliance that was formed under the guidance of the top Shia cleric in Iraq [Iranian born Grand Ayatollah al-Sistani], and that's a real threat to them. A lot of Sunnis are deeply distrustful of anyone involved with the Alliance and deeply distrustful of Sistani. Then you have Abdul Aziz al-Hakim, the head of SCIRI [Supreme Council for Islamic Revolution in Iraq], and you have Dawa, another Shia Islamic organization. Both of these parties have deep, deep ties to Iran. The Sunnis, including moderate Sunnis, are very suspicious that the Shias are moving toward theocracy—maybe not tomorrow, but eventually. The Sunnis are worried that the Shias are going to pursue a constitution that might have some sort of Trojan horse language that says, "Iraq cannot have laws contrary to Islam," which could mean that later on a council of clerics would be deciding what is contrary to Islam. The Shias totally deny this. They say they're looking for a government that will include all people and that they want to respect the Islamic identity of Iraq, but they recognize that Iraq also has a secular identity. But the perception among many Sunnis is that the Shias are going to try to take over. Because of that heightened sense of isolation, of being cornered, there's a lot of despondency among the Sunnis, and when things happen between Sunnis and Shias, especially at the neighborhood level, Sunnis tend to be more reactionary now. They might see fewer options than they did before and less hope for the political process. All of that has certainly sparked violence in other countries, and it seems to be doing it here as well.

Do you think that the Shias or their leader, Grand Ayatollah al-Sistani, could actually be proponents of a secular government?

Sistani is a hard guy to read. I've never spoken with him, and neither has any other journalist that I know. People in Iraq are left to interpret what Sistani wants and what he means by what he's done. He has certainly shaped the political process here. He pushed hard for elections and had a lot to do with the Americans abandoning this sort of caucus structure political system they had devised for holding free elections. In January of 2004 Sistani was getting very impatient with the time line, very impatient with the political process, and one day you saw over a hundred thousand Shias marching through downtown Baghdad. They just took downtown Baghdad. It was a peaceful demonstration, but it was a very obvious message: "I lift my finger and this is what it looks like. Let's work this out in a peaceful way."

But that didn't necessarily mean that he was hell-bent for democracy; that might just have meant that he wanted the process to go forward so the Shias could regain the power that they lost under Saddam.

I think it was clear he was bent on having free elections, and it's clear that those elections would deliver the majority of power to the majority population, which are Shias. What they intend to do with that power remains to be seen. Sistani has said through his fatwas[2] and through his intermediaries that he wants to back away from the political process, that it was just his duty to his followers to be sure that they had this freedom, and he's now going to back away and they can take over from here and be politicians. There are certainly suspicions in the Sunni community that that's not the case. There's a fundamental difference in the way Sunnis are structured and Shias are structured, and it's really important to understand this. Shias are structured under a *marja'iya*, which is a council of clerics. There are four grand ayatollahs in Najaf of which Sistani is the most senior, and their word is the law for Shias. It is an ingrained part of their identity, in terms of both religion and culture. The *marja'iya* is the beginning and the end of what one does in life. The Sunnis don't have anything like that. That's why the list that won was the "169 list" of parties and candidates that Sistani certainly guided to form. Those 169 election posters had pictures of Sistani on them, and people voted for that list because a lot of them thought that it was the *marja'iya*'s list so then it became a duty with a capital "D" to vote for it. There were a lot of complaints around the election that the United Iraqi Alliance abused the 169 list, that they had clerics in mosques saying that if you didn't vote for 169 you'll go to hell or you won't be able to touch your wife. I personally didn't hear an imam saying that, but a lot of folks said that they did. The Sunnis don't have anything as a whole to compete with that sort of focus. Beyond that, the Sunnis right now are really scattered and have no one who can deliver the Sunni vote. Even if they did, their best-case scenario just wouldn't compare to that Shia experience of the *marja'iya*. And that fundamental difference makes Sunnis suspicious that in Najaf, which is a small town that looks sort of like a small Mexican village with very dusty, low buildings, there's this guy Sistani who almost never leaves his house, and his word guides millions of people without question.

Does that spell democracy to you?

Sistani, I think, would say that his authority has to do with religious things; it has to do with how a Muslim should conduct himself in the personal sphere versus the political sphere. In fact, if you go to www.Najaf.org, there is a part of it called "Ask Sistani" in which people can do just that, ask Sistani questions about anything related to how inheritance should work and to what sexual acts are and are not permitted between man and wife.

What about whether women can work, whether women can drive a car, whether women can do all kinds of stuff men can do?

Right. That's where you get into the Sunni argument, which is that this personal sphere will expand into the political sphere, that it's all one system, much as in Iran, where you have councils of clerics that define everything. The clerics ultimately have the final say and that's what the Sunnis fear about Sistani, and it's all wrapped up in Iran and the war between Iraq and Iran. It's wrapped up in Sistani being Iranian-born, it's wrapped up in distrust between Sunnis and Shias, and it's wrapped up in Saddam oppressing Shias and favoring Sunnis. So there's a stew of things.

It almost feels like a potential repeat of history, of when the shah was replaced by Khomeini. As brutal as the shah was, and as brutal as Saddam Hussein was, they were both secularists. The shah was replaced by Khomeini, and while al-Jafaari, the new prime minister, may not be an Iraqi Khomeini, I don't think he's a secularist.

The best advice I've had about covering Iraq came from a Jordanian who said, "No matter what you write about Iraq, the opposite often will be true." Certainly what we've seen is people in the Alliance, the Shia political ticket, going to Najaf to consult with Sistani, and senior political leaders saying, "Of course we consult with Sistani about anything that's important," he is the head of *marja'iya*, the grand ayatollah. But again, they draw this distinction by saying that they're only asking for his advice and that Sistani is not controlling things or dictating how far they will go or where they'll draw the line in terms of Islam's influence on governance.

Ibrahim al-Jafaari is a man who literally recites poetry when you ask him about Iraqi politics. But people look at his background and find some concern that an offshoot of his Dawa Party has called for an Islamic republic in Iraq that looks an awful lot like Iran, where you have these councils of clerics. When Jafaari started out with Dawa he was, at one time, an undercover Dawa operative up at his university in Mosul. At that time, Dawa was headed by a cleric who very much wanted an Islamic republic in Iraq. My experience with Jafaari is that he will not answer directly the question about whether or not Iraq will be a theocracy, but he will talk about the evolution of politics in the Soviet Union and Russia from a totalitarian state to a state that's now moving more toward democracy. It sounds like he's saying that in his radical youth he pursued what some might see as a more extreme path, but now he's older, he's traveled, he's seen the West, he's seen things about democracy that he likes, and he wants to find a middle path.

Talk about the fight in Najaf and Sadr City; I think that situation encapsulates the problems going on among the different players.

That had to do with Muqtada al-Sadr. Sadr's father, before he was killed, was what Sistani is now, the senior Shia cleric. Sadr has pursued a very anti-American, very antioccupation line and has called several times for armed revolt against US forces. He did it in April of last year, and there was a lot of fighting. Then he pulled back, regrouped, and did it again in July and August of this year, and again there was a lot of fighting in Sadr City, a very large slum in Baghdad, which is really the center of his power. A lot of the fighters in Najaf were being bused down from Sadr City. The culmination of things in Najaf was this standoff at the Imam Ali shrine, one of the holiest sites in Shia Islam. Sadr's guys were holed up in the shrine, and you had a cordon of American forces around Najaf threatening to go get Sadr. It was, for a moment, a very tense situation in which the wrong tank shell through the wrong part of that shrine really could have sparked fighting that would have spread far more widely. They ended up dealing with it more or less through political negotiations. Sistani and the *marja'iya* in Najaf put a lot of pressure on Sadr to back down and not take Najaf down in flames with him. You get the sense that what Sadr really wants is the recognition that his father had, and he isn't getting it. The situation in Najaf also exposed the continuing problems with desertion among the Iraqi security forces. They were deserting in April during the fights in Fallujah and Najaf, and again in August in Najaf. What you're running into there are the sectarian lines in the security forces where the Shias did not want to go fight their fellow Shias holed up in the Imam Ali shrine.

The other side of that was, a couple of weeks ago I spent some time on Haifa Street, an area in Baghdad that's fairly violent. It's not as violent as it once was, but we still received sniper fire while on patrols. There, you have national guard troops who are largely Shia patrolling a Sunni neighborhood. The guards are very aware of the fact that the people who are sniping at them are Sunni, and you hear a lot of sectarian rhetoric. A lot of people are concerned about both Sunni and Shia members of the security forces carrying out sectarian agendas and the security forces ending up essentially turning into Sunni and Shia militias. The Sunnis are really concerned about this with the Iraqi Alliance coming into power. They're worried that the Shia are going to come in and, to use al-Jafaari's word, "cleanse," or de-Baathify, the Iraqi security forces.

Is that possible? There are so many of them.

Sure it's possible. The concern is that those people will be replaced with Shia militia members. The militant arm of SCIRI is the Badr brigade which during the war between Iraq and Iran was notorious for being vicious in its attacks against Iraqis. The Sunnis fear that this Badr brigade, would in a lot of ways become part of the national security apparatus, that they would become the police, that they would become the army. There's a general fear across the board about soldiers coming in to the national guard and the Iraqi army with real sectarian bents. I saw a group of Shia soldiers just beat the hell out of a suspected Sunni insurgent in the Haifa Street area, and what they were yelling as they were doing it was "Revenge." One got the sense that the revenge wasn't just against the insurgency but was against the Sunni insurgency that often targets Shias. It's very volatile stuff.

How does the average citizen view the insurgency? Is there a consensus or does it depend on who you ask?

It depends a lot on who you ask. In the Sunni population, a lot of people distinguish between insurgents and terrorists. To them, insurgents are nationalists; they're people fighting the US occupation. Terrorists are foreign jihadists who set off car bombs in crowded markets. Among some Shias, there's sympathy for what they see as anti-US insurgents, but there's absolutely no sympathy for insurgents or terrorists who target Shias. An awful lot of these mass bombings are against Shia army and police recruits who come from down south or Shia neighborhoods in Baghdad. They're sons and fathers and brothers, and it certainly becomes very personal for the Shia.

Do you think the Americans will be OK with al-Jafaari as prime minister?

Sure. American diplomatic sources say that Jafaari's election as prime minister is proof that they've stayed out of the process. I think it's safe to say Jafaari probably is not the guy that the US diplomatic community would have chosen to be prime minister.

Who would the Americans have preferred?

I think it's fair to say that Allawi is friendlier toward the US administration than Jafaari might be. At the very least, he's a far more Western man than Jafaari and far more secular. Jafaari has deep ties to religious organizations with deep ties to Iran.

If Jafaari becomes the next prime minister and it looks like he wants to establish a theocracy, do you think he'll last in power?

I have no idea. I really try to stay away from predicting things about Iraq. I think that the only thing that you can predict right now is that there's going to be more fighting and more people killed. The scope and nature of the fight could take a lot of turns.

Do you think a significant US troop withdrawal is in the offing? I'm asking for your assessment based on what's happening on the ground over there because it's always said that what's happening on the ground is what's going to determine how long we stay.

What I see on the ground is less violence against the US military and more Iraqi versus Iraqi violence. Whether that equals the same number of US forces staying in place to act as a safeguard between those communities or whether that equals a US military that's not being attacked as often, allowing it to reduce its forces, I just don't know. I think that if the United States were to substantially reduce its numbers, you would see a lot more fighting. It's so difficult to say, but if the US military left tomorrow, I think there would be an awfully big fight in Iraq between groups who have been waiting a long time to fight each other.

Is that going to change with the prolonged presence of the United States?

It's really hard to say. Maybe next week everyone will work out their differences.

Do you really believe that, given what you've seen?

It is an awfully topsy-turvy place and it's difficult to say. You can go spend a day in Baghdad and have a nice lunch if you keep a low profile and go through all the security protocols. You can go visit a family in a garden. Then you can go out the next day and mortars can be thudding around, or a rocket can go over, or terrible violence can break out, and suddenly the things that seem possible become pretty dark.

How do the Iraqis perceive Americans and America?

It depends on who you're talking to. A Shia family whose sons were killed brutally by Saddam and never had anything is going to view the force that removed Saddam a lot differently than a Sunni family that lived under a harsh dictatorship but still had more options than it does now. That Sunni family sees the American forces a lot differently than the Shias. The Kurds, who I haven't talked about much here, exist in a lot of ways because of the Americans. Had the Americans not drawn the line, Saddam would have killed a whole lot more Kurds than he did. The Kurds have a much more favorable impression of Americans than the Sunnis do because, since the early 1990s, they've been able to cultivate and develop a society and a government. It's amazing to go up to Kurdistan. There are mountains and green pastures and families go on picnics and couples stroll hand in hand at night. They're having a much better time of it than a Sunni family in Ramadi, so the Kurds see the American presence in a significantly different way.

Given your experience over there, are there things that you think Americans don't understand about this situation and about the Middle East?

I think that they don't understand how complicated Iraq is. When I think about it, I think of Fallujah. In the summer of 2003 I was in Fallujah a lot. We would get in a car and drive out there. I had dinner with many families and learned about this tribal system where if you cross these people they will kill you. They will not threaten you; they will kill you. But if you come as their guests, they offer this incredible protection. Fallujah was a very angry place, and at that time it was the most violent place in Iraq. I spent a lot time out there with the soldiers of the Third Infantry Division. They had one view about how things were going in Fallujah, and when I talked to the people living in Fallujah, they had an opposite view. The Americans thought things were going well. I always asked Fallujahns, "If the Americans stay here, what will happen?" If I was talking to a guy who sold fish in the market for a living, or to an attorney, or to a guy who sold cigarettes, they would all say, "There will be more violence; there will be a big fight." So we would go out there and do all this and go have a kabob and it was a very interesting place.

When I came back in December of 2003, Fallujah had become significantly more violent, but I still went with my translator and we were always sure to be the guest of a sheikh so that if guys with guns stopped us, we could say, "We're this guy's guests," and it would smooth things over. In November of 2004 I went in with the American military during the fight for Fallujah and I went through a week of fighting unlike any other fighting that I've ever seen in its intensity. The US military said it was the most intense urban combat since Vietnam. I saw an awful lot of destruction. A US Army captain who I'd become buddies with was killed in a house, and I was in vehicles that were hit with RPGs [rocket-propelled grenades] and took shrapnel from IEDs [improvised explosive devices]. It was the same place and the same road that we drove down on our way to get kabobs. I saw the road from a roof, and it had just been pummeled. We were up on the roof taking sniper fire from all over. It was the same town; the same place. It's just complicated.

Do Americans understand the nature of these tribal areas? I'm asking you that in the context of George W. Bush announcing that democracy is on the march in Iraq and the Middle East. Is a US–style democracy really possible there?

I'm going to give you another "it depends on where you are" answer. The tribalism I was talking about is very distinct to western Iraq. The Dulemi tribe that controls that section of the country is distinctly different from the tribal system in other areas of the country. I don't think Americans understand that kind of tribalism and I don't expect them to, it's unlike anything that you would encounter in the United States. I don't think that US diplomats on the ground here expect US-style democracy to take root in Iraq. Out west, it runs into this sort of orthodox Sunni tribalism. Down south, it runs into Shia ideas of the *marja'iya*. Up in Kurdistan it seems more possible, but Kurdistan is one of those places where you also have a very large militia, the *peshmurga* Kurdish militia, who are very fierce fighters. This kind of militia could not exist in the United States the way that they exist there.

I think US diplomats are looking for Iraqi democracy to take root. Diplomatic sources have said to me that the goal is to have a country where minorities are respected, where their physical safety is not threatened by the majority; where people who are secular are able to exist and operate freely just as those who are religious would, where Sunnis would be able to operate as Shias do and vice versa; and that while certainly there would be religious overtones to the Iraqi national government, which you would not find in the United States in terms of structure and guidance of government, people would be able to coexist.

Is there an understanding of what democracy is and do they want it?

I think the question, "do they understand what it is," is the more immediate one right now. I think that for a lot of Iraqis, the answer is no, they
don't know what democracy is. They have lived under a dictatorship for
thirty years. Even people who had it good here lived under a very strict
authoritarian dictator who killed members of their families. That experience is obviously very different from the recent experience of having had
the second meeting of the national assembly. The political process that the
Iraqis are in right now is still in the very early stages. Then, there are a lot
of Iraqis who don't want democracy. There certainly are some Shias—not
all, but some—who want Islam to be the guiding force of everything.

**How big a percentage of the Shias do you think want some sort of
theocracy?**

It's really hard to say, and again, it depends on where you are. You will
find more people in the southern towns of Najaf and Karbala who would
be willing to accept a theocracy than you would find Shias in Baghdad
willing to accept theocracy. In Iraq there's a sort of dynamic that happens
in the United States as well, which is that rural populations are sometimes
more religious than city populations.

Iraq is mostly rural, but you're talking about a country where in
recent history much of the power has been based in bigger cities like
Baghdad, Mosul in the north, and Basra in the south. There's a shift that
might be happening right now, which is that, functionally, Najaf may
become the capital of Iraq, and by capital I mean the place where important decisions that guide the political process will be made. This would
represent a seismic shift. But for now, if you ask the Shia politicians in
Baghdad about this, they say no, that they will consult with people in
Najaf, but decisions will be made in Baghdad.

There are a lot of Sunnis who fear it will be a hard-line theocracy, but
the Shias say, "No, it will be a free and open country that respects everybody's rights.

Talk about the security situation and how you handle it as a reporter.

Right now, I would not think about getting into a car and going much west
of Baghdad. When I go to safe places in Baghdad, it's with two cars, and
I have drivers who have radios. We have a security consultant who lives
with us, and he goes out with us only when we go to the airport. We consult with him; we map out the trip and talk about where we're going. We

go to places where we have interviews with people we know and trust but, that said, four or five months ago, there were a lot of places in Baghdad that you just didn't go to, period. Things have softened up a little bit and the kidnapping threat is not quite as bad or vicious as it was. It's certainly still there for Iraqis and it's definitely there for Westerners and doubly so for non-Muslim male Americans. So there's certainly a very real threat, but I'm able to get around Baghdad.

Trips outside of Baghdad are with the military or on a helicopter. It's the trip to wherever you're going that's bad. I would feel fine spending the next week in Najaf with just my translator, but it's the drive to Najaf that's the problem. There are some really nasty towns on the way there, and I should say that I mean "nasty" only in that they are violent. There's the town of Mahmoudia, where one of the last times that we were going down there we had gotten just south of Mahmoudia and traffic was stopped in front of us because there was a bomb on the road, an IED. As the Iraqi national guards came up from behind to see what was going on with the IED, the people who had laid the IED and had been waiting in a ditch along the road jumped out and started shooting at the national guards and everyone around the IED. A lot of guys in cars around us jumped out with guns; some were shooting at the national guards and some were shooting at the insurgents. We were sitting there in our car in a place with a real high kidnapping threat and we had to get out of the car because there was fire. My translators and drivers spoke Arabic to me the whole time so that everyone would think I wasn't a foreigner. I just nodded along like we were having a conversation.

The ride down south is a problem. The same is true with Kurdistan. You can run through Sulemania with an American flag on your back and you'll be fine, but going up to Sulemania, you go near Baquba, which is a very dangerous place, and near Kirkuk, which is a dangerous place, and near Mosul, which is a dangerous place, so it's the ride up that's hair-raising. It's navigating through these Sunni areas where you have a real severe intimidation campaign and a lot of insurgent activity that is the problem.

You're going to Kirkuk this weekend, right?

I am, and I'm going with the military. In times past, we would just jump in a car and go up to Kirkuk, but it's just not worth the risk now. The difference is like going from being in a field where you know that there are some mines, but if you watch for the signs and you're careful you can avoid them, to being in an actual minefield. If you start on one side of that minefield and sprint and get to the other side and you're safe, you're not smart or brave; you're just stupid and lucky. What you've just done is dumb. You've put yourself at risk, put the people who work with you at risk, and you could get in a situation that affects the entire journalistic community. If you get kidnapped or killed, it could prompt other news organizations to clamp down or pull out.

I embedded on Haifa Street a couple of weeks ago with a patrol of about thirty-five Iraqi national guards and four American soldiers, and there you take sniper fire. It's a really nasty place, and there's a lot of raw sewage in the streets, but it's a place where you can navigate the risk, where you can try to be smart and try to know what's going on. But driving up to Kirkuk, you can't control whether or not an insurgent checkpoint is going to pop up. Professionally, it's very frustrating and humbling to not be able to just get in a car and go to Kirkuk. The story that I would get by just going to Kirkuk and staying in a hotel and going and knocking on the military's door and interviewing them and then going and interviewing people in the town would be richer and more nuanced than the story that I'll get embedded.

> **Everyday when you wake up, you wake up knowing that you're going to stare your mortality in the face. How do you handle that? Some war correspondents admit that they're adrenaline junkies.**

Getting shot at sucks. It is no fun. Seeing people killed is awful and seeing dead bodies is awful and it is a bad deal to see or experience that sort of stuff. That said, I think you have to be careful not to fall into the bullshit of "I am a dark knight who has seen things you would not understand." We're all here because we're journalists; we're here because we decided to be here and it's just part of the deal that it's a dangerous place. Bad things happen in Iraq, and if you come to Iraq and something bad happens to you, you might end up wishing that you hadn't come, but you did.

I came during the war as an embed with the 101st Airborne Division because the United States was going to war and I'm a reporter and it was an awfully big and interesting story. Then I kept coming back. Now I live here because it's an important story and how history judges this in both the near and far term might have a lot to do with America and what America means in the world. It's an important story on so many levels. It's an important story for the region, for what it means to Iraqis, and certainly for what it means for the Middle East, for American foreign policy, and for the American military—how the military is structured and what sorts of threats it faces.

There certainly are dangers involved in reporting the story. We went to an art gallery a couple of days ago and we were standing there talking with these Iraqi private security guys who were patting us down and then all of a sudden there was the "boom, boom, boom" of three mortars. You learn to hear that the mortars are far enough away that you don't have to be worried about them. You just keep doing what you're doing, and you try to be as smart about it as you can and not invite risks or threats. You try not to be cavalier about things and to be prepared for anything. Embedding with the military makes you such a target in some places, so you try to prepare yourself to be able to see through the smoke and you say to yourself, "This thing that you're worried about has happened. Now what will you do?" I've learned over here that in bad situations, it's not always the big strong brave guy who makes things OK, but it's the person who is able to see through the smoke and the panic and the noise and who is able to—I don't quite know how to put it—see the situation and to move the right way in the right direction. But being here for the adrenaline, I'm sure on some level that's it; I mean there's certainly some ego involved with it, but I just can't express to you enough how much it sucks to be shot at and to be in situations that are just bad. It's not fun. Your only thought is to get out of them or to survive them. Your thought is not, This is really cool, I hope someone's taking a picture of me right now.

When they would see news correspondents walking by, the guys I was embedded with in the 101st would get this voice and say, "No shit, there I was." They would mock the self-aggrandizing attitude that some of the reporters have. I think it's important to try to stay even and to stay away from that.

You must have learned some fairly interesting things about yourself by now in these extreme circumstances.

I've learned that if I'm not embedded, that if I have to choose between body armor and tennis shoes, I'll take tennis shoes because sometimes running fast is what is important.

You go to the States and you see these guys with these high-tech watches and all that stuff and you think, "That stuff is the first thing that is going to get you killed." All this sort of soldier of fortune stuff—just give me some tennis shoes. Tennis shoes, snugly tied, and I'll be all right. A reporter came over here one time with his GPS tracker and I was like,

'Man, that is the last thing you're going to be thinking about. If you are off a major thoroughfare in Iraq and trying to figure out which way is which, considering the immediate danger, my advice to you is throw that thing as far away from you as you can and start running. What you need, brother, is not a GPS tracker, it's good running shoes."

If you were going to give somebody a set of rules for reporting in Iraq right now, what would they be?

My first one would be to talk to Iraqis. If you're wondering what's going on in Iraq, check out what the Iraqis are saying. Part of talking to Iraqis is knowing the difference between being someone's guest and not being someone's guest, so pay attention to whether somebody is serving you tea in their house or whether they're not. Pay attention and be careful. Try to do your job as evenly as possible. Respect the risk and danger of the assignment; don't turn it into the "No shit, there I was."

Just listening and watching are pretty important. An awful lot of what's important to do here is the same as what you would do as a good reporter anywhere, which is to talk to lots of different folks about what's going on, to bear in mind their agendas, and to get their quotes right. You have a lot of responsibility to be fair to whomever you're writing about and to be fair to them in all the ways that you would be fair to your sources in any story you are covering.

Have enough notebooks and pens and good tennis shoes. Don't forget your sneakers—that's key. In one of my rooms, there's a cabinet, and in that cabinet there's all of my embed stuff. That stuff never comes out unless I am embedding. The boots that I wear on embeds I would never, ever wear anywhere other than when I'm embedded. I also have a different flak vest that I wear at embeds. The vest I would wear on the streets of Iraq is different, and I would wear it only if something pretty special was happening. The cargo pants I wear on an embed I don't ever, ever, ever wear on the streets of Iraq. The shirts I wear in the streets are shirts that I've bought here in Iraq. They're Western-style shirts; I'm not running around in a dishdasha or with a keffiya on my head. I wear shoes that I've bought here and khaki pants that I've bought here and button-up shirts that I've bought here. I wouldn't wear cargo pants with my best safari khaki shirt and boots to run around Baghdad. You don't want to stand out. You don't want to call any attention to yourself, and every little small thing helps.

**Are you paying any attention at all to any of the reporting from othe
sources on what's going on in Iraq?**

I probably don't pay as much attention as I should to what other folks are
doing. We get a daily feed from our DC bureau. That feed comes in the
afternoon Iraq time. I don't spend a lot of time in the morning looking at
other news services. I'll check the wires to see if some large act of violence
has happened that we need to pay attention to, but in terms of working on
a trend story about the insurgency, I don't typically do clip searches. I typically go talk to folks, to US military sources, to Iraqi analysts, to people
in the neighborhoods, and to whoever makes sense. Then I get the feed
later in the afternoon and I read it and I see what folks are doing.

There are a lot of nonreporting things to pay attention to. The letter *H*
came off my keyboard today, so I'm going to think a lot more about that
today than what other people are writing.

Any final thoughts?

I hope I didn't come off as too evasive. So much over here just depends
on who you're talking to. Also, I guarantee you that by the time this is
printed, everything will be different. All that stuff I just said about Sunnis
and Shias will be different in some powerful and dynamic way.

I have a translator I worked with for a while—he is our office manager now—and when we went out to some massive car bombing site, or
something absurd or violent was happening in traffic, I would ask him,
"Omar, what's going on?" And he'd say, "Iraq is a place of much mysteriousness."

TOM LASSETER is a correspondent for Knight Ridder Newspapers
assigned to Iraq. Lasseter grew up in Atlanta and attended the University
of Georgia. He interned at the *Anniston (AL) Star* and the Atlanta bureau
of the *New York Times*, then joined the *Lexington Herald-Leader* in 1999,
where he covered a variety of issues, including drug trafficking and corruption in eastern Kentucky. He was part of the Knight Ridder team of
reporters embedded with the army's 101st Airborne Division in Iraq
during the initial stages of the war in March and April of 2003 and was
detailed to Iraq three times after that. In October 2004 he became a full-
time correspondent, reporting to the Knight Ridder Washington bureau.

NOTES

1. The Baath Party follows a secular ideology that advocates pan-Arabic unity, Arab socialism, nationalism, and militarism. http://en.wikipedia.org/wiki/Ba'ath _Party.

2. A fatwa is an Islamic religious edict or proclamation.

INDEX

INDEX

INDEX

INDEX